THE LAST EMPIRES

To Bob,

Many thanks for encouraging me to talk about one.

very sincerely

Beauy.

30/xii/86

THE LAST EMPIRES

A Music Hall Companion

EDITED BY BENNY GREEN

PAVILION
MICHAEL JOSEPH

To Henry Shaw in gratitude

First published in Great Britain in 1986 by
Pavilion Books Limited
196 Shaftesbury Avenue, London WC2H 8JL
in association with Michael Joseph Limited
27 Wrights Lane, Kensington, London W8 5TZ

Introduction, notes and selection © Benny Green 1986
Other copyright holders are acknowledged on page 321
Designed by Lawrence Edwards

The Last Empires
1. Music-halls (Variety-theatres, cabarets,
etc.)—Great Britain—History
I. Green, Benny
792.7'0941   PN1968.G7

ISBN 1-85145-061-0

Typeset by Dorchester Typesetting, Dorchester
Printed and bound in Great Britain by
Biddles Ltd, Guildford and King's Lynn

DEDICATORY OVERTURE

My father's mother, Deborah Slovis, was a shortish, dumpy old lady with a disposition so genial that even her own children quite liked her. By the time I became aware of the world, she had already settled into the final role of her career, an obese matriarch swathed in long, shapeless black dresses which somehow gave her the aspect of a pantomime charlady. Never dressing in any other colour, never venturing out into the street, half-crippled by arthritis, rendered stoic by the loss of too many children, she remained a cheerful, affectionate, lovable old woman in whose lively brown eyes the twinkle was unquenched by the hardships imposed upon her by an indifferent world. In my early years I spent a great deal of time alone with her in the great subterranean kitchen of the house in Greenwell Street, observing her style as she shuffled across the rush matting from table to stove, stove to sink, sink to table. I was her first grandchild, indeed the only one she survived for long enough to enjoy, and the novelty of my status rendered me a protected species. On those occasions when my father was tempted to give me a corrective clip round the ear, she would forbid any such measure, saying that whatever misdemeanours I might have committed, they were nothing compared to the chaotic disruption of the whole neighbourhood he had wrought in his time. I can see her now, standing between us, shouting 'Davey, leave him alone', an instruction somehow so ludicrous that it never failed to clear the air by reducing all three of us to self-conscious laughter. She was, looking back on it, one of my best friends, an approving relative so ancient that I could not imagine how many years she had seen. When in the summer of 1936, after a Saturday evening spent in happy concentration breaking up firewood, she turned over in bed and died, I was astonished to learn that she was only in her mid-sixties. Had they told me she was a hundred I should have believed them, for she possessed that most exclusive of all the secrets of my world, recollections of a time before my own parents existed.

Being so small, I never thought of her in any context apart from the one she had chosen for herself. So far as I was concerned, she had no past, no acquaintances, no worldly experience, and must, I assumed almost without thinking about it, have spent her entire life padding around that kitchen, softening the lines of its flaking whitewashed walls with billows of steam on washdays, pervading it with the rare perfumes of her vegetable stews each evening and, surprisingly to me, providing her own musical accompaniment to the drudgery of her constrained life. As she worked at the sink, or fed the cat, or sat contentedly at the vast deal table, peeling potatoes or slicing apples, she would hum and sing. They were not the melodies I knew from my regular visits to the local picture palaces, or from my crude empirical experiments with the portable gramophone in the parlour cupboard, but seemed in some quaint way to be airs from another time, music in retrospect, a vocal analogue of the twin portraits on the back wall of King Edward and Queen Alexandra. It comes back to me that once, as she was serving me a bowl of steaming barley soup, she was singing something about dilly-dallying on the way. And another time, when the early winter dusk was gathering outside the window over the sink, and the sad winter rain drummed on the dustbin lids in the yard beyond, she made a cryptic reference to one

Dolly Daydream, a lady then unknown to me. There must have been dozens of songs conjured up by her in this way, but either the renditions were too sketchy to make much of an impression, or my mind was not yet capable of retaining the contours of more than two or three tunes at a time. All I sensed was that these vague fragments were a kind of vocal expression of my grandmother's sense of fun.

Or rather, of the ridiculous. She was, for example, given to slapping the palm of her hand on the table without warning and exclaiming in mock-anger. But they were never exclamations which made any sense, only crazy conglomerations of nonsense-syllables. The only one I can remember, the one she performed whenever she thought I needed a laugh, was 'Schmackel-de-bom-luxe-ee-ay', a neat compromise between ribaldry and the Lottie Collins school of vocalising. She also had the occasional habit of performing some mundane action as though it had never been seen before in the history of the world. One of her more bizarre affections was for the bright yellow residual liquid to be found at the bottom of the jars of Piccalilli. This deadly acidic draught, notorious as a bleacher of grubby pennies, was the elixir of life to her, the non-alcoholic equivalent of my grandfather's quaffs of rum taken straight from the bottle. For my benefit she developed the routine of holding the jar up to the light, squinting into its recesses with comical relish, and then smacking her lips. 'Now you see it, now you don't,' she would say, draining the contents of the jar at a single gulp, conscious with every movement she made that she had a rapt audience of one.

Yet it never occurred to me that she had the performer's instinct, that like several of her wayward children she had been half-endowed by nature with the sort of temperament which, impatient with the longueurs of humdrum existence, yearns to cut the traces and go in for vaguely artistic vagabondage. It was sad for all of them that they were no more than half-endowed, that this dream of exhibiting themselves in public was never quite strong enough to make a real artist out of any of them. Two of my uncles dabbled with musical instruments; one of them actually rose, for one brief summer in a Brighton dance hall, to a rickety professionalism, which soon collapsed before the blandishments of a career as a street bookmaker. My father went further than any of them, as I shall describe, and peering back down the perspective of the century at those long childhood interludes in my grandmother's kitchen, I can see that she too had a touch of the ham in her, some broad streak of mischief which tempted her to moments of slapstick indignity despite her age, her aching limbs, her mourning weeds.

Because of this realisation, I found the obsequies following her death painfully inappropriate. She had been a kindly, charitable woman, and yet here were all these related strangers, solemnly exercising their jaws on my Aunt Jane's maliciously unchewable pastries, pretending to be deeply moved by the passing of someone whom none of them had ever taken the trouble to visit, certainly not in my lifetime anyway, for I had seen hardly any of them before, and never did quite master the ramifications of the family tree comprehensively enough to be able to put names to faces and titles. To this day I am unsure who my great-aunts and great-uncles were, what they did, where they lived, where they went and why. My father, a connoisseur of eccentricity in its more harmless modes, later told me that this one was a self-confessed scoundrel and that one generally acknowledged to be very slightly off her head. But I cannot say for certain which of the inmates of this parrothouse of consanguinity constituted cousins of the deceased, or in-laws, or old friends, or old enemies, or nieces and nephews. The house that day was nothing more than a wild gallimaufry of cloche hats and bombazine, pot bellies, blue serge and watchchains, jade ornaments and elastic stockings, gold rings and gold fillings, avuncular hands slipping sixpences into my embarrassed pockets, booming old ladies taking my cheeks between gloved fingers and telling me I was 'Davey's boy'. There were Annies and Joes and Sarahs and Toms and Lilys and Lews, but which was which I had, and have, no idea. Nobody in the clan seemed to think it was of the slightest importance, with the effect that today our family tree is a pathetic specimen, blighted by wilful neglect and forgetfulness, and with only two or three newer branches strong enough to sustain memory and affection. This erasing of past ties has on occasions embarrassed and exasperated me so violently that I have cursed the shades of those indifferent ancestors of mine, who might so easily have unbent to the extent of telling me who we all were. One afternoon some years ago I stepped into a taxi in Tottenham Court Road and asked to be taken to Victoria Station. By this time I had made some small reputation as a musician and broadcaster, and was well known to a minority of enlightened strangers, among whom was my taxi driver, who began the conversation as a great many members of his generation and calling used to do, by claiming to be related to me. Or in this case, almost related to me. Seeing that my confusion was quite genuine, he then recounted a bizarre tale of how he had once fallen madly in love with a cousin of my father's called Fanny. They had become engaged to be married, but two days before the ceremony she had suddenly collapsed and died of a mysterious fever, which was how he came to be a lifelong bachelor. He found it incredible that nobody had ever told me this story, but was finally convinced when I told him that not only had I never heard it before, but that I had had no idea that my father had ever had a cousin called Fanny. I think this innocent confession must have offended him, for he grew suddenly silent, almost hit a van in Trafalgar Square, and dropped me at Victoria with a distinctly dubious expression on his face. Later, when I sought substantiation of his story, I found it to be true in every detail.

Although that was the most melodramatic of all the family revelations on which I stumbled in unguarded moments, it was not quite the most surprising. It must have been just before the start of the Second World War that my father, talking for once with some freedom of a family from which he had half-detached himself, dropped the great revelatory bombshell. We were coming home on the bus from the Metropolitan, Edgware Road, where we had been to see a comic called Ernie Lotinga masquerading as the king of some impossibly Ruritanian principality. Something about the ambience of the hall, the ribaldry of the entertainment, the warm, Londonish conviviality of the house, must have loosened his tongue, for while we were trundling through the shadows of Marylebone Road, he put down his newspaper and said, 'Did you know that grandma had a cousin who was in the music hall?' This casual remark so confounded me that I had to ask him to repeat it to confirm that I had not misheard. 'Yes. I went to see him once or twice. Chiswick Empire, I think. Long time ago.'

'What was he like? What did he do?'

'A sort of comic. He used to sing silly songs and dress up in silly clothes. Real old-time stuff. A bit old-fashioned, I thought.'

What happened next I cannot account for, except to say that real life is never very logical. Having been vouchsafed the precious information that we had a demigod in the family, I forgot about it; soon the information was buried so deeply under the mountains of experience as to be almost beyond retrieval. I never thought about it for twenty years, until one day, a picture in a magazine reminded me of my grandmother's funeral tea, and it suddenly occurred to me that perhaps one of those smiling, red-faced men who had gathered in the upstairs parlour on that long-lost afternoon may have been the great man. Perhaps he had steered gracefully through the minefields of bombazine and hatpins to the tea-trolly and choked over one of those pastries. Perhaps I had actually spoken to him, shyly shaken his hand, laughed dutifully at one of his little drolleries, touched the hem of history, so to speak, without knowing it? I asked my father, but he could not recall who was there on that sad and distant afternoon. When I asked my aunts and uncles, they seemed not to have any idea what I was talking about, and told me to ask my father, who, they said loftily, was interested in that sort of thing. Once or twice over the years since, the recollection of my celebrated ancestor has come wafting back as a momentary awareness which flits away almost before it has arrived, like the wisps of a dream on waking. A visit to the old Hackney Empire during its conversion to a television studio;

a Sunday night concert in my playing days at the old Met, not long before it was so shamelessly demolished to make way for a motorway intersection which was eventually sited a hundred yards further south. One day at Broadcasting House, after a long conversation with Bud Flanagan, I resolved to find out more about my relative, but there were a thousand other interesting and more pressing duties to be performed, and it was not until compiling this book that I was able to gratify my curiosity.

Sam Mayo, real name Cowan, anglicised from Cohen, was born in Lambeth in 1881, one of three sons of the proprietor of a second-hand shop. He made his professional debut at the Alhambra, Sandgate, in 1898, but it was some time before he found his own style, which was to deliver absurdities while keeping a perfectly straight face. By 1904 he had come into his own as 'Sam Mayo the Immobile One', a reference to his technique of sitting at the piano and singing his own droll songs without the flicker of an eyelid. It was in that year that he is said to have set a metropolitan record by playing twelve shows a night for four weeks, dashing from hall to hall in hansom cabs. Contemporary reports claim that he added a consummating touch of absurdity to his act by performing it swathed in a dressing-gown, but in the only portrait photograph I have been able to trace, he appears to be sporting an ankle-length overcoat. A cap with a shiny peak, a stiff white shirt collar and a tiny black bow-tie complete his costume, except for a strange-looking contraption dangling on his chest, suspended by a string looped around his neck. In each hand he holds a drumstick and looks likely to bang the contraption with them. This must be the action of his most celebrated song, 'The Old Tin Can', which he wrote and introduced in 1905. The composer of at least 250 other songs, including such whimsicalities as 'I Know Where the Flies Go' and 'I've Only Come Down for the Day', Mayo supplied Flanagan and Allen with one hit called 'Down and Out Blues', but in spite of his great success as a star who topped the bill, he never mastered the most difficult trick of all, which was to hang on to some of the money. A notorious gambler, he was bankrupted three times, and is said to have left this world holding exactly the same possessions as when he had entered it, all of which sounds very much like my family.

But to his distant descendent, by far the most significant things about him are his face and his voice. In that photograph, of the sad-eyed comic saddled with an old tin can, the line of resignation formed by the mouth, the disposition of the dimpled cheeks and the raised eyebrows, there is an echo of the corporate face of my father's family in its moments of exasperation with the world. Above all the eyes – slightly hooded, excessively bagged, with bright, dark, obviously brown irises – gazing out at the world with that air of comical disenchantment, they are the eyes of my aunts and uncles when they were trying to be dismissive. My father, had he ever resorted to stage make-up and sported a peaked cap, might easily have been taken for the comic in a dim light. Then there is the voice. Several of Mayo's recordings survive; indeed, one of them, 'Put That Gramophone Record On Again', was selected as the first example of coherent recorded vocal performance in 'The Wonder of the Age', a four-sided compilation illustrating the history of recorded sound, in which Mayo's overture heralds the arrival of Edison, Barnum, Bottomley, Gladstone, Florence Nightingale, Bernard Shaw, Arthur Sullivan and several others whose stage careers were less successful than Mayo's. The texture of his voice, the key in which it is pitched, its intonations and stresses, are all strongly reminiscent of the sound of smalltalk which comes floating back to me in waves of recollection, from my grandfather's workshop across the landing from the parlour, where the theme was racing, racing and racing, and where the ebb and flow of the voices followed with astonishing precision the nuances of Mayo's vocal style.

He died as late as 1938, and it suddenly occurs to me for the first time that perhaps on that night on the bus in Marylebone Road, returning home from an evening with Ernie Lotinga, the agency which so unexpectedly caused my father to put aside his paper and tell me about Mayo was an item in that paper reporting the old boy's death. It seems that he was as accomplished on the green baize as on the boards, and was several times Billiards champion of the music hall brotherhood. One afternoon in 1938 he was playing snooker in the Ascot Club in Charing Cross Road when he collapsed in mid-break. An ambulance rushed him to Charing Cross Hospital, but he was found to be dead on arrival. It is too late to administer the kiss of life, but I can at least, on behalf of his cousin my grandmother, my father and his musician manqué brothers, and all the rest of the clan which regarded its own component parts with such cavalier disdain, dedicate this book to him.

Benny Green
London, 1986

The rise of the music hall embodies one of the nicest ironies about the bibulous British, their discovery about half-way through the nineteenth century that man cannot live by booze alone and ought to spice his alcohol with a little rough art. The evolution of the public houses and supper rooms at the start of the Victorian age into the gilded palaces at the end of it is an evolution from eating and drinking, to eating and drinking to the incidental distraction of a singer or comic, to eating and drinking challenged as the main attraction by singers and comics, to professional entertainment at which food and drink were readily available, to professional entertainment patronised purely for its own sake. Anyone attempting to chart this process has to decide for himself at which precise point the old supper club or public house began to be recognisable as a music hall. Most historians settle for those West End boltholes immortalised by one of their most dedicated supporters, William Makepeace Thackeray. His particular favourites were the Coal Hole in the Strand, the Cyder Cellars in Maiden Lane, and especially Evans's Supper Rooms in Covent Garden. Not endowed with a particularly fascinating home life, Thackeray became reliant on such places for his socialising and entertainment, a nomadic clubman seeking out those all-male bastions where he could console himself with good food and good company, and even on occasion a good audience, for there were frequent nights when he would read extracts from work in progress to his closest cronies. Some say there was at least one instance of Thackeray actually writing material for the entertainers to sing.

Married to a Mermaid

There was a gay young farmer who lived on Salisbury Plain,
He loved a rich knight's daughter and she loved him again.
The knight he was distress-ed that they should sweethearts be,
So he had the farmer soon press-ed and sent him off to sea.
Singing Rule Britannia, Britannia rules the waves,
Britons never never never shall be married to a mermaid at the
    bottom of the deep blue sea.

'Twas on the deep Atlantic, midst equinoctial gales
This gay young farmer fell overboard among the sharks and whales.
He disappeared so quickly, so headlong down went he
That he went down a sight like a streak of light to the bottom of the
    deep blue sea.
Singing Rule Britannia, etc.

He said that as he went down, great fishes he did see,
They seemed to think as he did wink that he was rather free,
But down he went so quickly, saying 'Tis all up with me',
When he met the lovely mermaid at the bottom of the deep blue sea,
Singing Rule Britannia, etc.

ATTRIBUTED TO WILLIAM MAKEPEACE THACKERAY

1

Some of Thackeray's friends affected a mild distaste for such low haunts, but they found that if they desired Thackeray's company, then they had to accept the environment which went with it. John Cordy Jeaffreson (1831-1901) writes at great length about Thackeray in his memoirs, and although some of Thackeray's biographers have impugned both his motives and his accuracy, there is no mistaking the immediacy of his recollections.

I often met him on the pavements of the town, and when we met in a public thoroughfare he usually stopped to chat with me, and sometimes asked me to walk with him. It was at his request that I used to look for him at Evans's, when I was passing through or near Covent Garden at night, on my way to or fro between my home in Heathcote Street and the offices of the journals to which I contributed. Had he not asked me to seek him there, I should seldom have visited the supper room on the basement of Evans's Hotel, of which Thackeray was an habitué; for to me the hot, noisy cellar, in which journalists and gentlemen about town used to assemble and drink grog and toddy, and consume unwholesome suppers, when they should have been going to bed, was far from being a Cave of Harmony and Delight. Thackeray, on the contrary, enjoyed the music, the noise, and the hot smoky atmosphere of the crowded cellar, where Herr von Joel used to whistle and 'do the farm-yard' to the lively delight of young farmers from the country. Dropping into Evans's late for 'a finish' after 'the play', or a grand dinner or a rout, the author of *Vanity Fair* used also to go there early for the pleasure of hearing the musical boys sing glees, and madrigals, and quaint old ballads. He would listen to them song after song, for the hour – ay, for hours together, never speaking a word during the performances. Several of the singing-boys were church choristers and, in reference to their ecclesiastical employment, Thackeray once said to me, 'It does me more good to listen to them in this cellar than in Westminster Abbey.'

JOHN CORDY JEAFFRESON, *MEMOIRS*

Thackeray's first biographer was Herman Merivale (1836-1906), the son of one of the writer's close friends. Ill health prevented him from completing a life of Thackeray, but some of his work corroborates Jeaffreson's story.

When he treated boys, it was with no ungenerous views about bed. After the play he carried us off to Evans's to be greeted by Paddy Green with 'Dear boy, dear boy', to eat such baked potatoes as never have been baked since, and listen well into the small hours to the divine voices of the boys, in a framework of rich portraiture of bygone heroes of the stage. How Thackeray loved the boys' voices.

HERMAN MERIVALE

2

Evans's Supper Rooms were at 43 King Street, on the corner of the Covent Garden Piazza, part of the Grand, London's first family hotel. Evans, a one-time comedian at the Theatre Royal in Covent Garden, converted the hotel's great dining salon into a Supper Room, keeping it open each night into the small hours, and advertising his entertainment as of 'an erotic and Bacchanalian order'. The singers he hired were paid about one pound a week and free drink, but much of the vocalising was left to the patrons, who were generally only too eager to oblige. In spite of the claims to eroticism, the feature of the entertainment which gave Evans's some distinction was its comparative decorum, defined by one commentator as 'respectably bohemian'. On the programmes there appeared the Victorian London version of the later American invocation not to shoot the pianist, who was doing his best: 'Gentlemen are respectfully requested to encourage the Vocalists by attention, the Café part of the Rooms being intended for Conversational Parties'. The glees and madrigals which so delighted Thackeray usually came at the beginning of the recitals, whose second half was given over to a style of performance in distinct contrast.

The outstanding comedian of the day was Sam Cowell, the star of Evans's. He had a vivid personality. His father, the son of a colonel in the British Army, had been a popular actor in America, where Sam first appeared, and through his mother he was connected with the Siddons and Kemble families. 'Billy Barlow' was the song especially associated with his name; he also sang 'The Rat-Catcher's Daughter', 'Macbeth', 'Hamlet' and other doggerel burlesques. Other stars at Evans's included Charles Sloman, who was the original of Little Nadab in Thackeray's *The Newcomes*. His fame rested on his quickness in extemporising on any subject suggested by the audience. Then there was J. W. Sharp, who specialised in topical songs. At Evans's he got a pound a week and free drinks, but he made more by selling manuscript copies of his songs to the audience. There was also Sam Collins, the ex-chimney sweep, who made his first success at the Pantheon in Oxford Street in the early 1850s, and was to found the music hall which bore his name. Though London-born, he specialised in Irish songs, such as 'No Irish Need Apply', based on a supposed ban on Irish labour at the Great Exhibition. He became owner of the Welsh Harp at Hendon, the Rose of Normandy Tavern, which he turned into the Marylebone Music Hall, and the Lansdowne Arms at Islington, which he opened in 1862 as the Collins's Music Hall. He died in 1865, aged thirty-nine; his Irish hat and shillelagh are carved on his tombstone at Kensal Green. The epitaph reads:

> Farewell, good-natured, honest-hearted Sam,
> Until we meet before the Great I AM.

CHRISTOPHER PULLING, *THEY WERE SINGING*

Collins's early death was all too typical of the star turns of his generation. Even greater celebrity attached to Sam Cowell, who destroyed his own constitution with drink, and died in his forty-fifth year in of all places Blandford, in Dorset, to which he had been invited by a rural well-wisher anxious about the physical condition of the great comedian. Sam instantly became something of a landmark in that sleepy country town, bringing with him a lurid reputation, pervading its lanes and pothouses with a heady whiff of wicked metropolitan license. The waiters and chambermaids at the inn where he stayed 'regarded him with curiosity; the stablemen talked of him over their beer; his arrival made more or less sensation throughout the town'. It sounds rather like the setting for one of Dion Boucicault's town-and-country comedies of manners, except that this was grim reality and the hero died before the comedy could get under way.

In 1844 Evans retired and handed over control of the Rooms to one of his singers, John Greenmore, the Paddy Green of Merivale's reminiscence. In 1856 Greenmore reconstructed the place radically, converting the old hall into an art gallery featuring the work of Frith, Daniel Maclise, and the man often cited as the great-uncle of Sherlock Holmes, Horace Vernet (1789-1863). For the serious business of the evening Greenmore built a new hall with a raised platform on which the artists could enjoy the exaltation of elevation while performing.

The enlarged supper room was built in the garden at the rear of the hotel, and there under the blaze of gaslights from ten great chandeliers heavy suppers were consumed at 1 a.m. – chops and steaks and kidneys, poached eggs, oysters and Welsh rarebits. It was famous for its mealy potatoes baked in their jackets. Among the regular frequenters was Thackeray, who could walk along from the Garrick Club, just along the street. His Cave of Harmony in *The Newcomes* was probably a composite picture of Evans's and the Coal Hole, just as his Back Kitchen in *Pendennis* has been identified with the Cyder Cellars.

CHRISTOPHER PULLING, *THEY WERE SINGING*

Going to the play then, and to the pit, as was the fashion in those merry days, with some young fellows of my own age, having listened delighted to the most cheerful and brilliant of operas, and laughed enthusiastically at the farce, we became naturally hungry at twelve o'clock at night, and a desire for welsh-rabbits and good old glee singing led us to 'The Cave of Harmony', then kept by the celebrated Hoskins, among whose friends we were proud to count. We enjoyed such intimacy with Mr Hoskins that he never failed to greet us with a kind nod; and John the waiter made room for us near the President of the convivial meeting. We knew the three admirable glee-singers, and many a time they partook of brandy-and-water at our expense.

WILLIAM MAKEPEACE THACKERAY, *THE NEWCOMES*

Perhaps the most significant condition of all about life at Evans's, more telling than the food or the entertainment, was the fact that it was as resolutely all-male as any Gentleman's club. When in the late 1860s ladies were at last admitted, to boxes with latticework screens in front, business began to fall off. Then in 1872 a Licensing Act fixing 12.30 as the closing time for all public entertainments killed off what was a dying institution. In mourning their departure, posterity has often had the pleasure of measuring the real thing against projections of reality to be found in Thackeray. The young hero of *Pendennis* is a man-about-town with a tendency for crushes on fairly dissolute actresses. At a stage in his bachelor career when he ought to be concentrating on sterner matters, he reflects the tendencies of his creator by frequenting a supper room which appears to be a composite of Evans's and the Coal Hole.

. . . honest Mr Bows of the Chatteris Theatre, who was now employed as pianoforte player, to accompany the eminent lyrical talent which nightly delighted the public at the Fielding's Head in Covent Garden, and where was held the little club called the Back Kitchen. Numbers of Pen's friends frequented this very merry meeting. The Fielding's Head had been a house of entertainment almost since the time when the famous author of *Tom Jones* presided as magistrate in the neighbouring Bow Street; his place was pointed out, and the chair said to have been his, still occupied by the president of the night's entertainment. The worthy Cutts, the landlord of the Fielding's Head, generally occupied this post when not disabled by gout or other illness. His jolly appearance and fine voice may be remembered by some of my male readers. He used to sing profusely in the course of the harmonic meeting, and his songs were of what may be called the British Brandy-and-Water school of Song – such as 'The Good Old English Gentleman', 'Dear Tom', 'This Brown Jug', and so forth – songs in which pathos and hospitality are blended, and the praises of good liquor and the social affections are chanted in a baritone voice. The charms of our women, the heroic deeds of our naval and military commanders, are often sung in the ballads of this school; and many a time in my youth have I admired how Cutts the singer, after he had worked us all up to a patriotic enthusiasm, by describing the way in which the brave Abercromby received his death-wound, or made us join him in tears, which he shed liberally himself, as in faltering accents he told how autumn's falling leaf 'proclaimed the old man he must die' – how Cutts the singer became at once Cutts the landlord, and, before the applause which we were making with our fists on his table, in compliment to his heart-stirring melody, had died away, was calling, 'Now, gentlemen, give your orders, the waiter's in the room – John, a champagne cup for Mr Green. I think, sir, you said sausage and mashed potatoes? John, attend on the gentleman.'

WILLIAM MAKEPEACE THACKERAY, *PENDENNIS*

On the strength of passages like that, Thackeray is honoured as the literary patron saint of the old supper rooms, and rightly so. But in 1857 Dickens published *Little Dorrit*, whose heroine at one point visits the theatre where her uncle works as a musician in the pit orchestra. Most writers, then and since, have tended to assume that the life of the professional musician must be one endless whirl of pleasure. Just fancy, thinks the outsider in all his innocence, being paid a wage for so delightfully recreational a pursuit as playing tunes on an instrument. Dickens has been one of the very few novelists to perceive that music is a trade like any other, and that, so far from enjoying a life of subsidised self-indulgence, the professional musician might well come to regard the tools of his trade with the same weary distaste as that of the charlady for her mops and brushes. None of the members of Frederick Dorrit's family ever grasps this simple truth about him; when at last they come into their fortune and embark on the Grand Tour, they take care to include among old Frederick's luggage his clarinet, to be stuffed in his mouth in a crisis much as a solicitous parent might stuff a dummy into the mouth of a fractious baby. But Frederick would much rather be miserable than ever blow the thing again. He loathes that clarinet. He detests it with all the bitterness of a martyr who recognises it as the symbol of his long servitude. He wishes that the family had left either it or him behind. And the roots of his disenchantment lie in that orchestra pit where for interminable years he has sat in the shadows, puffing and squeaking his way through his life, utterly indifferent to what is going on just above his head. In a cheap, dusty, decrepit backstreet theatre whose fare could not have been so very far removed from what audiences might have found at the emergent music halls, Little Dorrit takes her seat, peers down into the pit and recognises her uncle . . .

. . . at the bottom of the well, in an obscure corner by himself, with his instrument in its ragged case under his arm.

The old man looked as if the remote high gallery windows, with their little strip of sky, might have been the point of his better fortunes, from which he had descended, until he had gradually sunk down below there to the bottom. He had been in that place six nights a week for many years, but had never been observed to raise his eyes above his music-book, and was confidently believed to have never seen a play. There were legends in the place that he did not so much as know the popular heroes and heroines by sight, and that the low comedian had 'mugged' at him in his richest manner fifty nights for a wager, and he had shown no trace of consciousness. The carpenters had a joke to the effect that he was dead without being aware of it; and the frequenters of the pit supposed him to pass his whole life, night and day, and Sunday and all, in the orchestra. They had tried him a few times with pinches of snuff offered over the rails, and he had always responded to this attention with a momentary waking up of manner that had the pale phantom of a gentleman in it: beyond this he never, on any occasion, had any other part in what was going on than the part written out for the clarionet; in private life, where there was no part for the clarionet, he had no part at all. Some said he was poor, some said he was a wealthy miser; but he said nothing, never lifted up his bowed head, never varied his shuffling gait by getting his springless foot from the ground.

CHARLES DICKENS, *LITTLE DORRIT*

Even as the supper rooms were drifting so nonchalantly towards their own extinction, the future of the music hall was already being secured by a man called Charles Morton, born in 1819 in Hackney, and dedicated since early youth, not to the cause of drink, but to the allure of entertainment. In his early twenties he became licensee of a public house in Pimlico, graduating to several other taverns before taking over the Canterbury Arms in Upper Marsh, Lambeth. Taking note that the premises included a parlour sometimes used for what was euphemistically described as 'Harmonic Meetings', Morton began installing those refinements which were eventually to lead to the great innovatory step of his life.

He first added several highly-polished Spanish mahogany tables, on which were many handsome brass candlesticks, with candles of the best wax, glasses for spills (and even for grog). These concerts here were at first held on Mondays and Saturdays, and were for 'Men Only'. The 'Sing-Song' or 'Free-and-Easy', however, soon proved so popular that mine host was ere long petitioned by his toiling clientele to provide a weekly Ladies' Night in order that the men-folk might bring their sweethearts and wives to add to the general joy, also to see how their lords and masters spent their evenings. In due course, therefore, the new proprietor instituted a series of 'Ladies' Thursdays', and highly successful the daring innovation became.

W. H. MORTON AND H. CHANCE NEWTON, *SIXTY YEARS' STAGE SERVICE*

Events were now beginning to move faster than Morton could keep up with. Already it was the entertainment rather than the drink which was making his public house more popular than the others. Already the idea that men should be able to drink in an exclusively male preserve was discredited. Already the premises were barely large enough to contain all the potential custom, nor specialised enough to accommodate performing artists as well as customers. Perceiving that he had perhaps stumbled on something quite new in popular entertainment-cum-catering, Morton now took that bold step which marks the birth of the genuine music hall as we tend to regard it. At the back of his tavern was some spare ground which had once been a skittle alley. On its site Morton speculated to the extent of building the Canterbury Hall, able to seat 700, with a platform at one end on which entertainers could perform. In this new venue ladies were allowed every night, a move which proved to accelerate Morton's fortunes. He opened his new hall on the most significant date in all the history of music hall, 17 May 1852.

'Give your orders, gentlemen, please!' The chairman cannot make himself heard. *'Orders, Gents.'* His tone insists that as the cost of the entertainment comes out of the sale of food and drink, there can be no more songs if there is no more supper. 'ORDERS, GENTS.' This is clearly a threat that unless tankards are more hastily emptied and refilled, he will stay the glees and catches. Somebody at his own table calms him by asking, yet again, what he will have; he answers, raps on the table with his hammer, and announces the next singer.

Most of the audience are tradesmen and mechanics; they smoke pipes, drink porter, and like to keep their money for their wives. But these Saturday nights at the Canterbury Arms, by the railway arch in Westminster Bridge Road, are so popular that the public house is crowded out. Charles Morton, the landlord, starts Thursday nights as well, and they too are crowded out. In less than a year he builds a hall over his skittle alley big enough for 700 people, admittance by ticket that pays for refreshment. It thrives so well it has to be grandly rebuilt. Henceforth the term 'music-hall' means the 'music hall of a tavern'. At the Canterbury music is taken very seriously – Gounod's *Faust* is sung for the first time in London, and Mme Tietjens comes to hear it.

M. WILLSON DISHER, WINKLES AND CHAMPAGNE

The admission to this Canterbury was by means of what was called a 'sixpenny refreshment ticket'. The new Mortonian hall – even at this low charge – of which, of course, part came back to the customer in drinks – was so great a success that after the first three months a sum was charged at the doors also. This sum was threepence per head, for any part of the house. Mr Morton's courteous consideration of the Dear Ladies soon began to place him somewhat in the position of the engineer who is hoist with his own petard. For, lo, the fair sex came in such abundance to the new Canterbury as to interfere somewhat with what is known in music hall establishments as the 'wet money'. The 'dry money' – the aforesaid threepences – was, of course, not sufficient of itself to pay for such a fine company as he now regularly engaged. He was therefore, he confessed, fain at times to descend to a little fiction, and to announce the Canterbury as being full, in order that gentlemen who had brought their feminine belongings might be sent off elsewhere in favour of gentlemen who had not been so gallant.

Soon Morton began to contemplate and to carry out a still larger and even more luxurious building. Thanks to the ingenious manager securing an equally ingenious architect and builder it was found possible to put up all the new stage and half the new hall without in any way interfering with the usual nightly entertainment. This half of the second Canterbury was therefore opened to the public on the Monday, as the first Canterbury was closed on the previous Saturday. Thus, the legend observed in sundry tavern windows, namely, 'Business carried on during alterations', was able to be utilised with especial emphasis on this occasion; and within a very short space of time the whole of Canterbury No. 2 was thrown open to the public. That is to say, on December 21st, 1856.

M. WILLSON DISHER, WINKLES AND CHAMPAGNE

In a relatively short span of time Morton had broken the two golden rules which had always obtained in haunts like Evans's and the Coal Hole. He had opened his doors to the ladies, and he had successfully established the precedent of charging an admission fee to people wishing to enjoy the entertainers. At the New Canterbury, the list of nightly attractions, the 'House Bill', was printed in much neater style than in any rival establishment, taking the form of a small book, complete with the lyrics of the glees and madrigals included. Before many weeks had passed, Morton's innovations had so dramatically transformed the public house into something subtly different that even the so-called respectable magazines began to acknowledge its existence.

Near the Bower Saloon in the Upper Marsh, has been erected the Canterbury Hall, one of a class of establishments affording the means of recreation for the respectable classes far above the entertainment proffered a few years since at establishments of this kind. The building is remarkable for its architectural merits, and the general propriety and beauty of its decorations. The distinguishing points are the careful blending of colour and the large amount of glass judiciously distributed over the building imparts lightness and character to a room of more than ordinary dimensions. The bas-relief at the further end of the room, effectively placed above the orchestra, is of tasteful design; the original drawing, by Mr Jeffs, a Belgian artist, was last year exhibited in the Royal Academy. The ventilation and lighting of the hall have been carefully superintended. The vast number of chandeliers are peculiarly graceful in form and character, and are by Messrs Weston and Curel. The musical entertainment which takes place nightly is under the careful control of Mr John Caulfield, late of the Haymarket Theatre. The customary evening attendance at this popular resort, we understand, extends to 1,000 persons.

ILLUSTRATED LONDON NEWS, DECEMBER 1856

A well-lighted entrance attached to a public-house indicates that we have reached our destination. We proceed up a few stairs, along a passage lined with handsome engravings, to a bar, where we pay sixpence if we take a seat in the body of the hall, and ninepence if we ascend into the gallery. We make our way leisurely along the floor of the hall, which is well lighted and capable of holding 1,500 people. A balcony extends round the room in the form of a horse-shoe. At the opposite end at that to which we enter is the platform, on which are placed a grand piano and a harmonium on which the performers play in the intervals when the previous singers have left the stage. The chairman sits just beneath them. It is dull work to him, but there he must sit drinking and smoking cigars from seven to twelve o'clock. The room is crowded, and almost every gentleman has a pipe or a cigar in his mouth. Evidently the majority present are respectable mechanics or small tradesmen with their wives and daughters and sweethearts. Now and then you see a midshipman, or a few fast clerks and warehousemen. Everyone is smoking, and everyone has a glass before him; but the class that comes here are economical, and chiefly confine themselves to pipes and porter.

J. E. RITCHIE, *THE NIGHT SIDE OF LONDON*

Among the other reputable magazines to nod approvingly in Morton's direction was *Punch*, whose correspondent, George Augustus Sala, dubbed the art gallery 'The Royal Academy over the Water'. Morton was tireless in his attempts to refine the amenities on offer; before long the gallery was also a reading-room of sorts. Soon his rivals were copying his every move, but at last he overstepped the bounds of the law, as his biographers describe.

It was open day and night – even on Sunday nights – to the public, who expressed themselves hugely delighted with this Fine Art Gallery, which was full of all kinds of provision for the comfort of patrons, including all sorts of amusing and instructive books, and all the current papers and periodicals, illustrated and otherwise.

On Sunday nights the number of visitors admitted on the then prevalent 'sixpenny refreshment ticket' was indeed very great. Quite a roaring trade was done in all kinds of 'creature comforts', which were dispensed at very moderate charges. For example, you could get a dozen native oysters and bread and butter for a shilling, and for the same sum the finest of chops and the flouriest of potatoes baked 'in their jackets'. Therefore it was not to be marvelled at that, in addition to the general public, such famous benefactors as Charles Dickens and William Makepeace Thackeray were wont to visit the Canterbury regularly, and to advertise far and wide its overwhelming superiority to the frowsy metropolitan 'Cider Cellars', and 'Coal Holes' of the period.

It is interesting to note that Preece at the Surrey Music Hall was advertising a 'Grand Picture Gallery' in 1853. This was also open on Sunday.

Morton's innovations were to bring him into trouble. In Christmas 1855 he produced a dramatic sketch *The Enchanted Hash*. This was a big success and envious local theatre managers instituted proceedings which ended in Morton being brought before the Magistrates. He was fined for allowing dialogue. The sketch had two speaking parts and infringed his licence, though later, when Edward Marshall, the star of *The Enchanted Hash*, played it as a 'one man show', speaking all the parts himself, nothing could be done to prevent it. Morton had trouble again with a condensed version of *The Tempest*. The magistrate went to see the offending piece and at the adjourned hearing announced: 'I am sorry, indeed, Mr Morton, to have to fine you for the production of such a splendid novel and pleasant entertainment. But the Law is very strong on this point; and enacts that you shall not perform a stage play, or any part of it, in an unlicensed place. . . . I must, therefore, fine you Five Pounds!'

Strangely enough, this decision, together with a full description of the entertainment, appeared in *The Times*, which had never before given any notice of any music hall. Moreover *The Times* had never inserted an advertisement of any such entertainment. Upon this, however, Morton offered *The Times* an advertisement, which was graciously accepted. In due course advertisements of other music halls were taken in that, and other papers; and thus Charles Morton became, as one may say, the pioneer of variety advertisements, as he had been the pioneer of the entertainments themselves!

W. H. MORTON AND H. CHANCE NEWTON, SIXTY YEARS' STAGE SERVICE

M orton invented something else too, something so vital to the concept of popular entertainment that it has survived even the demise of the music hall itself. He soon realised that if some performers are more gifted and more popular than others, then their advertised appearance at a hall might be a guarantee of packed houses. He had stumbled on the Star system, and once having perceived that it worked beautifully, began rewarding his leading attractions with a profligacy undreamed of in the old pound-and-all-you-can-drink days at Evans's. But the drink was still given free, if for a different reason.

There never has been another community like the old idols of the halls who drank champagne with princes in palaces, ate winkles with their old friends round street stalls, and among themselves swallowed champagne, whelks and winkles together. If kind hearts and simple faith are as precious as the poet declared them to be, these were the salt of mid-Victorian society. The *serio comic*, in her hours of ease, would not only smooth pillows, but scrub the floors for her sick friends, and the *lion comique* would fetch a sack of coal and another of potatoes in his own carriage-and-pair to an old penniless neighbour. That still happened in their hey-day in the 'nineties when Albert Edward, Prince of Wales, was glad to meet them, hear them sing, and give them jewelled tie-pins.

Among the *lions comiques* was the Great Vance, originally Alfred Peck Stevens, who walked out of a solicitor's office in Lincoln's Inn Fields and into a stage-door. When singing became more profitable than acting, he went on the boards with:

> I'm a chickaleery bloke with my one, two, three,
> Vitechapel was the willage I was born in ;
> To catch me on the hop, or upon my tibby drop,
> You must get up werry early in the morning.

That followed the Cockney style of Sam Cowell without any attempt to be leonine. The heavy swell who went on the spree was not invented until a mechanic from the Midlands came to London for work, sang in the East End as Joe Saunders, and was set by Charles Morton before the worshipping eyes of the Canterbury as George Leybourne or Champagne Charlie. On the stage he was as gilded as Lord Dundreary. Off the stage he was carried away by the industrial holiday fever of the wakes. 'The whole duty of man is to earn all he can in order to spend all he can,' would express his outlook on life. His year's engagement at the Canterbury at twenty-five pounds a week gave him a taste for champagne, a glistening topper, and a greatcoat with the largest fur collar in London. He rode with pretty creatures in his own carriage-and-pair – a carriage-and-four in times of advertisement. One of his rivals, to ridicule him, drove a cart and four donkeys.

In 'Champagne Charlie' he voiced sentiments so agreeable to rebels against Victorian respectability that his salary went up to £120 a week. Before his audience in the evenings he wore fantastic clothes of many colours, decorated his face with monocle and whiskers, and exhorted his hearers to be with the boys 'who make a noise from now till day is dawning'. At night he took his own advice. Every day was a holiday; his pockets filled as soon as they emptied.

The success of Vance, who imitated him with 'Clicquot, Clicquot, That's the Wine

11

for Me', increased his own. Together they went through the list with 'Moët And Chandon's The Wine For Me', 'Cool Burgundy Ben', 'Sparkling Moselle', and 'Our Glorious English Beer'. Then Vance began a craze for righteous fervour with 'Act On The Square, Boys, Act On The Square', one of many 'motto songs'. These were specially favoured by Harry Clifton, although he would unbend in 'The Weepin' Willer Or The Miller's Daughter', words and music by himself:

> Then she did prepare,
> Her mortal life to injure,
> Her head was bare and the colour of her hair
> Was a sort of delicate ginger——Auburn.

Harry Clifton had a holy fervour when singing about helping a weary brother in 'Pulling Hard Against The Stream', or loving your neighbour as yourself in 'Paddle Your Own Canoe'. Although there was a large number of comic songs in his repertoire, it was dominated by the exhortatory style of 'Work, Boys, Work, And Be Contented' and (still more unwearying in moral zeal) 'Try To Be Happy And Gay, My Boys'. This mood affected all the idols of the halls. They were strictly moral in principle, however reckless they might be in practice. Judged by virtues that are the heart's test, they were as good as bread.

Like the rest, Leybourne spent money as freely on the poor as on the champagne he drank out of pewter pots to wash down plates of whelks.

M. WILLSON DISHER, *WINKLES AND CHAMPAGNE*

Leybourne and Vance set the pace for each other, and it was generally agreed that honours were even. If Vance was the first to present the beau ideal of the music hall artist, it was Leybourne who became the great spokesman on behalf of champagne. Indeed, so potent was his effect on audiences that the firm of Moët & Chandon became his sponsors, providing him with a retainer and unlimited supplies of their product to be lavished by Leybourne on his audiences. But it was Vance who first created a neologism which soon passed into the common stock-pot of the English language and has remained there ever since.

Alfred Vance, ex-solicitor's clerk, was first with the stage portrait of the 'swell of the period'. Immaculate in dress and deportment, he was the Beau Brummell of the halls, with his fair hair, eyeglass, gold-knobbed cane, and jewellery. The tight trousers, crutch stick, and gold toothpick of the smart man-about-town gave such people the title 'the crutch and tooth-pick brigade', of whom Nellie Farren sang:

> How do you like London? How d'you like the town?
> How d'you like the Strand, now Temple Bar's pulled down?
> How d'you like the la-di-da, the toothpick, and the crutch?
> How did you get those trousers on, and did they hurt you much?

Vance satirised the type in such songs as 'The Style, by Jove!', 'The Young Man of the Day', 'The Languid Swell', 'The Dancing Swell', and 'The Continental Swell', and his fame was such that he was invited to Marlborough House by the Prince of Wales (later Edward VII). One of his best-known songs was 'Walking in the Zoo', sung by him in 1870. The Great Vance coined the word 'Zoo'; it affronted the Fellows, who up to then had always insisted on the full title 'Zoölogical Society's Gardens'; but what Vance said 'went' with the general public.

Ever since the Zoölogical Gardens had been opened in Regent's Park in 1827 Sundays were reserved for the Fellows and their guests: it was not until 1940 that the Zoo was thrown open to the general public on this day. Top-hats were a matter of unwritten law for those Sunday promenades, and Sunday passes were much sought after.

> The Stilton, sir, the cheese, the O.K. thing to do,
> On Sunday afternoon, is to toddle in the Zoo.
> Weekdays may do for Cads, but not for me and you,
> So, dress'd right down the road, we show them who is who.
>
> The walking in the Zoo, walking in the Zoo,
> The O.K. thing on Sunday is the walking in the Zoo,
> Walking in the Zoo, walking in the Zoo,
> The O.K. thing on Sunday is the walking in the Zoo.

M. WILLSON DISHER, *WINKLES AND CHAMPAGNE*

Although in retrospect the reputations of performers like Vance might seem to have been purely parochial, this appears not to have been the case. In the absence of those two deadly weapons of dissemination, the wireless and the gramophone, the repertoire of the *lion comique* still managed somehow to cross oceans and span continents. That most erudite and eminent of American literary critics, Edmund Wilson, always a man with an ear for the homely truths broadcast by the popular arts, offers proof of the international range of artists like Vance.

It comes back to me that Homer Collins, my father's devoted companion on his fishing expeditions, who had once been in the navy and had named his dog Funston after the general who had put down the Philippine rebellion and had captured their leader Aguinaldo, used to sing what must have been the most ancient comic song that I have ever heard at first hand. This song was popularised by 'The Great Vance' sometime after 1864:

> There is a school of jolly dogs,
> I've lately come across;
> They're game for any mortal thing,
> From this to pitch and toss.
>
> And they always seem so jolly, oh!
> So jolly oh! so jolly oh!
> They always seem so jolly oh!
> Wherever they may be.
> They dance, they sing, they laugh he, he,
> They laugh he, he, they dance, they sing,
> What jolly dogs are we!

Slap, bang, here we are again, here we are again,
Here we are again,
Slap, bang, here we are again,
What jolly dogs are we!

EDMUND WILSON, *UPSTATE*

S o pervasive is the image of Leybourne and Vance cheerfully singing of their own tendency to drunkenness on behalf of vested interests like Morton and the liquor trade that posterity is inclined to forget that not all the *lion comique* songs were about boozing. Not even the greatest performer can limit himself to a single recurring theme, and Vance, Leybourne and their imitators gradually began to extend the range of their repertoire.

Vance's principal rival was George Leybourne. Leybourne, a mechanic from the Midlands, was tall, handsome, elegant, with an infectious gaiety and charm. George Edwardes used to say that his personality would have been worth a thousand pounds a week to him at the Gaiety. He burst into fame in 1867 with 'Champagne Charlie', which started a series of competitive 'wine songs', Vance countering with 'Sparkling Moselle' and 'Clicquot, Clicquot, That's the Wine for Me' (to the tune of 'Funiculi Funicula'), Leybourne retaliating with 'Moët and Chandon', or 'Louis Renouf', or 'Pop, Pop, Pop, or Sparkling Wine,' while other favourite songs of his were 'Cool Burgundy Ben' and 'Lemonade and Sherry', a strange mixture which he assured his listeners was 'a first-class wet'.

They did not altogether neglect the tastes of the common man. Vance sang of 'Beer':

> The beer that you get
> When it's bitter and wet
> Is the same for a clerk and a peer.

It was the champagne-shippers, however, who subsidised the songs, making an allowance of twenty pounds a week to be spent at the bar on the brand to be popularised, and Leybourne soon developed the habit of calling for champagne on the slightest provocation. No wonder they burnt out their candles quickly!

A very popular song of Leybourne's, delivered in faultless evening dress, was 'After the Opera':

> After the opera's over,
> Attending the ladies is done,
> We gems of the very first water
> Commence with our frolic and fun.

The illustration on the cover of the song shows him sporting the long, flowing whiskers known as 'Piccadilly Weepers'.

14

He also sang 'I'm a Member of the Rollicking Rams':

> The only boys to make a noise
> From now till day is dawning;
> Out all night till broad daylight,
> And never go home till morning.

Vance capped this with 'The Roaring Boys'.
It was Leybourne who sang 'The Comet of the West; or, Stand Aside':

> I'm the Comet of the West;
> In the shade I put the rest;
> All others are my satellites, you see;
> But mooning's not my game;
> I've won my way to fame,
> And they all have to stand aside for me.
>
> Shout, boys, shout and let's be jolly;
> Stand aside and let this swell go past;
> I like to do the grand with a short cane in my hand,
> For, by Jove you see, the Comet's come at last.

M. WILLSON DISHER, *WINKLES AND CHAMPAGNE*

True to the pattern of the profession, neither Vance nor Leybourne lived into old age. Leybourne (1842-84) died having dissipated the enormous sums he earned as an entertainer. Vance, whose real name was Alfred Peck Stevens (1840-89), was a Londoner trained for a legal career; he collapsed and died on stage at the Sun Music Hall in Knightsbridge during a Boxing Day performance. Leybourne is generally credited with the lyrics of 'The Flying Trapeze', but all too often the writers of the popular songs of the period sold their work for a pittance, leaving the performers to take both the credit and the profit. In Leybourne's case, it seems likely that he did write those immortal words, 'that daring young man on the flying trapeze'. On the visit to the Alhambra in Leicester Square in 1860 of the great Leotard, half the town crowded in to see his act. Leybourne soon saw the possibilities in a song about this new sensation, and recruited his friend Alfred Lee to provide a melody. Posterity hopes that Lee was well rewarded for his part in the work. When he wrote his earlier hit, 'Champagne Charlie', he arrived in London with the manuscript early one morning, in so advanced a stage of penury that it was all he could do to find the small coin which could carry him through the toll gate at Waterloo Bridge. It was just as well that Leybourne was looking about for new themes to sing of, because it was not so long before the bottle-waving, glass-raising conventions of his type of entertainment were being made to seem quaint by younger artists looking further afield.

After a time the comic singers began to satirise and poke fun at the clerks and shopmen who made up the greater part of their audience. And so we come to songs like Nellie Power's 'The City Toff', with which she made a comeback in 1884, after seeming to have passed the zenith of her popularity. It was written by E. V. Page.

> Let me introduce a fellah,
> Lardy-dah! Lardy-dah!
> A fellah who's a swell, ah!
> Lardy-dah!
> Though limited his screw, yet
> The week he struggles through it,
> For he knows the way to do it,
> Lardy-dah! Lardy-dah!
> Yes, he knows the way to do 'the Lardy-dah!'
>
> He wears a penny flower in his coat, Lardy-dah!
> And a penny paper collar round his throat, Lardy-dah!
> In his hand a penny stick, in his mouth a penny pick,*
> And a penny in his pocket, Lardy-dah, Lardy-dah!
> And a penny in his pocket, Lardy-dah!

The crutch and toothpick had found their way down, it will be observed. That was before the days of 'male impersonators' wearing realistic male attire, and the cover of the song shows Nellie Power singing it in mauve tights and spangles, the whole crowned by one of the fashionable small curly-brimmed bowler-hats.

T. W. Barrett, who became known by the title of his song, 'The Nobleman's Son', sang:

> I tell them my father's a marquis,
> But wouldn't Society frown
> If they knew that he shaved for a penny a time
> In a little shop down Somers Town?
> I tell them he rides in his brougham,
> And is a big swell for the day;
> If they knew that my father
> Was Knight of the lather
> I wonder whatever they'd say!

Harry Rickards, who, after an up-and-down career, made a fortune as a manager in Australia, sang 'I Never Go East of Temple Bar' ('I stick to St James's and Belgravi-ah!') at the time when he was going through the bankruptcy courts. A voice from the 'gods' called out one night, 'How did you get to Basinghall Street, then?' – the site of the old bankruptcy court. Rickards had made an earlier success with 'Captain Jinks of the Horse Marines', first sung in 1870, which was immensely popular in America, and was quoted in a Senate debate, besides forming the title of Ethel Barrymore's first play:

> I'm Captain Jinks of the Horse Marines,
> I feed my horse on corn and beans,
> Which, of course, is a great deal beyond the means
> Of a Captain in the Army.

*The 'penny pick' was the Pickwick, the cheapest cigar in the glass-covered boxes on every tobacconist's counter.

M. WILLSON DISHER, *WINKLES AND CHAMPAGNE*

But what, meanwhile, had been happening to Morton? That restless spirit was hardly likely to sit back in the Westminster Bridge Road and watch an army of imitators stealing his thunder. Torn between pride at what he had initiated and dismay that the laurels might be snatched from him by those who had so speedily followed in his wake and who were learning so quickly from his mistakes, Morton decided that he must make further advances. For there could no longer be any doubt that as far as the drinking classes were concerned, Morton had started an avalanche.

Every publican would now try to lay violent hands on the building next door, whether workshop or stable-yard, school or church. No opera house was too grand for the purpose and no shanty too mean. Weston's was constructed out of the Holborn National School Rooms. The South London usurped the site of a Roman Catholic chapel. The London Pavilion had been a stable-yard until an exhibition of anatomical waxworks put a roof over it, and was next a skating-rink before the music hall chairman claimed it. Later, the Trocadero, named after a palace in the Paris Exhibition which had been named after a fort at Cadiz, took the place of the notorious Argyll Rooms at the top of the Haymarket. Even the Pantheon in Oxford Street, beneath whose eighteenth-century portico fifty gallants with drawn swords had escorted Mrs Baddeley from her sedan chair and forced the manager down upon his knees to crave pardon for barring actresses from the masquerades, was pressed into service.

M. WILLSON DISHER, *WINKLES AND CHAMPAGNE*

As every public house proprietor rushed to keep up with the new trend, a small but significant event took place in 1857 which spurred Morton to his next innovation. In that year a Holborn tavern called the Seven Tankards and Punch Bowl was transformed by a man called Edward Weston into Weston's Music Hall. Morton was quick to perceive this sudden westering drift of the business, and decided that the time was auspicious to attempt the realisation of the most grandiloquent of all his dreams, the conquest of the West End of London and its rich potential audiences, especially the ranks of the men-about-town and the sporting fraternity, groups which for the moment had no alternative for their nightly pleasures but the dying supper clubs. It was Morton who first saw that there was no good reason why the bohemian element should not mix with the respectable working classes in the same halls, and with this idea in mind he began to conduct a series of reconnaissances, all of them to the west of Weston's.

While thus prospecting, his attention was directed to the old Boar and Castle Inn, which stood near the junction of the Tottenham Court Road and Oxford Street, and with the adaptability of which to his requirements Mr Morton appears to have been immediately smitten. The inn formed one of those old roadside taverns which belonged essentially to the days of stage-coaches and post-chaises, and which the advent of the steam monarch had already begun to wipe out of existence. It dated back to a period prior to the Great Fire of London, when its spacious yard, around which ran the picturesque gallery peculiar to these old inns, doubtless afforded an excellent opportunity for the presentment of the theatrical and other entertainments which it was usual to give in these places. Down to the reign of Queen Anne, the inn retained all the characteristics of a genuine village hostelry and posting-house. Stage-coach drivers, postboys and carriers thronged its roomy yards, while the traveller found refreshment and accommodation after his twelve hours' tedious and rather hazardous journey from Oxford by the lumbering stage-waggon. Here nightly assembled the wit and wisdom of the rapidly growing district, with perhaps a 'gentleman of Oxford', or a Tony Lumpkin of the period come up from his paternal acres in some Buckinghamshire hamlet to 'see the town'. At this period the 'village' pound of St Giles stood nearly opposite the Boar and Castle, on the south side of the Oxford Road; and even at the end of the last century there might yet be seen from the back windows of the old hostelry such vestiges of rural scenery as an orchard, a pond, and a rustic windmill.

Mr Morton, it is perhaps unnecessary to say, took the first opportunity of acquiring the Boar and Castle, and on the ground mainly afforded by the old inn yard he built and opened on March 26th, 1861, the first Oxford music hall. The programme on that occasion contained the names of such prominent artistes as Mdlle Parepa, who afterwards became the wife of the late Carl Rosa, Mdlle Manietta, Miss Poole, Miss Russell, Miss Ernst and Miss Rosina Collins. In addition there were Messrs Santley, Swift, Genge, G. Kelly, C. Greville, Levy Hime and Jonghmann. Mr Sims Reeves, too, was offered his own terms to come and sing on that occasion, but although at first the celebrated tenor appeared to entertain Mr Morton's liberal proposal, he subsequently thought fit to decline it, expressing, however, at the same time, the greatest interest in the undertaking.

The first Oxford hall, in point of architectural beauty, was one of the finest then existing. It was a handsome structure, forty-one feet high, with a total length of ninety-four feet. One of its chief features was the system of lighting employed, which consisted of twenty-eight brilliant 'crystal' stars, a novelty thought very charming and effective in its day, but which was shortly afterwards superseded by four large chandeliers suspended from the roof, with smaller ones in the galleries. To the Oxford belongs the unenviable distinction of being the first London music hall to be destroyed by fire. Early in the morning of the 11th of February 1868, the night-watchman discovered that a fire had broken out in a corner of the gallery on the Oxford Street side. The fire was confined to the hall itself, and although some damage was sustained by their contents, the several promenade bars, supper-room, entrance hall, and even the private boxes in the gallery were not substantially injured; but the fine plate glass mirror fixed at the back of the stage, and which was a feature in the building, was totally destroyed. The hall was reconstructed and again opened to the public on the 9th August 1869.

W. H. MORTON AND H. CHANCE NEWTON, *SIXTY YEARS' STAGE SERVICE*

At Morton's Oxford there was a proper stage, but in the main body of the hall, with its brilliant gas-lighting, the restaurant element continued: there was a substantial 'ordinary', price half-a-crown, which included admission to the variety show; the bars and barmaids also were a feature. Morton revived the part-singing and operatic elements of the earlier tavern concerts, engaging Emily Soldene, later to star in opera bouffe under him at the Philharmonic, and Charles Santley, the baritone, to sing. (He wanted Sims Reeves, who had sung both at the Grecian and at the Canterbury under an assumed name.)

CHRISTOPHER PULLING, *THEY WERE SINGING*

Bars down the side were dressed with plenty of flowers, coloured glass, and any amount of bright, glittering, brass-bound barrels and bottles. But, after all, the brightest, most glittering, and most attractive thing about the bars, not counting the drinks, were the barmaids. Rows of little tables, at which people sat and smoked, and drank, filled the auditorium, and in and out the tables circulated the peripatetic, faded, suggesting, inquiring, deferential waiter, and the brisk, alert, 'cigar', 'programme' and 'book of words' boy. Many a night have I, by request, sung 'Home, Sweet Home' because I made them cry.

EMILY SOLDENE, *MY THEATRICAL AND MUSICAL RECOLLECTIONS*

So the Oxford remained until one February night in 1868. Charles Morton, while passing that way by chance, saw in a window the beginnings of a blaze that burned the building down.

M. WILLSON DISHER, *WINKLES AND CHAMPAGNE*

By this time a third great *lion comique* had arrived to eclipse the fame of Vance and Leybourne. Born in 1845 as G. H. Farrell, he had gone to work as a bricklayer and then as a seaman. At this point, he dropped the surname and used his two Christian names as a new identity, Gilbert Hastings, in preparation for his new career as an actor. From treading the boards he graduated to authorship, after which he became a well-known stage manager at the Grecian, the Britannia and the Islington Grand. He then blossomed as a music-hall singer, from which eminence he drifted into music-hall management and at last became an agent. But it was his spell as a professional singer that pushed him into the annals of social history as 'the Great Macdermott'. His fame was intimately linked with a songwriter called G. W. Hunt, a tiny man with the moustache of a very large one. He too had acquired experience as a music-hall manager, but in 1877 he became one of the most successful of popular composers with 'Dear Old Pals', a sentimental ballad whose clammy sentiments were a considerable departure for Macdermott, who up to this point had been noted for his lampooning of topical personalities. One of his earlier satires, called 'Captain Criterion', a joke at the expense of bibulous army officers, was considered so cutting that it was surreptitiously censored out of existence.

For I'm Captain Criterion of London,
Ready and never afraid.
Whenever some new juggins is d——d well done,
It's sure to be by one of our brigade.

The American long bar at the Criterion was famous – or infamous – for its *habitués*, and Cecil Raleigh composed some verses upon it which Teddy Solomon, a musician of no small ability and a popular figure of old Pelican Club days, set to a catchy air, and which, as sung at the Pavilion by Macdermott, at once caught the town. The words were a little too pointed in the estimation of Messrs Spiers and Pond, who bought the rights and killed the song.

J. B. BOOTH

It was Macdermott's good fortune to become the first music-hall star to establish what a later age would come to define as a hit song. In 1877 the knockabout farce referred to by historians as Russian foreign policy caused British public opinion to become faintly hysterical. By threatening to invade Constantinople on some trumped-up pseudo-religious pretext, the Russian bear was thought to be imperilling British control over the Mediterranean. The songwriter Hunt, his huge moustaches bristling in a frenzy of patriotic passion as he read his newspaper in bed one morning, sensed that the moment was ripe for an anti-Russian ditty. He then wrote his song very quickly and dashed round to Macdermott's house waving it like a banner. But Macdermott was still in bed, and so disinclined to listen to new songs before breakfast that when Hunt started to sing at him, Macdermott flung a boot at his head. But the persistent Hunt at last had his way, and Macdermott, who was by this time earning £100 a week, generously dipped deep into his wallet and paid Hunt one whole guinea for the song.

[It had] so strong an influence over the public that historians have noted it. In his *Disraeli*, D. L. Murray describes how the Tory Government triumphantly carried their vote of credit for six millions through Parliament to oppose Russia in the Near East, while 'in the Pavilion Music Hall the glasses leapt and rattled, and in all the streets the errand-boys went whistling truculently to the lilt of a new song'. It began:

> The Dogs of War are loose and the rugged Russian Bear,
> Full bent on blood and robbery has crawled out of his lair,

declared:

> As peacemaker Old England her very utmost tried,
> The Russians said they wanted peace, but then those Russians lied,
> Of carnage and of trickery they'll have sufficient feast,
> Ere they dare to think of coming near our Road unto the East,

and accused the Cossacks of atrocities in verses that fired patriots to sing the chorus:

> We don't want to fight, but by Jingo if we do,
> We've got the ships, we've got the men, and got the money too,
> We've fought the Bear before, and while we're Britons true,
> The Russians shall not have Constantinople.

At the time of Turkish successes Hunt prepared a new version in the autumn of 1877, with the last line of the chorus changed to 'The Turks have proved so true, the Russians can't get near to Constantinople'. But when the tide of battle turned, the singer revived the first version before bringing out a sequel, answering those who 'sneer about Jingoes' with 'If it's Jingo to love honour, then Jingoes sure are we', to the refrain of:

> So we're waiting for the signal; directly up it runs,
> Clear the decks for action, stand by the guns,
> Our Army and our Navy, true British dogs of war,
> Will make them cry 'Peccavi', the same as they did before.

20

Starting up-stage, Macdermott would come down to the footlights 'in a series of dramatic little hops', each hop emphasising bulldog determination which culminated in a threatening gesture at 'Shall not have Constantinople'. There were riots. Mobs sang 'By Jingo If We Do' in the streets, at peace meetings, and outside Gladstone's house before smashing the windows. The composer, who was called 'Jingo' Hunt until after his death over a quarter of a century later, has been credited with having coined that exclamation. It had been in use for centuries, and not he, but political opponents, gave 'Jingo' and 'Jingoism' their present meanings.

M. WILLSON DISHER, *WINKLES AND CHAMPAGNE*

But for all the furore, it should not be assumed that this was the music hall's last word on the crisis. This irreverent institution had already developed the convention of taking hold of its own biggest successes and lampooning them without mercy. Jingo Hunt's song for Macdermott had hardly begun to echo across the land before the comedian Herbert Campbell had parodied its sentiments with:

> I don't want to fight, I'll be slaughtered if I do,
> I'll change my togs, I'll sell my kit, and pop my rifle too;
> I don't like the war, I ain't a Briton true,
> And I'll let the Russians have Constantinople.

By now also, the performers and writers were using the social history of the moment in their work, reflecting trends in art, literature and drama. There is a good case to be made, for instance, that the halls saw comic potential in the posturing of the Aesthetes before Gilbert and Sullivan's *Patience*. But the Gilbertian touch can be seen clearly enough in the rhyming conventions of several songs popularised in the halls.

Macdermott's song 'Hildebrandt Montrose' (actually written and originally sung by Arthur Lloyd) dates from the seventies, and shows that the æsthetic movement of the pre-Raphaelites, Whistler, and Japanese art – the men's velvet coats, lace collars *à la* Little Lord Fauntleroy, knee-breeches, long hair, and broad-brimmed hats – had become a target for popular ridicule, if not resentment, before Gilbert's *Patience* in 1881 satirised Wilde in Bunthorne and the 'greenery-yallery' young man. The song which Macdermott sang in the halls stressed the fake in the assumed character:

> His scarf, unlike himself, is green,
> His gloves, 'no kid', are yeller,
> His washed-out pants are well strapp'd down,
> He carries a 'fake' umbrella.
> His hair is in Barber's ringlets,
> His eyes are made up dark,
> He walks upon his uppers
> While strolling in the park.

'*Au revoir*, ta ta!' you'll hear him say
To the Marchioness Clerkenwell while bidding her good-day.
'I'll strike you with a feather, I'll stab you with a rose,
For the darling of the ladies is Hildebrandt Montrose.'

The term 'masher', which came from America, belongs to the eighties. Charles Godfrey's 'Masher King', first sung at the London Pavilion in 1886, was another skit on the æsthete, delineated in George du Maurier's *Punch* drawings of Postlethwaite. The cover of Godfrey's 'Masher King' shows him in a velvet dress-suit with knee-breeches.

I used to be steady, I used to be staid,
And my toys were all bought in the Lowther Arcade;
I'd sit at the feet of my dearest Mama,
And recite little poems to fondest Papa;
Or go with my sister for walks in the park,
And get home quite an hour before it grew dark.
But now that's all changed, that is easy to tell;
I'm the latest invention, the Masher, the Swell!

I'm a strut up the Strand-ity, cane in my hand-ity,
Doing the grandity swellah;
Very much baronly, see Nellie Farrenly,
Row with the cab-ity fellah.
Smoke a cigar-ity, with the Majah-ity,
Dwiddle and dwaddle and dwawl;
I'm a rickity, rackity, trickity, trackity,
Prize-medal mashah of all!

George Byford parodied Godfrey's song with the 'Broken-down Masher'. ('I'm the used-up invention, the once Masher Swell'):

I'm a gone to the deuce-ity, not any use-ity,
Show flag of truce-ity fellah;
Crawl up the Strand-ity, matches in hand-ity;
'Pipe light, sir?' loudly I call.
Wear shabby clothes-ity, boots without toes-ity,
Cold in my dose-ity Swellah;
Wash at a pump-ity, doss in the lump-ity,
Bottled-up Masher of all.

M. WILLSON DISHER, *WINKLES AND CHAMPAGNE*

As the scope and popularity of the music hall extended, Charles Morton ironically was drifting away from it into what is sometimes laughingly defined as the legitimate theatre. It was almost as though having thrust his foot in the door of the West End by opening the Oxford, his ambition was revealed, not as wishing to establish music hall in central London but as wishing to establish himself there. After the débâcle of the fire, Morton pursued a succession of hares which, notable or not, had little to do with what he had instigated at the Canterbury Arms.

His next adventure (after the Oxford fire) was the North Woolwich Gardens, where 'he made and lost a lot of money', to use his own words. Then, in partnership with Mr Chas. Head, Mr Morton took the Philharmonic Hall, Islington, just vacated by the late Mr Sam Adams, and produced a version of *Chilperic*, which at once provoked litigation, instigated by theatrical managers. In order to regulate their position, Mr Head and Mr Morton turned the Philharmonic into a theatre, and produced an interesting series of opéra-bouffes, beginning with *Geneviève de Brabant*. A subsequent production was *La Fille de Madame Angôt*, which, in partnership with the late Mr John Hollingshead, Mr Morton brought into the Strand. Leaving Islington he interested himself in one theatrical adventure after another in the West End, and went to America in the pursuit of his business. In the Autumn of 1877 he was appointed manager of the Alhambra. His first production, in November, 1877, was a revival of *La Fille de Madame Angôt*, with Selina Dolaro for his prima donna. In December, 1882, the Alhambra was burned down. Mr William Holland had meanwhile become manager, and Mr Morton joined Mr Sefton Parry at the newly built Avenue Theatre, when again opéra-bouffe was the attraction. In the following autumn Mr Morton resumed the position of acting-manager at the New Alhambra, and here he remained until 1891, when he undertook the management of the reconstituted Tivoli in the interest of the Newsom-Smith Syndicate. His retirement from the Alhambra was the occasion of a gigantic benefit performance at which most of the celebrities in the theatrical and musical professions lent a willing hand.

The appointment of Mr Morton to manage the Palace, on its failure as an English Opera House, was the crowning point of his career. It was also a just tribute to his abilities and character. Under his management the Palace has become an institution quite by itself. The Palace audience is the most thoughtful audience in London. Hence the South African War, which told terribly on other variety houses, was a gold mine to the Palace. Mr Morton did not lose his head. He engaged Mrs Tree to recite 'The Absent-Minded Beggar' at £100 a week, and her salary and any contributions made during the evening went to swell the fund for the men at the front. He steered clear of all party questions, and his house was not divided against itself. He reproduced, too, by means of a biograph, the very best films procurable from the front. People who were not going out to the ordinary place of entertainment went to the Palace for information, well knowing that whatever their politics and feelings there they would be respected.

Mr Morton could never have done the work he did without the exercise of care and self-control. He was almost an abstainer, he was almost a vegetarian, and almost if not quite, a non-smoker. His life was of the simplest. His only indulgence was Ascot. He rarely, if ever, took a cab, and his greatest luxury was the cup of tea or cocoa and the single biscuit, which at half-past nine were always placed on the little table by which he, attired in a neat but rather old-fashioned dress suit, sat in the promenade. His short, spare figure was wonderfully agile up to nearly the end: he thought nothing when eighty-three of running upstairs to the topmost dressing-rooms two or three times in the course of the evening. Almost if not the very last time he was present at the Palace was on 11 August. It was the eighty-fifth anniversary of his birthday. All the evening telegrams of congratulation came pouring in; at some which came unexpectedly from friends whom the world once knew but has long forgotten he was visibly affected. He seems to have contracted a chill during that evening. He took to his bed. It was soon manifest that his work was done, and he resigned his post.

The management of the Palace Theatre, having made arrangements for a matinée performance as a farewell testimonial to Mr Morton, has decided that, notwithstanding his lamented death, the performance shall be given and the proceeds presented to Mrs Morton as a testimonial of the esteem and regard in which her husband was held.

W. H. MORTON AND H. CHANCE NEWTON, *SIXTY YEARS' STAGE SERVICE*

Morton had lived to see his modest innovations in the Westminster Bridge Road flower into the leading form of popular entertainment in Britain. Even more significant, the airs and vocabulary of the music hall world had so permeated the national consciousness that the better-known songs soon became symbols of a good time, of a night on the town, of a laugh and a drink. Like great secular hymns, they gave solace to the troubled. When Morton had so innocently attempted to elevate the tone of the bill at the old Canterbury by introducing Gounod's *Faust* he could hardly have suspected that a generation later, tribute would come from the most riotously successful comic book of the later Victorian age.

I began to get nervous myself. I looked again at the map. There was Wallingford lock, clearly marked, a mile and a half below Benson's. It was a good, reliable map; and besides, I recollected the lock myself. I had been through it twice. Where were we? What had happened to us? I began to think it must all be a dream and that I was really asleep in bed, and should wake up in a minute, and be told it was past ten.

I asked my cousin if she thought it could be a dream, and she replied that she was just about to ask me the same question; and then we both wondered if we were both asleep, and if so, who was the real one that was dreaming, and who was the one that was only a dream; it got quite interesting.

I still went on pulling, however, and still no lock came in sight, and the river grew more and more gloomy and mysterious under the gathering shadows of night, and things seemed to be getting weird and uncanny. I thought of hobgoblins and banshees, and will-o'-the-wisps, and those wicked girls who sit up all night on rocks, and lure people into whirlpools and things; and I wished I had been a better man, and knew more hymns; and in the middle of these reflections I heard the blessed strains of 'He's got 'em on', played badly on a concertina, and knew that we were saved.

I do not admire the tones of a concertina, as a rule; but oh! how beautiful the music seemed to us both then – far, far more beautiful than the voice of Orpheus or the lute of Apollo, or anything of that sort could have sounded. Heavenly melody, in our then state of mind, would only have still further harrowed us. A soul-moving harmony, correctly performed, we should have taken as a spirit-warning, and have given up all hope. But about the strains of 'He's got 'em on', jerked spasmodically, and with involuntary variations, out of a wheezy accordion, there was something singularly human and reassuring.

The sweet sounds drew nearer, and soon the boat from which they were worked came alongside us.

It contained a party of provincial 'Arrys and 'Arriets, out for a moonlight sail. (There was not any moon, but that was not their fault.) I never saw more attractive, lovable people in all my life. I hailed them, and asked if they could tell me the way to Wallingford lock: and I explained that I had been looking for it for the last two hours.

'Wallingford lock!' they answered. 'Lor' love you, sir, that's been done away with for over a year. There ain't no Wallingford lock now, sir. You're close to Cleeve now. Blow me tight if 'ere ain't a gentleman been looking for Wallingford lock, Bill.'

I had never thought of that. I wanted to fall upon all their necks and bless them; but the stream was running too strong just there to allow of this, so I had to content myself with mere cold-sounding words of gratitude.

We thanked them over and over again, and we said it was a lovely night, and we wished them a pleasant trip, and, I think, I invited them all to come and spend a week with me, and my cousin said her mother would be so pleased to see them. And we sang the 'Soldier's Chorus' out of *Faust*, and got home in time for supper after all.

JEROME K. JEROME, *THREE MEN IN A BOAT*

As a young actor-turned-journalist, Jerome was conversant with the nuances of the music hall, and had, on one famous occasion, been present at an historic incident when one of the performers, baited by a member of the audience, had turned upon him and casually dismembered him. Jerome turned up one night at the Star, Bermondsey, where a change in the programme had been made at the last minute, a local favourite dropping out and her place taken by a Hoxton rabbit-skinner called Bessie Bellwood. Miss Bellwood, whose real name was Mahoney, was announced by the chairman that night as Signorina Ballatino, the world-famous performer of the zither.

To a large coalheaver who at once protested, the chairman said, 'You sir, in the flannel shirt. I can see you. Will you allow this lady to give her entertainment?' 'No', was the answer.

'Then sir,' said the chairman, 'you are no gentleman.' The signorina took charge. Telling the chairman to shut up if that was all he could do, she came down to the footlights. Jerome goes on:

'Thereupon ensued a slanging match the memory of which sends a thrill of admiration through me even to this day. It was a battle worthy of the gods. He was a heaver of coals, quick and ready beyond his kind. But as well might the lamb stand up against the eagle when the shadow of its wings falls across the green pastures, and the wind flies before the dark oncoming. At the end of two minutes he lay gasping, dazed and speechless.'

After announcing her intention of 'wiping down the bloomin' 'all' with him, and making it respectable, she began, and the people sitting near him drew away, leaving him alone, surrounded by 'space and language'. She spoke for five and three-quarter minutes by the clock without a pause. Jerome says:

'At the end, she gathered herself together for one supreme effort, and hurled at him an insult so bitter with scorn, so sharp with insight into his career and character, so heavy with prophetic curse, that strong men drew and held their breath while it passed over them, and women hid their faces and shivered. Then she folded her arms and stood silent, and the house, from floor to ceiling, rose and cheered her until there was no more breath left in its lungs.'

M. WILLSON DISHER, *WINKLES AND CHAMPAGNE*

Miss Bellwood became, in her short, rowdy life, a legendary blasphemer adored for her charitable instincts. She would think nothing of giving her money away to those who needed it more, and she never stood on ceremony or bothered with the niceties of protocol. Her most famous song, composed by herself, went:

> What cheer, Riah!
> Riah's on the job.
> What cheer, Riah!
> Did she speculate a bob?
> Now Riah she's a toff,
> And she looks immensikoff,
> So it's what cheer, Riah, Riah,
> Hi! Hi! Hi!

This song, which depicts the plight of a seller of vegetables stepping out into society, was received in at least two different ways by the same audience.

Riah is very self-conscious that she is stepping out, not merely in the sense of stepping out for an evening, but also overstepping those indefinable but rigid boundaries that confine her to a particular way of life; and it is her own friends as well as the toffs who make her attempt to step briefly into another kind of society impossible. It would be silly to be portentous about Riah's ejection from the floor of the hall, but the fact that she doesn't fit is the theme of the song. It is significant that though she behaves with decorum – and she comically proves the fitness of her dress for the occasion by directing the audience's attention to 'these wery clothes you see' – it is everyone else who makes her position intolerable. There is too, a subtle – perhaps a sly – difference between the reactions of those in the gallery and those on the floor of the hall. Her friends up aloft still see her as one of them, and though she chaffs them back (and 'chaff' gives the right tone of jolly teasing, as well as being, for an audience of the time, a delightful understatement of Bessie's power of repartee), their horseplay makes it too warm for her so she begins to beat a discreet retreat. It is then that we have the pointed contrast between the behaviour of friends and toffs. The blame for the incident is put squarely on Riah. It is a comic song, yet in the song and the patter, the conflict of the classes is sharply presented.

PETER DAVISON, *THE BRITISH MUSIC HALL*

The fame of Bessie and her best-known song spread rapidly into every corner of the country. It became fashionable to be *au fait* with what Bessie did in the song, and nowhere was curiosity about the act more rampant than in those very sections of smart society which Miss Belwood was castigating.

Word was brought that Princess Louise and other members of the Court were just dying to hear her sing. A charity matinée was organised for the purpose, at the house of an enthusiast whose husband objected so strongly that he had himself locked in his library. When Bessie arrived bedraggled, the butler gazed at her in horror until she examined him with care and said sorrowfully, 'Gor' blimey! Where *'ave* they found it?' To see if he was real, she pinched his legs and stuck a pin through his wig, until he screamed like a frightened child and lost the key of the library.

'Surely a Jekyll and Hyde among comediennes', was how Arthur Roberts described her. Among the poor she was known for her kindness of heart in giving them literally all her worldly goods, nursing the sick, washing and scrubbing for them, and paying to have masses sung for the souls of the dead.

M. WILLSON DISHER, *WINKLES AND CHAMPAGNE*

It is clear enough from accounts of her private behaviour as well as her public persona that Bessie when she stepped on to the stage was merely presenting a cleverly heightened version of her true personality. Most of the anecdotes about her symbolise the confrontation between the classes which lies at the heart of 'What cheer, Riah!' The pinching of the butler's legs is one example, but there is another, altogether more extraordinary, which shows how the successful music-hall artist was able to span the social abyss which so routed poor Riah.

Little is remembered of Bessie Bellwood because her fame has been overshadowed. But she was the rowdiest daredevil of the lot. Within four hours of a conversation with Cardinal Manning about some Catholic charity, she was arrested for knocking a cabman down in Tottenham Court Road because he had insulted, or rather because she fancied he had insulted, her man.

M. WILLSON DISHER, *WINKLES AND CHAMPAGNE*

One of Bessie's friendly professional rivals was Jenny Hill, 'the Vital Spark', whose reputation grew to the point where New York demanded her appearance there. In order to arrange this engagement, the American showman Tony Pastor came to London, and was invited to a party at the Hermitage, the Streatham farm which Miss Hill had bought. Again, Miss Bellwood could not resist the desire to show the comic truculence of the lower orders when confronted by the niceties of polite behaviour.

To the Hermitage that summer Sunday went every music-hall celebrity of the day. The arrivals began at ten o'clock in the morning, and everyone was greeted under the Stars and Stripes with a freshly opened pint of champagne. There was a luncheon; there was afternoon tea in the grounds, there was a dinner, with many speeches, and there were early morning travellers to London by the workmen's trains. But, indeed, there was no note so human as Bessie Bellwood's shriek of delight when she heard a hawker crying winkles down the lane. His stock, on a japanned tea-tray slung round his neck, was promptly commandeered. The shocked footman, handing round tea, was despatched for pins; and the immortal singer of 'Wot cheer, Riah', whose real name was Mahoney, and who claimed to be a descendent of Father Prout but who, most certainly, began life as a rabbit-skinner in the New Cut, carefully divided her spoils among many applicants.

H. G. HIBBERT, *FIFTY YEARS OF A LONDONER'S LIFE*

In 1896 Bessie died at the age of thirty-nine, her reputation destined to be eclipsed by the great stars of the coming golden age of the music hall. She is remembered for her one nationally renowned song, and for a few spectacular acts of public defiance, the most celebrated of which was her acceptance of a wager that she would not run across the stage of the Tivoli without her skirt and petticoats. She performed the deed, telling 'the boys' as she did so to take no notice of her round-the-houses.

The realism lying just beneath the surface of songs like 'What cheer, Riah' is obvious enough to a later age, but very often the topical overtones of a popular song have been lost through the understandable selectivity of amateur singers who concentrate on the famous chorus at the expense of the more obscure verses. In his immortal celebration of the Thames, Jerome K. Jerome hints at this aspect of the popular songs of the day without bothering to be explicit. The three men in their boat, to say nothing of the dog, are almost at the end of their odyssey when George decides to serenade his fellows with a little banjo recital.

I will say for George that he did not want any pressing. There was no nonsense about having left his music at home, or anything of that sort. He at once fished out his instrument and commenced to play 'Two Lovely Black Eyes'. I had always regarded 'Two Lovely Black Eyes' as rather a commonplace tune until that evening. The rich vein of sadness that George extracted from it quite surprised me. The desire that grew upon Harris and myself, as the mournful strains progressed, was to fall upon each other's neck and weep; but by great effort we kept back the rising tears, and listened to the wild yearnful melody in silence. When the chorus came we even made a desperate effort to be merry. We refilled our glasses and joined in; Harris, in a voice trembling with emotion, leading, and George and I following a few words behind:

> Two Lovely Black Eyes,
> Oh! What a surprise!
> Only for telling a man he was wrong,
> Two –

There we broke down. The unutterable pathos of George's accompaniment to that 'two' we were, in our then state of depression, unable to bear. Harris sobbed like a child, and the dog howled till I thought his heart or his jaw must surely break. George wanted to go on with another verse. He thought that when he had got a little more into the tune and could throw more 'abandon', as it were, into the rendering, it might not seem so sad. The feeling of the majority, however, was opposed to the experiment. There being nothing else to do, we went to bed.

JEROME K. JEROME, *THREE MEN IN A BOAT*

Had George been allowed to proceed to further verses, he would have told his sobbing companions of a sad tale of political intolerance. The song was written in 1886 at a moment when Mr Gladstone was under acute pressure to resign from the premiership in the wake of his unsuccessful attempt to give a measure of Home Rule to Ireland. At last he did indeed resign and the Home Rule cause was shoved aside for a few more years. In the song the recipient of the two black eyes acquires them through an inability to distinguish a diehard from a Home-Ruler:

> Strolling so happy down Bethnal Green,
> This gay youth you might have seen,
> Tompkins and I with his girl between,
> Oh, what a surprise.
> I praised the Conservatives frank and free,
> Tompkins got angry so speedily.
> All in a moment he handed to me
> Two Lovely Black Eyes.

The familiar chorus follows, after which the singer describes his attempts at his own political reform:

> Next time I argued I thought it best
> To give the Conservative side a rest.
> The merits of Gladstone I freely pressed,
> When, oh, what a surprise!
> The chap I had met was a Tory true,
> Nothing the Liberals right could do.
> This was my share of that argument too,
> Two Lovely Black Eyes.

29

What have his experiences taught him? That nihilism is best:

> The moral you've caught I can hardly doubt.
> Never on politics rave or shout.
> Leave it to others to fight it out,
> If you would be wise.
> Better, far better it is to let
> Lib'rals and Tories alone, you bet,
> Unless you're willing and anxious to get
> Two Lovely Black Eyes.

The composer, Charles McCullam, had begun as a singing waiter and chucker-out at the Alhambra, in the Isle of Dogs. Typically the germ of the idea for the song had been a satiric one.

For over sixty years Charles Whitton McCullam has been known to the public as Charles Coburn. For just on fifty of them he has been singing 'Two Lovely Black Eyes'. Make no mistake about it, the success of that song was no accident. At first it was nothing more than a vague idea in his mind that 'My Nelly's Blue Eyes' of the Christie Minstrels ought to be parodied. Next came a determination to rewrite it comically. After that came the struggle, for such it was to him no matter how simple the words may seem now, of poetic composition. Nothing short of inspiration was needed to supply 'Oh, what a surprise!' as the second line to avoid 'Two Lovely Black Eyes' thrice in each chorus. All this is in his autobiography, where he confesses how he applied for his engagement at the Trocadero in the summer of 1866 while the too-critical manager was away:

> My turn was something after ten o'clock and I well remember how dear old Pony Moore, Gene Stratton, Sam Raeburn and others, members of the Moore and Burgess Minstrels at St James's Hall nearby, would come in every night, after they had done their work, and sit in the stalls and help me loyally with the chorus. On some nights they would seem to be almost the only people in the hall.

By working 'the chorus for all it was worth', he had his reward in less than a fortnight. Audiences came in simply to join in the chorus. One reveller who sang it right through the entire programme and was afterwards knocked down outside continued it in the gutter. As doors and windows were open because of the heat, massed voices from the Trocodero were wafted across Great Windmill Street to the London Pavilion, where the audience stopped their own show in order to take part. Titled swells at the tables in the side saloon caught the craze. It spread to the younger members of the Royal Family, and forty years later the Duke of Windsor, when Prince of Wales, echoed the refrain while the same singer was singing the same song.

M. WILLSON DISHER, *WINKLES AND CHAMPAGNE*

Every music-hall artist hoped and prayed for the kind of international fame which Coburn enjoyed with his song. Only a few ever achieved it, but Coburn is remarkable for having enjoyed hysterical adulation for a song not once but twice. The second success again had its roots planted firmly in reality, the celebrated scandal involving one Charles de Ville Wells, described by Henry Labouchère in *Truth* as the biggest swindler in Britain. The confidence trick which earned Wells this impressive reputation involved the taking out of provisional patents at the Patent Office and then inserting advertisements in the popular press asking for investors who believed in his 'inventions'. Money streamed in from readers convinced they were about to make their fortunes. Thriving in their donations, Wells rented vast palatial offices and bought a fleet of yachts, which proved useful when an adverse decision in the Civil Courts put his reputation in jeopardy. In 1892 Wells boarded one of the yachts and beat a strategic retreat to Monte Carlo, where he immediately began to play the tables. Unhandicapped by any infallible systems, he enjoyed a freakish run of luck. Twelve times in a single day the croupiers had to send out for more money, but in spite of these reinforcements, Wells managed to break the bank six times. Starting off with £400, he turned it into £40,000 in three days. The world's press began publishing daily bulletins of his good fortunes, broadsheets telling of his feats were peddled in the streets of London.

Wells, a small, balding man of fifty with a black beard and shabby clothes, was very far from the dashing swell of the song inspired by him. He must, however, have been an unusually plausible rogue, for among his victims was the sister of an English judge who was so convinced that he held the secret of reducing fuel consumption in steam yachts that she thrust £18,000 upon him. Ironically it was the huge success he enjoyed at the tables in Monte Carlo which led to his eventual downfall. Having fled to Monaco with the intention of lying low, Wells found himself at the centre of one of the most sensational publicity booms of his generation. It was now easy enough for the law to track him down, arrest him on his yacht, bring him back to England in January 1893 and charge him with obtaining £30,000 by false pretences. He was found guilty and served eight years' penal servitude. In 1906 he was imprisoned for a second time, and in 1912 was arrested in Paris for a third time. The only testimonial to his character was given by the Governor of Dartmoor Prison, who described him as 'the pleasantest and most unselfish of all the rascals that passed through my hands'. Long before his death in 1926 he and his crimes had been forgotten, but not his gambling exploits, which were perpetuated in the song which was to give Charles Coburn a fame which has lasted ever since.

There can be no doubt that the man we know as Charles Coburn was a pioneer of song-plugging, a craft which consists of persistently planting a song in one place until it takes root and spreads. He gained the name of Charles Whitton McCullum, which seems to explain his pertinacity, from his parents. He called himself Charles Lawrie when he began on the old Cockney halls, where Irish humour was welcome and Scottish humour unknown. Somebody advised him to try a crisper stage-name. He was standing, that moment, in Coburn Street, Poplar. A railway station is also named after it. He is still singing 'Two Lovely Black Eyes' and he is still singing 'The Man Who Broke the Bank at Monte Carlo'. Notice how complicated the chorus of the latter is compared with 'Two Lovely Black Eyes', which it replaced in popular fancy. The business of teaching it to the world was very hard work. Yet it was prompted by a sudden inspiration that could not be withstood. Tom Costello tells, more dramatically than can be told in print, how Fred Gilbert pointed to the words, 'Man Who Broke the Bank at Monte Carlo' on a poster in the Strand.

'There's rhythm there,' said Gilbert, and began to beat his right fist against his breast, like a gorilla, as he walked. After they had parted, he went on beating time thus to the unborn tune. He was in labour with it all day. At home his wife had a raging toothache. She suffered his obsession until nightfall, but when he beat his breast in bed, at last complained. Gilbert paced the floor in the throes of composition all that night. He worked at the same task all the next day. But when this heaven-sent song was complete, no one would have it. Many, including Albert Chevalier, had refused it before it was despairingly submitted to Coburn; and he, deciding that it was 'rather too highbrow for an average music-hall audience', so he says in the autobiography named after it, sent it back:

> But no sooner had the letter and song been posted than I began to fear I had made a mistake. I went up and down the house humming the chorus, which I could not get out of my mind. I said to myself, 'After all, it's only a guinea for the singing rights, apart from publication, and it certainly is a fine chorus'. At last I decided that I would have it, and then began to tremble for fear somebody else had snapped it up. Early next morning I went over the water to York Corner, found Fred Gilbert's address, and went after him. Shown into his room, where he sat at a table covered with papers, I said, 'Well, Fred, I've decided to have that song after all.' I waited for him to say, 'Sorry, old chap, but I've sold it.' But he didn't. He said, 'All right, you can have it,' and in a few seconds I became proprietor of that wonderful song.

The first time Coburn plugged 'The Man Who Broke the Bank at Monte Carlo' at the Oxford, he sang the chorus of the last verse ten times. He gagged for all he was worth in order to make the audience believe it was worth while to memorise the words. A critic declared the next day that the comedian's salesmanship made the audience disgusted and himself sick. 'I don't wonder', was Coburn's comment. But he did not possess the name of Colin Whitton McCallum in real life for nothing. One night the manager heard him saying to himself in the glass, 'It's a good song – I like it – and they'll have to like it. They've got it now, sir, haven't they?'

When it came to publication, the author-composer willingly accepted ten pounds for his share. Coburn handed the MS over for 'a fiver and a royalty'. Then it was sung by Maggie Duggan in a Gaiety show, and the receipts went up until Coburn's share alone amounted to six hundred pounds. At the Eden, a rough house on the site now occupied by the Kingsway Theatre, the audience were so rowdy one night that nobody on the stage could get a hearing. Charles Coburn got the band to strike up 'The Man Who Broke the Bank at Monte Carlo'. After the third verse, just to teach the ruffians a lesson, he kept repeating the chorus until they had to stop for sheer weariness.

M. WILLSON DISHER, *WINKLES AND CHAMPAGNE*

By the time Coburn came into his amazing good fortune, the music hall had already left the original Mortonian conception far behind. The public house which provided its customers with a little light entertainment was now superseded by something approaching a legitimate theatre. Even as Morton was hurrying to get his Oxford ready for the public, a pair of rivals called Loibl and Sonnhammer were converting their roofed-in stableyard into a music hall with the grandiloquent title of the London Pavilion, which opened in February 1861. By then the Alhambra had already been converted into an auditorium with proscenium and stage, which meant that elaborate dance spectacles could now be presented. The rebuilt Oxford was another bona fide theatre.

The turning point came in 1878 with the passing of two new bills. In London the Metropolitan Board of Works was empowered to issue a certificate 'of suitability' to every music hall when the manager made his annual application for a licence; among the new requirements was a safety curtain. In the same year the Board of Works, embarking on extensive street improvements, developed Piccadilly Circus and created Shaftesbury Avenue. Among the old buildings to go down was the London Pavilion, whose modest appearance should not mislead posterity into assuming that its early programmes were negligible; a photograph of the old Pavilion just before its demolition advertises the appearances of the Great Macdermott, Bessie Bellwood, and James Fawn, who became famous for 'If You Want to Know the Time Ask a Policeman'. The creation of Shaftesbury Avenue gave the proprietors a chance to build a new and magnificent London Pavilion, flagship of what came to be known as the Matchamite Empire, after Frank Matcham, the architect who designed dozens of theatres all over Britain for the syndicates now taking over control of the nation's scattered music halls. In 1885 the owners of the old Pavilion closed down; by November they were ready to reopen in the new premises.

This event inaugurated a fresh era in music-hall history. It marked the final and complete severance of the variety stage from its old association of the tavern and the concert saloon from the sphere of which it had, year by year, been gradually but perceptibly departing. Hitherto the halls had borne unmistakable evidence of their origin, but the last vestiges of these old connections were now thrown aside, and they emerged in all the splendour of their new-born glory. The highest efforts of the architect, the designer and the decorator were enlisted in their service, and the gaudy and tawdry music hall of the past gave place to the resplendent 'theatre of varieties' of the present day, with its classic exterior of marble and freestone, its lavishly-appointed auditorium and its elegant and luxurious foyers and promenades brilliantly illuminated by myriad electric lights. Hitherto the halls had been almost exclusively patronised by a class composed mainly, if not exclusively, of the lower and middle grade of society, that huge section of the public comprehensively summed up in the term 'the people'. Now, however, wealth, fashions and *ton* became attracted to these handsome 'Palaces' of amusement, and in the grand saloon of the West End halls the most prominent and distinguished representatives of art, literature and the law mingled nightly with city financiers, lights of the sporting and dramatic world, and a very liberal sprinkling of the 'upper crust', as represented by the golden youth of the period.

STUART AND PARK, *THE VARIETY STAGE*

The wonderfully comic snobbery of this description seems to be focussing attention, almost for the first time, on the audience rather than the entertainers. From this point on, the music hall was to become governed to an extent by social considerations quite unconnected with the grace and artistry of the performers, a contradiction which was to lead, inevitably, to royal patronage and the imbecility of the arrangements pertaining to the notorious first Royal Command Performance of 1912. But for the moment, all was rapture. Soon the new Pavilion was acquired by the Syndicate Halls Company, which speedily severed the last links with the old-time saloon-hall by removing the ground-floor tables. In 1886 the tables were removed, the Chairman dispensed with, and the new-fangled tip-up seats installed; one concession to tradition were the ledges at the back of each seat on which customers could place their drinking glasses. By 1890 developments were taking place at such a rate that *Harper's Magazine* sent one of its better-known reporters to make a survey. This was Thomas Anstey Guthrie (1856-1934), who wrote under the pseudonym of F. Anstey, and whose comic novel of role reversal, *Vice Versa*, had made him famous in 1882.

London music halls might be roughly grouped in four classes – first, the aristocratic variety theatre of the West End, chiefly found in the immediate neighbourhood of Leicester Square; then the smaller and less aristocratic West End halls; next, the large bourgeois music halls of the less fashionable parts and in the suburbs; last, the minor music halls of the poor and squalid districts. The audiences, as might be expected, correspond to the social scale of the particular place of entertainment, but the differences in the performances provided by the four classes of music halls are far less strongly marked.

Both externally and internally the bourgeois and suburban music hall differs considerably from its more fashionable rival. For one thing, it is generally dingier and gaudier of appearance; the entrance is covered with huge posters and adorned with tea-garden plaster statues bearing coloured lamps; the walls are lined with tarnished looking-glass, gilded trellis-work, or virgin cork. Sometimes there is a skittle-alley or a shooting-gallery in the 'Grand Lounge'.

The interior is as often rectangular as semicircular, and the scheme of decoration of the old gaudy crimson, plaster and gilding order. In many places, too, the chairman still lingers. This personage is, of course, a survival from the old 'Cave of Harmony' days, and his duties are now confined to sitting at a table either in front of the orchestra or in the centre of the stalls, from whence he rises at the conclusion of each 'turn' to announce 'Ladies and gentlemen, that celebrated comedian, Mr Paul Pongwell (or that favourite lady vocalist, Miss Peggie Patterville, as the case may be) will appear next', after which he resumes his seat and applauds himself with a little auctioneer's hammer. There is a melancholy dignity about him, however, which causes him to be approached with much deference and respect by the young clerks and shop boys who take their pleasure there, and who are proud to be distinguished by a shake of the hand from him, and flattered when he condescends to accept liquid refreshment or 'one of the best twopenny smokes in London' at their expense. Even the torrent of chaff from a lady artiste, with a talent for improvising light badinage which would render an archbishop ridiculous in two minutes, fails to rob him of his prestige.

The audience is not a distinguished-looking one; there are no dress-coats and caped cloaks, no dashing toilettes, to be seen here; but the vast majority are in easy circumstances and eminently respectable. You will see little family parties – father, mother, and perhaps a grown-up daughter or a child or two – in the stalls. Most of them are probably regular visitors, and have the entrée here in return for exhibiting bills in their shop-windows; and these family parties all know one another, as can be seen from the smiles and hand-shakes they exchange as they pass in or out. Then there are several girls with their sweethearts, respectable young couples employed in neighbouring workshops and factories, and a rusty old matron or two, while the fringe of the audience is made up of gay young clerks, the local 'bloods', who have a jaunty fashion in some districts of wearing a cigar behind the ear. Large ham sandwiches are handed round by cooks in white blouses, and when a young woman desires to be very stylish indeed, she allows her swain to order a glass of port for her refreshment. Taken as a whole, the audience is not remarkable for intelligence; it is seldom demonstrative, and never in the least exacting, perfectly ready to be pleased with dull songs, hoary jokes, stale sentiment, and clap-trap patriotism.

The character of the performances which find favour may be best illustrated by a description of part of the actual programme at a well-known music hall in South London when the writer was present. After a song and some feats by a troupe of acrobats, came an exhibition by a young lady in a large glass tank filled with water. She was a very pretty and graceful young lady, and she came on accompanied by a didactic gentleman in evening dress, who accompanied the announcement of each new feature of her performance by a little discourse. 'Opening and shutting the mouth under water', he would say, for example. 'It has long been a theory among scientific men that by opening the mouth while under water a vacuum is created, thereby incurring the risk of choking the swimmer. Miss So-and-so, ladies and gentlemen, will now proceed to demonstrate the fallacy of that opinion, by opening and shutting her mouth several times in succession while remaining at the bottom of the tank.' Which Miss So-and-so accordingly did, to our great edification. Then came 'gathering shells under water', which was accomplished in a highly elaborate manner, so that there could be no mistake about it. 'Sewing' and 'writing under water'. 'Eating under water', when the lady consumed a piece of bread with every appearance of extreme satisfaction. 'Drinking from a bottle under water. Most of you', remarked the manager, sympathetically, 'are acquainted with the extreme difficulty of drinking out of a bottle under any circumstances'. Then a cigar was borrowed from the audience, lighted, and given to the lady, who, shielding it with her hands, retired under the water and smoked vigorously for a minute or two, reappearing with the cigar still unextinguished. Lastly the manager announced, 'Ladies and gentlemen, Miss So-and-so will now adopt the position of prayer'; whereupon the lady sank gracefully on her knees under water, folded her hands, and appeared rapt in devotion, while the orchestra played 'The Maiden's Prayer', and the manager, with head reverently bent, stood delicately aside, as one who felt himself unworthy to intrude upon such orisons. Then the lady adopted a pose even more imploring, and a ray, first of crimson and then of green light, was thrown into the tank, presumably to indicate morning and evening in prayer respectively. After some minutes of this, the fair performer, a little out of breath from her spiritual exertions, rose, sleek and dripping, to the surface, hopped nimbly out, and bowed herself off.

After that there was a lady vocalist who informed us in song of her self-denial on a recent occasion, when

She wouldn't call for sherry; she wouldn't call for beer;
She wouldn't call for cham, because she knew 'twould make her queer;
She wouldn't call for brandy, rum, or anything they'd got;
She only called for Bovril – hot! hot! hot!

– a ditty to the moral of which not even the Brick Lane Temperance Association could reasonably take exception. Next we had an exposure of some familiar conjuring tricks by a gentleman with a foreign accent, who was genuinely amusing; some fantasias performed with hammers on a grisly instrument constructed of bones – veritable skeleton·music; and, to wind up, the great sensational sketch, *The Little Stowaway*, which apparently touches the hearts of the audience.

THOMAS ANSTEY GUTHRIE IN HARPER'S MAGAZINE, 1890

The trend for grandiose façades and lavish interiors was in full flow, and by the time Anstey conducted his readers on a guided tour, the two most significant events in the history of the Victorian music hall had already taken place, the construction of the two most richly gilded palaces of all. In 1854 in Leicester Square there had arisen the Panopticon, an educational institution which so failed to educate that it soon became a circus. In 1860 a proscenium and stage were installed and, renamed the Alhambra, it soon became famous as the stronghold of lavish ballets.

At one time an honoured part of the world of opera, the ballet had come on such hard times that its dancers and choreographers were seeking refuge in the halls, and it was the Alhambra which did most to keep the balletic tradition alive. The theatre then burned down, was swiftly rebuilt and reopened in 1883. Theatre fires had by now become so frequent that *The Saturday Review* was prompted to declaim against the slovenly fire precautions which so many music-hall managements appeared to regard as adequate.

Whatever may be said of the London theatres, they are fireproof as compared with the majority of the music halls. In comparing the music halls with the theatres, it must be remembered that, if the former are much smaller and do not contain as many people as the latter, they unquestionably make up the difference in size by a more than proportionate amount of danger. In the first place, drinking, which admittedly tends to excite the audience, goes on during the entire performance, and smoking is of common occurrence. Indeed, it is the rule, and not the exception, with the male portion of the audience. Smoking leads to throwing about lighted cigar ends and cigarette ends. And one muslin dress set on fire by a match or a cigar or cigarette end carelessly thrown would create just as great panic as would take place as a theatre wrapped in flames. The old Oxford music hall was, if we recollect rightly, burnt down through carelessness of this kind, and what has happened once may happen again. The entrance to the Oxford is in Oxford Street. In case of fire, the entire audience might have to leave, as they leave every night, by the one door by which they come in. There is another small exit, as the label says, 'in case of need', on the O.P. side of the stalls; but on the night of our visit it was locked. Another label directs the audience to another door on the Prompt side, which leads on to a small back-yard in Donaldson's Buildings and through a small, narrow court, blocked with shop-shutters, on to Tottenham Court Road. This door was also locked. Playful little jokes like these may possibly be amusing, but in our judgement should be sternly repressed. Twenty-one stairs lead on either side of the house to the balcony. At the very back of the hall, and quite close to the steps of the balcony, is, according to the label, another extra door. On examination, however, it turns out that the door in question leads down nineteen steps to the small yard in Donaldson's Buildings to which we have referred. In fire, there is but one real exit to the Oxford and that exit is no way sufficient.

Bad as is the Oxford, it cannot compare in any way with the Trocadero. This house is situated in Windmill Street, and its one entrance is divided into four doors. It is hardly possible to believe not only that all these four doors open inwards, but also that, even in this hot weather, three out of the four doors were firmly barred and bolted up.

THE SATURDAY REVIEW, 6 AUGUST 1887

The new Alhambra which rose from the ashes of the old became one of the most famous public buildings in England, and its style of entertainment familiar enough. But posterity can get a vivid impression of what the Alhambra was like before the fire through the eyes of a penniless would-be writer who had come to London in the 1870s to seek his literary fortune without the slightest success either artistic or financial. In his first novel, written in 1879, and not published for another fifty-one years, there occurs the following remarkable passage, in which the priggish hero is tempted by the allurements of the Alhambra ballet to buy a ticket, with alarming effects on his fevered imagination.

When he reached the street again, he felt that to spend the evening at home after such a parting would be impossible. He therefore started briskly towards the west end, and soon hailed an omnibus, which carried him to Hyde Park Corner. Here he alighted, and finding himself in a congenial frame of mind, passed the remaining hour of daylight pleasantly wandering by the Serpentine. Shortly before nine o'clock, having been expelled from Kensington Gardens by a policeman, he set his face to the east, and at half-past nine arrived in the half foreign, half theatrical region which surrounds Leicester Square. Infected by the prevailing atmosphere, he was seized with a desire to see some entertainment in harmony with the aspect of the place. He heard a young man who had just been stopped by an acquaintance say 'I am off to the Alhambra'.* Smith had heard the Alhambra spoken of as a wicked place, but had never visited it. Determining now to see it for himself, he made his way thither quickly, and paid a shilling for the privilege of admission. On entering, he found himself in a huge circular theatre, lighted by small lamps arranged in continuous lines around the auditorium. The centre of the floor was occupied by seats of various denominations, according to their degree of proximity to the stage, and surrounding these and separated from them by a barricade was a narrow strip forming the extreme circumference, which was unprovided with seats, and to which Smith discovered that he was limited by the modest sum he had disbursed for his ticket. As the curtain was down when he entered, and the crowd who shared this promenade with him either moving to and fro or drinking in the various holes containing bars which were placed around, he walked about, observing the throng, feeling uncomfortable, and hoping that he might not be discovered by any of his acquaintances in such a place. There were many old men present and many young ones, who looked on their seniors with that intolerance of dissipation which depraved

---

*The old Alhambra, on the site of the later Alhambra. It is proper to state here that the establishment of the London County Council, about ten years after Smith's visit, led to a municipal control which made the moral atmosphere of the new Alhambra quite different from that of the old, as truthfully described in the text. The controlled variety theatres of London are immeasurably more refined and artistic, even in their immoralities, than the old music halls and *opéra bouffe* theatres. The old Alhambra caught fire one night. I saw it burn gloriously.

youth exhibits when it perceives its own weaknesses reflected in old age. There were a few soldiers, a number of women, and some officials in uniform, whose chief duty seemed to be the protection of the edifice from conflagration by smokers. The atmosphere was hot, and flavored with gas, cigar smoke, and effervescing liquors. Just as Smith had concluded that a wicked theatre without a performance was quite as dull as a virtuous one would be under the same circumstances, the band assembled. He enjoyed their playing, which, though coarse and slovenly, was spirited, and reminded him of the orchestra at Covent Garden, although it was more enjoyable to him. He was obliged to confess that he liked Offenbach. Meyerbeer, on the authority of the French newspaper, he respected. But he could not deceive himself into supposing that he liked him: he could but feel ashamed of himself for not liking him. When the curtain rose, the last act of *Le Voyage dans la Lune* was performed by many robust young ladies with large voices, which they were endeavoring by all the means in their power to destroy. As the voices Smith had heard at Covent Garden had, for the most part, been destroyed already for the benefit of continental audiences, he could not help preferring the Alhambra artists; and he felt that this preference was an additional proof of his ignorance. He was moderately pleased by the gorgeous dresses and scenery; yawned at the long processions; and laughed at the horseplay; for he loved the humor of harlequinade.

When the curtain descended, it was late; but the audience was increasing; and Smith, on addressing an inquiry to one of the men in uniform, learned that the next entertainment would consist of a ballet entitled *The Golden Harvest*. The Alhambra was famous for its ballets; and Smith resolved to wait. At length a reedy prelude announced the pastoral atmosphere of the forthcoming spectacle. The curtain rose, and discovered a village, decorated as for a festival. Three young ladies with servants' caps and aprons, but otherwise prepared, as to costume, for the rite of confirmation, appeared and conversed by stamping, motioning with both hands towards the earth, combing their faces with their fingers, and slapping their persons in various places. They then danced. Interrupted by a sound of bells, they bent one knee at a right angle; rested an elbow on it and a cheek on the other, stretched the other leg as far as possible behind; and in this attitude, listened anxiously to the now deafening clamor. Satisfied that their ears had not deceived them, they ran away. A company of reapers with sickles entered, each reaper conducting a binder bearing a sheaf. They danced, the reapers sawing the air as though they were cutting the sheaves presented by the binders. Then a canopy appeared, beneath which were borne a bride and bridegroom. The bridegroom was attired in purple knee breeches, a white shirt, and a crimson sash in which was a tiny gold sickle. The bride was covered with a veil adorned with orange blossoms. As the orchestra paused on the chord of the dominant, she threw off the veil, and revealed a light nuptial costume consisting of a waistband and shoulder straps of white satin, to which was appended a skirt of about fifteen inches in length. In addition to the ordinary methods of locomotion, she has acquired the power of walking on the points of her great toes, and of poising herself on either one, and spinning herself about without becoming giddy. These feats admitted of but few combinations; and Smith thought the dancing resulting from them deficient in variety, destitute of charm, and no better than a painful and unmeaning species of gymnastics. Some unintelligible dialogue in gesture ensued; and after a tarantella concluding with more ringing of bells and the withdrawal of the procession, the scene shifted and disclosed a cornfield glowing in an autumn sunset. Here reappeared the reapers and binders, who celebrated the occasion by dancing around a maypole resembling a barber's sign decked with ribbons, which they carried in with them. In these rejoicings the bridegroom took an energetic part, and, long before they were ended, succumbed to weariness, and lay down at the base of a stack of sheaves, where he fell asleep. The bride presently missed him, and, having searched for him on her toes in every place but that in which he was, expressed distraction and ran off. The rest, after kneeling in obedience to the sound of the vesper bell, followed her; and night fell on the scene with tropical suddenness. The music became hushed and full of mystery. A powerful moon cast a halo on the sleeping figure of the bridegroom, and on the stack which sheltered him. Then the sheaves fell asunder, and a transcendent being, the spirit of the harvest field, appeared, enveloped in the hues of autumn, blood-red poppy lightening into gorgeous orange. Cornflowers and golden ears of wheat were twisted fantastically in her black hair. Her dark bright eyes flashed in the limelight. Smith forgot his surroundings. The audience, the lights, the cigar ends, the unpleasant bursts of laughter from the drinking bars, ceased to color his impression of the scene. The stage became an actual cornfield to him, and the dancer a veritable fairy. Her impetuosity was supernatural fire; her limbs were instinct with music to the very wrists; that walking on the points of the toes, which had given him a pain in the ankle to look at before, now seemed a natural outcome of elfin fancy and ethereality. He became infatuated as he watched her dancing in wanton overflow of spirits about the field, with the halo of the moon following her wherever she bounded. When she reminded him of her real circumstances by making a courtesy, he was irritated at the tameness of the applause which followed, cursing the indifference of the herd to refined art, and hammering with his walking-stick on the wooden barricade against which he stood. At one moment he fancied he had caught her eye, and that she was conscious of his presence. At another, he strove to establish a magnetic influence over her by fixing his gaze sternly on her face and holding his breath. He grudged all applause which was not addressed to her. He almost lost his temper when a woman stood up, and obstructed his view of the stage for a few seconds.

Meanwhile the story of the Golden Harvest unfolded itself as rapidly as the discursiveness of the saltatory illustration permitted. The fairy soon discovered the bridegroom; roused him; fascinated him; danced with him; languished in his arms, tantalisingly eluded him; and fell into graceful poses which he contemplated with as much astonishment as he could affect whilst supporting by her belt the hundred and twenty pounds avoirdupois which had no existence for Smith. Throughout a night of fifteen minutes' duration the bridegroom resisted the spells of the enchantress; but at the critical moment when he, overcome at last, was about to place a ring upon her finger, and thus deliver himself into her power for the ensuing century, the cock crew; the fairy vanished; the sun rose; the oboe on a drone bass discoursed in the spirit of the pastoral morning; and the reapers, returning to their work, found the now sleeping bridegroom, and restored him to his bride, whom he received (being, as Smith thought, a tasteless person) without making any disparaging comparisons. Then the curtain fell; and the audience dispersed slowly. Among them was a courtly old man, whose black silk stockings and studied gait proclaimed him a relic of a past generation. He was discussing the performance with a young officer, who had achieved the perfect gentility of the indescribable, having no individuality beyond the general characteristics of the class to which he belonged.

'Good, very good,' said the elder. 'Dancing is a lost art nowadays; but she has something of the old school about her. She is indeed the only one now who has. I have seen Cerito, Carlotta Grisi, Fanny Ellsler, and the great Taglioni. Taglioni was my *vis-à-vis* in a quadrille once, when I was sixteen years of age.' The old gentleman gave his shoulders a slight shrug, which Smith, who had overheard him with the deepest respect and pleasure, interpreted as the expression of tolerance opposed to that pang of mingled tenderness and despair which recollections call up, when they concern an order of things passed away for ever.

'She is a fine straight woman, all game, and no crumb,' replied the officer with energy. Smith cast a look of contempt at him, and passed out into the street. Here was a confusion of swift hansoms, clamorous vendors of obscene literature, violet sellers, and crowds of men and brilliantly attired women aimlessly wandering about with just sufficient motion to satisfy the urgent policemen, with a background of the gas-lighted windows of *cafés*, gin palaces, tobacconists, and eating-houses where lobsters predominated redly over the other edibles. Through this tumult Smith rapidly made his way, and reached Dodd's Buildings, as it seemed to him, almost immediately.

For half an hour after midnight he walked up and down his small room, thinking of the dancer, and inventing extravagant expedients by which he might make her acquaintance. He regretted that he had no skill in the art of picking pockets. How easy it would be, he thought, to wait at the stage door of the theatre in order to get near her, to steal her purse, and then to call on her and earn her gratitude by restoring it! This idea was followed by visions of runaway broughams, the Alhambra in flames, shipwrecks, and every disaster in which he could conceive himself united to her by a common danger. He repeatedly checked himself, and laughed at his indulgence in the very follies which he had often found trite in novels; but after each check of this kind, he relapsed again, and was only reminded of the advancing night by a knocking, which Mr Fenwick, umbrella in hand, clad in his nightshirt, and mounted on a chair, was indignantly making on the ceiling of his apartment, as a reminder to his fellow lodger that he could not sleep with a procession apparently passing overhead.

In the morning, Smith, reading the late Mr Mill's essay on religious liberty as an accompaniment to his breakfast, felt ashamed of himself. His pride in thinking comprehensively as a man, was wounded. He put on his boots, and then, finding he had still some minutes to spare before going to the office, he leaned back in his chair, and made his speech, telling off each section on his fingers.

'What are the facts of the case about this woman? (Forefinger.) In order to preserve her gymnastic skill she must pass hours every day in practice which has not one element of mental improvement in it. Therefore she must be utterly ignorant and narrow-minded. (Middle finger). She is disguised with masses of rouge and bismuth, and, deprived of them, would probably appear coarse looking. (Third finger.) As she certainly dances well, and as excellence in any art is only attainable by much experience, she must be pretty old. (Little finger.) Her profession is a guarantee of her low origin and indifferent character. Were I to observe her closely, I should be completely disillusioned. Consequently I will go again tonight and take up a position close to the stage – Psha!' he added, jumping up and putting on his hat. 'What gross sophistry! I shall never enter the Alhambra again.'

GEORGE BERNARD SHAW, *IMMATURITY*

The time was fast approaching when the writer of that passage would be paid to visit theatres like the Alhambra. By then the rebuilt bastion of the ballet would have a great rival, the Empire, a few yards from its door. Once again the vigilant Anstey went to report on his findings.

Its exterior is more handsome and imposing than that of most London theatres, even of the highest rank. Huge cressets in classical tripods flare between the columns of the façade, the windows and foyer glow with stained glass, the entrance hall, lighted by softened electric lamps, is richly and tastefully decorated. You pass through wide, airy corridors and down stairs, to find yourself in a magnificent theatre, and the stall to which you are shown is wide and luxuriously fitted. Smoking is universal, and a large proportion of the audience promenade the outer circles, or stand in groups before the long refreshment bars which are a prominent feature on every tier. Most of the men are in evening dress, and in the boxes are some ladies, also in evening costume, many of them belonging to what is called good society. The women in other parts of the house are generally pretty obvious members of a class which, so long as it behaves itself with propriety in the building, it would, whatever fanatics may say to the contrary, be neither desirable nor possible to exclude. The most noticeable characteristic of the audience is perhaps the very slight attention it pays to whatever is going on upon the stage. In the upper parts of the house the conversation renders it impossible to hear distinctly anything that is said or sung, through the same remark does not apply to the stalls, where the occupants, if not enthusiastic, are at least languidly attentive. There is a large and excellent orchestra, with just a tendency to overdo the drum and cymbals. Stage footmen, more gorgeous in livery but far meeker of aspect than their brethren in private service, slip a giant card bearing a number into a gilded frame on either side of the proscenium before each item of the programme. The electric bell tings, the lights are raised, the orchestra dashes into a prelude, and the *artiste* whose 'turn' it is comes on. The main and distinctive feature of the entertainment, however, is the *ballet divertissement*, for which all else is scarcely more than padding, and these ballets are magnificent enough to satisfy the most insatiate appetite for splendour. There are two in one evening, and each lasts about half an hour, during which time the large stage is filled with bewildering combinations of form and colour. Company after company of girls, in costumes of delicately contrasted tints, march, troop, or gallop down the boards, their burnished armour gleaming and their rich dresses scintillating in the limelight; at each fresh stroke of the stage-manager's gong they group themselves anew or perform some complicated figure, except when they fall back in a circle and leave the stage clear for the *première danseuse*.

To the writer this lady's proceedings are a source of never-failing enjoyment. There never was such artless *naïveté* in any other human being. To see her advance on the points of her toes, her arms curved symmetrically above her head, a smile of innocent childlike delight on her face, as if she had only just discovered the art of dancing and was quite surprised to find it so agreeable a pastime, is an experience indeed. Then her high-stepping prance round the stage, her little impulsive runs and bashful retreats, the astonishing complacency with which she submits to being seized and supported in every variety of uncomfortable attitude by the personage next in importance to herself, her final teetotum whirl, are all evidently charged with a deep but mysterious significance. It is not uninstructive, too, to watch the countenances of the *corps de ballet* during these evolutions. Some are severely critical, and obviously

41

of opinion that they could do it infinitely better themselves; others whisper disparagement to sympathetic ears; others again study the signorina's every movement until she is opposite them, whereupon they assume an ostentatious abstraction, as if she were really below their notice. And then she stops suddenly, amidst thunders of applause, the infantine smile giving place to a calm superiority as she haughtily makes her way to the wings through the ranks of *coryphées*. At last the end comes; the ballet girls are ranked and massed into brilliant parterres and glittering pyramids, the *première danseuse* glides on in time to appropriate the credit of the arrangement, and the curtain falls on a blaze of concentrated magnificence.

THOMAS ANSTEY GUTHRIE IN *HARPERS*

While the Alhambra and the Empire dominated Leicester Square, a third great palace arose a little further to the east, in the Strand. Some years before a café had been opened called the Tivoli Lager Beer Restaurant, named after the Tivoli Gardens in Paris. The restaurant was demolished in 1889 to make way for an altogether more splendid structure soon to become synonymous with the very best artistry the music hall had to offer. In its brief but brilliant career the new theatre set standards and created legends, and is generally remembered as the home of such scintillating brilliance that the facts of its early calamities are sometimes overlooked.

During the 1880s the music hall became the Theatre of Varieties, grander and more respectable. The Alhambra became the Alhambra Theatre of Varieties in 1884 and the Empire followed suit in 1887. As they went over to music hall, the houses were redecorated ever more flamboyantly. The Tivoli (1888-90) was extremely splendid. Emulating the Criterion in combining theatre and restaurant, the building presented to the Strand a glorious mixture. Plantagenet windows were separated by a giant order of French Empire pilasters, surmounted by an attic storey of Romanesque arcading and topped by a mansard roof. Walter Emden, the architect, had in fact conceived a similarly eclectic and extravagant central feature for the roof, but unfortunately this was omitted from the completed scheme.

The architect did not make provision for advertising; as a result, the neo-Romanesque style is somewhat obscured by the light-boxes which spell out the name of the theatre, while the clean ground floor lines are littered with prop-up billboards.

The Strand elevation was in fact that of the restaurant, while the theatre was behind. The term 'variety' described not only the kind of entertainment available but also the choice of décor. The buffet, at street level, was in Indian style. A staircase in François I style led to the Palm Room (walls and ceiling decorated with palm leaves) on the first floor and Flemish Room (oak carved in the Levant) on the second. Above were suites of private dining rooms, 'adorned in styles which their names convey, namely the Louis XV Room, the Japanese, the Arabian and the Pompeiian Rooms; and in addition there is a full-sized Masonic Room'. The kitchens were concealed behind the Romanesque arcading.

The Tivoli cost nearly £300,000, which was expensive considering that the Palace, Cambridge Circus, was done for £150,000 a little later. The Tivoli Company went bankrupt within a year and the building was sold for half its cost. Soon afterwards a new company was formed and the theatre went on to become the most famous of music halls.

The Tivoli became so synonymous with variety that its style of decoration created a vogue which influenced music halls all over Britain. Tivolis were built across the Empire. The Alhambra, even when it was the Panopticon, had been Saracenic; when it was rebuilt in 1883 after the fire of the previous year, it was tempered with the Moorish of Spain. The Tivoli was Indian; gods and goddesses were carved in high relief, coloured and gilt, while the boxes were swagged with Baroque opulence; elephants' heads topped the delicate iron columns supporting the ceiling. The elephant motif reappears in the Palace Music Hall, Glasgow (1907). The Moorish-Indian style became very contagious. Frank Matcham redecorated the Tivoli slightly in 1891. The onion-shaped Moorish arches of the set were a particular favourite of his; many of his Palaces of Variety sprouted onion domes in the 1890s.

VICTOR GLASSTONE, *VICTORIAN AND EDWARDIAN THEATRES*

With the rise of the great gilded palaces of the West End of London, and the organisation by the syndicates of chains of theatres all over the four kingdoms, the music hall had emerged at last from its embryonic stage, and was now equipped to cater, not just for the millions queuing at the box-office, but also for the astonishing stream of virtuosity pouring on to the stage. Although the nightly bills, often consisting of twenty-five or thirty acts, included necessarily a high percentage of dross, the bill-toppers were generally highly gifted artists who had evolved acts of genuine originality. It seemed that hardly a season went by without the rise of some new sensational performer, destined to remain a public hero or heroine for as long as the music hall itself survived. Through the sheer proliferation of its performers the profession could hardly help expressing many of those nuances of working-class life which until now had not been especially prominent in the courts of the artistic world, a fact which soon had the satisfying effect of attracting to the music hall a new generation of intellectuals whose predecessors would not in the general run of things have been expected to fritter away their precious cerebral energies in such plebeian pursuits. The music hall was about to be admitted to the cultural establishment, and its great artists to be lionised to the brink of deification.

In one respect the music hall was fortunate in that the legitimate theatre had for most of the century been at its lowest ebb. Between the comedies of Sheridan at the start of the nineteenth century and those of Shaw and Wilde at the end of it, no single work of dramatic art was produced on which a later age would waste much time, and it was this aspect of the music hall, its exciting vitality, which began to attract some of the better brains of the age. The case of the Irish novelist George Moore was a perfect example of a critic using the vigour and trenchant humour of the music hall as a stick with which to beat the solemn frivolities of the legitimate theatre. In a way it was a sort of inverted snobbery, the revelling in vulgar honesty at the expense of the twaddling teacup melodramas in cluttered make-believe drawing-rooms. In Moore's case the conviction of superiority was greatly enhanced by his extensive experience of continental culture. Returning to London from the Paris of Zola and the Impressionists in the spirit of a deep-sea fisherman peering into a goldfish bowl, Moore was able to adopt comfortably enough the pose of the detached man-of-the-world endowed by his Irishness and his cosmopolitanism with emancipation from the idiotic moral codes of the English stage, armoured by his past with an impregnable sense of superior judgement. Moore, affably contemptuous of West End problem plays, is teaching the English educated classes how to suck their music hall eggs.

There is one thing in England that reminds me of all the blithe humanities of the Continent, yet it is wholly and essentially English; its communal enjoyment and its spontaneity set us thinking of Elizabethan England – I mean the music hall; the French music hall lacks the vulgarity of the English hall – not the Pavilion, that is too cosmopolitan (dreary French comics are heard there) – let us say the Royal. I shall not easily forget my first evening at the Royal, when I saw for the first time a living house – the dissolute paragraphists, the elegant mashers (mark the imaginativeness of the slang), the stolid, good-humoured costers, the cheerful lights o' love, the extraordinary comics. What delightful unison of enjoyment, what unanimity of soul, what communality of wit; all knew each other, all enjoyed each other's presence; in a word, there was life. Then there were no cascades of real water, nor London docks, nor offensively rich furniture, with hotel lifts down which somebody will certainly be thrown, but one scene representing a street; a man comes on – not, mind you, in a real smock-frock, but in something that suggests one – and sings of how he came up to London, and was 'cleaned out' by thieves. Simple, you will say; yes, but better than a *fricassée* of *Faust*, garnished with hags, imps, and blue flame; better, far better than a drawing-room set at the St James's, with an exhibition of passion by Mr and Mrs Kendal; better, a million times better than the cheap popularity of Wilson Barrett – an elderly man posturing in a low-necked dress to some poor trull in the gallery; nor is there in the hall any affectation of language, nor that worn-out rhetoric which reminds us of a broken-winded barrel-organ playing *Ah, che la morte*, bad enough in prose, but when set up in blank verse shocking in its more than natural deformity – but bright quips and cranks fresh from the back-yard of the slum where the linen is drying, or the 'pub' where the unfortunate wife has just received a black eye that will last her a week. That inimitable artist, Bessie Bellwood, whose native wit is so curiously accentuated that it is no longer repellant vulgarity but art, choice and rare – see, here she comes with 'What cheer, Rea! Rea's on the job'. The sketch is slight, but is welcome and refreshing after the eternal drawing-rooms and Mrs Kendal's cumbrous domesticity; it is curious, quaint, perverted, and are not these the *aions* and the attributes of art? Now see that perfect comedian, Arthur Roberts, superior to Irving because he is working with living material; how trim and saucy he is! and how he evokes the soul, the brandy-and-soda soul, of the young men, delightful and elegant in black and white, who are so vociferously cheering him, 'Will you stand me a cab-fare ducky, I am feeling so awfully queer?' The soul, the spirit, the entity of Piccadilly Circus is in the words, and the scene the comedian's eyes – each look is full of suggestion; it is irritating, it is magnetic, it is symbolic, it is art.

Nor art, but a sign, a presentiment of an art, that may grow from the present seeds, that may rise into some stately and unpremeditated efflorescence, as the rhapsodist rose to Sophocles, as the miracle play rose through Peele and Nash to Marlowe, hence to the wondrous summer of Shakespeare, to die later on in the mist and yellow and brown of the autumn of Crowes and Davenants. I have seen music hall sketches, comic interludes that in their unexpectedness and naïve naturalness remind me of the comic passages in Marlowe's *Faustus*, I waited (I admit in vain) for some beautiful phantom to appear, and to hear an enthusiastic worshipper cry out in his agony:

> Was this the face that launched a thousand ships
> And burnt the topless towers of Ilium?
> Sweet Helen, make me immortal with a kiss.
> Her lips suck forth my soul; see where it flies!
> Come, Helen, come; give me my soul again.
> Here will I dwell, for heaven is in these lips,
> And all is dross that is not Helena.

And then the astonishing change of key:

> I will be Paris, and for love of thee,
> Instead of Troy shall Wittenberg be sacked, etc.

The hall is at least a protest against the wearisome stories concerning wills, misers in old castles, lost heirs, and the woeful solutions of such things – she who has been kept in the castle cellar for twenty years restored to the delights of hair-pins and a mauve dress, the *ingénue* to the protecting arm, etc. The music hall is a protest against Mrs Kendal's marital tenderness and the arbortive platitudes of Messrs Pettit and Sims; the music hall is a protest against Sardou and the immense drawing-room sets, rich hangings, velvet sofas, etc; so different from the movement of the English comedy with its constant change of scene. The music hall is a protest against the villa, the circulating library, the club, and for this the ' 'all' is inexpressibly dear to me.

GEORGE MOORE, *CONFESSIONS OF A YOUNG MAN*

In that observation of the state of English culture generally and its theatres in particular, Moore was, in the opinion of some, coming it a bit strong, as his music hall heroes would have been inclined to put it. By no means all of the erudite critics of art and society who ventured into the halls were as enraptured by what they found there. Twelve years after having completed his novel about the puritannical Smith who dares one visit to the Alhambra ballet and is utterly seduced by the grace of the dancers, Bernard Shaw, having transformed himself into a metropolitan music critic, developed the habit, uncommon if not unknown among his fellow-reviewers, of occasionally devoting some space to the music hall. Unlike Moore, Shaw felt that the cultural level of the serious stage, abysmal though it certainly was, remained far too elevated for the idlers who frequented the halls. What fascinated Shaw most of all was the different standards of etiquette obtaining in a music hall, where, instead of agreeing to maintain a reverent silence while the entertainment was proceeding, the customers felt free to do and say whatever they pleased at any given moment. In retrospect, this refusal to take for granted the dramatist's right to bore or hector his audience through the agency of the actors and actresses, and the willingness to turn away or make rude noises when displeased, seem much the more ethical stance of the two.

As to the general question of the quality of music hall entertainment, I have nothing to say about that: I am not a representative of the true music hall public, which consists partly of people whose powers of imaginative apprehension and attention are too limited to follow even the most incoherent melodrama, and partly of people who like to sit smoking and soaking in lazy contemplation of something that does not greatly matter. What astonishes a theatre-goer at a music hall, or an educated woman when she realises one of her most cherished dreams by at last persuading either her husband or the man-about-towniest of his friends to take her to the London Pavilion or the Empire, is the indifference of the audience to the performance. Five out of six of the 'turns' are of the deadliest dullness: ten minutes of it would seal the fate of any drama; but the people do not mind: they drink and smoke. Under these circumstances the standard of interest, much less of art, is low,

45

the strain on the management or the artists to keep it up being of the slightest. It is rising slowly, in spite of the influence of that detestable product of civilisation, the rich man's son, who now represents a distinct class, technically described as 'masher', and growing with the accumulation of riches in idle hands produced by our idiotic industrial system. If left to develop freely, our best music halls would in course of time present a combination of promenade concert, theatre, and circus (minus the horses): that is, you would have a good band, decent concert singers, acrobats, jugglers, ballets, and dramatic sketches, all in the same evening. And the refreshment department will probably develop also, as 'Arry develops into the noble Juggins, and begins to prefer the aerated bread shop to the public-house.

GEORGE BERNARD SHAW IN *LONDON MUSIC*, 18 OCTOBER 1889

The fate of Shaw's Smith, obliged by his own aesthetic inclinations to banish himself from a theatre whose leading dancer has captured his heart without even being aware of his existence, had a curious real-life counterpart in the experiences of a young undergraduate whose vacations from Oxford fortunately enabled him to educate himself in the ways of the world. In the 1870s one of the new stars to create an impression at the Oxford Music Hall was Marie Loftus, whose genteel ballads, ornate gowns and towering fruitarian millinery encouraged her to bill herself as 'The Sarah Bernhardt of the Music Halls'. She eventually married a fellow-artist, the comedian Ben Brown. In 1893 their teenaged daughter made her London début at the Oxford and caused an immediate sensation as an impersonator. But impressive though her effect on London audiences undoubtedly was, it was nothing compared to the romantic devastation she wrought on the young man destined within a few years to take over from Shaw as drama critic of *The Saturday Review*.

Back in London after term, Max once more haunted the music halls. During his absence a new star had appeared at the Tivoli, Cissey Loftus, 'the Mimetic Marvel'. Only fifteen years old, unrouged, in a pink frock and yellow strapped shoes, and with her straight hair falling Alice-in-Wonderlandlike on her shoulders, she stepped demurely forward, made a little bow and proceeded to imitate various popular comedians of the day. She did it with a diabolical skill rendered all the more piquant by her childlike appearance.

Max saw her and was conquered. This odd, charming blend of youth and sophistication appealed exactly to his taste: was it not a blend to be found in his own art? But indeed he liked everything about Cissey Loftus; her little bow, her unrouged cheeks, her strapped shoes, and the satiric force of her mimicry: and he thought her exquisitely pretty. Accordingly, night after night found him at the Tivoli standing at the end of a row of stalls applauding her act: after the performance he waited at the stage door to get a glimpse of her driving off in a shabby little carriage attended by her actress mother, Miss Marie Loftus. For, so he learnt, she had only just left a convent school and lived with her family, strictly chaperoned, in the respectable residential suburb of Herne Hill. Max took to haunting Herne Hill of an afternoon.

46

Now and again after her act she and her mother would come down into the audience and hold a little court. Max plucked up courage on one such occasion to scrape acquaintance with her on the pretence that he was a journalist asking for an interview. She proved just as attractive as on the stage and graciously promised to sign a photograph of herself for him. Altogether he thought her the most delightful object he had ever beheld. He made up his mind to be in love with her.

DAVID CECIL, *MAX*

The English music halls attracted a more literary and artistic crowd than did American vaudeville houses; Arthur Symons, Ernest Dowson, Herbert Horne (who was not only the biographer of Botticelli but the architect of the Savoy Hotel), Oscar Wilde, Selwyn Image, Walter Sickert, and Max were habitués. It was at one of the famous English halls, the Tivoli, that Max first saw, and fell in love with, 'the Mimetic Marvel', as she was billed in the advertisements, Cissie Loftus. When Max encountered Cissie, she was a little girl of sixteen, who had made a sensation singing songs and doing imitations.

The griefs and ecstasies of Max's love affair are recorded in a long series of letters he wrote to Reggie Turner. As Cissie was a mere child, though already famous when Max first saw her, he constantly refers to her in these letters as Mistress Mere. In the fantasy he wrote later, *The Happy Hypocrite*, the heroine with whom Lord George Hall falls in love is also a music-hall artist, and her name is Jenny Mere. The White Child and Small Saint are other pseudonyms Max provides for Cissie. Max had many chances to meet Cissie and talk with her, but for a very long time he was too shy; he risked it only after he had gone through agonies of pain and foreboding. Night after night, Max went *au Tivoli* to see Cissie, building up the minutiae of memory to last him until her next appearance. Max permits himself, in the privacy of his correspondence with Turner, to indulge in all sorts of fantasies about Cissie. She imitated, with exquisite delicacy, popular singers of indelicate songs; Max is riven by the thought of these ribaldries emerging from the lips of innocence. Max's passion for Cissie was epistolary; it was sincere and deep, and Max was absorbed in it, but it is evident that he extracted from the letters he wrote to Turner the vicarious delights of a rendezvous. How long this passion would have lasted without Turner to write to about it, one cannot tell. But Turner was also a writer, and would appreciate the chimes and changes of the serial novel Max was spinning for him about Mistress Mere. He kept up the correspondence that kept up Max. Max got, as he always got from Turner, many more than the few words of sympathy he asked for, and went on to the Tivoli to indulge again in the pleasures of self-laceration. Max finds the crowds' adulation of his sweetheart unbearable; he wishes she could perform just for him, and he is exacerbated by the suspicion that possibly Mistress Mere understands the suggestive references in the songs she is singing.

S. N. BEHRMAN, *CONVERSATIONS WITH MAX*

Max's persistence in indulging in his romantic reveries while resolutely refusing to put them to any sort of test of reality was typical of the man and may well have been typical also of many of the intellectuals who seemed determined to adore women from afar. One of Beerbohm's biographers, although never directly referring to the epistolary affair, not with, but about, Miss Loftus, puts his finger on the heart of this odd convention.

The addiction to music halls in the nineties had the force, for Beerbohm, of a vital aesthetic convention. He wrote an early essay, several reviews, and a 1942 reminiscence about the Pavilion, the Tivoli, names like Albert Chevalier, Gus Elen, Dan Leno, Marie Lloyd, George Robey, and he had by heart whole stanzas of songs. What he liked about music halls was the fatuous bawling humour, the talentless rendition of song after song 'instilling a sense of deep beatitude – a strange sweet foretaste of Nirvana'. The music hall may have been a kind of brothel for the man who did not want exactly that and a place to catch life's sordidness in humorous, unpretentious form.

JOHN FELSTINER, *THE LIES OF ART*

I t is with the 1890s that music hall begins to acquire a literature of its own, as the impressionable young men of the day followed Shaw and Beerbohm into the stalls, and the small boys destined one day to be professional writers stored up their impressions for future use. Motives were often mixed. While Beerbohm seems to have attached himself to the Tivoli for personal, romantic reasons, Shaw was drawn to the great Leicester Square houses in search of the fugitive art of ballet (although when it came to the serious theatre he was to display a talent for public love affairs with renowned actresses which reduces Max's longing for Miss Loftus to a mere twitch of the ego). When it came to the music hall, the views of Shaw and Beerbohm were violently opposed just as they were in almost all things. Max cherished the recollection of the *lions comiques* of his boyhood; Shaw was thankful that that period in the development of the art had passed away.

The last place a musical critic ordinarily thinks of going is to a music hall. I should probably not know what a music hall is like, if it were not for the transfer of the ballet in London from the Opera to the Alhambra. The effect of this transfer has been to confront music-hall audiences, nursed on double meanings, with an art emptied of all meaning – with the most abstract, the most 'absolute', as Wagner would have said, of all the arts. Grace for the sake of grace, ornamental motion without destination, noble pose without *locus standi* in the legal sense: this is the object of the tremendous training through which the classical dancer goes before figuring as *assoluta* in the Alhambra programme.

Some years ago, a section of the Church of England made the discovery, then rather badly needed in this country, that '*laborare est orare*' is true of labour devoted to the acquisition of money without regard to ulterior social consequences. This came with the shock of a blasphemous violation of vested interests to the section which had obligingly handed over the whole beauty-producing department of human industry to the devil as his exclusive property.

One discovery generally leads to another; and the clergymen who took up the new ideas had no sooner opened their minds resolutely to the ballet than they were greatly taken aback to find that the exponents of that art, instead of being abandoned voluptuaries, are skilled workers whose livelihood depends on their keeping up by arduous practice a condition of physical training which would overtax the self-denial of most beneficed clergymen. Strange doings followed. Clergymen went to the music halls and worshipped the Divine as manifested in the Beautiful; and a deputation of dancers claimed their rights as members of the Church from the Bishop of London,

48

who, not being up to date in the question, only grasped the situation sufficiently to see that if it is a sin to dance, it is equally a sin to pay other people to dance and then look on at them. He therefore politely and logically excommunicated the deputation and all its patrons, lay and clerical.

Matters have smoothed down a little since that time; and whilst nobody with any pretention to serious and cultivated views on art would now dream of ridiculing and abusing Mr Stuart Headlam as the fashion was in the early days of the Church and Stage Guild, the enthusiasts of that body would not now, I imagine, dispute the proposition that the prejudices against which they fought could never have obtained such a hold on the common-sense of the public had not too many music-hall performers acquiesced in their own ostracism by taking advantage of it to throw off all respect for themselves and their art. The ideas of the Guild have by this time so far permeated the press, that the present tendency is rather to pet the halls, and give free currency to knowing little paragraphs about them, the said paragraphs often amounting to nothing more than puerile gushes of enthusiasm about exploits that ought to be contemptuously criticised off the face of the earth.

Last week I devotedly sat out the programme at the Empire; and I am bound to say that I was agreeably surprised to find the 'lion comique' and the wearisome 'sisters' with the silly duet and the interminable skirt dance quite abolished – for that evening, at all events. Instead, we had Poniatowski's Yeoman's Wedding, 'I fear no foe', and some of Mr Cowen's most popular drawing-room songs. I took what joy I could in these; in the inevitable juggler who had spent his life practising impossibilities which nobody wanted to see overcome; in the equally inevitable virtuoso, who, having announced his intention of imitating 'the oboy', seized his own nose and proceeded grossly to libel the instrument; and in 'the Beduins', the successors of the Bosjesmen who turned somersaults round my cradle, and of the Arab tribes who cheered my advanced boyhood in flying head-over-heels over rows of volleying muskets.

I heard also the Brothers Webb, musical clowns who are really musical, playing the Tyrolienne from William Tell very prettily on two concertinas – though I earnestly beg the amateurs who applauded from the gallery not to imagine that the thing can be done under my windows in the small hours on three-and-sixpenny German instruments. The concertinas on which the Webbs discourse are English Wheatstones of the best sort, such as are retailed at from sixteen to thirty guineas apiece. There are two frankly odious items in the programme. One was a Hungarian quartet, in which the female performers did their worst to their chest registers in striving to impart the rowdiest possible entrain to some Hungarian tunes and to 'Le Père la Victoire'. The other was 'Ta-ra-ra', etc., sung by a French lady, whose forced abandonment as she tore round the stage screaming the cabalistic words without attempting to sing the notes, was so horribly destitute of any sort of grace, humour, naïveté, or any other pleasant quality, that I cannot imagine any sober person looking on without being shocked and humiliated.

Let me now hasten to admit that as the words of the refrain were perfectly harmless, and the lady dressed with a propriety which none of her antics materially disturbed, the most puritanical censor could have alleged nothing in court against the performance, which was nevertheless one of the least edifying I have ever witnessed. I have not had the pleasure of hearing Miss Lottie Collins sing this ancient piece of musical doggerel; but I should be sorry to believe that it 'caught on' originally in the unredeemed condition to which it has been reduced at the Empire.

All this, however, was by the way. What I went to see was the ballet. I have already said that classical dancing is the most abstract of the arts; and it is just for that reason that it has been so little cared for as an art, and so dependent for its vogue on the display of natural beauty which its exercise involves. Now the ballet, as we know it, is a dramatic pantomime in which all sorts of outrageous anomalies are tolerated for the sake of the 'absolute' dancing. It is much worse than an

49

old-fashioned opera in this respect; for although the repeated stoppages of the dramatic action in order that one of the principal dancers may execute a 'solo' or 'variation' is not more absurd than Lucrezia Borgia coming forward from the contemplation of her sleeping son, under thrillingly dangerous circumstances, to oblige the audience with the roulades of *Si volo il primo*, yet Lucrezia is allowed, and even expected, to wear an appropriate costume; whereas if the opera were a ballet she would have a dress such as no human being, at any period of the earth's history, has worn when out walking.

But this advantage of the *prima cantatrice* over the *prima ballerina* is counterbalanced by the fact that whereas dancers must always attend carefully to their physical training, singers are allowed, as long as their voices last, to present themselves on the stage in a condition ludicrously unsuitable to the parts they have to play. Twenty years or so ago you might have seen Titiens playing Valentine, just as you may today see Signor Giannini playing Radames or Manrico, with a corporeal opulence which is politely assumed to be beyond voluntary control, but which, unless it culminates in actual disease – as of course it sometimes does – is just as much a matter of diet and exercise as the condition of the sixteen gentlemen who are going to row from Putney to Mortlake next Saturday. Everything in opera is condoned, provided the singing is all right; and in the ballet everything is condoned, provided the dancing is all right.

But, as Rossini said, there are only twelve notes in European music; and the number of practicable vocal ornaments into which they can be manufactured is limited. When you know half-a-dozen *caballettas* you have no more novelty to look for; and you soon get bored by repetitions of their features except when the quality of the execution is quite extraordinary. My recollection of Di Murska's Lucia does not prevent me from yawning frightfully over the *fioriture* of the dozens of Lucias who are not Di Murskas. In the same way, since the stock of *pas* which make up classical dancing is also limited, the solo dances soon become as stale as the *rosalias* of Handel and Rossini.

The *entrechats* of Vincenti at his entry in the ballet of Asmodeus were worthy of Euphorion; but the recollection of them rather intensifies the boredom with which I contemplate the ordinary *danseuse* who makes a conceited jump and comes down like a wing-clipped fowl without having for an instant shown that momentary picture of a vigorous and beautiful flying feature which is the sole object of the feat. In short, I am as tired of the ballet in its present phase as I became of ante-Wagnerian Italian opera; and I believe that the public is much of my mind in the matter. The conventional solos and variations, with the exasperating teetotum spin at the end by way of cadenza and high B flat, are tolerated rather than enjoyed, except when they are executed with uncommon virtuosity; and even then the encores are a little forced, and come from a minority of the audience. Under such circumstances, a development of the dramatic element, not only in extent but in realistic treatment, is inevitable if the ballet is to surive at all.

Accordingly, I was not surprised to find at the Empire that the first and most popular ballet was an entertainment of mixed *genre* in which an attempt was made to translate into Terpsichorean the life and humours of the seaside. Maria Giuri, a really brilliant dancer, condescended to frank step-dancing in a scene set to national airs, which, however, included one brief variation on 'Yankee Doodle' which the most exclusive pupil of the grand school need not have disdained. Vincenti himself had an air of being at Margate rather than in the Elysian Fields as usual. I am afraid he is rather lost in Leicester Square, where the audience, capable of nothing but cartwheels, stare blindly at his finest *entrechats*; but that is the fate of most artists of his rank. He confined himself mainly to mere *tours de force* in the second ballet, *Nisita,* in which Malvina Cavallazzi, as the Noble Youth, was nobler than ever, and Palladino, who reminded me of the approaching opera season, hid her defects and made the most of her qualities with her usual cleverness.

Perhaps by the time I next visit a music hall the ballet will have found its Wagner, or at least its Meyerbeer. For I have had enough of mere ballet: what I want now is dance-drama.

GEORGE BERNARD SHAW IN *MUSIC IN LONDON*, 6 APRIL 1892

The case of Vincenti illustrates the impossibility of defining music hall. The artists who were engaged by the managements of the Alhambra and the Empire were certainly prepared to face what was a typical music hall audience, but the route by which they had arrived in the building was often in stark contrast to those of the generation of Vance and Leybourne, or to those of a young lady like Cissie Loftus. The music hall by the 1890s was a kind of central stockpot bounded by the other theatrical arts, within whose limits anyone might drift, from a ballerina to a matinée idol, from a balladeer to a reciter of literary monologues, from a hero of operetta to a sweetheart of musical comedy. Vittoria de Vincenti was evidently a great virtuoso, who one night so impressed Shaw that the latter's attempts to define his reactions quickly developed into a riotous mélange of hard fact and pure moonshine.

When I arrived at my door I found Fitzroy Square, in which I live, deserted. It was a clear dry cold night, and the carriage way round the circular railing presented such a magnificent hippodrome that I could not resist trying to go round just once in Vincenti's fashion. It proved frightfully difficult. After my fourteenth fall I was picked up by a policeman. 'What are you doing here?' he said, keeping fast hold of me. 'I bin watching you for the last five minutes.' I explained eloquently and enthusiastically. He hesitated a moment and then said, 'Would you mind holding my helmet while I have a try? It don't look so hard.' Next moment his nose was buried in the macadam and his right knee was out through his torn garment. He got up bruised and bleeding, but resolute. 'I never was beaten yet,' he said, 'and I won't be beaten now. It was my coat that tripped me.' We both hung our coats on the railings, and went at it again. If each round of the square had been a round in a prize fight, we should have been less damaged and disfigured; but we persevered, and by four o'clock the policeman had just succeeded in getting round twice without a rest or fall, when an inspector arrived and asked him bitterly whether that was his notion of fixed point duty. 'I allow it ain't fixed point,' said the constable, emboldened by his new accomplishment, 'but I'll lay half a sovereign *you* can't do it.' The inspector could not resist the temptation to try (I was whirling around before his eyes in the most fascinating manner); and he made rapid progress after half an hour or so. We were subsequently joined by an early postman and by a milkman, who unfortunately broke his leg and had to be carried to hospital by the other three. By that time I was quite exhausted, and could hardly crawl into bed. It was perhaps a foolish scene; but nobody who has witnessed Vincenti's peformance will feel surprised at it.

GEORGE BERNARD SHAW IN *THE STAR*, 21 FEBRUARY 1890

During the time of his introduction to the technicalities of Vincenti's art, Shaw took the trouble to acquaint himself with the technicalities of someone else's. 1892 was the year of one of those astonishing crazes for a chorus song whose words mean absolutely nothing. Whole continents fell before the incomprehensible blandishments of this song, and there is a comic contrast between the earnest analysis of the performance by a learned critic and the brief, brisk practicalities of the artist's own impressions of herself.

I took an opportunity the other night of acquainting myself with Miss Collins's interpretation of 'Ta-ra-ra', etc. It is a most instructive example of the value of artistic methods in music-hall singing, and may be contrasted by students with Violette's crude treatment of the same song. Violette's forced and screaming self-abandonment is a complete failure: Miss Collins's perfect self-possession and calculated economy of effort carry her audience away. She takes the song at an exceedingly restrained *tempo*, and gets her effect of *entrain* by marking the measure very pointedly and emphatically, and articulating her words with ringing brilliancy and with immense assurance of manner. The dance refrain, with its three low kicks on 'Ta-ra-ra' and its high kick on 'Boom' (with *grosse caisse ad lib.*), is the simplest thing imaginable, and is taken in even a more deliberate *tempo* than the preceeding verse.

Miss Collins appears to be in fine athletic training; and the combination of perfect sang-froid and the unsparing vigor with which she carries out her performance, which is so exhaustively studied that not a bar of it is left to chance or the impulse of the moment, ought to convince the idlest of her competitors and the most cynical of music-hall managers that a planned artistic achievement 'catches on' far more powerfully than any random explosion of brainless rowdiness. I do not propose to add to the host of suggestions as to the origin of the tune. As it is only a configuration of the common major chord, it is to be found almost wherever you choose to look for it. In the last movement of Mozart's finest pianoforte sonata in F, in the opening *allegro* of Beethoven's Septuor, and even in the first movement of Mendelssohn's Violin Concerto, it will henceforth make itself felt by all those who continue obsessed by it.

GEORGE BERNARD SHAW IN *MUSIC IN LONDON*, 11 MAY 1892

It was, I think, the mad rush and whirl of the thing that made it go. I got round a 40ft circle twice in eight measures. I first sang it at a matinée and such a storm of applause followed it I didn't know what I'd done.

LOTTIE COLLINS, 1891

Another prominent young writer who achieved intimacy of a sort with the art of the music hall was Rudyard Kipling, who, through the accident of the location of his London rooms, met the people of the halls and learned to listen to their songs so well that the time would come when he would define what he had heard as 'the very stuff of social history'. During the Boer War he was responsible for the raising of large sums of money through the setting of his verses 'The Absent-Minded Beggar' by Sir Arthur Sullivan, who 'wedded the words to a tune guaranteed to pull teeth out of barrel-organs'. Later one of his ballads, 'The Road to Mandalay', became popular in the halls when it was sung by a succession of gentlemen-tenors who sounded as though they were trying to swallow a pound of plums. But it was Kipling's exposure in youth to the rowdy company of his neighbours which first gave him the idea for one of the best-known publications of the decade.

Meantime, I had found me quarters in Villiers Street, Strand, which forty-six years ago was primitive and passionate in its habits and population. My rooms were small, not over-clean or well-kept, but from my desk I could look out of my window through the fanlight of Gatti's Music-Hall entrance, across the street, almost on to its stage. The Charing Cross trains rumbled through my dreams on one side, the boom of the Strand on the other, while, before my windows, Father Thames under the Shot Tower walked up and down with his traffic.

At the outset I had so muddled and mismanaged my affairs that, for a while, I found myself with some money owing for work done, but no funds in hand. People who ask for money, however justifiably, have it remembered against them. The beloved Aunt, or any one of the Three Old Ladies, would have given to me without question; but that seemed too like confessing failure at the outset. My rent was paid; I had my dress-suit; I had nothing to pawn save a collection of unmarked shirts picked up in all ports; so I made shift to manage on what small cash I had in pocket.

My rooms were above an establishment of Harris the Sausage King, who, for tuppence, gave as much sausage and mash as would carry one from breakfast to dinner when one dined with nice people who did not eat sausage for a living. Another tuppence found me a filling supper. The excellent tobacco of those days was, unless you sank to threepenny 'Shag' or soared to sixpenny 'Turkish', tuppence the half-ounce, and fourpence, which included a pewter of beer or porter, was the price of admission to Gatti's.

It was here, in the company of an elderly but upright barmaid from a pub near by, that I listened to the observed and compelling songs of the Lion and Mammoth Comiques, and the shriller strains – but equally 'observed' – of the Bessies and Bellas, whom I could hear arguing beneath my window with their cab-drivers, as they sped from hall to hall. One lady sometimes delighted us with viva-voce versions of – 'what 'as just 'appened to me outside 'ere, if you'll believe it'. Then she would plunge into brilliant improvisations. Oh, we believed! Many of us had, perhaps, taken part in the tail of that argument at the doors, 'ere she stormed in.

Those monologues I could never hope to rival, but the smoke, the roar, and the good-fellowship of relaxed humanity at Gatti's 'set' the scheme for a certain sort of song. The Private Soldier in India I thought I knew fairly well. His English brother (in the Guards mostly) sat and sang at my elbow any night I chose; and, for Greek chorus, I had the comments of my barmaid – deeply and dispassionately versed in all knowledge of evil as she had watched the zinc she was always swabbing off. (Hence, some years later, verses called 'Mary, pity Women', based on what she told me about 'a friend o' mine 'oo was mistook in 'er man'.) The outcome was the first of some verses called 'Barrack-Room Ballads' which I showed to Henley of the 'Scots', later 'National Observer', who wanted more; and I became for a while one of the happy company who used to gather in a little restaurant off Leicester Square and regulate all literature till all hours of the morning.

RUDYARD KIPLING, *SOMETHING OF MYSELF*

M eanwhile, Bernard Shaw had returned to the Empire, where he had encountered for the first time a rising star destined to become the most legendary and the best-loved music hall artist of all time. Shaw perceived her virtues in an instant, and seems to have been the first musician with any sort of legitimate training to do so and to commit his conclusions to print. But there is some slight doubt whether he quite grasped all the overtones of 'Oh, Mr Porter', whose innuendo regarding the plight of the young lady obliged by the accident of circumstance to go much further than she desires, may have escaped the great ascetic.

Now that the new English Opera House is about to be turned into a music hall, and that the Theatre of Varieties is supposed to be swallowing up all other theatres, I have resolved to keep myself up to date by visiting the halls occasionally. The other evening I went to the Empire, where I immediately found myself, to my great delight, up to the neck in pure classicism, siècle de Louis Quatorze. To see Cavallazzi, in the Versailles ballet, walk, stand, sit, and gesticulate, is to learn all that Vestris or Noblet could have taught you as to the technique of doing these things with dignity.

In the stage management too – in the colouring, the costuming, the lighting, in short, the stage presentation in the completest sense – an artistic design, an impulse towards brilliancy and grace of effect, is always dominant, whether it is successful or not; and in some scenes it is highly successful. Now is it not odd that at a music hall to which, perhaps, half the audience have come to hear Marie Lloyd sing 'Twiggy voo, boys, twiggy voo?' or to see Dr Darby jump a ten-barred gate, you get real stage art, whereas at the Opera the stage is managed just as a first-rate restaurant is managed, with everything served up punctually in the most expensive style, but with all the art left to the cook (called 'prima donna'), helped by the waiters (otherwise the chorus).

Wagner noticed long ago that the supremacy of the ballet-masters, who are all enthusiasts in the ballet, made it the most artistic form of stage representation left to us; and I think that anyone who will compare Versailles at the Empire with Orfeo at Covent Garden from this point of view, will see what Wagner was driving at, and what I have driven at pretty often without any further effect so far than to extract from my friends many goodnatured but entirely irrelevant assurances that our operatic impresarios are the best fellows in the world when you come to know them. As to which I may observe that I am a capital fellow myself when you come to know me.

One performance at the Empire exhibited the audience to pitiful disadvantage. A certain Senorita C. de Otero, described as a Spanish dancer and singer, danced a dance which has ennobled the adjective 'suggestive' to me for ever. It was a simple affair enough, none of your cruel Herodias dances, or cleverly calculated tomboyish Ta-ra-ras, but a poignant, most meaning dance, so intensely felt that a mere walk across the stage in it quite dragged at one's heart-strings. This Otero is really a great artist. But do you suppose the house rose at her? Not a bit of it: they stared vacantly, waiting for some development in the manner of Miss Lottie Collins, and finally grumbled out a little disappointed applause. Two men actually hissed – if they will forward me their names and addresses I will publish them with pleasure, lest England should burst in ignorance of its greatest monsters.

54

Take notice, oh Senorita C. de Otero, Spanish dancer and singer, that I wash my hands of the national crime of failing to appreciate you. You were a perfect success: the audience was a dismal failure. I really cannot conceive a man being such a dull dog as to hold out against that dance. Shall it be said that though Miss Collins could stimulate us cleverly but mechanically, Otero, an immeasurably greater artist, cannot touch us poetically? If so, then let the nations know that dancing in England is measured simply by the brightness of the scarlet and the vigor of the kicking. But I wax too eloquent.

There was a second ballet, called *Round the Town*, mostly mere drill and topical spectacle, plus a few excellent pantomime episodes in which Cavallazzi again distinguished herself, as did also Mr W. Warde, a skilful and amusing comic dancer, who played the swell (archaic name for a Johnny). Vincenti has given up the British public in despair, and treats them to unlimited cartwheels and teetotums instead of to the fine classic dancing he used to give us in *Asmodeus*. Both ballets, I may remark, became tedious at the end through the spinning-out of the final scenes by mechanical evolutions involving repeats in the music almost beyond endurance.

One other performer must not go unnoticed. Miss Marie Lloyd, like all the brightest stars of the music hall, has an exceptionally quick ear for both pitch and rhythm. Her intonation and the lilt of her songs are alike perfect. Her step-dancing is pretty; and her command of coster-girls' patois is complete. Why, then, does not someone write humorous songs for her? 'Twiggy voo' is low and silly; and 'Oh, Mister Porter', though very funnily sung, is not itself particularly funny. A humorous rhymester of any genius could easily make it so.

I am greatly afraid that the critics persisted so long in treating the successes of music-hall vocalism as mere impudent exploitations of vulgarity and indecency (forgetting that if this were more than half-true managers could find a dozen Bessie Bellwoods and Marie Lloyds in every street) that the artists have come to exaggerate the popularity of the indecent element in their songs, and to underrate that of the artistic element in their singing. If music-hall songs were written by Messrs Anstey, Rudyard Kipling, W. S. Gilbert, etc., our best music-hall singers would probably be much more widely popular than they can ever become now. Twiggez vous, Miss Lloyd?

GEORGE BERNARD SHAW IN *MUSIC IN LONDON*, 19 OCTOBER 1892

Not all writers were as indifferent to sexual innuendo as Shaw. Although only eight years old in 1891, when he was first exposed to the allure of Marie, Compton Mackenzie became so excited by a glimpse of the great lady's underwear that at the end of a long lifetime he could remember every detail with the enthusiasm of the born hedonist.

Just before our new governess Miss Stanwell arrived, Frank, Viola and I were taken by our old nurse to the pantomime for the last time. I remember that it was we in a way who were taking her to Drury Lane, so much in my own opinion had I been aged by a term of school. We sat again in the stage box on the prompt side on the other side of the footlights. The pantomime was 'The Yellow Dwarf' in which Little Tich, that comedian of grotesque genius, appeared as the Dwarf. What I remember most vividly was Marie Lloyd's performance as principal girl. She could not have been much more than nineteen at this date, and had had a resounding success in singing and dancing 'Ta-ra-ra-boom-de-ay'. The creator of 'Ta-ra-ra-boom-de-ay' was Lottie Collins, who had been singing it through that autumn in various music-halls. In those days the popular songs of the year were heard again in pantomimes all over the country. Marie Lloyd sang her most successful number just before the Transformation Scene and as she started Harry Paine, the last of the great clowns, came into our box before appearing at the end of the Transformation Scene with a great packet of crackers to give the time-honoured greeting of 'Here we are again', a greeting which had been given year in, year out, since the days of the famous Joseph Grimaldi, the original 'Joey', the name of every pantomime clown for over a century. After which, and before the first scene of the Harlequinade, he would toss these crackers to delighted children in stalls and pit and circle. Marie Lloyd was doing the high kicks which punctuated the singing of the chorus with glorious verve and revealing a great display of amber silk petticoats and long amber silk drawers frilled below her knees. I turned to Harry Paine in surprise and said, 'She's showing her drawers!'

From that surprised ejaculation of mine do not suppose I was shocked. If I had been shocked I should have said nothing and surrendered to a puritan's private enjoyment of the display while pretending to be shocked. No, I was not shocked, but I *was* greatly surprised that any girl should have the courage to let the world see her drawers as defiantly as Marie Lloyd. Harry Paine laughed so loudly that Marie Lloyd heard him and with a wink turned towards the stage-box and gave a terrific high kick almost into it.

'Wait when the curtain comes down after the Harlequinade,' said the clown, as he left the box to be ready for his entrance. And when the curtain fell Harry Paine came back and asked Nanny to wait with my brother and sister in the box while he took me to meet somebody. That somebody was Marie Lloyd herself, who was already dressed to leave the theatre by the time the Harlequinade was over, trim and tight-laced, bustled and bonneted.

'Here's the young gentleman who was shocked by seeing your drawers, Marie.'

Of course I was incapable of explaining that I had been surprised but not shocked at all, and Marie Lloyd, realising my embarrassment, took me by the arms and gave me a kiss and a hug.

COMPTON MACKENZIE, *MY LIFE AND TIMES*

Mackenzie, endowed with the most phenomenal powers of memory of his generation, or perhaps any generation, was fond of looking back at the music halls he had been taken to as a schoolboy. He seems to have forgotten not a single encore, no demon king, no string of sausages, no red nose, no clown floundering in the backwash of a bucket of paste, no ingenue with pink thighs and apple cheeks. Had the Victorian music hall been wiped out of existence and all its annals destroyed, most of it could have been reconstructed from the recollections of a few memoirists, among whom Mackenzie was supreme.

The first pantomime to which I was taken was *The Forty Thieves* at Drury Lane matinée in January 1887 when I was on the edge of four years old. I remember that long journey by District Railway from Kensington to the Temple, the fresh air of the Embankment when one emerged from the choking fumes of the underground, the adventurous crossing of the Strand, the rather frightening walk through the narrow thronged streets round Drury Lane, long since cleared away, the orange girls crying their wares in the colonnade as they had cried them since the days of Nell Gwynn. Then the sight of the crowded auditorium from a box in the dress-circle tier on the O.P. side – that is on the left as you look at the stage – the unforgettable pantomime smell of the past, a mixture of gas, oranges, human beings and dust, the noise of excited children and grown ups in the gallery and upper boxes (as the upper circle was called then), in pit and stalls and dress circle, and in the private boxes too, and finally the great gasp of anticipation as the curtain rose on the immemorial first scene of the Demon King announcing his villainous projects by the illumination of fizzy blue and red limes until the Fairy Queen entered from the prompt side and, standing in the holy circle cast by a fizzy white lime, vowed she would thwart his villainy. It was in one of those Drury Lane pantomimes of about sixty years ago that the Demon King sang:

> Hush, hush, hush!
> Here comes the bogey man,
> Be on your best behaviour,
> For he'll catch you if he can.

At these words children were fain to clutch parent or nurse or governess in panic, and I remember hearing it debated whether a theatre management was justified in terrifying children with such songs at a pantomime. Can you fancy children being terrified by such a song to-day?

My most vivid memory of *The Forty Thieves* is when Charles Lauri, as a donkey, and Paul Martinetti, as a monkey, climbed up from the stage to the boxes on the prompt side and ran, yes, ran all the way round the plush-covered parapet of the dress circle, raising shrieks from all the children in the front rows. When the two animals reached our box my young brother – still four months away from two – let out a yell so loud and continued to yell so loudly that our nurse had to take him out of the box; I was left alone, a rather apprehensive child, for the rest of the scene.

The Drury Lane pantomime in 1888 was *Puss in Boots*, and for me it was a tragedy because just as Letty Lind, the principal girl, came on in a coach and Charles Lauri, as the enterprising cat, was crying that his master the Marquis of Carrabas was drowning, my nurse suddenly decided that it was time to go home. We were in a circle box on the prompt side – she, an elderly woman who looked like a withered Chinese, a little girl friend, and myself. I implored Nanny to stay, but she insisted on leaving the theatre. At the time her behaviour was inexplicable; I realised later that she must have been seized by an overwhelming desire to get back to the gin which she imbibed for years before she was found out. I can hear now from long ago the echoes of my sobbing as I was led from the theatre, and I can see now through the glass doors of the circle lobby with a last despairing backward glance the glittering silver of Letty Lind's coach.

The pantomime of 1889 was the first in which the immortal Dan Leno appeared at Drury Lane. He played the Baroness in *The Babes in the Wood*. The laughter at his entrance, wheeling on the Babes – Herbert Campbell and Harry Nicholls – in a huge perambulator resounds in my ears from over sixty years ago. *Jack and the Beanstalk* followed in 1890. Harriet Vernon, a very handsome woman not far from six foot tall, was Jack, and I fell madly in love with her, being then on the edge of seven. When we got home from the matinée, I announced my intention of marrying her one day. 'You won't,' proclaimed my brother, four months away from five, 'I'm going to marry her.' In a trice we were locked in a furious duel, rolling over and over one another on the front door mat like a couple of cavemen. In the end, with the advantage of weight, I compelled my brother to renounce his ambition to marry Harriet Vernon.

By this date the Harlequinade had shrunk to a couple of scenes: no longer did the Clown go right through the pantomime as in the days of Grimaldi. At the end of what was called the Transformation Scene, which consisted of raising one by one a series of gauzes to reveal fairies, reclining in enormous roses and water-lilies and that kind of thing, Clown, Pantaloon, Columbine and Harlequin appeared, the Clown opening with the time-honoured greeting of 'Here we are again!' and proceeding to throw crackers to the children in the audience – often able to reach as far as the dress circle, which was a pretty good throw from the stage at Drury Lane. This was followed by a front-cloth street-scene in which the Clown always burnt everybody with a red-hot poker and always stole a string of sausages from a butcher's shop. Columbine was continually pirouetting backwards and forwards along the street and Harlequin playing all sorts of tricks on shopfronts with his wand. The Pantaloon and a gawky Policeman were always the butts of every joke and they were always being burnt more than anybody else by the Clown's red-hot poker. Then the street-scene gave way to an interior which ended in a riotous trap-act with Harlequin whizzing up ten feet in the air through a star-trap and diving head foremost through a wall just as the Clown was going to catch him. That second scene vanished early in the 'nineties, and by the beginning of this century nothing was left of the Harlequinade except a brief street scene. In a few years or so even that vanished, and the Harlequinade, as far as I know, is now extinct.

For the Drury Lane pantomimes of 1890 and 1891 we had the stage-box on the prompt side. In those days the stage-box was behind the orchestra and actually flush with the front of the stage – a most exciting place to be. I remember Marie Lloyd singing and dancing 'Ta-ra-ra-boom-de-ay' – no, not Lottie Collins who sang and danced it at the music halls – and, while she was high-kicking from a cloud of amber underclothes, Harry Payne, the last of the great clowns, came into our box all dressed to go on and cry 'Here we are again' when his cue came. That seemed the most tremendous encounter I had ever had with the great of this world. If Dick Barton stepped out of a loudspeaker and shook hands all round the room it would hardly provide a greater thrill for a boy of to-day.

Other pantomimes we used to visit in those far off days were at the old Surrey Theatre in the Blackfriars Road. It was a great adventure walking over the bridge from the underground station, and as I look back to the Thames as it then appeared to my childish eyes it seems rather larger than the Atlantic Ocean. The giant Blunderbore was a formidable figure in *Jack the Giant Killer*, for he was able to put his head into the two circle-boxes on either side of the proscenium and champ at us, and in *Valentine and Orson* the fight between the two brothers spilt so much red paint that the stage looked like the floor of a slaughter-house. Nowadays the psychosis ramp would attribute the most fearful consequences to a childhood exposed to such horrors, but I cannot say I have discovered any psychosis in myself.

It was in the mid 'nineties that the great boom in building suburban theatres was in full swing. Most of them are picture palaces to-day or, like the Grand Theatre, Fulham, empty and silent. Pantomimes there were almost our favourites, in spite of having to endure the spectacle of a little boy in an Eton collar standing up in the dress circle to sing a duet with Aladdin or Prince Charming. How we loathed that little boy! I remember one song which went:

> Your lips are red as rubies,
> Your eyes are diamonds rare.
> So while I have you,
> My lovely Sue,
> I'm as rich as a millionaire.

While this odious little boy was singing his first part Aladdin would go mincing about the stage, holding her hand to her ear – or I suppose I should say *his* hand, because she was the principal boy, and to our consternation and disgust we could hear elderly women all round exclaiming, 'Oh, what a little love! Oh, isn't he lovely!

Oh, I do think he's lovely.' We used to scowl our disagreement, but it was no use. To that audience of long ago this chorister was another Stewart Granger or Michael Wilding.

Those were the days when the telephone was still a novelty and Millie Legarde sang:

> Hello, my baby, hello, my honey,
> Hello, my ragtime girl.
> Send me a kiss by wire,
> Honey, my heart's on fire,
> If you refuse me, honey, you'll lose me
> Then you'll be left alone.
> So telephone, and tell me I'm your own.

We thought that this lyric touched the ultimate heights of passionate expression. To sing 'Drink to me only with thine eyes' or 'My love is like a red, red rose' after that would have seemed a descent to utter banality.

There were great houses for pantomime before the eruption of suburban theatres. The Grand, Islington, with Harry Randall as the Dame, the Standard, Shoreditch, and – more tremendous than any – the Britannia, Hoxton. If I were asked to name the audience that expressed beyond any other the spirit of London I would say the audience of the Britannia Theatre, Hoxton, at a pantomime. This was the apotheosis of the Cockney. This was the incarnation of his humour and gaiety and warm humanity. The women in their plumed hats! The costers in their pearlies! The oranges and nuts! That immense audience would seethe with enjoyment: it was a vast bubbling kettle of mirth. This was the stuff out of which came the London able to 'take it' forty years on. I used to have tears in my eyes just from the pleasure of being one in such a gathering. The man who was never one of an audience at the Britannia, Hoxton, has missed something in the life of London.

COMPTON MACKENZIE, *ECHOES*

Not all the available entertainment was quite as innocent as the Christmas pantomime. The Alhambra and the Empire in particular were by the early 1890s as famous for their Promenades as for the acts they presented on stage. That these promenades were an open invitation to prostitution there is little doubt. On the other hand, there will always be prostitution in great cities, and apologists at the time pointed out quite rightly that at least inside the two theatres everything was decorous, regulated, and calculated not to give offence. However, since the convention had been established that music-hall managers must apply for a license to open, the vulnerability of the Alhambra and the Empire was obvious enough. The real danger loomed with the creation in 1888 of the London County Council, some of whose functionaries took it upon themselves to be scandalised by the open parade of scarlet women on view each night at places which were catering for families and the young.

The moral wrath of the newly-founded council was personified in a Mrs Ormiston Chant, who by 1892 was embarked on her campaign to clean up the music hall in general and the Leicester Square promenades in particular. In retrospect it seems uncertain what she hoped to gain for the forces of moral righteousness. By having the promenades closed down she could not believe that she was reducing the amount of prostitution in the West End. Presumably she hoped to see it deinstitutionalised and divorced from the theatres. By 1894 the battle raged to its comic climax, raising, not for the first time, nor the last, the vexed question of how far censorship of an improvisatory art is possible, let alone desirable. Innuendo was there for those who chose to savour it; for the rest, everything seemed quite innocent. But without the innuendo and the double entendre, the wit of the halls might shrivel up and die altogether. As for Mrs Chant, she soon received the accolade of being quoted in a popular song which was itself a riot of innuendo.

And Her Golden Hair Was Hanging Down Her Back

There was once a country maiden came to London for a trip,
And her golden hair was hanging down her back:
She was weary of the country so she gave her folks the slip
And her golden hair was hanging down her back.
It was once a vivid auburn but her rivals called it red,
So she thought she could be happier with another shade instead.
And she stole the washing soda and applied it to her head,
And some golden hair came streaming down her back.

Chorus
But oh, Flo! such a change, you know,
When she left the village she was shy.
But alas and alack, she's gone back
With a naughty little twinkle in her eye!

She had a country accent and a captivating glance,
And her golden hair was hanging down her back.
She wore some little diamonds that came from sunny France,
And her golden hair was hanging down her back.
She wandered out in London for a breath of ev'ning air,
And strayed into a Palace that was fine and large and fair,
It might be in a Circus or it might be in a Square,
But her golden hair was hanging down her back.

Chorus

And London people were so nice to artless little Flo,
When her golden hair was hanging down her back,
That she had been persuaded to appear in a tableau,
Where her golden hair was hanging down her back.
She posed beside a marble bath upon some marble stairs,
Just like a water nymph or an advertisement for Pears,
And if you ask me to describe the costume that she wears,
Well, her golden hair is hanging down her back.

Chorus

She met a young philanthropist, a friend of Missus Chant,
And her golden hair was hanging down her back,
He lived in Peckham Rye with an extremely maiden aunt,
Who had not a hair a-hanging down her back.
The lady looked upon him in her fascinating way,
And what the consequences were I really cannot say,
But when his worthy maiden aunt remarked his coat next day,
Well, some golden hairs were hanging down the back.

These lyrics, written by one Felix McGlennon, may strike a more salacious age as innocent enough, but in the hands of the light comedian Seymour Hicks, they could be made rather more suggestive than on paper. With reference to the art of innuendo generally, the observations on the lyric by a postwar critic are interesting.

In the music hall, precisely what is assumed is left to the imagination of each member of the audience, but the implication is invariably of a kind delightfully described by Chance Newton as 'cerulean', or 'a touch of the blue bag'. It was a favourite comic device of Max Miller's. By means of stressed rhymes he would lead an audience to expect a blue joke, but would so time what he said that he could rely on being interrupted by the loud laughter of the audience before he reached the significant word. He would then feel free to upbraid the audience vigorously for having dirty minds and giving him a bad name – and this technique was far from peculiar to Max Miller.

This device, like any other, can be badly done, or it can be carried through with the downright cheek and superb sense of timing of a Max Miller. The performer's approach to the innuendo song varies. Slightly more teasing songs than 'And Her Golden Hair Was Hanging Down Her Back' are 'The Bird in Nellie's Hat' and 'Mother's Advice', but they must be presented quite differently. The former must be sung knowingly, while the latter depends on childlike innocence of presentation.

'And Her Golden Hair' was originally sung by Alice Leamar, but it was taken up by Sir Seymour Hicks, and was sung for some six hundred nights in the musical *The Shop Girl* in 1894-5. Hicks was not a music-hall artiste, but from time to time he performed on the halls with his wife, Ellaline Terriss, usually in sketches.

This song is one of the many that tells the story of the young innocent maiden who comes to the great city, and her golden hair was hanging down her back. Marie Lloyd had several such. Despite some padding, the song rises above the mundane for several reasons. It makes skilful use of the reiteration of the refrain, partly descriptive, partly an invitation to innuendo, but partly also a nice deflation of that very golden hair we are asked to admire – it was once a vivid auburn but her rivals called it red. There is also a neat variation in the refrain when it is used for the maiden aunt and there is a nice turn of phrase in calling her 'extremely maiden'.

It ought to be explained that a popular advertisement for Pears soap in the late Victorian period showed a naked child; and that 'Missus Chant' was Mrs Ormiston Chant who in 1892 began a campaign described even by that violently anti-Ibsen drama critic Clement Scott as 'Prudes on the Prowl'.

PETER DAVISON, *THE BRITISH MUSIC HALL*

In 1895 Mrs Chant was mentioned in another popular music hall song, by which time her campaign had been elevated to farce and the dangers of her campaign to the music hall somewhat reduced. She became a target for the wits, including the lyricist Basil Hood, who wrote a song for Arthur Roberts to sing in the musical comedy *Gentleman Joe* at the Prince of Wales. It consisted of the reminiscences of a London cab driver and was called 'In My 'Ansom'. The final verse read:

> In my 'ansom! in my 'ansom!
> Oh, it's no affair of mine to go an' blab.
> For it might ha' been 'is aunt
> Or another Mrs Chant,
> 'E was drivin' in my 'ansom cab!'

The Daily Telegraph, which constituted itself the champion of the halls through its drama critic Clement Scott, took some pleasure in publishing straight-faced verbatim reports of proceedings which held up the crusaders to great ridicule. The following extract from the paper dated 11 October 1894 introduces an unwitting comedian called Mr Collins, whose testimony must have caused more laughter in the West End bars and clubs than many a professional comic's nightly routine.

Mrs Chant stated that her attention was first called to the Empire early in the year by two American gentlemen. They were so shocked that she determined to visit the theatre, but did not do so until July, when the Living Pictures had made so much stir. Early in the evening there were comparatively few people in the promenade, but after nine o'clock the number increased. She noticed young women enter alone, more or less painted, and gorgeously dressed. They accosted young gentlemen who were strangers to them, and paid little attention to the performance. She herself was so quietly attired that one of the attendants exclaimed to a woman, 'You had better mind how you behave tonight, there are strangers about' (*laughter*).

Mrs Annie Hicks gave evidence on behalf of the opposition.

'Do you object to women going to places of entertainment alone?' 'No, I think that women ought to be able to go into any assembly alone.'

'Exactly on the same footing as men?' 'Quite so.'

'And not be interfered with so long as they conduct themselves with propriety?' 'Yes.'

Mr Collins, described as a tea merchant in London and Liverpool, deposed that he had gone to the Empire nearly twenty times during the last three months, and on one occasion counted well-nigh 180 women of objectionable character. The Empire was, he thought, notoriously a show place for that kind of thing.

Mr Gill, opening the case for the applicant, commented upon the testimony which had been produced in opposition to the license. Though well-meaning people, perhaps, the witnesses were persons of the most violent and extreme views, who, instead of attending to their own affairs, presumed to look after the morals of others and dictate what sort of entertainment should be offered to the London public. A number of gentlemen of large capital and great enterprise had been lavish in their expenditure in order to put on the Empire stage the best performance that money could possibly produce, with the result that the theatre was constantly full, so that any reflection upon the entertainment was equally a reflection upon the spectators.

Immoral characters were perfectly entitled to go to the promenade, and so long as they conducted themselves with propriety they ought not to be interfered with. There had not been the slightest complaint of their behaviour since the renewal of the license by the County Council. The authorities at the Empire took every possible precaution in the interests of the proper management of the theatre, and he urged the committee not to be led away by the extremely improbable stories that had been told them.

Mr George Edwardes, managing director of the Empire, said: 'In front of the house we have a large staff responsible for the good conduct of the people entering the theatre. It is nearly 100 strong, and headed by a retired inspector of police and several sergeants. Practically everybody is inspected before being allowed to enter, and nobody goes in without paying for admission. A sergeant and detective are in the promenade seeing that the women there behave themselves properly. If anything like marked accosting is observed, first the woman is cautioned, and for a second offence she is taken out of the house. The same thing applies to men. Women are frequently prevented from entering.'

THE DAILY TELEGRAPH, 11 OCTOBER 1894

The argument became more heated by the day, and the more heat that was generated, the more convoluted grew the arguments for and against. The Theatrical and Music Hall Operatives Union denounced the campaign to close the promenade on the grounds that it would force the theatre to close and bring about unemployment. George Edwardes claimed that the closing of the promenade and the banning of alcohol would oblige him to dismiss 670 employees. Advanced churchmen came out against the clean-up campaign, and the London Cab Drivers' Trade Union claimed that cab drivers would be deprived of a substantial slice of their income should the promenade go down. At last Mrs Chant, confused by the attacks, decided to restate her case.

All I want is to clear certain of the music halls of the unclean features which debar decent folks from attending and enjoying the performances. A short time ago I was at the Palace Theatre of Varieties in London, and I was charmed and delighted with what I saw. As to the living pictures, they were beautiful, and there were only three to which I objected. It is significant that these were received almost in silence by the audience. All the rest were enthusiastically cheered.

Do I object to ballet? Nothing is further from my mind. I don't object to tights, as such I know that when you dance very vigorously you must not be impeded by clinging petticoats about your ankles, or even about the knees. If need be, I think I could devise a costume which would give this freeness and yet clothe the limbs, although I am not one of those who think it a shame to have legs. It is the motive at the back of it all, and the obvious suggestiveness, which makes the thing evil. We have no right to sanction on the stage that which if it were done in the street would compel a policeman to lock the offender up. The whole question would be solved if men, and not women, were at stake. Men would refuse to exhibit their bodies nightly in this way.

THE DAILY TELEGRAPH, 18 OCTOBER 1894

osterity, regretting bitterly the failure of the theatrical costumiers to take up Mrs Chant's generous offer of a new design for a ballet costume, may marvel at the infallible way that do-gooders of all epochs reduce themselves to absurdity by claiming to be good sports with no objection to a little healthy fun. The Licensing Committee soon ruled that certain changes must take place at the Empire. On 26 October 1894, at the end of the evening's entertainment, Mr Edwardes came before the footlights and informed the audience that owing to the judgement of the council, he would be closing the theatre as from this night in order that alterations could be carried out in compliance with the new rulings. Amid cries of 'The dirty dogs', 'Out with them', and 'Foul bigots', Mr Edwardes calmly wished his audience good night. According to *The Star*, 'Strong men went pale and ghastly with rage, while dilettante youths tried to emulate their demonstrativeness, and succeeded to the extent of a shrill cry of "Dem'd shame".' On 3 November, alterations having been made, the Empire reopened, to a demonstration destined by a fluke of circumstances to become part of the history of English oratory.

In my last term at Sandhurst my indignation was excited by the Purity Campaign of Mrs Ormiston Chant. This lady was a member of the London County Council and in the summer of 1894 she started an active movement to purge our music halls. Her attention was particularly directed to the promenade of the Empire Theatre. This large space behind the dress circle was frequently crowded during the evening performances, and especially on Saturdays, with young people of both sexes, who not only conversed together during the performance and its intervals, but also from time to time refreshed themselves with alcoholic liquors. Mrs Ormiston Chant and her friends made a number of allegations affecting both the sobriety and the morals of these merrymakers, and she endeavoured to procure the closing of the promenade and above all of the bars which abutted on it. It seemed that the majority of the English public viewed these matters in a different light. Their cause was championed by *The Daily Telegraph*, in those days our leading popular newspaper. In a series of powerful articles headed 'Prudes on the Prowl', *The Daily Telegraph* inaugurated a wide and spirited correspondence in which persons were wont to contribute above such pseudonyms as 'Mother of Five', 'Gentleman and Christian', 'Live and Let Live', 'John Bull' and so forth. The controversy aroused keen public interest; but nowhere was it more searchingly debated than among my Sandhurst friends. We were accustomed to visit this very promenade in the brief leave allowed to us twice a month from Saturday noon till Sunday midnight. We were scandalised by Mrs Chant's charges and insinuations. We had never seen anything to complain of in the behaviour of either sex. Indeed the only point upon which criticism, as it seemed to us, might justly be directed was the strict and even rough manner in which the enormous uniformed commissionaires immediately removed, and even thrust forcibly into the street, anyone who had inadvertently overstepped the bounds of true temperance. We thought Mrs Ormiston Chant's movement entirely uncalled-for and contrary to the best traditions of British freedom.

In this cause I was keenly anxious to strike a blow. I noticed one day in *The Daily Telegraph* that a gentleman – whose name escapes me – proposed to found a League of Citizens to resist and counter the intolerance of Mrs Chant and her backers. This was to be called 'The Entertainments Protection League'. The League proposed to form committees and an executive, to take offices and enrol members, to collect subscriptions, to hold public meetings, and to issue literature in support of its views. I immediately volunteered my services. I wrote to the pious Founder at the address which he had given, expressing my cordial agreement with his aims and my readiness to co-operate in every lawful way. In due course I received an answer on impressively-headed notepaper informing me that my support was welcomed, and inviting my attendance at the first meeting of the Executive Committee, which was to be held on the following Wednesday at six o'clock in a London hotel.

Wednesday was a half-holiday, and well-conducted cadets could obtain leave to go to London simply by asking for it. I occupied the three days' interval in composing a speech which I thought I might be called upon to deliver to a crowded executive of stern-faced citizens, about to unfurl that flag of British freedom for which 'Hampden died on the battlefield and Sidney on the Scaffold'. As I had never attempted to speak in public before, it was a serious undertaking. I wrote and rewrote my speech three of four times over, and committed it in all its perfection to my memory.

It was a serious constitutional argument upon the inherent rights of British subjects; upon the dangers of State interference with the social habits of law-abiding persons; and upon the many evil consequences which inevitably follow upon repression not supported by healthy public opinion. It did not over-state the case, nor was it blind to facts. It sought to persuade by moderation and good humour, and to convince by logic tempered with common sense. There was even in its closing phrases an appeal for a patient mood towards our misguided opponents. Was there not always more error than malice in human affairs? This task completed I awaited eagerly and at the same time nervously the momentous occasion.

As soon as our morning tasks were done I grabbed a hasty luncheon, changed into plain clothes (we were taught to abhor the word 'mufti', and such abominable expressions as 'civvies' were in those days unknown) and hastened to the railway station, where I caught a very slow train to London. I must mention that this was for me a time of straitened finance; in fact the cost of the return railway ticket left me with only a few shillings in my pocket, and it was more than a fortnight before my next monthly allowance of £10 was due.

I whiled away the journey by rehearsing the points and passages on which I principally relied. I drove in a hansom cab from Waterloo to Leicester Square, near which the hotel appointed for the meeting was situated. I was surprised and a little disconcerted at the dingy and even squalid appearance of these back streets and still more at the hotel when my cab eventually drew up before it. However, I said to myself, they are probably quite right to avoid the fashionable quarters. If this movement is to prosper it must be based upon the people's will, it must respond to those simple instincts which all classes have in common. It must not be compromised by association with gilded youth or smart society. To the porter I said, 'I have come to attend the meeting of the Entertainments Protection League announced to be held this day in your hotel.'

The porter looked rather puzzled, and then said, 'I think there's a gentleman in the smoking-room about that.' Into the smoking-room, a small dark apartment, I was accordingly shown, and there I met face to face the Founder of the new body. He was alone. I was upset; but concealing my depression under the fast-vanishing rays of hope, I asked, 'When do we go up to the meeting?' He too seemed embarrassed. 'I have written to several people, but they have none of them turned up, so there's only you and me. We can draw up the Constitution ourselves, if you like.' I said, 'But you wrote to me on the headed paper of the League.' 'Well', he said, 'that cost only five shillings. It's always a good thing to have a printed heading on your notepaper in starting these sort of things. It encourages people to come forward. You see it encouraged you!' He paused as if chilled by my reserve, then added, 'It's very difficult to get people to do anything in England now. They take everything lying down. I do not know what's happened to the country; they seem to have no spirit left.'

Nothing was to be gained by carrying the matter further and less than nothing by getting angry with the Founder of the League. So I bade him a restrained but decisive farewell, and walked out into the street with a magnificent oration surging within my bosom and only half a crown in my pocket. The pavements were thronged with people hurrying to and fro engrossed upon their petty personal interests, oblivious and indifferent to the larger issues of human government. I looked with pity not untinged with scorn upon these trivial-minded passers-by. Evidently it was not going to be so easy to guide public opinion in the right direction as I had supposed. If these weak products of democracy held their liberties so lightly, how would they defend the vast provinces and domains we had gained by centuries of aristocratic and oligarchic rule? For a moment I despaired of the Empire. Then I thought of dinner and was pallidly confronted with the half a crown! No, that would not do! A journey to London on a beautiful half-holiday, keyed up to the last point of expectation, with a speech that might have shaped the national destinies undelivered and undigested upon my stomach, and then to go back to Sandhurst upon a bun and a cup of tea! That was more than fortitude could endure. So I did what I have never done before or since. I had now reached the Strand. I saw the three golden balls hanging over Mr Attenborough's well-known shop. I had a very fine gold watch which my father had given me on my latest birthday. After all, the Crown Jewels of great kingdoms had been pawned on hard occasions. 'How much do you want?' said the showman after handling the watch respectfully. 'A fiver will do', I said. Some particulars were filled up in a book. I received one of those tickets which hitherto I had only heard of in music-hall songs, and a five-pound note, and sallied forth again into the heart of London. I got home all right.

The next day my Sandhurst friends all wanted to know how the meeting had gone off. I had imparted to them beforehand some of the more cogent arguments I intended to use. They were curious to learn how they had gone down. What was the meeting like? They had rather admired me for having the cheek to go up to make a speech championing their views to an Executive Committee of grown-up people, politicians, aldermen and the like. They wanted to know all about it. I did not admit them to my confidence. Speaking generally I dwelt upon the difficulties of public agitation in a comfortable and upon the whole contented country. I pointed out the importance of proceeding step by step, and of making each step good before the next was taken. The first step was to form an Executive Committee – that had been done. The next was to draw up the constitution of the League and assign the various responsibilities and powers – this was proceeding. The third step would be a broad appeal to the public, and on the response to this everthing depended. These statements were accepted rather dubiously; but what else could I do? Had I only possessed a newspaper of my own, I would have had my speech reported verbatim on its front page, punctuated by the loud cheers of the Committee, heralded by arresting headlines and soberly sustained by the weight of successive leading articles. Then indeed the Entertainments Protection League might have made real progress. It might, in those early nineties, when so many things were in the making, have marshalled a public opinion so vigilant throughout the English-speaking world, and pronounced a warning so impressive, that the mighty United States themselves might have been saved from Prohibition! Here again we see the footprints of Fate, but they turned off the pleasant lawns to a stern and stony highway.

I was destined to strike another blow in this crusade. Mrs Chant's campaign was not unsuccessful, indeed so menacing did it appear that our party thought it prudent to make a characteristically British compromise. It was settled that the offending bars were to be separated from the promenade by light canvas screens. Thus they would no longer be technically 'in' the promenade; they would be just as far removed from it in law if they had been in the adjacent county; yet means of ingress and egress of sufficient width might be lawfully provided, together with any reductions of the canvas screens necessary for efficient ventilation. Thus the temples of Venus and

Bacchus, though adjacent, would be separated, and their attack upon human frailties could only be delivered in a successive or alternating and not in a concentrated form. Loud were the hosannas which arose from the steadfast ranks of the 'Prudes on the Prowl'. The music-hall proprietors for their part, after uttering howls of pain and protest, seemed to reconcile themselves quite readily to their lot. It was otherwise with the Sandhurst movement. We had not been consulted in this nefarious peace. I was myself filled with scorn at its hypocrisy. I had no idea in those days of the enormous and unquestionably helpful part that humbug plays in the social life of great peoples dwelling in a state of democratic freedom. I wanted a clear-cut definition of the duties of the state and the rights of the individual, modified as might be necessary by public convenience and decorum.

On the first Saturday night after these canvas obstructions had been placed in the Empire promenade it happened that quite a large number of us chanced to be there. There were also a good many boys from the Universities about our own age, but of course mere bookworms, quite undisciplined and irresponsible. The new structures were examined with attention and soon became the subject of unfavourable comment. Then some young gentleman poked his walking-stick through the canvas. Others imitated his example. Naturally I could not hang back when colleagues were testifying after this fashion. Suddenly a most strange thing happened. The entire crowd numbering some two or three hundred people became excited and infuriated. They rushed upon these flimsy barricades and tore them to pieces. The authorities were powerless. Amid the cracking of timber and the tearing of canvas the barricades were demolished, and the bars were once more united with the promenade to which they ministered for so long.

In these somewhat unvirginal surroundings I now made my maiden speech. Mounting on the debris and indeed partially emerging from it, I addressed the tumultuous crowd. No very accurate report of my words has been preserved. They did not, however, fall unheeded, and I have heard about them several times since. I discarded the constitutional argument entirely and appealed directly to sentiment and even passion, finishing up by saying, 'You have seen us tear down these barricades tonight; see that you pull down those who are responsible for them at the coming election.' These words were received with rapturous applause, and we all sallied out into the Square brandishing fragments of wood and canvas as trophies or symbols. It reminded me of the death of Julius Caesar when the conspirators rushed forth into the street waving the bloody daggers with which they had slain the tyrant. I thought also of the taking of the Bastille, with the details of which I was equally familiar.

It seems even more difficult to carry forward a revolution than to start one. We had to catch the last train back to Sandhurst or be guilty of dereliction of duty. This train, which still starts from Waterloo shortly after midnight, conveys the daily crop of corpses to the London Necropolis. It ran only as far as Frimley near Aldershot which it reached at three o'clock in the morning, leaving us to drive eight or ten miles to the Royal Military College. On our arrival at this hamlet no conveyances were to be found. We therefore knocked up the local innkeeper. It may well be that we knocked him up rather boisterously. After a considerable interval in which our impatience became more manifest, the upper half of the door was suddenly opened, and we found ourselves looking down the muzzle of a blunderbuss, behind which stood a pale and menacing face. Things are rarely pushed to extremes in England. We maintained a firm posture, explained our wants and offered money. The landlord, first reassured and finally placated, produced an old horse and a still more ancient fly, and in this seven or eight of us made a successful journey to Camberley, and without troubling the porter at the gates, reached our apartments by unofficial paths in good time for early morning parade.

This episode made a considerable stir, and even secured leading articles in most of the newspapers. I was for some time apprehensive lest undue attention should be focussed upon my share in the proceedings. Certainly there was grave risk, for my father's name was still electric. Although naturally proud of my part in resisting tyranny as is the duty of every proud citizen who wishes to live in a free country, I was not unaware that a contrary opinion was possible, and might even become predominant. Elderly people and those in authority cannot always be relied upon to take an enlightened and comprehending view of what they call the indiscretions of youth. They sometimes have a nasty trick of singling out individuals and 'making examples'. Although always prepared for martyrdom, I preferred that it should be postponed. Happily by the time my name began to be connected with the event, public interest had entirely died down, and no one at the College or the War Office was so spiteful as to revive it. This was one of those pieces of good luck which ought always to be remembered to set against an equal amount of bad luck when it comes along, as come it must. It remains only for me to record that the County Council Elections went the wrong way. The Progressives, as they called themselves, triumphed. The barricades were rebuilt in brick and plaster, and all our efforts went for nothing. Still no one can say we did not do our best.

WINSTON CHURCHILL, *MY EARLY LIFE*

Who was right, Winston Churchill or Mrs Chant? There is copious evidence to support both sides in the argument. In 1912 Compton Mackenzie, looking back to his youth in the West End theatre, published a novel about one Jenny Paul, a young dancer who joins the corps de ballet at the Orient Theatre, where she is exposed to the gaze of hundreds of male admirers, one of whom at last persuades her to retire from the dance and come and be his country wife, with tragic results. The Orient is clearly recognisable as an overpainted amalgam of the Alhambra and the Empire. It is surprising that Mackenzie, something of a moral realist, and a man with practical experience of writing for the popular theatre, should have conveyed such distaste.

The Orient Palace of Varieties rose like a cliff from the drapery shops of Piccadilly. On fine summer dusks, in a mist of golden light, it possessed a certain magic of gaiety; it seemed to capture something of the torch-lit merriment of a country fair. As one loitered on the island, lonely and meditative, the Orient was alluring, blazed upon the vision like an enchanted cave, or offered to the London wanderer a fancy of the scents and glossy fruits and warblers of the garden where Camaralzaman lost Badoura; and in autumn stained by rosy sunsets, the theatre expressed the delicate melancholy of the season. But when the rain dripped monotonously, when the fogs transformed the town, when London was London vast and grey, the Orient became unreal like the bedraggled palaces of an exhibition built to endure for a little while. After all, it was an exotic piece of architecture, and evoked an atmosphere of falseness, the falseness of an Indian gong in a Streatham hall. Yet it had stood fifty years without being rebuilt. In addition to having seen two generations pass away, something in the character of its entertainment, in the lavishness of its decoration, lent it the sacred permanence of a mausoleum, the mausoleum of mid-Victorian amusement.

The Orient did not march with the times, rising from insignificance. It never owned a chairman who announced the willingness of each successive comedian to oblige with a song. Old men never said they remembered the Orient in the jolly old days, for they could not have forgotten it. In essentials it remained the same as ever. Dancers had gone; beauties had shrivelled; but their ghosts haunted the shadowy interior. The silver-footed coryphees now kept lodging-houses; the swan-like ballerinas wore elastic stockings; but their absence was filled by others; they were as little missed as the wave that has broken. The lean old vanities quizzed and ogled the frail ladies of the Promenade and sniffed the smoke-wreathed air with a thought of pleasures once worth enjoyment. They spent now an evening of merely sentimental dissipation, but because it was spent at the Orient, not entirely wasted; for the unchanged theatre testified to the reality of their youth. It may not have been able to rejuvenate them, but, as by a handkerchief that survives the departure of its owner, their senses were faintly stimulated.

The Orient was proud because it did not enter into competition with any other house of varieties; preened itself upon a cosmopolitan programme. With the snobbishness of an old City firm, it declined to advertise its wares with eye-arresting posters, and congratulated itself on the inability to secure new clients. Foreigners made up a large proportion of the audience, and were apparently contented by equestrian mistresses of the *haute école*, by bewildering assemblages of jugglers, even by continental mediocrities for the sake of hearing their native tongue. They did not object to interminable wire-acts, and put up with divination feats of the most exhausting dullness. After all, these incidental turns must occur; but the ballets were the feature of the evening. For many who visited the Orient, the stream of prostitutes ebbing and flowing upon the Promenade was enough. Yet the women of the Orient Promenade would strike a cynic with uneasiness.

Under the stars, the Piccadilly courtesans affect the onlooker less atrociously. Night lends a magic of softness to their fretful beauty. The sequins lose their garishness; the painted faces preserve an illusion of reality. Moonlight falls gently on the hollow cheek; kindles a spark of youth in the leaden eye. The Piccadilly courtesans move like tigers in a tropic gloom with velvet blazonries and a stealthy splendour that masks the hunger driving them out to seek their prey. On the Orient Promenade the finer animalism has vanished; it was never more than superficially aesthetic. The daughters of pleasure may still be tigers but they are naphtha-lit, pacing backwards and forwards in a cage. They all appear alike. Their hats are all too large; their fingers are too brutal, their cheeks too lifeless. They are automatic machines waiting to be stirred into action by pennies.

Under the stars they achieve a pictorial romance; but on the carpet of the Promenade they are hard and heartless and vile. Their eyes are coins, their hands are purses. At their heels patter old men like unhealthy lapdogs; beefy provincials stare at them, their foreheads glistening. Above all the Frangipani and Patchouli and Opoponax and Trèfle Incarnat steals the rank odour of goats. The orchestra thunders and crashes down below; the comfortable audience lean back in the stalls; the foreigners jabber in the gallery; the Orient claque interrupts its euchre with hired applause. The corks pop, the soda splashes; money chinks; lechery murmurs; drunkards laugh; and down on the stage Jenny Paul dances.

The night wears on. The women come in continually from the wet streets. They surge in the cloak-room; quarrel over carrion game, blaspheme, fight and scratch. A door in the cloak-room (locked of course) leads into the passage outside the dressing-room, where Jenny changes five or six times each night. Every foul oath and every vile experience and every detestable adventure is plainly heard by twenty ladies of the ballet.

Dressing-room number forty-five was a long low room with walls of whitewashed brick. There was one window, seldom opened. There was no electric light and the gas-jets gave a very feeble illumination, so feeble that everybody always put on too much grease paint in their fear of losing an effect. The girls dressed on each side of the room at a wide deal board with forms to sit upon. There was a large wardrobe in one corner, and next to Jenny's place an open sink. The room was always dark and always hot. There were about eighty stone stairs leading up to it from the stage, and at least half a dozen ascents in the course of the evening. The dresser was a blowsy old Irishwoman more obviously dirty than the room, and there were two ventilators which gave a perpetual draught of unpleasant air. The inspectors of the London County Council presumably never penetrated as far as Room 45, a fact which seems to show that the extent of municipal interference has been much exaggerated.

The dressing-rooms were half on one side of the stage, half on the other. Those on the side nearer to the stage door were less unpleasant. The architect evidently believed in the value of first impressions. Anybody venturing into either warren without previous acquaintanceship would have been bewildered by the innumerable rooms and passages tucked away in every corner and branching off in every direction. Some of the former seemed to have been uninhabited for years. One in particular contained an ancient piano, two daguerrotypes and a heap of mouldering stuffs. It might have been the cell where years ago a Ballerina was immured for a wrong step. It existed like a monument to the despair of ambition.

The Orient stifled young life. The Corps de Ballet had the engulfing character of conventual vows. When a girl joined it, she cut herself off from the world. She went there fresh, her face a mist of roses, hope burning in her heart, fame flickering before her eyes. In a few years she would inevitably be pale with the atmosphere, with grinding work and late hours. She would find it easy to buy spirits cheaply in the canteen underneath the stage. She would stay in one line, it seemed for ever. She would not dance for joy again.

When Jenny went to the Orient first, she did not intend to stay long. She told the girls this, and they laughed at her. She did not know how soon the heavy theatre would become a habit; she did not realise what comfort exists in the knowledge of being permanently employed. But not even the Orient could throttle Jenny. She was not the daughter and granddaughter of a ballet girl. She had inherited no traditions of obedience. She never became a marionette to be dressed and undressed and jigged, horribly and impersonally. She yielded up her ambition, but she never lost her personality. When soon after her arrival the Maître de Ballet took her in his dark little corner and pinched her arm, she struck him across the mouth, vowed she would tell the manager and burnt up his conceit with her spitfire eyes. He tried again later on, and Jenny told his wife, a yellow-faced fat Frenchwoman. Then he gave her up, and being an artist, bore her no malice, but kept her in the first line of boys.

It is not to be supposed that the eighty or ninety ladies of the ballet were unhappy. On the contrary, they were very happy and so far as it accorded with the selfishness of a limited company, they were well looked after. The managing director called them 'Children', and was firmly convinced that he treated them as children. Actually, he treated them as dolls, and in the case of girls well into the thirties, with some of the sentimental indulgence lavished on old broken dolls. Perhaps it was the crowd of men who waited every night at the end of the long narrow court that led from Jermyn Street down to the Orient stage-door which has helped to preserve the vulgar and baseless tradition of frailty still sedulously propagated. Every night, about half past eleven, the strange mixture of men waited for the gradual exodus of the ladies of the ballet. A group of men, inherently the same, had stood thus on six nights of the week for more than fifty years.

They had stood there with Dundreary whiskers, in rakish full capes and strapped overalls. They had waited there with the mutton-chop whiskers and ample trousers of the 'seventies. Down the court years ago had come the beauties, with their striped stockings and swaying crinolines and velvety chignons. Down the court they had tripped in close-fitting pleated skirts a little later, and later still with the protruding bustles and skin-tight sleeves of the 'eighties. They had taken the London starlight with the balloon sleeves of the mid-nineties. They took the starlight now, as sweet and tender as the fairs of long ago. They came out in couples, in laughing companies, and sometimes singly with eager searching glances. They came out throwing their wraps around them in the sudden coolness of the air. They lingered at the end of the court in groups delicate as porcelain, enjoying the freedom and reunion with life. Their talk was hushed and melodious as the conversation of people moving slowly across dusky lawns. They were dear to the imaginative observer. He watched them with pride and affection as he would have watched fishing-boats steal home to their haven about sunset. Every night they danced and smiled and decked themselves for the pleasure of the world. They rehearsed so hard that sometimes they would fall down after a dance, crying on the stage where they had fallen from sheer exhaustion. They were not rich. Most of them were married, with children and little houses in teeming suburbs. Many, of course, were free to accept the escort of loiterers by the stage-door. The latter often regarded the ladies of the ballet as easy prey, but the ladies were shy as antelope aware of the hunter crawling through the grasses. They were independent of masculine patronage; laughed at the fools with their easy manners and genial condescension. They might desire applause over the footlights, but under the moon they were free from the necessity for favour. They had, with all its incidental humiliations, the self-respect which a great art confers. They were children of Apollo.

The difference between the gorgeousness of the ballet and the dim air of the court was unimaginable to the blockheads outside. They had seen the girls in crimson and gold, in purple and emerald, in white and silver; they had seen them spangled and glittering with armour; they had heard the tinkle of jewellery. They had watched their limbs; gloated upon their poses. They had caught their burning glances; brooded on their lips and eyes and exquisite motion. Inflamed by the wanton atmosphere of the Orient, they had thought the ladies of the ballet slaves for the delight of fools; but round the stage-door, all their self-esteem was blown away like a fragment of paper by a London night wind. Their complacent selves were brushed aside like boughs in a wood. Some, Jenny and Irene amongst them, would ponder awhile the silly group and gravely choose a partner for half an hour's conversation in a café. But somewhere close to twelve o'clock Jenny would fly, leaving not so much as a glass slipper to console her sanguine admirer. Home she would fly on the top of a tram and watch in winter the scudding moon whipped by bare blown branches, in summer see it slung like a golden bowl between the chimney stacks. The jolly adventures of youth were many, and the partnership of Jenny and Irene caused great laughter in the dressing-room when the former related each diverting enterprise.

The tale of their conquests would be a long one. Most of the victims were anonymous or veiled in the pseudonym of a personal idiosyncracy. There was Tangerine Willy who first met them, carrying a bag of oranges. There was Bill Hair and Bill Shortcoat and Sop and Jack Spot and Willie Eyebrows and Bill Fur. They all of them served as episodes mirthful and fugitive. They were mulcted in chocolates and hansoms and cigarettes. They danced attendance vaguely dreaming all the time of conquest. Jenny held them in fee with her mocking eyes, bewitched them with musical derision, and fooled them as Hera fooled the passionate Titan. In winter-time the balls at Covent Garden gave Jenny some of the happiest hours of her life. Every Tuesday fortnight, tickets were sent round to the stage-door of the Orient, and it was very seldom indeed that she did not manage to secure one. On the first occasion she went dressed as a little girl with a white baby hat and white shoes and socks and, wherever they might attract a glance, bows of pink silk. When the janitors saw her first, they nearly refused to admit such youthfulness; could not believe she was really grown up; consulted anxiously together while Jenny's slanting eyes glittered up to their majesties. They were convinced at last, and she enjoyed herself very much indeed. She was chased up the stairs and round the lobby. She was chased down the stairs, through the supper-room, in and out of half a dozen boxes, laughing and chattering and shrieking all the while. She danced nearly every dance. She won the second prize. Three old men tried to persuade her to live with them. Seven young

71

men vowed they had never met so sweet a girl.

To the three former Jenny murmured demurely, 'But I'm a good little girl; I don't do those things.' And of course they pointed out that she was much too young to come to so wicked a place as Covent Garden. And of course, with every good intention, they offered to escort her home at once.

With the seven young men's admiration Jenny agreed. 'I am sweet, aren't I? Oh, I'm a young dream, if you only knew.'

And as a dream she was elusive. She glorified in her freedom. She was glad she was not in love. She had no wish but to enjoy herself to the top of her bent. And she succeeded. Then at half past six o'clock on a raw November morning, she rumbled home to Hagworth Street in a four-wheel cab with five other girls – a heap of tangled lace. She went upstairs on tip-toe. She undressed herself somehow, and in the morning she woke up to find on each wrist, as testimony of the night's masquerade, a little pink bow, soiled and crumpled.

COMPTON MACKENZIE, *CARNIVAL*

The abolitionists would seem to have won the day. And yet it is revealing that neither Mackenzie nor Mrs Chant nor any of the other members of the clean-up brigade were themselves frequenters of the great theatres to which they took such strong objection. Churchill, young as he was, sensed that the promenades were only as deplorable as the male customers cared to make them, and that there must be thousands of males like himself who enjoyed the theatre, including its promenade and its bars, for reasons which might have surprised Mrs Chant. The point is made by J. B. Booth, the great annalist of West End bohemia in the years before the Great War. Booth was a journalist on 'The Pink 'Un', and in his endless volumes of reminiscence gives the impression of having known everybody in London whom Mrs Chant would rather not have known. He probably did too. Booth and his crowd revolved around the great West End showplaces, drifting into the Empire or the Alhambra or the Tivoli, not always to savour the art, sauntering down the Strand for supper at Romanos, celebrating a kill at the races, writing reams of gossipy, chatty journalism about their shamelessly self-indulgent lives. To men like Booth and his more gifted associate Arthur Binstead, institutions like the Empire and the Alhambra were not to be defiled by contact with the likes of Mrs Chant, and there is some bitterness in his argument in favour of the old days and the old ways.

Up to the end of, say, Hitchins' days as manager, the Empire was club as well as music hall. Men went there not so much for the entertainment as for companionship, and the companionship, be it noted, of other men. To the habitué, the feminine lure of the promenade made small appeal. Twenty years ago it was said that there were three places in the world in which one was bound to meet the returned wanderer from the waste places if one waited long enough – the Salon Carré of the Louvre, Charing Cross Station, and the Empire Promenade. When one said goodbye to a friend on his way to India, China, Singapore, or the backblocks of Empire, nine hundred and ninety times out of one thousand his last words were: 'So long, old man, see you in London again. Sure to run across you in the Empire.' So, in one sense, the music hall in Leicester Square was not ill-named. It was a gathering and meeting place for the men of the Empire.

During the years immediately preceding the war the club tone had dwindled, and probably the first signs of a break from the old tradition came when 'Prudes on the Prowl' agitated for the closing of the bar in the promenade. One restriction followed another, and after the death of Harry Hitchins many of the old associations were broken up. Before the days of the big salon at the back of the stalls on the ground floor, there was a foyer on the O.P. side of the circle which was like a clubroom – a tape-machine clicked off all the news of the evening, and on the eve of a big race much business was transacted there. And the liquor sold was of the best in London. That was one of the features of the Empire. One was sure of pure, wholesome whisky, and the old brandy was the real old brandy, while the cigars, which were bought through Mr Alfred de Rothschild, were of the highest quality. I remember one could get a Bock 'Cabinet' at the Empire for a shilling which even in the economical pre-war days would cost eighteenpence elsewhere. What it would cost nowadays goodness only knows.

In 1894 the LCC insisted on the foyer at the back of the circle being closed, and the regular habitués protested in forcible manner. There was a small riot, and the barriers were torn down by a group of young fellows about town, at the head of whom was a young fellow about town named Winston Churchill, who marched in procession round Leicester Square carrying the debris as trophies.

None of the music-hall managers themselves know the extent of the never-ending interferences of the County Council officials, but a C.C. gentleman in the days of the promenades made occasional compensating blunders. A certain door in the old Empire promenade was being redecorated. 'Here, this won't do,' announced the official. 'These painted panels must be replaced by plain white glass so that your officials can see what's going on inside at all times.'

'I'm afraid that wouldn't answer,' returned stately old Hitchins quietly.

'And why not, pray?'

'Because', said Scratchums, with an unchecked yawn, 'it's the ladies' lavatory.'

J. B. BOOTH, *OLD PINK 'UN DAYS*

So far from being distressed by the moral decline of the music hall as represented by the courtesans of the Empire, Booth and his friends actually considered the new style to be a vast improvement on the rough-and-ready emergent days of the halls, when rowdiness and drunkenness were more in evidence than would have been allowed in the great West End houses. It is clear enough from the foregoing reminiscence by Booth that the bohemian element regarded the great halls as amended versions of the gentlemen's clubs, and selected their favourite haunt accordingly.

The last idea with which one turned into a hall, whether it was the Pavilion, or the Empire, the Tivoli, or the Alhambra, somewhere about nine, was the idea of sitting penned in one's stall among total strangers. Each hall had its habitués; the habitués were typical of the hall, and there were subtle distinctions. The black-coated, white-shirted, silk-hatted crowd of young bloods who filled the promenades of the great Leicester Square houses in the intervals differed vastly from those one found in the Strand or in Piccadilly Circus; but in each crowd there was an intimacy, the intimacy born of coteries which frequently meet and whose aim is to enjoy life.

In the 'seventies, for the sum of sixpence you could put your elbows on the stage of the London Pavilion. Seats at marble tables at the sides of the stage cost sixpence, while for half-a-crown you could reserve a seat at the chairman's table. The chairman, Harry Cavendish, the absolute controller of stage and audience, was of superb presence and incredible cubic capacity. In those days the programme at the Pav was merely the current number of 'The Entre'Acte', with the names of the performers – afterwards to be loudly announced by 'The Chair' – printed on a full page facing one of Alf Bryan's cartoons, and the cost was one penny – a newspaper and programme for one penny! There were invariably eighteen or twenty turns, and the performance began at 7.30 and finished just at midnight. There were bars and waiters everywhere; excellent bitter ale was sold at tuppence a glass, and the frugal-minded could be uproarious on eighteenpence.

In the 'seventies there was no Empire, no Alhambra, and no Palace. Most of the music halls in London were attached to a public house, and the entertainment offered would be thought incredibly vulgar. Where the Victoria Place now stands was the Standard, a popular resort, where the stage jutted into a room, on the first floor, and the performers were able to exchange pleasantries with the audience, who sat around little tables in the French *café chantant* style. The original Pav was little more than a barn, oblong in shape, with a gallery on one side and boxes on the other. It was supposed to have occupied the site of Dr Kahn's Anatomical Museum. The original building had been a swimming bath – and looked it: the old dressing cabins must have been utilised for the private boxes. The proprietor was a Mr Loibl, who was reported to have been a waiter at Scott's.

J. B. BOOTH, *OLD PINK 'UN DAYS*

To balance this enlightened contemporary view, there is the distaste of the social historians who followed. The following description of the Chant campaign, besides taking the part of the reformers, suggests how the frontal assault demonstrated by young Churchill and his fellow-cadets may not quite have been the most effective way of proceeding, and that the cagey politicising of George Edwardes was much more effective. The curious circumstances attaching to the final closure of the promenades and the expulsion from the halls of the prostitutes offers a revealing insight into the morality of an age which encouraged its young men to kill Germans in their beds while doing whatever it could to prevent them from making love to English women in theirs.

The last great flare-up about the moral standing of the music hall occurred in 1894 over the scandal of the 'promenade' of the Empire Theatre of Varieties, Leicester Square, which was under the management of George Edwardes, and, like the nearby Alhambra, which also had a notorious promenade, was otherwise notable as having preserved interest in the ballet throughout the generation that preceded its return to glory with Diaghilev's 1911 season at Covent Garden. The promenades of both were notorious as resorts of high-class prostitutes (they had to be high-class since the entrance charge was five shillings). A high proportion of the male clientèle of the Empire went there primarily at the very least to mingle with these evidently fascinating, if to modern taste excessively over-fleshed, over-dressed and over-perfumed charmers.

A vigorous attempt was made by a group of courageously high-minded women to get the Empire's licence withdrawn on the double charge that it was a known resort of prostitutes and that the ballet dancers were too scantily clothed. As a result of the agitation, and despite a furious counter-agitation, which included a claim by London cab-drivers that a lucrative element in their business would be imperilled, the London County Council decreed that the promenade be abolished and drinks no longer sold in full view of the stage. George Edwardes, the manager, therefore constructed the minimum necessary alterations and cut off the promenade and bar from the auditorium by means of canvas screens. These were shortly afterwards pulled down by angry young men, who then paraded through Piccadilly waving portions of the partitions and crying 'Long Live Edwardes!' A group of army cadets from Sandhurst took a prominent part in the proceedings, one of their number being Winston Churchill, who preceded the operations by favouring the applauding promenaders with what he later claimed to have been his first public speech. As a result the partition had to be rebuilt in brick; but in 1894 Edwardes had his licence renewed unconditionally, and the promenades, both at the Empire and the Alhambra, continued until voluntarily closed down in 1916 because at that date they offered too flagrant a temptation to young officers on leave from the First World War. Both establishments, it is sad to report, appear to have suffered financially as a result.

L. C. B. SEAMAN, *LIFE IN VICTORIAN LONDON*

It seems clear enough that the great Leicester Square houses were an open invitation to prostitution, but that both of the great houses were careful to regulate proceedings as strictly as, and perhaps even more strictly than, any gentlemen's club. No rowdiness or offensive drunkenness was allowed, and according to one later account, methods of detecting and marking out potential rowdies were as ingenious as they were effective.

The Empire was luxurious with deep pile carpets and footmen in blue and gold livery. It advertised itself on a programme as 'The Cosmopolitan Club of the World' and when an Englishman arrived back from some far-flung corner of the Empire he headed straight to the other 'Empire' in Leicester Square. Great care was taken to avoid trouble. On Boat Race night, the rowdiest in the year, they cleared the tables of bottles, glasses and anything breakable. Bodyguards were stationed all round the hall and the Manager wearing full evening dress and white kid gloves would go up to any young man causing trouble and pat him politely on the shoulder; then he'd be thrown out. Concealed in the Manager's white glove was a piece of chalk which left its warning mark and if the young man staggered round to another entrance he was recognised as a trouble-maker and thrown out again.

DAN FARSON, *MARIE LLOYD AND THE MUSIC HALL*

Among those tens of thousands of young men who would much have preferred the ladies of the promenade to Mrs Chant was a poet called Arthur Symons (1865-1945), who, by insisting on his Welsh birthplace, his Cornish antecedents and his Parisian experiences, contrived to rid himself of the tiresome label of

Anglo-Saxon. Symons, a prominent figure among the Decadent Movement of the 1890s, found in the cheap perfume and contrived exoticism of the courtesans of the West End halls the perfect theme for his febrile imagination. What to Mrs Chant was loathsome, and to young Churchill pleasant decoration, was to young aesthetes like Symons the spur to romantic poetry. Some of his fellow-intellectuals saw the music hall as an important addition to the enjoyable side of life; others regarded it as even more significant, but only Symons conceived the halls as an allegory of all existence as he knew it.

Prologue

My life is like a music hall,
Where, in the impotence of rage,
Chained by enchantment to my stall,
I see myself upon the stage
Dance to amuse a music hall.

'Tis I that smoke this cigarette,
Lounge here, and laugh for vacancy,
And watch the dancers turn, and yet
It is my very self I see
Across the cloudy cigarette.

My very self that turns and trips,
Painted, pathetically gay,
An empty song upon the lips
In make-believe of holiday;
I, I, this thing that turns and trips!

The light flares in the music hall,
The light, the sound, that weary us;
Hour follows hour, I count them all,
Lagging, and loud, and riotous:
My life is like a music hall.

ARTHUR SYMONS, *LONDON NIGHTS*

Symons seems to have been less interested in the art of music hall than in the erotic possibilities of the young ladies who earned their living there. None of his poetic effusions is about the great clowns and coster comics of the day, but always concerned with pairs of rose-bud lips and flowers of innocence glimpsed in the fleshly ravine sundering a pair of gleaming breasts. In a short cycle of poems called *Décor de Théâtre*, Symons is sometimes emboldened to dedicate his lines to a particular goddess. This one suggests both the allure of the footlights and the hard realities hinted at in Compton Mackenzie's fictions.

Behind the Scenes, Empire

To Peppina

The little painted angels flit,
See, down the narrow staircase, where
The pink legs flicker over it!

Blonde and bewigged, and winged with gold,
The shining creatures of the air
Troop sadly, shivering with cold.

The gusty gaslight shoots a thin
Sharp finger over cheeks and nose
Rouged to the colour of the rose.

All wigs and paint, they hurry in:
Then, bid their radiant moments be
The footlights' immortality.

ARTHUR SYMONS, *DÉCOR DE THÉÂTRE*

Symons evidently knew all the degrees of acceptance in the tight, tiny world of the musical theatre. Peppina clearly allows him to come back-stage. In another poem, inspired by a night at the Foresters Music Hall, Symons is watching the show from the wings, where he can observe the 'mock roses' in his young lady-friend's face. But on the other nights he sits in the stalls with the ordinary mortals and weaves the fantasy that one dancer among the troupe is performing for his eyes alone. On still others he waits at the stage-door, watching the bright faces of the emerging dancers with predictably 'rose-leaf cheeks and flower-soft lips'. But the most comforting fantasy for Symons is to imagine that the whole show has been staged purely for his benefit.

On the Stage

Lights, in a multi-coloured mist,
From indigo to amethyst,
A whirling mist of multi-coloured lights;
And after, wigs and tights,
Then faces, then a glimpse of profiles, then
Eyes, and a mist again;
And rouge, and always tights, and wigs, and tights.

You see the ballet so, and so,
From amethyst to indigo;
You see a dance of phantoms, but I see
A girl, who smiles to me;
Her cheeks, across the rouge, and in her eyes
I know what memories,
What memories, and messages for me.

ARTHUR SYMONS, *DÉCOR DE THÉÂTRE*

Holbrook Jackson, historian and annalist of the 1890s, defines this sort of thing as 'a Pagan revolt by Symons against Puritanism', but, as the Victorian age drew to a close with the débâcle of the Boer War and the Oscar Wilde trials, there were other, more dominant aspects of the evolving art of the halls, over which observers and analysts have been puzzling ever since. Beerbohm, perverse as always, was almost alone in mourning the disappearance of the old naïveté. Defending himself from ridicule with an invisible shield of facetiousness, Max looks back with a meticulously manufactured sigh to the great days of Vance and Leybourne.

The Blight On The Music Halls

O Love! When you're in love –
Love makes a man
Feel awf'lly peculiar.
O Love! When you're in love –
With a Jane or a Julia
Man falls in love!

These words, and their music, not less exquisite, I owe to the erudition of a certain painter, who seems to have spent most of the evenings of his life in Music Halls and can bring forth from the storehouse of his memory many fatuous, forgotten choruses. Through the old 'Oxford' these words resounded from the throat of the great George Leybourne, nightly, years ago. Now they are not remembered. They buzz no longer in brains that are fulfilled with later melodies; and save, haply, in a far county, by an old farmer, whose quiet life has not expunged the memory of his visit to the town, you do nowhere hear them carolled. I am glad to ressuscitate their rhythm: bugle-notes to wake sleeping memories in some breasts; more melancholy for me, fainter, than scent of soever long-kept lavender.

They belong to the unregenerate period of the Music Halls. In sense and sentiment and syntax, they differ vastly from anything that one hears now. Yet, in their day, they were vastly popular, were typical, indeed, of all the songs sung in the old 'Oxford' or the 'Albert' or the 'Hoxton Palace of Varieties'. To that sea of billicocks, the audience, through a fog of cheap tobacco-smoke, with the glare of footlights cast up on to his crumpled shirt-front and making a dark cavern of his mouth, the *Lion Comique* bawled out always some such crude, conventional ditty. And, when his turn was done, and he had swaggered off that stage whose backcloth was ever a green glade with a portico or two of white marble, on tripped his sister-artist, the badly-rouged Serio, gaudy in satinette, energetic, hoarse, and without any talent. Young or old she might be, gracious or uncomely, might trip off at last, *non sine pastoricia fistula* or in a storm of approval – what matter? She was ever the same Serio. The convention was never broken.

Well! I know these things only by tradition. If I fare to the Transpontine Halls, I find but an embarrassed remnant of the old performers, striving to live up to the imitators of Chevalier and Marie Lloyd. Reason, variety, refinement have crept gradually in, till one shall sigh in vain for the fatuous and delightful days of:

> Oh the Fairies! Oh the Fairies!
> They are so tender,
> The feminine gender,
> Oh the Fairies! Oh the Fairies!
> Oh for the wings of a Fairy Queen!

But one must not marvel that those days are over. With sumptuous palaces erected in the heart of London, and with the patronage of fashion, new modes were bound to come in, sooner or later. The homely humour of James Fawn and Bessie Bellwood was superseded, ere long, by Chevalier, with his new and romantic method; by Gus Elen, with his realistic psychology and his admirably written songs; by Marie Lloyd, with her swift *nuances*. Meanwhile – a new art! Every one was interested. Every one had seen Mr Sickert's paintings. Soon other painters began to frequent the Halls. Mr Arthur Symons cut in, and secured the Laureateship. Mr Anstey wrote satires. Mr Frederick Wedmore began to join in the choruses with genteel gusto. And now, when forewearied with the demands of an intellectual life, I stray into the Tivoli, and would fain soothe my nerves with folly, I find an entertainment that is not only worthy of attention, but is even exigent of all my aesthetic faculties. There is a swift succession of strongly, variously defined personalities, all trained and talented and self-conscious; all in pretty or appropriately grotesque costumes; all imitating this or that phase of modern life within the limits of their new art. The words of their songs are quite pregnant with character and wit. The music to which they are set is no longer the eternal variation on one or two themes, but is often novel and always adapted to the words' meanings. When fatuousness and vulgarity take their turn, themselves are in the nature of a surprise, startling, not soothing. I find no repose for my faculties in the Tivoli. The atmosphere from the stage of it is surcharged with artistic conscience. One knows that every performer is, in private life, a charming and serious person, whose photograph is reproduced in the illustrated paper from time to time, with a description of his domestic life and his valuable collection of proof-engravings, press-cuttings, and what not. The interviewer has told one that he has a grand piano in his drawing-room and often composes his own songs, and 'will sing no words that he could not individually express'. And one compares him, as he stands there, with that humble creature who sang, with very great success, years ago,

> Then say was he a coward?
> Had he a coward's heart?
> By acting in this manner, did
> He play the coward's part?
> It was his earnest wish
> One day nobly to behave –
> And he proved himself at last to be
> The Bravest of the Brave.

Does one, as I do, wish only for relaxation in Music Halls, he must needs go to Paris. There the Music Halls have been always kept in their proper perspective. Yvette Guilbert is but an accident. She was never *du café chantant*, and I hope she will soon retire to the legitimate stage. It is creditable to the Parisians that, despite her talent and individuality, she never found an imitatress. She was, indeed, the one jarring note in the *Ambassadeurs*, where, in a pale-green avenue, brilliant with white lights, one sought the restfulness of a fatuous convention; sought to be lulled by the eternal fat men, telling of *La Patrie* or of their *amourettes*, and by the voiceless, sprightly baggages, who sing eulogies of *Les Militaires*. Part of their charm for me is that, unless I listen, I know not what they are saying in their alien tongue. But they caper and gesticulate gracefully, and the light, familiar music soothes me. I have often thought that a man might end his days very pleasantly in the *claque*.

Between the French and the old English convention there are several points of difference, but each is based on a monotonous vulgarity. Perhaps some person, who understands the charm of monotony, will say that in time our music halls will reach a plane of monotonous refinement, and that all will then be well. All would then be better, doubtless. But we have already the Italian Opera, and we have the Albert Hall. I insist that vulgarity is an implicit element of the true music hall. Why should we have sought to eliminate it? Out of the vulgarity of the people did the music hall arise, nor will anyone be so foolish as to contend that, by tampering with its foundations, we shall go one step towards refining the people. In its early stage, the music hall was a very curious and interesting phenomenon, a popular art. What better outlet for the people's vulgarity? For cultured persons, what better expression of that laughing and contemptuous spirit, which Aristotle knew to be a danger? Vulgarity will, of course, last till the next Glacial Epoch, and we shall always be able to contemplate it. But we are fools to drive it from its most convenient haunt. Oh, for the wasted glories of the old Oxford! Oh, for one hour in the Hoxton Palace of Varieties! I must be glad that a few fragments have been snatched for me from their irrepleviable ditties. And, for my part, I do rejoice, in Summer and in Spring, in Autumn and in Winter, this sweet refrain to sing:

> He's a dear old pal of mine,
> He helped me when I was down,
> Lent me his aid,
> Willingly,
> With a smile, not a frown.
> And if the day should come,
> And my lucky star should shine,
> I shall always be
> Most happy to say
> 'He's a de-ar old pal of mine!'

MAX BEERBOHM, *MORE*

But there was an aspect of the halls which Max would have been inclined to mock, and which would hardly have commended itself to Symons even had it occurred to him, and that was the mingling of the classes. Unlike the serious theatre, where certain styles of dress were *de rigueur*, and where the customer had to go through the often inhibiting ritual of booking a ticket in advance, the music hall was a relaxed communal arena. Although, as the years went by, it too was increasingly inclined to ritualise its own proceedings, by the end of the century the music hall could be said to constitute a genuinely democratic theatre. In spite of the divine afflatus which hit Symons every time the curtain rose, and for all the erudite annotations in French and Latin with which Max might dignify a music-hall review, the halls remained not quite respectable, and for that reason tremendously popular with *all* classes.

The Victorian music hall was always rooted in the national culture. Its significance lies in its function as a bridge between the less deprived among the lower classes, and the otherwise distant middle and upper classes. But although music halls at the end of the reign were something of a cult among a limited part of the aristocratic and literary worlds and were no longer thought exclusively working class or 'low', they cannot be said ever to have been looked on as really reputable places. They were regarded throughout their history as being in questionable taste and never completely lived down their early reputation as 'unsuitable' for serious-minded, thoughtful people as, in the end, the cinema managed to do. The very intensity with which the legend of 'the halls' was and is cultivated suggests a strenuous effort to compensate for their always dubious state even in their heyday. Their great quality was that they were a wholly native institution and that in some degree they succeeded in presenting the working-class people of the British Isles to the rest of society in a warmer and more human way than the social reformers, rescue workers and investigators of the Victorian age could do; and to that extent they lowered, just a little, the barriers that divided class from class in that age. True, they bowdlerised themselves on stage and often sentimentalised themselves excessively; but any cultural activity with a wide following that caused metropolitan audiences to feel at one with costermongers from Kennington or with Irish immigrants as well as, in due time, the working class of Lancashire, Yorkshire and the Clyde, was performing a valuable service to the society at large. The halls also spoke for the working classes themselves, deepening their own sense of community, enabling them to laugh in public at their own weaknesses as well as those of the 'swells' and 'toffs' they so frequently burlesqued.

L. C. B. SEAMAN, *LIFE IN VICTORIAN LONDON*

In 1898, moving into the chair vacated by Bernard Shaw at *The Saturday Review*, Max Beerbohm immediately published an essay about the music hall in which he took his predictably perverse stance against improvements in presentation and technique. Max professed to hunger for the sentimental *naïveté* of the good old days, for love-lorn maidens and strong jingo moustaches. In this essay he is one of the first observers to spot the social pretensions of George Robey and cannot forgive him what he is prepared to wink at in his idol, Dan Leno. Today this essay is perhaps most remarkable for the beautiful anecdote relating to song-writers and their rates of pay.

At the Tivoli

A lady of heroic proportions, accoutred as a life-guardsman, strode upon the stage just as I was edging my way to my seat. There was patriotism in her every curve, and I presume that her song, to which I did not listen, was about the Twenty-First

81

Lancers. My thoughts were far away, coursing sentimentally through the Past and lingering among the many evenings I had frittered at the Tivoli in the period of earlier youth. Here, in these very stalls, I would often sit with some coæval *in statu pupillari*. Lordly aloof, both of us, from the joyous vulgarity of our environment, we would talk in under-tones about Hesiod and Fra Angelico, about the lyric element in Marcus Aurelius and the ethics of apostasy as illustrated by the Oxford Movement. Now and again, in the pauses of our conversation, we would rest our eyes upon the stage and listen to a verse or two of some song about a mother-in-law or an upstairs-lodger, and then one of us would turn to the other, saying 'Yes! I see your point about poor Newman, but...' or 'I cannot admit that there is any real distinction between primitive art and...' Though our intellects may not have been so monstrous fine as we pretended, we were quite honest in so far as neither of us could have snatched any surreptitious pleasure in the entertainment as such. We came simply that we might bask in the glow of our own superiority – superiority not only to the guffawing clowns and jades around us, but also to the cloistral pedascules who, no more exquisite than we in erudition, were not in touch with modern life and would have been scared, like so many owls, in that garish temple of modernity, a Music Hall, wherein we, on the other hand, were able to sit without blinking. Were we, after all, so very absurd? It was one of our aims to be absurd. Besides, does not every man see something absurd in the things he did four or five years ago? Assuredly, that is a law of nature. A man may not have progressed in intellect – he may even have deteriorated – but he cannot regard himself, as he was, without some measure of contempt. I fancy that even an octogenarian must (if his memory be unimpaired) think that he was rather an ass at the age of seventy. Men who paint pictures or write books or produce anything that abides tangibly with them, may look at their old work and find much that is good in it; but, the greater their admiration, the greater their wonder that they, being what they were, contrived to do it. I myself was reading lately a little essay on Music Halls, written by me in the period to which I have alluded. I find it excellent. Yet I can but blush for the fatuous creature I was in the days when I wrote it – just as I shall be blushing, five years hence, at my present personality, in which I cannot now detect any flaw.

The foregoing words are a more or less amplified version of the reverie I indulged in while the lady of heroic proportions held the rest of her audience in spell. The loud applause in which, at length, she marched off the stage, also put a term to my reverie. I remembered that I had come, not for the old purpose of being superior, but to lay the foundations for an article. And so I listened attentively to Mr Tom Costello. I do not remember what either of his songs was about. I remember only that he wore two false noses, one for each song. It is one of the old traditions of an English Music Hall that the male comedians must make themselves as unsightly as they can. Indeed, ugliness, physical or moral, always seems to be the chief feature of the characters represented by the male artists. The aim of the Music Hall is, in fact, to cheer the lower classes up by showing them a life uglier and more sordid than their own. The mass of people, when it seeks pleasure, does not want to be elevated: it wants to laugh at something beneath its own level. Just as I used to go to Music Halls that I might feel my superiority to the audience, so does the audience go that it may compare itself favourably with the debased rapscallions of the songs. Perhaps this theory would apply even better to the case of the outlying Music Halls, where there is no prosperous element in the audience. At the Tivoli most of the audience is prosperous. Music Halls have become, in recent years, a feature of the 'West End', a rival to the theatres. Gradually, they are becoming less and less Music Halls in the old sense – places, I mean, where songs are sung in succession throughout the evening. The 'turns' are now interspersed with such items as juggling, bell-ringing, limb-contorting. The Tivoli is in a state of transition. But the old convention – the convention of unalloyed ugliness – still lingers and will, I fancy, die hard. It is significant that most of the younger men on the Music Hall stage adhere strictly to the old convention. The most gifted and popular of these younger men, Mr George Robey (who was educated at Cambridge and is, in my opinion, one of the few distinguished men produced by Cambridge within recent years), nightly presents himself in the most hideous guise and makes the most hideous noises. Shortly after Mr Robey's 'turn', the other night, appeared Mr T. E. Dunville, whom I saw for the first time. He is, in all respects, a replica of Mr Robey. He has the same kind of make-up, the same kind of manner – the Cambridge manner, I suppose – and the same kind of songs. Evidently the old convention has life in it. Personally, I do not like it. I can bear it from Mr Dan Leno – genius reconciles one to anything. From Mr Robey, clever as he is, and from Mr Dunville, it jars on me. At the same time, it is interesting; also, it seems to give great pleasure; and so no student of life can afford to ignore it. And I feel that, in saying that I dislike it, I may be betraying my own limitations. I hasten, therefore, to say that I yield to none in my enjoyment of that fatuousness which, in the old convention, is as necessary to the songs sung by women as is ugliness to the songs sung by men. Who (I have often wondered) writes the words? Of the rate at which they are written I had an interesting glimpse not long ago, in the report of a case in the County Court at Brighton. The defendant, asked by the Judge to state his occupation, said that he wrote the words of songs for Music Halls, receiving the sum of one pound for every song. Asked how much he made in the course of a year, he replied simply, 'Three hundred and sixty-five pounds'. I blame the Judge for not having pushed his inquiries further. I should have liked to know something of the spirit in which the defendant wooed his Muse. Was it a rough wooing, for the most part, or a timid? Was she never coy? Would he say that on some days she yielded to him with greater ardour than on others? Did he discriminate between the fruits of their union, regarding this one as fine, that one as puny? Would he hotly maintain that some of his songs were underrated by the public, and others esteemed beyond their deserts? Would he give a fig for what the public thought of his work, or did he, in the silence of his Study, strive only to please himself and to satisfy his own conscience? If he did sometimes write merely to tickle the ears of the groundlings, did he find the groundlings knowing by some subtle instinct of their own that he had trifled with them, and refusing to react to his humour or his pathos? I think it probable that all the really successful songs are written in straight sincerity, to the utmost of the writers' powers. And yet – I don't know.

> In the lane where the violets nestle,
> In the lane where the lilies grow,
> When Jack comes home from his vessel
> He will meet me again, I know.
> Hand in hand we will wander together,
> For his heart beats true, it is plain;
> On the deep blue sea he is waiting for me
> And the day when we'll meet in the lane.

That was the song sung by Elementary Jane, in Mr Richard Pryce's delightful novel; and in real life, I am sure, it would go as straight to the heart of the public as it did in the book. Yet Mr Pryce is far from being an unsophisticated writer. 'Since I came to London' was sung by one of Jane's elder rivals, and I wish Mr Pryce had not kept it to himself. Its sprightliness must have been so traditional, so restful – something in the manner of what Miss Alice Lloyd was singing at the Tivoli the other night:

You don't know you're alive!
That's so – oh, no!
A girl like you of twenty-one,
Nothing done, and had no fun!
You say you've never heard
How many beans make five?
It's time you knew a thing or two –
You don't know you're alive!

That is exquisitely in the tradition. But for my own part I adore the sprightly style less than the pathetic.

MAX BEERBOHM IN *THE SATURDAY REVIEW*, 3 DECEMBER 1898

As the new century dawned, in military fiasco and the aftermath of sexual disgrace, the very greatest talents in the halls had already matured. The artists who were to dominate music hall in the golden age leading up to the Great War were all products of the preceding years. Now, as the great Palaces and Empires towered over the main street of every sizeable town in Britain, the music hall, not so long ago a minor form of local entertainment, had become a vast and highly profitable industry, with all the refinements that such a development implies. It had its own managers and agents, its own scouts and touts, its own newspapers, its own popular restaurants and pubs, its own slang, fashions, charitable institutions, even its own trade union. But its greatest glory, and its only real asset, was its stars, one of the very brightest of whom was fated to see very little of the new age.

With a quick, timid look over his shoulder into the wings to make sure he is *not being overheard*, the little figure in front of the scene of shops in a street so deserted that it seems always Sunday afternoon, takes all the hundreds of us completely into his confidence about family affairs. There is a perpetually startled look in his bright, merrily gleaming eyes, framed in semi-circular brows, and in his jerky movements; there is eagerness in every part of him from the disconcerting legs to the straight, strained mouth set in the curious double-rim formed by the lines of the cheeks. He wants to tell us his secrets. He must tell us. For the sake of his own peace of mind he wants to explain how he is related to somebody or other who has become involved in a scandal. 'It's like this,' he begins, only to realise it is not so, for he has become thoroughly confused over his uncles, cousins, father and grandfathers. Then he pauses with his fingers over his mouth and suddenly croaks, 'There's a postman mixed up in all this.'

That was Dan Leno. In the midst of wildly fantastic fun, he would mutter some half-spoken thought like that and relate it all to reality. Then, as a critic said in a happy moment, 'whole breadths of London rushed into view, all the flickering street corners on Saturday nights, all the world of crowded door-steps and open windows'. In him Cockney comedy came to full bloom. He created the humour of the humble home – the mockery of hardships, the laughter at squalor, the mirth over domestic drudgery, born of endurance. These jokes of desperation came naturally to him because he had experienced the miseries of poverty almost from the time of his birth in 1860 at a spot now covered by St Pancras Station. His parents, whose real name was Galvin, were appearing at concerts as Mr and Mrs John Wilde. When his father died, his mother married a performer named William Grant whose stage name was Leno. The infant made his first public appearance at the age of four, as the partner of his brother Jack. Next he had to perform with his uncle, Johnny Danvers, who was the elder by four weeks. Together these two children danced for hours in public-houses to earn a handful of coppers. If lucky, they were allowed to lie down on the bare boards of a garret afterwards – but not to sleep. According to Sir Seymour Hicks, who had the story from Leno himself, they then performed for one another's benefit. Each would tell the other stories. The one who made the other laugh got up from the floor, rolled up the blind as though it were an act-drop, and bowed to an imaginary audience on the tiles.

Forming a company of four with Dan's parents, they travelled round the country with an old iron bedstead as the apparatus of their turn. Each Sunday the two boys took this on to the stage to see that it could be well secured. One night they had to bore a hole to manage this, each in turn striking a match as a light for the other to work by. Presently they saw a gleam in the mezzanine below. Dan said, 'We've set the theatre on fire,' and Johnny emptied a bucket down the hole to put it out. Actually it was the lantern of the groom who was a feeding a pony, and as the water had dropped down his neck they had to run for their lives.

At Pullan's Theatre of Varieties, Brunswick Place, Bradford, on Monday, May 20, 1878, the champion dancer, at the bottom of the bill in the smallest type, was having a hard time of it. He danced until there was hardly any sole left under his clogs. In 1880 he won a championship belt, and retained his title until a judgement was unfairly given against him. For some months after that he sang a libellous song describing how the belt had been stolen while he was executing the winning dance. In 1883 he won a handsome belt as champion clog dancer of the world after a six nights' contest against all-comers. When his youthful energy slackened he no longer danced, although he could casually take a stride of six feet or slap the sole of his shoe on the stage with a report like a pistol shot.

While Leno was touring the provinces, George Conquest heard his song, 'Milk For Twins', and engaged him for two pantomimes at the old Surrey. There he caught the eye of Augustus Harris and went to Drury Lane, in 1888, as the Baroness in 'The Babes In The Wood And Robin Hood And His Merry Men And Harlequin Who Killed Cock Robin'. According to Hickory Wood, wittiest of pantomime authors, Dan Leno could be 'quite a possible queen' when he chose, even though she lived under such conditions that a pair of braces was the natural thing to buy the king on his birthday, while the mistake of handing him a parcel of lingerie by mistake, to be opened in full view of the Court, was one that any royal lady might make. In his studies of women in a humble walk of life, said Hickory Wood, Dan Leno's gait, manner and expression were altered, and all his dignity vanished:

'He was homely, discursive and confidential, not to say occasionally aggressive. His own personality was, of course, ever present, but when I saw him playing this kind of parts, the impression he left on my mind was not so much a picture of Dan Leno playing the part of a woman in a particular walk of life as the picture of what Dan Leno would have been if he had been that particular woman.'

Wash-tubs filled with tattered underwear, and kitchen tables loaded with a mess of uncooked, adhesive pastry, were not necessary to Dan Leno. As a designing Sister Anne, who wondered 'did she push' herself too much, but tried all the same to capture the heart of Bluebeard with 'When The Heart Is Young' until her hair got caught in the strings of her harp; as Widow Twankey, making fatuous observations upon the tricks of the Slave of the Lamp (who was Cinquevalli); as Cinderella's stepmother mocking the flunkey who tried to stop her from coming to the ball, his humour was so closely related to real life that people who wanted pantomime to be really childish nonsense protested. Childish nonsense was what Dan Leno revelled in off the stage. When he learned that Whimsical Walker was expecting a dog by train, he entered the Clown's house in his absence, waited there with a box, abused Walker on his arrival for cruelty because the dog had not been given a drop of water, and swore that the RSPCA should be informed. When Walker put his hand inside the box, he found the poor beast was stone cold. 'It's dead, Dan,' he said before he found it was a pantomime dog from the property-room.

M. WILLSON DISHER, *WINKLES AND CHAMPAGNE*

Perhaps more than any of his contemporaries Leno suffered from the lack of any technology to preserve his art. Neither on gramophone recordings nor in the written words of his material nor in the descriptions of witnesses does his sense of humour and its cleverly concerted effect on an audience come across fully. Leno orchestrated his effects, using each audience as an instrument on which to gain his comic impact. Like so many great clowns he was a small, pathetic-looking man with an oddly wizened face and a look of vulnerability from which glowed a spirit of comic defiance. Many of the most popular solo pieces consisted of a comic song whose verses were broken up by interludes of patter consisting of non sequiturs, malapropisms, puns and incongruities pursued with an unshakable air of illogic. Posterity, confronted by the mildness of the printed words, has been obliged to take on trust what was evidently a riotous comic experience.

Without his personality to go with them, Leno's songs and acts, even more than those of other artists, are clearly but a shadow of what he made them. As he died in 1904, his recordings were made when techniques were very crude, so that although it is possible to hear his voice and gauge in some little way his approach, these recordings cannot do him even such justice as the restrictions of that medium would permit. Even without his personality to give it the inimitability of which every single writer who mentions him speaks of with a mixture of wonder and reverence, I have known a crude amateur performance of his monologue, 'The Robin', to give considerable delight.

Yet even without such a vital element of his act, the words that Leno sang and spoke may sometimes have considerable interest. 'The Huntsman' is far more act than it is song, and the song indeed is virtually no more than a hunting cry. The patter is largely, but not entirely, absurd humour based on the association of ideas, and it makes possible the kind of scene painting in words in which Leno specialised. Taken in isolation, the humour is not very remarkable. For example, there is nothing excruciatingly comic about this:

> Then the Baron said, 'Now we will go to the meet'.
> I couldn't see any meat.
> I looked round, but only saw a lot of empty plates;
> I think they must have eaten all the meat for breakfast.

PETER DAVISON, *THE BRITISH MUSIC HALL*

'The Huntsman', written for Leno by the team of George Stevens and Albert Perry, with music by Fred Eplett, was an exercise in Cockney humour at the expense of the huntin', shootin' and fishin' classes. Just as Bessie Bellwood had extracted working-class laughter from audiences well aware of the vast gulf in wealth and creature comforts between themselves and the upper classes, so Leno reduced the Huntsman to absurdity by manufacturing confusions between the vocabularies of the two classes as well as marking the contrasting conventions of dress and manners. 'The Huntsman' is set up with a sung quatrain which immediately scores a laugh by likening the red of the hunting field to something rather more mundane:

> I'm not a fireman or a 'tec, as some folks may suppose,
> Although perhaps you'd think so, when you gaze upon my clothes.
> At present I'm a huntsman gay, a huntsman gay am I,
> And all the ladies smile at me, as through the air I fly.

The last word in that verse is the springboard from which Leno dives into a sea of misunderstandings.

'Fly! Fly! Fly! Now, when you come to think of it, what a harmless little creature the fly is. You see the other day I was invited down to the Duchess of Piccadilly Circus's country seat to attend the meet. Now when I say "attend the meet", I don't wish you to mistake me for a pork butcher. No! I mean hunting the hares. Now, by hunting the hares, I don't wish you to mistake me for a hairdresser. To be explicit, hunting the hares means following the hounds. And they *were* a lot of hounds, especially Lord de No Oof, because just to show that I was used to hunting, I shouted in his ear, "Tally ho!" He turned pale and nearly fainted. He thought I said, "Tally-man". But after all, following the hounds is a splendid life. The bugles buge, the post-horns horn, and the horses horse.'

DAN LENO

After riding off in pursuit of the hares in borrowed clothes, Leno commits the *faux pas* of shooting a cat by mistake, after which he reaches the conclusion that life would be far simpler if the hunters would agree to purchase their meat in the local butcher's shop. Altough the entire routine is a gesture of derision aimed at what the audience sometimes thought of as their betters, Leno's absurdities were by no means restricted to the enemy. Having been raised in Somers Town, one of the most notorious rookeries in the whole of London, Leno was under no illusions as to the probity of the working classes, and knew as well as any man that crime was a normal source of income among the under-privileged. His definition of London, rarely quoted outside the context of the music hall, is nevertheless one of the most pertinent ever made. Allowing for the comicality of the exaggeration, and for the specialised context in which the remark was used, Leno's view of things contains much truth: 'London is a large village on the Thames where the principal industries carried on are music hall and the confidence trick.' In another patter song, 'The Swimming Master', Leno casually throws away a joke about the extent to which the poor sometimes prey on each other by selling food which might not quite be what it appears; it is typical that the joke should come without warning at so oblique an angle to the main dissertation.

'You wouldn't believe how strong you get having so much to do with water. Before I taught swimming I was a poor, weak little chap, with no chest and thin arms. Well, now look at me! Oh, I love the water. All our family love water. I've seen my father drink quarts of water – of course with something in it. And my brother, he's passionately fond of water. He's a milkman.'

DAN LENO

Each of Leno's songs was an impersonation of a type familiar to his audience. Whether as huntsman or swimming master, or the lodger at the mercy of a voracious landlady, character delineation was at the heart of every gesture and every vocal nuance. Before audiences ever saw a new Leno character, the comedian had already worked tirelessly, often for months on end, to find the heart of the performance. There were times when he never found it.

The characters in my songs are all founded on fact. To get the effect out of songs is not as easy as it looks. In the first place you've got to catch your song, and you'll understand the difficulty when I tell you I've over 150 songs at home for which I've paid from one to five guineas each, and which are utterly worthless. Sometimes I sit up all night studying a song, trying to see chances of effect in it, till I get out of temper and chuck it in the fire. I study hard for all my songs; my favourite way is to walk a few miles in the rain, keeping time to the tune with my feet.

DAN LENO

One of the first lessons which every music-hall artist learned was that London was a huge city and that each music hall had its own regular clientèle whose tastes in humour might be specialised. Artists were often depressed by the failure of a proven piece of material when it was used in a different town, or even a different district. One of the most famous confrontations between artist and audience, between Marie Lloyd and the city of Sheffield, came about because of this regional differentiation. Leno, too, was sensitive to the gradations of humorous reaction in the London halls, and knew perfectly well that because a song failed in the glitter of the West End, that did not mean it could not be made to work in more modest surroundings.

Here is the chorus of an early song, sung in the character of a workman's wife:

> I can do what I like with dear old Mike,
> All the days of the week but one day.
> He's as happy as you please, with a bit of bread and cheese,
> But he likes his bit of meat on Sunday.

Already with him the words of a song were to do little but serve as an introduction to one of the character studies he made so famous, and Horace Lennard had a curious story about this particular song. Leno sang it first one night at the Empire, and Lennard went round to see him in his dressing-room. The new song had not gone particularly well.

'Come round with me and hear me sing it at the Mo,' said Dan, 'this audience doesn't know the type, but they'll see it all right at the Mo.'

He drove Lennard in his Brougham to the old Mogul, where on his appearance he had the usual tremendous reception. He let himself go, as only Leno could, and when, as the frowsy yet lovable old harridan he produced from his marketing basket Mike's little bit of meat in the shape of a belly-piece of pork, which he referred to as 'the waistcoat piece with the buttons', the house became hysterical with delight.

From Christmas 1888 until his death, Leno joined forces annually with two other comics, his uncle, Johnny Danvers, and the elephantine Herbert Campbell, to animate the Drury Lane pantomimes. Leno played one of the Forty Thieves, or Mother Goose, or one of the Ugly Sisters, or whichever traditional role gave him the best chance of dispensing his art. The reminiscences of the Georgians are cluttered with accounts of childhood visits to Drury Lane, and especially of Leno's triumphant assertion of his comic genius. But there was one voice of dissent in particular, which suggests that perhaps the felicities of the Drury Lane pantomimes faded when the audience had passed a certain age. One of the bitterest enemies of this beloved institution was Bernard Shaw, who opened one of his weekly *feuilletons*: 'Not having seen a pantomime for fourteen years, I decided to drop into Drury Lane. I do not think I shall go for another fourteen.' In January 1897 Shaw used the pantomime as a pretext for continuing his long onslaught on the sensibilities of the grandee of the Drury Lane Theatre, Sir Augustus Harris. Sir Augustus had recently died, but this was no impediment to the critic.

As it happens, being no great pantomime goer, I never saw one of Mr Oscar Barrett's pantomimes until I went to *Aladdin*; so I am perhaps unwittingly disparaging his former achievements when I say that it is the best modern Christmas pantomime I have seen. Not that it is by any means faultless. It is much too long, even for the iron nerves of childhood. The first part alone would be a very ample and handsome entertainment. But if thirteen changes and a transformation are *de rigueur*, the surfeit might be lightened by a little cutting; for one or two of the scenes, especially the laundry scene in the first part, are dragged out to a tediousness that defies even Mr Dan Leno's genius. The instrumentation of the ballet in the second part, too, unaccountably discredits the musical taste and knowledge which are so conspicuous in the first part. For here, just at the point when about two and a half hours of orchestration have made one's nerves a little irritable, this big, glittering ballet begins with a reinforcement of two military bands, coarse in tone, and with all the infirmities of intonation produced by valves in brass instruments. The result is a pandemonium which destroys the hitherto admirable balance of sound, and sets up just that perilous worry – the bane of spectacular ballets – which Mr Barrett up to that moment triumphantly avoids. This is the more unexpected because the ballet scene in the first part is a conspicuous example of just the kind of musical judgement that fails him afterwards. In it Mr Barrett fills the back of the stage with trumpets, and overwhelms the house with their ringing clangor, the effect, though of the fiercest kind within the limits of music, being magnificent. But this clarion outbreak is the climax of a long series of effects beginning quietly with a unison movement for the bass strings, and gradually leading up to the *coup de cuivre*. It is astonishing that the same hand that planned the music of this scene should afterwards begin a similar one by flinging those two horrible extra bands at our heads.

Let me add, so as to get my faultfinding all together, that I do not see why the traditional privileges of vulgarity in a pantomime should be so scrupulously respected by a manager whose reputation has been made by the comparative refinement of his taste and the superiority of his culture in spectacular and musical matters. Why, for instance, is the 'principal boy' expected to be more vulgar than the principal girl, when she does not want to, and when there is not the slightest reason to suppose that anyone else wants her to? I cannot for the life of me see why Miss Ada Blanche, who at certain moments sings with a good deal of feeling and speaks with propriety, should not be as refined throughout as Miss Decima Moore. But as that would not be customary, Miss Blanche takes considerable trouble, which is probably quite uncongenial to her, to be rowdy and knowing. Again, Mr Herbert Campbell, though he is incapable of the delicate *nuances* of Mr Leno, is an effectively robust comedian, whose power of singing like a powerful accordion, which some miracle-worker has got into perfect tune, is not unacceptable. But why should it be a point of honour with him to carry the slangy tone and street-corner pronunciation of his music-hall patter into those lines of his part in which he is supposed for the moment to be, not the popular funny man, but the magician of the fairy tale. Mr Campbell can say 'face' instead of 'fice', 'slave' instead of 'slive', 'brain' instead of 'brine', if he likes; and yet he takes the greatest possible pains to avoid doing so lest his occupation as a comically vulgar person should be gone. Naturally, when this occurs in a classic passage, it destroys the effect by suggesting that he mispronounces, not as a comic artist, but because he cannot help it, which I have no doubt is the last impression Mr Campbell would desire to convey. There are passages in his part which should either be spoken as carefully as the speech of the Ghost in *Hamlet* or else not spoken at all. Pray understand that I do not want the pantomime artists to be 'funny without being vulgar'. That is the mere snobbery of criticism. Every comedian should have vulgarity at his fingers' ends for use when required. It is the business of old Eccles and Perkyn Middlewick to be vulgar as much as it is the business of Parolles and Bobadil to be cowardly or Coriolanus to be haughty. But vulgarity in the wrong place, or slovenliness of speech in any place as a matter of personal habit instead of artistic assumption, is not to be tolerated from any actor or in any entertainment. Especially in a pantomime, where fun, horseplay, and the most outrageous silliness and lawlessness are of the essence of the show, it is important that nothing should be done otherwise than artistically.

Fortunately the Drury Lane pantomime offers more positive than negative evidence under this head. The knockabout business is not overdone; and what there is of it – mostly in the hands of Mr Fred Griffiths as a Chinese policeman – is funny. Mr Leno only falls twice; and on both occasions the gravest critics must shriek with merriment. Mr Cinquevalli's juggling need not be described. It is as well known in London as Sarasate's fiddling; and it fits very happily into the pantomime: indeed, it would be hard to contrive a better pantomime scene of its kind than that in which Cinquevalli, as Slave of the Lamp, appears in the Aladdin household and begins to do impossible things with the plates and tubs. His wonderful address and perfect physical training make him effective even when he is not juggling, as when he is flinging two plates right and left all over the stage, and fielding them (in the cricketing sense) with a success which, though highly diverting, is, no doubt, contemptibly cheap to him. Madame Grigolati's aerial dancing is also, of course, familiar; but it, too, fits perfectly into the pantomime, and is the first exhibition of the kind in which I have seen the aerial device used to much artistic purpose, or maintain its interest after the first novelty of seeing the laws of gravitation suspended in favour of a dancer had worn off. In short, nobody is allowed to take a prominent and independent part in the pantomime without solid qualifications. The second-rate people are not allowed to stand in the corner improvising second-rate tomfooleries. The rank and file are well disciplined; and there is not only order on the stage, but a considerable degree of atmosphere and illusion – qualities which the only Harrisian pantomime I ever saw signally failed to attain. The comedians do not pester you with topical songs, nor the fairy queen (who is only present in a rudimentary form) with sentimental ones. Indeed, the music shews the modern tendency to integrate into a continuous score, and avoid set 'numbers'. The point reached in this respect is not Wagnerian; but it is fairly level with Gounod, who, by the way, is profusely, and sometimes amusingly, quoted. Mr Barrett is catholic in his tastes, and takes his goods where he can find them, Wagner and Bellini being equally at his command. Thus, Abanazar's exhortation to Aladdin to take the magic ring leads to an outburst of 'Prendi l'anell' ti dono' from *La Sonnambula* (not recognised, I fear, by the present generation, but very familiar to fogies of my epoch); and a capital schoolboy chorus in the second scene is provided by a combination of the opening strains of the Kermesse in Gounod's *Faust* with a tune which flourished in my tenderest youth as 'Tidd yiddy ido, Chin-Chon-Chino', and which was used freely by Mr Glover in last year's pantomime.

The best scenic effect is that achieved in the last scene of the first part, where the stage picture, at the moment when the procession of bearded patriarchs is passing down from the sun, is very fine. In some of the other scenes, especially those in which a front scene opens to reveal a very luminous distance, the effect is generally to make the foreground dingy and destroy its illusion. No doubt people seldom attend to the foreground under such circumstances: all the same, the effect on them would be greater if the foreground would bear attention; and it seems to me that this could be managed at least as well on the stage as in the pictures of Turner, who also had to struggle with a tradition of dingy foregrounds.

Mr Barret does not consider the transformation scene and harlequinade out of date. His transformation scene is very pretty; and the harlequinade is of the kind I can remember when the institution was in full decay about twenty-five years ago: that is, the old woman and the swell have disappeared; the policeman has no part; the old window-trap, through which everybody jumped head foremost except the pantaloon (who muffed it), is not used; the harlequin and columbine do not dance, and the clown neither burns people with a red-hot poker nor knocks at the baker's door and then lies down across the threshold to trip him up as he comes out. But there *is* a clown, who acts extensively as an advertisement agent, and plays the pilgrim's march from *Tannhäuser* on the trombone until a hundred-ton weight is dropped on his head. His jokes, you see, are faithful to the old clowny tradition in being twenty years out of date. His name is Huline; and he is exactly like 'the Great Little Huline' of my schooldays. And there is a pantaloon, another Huline, whose sufferings and humiliations are luxuries and dignities compared to those which pantaloons once had to undergo.

Let me add, as a touching example of the maternal instinct in Woman (bless her!), that the performance I witnessed was an afternoon one, and that though the house

91

was packed with boys and girls trying to get a good peep at the stage, I never saw the *matinée* hat in grosser feather and foliage. The men, on the other hand, took their hats off, and sacrificed themselves to the children as far as they could. Brutes!

GEORGE BERNARD SHAW IN *LONDON MUSIC*, 23 JANUARY 1897

Shaw could not resist the temptation to return to the Drury Lane panto in order to castigate its stars for not being serious artists and its impresarios for betraying weaknesses of judgment. In the following year he went back and was particularly incensed by the theme of the humour based on *Hamlet*. After opening with his historic broadside at the institution of Christmas, and pausing briefly to take a sideswipe at poor posthumous Sir Augustus, Shaw gets down to business and attacks the pantomime for doing so jocosely what he himself had been doing for some time with great brilliance, making Shakespeare seem ridiculous.

PEACE AND GOODWILL TO MANAGERS
The Babes in the Wood. The Children's Grand Pantomime.
By Arthur Sturgess and Arthur Collins. Music by J. M. Glover.
Theatre Royal, Drury Lane, 27 December 1897.

I am sorry to have to introduce the subject of Christmas in these articles. It is an indecent subject; a cruel, gluttonous subject; a drunken, disorderly subject; a wasteful, disastrous subject; a wicked, cadging, lying, filthy, blasphemous, and demoralising subject. Christmas is forced on a reluctant and disgusted nation by the shopkeepers and the press: on its own merits it would wither and shrivel in the fiery breath of universal hatred; and anyone who looked back to it would be turned into a pillar of greasy sausages. Yet, though it is over now for a year, and I can go out without positively elbowing my way through groves of carcases, I am dragged back to it, with my soul full of loathing, by the pantomime.

The pantomime ought to be a redeeming feature of Christmas, since it professedly aims at developing the artistic possibilities of our Saturnalia. But its professions are like all the other Christmas professions: what the pantomime actually does is to abuse the Christmas toleration of dullness, senselessness, vulgarity, and extravagance to a degree utterly incredible by people who have never been inside a theatre. The manager spends five hundred pounds to produce two penn'orth of effect. As a shilling's worth is needed to fill the gallery, he has to spend three thousand pounds for the 'gods', seven thousand five hundred for the pit, and so on in proportion, except that when it comes to the stalls and boxes he caters for the children alone, depending on their credulity to pass off his twopence as a five-shilling piece. And yet even this is not done systematically and intelligently. The wildest superfluity and extravagance in one direction is wasted by the most sordid niggardliness in another. The rough rule is to spend money recklessly on whatever can be seen and heard and recognised as costly, and to economise on invention, fancy, dramatic faculty – in short, on brains. It is only when the brains get thrown in gratuitously through the accident of some of the contracting parties happening to possess them – a contingency which managerial care cannot always avert – that the entertainment acquires sufficient form or purpose to make it humanly apprehensible. To the mind's eye and ear the modern pantomime, as purveyed by the late Sir Augustus Harris, is neither visible nor audible. It is a glittering, noisy void, horribly wearisome and enervating, like all performances which worry the physical senses without any recreative appeal to the emotions and through them to the intellect.

I grieve to say that these remarks have lost nothing of their force by the succession of Mr Arthur Collins to Sir Augustus Harris. In Drury Lane drama Mr Collins made a decided advance on his predecessor. In pantomime he has, I think, also shewn superior connoisseurship in selecting pretty dummies for the display of his lavishly expensive wardrobe; but the only other respect in which he has outdone his late chief is the cynicism with which he has disregarded, I will not say the poetry of the nursery tale, because poetry is unthinkable in such a connection, but the bare coherence and common sense of the presentation of its incidents. The spectacular scenes exhibit Mr Collins as a manager to whom a thousand pounds is as five shillings. The dramatic scenes exhibit him as one to whom a crown-piece is as a million. If Mr Dan Leno had asked for a hundred-guinea tunic to wear during a single walk across the stage, no doubt he would have got it, with a fifty-guinea hat and sword-belt to boot. If he had asked for ten guineas' worth of the time of a competent dramatic humorist to provide him with at least one line that might not have been pirated from the nearest Cheap Jack, he would, I suspect, have been asked whether he wished to make Drury Lane bankrupt for the benefit of dramatic authors. I hope I may never again have to endure anything more dismally futile than the efforts of Mr Leno and Mr Herbert Campbell to start a passable joke in the course of their stumblings and wanderings through barren acres of gag on Boxing-night. Their attempt at a travesty of *Hamlet* reached a pitch of abject resourcelessness which could not have been surpassed if they really had been a couple of school children called on for a prize-day Shakespearean recitation without any previous warning. An imitation of Mr Forbes Robertson and Mrs Patrick Campbell would have been cheap and obvious enough; but even this they were unequal to. Mr Leno, fortunately for himself, was inspired at the beginning of the business to call Hamlet 'Ham'. Several of the easily amused laughed at this; and thereafter, whenever the travesty became so frightfully insolvent in ideas as to make it almost impossible to proceed, Mr Leno said 'Ham', and saved the situation. What will happen now is that Mr Leno will hit on a new point of the 'Ham' order at, say, every second performance. As there are two performances a day, he will have accumulated thirty 'wheezes', as he calls them, by the end of next month, besides being cut down to strict limits of time. In February, then, his part will be quite bearable – probably very droll – and Mr Collins will thereby be confirmed in his belief that if you engage an eccentric comedian of recognised gagging powers you need not take the trouble to write a part for him. But would it not be wiser, under these circumstances, to invite the critics on the last night of the pantomime instead of on the first? Mr Collins will probably reply that by doing so he would lose the benefit of the press notices, which, as a matter of Christmas custom, are not criticisms, but simply gratuitous advertisements given as a Christmas-box by the newspaper to the manager who advertises all the year round. And I am sorry to say he will be quite right.

It is piteous to see the wealth of artistic effort which is annually swamped in the morass of purposeless wastefulness that constitutes a pantomime. At Drury Lane many of the costumes are extremely pretty, and some of them, notably those borrowed for the flower ballet from one of Mr Crane's best-known series of designs, rise above mere theatrical prettiness to the highest class of decorative art available for fantastic stage purposes. Unhappily, every stroke that is at all delicate, or rare, or precious is multiplied, and repeated, and obtruded, usually on the limbs of some desolatingly incompetent young woman, until its value is heavily discounted. Still, some of the scenes are worth looking at for five minutes, though not for twenty. The orchestral score is very far above the general artistic level of the pantomime. The instrumental resources placed at the disposal of Mr Glover – quite ungrudgingly as far as they consist of brass – would suffice for a combined Bach festival and Bayreuth

Götterdämmerung performance. To hear a whole battery of Bach trumpets, supported by a park of trombones, blasting the welkin with the exordium of Wagner's *Kaisermarsch*, is an ear-splitting ecstasy not to be readily forgotten; but these mechanical effects are really cheaper than the daintiness and wit of the vocal accompaniments, in which Mr Glover shews a genuine individual and original style in addition to his imposing practical knowledge of band business.

If I were Mr Collins I should reduce the first four scenes to one short one, and get some person with a little imagination, some acquaintance with the story of the Babes in the Wood, and at least a rudimentary faculty for amusing people, to write the dialogue for it. I should get Messrs Leno and Campbell to double the parts of the robbers with those of the babies, and so make the panorama scene tolerable. I should reduce the second part to the race-course scene, which is fairly funny, with just one front scene, in which full scope might be allowed for Mr Leno's inspiration, and the final transformation. I should either cut the harleqinade out, or, at the expense of the firms it advertises, pay the audience for looking at it; or else I should take as much trouble with it as Mr Tree took with *Chand d'Habits* at Her Majesty's. And I should fill up the evening with some comparatively amusing play by Ibsen or Browning.

Finally, may I ask our magistrates on what ground they permit the legislation against the employment of very young children as money makers for their families to be practically annulled in favour of the pantomimes? If the experience, repeated twice a day for three months, is good for the children, I suggest that there need be no difficulty in filling their places with volunteers from among the children of middle and upper-class parents anxious to secure a delightful and refining piece of education for their offspring. If it is not good for them, why do the magistrates deliberately license it? I venture to warn our managers that their present monstrous abuse of magistrates' licences can only end in a cast-iron clause in the next Factory Act unconditionally forbidding the employment of children under thirteen on any pretext whatever.

GEORGE BERNARD SHAW IN *LONDON MUSIC*, 1 JANUARY 1898

But Shaw, when he writhed at the fatuities of the Shakespearean parodies of Leno and company, was already over forty years old and just approaching that watershed of his life when his red beard turned white from sheer intellectual power. The right age to revel in the Drury Lane shows was not forty but seven or eight, preferably in the company of your contemporaries, and at a stage of worldly experience when a visit to the theatre, so far from being an incident in the weekly drudgery, was an adventure cloud-capped and breathtaking. Ernest Shepard, the illustrator who never, in a life even as long as Shaw's, was to lose his path back to childhood, and whose drawings of the folk at Pooh Corner and Toad Hall endeared him to generations of the children who came after him, gives a very different picture of what it was like to sit in the vast theatre and be transported into some other world of fancy and tomfoolery.

Near the end of January, on one particularly murky morning when it was dark enough to have the gas light in the schoolroom, I was glooming over my work in class when I was called out by Miss Gardner. She told me that we had been sent for. I hurried out to find Martha waiting below. Cyril came out from his classroom, and Martha told us

94

that we were to go home at once on account of something important. While we scrambled into our coats and mufflers we tried to get Martha to tell us what it was. All she would say was: 'You must wait till we get Miss Ethel from the High School.' When we were all gathered together she told us that we were to go to Drury Lane Pantomime that *very* afternoon!

It is difficult to describe the state this put us in. Cyril and I shouted and sang all the way along the Park Road and the fishmonger wanted to know what it was all about. When we arrived home Mother was waiting. She told us that Mr Oliver, who had the theatre agency in Bond Street, had lent us his box for the afternoon performance at Drury Lane. Cyril and I, overcome with joy, turned somersaults round the dining-room table and were then packed off to lie down – *'Lie down,* mind!' – and told that we would have a light lunch and then go by cab to Drury Lane. Though we obediently lay down, neither Cyril nor I could sleep; we just lay there exchanging speculations on the glories to come. We had never been to a pantomime before. We had seen Hengler's Circus the previous year and also the Minstrels, but this was far, far more thrilling.

At midday we were told to get up and put on our best velvet suits. This usually irksome task, normally done under protest, was performed with quite unheard-of speed and we were soon ready to sit down at table. Appetite seemed to have deserted me; I was much too excited; but I was made to eat something. Lizzie was shaking her head over our chances of ever reaching the theatre. She recalled how once, years before, in just such a fog, Grandma had failed to arrive at a concert at which she was to sing. We were glad when Father came home from the office. He was just as pleased as we were, though he said we must allow plenty of time, for the fog was even thicker down in the West End. The old messenger man was summoned from his seat at the end of the Terrace and sent to find a four-wheeler. It was agony waiting while he was gone, but he came back seated inside and the horse all steaming in the cold foggy air. We started off, our progress getting slower and slower as the fog grew thicker. It was worse by the time we reached Marylebone Road, and along Tottenham Court Road gas flares were burning and the traffic moving at a snail's pace. Two or three times we nearly mounted the curb and it seemed as if we should never get to the theatre. Boys with flaring torches were guiding people along the streets. Oh, dear! suppose we should be too late! At last we reached Long Acre and, turning into Drury Lane, came in sight of the gas torches burning under the great portico of the theatre. There were crowds of carriages and cabs in the street, with touts running among them to guide people and earn a few pence. We left our cab and, struggling through the press of people and clinging to each other, made our way up the steps.

Two Grenadier sentries in overcoats and busbies were standing at attention, a strange contrast to the heaving crowd. Dodging among the people were boys dressed as pages, in bright blue suits with buttons and pill-box caps, giving away little bottles of scent. I grabbed one of these, but after the first whiff it began to smell very nasty and I threw it away. Waiting while Father fumbled for the tickets was misery . . . Suppose he had lost them! Or suppose they were for the wrong day! But all was well, and we crowded inside and along the passage, where a woman in an apron opened a small door and we were shown into our box. There the full glory of the place burst upon us. I stood looking at the auditorium, fast filling up, trying to take it all in. There were pegs at the back of the box and the woman helped us hang up our coats and mufflers. The box contained only four chairs but that didn't matter as I was far too excited to sit and kept hopping up and down. Somebody brought a programme and the orchestra began to tune up. Then the great big circle of gas in the roof was turned up and the limelights in the wings began to fizz. A general hush descended on the audience. Threading his way among the orchestra came the conductor.

At this point Cyril was sick. He generally was when he got over-excited and it always happened at an inconvenient moment. However, the woman in the apron was most sympathetic and tidied everything up. My chief concern was that Cyril might miss something, but, having done his bit, he seemed to be all right. Then the curtain rose and I became lost to all around me, translated to another land, borne aloft on magic wings into another world.

The story must have been *The Babes in the Wood*, for otherwise why should Harry Nicholls and Herbert Campbell, both outsize Babes, have appeared seated side by side in an enormous double perambulator and proceeded to sing a duet?

Two bandits, though hired for the purpose of making away with this innocent pair, spent most of their energies in knock-about comedy. Can they have been the Griffiths brothers, the famous inventors of Pogo the horse? The scene in the kitchen of the wicked Baron's house was a riot below stairs, with a cat who jumped over a large kitchen table, all laid ready for a meal; he jumped like a real animal and landed on his forelegs, a thing no one but Charles Laurie could do. This was before Dan Leno's day; he did not come to Drury Lane till a year or two later. But I remember a gay young woman with prominent teeth and a flaxen wig who sang and danced bewitchingly. She could only have been Marie Lloyd, the unforgettable, aged seventeen and in her first Pantomime at 'the Lane'. In the Harlequinade the clown was an old favourite, Harry Payne, so Father told us, who had been clowning for years and was shortly to give place to another famous clown, Whimsical Walker.

It was all such a feast of colour, music and fun, and it would be quite impossible to express all the emotions that were aroused in a small boy's breast. I know that I stood gripping the velvet-covered front of the box, lost in a wonderful dream, and that when the curtain fell at the end of the first act and the lights in the auditorium went up, I sat back on Mother's lap with a sigh. I could not speak when she asked me if I was enjoying the show. I could only nod my head. I did not think it possible that such feminine charms existed as were displayed by the Principal Boy. Ample-bosomed, small-waisted and with thighs – oh, such thighs! – thighs that shone and glittered in the different coloured silk tights in which she continually appeared. How she strode about the stage, proud and dominant, smacking those rounded limbs with a riding crop! At every smack, a fresh dart was shot into the heart of at least one young adorer. I had a grand feeling that it was all being done for my especial benefit: the whole performance was for *me*; the cast had all been told that they were to do their best because *I* was there. Nobody else, not even Mother, could feel exactly the same as I did.

I had one dreadful moment when I happened to look round while the adored one was singing one of her songs . . . Father, at the back of the box, was reading a newspaper. I could hardly believe my eyes. Could it be that he was so overcome that he was trying to conceal his emotion by this show of indifference? Yes, no doubt that was it; but I have since wondered if I was right.

The spectacle reached a climax with the transformation scene. Glittering vistas appeared one behind the other, sparkling lace-like canopies spread overhead, a real fountain poured forth in the background. On either side golden brackets swung out from the wings, each with its reclining nymph, solid and spangled and in a graceful attitude. Flying fairies, poised but swaying gently, filled the air and formed a sort of triumphal archway, below which the performers gathered. The Good Fairy, stepping forward, invoked in rhymed couplets the Spirit of Pantomime, and out from the wings burst Joey the clown, Pantaloon, Columbine and Harlequin to complete the tableau. Not quite, for, led by the Principal Boy, there came Augustus Harris himself, immaculate in evening dress with white waistcoat, to receive the plaudits of a delighted audience.

There was still the Harlequinade to come. The red-hot poker (that kept hot for a remarkably long time), the strings of sausages, the stolen goose, the Pantaloon always in difficulties, the Policeman, blown up and put together again. Oh, how I longed for it to go on for ever! Then Harlequin, with a wave of his wand, brought on his Columbine, so fair and dainty, but not so lovely as to steal one's heart, though she helped to rob the shopman. On came the tall thin man who sang and sang the while he was belaboured by Joey and Pantaloon. And then – the end!

It was really over at last. No use to gaze at the dropped curtain, the dimming lights or the emptying theatre. I was speechless as we muffled up for the journey home. Speechless as we sat in the cab and crawled slowly through the same fog which seemed so much blacker than it was before. Speechless as I tried to eat the unwanted supper, while the others prattled of all the lovely things they had seen. 'Do you remember when the cat...?' and 'Did you see those two men fight and their swords come to pieces...?' I could only see one vision: *she* floated before me, superb and feminine.

My tongue was loosed when Mother came up to kiss me good night. 'Darling,' she said, 'did you really enjoy it?'

'Yes, oh yes!' Then, rather breathlessly, 'Wasn't she lovely!'

I did not want Mother to go, so I took her hand as she sat beside me on my bed. I asked her if she had been to a pantomime when she was a little girl. 'There were very few pantomimes when I was your age,' she replied, 'and none anything like so grand as this one. I remember a clown and a harlequin, but all the girls wore skirts to their knees' (this was a smile at me). Then she said: 'I must have been twelve years old before Grandma took me to one, but not in a box, we had quite humble seats.'

I thought about this for a moment or two and then said: 'Do you think we shall be able to go to one again next Christmas?'

She laughed and replied: 'Why, that *is* a long way off, but perhaps we may be able to.' Then she kissed me good night and went downstairs.

I lay back in bed and made up my mind that I would draw all I had seen, using my new coloured chalks, red, blue and yellow for the clown and pantaloon, the choice sky-bue tint for the spangled corsage of my beloved's costume which she wore when she came on at the end. Yes, and primrose yellow for her little short cloak and those shining legs. The hat, bedecked with ostrich feathers, should be pink. But oh! could I ever draw her as she really was? Sleepily, with my head on the pillow, I thought all this over and tried to decide where I should begin. Overcome with drowsiness, I lay there watching the faint light from the gas lamp on the stairs. The door was open and I could hear the cistern making its usual dripping noise. Then Mother's voice came to me from below. She was singing in the drawing-room, 'Robin, lend to me thy bow'. I think she knew it was my favourite song.

ERNEST SHEPARD, *DRAWN FROM MEMORY*

Shaw appears to have been in a minority of one. Audiences seemed to care very little what Leno did so long as he did it in his own style, cutting across class divisions with great success most of the time, especially at Drury Lane, where he was seen by a rather more genteel clientèle than he might have found in the suburban London halls. Children especially were inclined to adore him in pantomime, which has much to do with the lingering bouquet of his reputation. The small boys and girls who watched him as Widow Twankey or the Ugly Sister never forgot the experience, and waxed eloquent about it in their memoirs, in the years after not only Leno but the music hall itself were long gone. Leno's reputation embraced the intellectuals, the mob, children, even the kind of old ladies whose mannerisms he might be parodying in his patter-songs. For the most part he was above criticism.

He was patient – yet impatient. 'Don't look so stupid!' he would plead: and the house roared, at its own imputed lack of uptake. Like the other great artists of his era, Marie Lloyd, Arthur Roberts, Harry Randall, Eugene Stratton and Coburn, he pervaded stage and auditorium; he gathered his audience in his hands, and drew them to him; they were his, part of him, and he played with them as he pleased. As time went on, the actual song seemed to matter less and less. He came to content himself with a solitary verse, used as an introduction, and a chorus. The song was merely an excuse for the presentation of a type, a type which, however extravagant, had an instant appeal, and bore a mad relation to actuality. Leno's humour was wild and inconsequent, yet, at the same time, sane and keenly observant, an impossible paradox to anyone who never saw him. In the apparent wildness and extravagance there were acute observation and criticism. His wildest types were living, human beings, with outlooks and idiosyncracies that had a fundamental appeal. His criticism took the form of caricature, and the most ridiculous non sequitur conveyed a meaning.

M. WILLSON DISHER, *WINKLES AND CHAMPGNE*

In pantomime, it was Dan Leno first and the rest of the field nowhere. Of course, I liked it all, but I knew the difference. We generally did at least two pantomimes a year, the one at Drury Lane and the one at the Islington, where we saw Dick Whittington in the year of Lottie Collins. Harry fell for her. She and her Ta-ra-ras became his. I liked, but not adored her – and of this pantomime, apart from her big hat and tossing skirts, I chiefly remember clapping a song by the Principal Boy – well, one clapped everything, didn't one? The song was called 'Oh, What a Difference in the Morning!' I didn't understand it much, but it had a lively tune, and there was a lot of grown-up laughter; so naturally when the song was done I clapped. Over my shoulder came Papa's warm, firm hand; he was sitting behind me. His fingers closed on mine, and held them still for a moment on the box-ledge. I looked round enquiringly, and he smiled at me, and took his hand away. I asked no question, and did not clap any more.

ELEANOR FARJEON, *A NURSERY IN THE NINETIES*

That was, perhaps, Dan Leno's greatest triumph, that the grimy sordid material of the music-hall low comedian, which, with so many singers, remains grimy and sordid, in his refining hands became radiant, joyous, a legitimate source of mirth. In its nakedness it was still drunkenness, quarrelsomeness, petty poverty, still hunger, even crime; but such was the native cleanness of this little, eager, sympathetic observer and reader of life, such his gift of showing the comic, the unexpected side, that it emerged the most suitable, the gayest joke. He might be said to have been a crucible that transmuted mud to gold.

E. V. LUCAS

. . . Leno's pathetic little Cockney, just married, the victim of a building society; he had bought a house, and he leant over the footlights to tell us in husky confidence of his pride of possession. It was a nice house, with the river at the bottom of the garden; that is, when the garden wasn't at the bottom of the river.

NEVILLE CARDUS, *SECOND INNINGS*

S haw's strictures regarding the lampoon of *Hamlet* had a tragic sequel some years later. Leno was not the first comic idol to strain his own sanity to the breaking point, nor will he be the last. His art, balanced on a knife-edge between perceptive insight and hysterical illogicality, required the perfect environment for its full expression and a friendly reception. In 1901 an honour came to him so great that it is said to have unnerved him once and for all. He was summoned by royal command to entertain the King at Sandringham. The ordeal of taking the humours of Somers Town to the very apex of society preyed on his mind and, it was generally recognised, did him some sort of permanent psychological damage.

A very old friend, Mrs Helen Tresahar, who acted under the name of Daisy Thimm, travelled to Sandringham in the same train as did Leno. She had a small part in the sketch 'Scrooge', which was being presented by Sir Seymour Hicks in the same programme before King Edward VII as that in which Leno was performing 'The Huntsman'. Leno, though the idol of the halls, suffered agonies of nervousness especially in the course of working up his acts. The importance of this occasion so worried him that throughout the journey he was sick time and again.

PETER DAVISON, *THE BRITISH MUSIC HALL*

N ot all the commanded artists took the occasion quite with Leno's seriousness. Also on the bill was a contingent from that Bohemia represented by the men-about-town of the variety world, those sophisticates whose work and art were familiar fixtures at the larger West End halls. To these men, the occasion was not only an honour and an ordeal, but also a bit of a lark. The performers involved were experienced enough to know that in a theatre as incongruous as Sandringham, some of the arrangements were bound to go awry, and that consequently, with a little bit of luck, some enjoyably farcical overtones might result. The men-about-town were not to be disappointed. The sequence of events which might have driven a delicate soul like Leno screaming from the premises only served to make a cherished anecdote in the careers of the showmen.

It was through a command performance that Herman Finck accidentally overheard King Edward's personal and private opinions on Germany and things German. To celebrate Queen Alexandra's birthday the King had commanded a performance at Sandringham, and amongst the folk who went down were 'The Follies' – who were then at the Palace Theatre – Alfred Butt, and Herman Finck. As the company left town at noon and were not to ring up until 10 p.m., the wait was long and trying. Poor Harry Pelissier worked himself into a state of semi-idiocy, and by the time 10 o'clock drew near hardly anyone was in a state of calm dignity which seems to prevail in all royal establishments. Meanwhile, Finck had made a discovery for himself. It appeared that the Queen objected to an orchestra between herself and the stage, and that all the music was to be behind the scenes. Imagine, therefore, the duettists, Finck and Pelissier, who were to play the overture to the Follies, seated at a cottage-piano, in semi-darkness, peering anxiously at the conductor of the royal band, who, on the other side of the stage, was awaiting the entrance of the Royal party to strike up the National Anthem.

Several nerves cracked, and one member of the Follies, Lewis Sydney, went for a walk to endeavour to compose himself. He returned looking scared, and somewhat uncertain as to what had happened. It seemed that he had found himself in a long gallery, hung with pictures, and, to compose his nerves, began to take an interest in art, when folding doors opened, and a personage in what at a hurried glance appeared to be a Field Marshal's uniform, his breast covered with medals, entered with stately step. Sydney stared at a picture, and wondered frantically whether it was the etiquette to drop on one knee or both, when the Field Marshal stopped, stooped, and, from a tiny cupboard in the wainscot, extracted a duster and small brush, turned and left.

Nor was this all.

Through another pair of doors appeared a procession – this time of two Field Marshals, one bearing in his extended arms a long white object which the startled onlooker afterwards vowed to be a Royal Infant on its way to a State baptism. The doors closed behind the pomp, and Sydney fled back to his companions.

Meanwhile, the duettists sat perspiring in the dark, and at last Pelissier could stand it no longer. 'For God's sake,' he appealed to Finck, 'go and ask the royal conductor what's the matter. Something awful has happened.'

Finck went across. 'No,' replied the royal conductor, 'nothing awful. The King spilt some soup at dinner and is changing his shirt.' Sydney's 'Royal Infant' was the 'Royal Shirt'.

At last the performance commenced. The duettists came to the Follies skit on German Opera, and even from where the players sat in darkness, pounding at the cottage piano, they could hear King Edward's great laugh, and his deep-voiced explanations and comments upon things German. He knew his Germany, and his hearers gathered that his admiration for it was not excessive.

After the Follies' performance came Finck's special trial. During the change of scene, the Bioscope – then more or less a novelty – was to be shown, and from the little corner in the darkness the composer was to play descriptive music to the pictures. As he could see nothing of the screen George Ashton stood in the wings and called the subjects to him.

'River', hissed Ashton, and the river music rippled.

'Train', came the voice, and the journey started, but hardly was steam up when the voice sounded again, 'Cavalry, quick. Train's over'.

The piano player was rapidly approaching nervous collapse when he became conscious of strange things happening around him in the darkness, of dim forms moving, of muffled thumps, and a strained whispering.

'Boats', murmured Ashton appealingly, when another voice broke in, in tense fury: 'Where the devil is that table? Put it here, you –!'

'Zoological Gardens, quick', pleaded the prompter, and '*Will* you put that infernal chair down here', continued the irate whisper.

'Review', and on pounded the musician, when, 'Oh, for god's sake take that infernal piano out of the way!' cried a spirit voice, and the piano rose on invisible hands and started to move, the pianist following it into the darkness, tripping, stumbling, perspiring, but playing, always playing, till the pace grew too hot, just as Ashton cried, 'Curtain!'

Then the lights went up and revealed the stage hands hard at work setting the stage for 'Pantaloon'. Exhausted, nerve-wracked, Finck staggered into the artistes' room, where stood Sydney's Field Marshal beside a table bearing things on it. 'First aid!' he gasped.

100

'Orangeade, sir?' repeated the Field Marshal approvingly. 'Most certainly. It is Her Majesty's favourite refreshment.' And not daring to correct the mistake, Finck suffered him to select the orangeade decanter from the goodly ranks.

But, as at all commands, everything ended happily, in compliments, kudos, and presentation scarfpins.

J. B. BOOTH, OLD PINK 'UN DAYS

But the joke eluded poor Leno, who was never the same man again. Having become a national idol, both as a solo act topping the bill, and as part of a beloved annual pantomime trio, Leno, emerging from his encounter with the reigning monarch in a state of some confusion, developed the idea that his career must take a new turn. The jolly coarsenesses of his old lampoon of *Hamlet* evidently forgotten, the clown conceived the idea of doing the play again, only this time seriously.

In the November of 1901 he sang 'by command' before Edward VII at Sandringham. The honour was too much for him. There have been many attempts to describe how his mind snapped under the strain – how he gave away jewellery and money to odd strangers, how he raged against his friends one moment and begged their forgiveness the next, how his malady finally made itself known to all when he was seen capering near the stage-door of His Majesty's Theatre. The explanation of these seemingly disjointed episodes is given by Miss Constance Collier in *Harlequinade*. While acting at His Majesty's in 'The Eternal City', she lived with her parents in Shaftesbury Avenue. Their little flat was at the top of a building. One night, on returning to it at about one o'clock, she and her mother happened to look into their sitting-room. There they saw, in 'a little bit of moon under the window', Dan Leno. That was their first meeting. He had arrived two or three hours earlier and his brougham was still waiting outside. When he took her hand eagerly in a painful grip she felt he was trembling from excitement. With the moonlight on his face, for no one thought to light the gas, he 'burst into his life story', saying that his father was a Scottish marquis and his mother a housemaid. 'And then he told me the ambition of his life was to play Shakespeare' – Richard III and Hamlet.

Being advised by her to see Sir Herbert Tree at His Majesty's in the morning, he was happy when he went away, and at the theatre the next morning she found he had been there for about two hours, giving the stage-doorkeeper money to buy a silk hat; drawing up contracts for players in his Shakespearean company, and bestowing handfuls of money on newspaper boys, while a happy crowd looked on. The rehearsal of a curtain-raiser began. Miss Collier went through her part with Dan Leno constantly at her side until Tree entered and took him into the stalls. They talked there, 'face to face, excitedly nodding and agreeing', until somebody was called to take charge of the poor little man.

On her return home that afternoon, she found him waiting there to offer her a diamond plaque, with a contract to be his leading lady. When she declined, as gently as she could, he left 'with tears pouring down his face' – and on his way home gave the plaque to a barmaid. Just before the next Christmas he was well enough to join the pantomime company at Drury Lane. The next year Miss Collier saw him at a music hall, where he looked bewildered because the audience didn't laugh. 'I wish he had never come back,' she writes. 'He died soon after.'

M. WILLSON DISHER, *WINKLES AND CHAMPAGNE*

Between Leno's calamitous night of honour at Sandringham and his death three years later, he remained as the recognised head of the comic profession, even though his health was so poor that it was evident to some that he would never regain his old flair and confidence. In 1903, by which time he had recovered sufficiently to take his place once more at Drury Lane for the Christmas pantomime, his idolator among the intellectuals, Max Beerbohm, published an essay which demonstrates his curious gift for seeming to be old and bent. It had already been said of Max that he was born with the gift of eternal old age, and certainly in his periodic grumblings about the evolving stages of the music hall he harps perversely on the passing of an age of *lions comiques* and sentimental balladry which almost all other connoisseurs would have dismissed as markedly inferior to the artistry displayed by the great coster comics and the rumbustious ladies of song. It is in the course of this essay that Max, in exempting Leno from his strictures, celebrates the discovery of what must have seemed to him a desperately remote and dangerous metropolitan outpost, but which was in fact no more than five minutes' walk from Marble Arch.

The Older and Better Music Hall

'An octogenarian in the hunting-field' is the title of annual paragraphs in the daily press. Annually one reflects that 'an octogenarian in bed' were better news. One may be wrong. There are men incapable even of growing old – men so insignificant that Time overlooks them. Let such men pursue foxes even to the brinks of their own graves. As with the body, so with the mind. There are they who never cease to be intellectually receptive. A new idea, or a new movement, appears in their senile course, and lightly they 'take' it, undaunted by the five bars or so, and gallop on. One admires them as showy exceptions to the law of nature. But one knows that they could not be so receptive if in their youth and prime they had ever deeply understood, or felt strongly, anything. They are shallow, and they are cynics, these genial old souls. What shall be said of those others who, having long ago exhausted their curiosity and keenness, do yet, in sheer vanity, pretend themselves keen and curious? How graceless an eld is theirs! See them riding to the meet, laced and stayed to a semblance of jauntiness! See them furtively leading their horses through the gaps, and piping, at last, a husky 'view holloa' over the fallen fox! (Any reader who is also a sportsman will amend my metaphor if it is wrong.) Such imposters deserve no mercy from us. To us the prejudices of eld are sacred, and should be yet more sacred to their holders. I, for one, in the fulness of time, shall make no secret of them. I am too closely in touch with things now, too glad and eager, to be elastic in the dim future, and as for pretending to be elastic . . . no! I look forward to a crabbed and crusty old age. I mean to be a scourge of striplings.

The history of a keen soul in relation to a live art falls usually into three parts: (1) The soul lives in the future, the art lagging behind. (2) The soul lives in the present, the art having caught it up. (3) The soul lives in the past, left behind by the art. My soul, in relation to dramatic art, is still in its first stage. (Or rather, dramatic art, in relation to my soul, is still in its first stage. For the soul itself is always static.) So far as the theatre is concerned, I am still a beckoner, a 'progressive'. But in the manner of music halls, I am already a staunch, even a passionate, reactionary – not a beckoner, but a tugger-back. There never was a time when the music halls lagged behind my soul. To me, as stripling, they seemed perfectly delightful. I dislike the fashion that now dominates not merely the specific 'palaces of varieties' but also such places as the Pavilion, the Tivoli, and even that titular home of lost causes and impossible loyalties, the Oxford. The stripling reader tries politely to repress a sneer. Let him sneer outright. I can justify my prejudice. I may be old-fashioned, but I am right. The music-hall entertainment ought to be stupid, as surely as the drama ought to be intelligent. In every human creature is a mixture of stupidity and cleverness, and for both qualities we need nutrition. How can we satisfy our cleverness in a music hall? What comes to us but a sense of confusion and fatigue from the fashionable gallimaufry of clever poodles, clever conjurers, clever acrobats, clever cinematographs, clever singers and clever elephants? No good can be done to the intellect where no mental effort can be sustained and concentrated. A music hall, by its inherent nature, precludes such good. On the other hand, it can appeal very pleasantly to the stupid, or sensuous, side of us. It did this in the good old days, when there was an unbroken succession of singers, alternate males and females, each singing a couple of songs written and composed in accord to certain traditional conventions. We did not come away wiser and better men; but an inward unity in the entertainment had formed for us a mood. All those so similar songs were merged into our senses, pleasing and amusing, subtly sedative, warm. That old lilt in the veins of us – how bitterly we miss it! Even such songs as are still sandwiched in at the modish halls have lost all their charm. Patter leaves but a corner to tune. Like many other men of original genius, Mr Dan Leno broke the form provided for his expression. We gladly barter tune for a full sense of so delightful a personality and so accomplished an actor as Mr Dan Leno. But the others, the imitators, do not make good our loss. Clever they are, more or less, but we – we who are not of a generation that knows no better – would gladly sacrifice their cleverness in return for straightforward tunes.

Can we anywhere recapture the olden pleasure? Indeed, yes. I have found a place. Let me guide you to it. Half way up the Edgware Road we come to a very signally illuminated building. Nothing could seem more brand-new than the front of this Metropolitan Music Hall; but enter, and you will be transported, deliciously, into the past. The system of ventilation is quite perfect, yet the atmosphere is the atmosphere of a decade since. Look, listen!

> If *you* don't trouble trouble
> Trouble doesn't trouble *you*,
> So don't – you – worry over me!

Is it – no – yes – it must be – it *is* Mr Harry Freeman. That simple, jolly, straightforward singer, dancing as he sings – how long is it since we saw him? We tremble lest he have truckled to changing fashion. Not he! No patter: just a short, sharp phrase uttered through the music between the chorus and the next verse – no more. A thousand memories sweep back to us from that beaming face under the grey bowler hat. That face radiates the whole golden past, and yet, oddly enough, seems not a day older than when last we looked on it. We – we have changed. Our taste, however, is as of yore, and we always did delight in Mr Harry Freeman. We beat time to his familiar music. We sit again at his ever-moving feet. He always was a

103

philosopher, in his way. He was always a Stoic. A Stoic he remains. As of yore, he is overwhelmed with misfortune. Fate still smites him hip and thigh. He has just been robbed by one man and knocked down by another. His home has been broken up. He has been recently in prison. But

> If *you* don't trouble trouble
> Trouble doesn't trouble *you*,

and no sympathy is craved by this joyous dancer. This attitude has a more than personal significance. Not long ago, Mr Arthur Symons wrote an essay about the very thoroughfare whose inhabitants Mr Freeman is now delighting. He suggested that the dominant characteristic of these inhabitants was a dull acquiescence in the sordidness of their lives. Acquiescent they are, but not dully so. Mr Symons, very naturally, cannot imagine a man leading with pleasure their kind of life. They who have to lead it, however, take it as a matter of course, and are quite cheerful about it. They are, in fact, Stoics. This is one of the advantages of the old music hall over the new: it does reflect, in however grotesque a way, the characters of the class to which it consciously appeals. And so, after all, accidentally, one gets from it a mental stimulus. . . . Who is this vast man in evening dress? A 'Lion Comique'? Not quite that. But something contemporaneous: a 'Basso Profondo'. He urges us to tak' the high road; he himself is going to tak' the low road. Loch Lomon', in 1903! Delightful! . . . And here is a 'Serio', with the true Serionian voice and method:

> Do not complain,
> I'll single remain,
> Of sweethearts I want no other.

The gallery-boys take the chorus from her, and she sways silently from side to side in measure to the waltz, smiling the smile of triumph. Comes a 'Burlesque Actress', dressed daringly. The diamonds flash, but the heart is in the right place, and the song is about some one whose

> Sweet face so glad
> Brings smiles to the sad.

Comes a 'Comedienne'. She strikes a rather more modern note. There is, according to her, one, and only one, way of putting the War Office on a sound basis, and that is the instant instalment of Sir Redvers Buller. The audience unanimously endorses her scheme, and she is, no doubt, right; but we regret the introduction of any names that were not names to conjure with in our boyhood: they are anachronisms here. Mr Harry Randall, with his patter, is another anachronism. Several other turns, admirable though they are, we could spare also for that they interrupt in us the luxurious development of the true music-hall mood.

But, certainly, the Metropolitan is a great discovery. Let us go to it often, magically renewing there our youth. And in those dreary other halls let us nevermore set foot.

MAX BEERBOHM IN *THE SATURDAY REVIEW*, 14 NOVEMBER 1903

The Metropolitan proved almost as durable as Max evidently hoped it would. It outlived him, and Shaw, and Arthur Symons, and all the rest of the scholars and aesthetes whose curiosity was stimulated by the bright hope of the halls. Indeed, it survived for so long into an age crudely antipathetic to its art that the present writer made one professional appearance on its stage, in the spring of 1953, when the last of the suburban Empires were beginning to be sold off. The Met by that time was decrepit but defiant. From its stalls bar you could still hold your glass and watch the acts, still get a superb sense of the proximity of artist and audience. Even by the time I worked there, those audiences were as staunch supporters as ever of the medium of music hall generally but of one god in particular. The Met was one of the last halls where Max Miller could draw the town. When his name was advertised, in streamed the doggish young men, from the local back streets, from the quiet avenues of suburbia, even sometimes from provincial outposts, whooping with rabelaisian delight at the defiant broadsides of humour being fired by Max at a nation whose staple diet had for so many years now been provided by Hollywood. It was very nearly a case of religious idolatry, with the baying, shrieking pit, stalls and gallery genuflecting with laughter before their dearest hero. Nobody who was a part of a Max Miller audience ever forgot it.

When at last the Metropolitan came down, it became the centre of a farcical bureaucratic bungle which was itself pure music hall. A fly-over was planned to carry motorists from Marylebone Road to Shepherd's Bush in double-quick time. The route of the fly-over lay directly across the site of the Met. Like some last obstinate bastion of a defeated army, the building fell. Like some huge, impersonal conquerer the fly-over rose – in the wrong place. Some learned donkey had erred with his blueprints, and the fly-over as it was finally constituted by-passed the site of the Met by about a hundred yards. In its place there stands today a police station. What might the wags of Leno's day have made of that? What laughter might have been extracted out of it by Dan and his pantomime accomplices Danvers and Campbell? When Leno died the tributes proliferated. None reads better than the one published in *The Saturday Review* by his most loyal booster, Max Beerbohm.

So little and frail a lantern could not long harbour so big a flame. Dan Leno was more a spirit than a man. It was inevitable that he, cast into a life so urgent as is the life of a music-hall artist, should die untimely. Before his memory fades into legend, let us try to evaluate his genius. For mourners there is ever a solace in determining what, precisely, they have lost.

Usually, indisputable pre-eminence in any art comes of some great originative force. An artist stands unchallenged above his fellows by reason of some 'new birth' that he has given to his art. Dan Leno, however, was no inaugurator. He did not, like Mr Albert Chevalier, import into the music hall a new subject-matter, with a new style. He ended, as he had started, well within the classic tradition. True, he shifted the centre of gravity from song to 'patter'. But, for the rest, he did but hand on the torch. His theme was ever the sordidness of the lower middle class, seen from within. He dealt, as his forerunners had dealt, and his successors are dealing, with the 'two pair-back', the 'pub', the 'general store', the 'peeler', the 'beak', and other such accessories to the life of the all-but-submerged. It was rather a murky torch that he took. Yet, in his hand, how gloriously it blazed, illuminating and warming! All that trite and unlovely material, how new and beautiful it became for us through Dan Leno's genius! Well, where lay the secret of that genius? How came we to be spell-bound?

Partly, without doubt, our delight was in the quality of the things actually said by Dan Leno. No other music-hall artist threw off so many droll sayings – droll in idea as in verbal expression. Partly, again, our delight was in the way that these things were uttered – the gestures and grimaces and antics that accompanied them; in fact, in Dan Leno's technique. But, above all, our delight was in Dan Leno himself. In every art personality is the paramount thing, and without it artistry goes for little. Especially is this so in the art of acting, where the appeal of personality is so direct. And most especially is it so in the art of acting in a music-hall, where the performer is all by himself upon the stage, with nothing to divert our attention. The moment Dan Leno skipped upon the stage, we were aware that here was a man utterly unlike any one else we had seen. Despite the rusty top hat and broken umbrella and red nose of tradition, here was a creature apart, radiating an ethereal essence all his own. He compelled us not to take our eyes off him, not to miss a word that he said. Not that we needed any compulsion. Dan Leno's was not one of those personalities which dominate us by awe, subjugating us against our will. He was of that other, finer kind: the lovable kind. He had, in a higher degree than any other actor that I have ever seen, the indefinable quality of being sympathetic. I defy any one not to have loved Dan Leno at first sight. The moment he capered on, with that air of wild determination, squirming in every limb with some deep grievance, that must be outpoured, all hearts were his. That face puckered with cares, whether they were the cares of the small shopkeeper, or of the landlady, or of the lodger; that face so tragic, with all the tragedy that is writ on the face of a baby-monkey, yet ever liable to relax its mouth into a sudden wide grin and to screw up its eyes to vanishing point over some little triumph wrested from Fate, the tyrant; that poor little battered personage, so 'put upon', yet so plucky with his squeaking voice and his sweeping gestures; bent but not broken; faint but pursuing; incarnate of the will to live in a world not at all worth living in – surely all hearts went always out to Dan Leno, with warm corners in them reserved to him for ever and ever.

To the last, long after illness had sapped his powers of actual expression and invention, the power of his personality was unchanged, and irresistible. Even had he not been in his heyday a brilliant actor, and a brilliant wag, he would have thrown all his rivals into the shade. Often, even in his heyday, his acting and his waggishness did not carry him very far. Only mediocrity can be trusted to be always at its best. Genius must always have lapses proportionate to its triumphs. A new performance by Dan Leno was almost always a dull thing in itself. He was unable to do himself justice until he had, as it were, collaborated for many nights with the public. He selected and rejected according to how his jokes, and his expression of them 'went'; and his best things came to him always in the course of an actual performance, to be incorporated in all the subsequent performances. When, at last, the whole thing had been built up, how perfect a whole it was! Not a gesture, not a grimace, not an inflection of the voice, not a wriggle of the body, but had its significance, and drove its significence sharply, grotesquely, home to us all. Never was a more perfect technique in acting. The technique for acting in a music hall is of a harder, perhaps finer, kind than is needed for acting in a theatre; inasmuch as the artist must make his effects so much more quickly, and without the aid of any but the slightest 'properties' and scenery, and without the aid of any one else on the stage. It seemed miraculous how Dan Leno contrived to make you see before you the imaginary persons with whom he conversed. He never stepped outside himself, never imitated the voices of his interlocutors. He merely repeated, before making his reply, a few words of what they were supposed to have said to him. Yet there they were, as large as life, before us. Having this perfect independence in his art – being thus all-sufficient to himself – Dan Leno was, of course, seen to much greater advantage in a music hall than at

Drury Lane. He was never 'in the picture' at Drury Lane. He could not play into the hands of other persons on the stage, nor could they play into his. And his art of suggestion or evocation was nullified by them as actualities. Besides, Drury Lane was too big for him. It exactly fitted Mr Herbert Campbell, with his vast size and his vast method. But little Dan Leno, with a technique exactly suited to the size of the average music hall, had to be taken, as it were, on trust.

Apart from his personality and his technique, Dan Leno was, as I have said, a sayer of richly grotesque things. He had also a keen insight into human nature. He knew thoroughly, outside and inside, the types that he impersonated. He was always 'in the character', whatever it might be. And yet if you repeat to any one even the best things that he said, how disappointing is the result! How much they depended on the sayer and the way of saying! I have always thought that the speech over Yorick's skull would have been much more poignant if Hamlet had given Horatio some specific example of the way in which the jester had been wont to set the table on a roar. We ought to have seen Hamlet convulsed with laughter over what he told, and Horatio politely trying to conjure up the ghost of a smile. This would have been good, not merely as pointing the tragedy of a jester's death, but also as illustrating the tragic temptation that besets the jester's contemporaries to keep his memory green. I suppose we shall, all of us, insist on trying to give our grand-children some idea of Dan Leno at his best. We all have our especially cherished recollection of the patter of this or that song. I think I myself shall ever remember Dan Leno more vividly and affectionately as the shoemaker than as anything else. The desperate hopefulness with which he adapted his manner to his different customers! One of his customers was a lady with her little boy. Dan Leno, skipping forward to meet her, with a peculiar skip invented specially for his performance, suddenly paused, stepped back several feet in one stride, eyeing the lady in wild amazement. He had never seen such a lovely child. *How* old, did the mother say? Three? He would have guessed seven at least – 'except when I look at you, ma'am, and then I should say he was one at most.' Here Dan Leno bent down, one hand on each knee, and began to talk some unimaginable kind of baby-language. . . . A little pair of red boots with white buttons? Dan Leno skipped towards an imaginary shelf; but, in the middle of his skip, he paused, looked back, as though drawn by some irresistible attraction, and again began to talk to the child. As it turned out, he had no boots of the kind required. He plied the mother with other samples, suggested this and that, faintlier and faintlier, as he bowed her out. For a few moments he stood gazing at her, with blank disappointment, still bowing automatically. Then suddenly he burst out into a volley of deadly criticisms on the child's personal appearance, ceasing as suddenly at the entrance of another customer. . . . I think I see some of my readers – such as them as never saw Dan Leno in this part – raising their eyebrows. Nor do I blame them. Nor do I blame myself for failing to recreate that which no howsoever ingenious literary artist could recreate for you. I can only echo the old heart-cry 'Si ipsum audissetis!' Some day, no doubt, the phonograph and the bioscope will have been so adjusted to each other that we shall see and hear past actors and singers as well as though they were alive before us. I wish Dan Leno could have been thus immortalised. No actor of our time deserved immortality so well as he.

MAX BEERBOHM IN *THE SATURDAY REVIEW*, 5 NOVEMBER 1904

There is no question that Leno was an original whose humorous tendencies were far in advance of the age over which he presided. Some of his comic ideas have a surprising modernity, even a surreal ring about them, almost as though he is preparing the way for strivers after nonsense like Stephen Leacock and Ring Lardner.

In proof of his freakish originality, after Leno's death a MS book was discovered, which it had been his custom to carry about with him, and note down any idea that occurred to him. Many of the notes are naturally disconnected, but some ideas he carried to a conclusion, notably a 'melodrama' in four acts and eight scenes. Here are one or two scenes in full:

Scene: The Docks. Enter Sailor
Sailor: 'Here's a fine go. I've been and lost my bacca box.'
Enter Press Gang. They take no notice of him so he volunteers.
CURTAIN.

Scene: *A Fried Fish Shop. Enter a Crowd, who borrow eightpence, and exit. Enter Villain.*
Villain: 'I know not how it is with me, and I'm blessed if I know how it would be without me.' *Exits.*

Scene: *Italy, or as near as possible. Enter Maiden and Sailor, followed by Brigands, armed with bowls of soup.*
Maiden: 'At last we meet.'
Sailor: 'Yes, but I wonder why we walked here from Swansea.'
All exit, wondering.

J. B. BOOTH, *THE DAYS WE KNEW*

But there remained tiny pockets of resistance to Leno's muse. For some excessively refined folk, the music hall, which was good enough for the King, was not quite good enough for them. There was too much vulgarity in the popular arts, and the children of the rich, who might themselves grow up to be crashing snobs one day, must be protected from any danger of contamination. There is a curious moment in a famous novel of the 1920s in which Leno, separated from readers by the death of kings and the slaughter of a world war, is suddenly evoked as a symbol of the unacceptable.

Nurses and governesses looked after the children. Mrs Bidlake superintended their upbringing simply and as though from a distance. From time to time she swooped across the border dividing her private country from the world of common fact; and her interference with the quotidian order of things had always a certain disconcerting and almost supernatural quality. Incalculable things were liable to happen whenever she descended, a being from another plane and judging events by other standards than those of the common world, into the midst of the children's educational routine. Once, for example, she dismissed a governess because she heard her playing Dan Leno's song about 'The Wasp and the Hard-Boiled Egg' on the school-room piano. She was a good girl, taught well, and supported a paralytic father. But great artistic principles were at stake. Elinor's musical taste might be irretrievably ruined (incidentally Elinor resembled her father in detesting music); and the fact that she was very fond of Miss Dempster made the danger of contamination even greater. Mrs Bidlake was firm. 'The Wasp and the Hard-Boiled Egg' could not be permitted. Miss Dempster was sent away.

ALDOUS HUXLEY, *POINT COUNTERPOINT*

Poor Mrs Bidlake was hopelessly behind the times. The more lavish halls, and certainly places like the Tivoli and Drury Lane, where Dan Leno was a great hero, had become to some extent classless. While the ordinary working citizens of the town attended the halls because it was there rather than in the legitimate theatre that they could be genuinely entertained, their social betters also attended, partly to be in the swim, but generally because some instinct informed them that it was here and not at the Opera House or the theatre that a great age of creative brilliance was in flower. While not every comic was a Leno, or every *chanteuse* a Marie Lloyd, the twenty or thirty acts in the West End bills almost always included at least half a dozen which were as entertaining as they were inimitable.

By the time Edward came to the throne the more lavish music halls had become 'Palaces of Variety' and the resort of 'wealth, fashion and *ton*' where could be seen, according to one authority writing in 1895, 'the most prominent and distinguished representatives of art, literature and the law' together with 'city financiers, lights of the sporting and dramatic world and a very liberal sprinkling of the "upper crust", as represented by the golden youth of the period'. Thus the Palace of Varieties became the medium by which the wealthy could make contact with talented members of the lower orders of society in a less intimate but also less sleazy way than they had done in the early Victorian years, at the racecourses, the bare-knuckle prize-fight and the gambling, cock-fighting or ratting den. Little was lost by the change; the relationship was no longer tinged with criminality, even if it was overlaid by a great deal of sentimentality.

L. C. B. SEAMAN, *LIFE IN VICTORIAN LONDON*

The writer was looking back down the long perspective of the century. Earlier social historians, sensing that the music hall was too valuable a source of popular psychological mood to be overlooked, or rejected on piddling grounds of class, perceived a rather different landscape. J. A. Hobson, in evoking recollections of the Jingo school headed by the Great Macdermott, may not altogether have been aware that he was a full generation in arrears. But there remained much truth in his claims. Fashions in jingoistic songs came and went, ebbed and flowed with the prevailing political winds. It is revealing that one of the most stirring of all demagogic ditties, 'Soldiers of the Queen', was written as early as 1881. When fourteen years later it was sung by Haydon Coffin in a West End musical called *An Artist's Model*, the words were altered to give them a cynical twist. Not till the patriotic convulsions of the Boer War did that song really come into its own as an assertion of the primacy of the red, white and blue, as originally intended by its composer Leslie Stuart, a Lancashire church organist whose melodies were to have a profound effect on both the music hall and the musical theatre. Among his idolaters was the Broadway master Jerome Kern (1885-1945), whose working visits to London during the Edwardian age left him with the conviction that Stuart was a supreme master of his craft and a man worthy of emulation. Traces of the Stuart influence are to be found in several of Kern's early tunes, and of the London music hall in his first published song, 'How'd'ya Like to Spoon With Me?' (1905), later revived and incorporated into the amorphous mass of *Show Boat*.

Stuart, composer of one of the most durable and adored melodies ever to come out of the halls, 'Lily of Laguna', embodies so many of the clichés of the music-hall life as to be a symbolic figure: the ecclesiastical obscurity of his provincial beginnings, the sudden triumphal assertion of a more secular gift, the speedy conquest of the West End of London, the debonair profligacy, and then the breach of the Great War, obscurity again, and a last brief attempt at a come-back before premature death in 1927. Nothing about Stuart speaks more eloquently of his type and epoch than the fact that in his great days he left a standing order at the Savoy Hotel that any friend of his who asked should be given a free meal. For that casual expansiveness he must have been toasted frequently in his own absence. Perhaps he still is.

Among large sections of the middle and the labouring classes, the music hall, and the recreative public-house into which it shades off by imperceptible degrees, are a more potent educator than the church, the school, the political meeting, or even than the press. Into this 'lighter self' of the city populace the artiste conveys by song or recitation crude notions upon morals and politics, appealing by coarse humour or exaggerated pathos to the animal lusts of an audience stimulated by alcohol into appreciative hilarity.

In ordinary times politics plays no important part in these feasts of sensationalism, but the glorification of brute force and an ignorant contempt for foreigners are ever-present factors which at great political crises make the music hall a very serviceable engine for generating military passion. The art of the music hall is the only 'popular' art of the present day: its words and melodies pass by quick magic from the Empire or the Alhambra over the length and breadth of the land, re-echoed in a thousand provincial halls, clubs and drinking saloons, until the remotest village is familiar with air and sentiment. By such process of artistic suggestion the fervour of Jingoism has been widely fed, and it is worthy of note than the present meaning of the word was fastened upon it by the popularity of a single verse.

Nicer critics may even be disposed to dilate upon the context of this early use of the new political term – the affected modesty of the opening disclaimer, the rapid transition to a tone of bullying *braggadocio*, with its culminating stress upon the money-bags, and the unconscious humour of an assumption that it is our national duty to defend the Turk. Indeed, without descending to minute analysis, we may find something instructive in the crude jumble of sentiment and the artistic setting which it finds –

We don't want to fight, but by Jingo if we do,
We've got the men, we've got the ships, we've got the money too

crowned by the domineering passion blurted out in the concluding line –
The Russians shall not have Constantinople!

J. A. HOBSON, *THE PSYCHOLOGY OF JINGOISM*

A more benign view was taken by Charles Booth, a shipowner turned social historian whose *Life and Labour of the People in London* is the most monumental work of its kind ever undertaken. An attempt to encompass in seventeen volumes 'the numerical relation which poverty, misery, and depravity bear to regular earnings and comparative comfort, and to describe the general conditions under which each class lives', Booth's book wielded such influence that it was largely instrumental in the introduction and passing into law of the Old Age Pensions Act of 1908. In his exhaustive exploration of the lives of the urban poor, Booth could hardly have ignored the music hall. Nor did he.

There has been a great development and improvement upon the usual public-house sing-song, as to the low character and bad influence of which there are not two opinions. The story of progress in this respect may be traced in many of the existing places which, from a bar parlour and a piano, to an accompaniment on which friends 'obliged with a song', have passed through every stage to that of music hall; the presiding chairman being still occasionally, and the call for drinks in almost every case, retained. But the character of the songs on the whole is better, and other things are offered: it becomes a 'variety' entertainment. The audiences are prevailingly youthful. They seek amusement and are easily pleased. No encouragement to vice can be attributed to these local music halls. The increase in the number, as well as the size, of these halls, has been rapid. The profits made by the proprietors have been great, and the favourite performers, being able to appear before a succession of audiences, passing rapidly with their repertoire from hall to hall, can be and are very highly remunerated. The performances also can be continually varied, for the supply of artistes is without end. The taste becomes a habit, and new halls are opened every year; soon no district will be without one. Then theatres follow. But meanwhile, and especially in poor neighbourhoods, the old-fashioned style of sing-song still continues in force.

In the central districts all places of amusement are very largely supported by the rich or by strangers visiting London. People from the outskirts come occasionally, but it is the music hall or theatre of their own neighbourhood that they frequent, and of which the influence has mainly to be considered. It is, perhaps, too much to ask that the influence of music halls and theatres should be positively and entirely good; at any rate no one claims that it is so. If it is not directly, or in the whole, evil, or if one can hope that it takes the place of something worse, a measure of improvement may be indicated. This can, I think, be claimed. It is not very much. A tendency in the direction of the drama, which is certainly an advance, may be noticed in music-hall performances, and it is to be regretted that questions arising from the separate licensing of playhouses should check the freedom of development in this direction amongst the halls. Excluding the dramatic pieces or 'sketches', the production of which is hampered in this way, the attractions most usually offered are those of a low form of art or of blatant national sentiment, neither of which can be carried further without becoming worse; or of displays of physical strength and skill on the part of acrobats and gymnasts, or of performing animals; all representing, indeed, a background of patient and unwearied effort, but involving, it cannot be supposed, not a little cruelty in the training of children and animals necessary to secure the rewards of popularity. But the 'variety' of the entertainments increases. In addition to conjuring and ventriloquism, which are old-fashioned, we have now, for instance, the cinematograph and various forms of the phonograph, and there has been much development in the forms of stage dancing.

Limitations in the form of entertainment apply less to the halls in Central London, where, for instance, beautiful and elaborate ballets are produced. These fashionable resorts have the best of everything that can be offered, and the performances, consequently, reach a perfection which silences criticism in that respect, though in some cases there may remain ground for attack on the score of encouraging vice. In these palaces of amusement even music is not neglected. The orchestra at the Alhambra is very famous, whilst those at the Empire and the Palace are also excellent. But in the minor halls, development is never in the direction of music. Strange as it may sound, anything that can rightly be called music is seldom produced at a local music hall. The only exceptions I call to mind are a performance of Lancashire bell ringers and the vagaries of a musical clown on his violin. In this respect, the efforts of negro minstrelsy have been far superior. Perhaps music might some day find its way in through operatic sketches, if these were encouraged.

C. BOOTH, *LIFE AND LABOUR OF THE PEOPLE IN LONDON*

Understandably it was the Boer War which reinvigorated the lust for jingo sentiments in the halls, although the appetite had been working up steadily through the strident imperialistic mood of the 1890s. The publication in 1897 of 'Sons of the Sea' was one landmark, and the reinstatement of the original text of 'Soldiers of the Queen' another. But when real soldiers began firing real bullets at a tangible enemy, then the jingoism of the halls became so respectable that some of the most distinguished artists in the kingdom decided to take a hand.

Money was wanted to procure small comforts for the troops at the Front, and, to this end, the *Daily Mail* started what must have been a very early 'stunt'. It was agreed that I should ask the public for subscriptions. That paper charged itself with the rest. My verses 'The Absent-Minded Beggar' had some elements of direct appeal, but, as was pointed out, lacked 'poetry'. Sir Arthur Sullivan wedded the words to a tune guaranteed to pull teeth out of barrel-organs. Anybody could do what they chose with the result, recite, sing, intone, or reprint, etc; on condition that they turned in all fees and profits to the main account – 'The Absent-Minded Beggar Fund' – which closed at about a quarter of a million.

RUDYARD KIPLING, *SOMETHING OF MYSELF*

But there were dissentient voices. A sizeable minority of the electorate suspected that the war was not quite the pristine crusade it was cracked up to be, and even in the boisterous bonhomie of the halls there was always the danger that this minority might make itself heard. The most vivid example in fiction is to be found in the works of that scandalously underrated writer, Henry Major Tomlinson (1873-1958), whose novel, *All Our Yesterdays*, published in 1928, covers the years between the outbreak of fighting in South Africa and the disillusion of the immediate post-war period after 1918. At the start of the story Mr Bolt, a sturdy ship-worker from Tomlinson's own borough of Poplar, decides to go with a few of his cronies to the local music hall to genuflect before that great favourite Dolly Mashem, whose amplitude of thigh and resonance of voice are perfectly suited to the martial demagogy of the hour. But the potent brew of those thighs and that voice, the smoky, boozy atmosphere and Leslie Stuart's stirring musical bellicosity proves to be a little too much for the pacifistic tendencies of the Little Englanders in the audience.

Mr Bolt gazed round him to collect his thoughts. Then he saw the brightly lighted entrance to the Theatre of Varieties. 'Here we are,' he remarked with relief. 'Come on, or we shan't see Dolly.'

In we went. Mr Bolt was notably wide and bulky across the shoulders. His brooding grey eyes, I could see now, were humane as well as truculent, and his clean-shaven face was massive and candid, and had a leathery texture which gave confidence in his lasting power. There was sardonic tenacity in his mouth and chin, but beer had pouted his lips that night into a little petulance. One could be sure he was a cunning craftsman, and could handle refractory steel with casual firmness. We found the hall was full, and that we must watch from the promenade. Mr Bolt took his hat off, glanced round as though to be sure trouble was absent, ran a hand over his turbulent sandy hair, which suggested romantic generosity as well as promptitude to heat, and then signed to me with a twist of his mouth and a thumb which pointed backwards to the bar. We had one, and then another, and then went to lean on the bulwarks of the promenade.

'The house is full,' I said.

'Of course,' replied Mr Bolt quickly and respectfully. 'Dolly's on tonight.' There was something in the air of that music hall, its depth murky with the incense of tobacco smoke, which had a soothing effect on my companion. Perhaps it was because he was within the influence of art. He became peaceful with devotion in this temple. A wizard was before us, dressed as a Chinese mandarin, who juggled with silver balls, keeping a hypnotising stream of them weaving through the air with but slight movements of his hands. We watched him, and were as still as the buxom statues of the Muses that posed by the proscenium, on whose semi-nudity the plaster drapery was set at a moment of danger. There was not a stir in the spread of heads between us and the performer. That the balls should continue in unbroken circuit was of grave concern to us all. The Chinaman brought them deftly to a halt, and our feet thundered. The heads before us were released on their necks. A man below me stooped to fumble under his seat, hauled out a demijohn, and raised it above his lips. Then he rubbed his cuff over the mouth of the jar, and handed it to the lady sitting beside him, and she tilted it above her face, while the bangles of her bonnet danced to the happy rhythm of her refreshment.

We waited, though not for long, for soon an expansive lady in a corsage at high tension tripped saucily before us on high-heeled shoes. Her lusty thighs, and the

113

immediate uproar, told me who she was. Dolly was an endearing name for one with a wink intimate with full liberty. Mr Bolt nudged me, but there was no need for it. For some moments Dolly was permitted only to nod brightly to us like a sister and distribute favours with her eyes. Then she sang that song, a little hoarsely, which Mr Bolt had promised, and the jovial house helped with the chorus. Dolly retired; and the jaunty poise of elderly curves so ample on feet so diminutive was sensational. But soon the singer came back bringing with her a soldier of the line in the uniform of South African work. He smartly raised his hand to his solar helmet when we cheered him. Dolly flourished a Union Jack in each hand, and this was almost too much for us. It released the emotions with which the news of the day had filled us. She sang 'Soldiers of the Queen' while the man in khaki stood to stern and unblinking attention even when the flags were waved in his face.

It must have been during the last verse, which we sang with her, that a surly fellow near me made a comment. Perhaps it was merely to himself; he may have supposed it would have been drowned unnoted in the noise of our common enthusiasm. He grumbled, I thought, that we were likely to be rewarded in a way which would be unenjoyable, though we had asked for it. The lady with the bangles in her bonnet must have heard him, for she bounced round menacingly. ''Ere,' she cried, 'yore name Kruger?' Her companion turned also, though more carefully, for he was nursing his amphora of beer. 'What's more,' he added slowly, 'you can get what trouble you want by asking for it, and 'ave it now.' But the critic, who was a young man, already was disappearing. Mr Bolt, I noticed, eyed the vanishing interrupter with louring disfavour.

'It'd do me good,' he muttered darkly.

'What's that?' I asked.

'Dot him one. I haven't hit a man because he wanted it for years and years.' The approach of a lank and lugubrious apparition to the footlights, whose nose was remarkable in a chalky face, composed the interlude. He was a comedian. He wore a tiny hat with difficulty. He gulped a song abruptly, in but one note, and occasionally interrupted it with an anecdote. He told us that once he had an African parrot. Its name was Kruger, for its origin was low, and the audience laughed derisively. It was always fooling the dog with false calls, a bright little terrier named Joe. 'Good ole Joe,' we cried. 'That's right,' agreed the comedian; 'He had such a sharp nose for rats that I had named him Joe,' and we applauded so good a reason for a Christian name. But one day, he told us, the artful African bird called mockingly to Joe once too often. It was therefore found under the table, disfeathered and repentant, saying to itself, 'I know what's the matter with me. I know what's the matter with me. I talk too damn much.'

The comedian maintained his calm pause beyond our merriment. He was sure of us. He was leisurely giving his hat the right groggy tilt, before telling us another story, when a discordant cry shocked us.

'To hell with Chamberlain!'

The comedian only started, in an attitude of sincere woe, with his hand on his hat. He had no wit ready for this. The blasphemy stilled us. Then the pit and stalls began to move confusedly. Unhappy howls arose in the remote gallery, where it was known the next performance might be out of its view. The heads below me, which had been expressionless, were now reversed, for the entertainment was in the opposite direction. I was looking at angry faces swarming. They were mounting the back of the seats and were coming towards me. I dodged a missile in flight. The man with the demijohn was peering about eagerly for someone to whom he could give it. We were all looking for whoever deserved to have it, when another voice cut the confusion clearly and with sombre warning: 'Make your peace with God.' I could see that fellow, an elderly crank who paraded our streets whenever the Sunday was fine and he was persuaded that his neighbours might be enjoying themselves, and who then bore sandwich boards advertising wrath and the latter end of people such as we.

Mr Bolt marked the last interrupter. 'Silly old fool,' he breathed aloud, in wonder at such courage in the aged. But the grey-haired prophet was already submerged. There was no need to do more to him. He foundered in a surging current of heads; though certainly he was not the offender, for the first voice bawled provocatively again, 'It's a mug's war!'

There he was; there he was for but a brief glimpse. But he did not completely founder, like the elderly peace-maker. He came to the surface again and disturbed it vehemently. Eager advice was cried from those who were too distant to aid to those who were near enough. 'Wring his neck.' We were told where we ought to kick him. The offender was propelled through the riot. A woman's market basket, which rose and fell with regularity about the place where probably he was, marked his progress. He came clear of the press, disarranged but active, still gasping taunts. Many were trying to grapple him.

'Hand him over,' shouted Mr Bolt. But nobody showed readiness to surrender a gratification so unusual. Mr Bolt therefore took the young man, and lightly whirled him free from his other assailants. The response of the rebel in his gyration was so agile and unexpected that the shipwright's face was jarred and his hat took flight. A hurtling bottle brought down the plate-glass of the bar in a shocking avalanche.

Now I had lost Mr Bolt. A woman stood near me clasping her child rigidly and with her frightened face bleeding. I could see only that woman, and the storm raised by an unlucky word cast into the peace of our hearts. I was part of it, crunching over broken glass in a weight of straining bodies. 'You one of the swine?' demanded a whoop near me. I saw the fellow and wondered if I were his target, for his malignant squint misdirected his cry, and then he vanished as he slipped on glass. The torrent brawled down a corridor and shot me outside into the night.

H. M. TOMLINSON, *ALL OUR YESTERDAYS*

Mr Bolt and his pals would not have had to walk very far to find the formidable Miss Mashem. Every district had its hall, and every hall its own favourites, procedures, conventions. In 1900 *The Era Almanack*, issued by the most popular of the weekly publications covering the world of music hall, published a list of London halls:

The Albert, Alhambra, Bedford, Camberwell Palace, Cambridge, Canterbury, Collins's, the Eastern Empire, the Empire, the Empire Holloway, the Empire New Cross, Empress Palace Brixton, Euston Varieties, Foresters', Gatti's (Charing Cross), Gatti's (Westminster Bridge Road), Grand Hall Clapham, Granville Walham Green, Hammersmith Palace, Kilburn Varieties, the London, London Hippodrome, London Pavilion, Marylebone, Metropolitan, Middlesex, the Oxford, Palace, Paragon, Parthenon Greenwich, Queen's Poplar, Royal, Sadler's Wells, Sebright, the South London, Standard, Star, Stratford Empire, Tivoli, Varieties Hoxton, Victoria Coffee Palace.

The list is followed in the *Almanack* by a parallel list of provincial halls. In all there were 226, but the conventional pattern for provincial turns and artists with a regional appeal was the journey south and an attempt at the conquest of London. As for the capital itself, it inspired one of the most famous of all theatrical types, the coster comic, the backstreet poet with pearly buttons stitched on to his clothes, and an act usually compounded of rough humour and a sentiment sometimes so powerful as to evoke tears as well as laughter. The most renowned of these was Albert Chevalier, two of whose songs, 'Knocked 'em in the Old Kent Road' and 'My Old Dutch', have passed into the folklore of the British. Chevalier was untypical of the music hall of his day in that he graduated to it not from the street and the saloon bar but from the legitimate stage, where he had worked as an actor since 1877. It was fourteen years before he ventured on to the halls, where his long experience in delineation of character served him well in his musical sketches of London types.

But Chevalier was a curious case of the manufactured article being preferred to the real thing. So far from being a rough street type from the working classes, he possessed sensibilities which might have surprised some of his most ardent followers, and which his rivals were at first inclined to dismiss as delusions of grandeur. Born in Notting Hill into the lower middle-class, he had at one time considered becoming a Roman Catholic priest, before the lure of the coster scene proved too strong to resist. When he finally took the plunge into music hall at the London Pavilion in 1891, he followed Bessie Bellwood on the bill, and was understandably worried that so rumbustious a performer might create an atmosphere unsympathetic to his quieter, more refined art. That he was proved wrong owed much to the song he sang that night. 'The Coster's Serenade', sometimes known as 'Down at the Welsh Harp', a heartbreaking hymn to unrequited love. In the following year his brother, masquerading under the pseudonym of Charles Ingle, composed a melody to which Chevalier fitted words destined to become famous. It is often forgotten today that when Chevalier performed 'My Old Dutch', it was against a backdrop showing the workhouse, which helped to make the point that when married couples had sunk to that level, they were segregated by the authorities. In the previous year he and Ingle wrote the song which has lasted best of all, the tale of the south Londoner who inherits a donkey cart but no money.

Chevalier's great champion was Max Beerbohm, who, in an essay written at the start of the century, measured Chevalier's essentially London art against that of a performer from a very different world indeed.

Yvette Guilbert and Albert Chevalier

I went one afternoon this week to the Duke of York's Theatre, and saw Mme Yvette Guilbert and Mr Albert Chevalier in juxtaposition. It seemed appropriate that these two should be together. The name of each conjures up visions of the early 'nineties. Both were innovators in method and in subject-matter, Mr Chevalier weaving a network of romance around costermongers, Mme Guilbert depicting in hard, sharp outline the tragedies and comedies of the least pleasant persons in Paris. Years have passed, revising somewhat the aspect of both artists. Both were ethereal. Both are normally plump. And their outlook, not less than their aspect, has expanded. Mme Guilbert's is no longer confined to 'les trous dangereux', though she still keeps an eye on them. She ranges over the gay and harmless provinces of France, in the gay and harmless past. Poudrée, she sings of Brittany; and in a crinoline she warbles of Parthenay; and in a peculiar costume meant to suggest that of a bygone English peasant she essays the folk songs of our own counties. Mr Chevalier, in like manner, is unfaithful to the Old Kent Road, and deems alien from himself nothing that is human. He does not, like Mme Guilbert, dally with the past; but his range over the present is unbounded. Altogether, there is a distinct kinship between these two artists. And thus the differences between them have a certain significance, as illustrating the differences between French and English art.

No one, I imagine, will dispute the platitude that French acting is better than English. The points of superiority are many; but the most noticeable of them all is the quickness and apparent ease with which (I speak, of course, generally) French mimes express as much as can by English mimes be expressed only with much deliberation and apparent effort. I cannot conceive a better illustration of this difference than is offered by Mr Chevalier and Mme Guilbert in double harness. Mr Chevalier is not, of course, thoroughly English. He has Italian as well as French

116

blood in his veins. And this admixture accounts for the vivacity of face and figure that surprised us so much in the early 'nineties, setting him so far apart from the ordinary music-hall artists that we had known. But, despite his cosmopolitan breeding, it was only on the English stage that he graduated. And so, despite his vivacity, he has never picked up the knack of ease and quickness. Indeed, his vivacity itself seems to act as a stumbling-block. He makes a dozen gestures, a dozen grimaces, when one would be ample. He suits the action to the word so insistently that every word, almost, has an action to itself. Often the action is a very elaborate one, insomuch that when the way is clear, at length, for the next word, you have quite lost sight of the last word but one. In one of his rustic songs – 'Wot vur do 'ee lov oi?' – he speaks of a kiss and of holding hands. Before he comes to the word 'kiss' he violently kisses the air for quite a long time; and when he illustrated the holding of hands I feared that he would never, never unclasp them. Mr Chevalier might reply that in this song he is merely illustrating the slowness of an agrestic mind. To which I should retort that every one of his other very diverse impersonations is marred by just that same extremity of slowness. Every one of them is admirably conceived; and the words, written by Mr Chevalier himself, admirably express the conception. If only Mr Chevalier would allow them and the conception a certain amount of liberty to take care of themselves! If only he would not overwhelm them with illustration! We may be fools, but we are not such fools as he takes us for. His points do not need such an unconscionable amount of hammering, to drive them home for us. If he were the owner of an inexpressive face and voice and hands, then, perhaps, all this strenuousness of his would be indispensable. As a matter of fact, every part of him happens to be mercurial. Evidently he under-rates himself as much as us.

One reason why I deplore his passion for over-emphasis is that the songs, as songs, lose thereby their savour. The lilt of the music disappears. The accompanist sits at the piano, waiting patiently till Mr Chevalier will sing another half bar or so; and we sit patiently wondering what sort of a tune it is. One of Mme Guilbert's virtues is that she never forgets that a singer's first duty to a song is to sing it. Always she obeys the rhythm of the music. All her acting is done within that right limitation. Yet is not lost one tittle of the acting necessary to express the full meaning of the words. I do not think that her face, voice, and hands are more naturally eloquent than Mr Chevalier's. But she knows just how much use to make of them. Notice, in the famous 'Ma Grandmère', how perfectly she differentiates the words of the girl from those of the old woman, yet with hardly a perceptible pause, with hardly a perceptible change of key. Something happens in her eyes, and we know that it is the girl speaking: we see the girl herself; and then again, in another instant, we see the old woman. One can imagine the pauses with which Mr Chevalier would mark these transitions, and the violent contortions he would go through before he got under weigh. And yet he would not make us realise the old woman and the girl half so vividly as does Mme Guilbert. We should realise that he was performing an ingenious feat of character-acting. We should think him frightfully clever. But – well, it never strikes us that Mme Guilbert is clever. She does but fill us with a perfect illusion of whatsoever scene she sings, of whatever type she apes. How she does it is (at the moment of watching her) a mystery. And but for that mystery she couldn't do it.

Mme Guilbert's restraint is so exquisite, she so perfectly effaces herself in the subjects of her songs, that I cannot understand how she has let herself fall into the habit of flinging restraint to the winds and luridly revealing herself when she sings the last line. In some of her songs this habit is absolutely fatal to the effect. Obviously, for example, 'La Grandmère' ought to end on the note of quiet melancholy that has been struck throughout. (You remember the refrain:

'Combien je regrette
Mon bras si dodu,

Ma jambe bien faite,
Et le temps perdu.')

When Mme Guilbert sings this refrain for the last time, she pauses after the third line, throws back her head, spreads out her arms to the audience and utters 'et le temps perdu' in a tone of radiant ecstasy, as much as to say *'Haven't* I sung that well?' Again, at the end of 'La Glu', – 'le cœur disait, en pleurant, "T'es tu fait mal, mon pauvre enfant?"' – it is obvious that the words ought to be spoken quite faintly. Mme Guilbert drives them home with an emphasis which not Mr Chevalier himself could surpass. We lose all sense that it is the heart of the murdered mother that is speaking. We lose all the piteousness of the song. We are conscious only of Mme Guilbert demanding applause. I have often heard her sing both these songs. I am sure she used not to spoil them thus.

MAX BEERBOHM IN *THE SATURDAY REVIEW*, 23 JUNE 1906

Beerbohm's dissertation on Yvette Guilbert is a timely reminder that there were some music hall stars whose reputations were international, or at least binational. Miss Guilbert had developed a large British following long before the publication of Beerbohm's essay. Back in the 1890s she had attracted the attention of one of the most relentless seekers after artistic experience in the literary world, Arnold Bennett. At this stage in his life, still with a reputation to make, and utterly convinced that if it was real art you wanted, then the only place was France, Bennett was bound to be drawn to Miss Guilbert, and, with typical Five-Towns knowingness, took care to display inside information about money. Bennett never failed to be seduced by the romance of money, and was indeed so eager to locate it that he proved at times to be comically gullible in the matter of the salaries of the stars. Many years later, by which time he should have known better, he confided to his journal details of the wages of the resident orchestra at the Savoy Hotel which were so ludicrous as to cast a shadow of doubt over his assessment of Miss Guilbert's income. She was, at any rate, not underpaid.

Friday, May 8th, 1896

Tonight I heard Yvette Guilbert sing five songs – including 'La Soularde', Berenger's 'Grand'mère', 'Her Golden Hair was Hanging down her Back', and 'I Want you, Ma Honey' (alternate verses in French and English). The performance took about 23 minutes, and she received £70 a night (ten nights). My father, who had seen her on the previous evening, said to me at dinner at Gatti's, 'I can't see £70 in what she does'. 'No,' I said, 'perhaps you can't; but you can see it in the audience which pays to listen to her.'

I think I never saw the Empire so full. Yvette wore a gown of bluish-green flowered silk, and the unchangeable black gloves. To the back of the pit, where I stood, her voice came as if from an immense distance, attenuated, but clear and crisp.

ARNOLD BENNETT, *JOURNALS*

I f Albert Chevalier, in perfecting his impersonations of Cockney life, raised the art of contrivance to the highest point reached by a performer of his type in the music hall, his strongest rival for the title of pre-eminent stage coster, Gus Elen, was the genuine article. Elen studied his songs with such minute attention to detail, and immersed himself so utterly in each character he portrayed, that one of the most telling of all music-hall anecdotes attaches to this intensity of his. It is recounted how, late in life, when making a sort of comeback by broadcasting for the BBC, he prepared himself for this early sound transmission by dressing in costume and applying full stage make-up. The same dedication to duty may be seen from a different perspective in a remarkable essay published in the national press long after Elen's death. It gives perhaps a deeper insight into the struggle for mastery over music-hall technique than any piece of prose ever published.

A critic of the 1890s, George Gamble, explained his distaste for Gus Elen: 'He too much resembles the real thing to be wholly pleasing. To measure the little by the great, he is the Zola of costermongers, as his forerunner was the Dickens.' It was not quite fair to call Albert Chevalier the forerunner of Elen, since both men started singing coster songs in the music halls at about the same time. Chevalier sang 'The Coster's Serenade' at the London Pavilion on February 5th, 1891; Elen introduced 'Never Introduce your Donah to a Pal' at Harwood's Varieties, Hoxton, on June 4th the same year. There had been Cockney character comedians, as they were billed, before, but Elen and Chevalier were unrivalled.

They admired each other, though their styles were as different as their origins. Chevalier was a gent, born in Notting Hill and trained in the legitimate London theatres to which he always returned from time to time. He had good songs, and a superb technique; but the attitudes reflected in numbers like 'My Old Dutch' or 'The Coster's Serenade' were incorrigibly romantic and sentimental, aimed at the middle-class audiences who patronised his smart recitals. Seymour Hicks praised 'the subtlety, the sweetness, and the superlative tenderness of one who understood to the full the heart that beats beneath the pearlies'. Elen, who never wore pearlies, perhaps understood more than Chevalier about working-class London. He was born Ernest Augustus Elen in Pimlico on July 22nd, 1862, and worked variously as a programme boy, a barman, a draper's assistant, and an egg-packer at the Co-op before appearing at public house sing-songs at the age of 20. For years he plodded about the 'smalls' as a 'negro impersonator and eccentric character delineator' before he discovered success with his Cockney songs. There was little of Chevalier's 'sweetness and tenderness', nothing easily ingratiating about Elen's characters, who generally slouched on stage with faces twisted in a variety of scowls of resentment or anger or incomprehension, and gave forth their complaints in sharp, incisive aggressive tones. (Elen's is the only living voice in which we can still hear the authentic London speech of Dickens's time, with the Wellers' indiscriminate alternations of v's and w's.) He was caustic and realistic. His songs were richly comic, but the comedy was created out of a real world of poverty and violence and inequality, of basic social loyalties and meagre physical pleasures. A song he sang in 1892 made his position quite plain:

I ain't at all the coster wot yer 'ears about in songs,
As allus talks about 'is girl, 'er beauty and 'is wrongs,
And then a-serenading when the night is freezing 'ard
Is a kind of sport the costers you will find 'ave always barred.
When the elements is wicious on the landlord we will sub,
And drink and smoke (and sometimes fight) inside the nearest pub.
But it sounds so wery pretty in a sweetly warbled ditty
With footlights, limelights, pearlies to the ground:
Now I gives yer all my word, it's a fable wot yer've 'eard,
For there ain't a coster like it to be found.

Subsequent verses leave no doubt that Chevalier is Elen's target. Elen's costers live in a London of grimy tenements. The Cockney gardener boasts about his view: 'With a ladder and some glasses, You could see to 'Ackney Marshes – if it wasn't for the 'ouses in between'. In 'The Coster's Mansion':

If yer wants to see the dining room or step into the parlour
Or my orfice where I contracts all my biz;
If you wants to see the bedroom or the place we call the larder
Why! You've only got to stop just where you is!

In this world there was no room for 'My Old Dutch' sentiment in marital relationships. In 'Mrs Carter', the husband bemoans his wife's equanimity: 'What's the use of couples getting married at all if they never 'as a blooming row?' The luckier husband of 'An 'Andle to 'Er Name' gives his wife a couple of black eyes every night, though the marital war was two-sided:

It's a great big Shame, and if she belonged to me
I'd let 'er know 'oo's 'oo.
A nagging at a feller wot is six foot four
And 'er only four foot two.
They 'adn't been married not a munf nor more
When underneaf 'er fumb goes Jim.
Oh, isn't it a pity as the likes of 'er should put upon the likes of 'im?

Love meets other obstacles in 'Cupid in Jail and Out'; the couple can never get married because no sooner is one out of jail than the other is in: 'When I came out I found that Liza was in prison still. For when ordering of 'er wedding cake she'd simply pinch the till.' Elen's characters were often on, or over, the verge of criminality. 'Down the Dials' describes a cardsharper and thief:

We're the champions at doing what you call the Three Card Trick,
We goes down on our knees just so, and does it wery quick,
And if the Josser finds the card we bang him with a brick
Down the Dials, Down the Dials, Down the Dials.
Pleasures were few and mostly drink:
If I could do what the camel does,
Drink seven days supply upon the spot,
I'd get loaded up each Saturday and sleep until the next –
If I only 'ad the tank the camel's got!

No wonder that The Publican congratulates himself that:

The neighbourhood supports me, though they can't support themselves.

The coster's world imposed codes of strict social loyalty. It was unforgiveable to step outside your class, like Jack Jones, who, since he's had the bullion left, 'Dunno Where 'E Are':

When I see the way 'e treats old pals I am filled with nuffing but disgust,
'E says as 'ow we isn't class enough, sez as 'ow we ain't upon a par,
Wiv 'im just because 'e's better off; won't smoke a pipe, must take on a
    cigar.

''E Grumbles' pokes fun at a father who cannot understand his son's reluctance to live up to their new-found wealth:

And I've told him eddicated folks sneer at such wulgar ways,
And yet somehow 'e just doesn't seem to tumble.
Our parlour paper's 'eliotrope and streaked with amber pink,
But still 'e wants to wash in there instead of in the sink.
And 'cause I wouldn't let him toss the housemaid for a drink
'E 'as the ascer-dacity ter grumble.

The ability to characterise a particular social class was one thing. The technical accomplishment required to hold one's own as a star of the late Victorian music halls was another. In retrospect it is clear that this was one of the great peaks of popular theatre. One of the few serious stage people to perceive this at the time, Vsevolod Meyerhold, pointed out in 1912 that 'although two-thirds of the acts in any of the better theatres of this type (that is, the English music halls and Parisian *variétés*) have no right to be called art, there is more art in the remaining third than in all the so-called serious theatres which purvey "literary drama"'.

The halls were the only entertainment for the great new urban masses of the late industrial revolution, who were no great readers, had not patience or the money for the legitimate theatres, and were as yet undistracted by mechanical home entertainments. Music halls proliferated throughout the English-speaking world, providing work for thousands of performers. A wide choice sharpened the audience's discrimination and spurred competition among artists. The vast number of theatres meant that a performer could use the same material on tour for years with a constant compulsion to refine and perfect it to prevent it becoming stale by repetition.

One of the difficulties of assessing the music hall's achievement in terms of theatre art is that, though a mass of gossip and anecdote has survived, there is very little concrete evidence about the great days. Most of the great performers were at work too early to be adequately recorded on film or even on gramophone records. Few of them were literary-minded or articulate about their work. Apart from scattered essays by Shaw and Beerbohm, no serious critics thought this proletarian theatre worth their attention. It is very hard to find anyone who can tell you just what Marie Lloyd or Vesta Tilley did on stage, or why they were so good.

But we can discover what Gus Elen did, thanks to a unique document which has recently come to light in a private collection – his personal song book. Many artists kept such manuscript records of the words of their songs, but Elen seems to have been an obsessively meticulous man. In addition to the words of his songs, for instance, this shabby foolscap volume records all kinds of professional information such as how to get from his home in Balham to the principal London halls. 'Kilburn Empire: No 88 bus from Nightingale Lane to Marble Arch (Edgware Road), take 8 to Kilburn Empire or taxi about 2s.2d. fare or tram to Plough, then Underground railway to Kilburn. This is a very stuffy journey.'

The script is a good, rapid Victorian hand with only a few mis-spellings and an eccentric use of parentheses to betray Elen's limited formal education. He heads the book: 'Business Make-ups (Invented and Arranged) by Gus Elen, containing also the

121

words and the names of the various Publishers, Authors and Composers of GUS ELEN's Songs.' The lyrics appear on the right-hand pages; facing them are details of business, costume and make-up, sometimes illustrated by a photograph or song-cover illustration, and sketches of props. The record was apparently begun about 1900, since the songs created between 1882 and this date are arranged in no particular order. Elen was still using it as late as 1938, when he stuck in a news item which amused him by its relevance to 'The Postman's Holiday'. Thus it provides a sort of creative autobiography as well as a manual of stage techniques.

Elen's approach would have delighted Meyerhold, whose acting method was based on principles of controllable external observation, in aggressive reaction against the interior, emotive system of the Stanislavski school. 'Only a few exceptionally great actors', Meyerhold said, 'have succeeded instinctively in finding the correct method, that is, the method of building the role not from inside outwards but vice versa.' While many of his contemporaries in the halls advocated the 'emotive' method, Elen clearly created from the outside. The last verse of 'Down the Road', describing the death of the coster's mare, was one of Elen's rare appeals to emotion, and famous for never leaving a dry eye in the house. The song book reveals that even in this, Elen's acting was calculated and externalised to the last gesture. He wrote:

> During 3rd chorus which must be rendered (pathetically) & slower time:
> 1st line. (right hand outstretched-pointing right) sing Down the Road – Away went Polly, not a face was jolly, 'twould have seemed a sin.
> 2nd line. (Head dropped, looking at ground) sing Down the road – the pace not killing, the dead mare willing – For the final spin.
> 3rd line. (Hands outstretched towards the audience) sing – Everybody looked so sad and I felt quite forlorn.
> 4th line. (Drop on right knee, kneeling, removing cap same time with left hand – and with right hand as if stroking the dead mare) sing – Whoa, mare (slowly) Whoa mare (slowly). Then gradually to quickened time, as if you will go crazy – sing – You've earned your little bit 'o corn.
> Slow, slow, gradually to quick time. Then up on feet (repeat chorus to maddened quick time)

The only surviving film of Elen shows him singing 'It's a Great Big Shame'; we can compare the precise, even balletic pantomime he performs during the 'symphony' (as he correctly calls the orchestral introduction to each verse) with little sketches in the song book which indicate how the action – miming the respective heights of 4 foot 2 and 6 foot 4, and suddenly producing a hammer to indicate what he would do to such a wife – must fall on the exact beat of the music. Nothing was left to chance. Every odd pronunciation and enunciation is specified:

> When singing lines – at scrappin' 'e 'ad won some great renown.
> It took two coppers for to make 'im move along.
> And annover six to 'old the feller dow-own.
> On word 'renown' Jerk this out-latter part of word like double note (Re-now-own) – an extra Jerk out word (down).

If he introduced a topical line or gag, that also was recorded (the song book was clearly a form of registration of material, as well as an aid to memory). The manuscript of 'The Pavement Artist' shows five progressive attempts at a new couplet about the Kaiser. The first four are deleted, with initials G.E. and explanations of their unsuitability ('Not clear, and pointless'. 'Better – but weak').

The music-hall artist was his own *metteur-en-scène*. Elen gives elaborate stage plans and directions for the tiny scene that went with 'Wait Till the Work Comes

Round', even including, confidently, ('laugh from audience'), or ('audience usually laughs here'). The setting for the character of the idle workman shows a Stanislavskian concern for realist detail. The props include 'An orange box to serve as a cupboard', and inside it 'Few old plates (dust-covered), cup and saucer'. This was his most elaborate presentation, but every song had its individual *mise-en-scène*. Entrances are always very precisely plotted, and we find Elen observing the tradition of the Victorian music hall that the artist entered up-stage, walked to the middle of the cloth before turning to walk down-stage, and only then acknowledged the audience's presence. For 'It's a Great Big Shame' he wrote:

> Enter, last line of chorus, hands in pockets, sideways, keeping face from audience's view, walk right across to centre stage and stand looking at scenery, till Symphony commences then turn and walk down to footlights; at end of Symphony commence 1st Verse.

Exits were more perfunctory ('exit with last line of chorus'). The performers of the great days scorned to ask for applause and Hetty King still advises: 'Take what's coming to you and get straight off'.

The *mise-en-scène* and technique are all aimed towards one end – the creation of character, which the music-hall singer saw as his principal object. Like the play-goer or the novel reader, the music-hall audience wanted to see the depiction of interesting, recognisable truthful characters. Elen often heads the manuscripts of his songs with brief definition of the character delineated: 'A workman moocher', 'A horsey or racy character'. Every song presented a different character; every character required a different costume. Only rarely will the need for a quick change persuade Elen to a compromise like using, for 'The 'Ouses in Between', 'a sort of old short (night-shirt) over "Coster's Muvver" coat'.

Yes, Gus Elen's song book already foreshadows the decline, the days when twice-nightly variety and different fashions would leave no time for the expansive methods, the meticulous craftsmanship and artistry of his generation. Twice he retired to devote himself to his favourite pastime of fishing, and a loose sheet in the song book plans his packing for a week's fishing trip (trout-net, toe-clippers and towel for front in green trunk; brandy, Johnny Walker, large thermos and slippers in the car). He came back in 1916 and again, in ripe but undiminished age, in 1931. The song book records the new, abbreviated business which he was now obliged to adopt for 'Arf a Pint of Ale' in order to keep up with the times and with variety theatre schedules. Long before his death in 1940 he must have been conscious that the great days – to which in his song book he had unwittingly composed so vivid a memorial – were over.

ADRIAN NEW IN *THE TIMES*, 19 DECEMBER 1970

Elen (1862-1940) had an apprenticeship as protracted as Chevalier's if very different in kind. He had started as a street busker, working in pubs before graduating to the minstrel seaside troupes. It was Chevalier's success that encouraged him to abandon his other styles and concentrate on coster songs. Elen was fortunate in his writers. The lyricist Edgar Bateman and the composer George Le Brunn gave him what is one of the greatest of all music hall songs, a fragment of social history which tells posterity what it was like for the Londoner to yearn for pastoral delights at a moment when the most violent urban explosion in history was taking place. At the start of the nineteenth century there were one and a half million Londoners; by 1851 for the first time in the history of any nation Britain had more townees than country dwellers; by the time Elen was singing his song, the population of London was edging towards six million.

If you saw my little backyard, 'Wot a pretty spot!' you'd cry,
It's a picture on a sunny summer day;
Wiv the turnip tops and cabbages wot peoples doesn't buy
I makes it on a Sunday look all gay.
The neighbours finks I grow 'em and you'd fancy you're in Kent,
Or at Epsom if you gaze into the mews.
It's a wonder as the landlord doesn't want to raise the rent,
Because we've got such nobby distant views.

Oh it really is a wery pretty garden, and Chingford to the eastward could be seen;
Wiv a ladder and some glasses
You could see to 'Ackney Marshes,
If it wasn't for the 'ouses in between.

We're as countrified as can be wiv a clothes-prop for a tree,
The tub-stool makes a rustic little stile;
Ev'ry time the bloomin' clock strikes there's a cuckoo sings to me,
And I've painted up 'To Leather Lane a mile'.
Wiv tomatoes and wiv radishes wot 'adn't any sale,
The backyard looks a puffick mass o' bloom;
And I've made a little beehive wiv some beetles in a pail,
And a pitchfork wiv a handle of a broom.

Oh, it really is a wery pretty garden, and Rye 'ouse from the cock-loft could be seen;
Where the chickweed man undresses
To bathe 'mong the watercresses,
If it wasn't for the 'ouses in between.

There's the bunny shares 'is egg box wiv the cross-eyed cock and hen
Though they 'as got the pip and him the morf;
In a dog's 'ouse on the line-post there was pigeons nine or ten,
Till someone took a brick and knocked it orf.
The dustcart though it seldom comes, is just like 'arvest 'ome
And we mean to rig a dairy up some 'ow;
Put the donkey in the washouse wiv some imitation 'orns,
For we're teaching 'im to moo just like a cah.

Oh, it really is a wery pretty garden, and 'Endon to the Westward could be seen;
And by climbing to the chimbley,
You could see across to Wembley,
If it wasn't for the 'ouses in between.

Though the gas works isn't wilets, they improve the rural scene,
For mountains they would very nicely pass.
There's the mushrooms in the dust-hole with the cowcumbers so green,
It only wants a bit o' 'ot-'ouse glass.

I wears this milkman's nightshirt, and I sits outside all day,
Like the ploughboy cove what's mizzled o'er the Lea,
And when I gets indoors at night they dunno what I say,
'Cos my language gets as yokel as can be.

Oh, it really is a wery pretty garden, and soap works from the 'ousetops could be
    seen,
If I got a rope and pulley,
I'd enjoy the breeze more fully,
If it wasn't for the 'ouses in between.

Many of the more accomplished artists of the period up to the Great War, well-known players not quite in the class of Leno, Chevalier and company, are in danger of being forgotten altogether. In the spring of 1974, while working on a radio series about popular music in Britain, I went on behalf of the BBC to the village of Angmering in Sussex in the hope of excavating some recollections from the area's most celebrated resident, Stanley Holloway. No excavation was required. Stanley, a mere eighty-two at the time, was a positive volcano of existence, erupting every three or four minutes. He sat in an armchair in the drawing-room, with the English Channel whispering away just over the garden wall, and conjured impressions of whole routines, whole acts, going back fifty years, sixty, seventy. Sometimes, when he had evoked a picture too powerful to resist, he would leave his chair and demonstrate entrances and exits, perform deft little steps, twirl around in imitation of some long-forgotten comic choreography, his eyes twinkling, his laugh booming the whole time. In the course of this brilliant dissertation, he suddenly began impersonating an act called 'Phil Ray, the Abbreviating Comic'. Standing on stage against a backdrop of bathing-machines, rampant crabs, hour-glass figures, jolly fishermen and the rest of the gallimaufry of the music-hall seaside, this unusual comic had leaned against a conspicuously two-dimensional fishing smack, and....

.... then there was Phil Ray, who used to sing this song. Let me see...

> I weren't feeling right
> so I went down to Bright;
> to spend a few mins by the sea.
> On Victoria plat
> I patiently sat
> with my little portmant on my knee.
> Then in from the junc
> came the 3.30 punc,
> as they shunted it in from the staysh.
> Said the guard, 'Make a start,
> room for one, this compart.'
> I said, 'Thanks for the kind informaysh.'
> So I journed to Ostend
> with a pash lady friend

and we posed as Watt nymphs on the rocks.
She'd a rather swag rig
and a very fine fig;
and her hair was no stranger to perox.

BBC SOUND ARCHIVES

Ray abbreviated words. Nature abbreviated Harry Relph, one of the most extraordinary figures ever to appear on any stage anywhere. The sixteenth child of a father who was seventy-seven years old when the child was born, Relph had five fingers and a thumb on each hand, with fingernails which never grew. His palms were unlined, and half of each hand, from little finger to centre joint, was slightly webbed. After reaching a height of four feet six he stopped growing, but succeeded so well in overcoming his disabilities, psychological as well as physical, that he taught himself to be an accomplished musician and sketcher. But it was his comic genius which made him one of the best-loved Englishmen of his day. He was also one of the few comics who went to Paris and so triumphed in that most sophisticated of cities that its intellectuals embarrassed him with the extravagance of their eulogies. A performer from childhood, Relph at first enjoyed his biggest successes in America, but finally established himself at home in his twenty-third year when he appeared in Manchester in the pantomime 'Babes in the Wood'.

He goes through several wild and wonderful step-dances, knocking himself down and flinging his legs about with an awkward gravity that makes his movements extremely laughable. His dance in long flat wooden shoes is a triumph of eccentric step-dancing – accurate, elaborate with many different gymnastic contortions, and full of whimsical and extravagant antics. It is certainly the most striking thing in the pantomime, and was loudly encored.

MANCHESTER GUARDIAN

Relph, known as Little Tich after the notorious Tichborne Claimant, was brought to London by Augustus Harris to appear at the Drury Lane pantomime, from which point he was acknowledged as one of the brightest stars in the profession.

This wonderful little comedian figures first as a two-year-old babe, with his feeding bottle, and in the course of the story he matures to manhood. The idea is a most amusing one, and offers him opportunities of appearing as a baby who can vault into his cradle, as the 'dirty boy' who requires washing, as the precocious youth in a Lord Fauntleroy velvet suit and ruffles, and of displaying 'the education of the feet' with the most droll and mirth-provoking humour.

THE ERA

With a head as bald as polished ivory, with his diminutive proportions, his infantile costume and a peculiarly bland smile rivalling that of the Heathen Chinee, Little Tich is surely the oddest and one of the most diverting figures seen upon the stage. He is a droll in the best sense of the word, and had he lived half a century ago he would have left a mark in English dramatic history as one of our leading English clowns. Let it not be said that true pantomime is dead or that the art of mimicry is lost while it is possible to enjoy the whimsicalities of such a mime as Little Tich. Such a performance is inimitable. All Lancashire will feel bound to see it.

MANCHESTER GUARDIAN

No one can have any idea of the variety of steps until he has seen Little Tich's galvanic legs. One of his songs says he is 'highly educated in the feet'. But that underestimates his powers. Highly educated! He is far away the most marvellous dancer the stage knows. But any description of his movement is impossible.

SUSSEX DAILY NEWS

L ionised in Britain, Little Tich was positively idolised in France, where he was treated not so much as a slapstick clown as a genius of the theatrical arts. Some of the effusiveness rather embarrassed Relph, but he was certainly proud of one admirer among the Parisian intelligentsia.

More to Harry's taste was the admiration of Toulouse-Lautrec. The painter and the performer were almost of an age, and were exactly the same height: four feet six. It is not known when Lautrec first saw Harry's act; perhaps on his visit to London in 1894. But as an Anglophile and an habitué of the music halls, he would have seen Tich for himself in Paris soon after Harry's 1896 debut there. They became friends for a few years before in 1899 the Count went into a mental home, an old man at thirty, 'always on the verge of delirium tremens, never sober, scarcely sane'. They were seen together in Paris and in Dieppe, where, so Walter Sickert told Sacheverell Sitwell, they frightened women on the pier by their deliberately offensive behaviour. Harry went to Lautrec's studio in the Avenue Prochet, and was invited to his château. Lautrec made at least one drawing of him, as a Spanish dancer, according to C.B. Cochran. This cannot now be traced, although Lautrec's portraits of several other forgotten English performers – like May Belfort, May Milton and Cissie Loftus – survive; and no further detail of their relationship has been discovered. One painting from that period which *has* survived is by the Belgian artist Jan van Beers, who in 1898 sought out Tich in order to paint his portrait, partly, as he explained, because he wanted to capture on canvas the sitter's Punch-like smile. He painted Harry in his big boots, leaning forward, and signed it: 'To the great comic – Little Tich'.

RICHARD FINDLATER, *LITTLE TICH*

Not all Tich's Parisian admirers were so controlled. In certain sectors of the acting profession, his technique and his peculiarly pathetic strain of humour inspired an enthusiasm not so very far short of hysteria. Nor was it a passion of the moment. For as long as Tich cared to work in Paris, his distinguished boosters remained faithful to him.

Two of Little Tich's most eminent Parisian admirers were Lucien Guitry and his son Sacha. When Lucien was at the top of his profession, he used to make a point of coming to see Tich's act, night after night, when Tich was in Paris. The elder Guitry used to sit, it is said in the front row of the stalls, leaning forward on his cane, watching Tich intensely – in quite a different way from the rest of the audience. He was, said Maurice Verne, taking lessons in humanity. Sacha was, perhaps, even more enthusiastic than his father, and his enthusiasm was no merely modish attitude, as it persisted for some thirty years. In 1907 we find Sacha saying to 'Gil Blas' of Tich that *'il est impossible d'avoir plus de mesure et plus de tact dans la bouffonnerie'.* In 1909, on a visit to England, he was quoted by *The Daily Telegraph* as saying, 'There is nothing I enjoy more than to spend an evening at the Tivoli in the company of artists like George Robey, Wilkie Bard and Little Tich. Shall I surprise you by saying that the last-named strikes me as the very embodiment of grace itself?' And Guitry later praised Tich for his inventiveness, witnessed by a thousand *droleries* copied a thousand times since, his good taste *('Jamais une vulgarité, jamais une faute de goût'),* his ability to make both the coarsest and the most cultivated members of the audience laugh at him and with him. Tich was, said Sacha, remarkable not only as a performer but as an author, a director, a complete artist – and a gentleman.

Guitry's admiration was unflagging. In 1920 C.B. Cochran's 'Grande Saison Parisienne' in London was inaugurated by a reception given by Lady Cunard, the supreme professional hostess of the day, at her home in Carlton House Terrace. According to James Harding, Guitry's biographer, 'Sacha electrified the 400 guests by stating that his favourite actor was Little Tich, whom he described as the quintessence of art.' Lucien attended Tich's first night at the Alhambra when he returned to Paris in the 1920s. Henry Sherek, whose father booked the acts for that music hall and who sat next to Guitry, recalled in his reminiscences that:

'When Little Tich made his entrance, Guitry, dressed in his famous black cloak, jumped to his feet, turned to the audience, waved his broad-brimmed black-brimmed hat, and with something akin to madness in his voice shouted: "Get up, all of you, in homage to the world's greatest genius." This was perhaps a slight exaggeration, but to my surprise the audience did actually all get up, and, led by Lucien, cheer for a considerable time.'

This was not all, according to Sherek. Just when Little Tich thought he had finished his act Lucien Guitry bounced up in his seat and begged him to do the Big Boots dance, a plea in which he was loudly applauded again by the audience. When Tich, after some reluctance, went off to find the boots and put them on once again (he had rashly brought them, with no intention of using them in the act), Guitry harangued the audience about him. After the dance was over, Sherek says, 'Guitry kissed me on both cheeks and then rushed backstage and kissed Little Tich on both cheeks. To do this he had to kneel.'

RICHARD FINDLATER, *LITTLE TICH*

In reading this and other accounts, posterity cannot help wondering to what extent the modest Kentish soul of the tiny clown was ever embarrassed by the idolatry of the *boulevardiers*. After all, if his genius was universal, his material was mundane enough, and certainly very English. No doubt Parisian audiences could infer the meaning, but it seems to have been his bodily control and the eccentric grace of his dancing which they found most intoxicating. In the following song, for example, one of Tich's biggest successes, the style of the language is so English as to be virtually untranslatable. There is more than a hint here of the surreal wordplay of Dan Leno, and, in the echoing nonsense of the non sequiturs, a portent of Billy Bennett.

One of the Deathless Army

I am a bolger sold – I mean a soldier bold,
I'm not so young as I used to be before I got so old.
I am a regular toff, I am, I am, I say, I am,
But you can't tell what's inside the jar by the label on the jam.
For I'm a soldier, a Territorial.
The girls will say when I'm on parade,
'There's one of the boys of the Old Brigade'.
If I ever go to war, I'll drive the enemy barmy,
Hi! Hi! Never say die!
I'm one of the deathless army.

Patter (to pathetic music)
Would you like me to tell you the story, sir, of the horribleness of war?
Well, it was half past six in the morning, sir, when the clock struck five to four.
There was something went wrong with the works, sir, but the enemy wanted a fight.
Why, they lay with our right on their left, sir, and we lay with our left on their right.
And I wanted a Turkish Bath, sir, but the Colonel said, 'Lad, there's no hope,
For the drummer-boy's drunk all the water and the bugler's swallowed the soap.'
I lay down and shrieked in my anguish, but the Colonel said, 'Lad, never mind.
Why, you haven't got on any trousers! Huh! So I went and pulled down the blind.
Then the bugler tootled his tooter, and I knew that the foeman was nigh,
So I rushed out to buy some tobacco, when a cannonball flopped in my eye.
You know, I could scarcely see for a moment, and I thought it was very unkind.
Then the Colonel's wife dropped in to see me and said, 'Er, shall we, er, pull down the blind?'
Then the enemy clustered around us and the Colonel went clean off his chump.
And the horses drew horse and stampeded and the camels had all got the hump.
Well, I was having a whisky and soda, sir, when a shot struck me, er, somewhere behind.
As I could not pull it out in the street, sir, I went in and pulled down the blind.
And the shells lay around me in thousands, and still they continued to drop.
So I paid for the dozen I'd eaten and walked out of the oyster shop.
And the shots they were buzzing around me, and one nearly blew off my head.
There were cannons to right of me, cannons to left of me, so what did I do? Went in off the red.

WORDS BY T.W. THURBAN, MUSIC BY G. WELLS, W. TERRY AND V.R. GILL

Audiences were content to wait all night so long as they knew that this sort of moment was coming. Tich topped the bill. It was usually he that the packed houses had turned out to see. They knew many of his characterisations, most of his songs, above all they knew about the Big Boots. It was the anticipation of these familiar delights to come which kept them on edge, until, in the last moments before he was due to appear, the pressure of expectation rose to bursting point, and exploded in a great roar of delight the instant he made himself visible.

———————————

Nearly a score of turns have come and gone, greeted with varying degrees of apathy and approval, on the stage of one of the long-lost Empires of a buried England. It is about 10.15 on a Saturday night, before the First World War, at the Tivoli, the London music hall behind the restaurant in the Strand. Indian gods and goddesses in their more chaste poses decorate the walls of this temple of pleasure. Expectation soars as the moment approaches for the top of the bill to make his entrance. An electric thrill passes through the audience, packed beneath the baroque opulence of the boxes, and as the illuminated red numbers change in the frames on each side of the stage, whose flanking pillars are topped by elephants' heads, the band in the orchestra pit starts up a catchy tune. People start to clap. The applause rises in a swell of excitement. It ebbs away; the house holds its breath; a bell buzzes; the band plays the tune again; the curtains swing up; the limes focus on the left of the stage; and a little man – a *very* little man – hurries on at high speed into a noisy gale of welcome, slides to a halt facing the audience, and receives their homage with an incomparable mixture of frank delight, elfish dignity and knowing amusement. Little Tich is on.

The Tivoli applause is immediately charged with laughter, although Tich has not yet said a word or sung a note or done a thing. There is nothing especially comic about his make-up (reddened nose and chin) or his costume: he is wearing a somewhat battered gibus, a very short jacket in large black-and-white checks, and baggy trousers, but this outfit – though scarcely naturalistic – is restrained when compared with the grotesque gear of some of his predecessors on the bill. This man is wearing something much more important, a mischievous, sweet, immensely infectious grin, as he eyes the house with a conspiratorial relish that invites them all to share the joke that he soon can scarcely contain, shaking with suppressed laughter, spluttering asides that he chokes on guiltily, swivelling a fearful eye at the boxes that suggests a pilferer caught in the act – till the smile comes back, as it always shines through all Tich's stage adversities, blandly menacing but irresistibly winning.

Why is the house laughing before Little Tich has apparently started? Because of his reputation – he has been a bill-topping byword since 1890. Because he is advertised (in succession to Dan Leno) as The Funniest Man on Earth. Because he is uncommonly short. Because they have been *waiting* to laugh. And because a lot of them have had a lot to drink. There is another reason: contrary to appearances, he *has* already started working. As soon as he came on the stage he connected with the emotional voltage in the auditorium, concentrated it and somehow intensified it, by the power that great performers often apply, that lucky audiences sometimes experience, and that nobody has ever satisfactorily explained; which is why people still call it magic. He has galvanised the Tivoli audience with a two-way charge of affection and sympathy that, if the gods are willing, and if neither his prodigious vitality nor his technical expertise nor his artist's instinct fails, will carry him through his turn. And it all scarcely takes a minute: Little Tich can't afford more, because he has barely fifteen minutes at the most, although he is topping the Tivoli bill and is the highest paid artist of his kind in the world. *Of his kind?* There's nobody quite like him on the halls.

During his first number Tich shows why he is still a popular idol after twenty years: not so much in the song itself or in the patter, but rather in the comic intensity of his characterisation, the finesse of his 'business', the impish, quicksilver energy with which he darts around the stage, as if continually improvising, as if *at play*. When he starts off he has the air of a man who has just had an exceptionally good dinner, topped off by a fine brandy and a splendid cigar. He looks as if he has every reason to feel pleased with himself. Then everything begins to go wrong. Things revolt against him. Twirling his cane, like a would-be swell, he manages to poke himself in the eye with it. Recovering quickly, with the same ineffable smile that he wore at his entrance, he shortly afterwards drops it on the stage – and pounces on it, snatching it up as if it were a naughty child. Then his hat falls off, and – taking a life of its own – refuses to be recaptured. His shoes, too, rebel against him; they trip him up and behave very oddly. At first he shrugs his shoulders at these misfortunes, and ignores them: the effects of the dinner and the cigar have not yet worn off. But gradually his morale is affected. He tries to quell the rebellious elements, *tame* them, plead with them. He chases his hat unavailing around the stage, smiling apologetically at the audience, until he suddenly hits on the idea of carrying out an encircling movement, which he does with ostentatious insouciance, and claps the hat back on his head. But a moment later, when he drops both the hat and the cane, he is plunged into a terrible dilemma: *which one will he pick up first?* He starts to move towards the cane, but breaks off half-way to head for the hat. He wavers again, and again, and again, miraculously taking the audience with him in what he calls 'the business of being undecided', but never stretching out the game for a moment too long. Suddenly his cane begins to slip down a hole in the stage, drilled for that purpose, and he goes with it, 'his eyes glaring, his face a study in epileptic dismay, his mouth a horrified little jam-puff,' carrying on an imaginary struggle with the demons below.

In the course of his turn Little Tich goes off three times to the quick-change booth in the wings, returning as a waiter and a gamekeeper, grotesques in extravagant make-up and costume who are nevertheless imbued with instantly recognisable humanity, miniatures brought to life in a song and patter for their few minutes on the stage with a hundred comic touches, movements, vocal inflections. Off he goes after the last song, to be recalled by furious applause, and whistles, and shouts of 'Boots!' 'Big Boots!' Obediently, after some byplay of protest, he kneels down on the stage. While the band repeats that catchy little piece of music over and over again, out of the wings towards him come hurtling two large, flat, heavy, narrow clogs, each twenty-eight inches long, more than half Tich's height. These are the Big Boots, and as each arrives it is greeted with an enthusiastic round of applause. Slowly, carefully, spinning out the ritual, Little Tich puts the boots on, chuckling obscurely to himself, pausing to struggle with a supposedly refractory lace or to tap out a syncopated coda to the never-ending music with one clog before he tries it for size. At last they are both on, and he begins his grotesque 'dance', a showpiece of acrobatic strength and skill as well as comic timing, slapping his feet down so vigorously to the rhythm that the dust rises in clouds. When his hat falls off, he leans forward at a perilously acute angle and scoops it up without bending his knees. He slides across the boards, doing the splits fast or slow. He falls over on his nose, with his feet still flat on the floor, then turns his face round and up to the audience to show that he's laughing. He sits down, bringing his legs together so that his face is hidden from the stalls by the boots. Then he slowly opens his legs again, beams out coyly at the audience, snaps the boots shut and cries out with pain ('Oo-er!') as if his fingers had somehow got caught between. He leans forward to take a bow, so very far forward that it seems

131

certain he will topple over into the orchestra pit; he doesn't, but he hits his forehead on the stage in a near-horizontal position, then raises himself to the upright position again, straight-legged, with magical rapidity. Then, finally, he reaches the longed-for consummation of the 'dance'. Slowly, winking knowingly at the house as if he were inviting them to share in another of his minor debacles, Little Tich rises up on the toes of his elongated wooden feet. Defying the laws of gravity, the manikin has become—for a moment of delicate balance—a giant nearly seven feet tall.

In a minute the dance is over. To tumultuous applause from the Tivoli audience Little Tich goes off; the red numbers change in the proscenium frames; a bell buzzes; the conductor strikes up a new signature tune. Not long afterwards, a serious, dandyish, dignified little man slips quickly out of the stage door, followed by his driver, into his waiting limousine, where he occupies a special high seat in the back. Mr Harry Relph is resuming his private life, a life that he kept rigidly separate from his professional career, and about which he maintained a secrecy that has persisted since his death fifty years ago.

Some attentive readers of the trade press may have known that Tich had unusual off-stage hobbies. He was a skilful, assiduous artist in oils, water colour and black-and-white; he enjoyed photography; he read widely, in religion, philosophy and literature. ('A knowledge of the best in literature,' he said, 'can help even a comedian'); he loved to play the 'cello (as well as billiards, chess and golf) and he both composed and arranged music for his act; he was a versatile linguist. He had other hobbies, too. But a great deal of his private life must remain today as much of a mystery as his comic genius. This word 'genius' is, of course, a dangerously devalued superlative, wrecked by generations of show business publicists; but it was used frequently in Tich's lifetime by discriminating observers, and we use it advisedly here because (so it appears to us) no other term will quite do.

RICHARD FINDLATER, *LITTLE TICH*

Descriptions of this kind, which attempt to portray in words what, in a later age, the television camera would have captured once and for all, achieve a correlation which suggests that a high degree of accuracy pervades them all. Somewhere between the flushed madness of a Guitry and the cool analysis of the following account, that chimera, the truth, probably hovers.

The scene tonight was a familiar one – a street with a background of houses and trees. On the right hand wing, a corner house with an area and a grating. Tich has on his fantastic boots and his little comic hat and he waves and waggles his little swagger cane. With this equipment he can make you laugh and can fascinate you endlessly with his nimble dancing and his twittering songs. Presently he will inadvertently hit his long boot with his cane, and his surprise and pain will be unbearably funny. Suddenly he sees the grating. At once the gay, innocent comic becomes a mischievous little monster, all leers and terrible chuckles. Turning his back he leans over his boots – which is funny enough in itself – he peers through the grating and begins to show signs of naughty excitement, his little stick held casually behind his back somehow begins to look like a little dog's tail which begins to wag with pleasure. The audience is not slow to get all these signs and they laugh and hoot and whistle rude noises. Tich is delighted with his peep show and, as the band begins to play its catchy tune again, he begins to sing:

Curi-uri-osity, curiosity,
Most of us are curious,
Some of us are furious,
I do think it's most injurious,
Curious to be.
What did I get married for?
Curiosity.

After this Tich makes some patter, and when the chorus breaks out again there is a crescendo of laughter and applause. Tich becomes tremendously animated and does a wonderful little dance, slapping his boots together in mid-air.

PAUL NASH, *OUTLINE*

One possible explanation for the striking contrast between French and British comment on Tich is that the French saw the very best of him. This seems a dubious premise on which to build a critique, for it seems very unlikely that once he won acceptance Tich ever improved or declined to any degree. He was a consummate artist from the very start, and he remained one to the very end. But one impresario who probably knew the relative merits of French and British artists and audiences better than anyone, was C.B. Cochran, who does suggest that by the time the Guitrys were throwing their cloaks over the local windmills, Tich had achieved an altitude of virtuosity almost too rarified to contemplate without suffering loss of breath.

I have thought that the French went to excess in their extravagant acclaim of Little Tich. It should be realised, however, that Paris saw Little Tich at his very best; as an incomparable gnome of fantasy. Even in England he had not then begun to follow the technique of Dan Leno and other comedians of this epoch by making a long monologue between a short verse and a short chorus the outstanding feature of his turn. Although he chatted away glibly in French, with the accent of Birmingham, he relied mainly on indescribable and truly inimitable movements. Got up as a grand lady, in court dress with a long train, he hurled himself upon the stage of the Folies Bergère.

'*Je m'appelle Clarice*', said Tich, with that chuckle which I recall when I hear Charlie McCarthy, the human wooden doll of Edgar Bergen. Continuing, in French – more or less: 'I am an admiral's daughter – I've just come from the Court ball – oh, my success! – what a *succès fou! – beaucoup de succès* – very nice!' – the 'very nice' always in English.

By this time the customers in the seats of the Folies Bergère were rolling in the aisles, and the ladies of the promenade had left the bars and crowded to get a view of the stage. Tich waved his large feather fan, got tied up in his train (as Lupino Lane did in the peer's robe in 'Me and My Girl'), and by this time everything done or said by the strange little figure was greeted with shouts of laughter. Old Parisians tell me that the success of Tich as a laughter-maker has never been equalled in Paris.

To the Parisians, Tich was the reincarnation of the dwarf court jesters of the Middle Ages – the little English Don Antonio of Velasquez; the poet Jean Lorraine saw in him all the grotesquerie of the low-life characters from the novels of Dickens. Toulouse-Lautrec drew him in his costume of a *danseuse espagnole;* it was the epoch

133

of La Belle Otéro, which intensified the drollery of the inhuman caricature. La Loie Fuller had recently captivated Paris with *la danse serpentine,* and when Tich, at the end of his turn, appeared in the voluminous skirts of La Loie, chasing the coloured lights from the projectors, the delight of the spectators surpassed all bounds.

Tich was the king of Paris.

C.B. COCHRAN, A SHOWMAN LOOKS ON

In a sense, Tich's triumph was his tragedy. Unlike most of his fellow-artists, he could not take off his make-up once the act was finished. His whole comic persona was built on his tiny body. When he left the stage-door, his freakishness went with him, even though no genetic sport ever fought harder to achieve a normal private life. He died in 1928 in his sixty-first year, and there is copious evidence to show that throughout all those years he dreamed of physical normality. Most of this evidence comes from Tich himself, who had the artist's perception for the telling anecdote, the self-revelatory aside, the accidental, unintentional reduction to absurdity of a man's life through a slip of a stranger's tongue.

'It is the lesser of two evils to be as I am. People don't realise the amount of problems giants have.'

'I had no coppers, so I gave the man a shilling, declined the butterflies and wished him a good night. He returned me my shilling and said, "Thanks, I don't take money from boys." Somebody then informed him that I happened to be Little Tich, so he chased me and said, "Mr Tich, I have made a mistake. I do take money from boys."
I said, "You do?"
He said, "Yes sir, I do."
I said, "That won't work. Since you left me I have grown up."'

When his son was born he was in a state of great anxiety, and he was sitting on the stairs, with his head bowed in his hands and wondering how everything was going, and presently the doctor came along and comforted him. 'It's all right, my little man,' he said, 'you've got a baby brother.'

MAX BEERBOHM

'I remember him standing on a little stool and saying, "That's the height I should like to be".'

WINIFRED RELPH, TICH'S THIRD WIFE

The one riddle which neither Tich nor any other performer ever resolved was the one represented by the audience. As an artist and a perfectionist, Tich was more troubled than most by the ineradicable unknown factor in an act. Having striven so effectively for technical perfection, he would have liked to assume, from his

134

bastion of virtuosity, that every time he stepped on to a stage, the magic of the blend between personality and technique would take its effect. But this was not always so, and Tich tended to agonise over it.

'The music hall audience is terribly trying to the artiste. One night they are all applause and the next night, for no apparent reason you find them perfectly cold and sometimes spiteful. I could not get a hand at first for the song, "I Could Do With a Bit". I threw it aside, and a year later when I tried it again it was a tremendous success. How do you account for that?'

Tich made the cardinal error of assuming that there was something called 'the Audience', a factor as constant as the act he brought to them. But this was not so. Every night, every performance, while the act changes in only the most microscopic details, the audience is a new one, composed of different elements. Perhaps on some nights there might be a few too many bilious or slow-witted onlookers for the fusion of artist and spectators to take place. Even after his reputation was secure, even after death, there were one or two minority voices which questioned his irresistibility. J. B. Priestley, while expressing great affection for him, suggested that the songs he sang were commonplace, and of course there was always the knowing Arnold Bennett, bristling with worldliness and delighted to play devil's advocate when it came to apportioning the music-hall laurels. But for the most part Tich received the respect and love his performances merited.

Sunday 2 January 1910

On Friday night, our last night in London, we went to the Tivoli. There were no seats except in the pit, so we went in the pit. Little Tich was very good, and George Formby, the Lancashire comedian, was perhaps even better. Gus Elen I did not care for. And I couldn't see the legendary cleverness of the vulgarity of Marie Lloyd. She was very young and spry for a grandmother. All her songs were variations of the same theme of sexual naughtiness. No censor would ever pass them, and especially he wouldn't pass her winks and her silences. To be noted also was the singular naïveté of the cinematograph explanation of what a vampire was and is, for the vampire dance. The stoutest and biggest attendants laughed at Little Tich and G. Formby. Fearful draughts half the time down exit staircases from the street. Fearful noise from the bar behind, made chiefly by officials. The bar-girls and their friends simply ignored the performance and the public. Public opinion keeps the seats of those who go to the bar at the interval for a drink. Going home, stopped by procession of full carriages entering the Savoy and empty carriages coming out of it.

ARNOLD BENNETT, *JOURNALS*

Genius is not too big a word to use of Little Tich. He has that strange and incalculable endowment, that thing which you cannot acquire and to which all else is added.

THE MANCHESTER GUARDIAN, 1928

Little Tich was a wonderful artist, with a deep rich voice and with great command. He presented a creature partly human, partly animal. His huge feet belonged to another world, not quite human. Sometimes they embarrassed him, sometimes they applauded him, and he could stand up on them elevated into a victory. This was an extremely bizarre act, but he was accepted by the rather simple music-hall audience as being no more than a trifle odd. Little Tich was *enormous*.

SIR RALPH RICHARDSON, LETTER QUOTED BY R. FINDLATER

It has gone largely unperceived by posterity that Little Tich's influence was so profound as to affect artists and art forms long after his death. The greatest tributes of all were those paid by his fellow-performers. Tich would have especially appreciated the remark of one of the very few performers to have a greater reputation even than his, Marie Lloyd, who, in asserting her primacy, said, 'I am sole top of the bill – or not at all. There are only two artists I would ever share with – Little Tich and George Robey.' Marie saluted Tich's genius and went on pursuing her own. Others paid Tich the more oblique tribute of imitation, not always with acknowledgement to the source. One young aspiring French artist was honest enough in his admiration.

The young Chevalier, who had been working hard, trying to perfect his act in the provinces, travelled to London in the hope of inspiration from the London stage. He was not to be disappointed. On his arrival he went immediately to the Victoria Palace, one of Britain's best Edwardian music halls at the time, and there he was overwhelmed by the performance of its star, George Robey, with his deep voice, wide smile and giant-sized eyebrows. He also saw performances by Harry Relph, 'Little Tich', whose act Charlie Chaplin was to parody and make so famous, and Wilkie Bard, who brought the house down night after night. They were all from poor backgrounds similar to Chevalier's own; each had a unique visual style which, back in his hotel room, the young comic tried to dissect and practised in front of the mirror.

CHARLES CASTLE, *THE FOLIES BERGÈRE*

But there was another case, altogether more peculiar than Chevalier's, involving the greatest reputation ever to emerge from the halls, of a world star, a man whose genius has been acknowledged by every group in every society the world over, whose symbolic importance has transcended language and culture, religion and geography. With the possible exception of Mickey Mouse, no performer in the world's history is more widely known and more deeply loved than Charlie Chaplin and his silhouette of the Little Tramp, sporting his armour of jaunty bowler hat, toothbrush moustache, flat feet and swagger cane. Yet it would seem that the contrivance of the Tramp was lifted bodily from Little Tich, who was to live long enough to endure the ultimate irony of being accused of plagiarising his plagiariser.

136

Touring with Fred Karno's Troupe, Charlie Chaplin made his debut at the Folies Bergère in 1909 at the age of fourteen, where he was paid £6 a week for the ten-week season. He was a small, thin lad, almost cadaverous, with long hair and a sulky expression. He staggered about the stage in a frock-coat several sizes too large for him, tripping over himself in a frenzy of inspired buffoonery, and soon all Paris was flocking to see him. It is no exaggeration to say that but for that visit to the Folies Bergère, Charles Chaplin would not have become the Charlie Chaplin the world came to know and admire. It was in Paris that he met the two men who had a predominant influence on his career: Max Linder and Little Tich. Max Linder was the greatest French comedian of his day. Chaplin would dash in to see his act whenever he could. He learnt all his gags, his wistful good humour, his pathetic helplessness and when Hollywood made him an offer two years later, he declared, 'I want to be America's Max Linder.'

Chaplin adored Little Tich's walking stick, his enormous boots and his little bowler hat. In fact, it was at the Folies Bergère that Chaplin discovered his famous silhouette. A few years later, after the first war, Little Tich returned to appear at the Folies Bergère. In the meantime, Charlie Chaplin's antics had set the whole world laughing and the dwarf who had been so adulated ten years before was slated for imitating Charlie Chaplin.

CHARLES CASTLE, *THE FOLIES BERGÈRE*

Of course there is nothing wrong in paying the tribute of imitation, especially if it is acknowledged. No doubt there were faint traces of Dan Leno in Tich's own convention of making the English language stand on its head. But the greatest surprise of all, and one of the deepest significance, as we shall see, was Chaplin's blatant refusal ever to nod in Tich's direction. For the moment, in the years leading up to the Great War, Tich was in the ascendant and Chaplin a mere rising young juvenile. It was in this period that the richness of the reminiscences matches the richness of the talent which inspired it. Of those audiences whose constituents included the occasional misanthrope resistant to the wiles of Little Tich, none has left a more affectionate impression than Frederick Willis, a tireless annalist of the old, lost London. Willis, a professional hatter whose retrospective volumes of a suburban life in Victorian and Edwardian London are a priceless storehouse for the social historian, travelled up as a young married man each day from his home in Camberwell to a firm of hatters not far from Ludgate Circus. He was a man in love with his own past and the town in which he had spent it, and in his own modest way he was attempting to save from oblivion the myriad facts and sights and sounds forever gone. In publishing *A Book of London Yesterdays,* he prefaced his recollections with a deft sketch of the kind of Londoner he had in mind. If the following passage is not, strictly speaking, about the music hall, it is about the type of man who attended the halls and found there a refuge from petty cares.

This book is no glorification of the past but a reconstruction, based on my experience, of the life lived by the Little Man who crowded the streets, the trains, the buses, and trams; who applauded Irving and Ellen Terry, Dan Leno and Marie Lloyd. He was always hard up but as optimistic as Mr Micawber. He was as obscure as the other side of the moon, and the only time he got his name into the papers was in the casualty list of the First World War. I ought to know, for I was such a one myself.

This then is the London of the Little Man; it is a London which is normally unnoticed by the professional historian. The London of the first three generations from the old board schools. The Londoner I have in mind was God-fearing, although he seldom went to church; patriotic, but he seldom waved a flag. He was blessed with a humorous cynicism and patient endurance, and his natural shrewdness was mixed with naïveté which made him an easy victim of humbug. He was the man the New Journalism was made for, and the gorgeous oleographs in the Christmas numbers of *Pear's Annual* and other publications. The Thirty Shilling Tailors sprang into existence especially for him, and the smart teashops did likewise. He was the lifeblood of the Palace of Varieties and the respected gallery boy of the West End theatres. He was hard-working, cheerful, and expected help from nobody, which was lucky, for he certainly did not get any. Shakespeare has said, 'Security is mortals' chiefest enemy'. If this is true, how happy was the pre-1914 Londoner, for security to him was unknown. Of course I mean economic security, for he had any amount of physical security, since London was the safest city in the world. He took his ease in hundreds of obscure little taverns on Saturday night, and he did not suffer from inhibitions, complexes, and frustrations, so was a headache to nobody.

Rattle him out of bed early in the morning, keep his nose to the grindstone for from eight to twelve hours a day, give him a little six-roomed house and a wife and children to go home to at night, and he was as happy as we poor mortals can hope to be. Provided he managed to pay his rent he was as safe in his little house as William the First was in his Tower of London. Probably he was much safer, and I suspect he loved his little castle much more than William loved his great one.

Over one hundred thousand of these little houses were wholly destroyed in the last war, and in many cases the Londoners they sheltered went with them. The majority of those little houses were not much loss, and as I see the fine new blocks of flats arising on their sites I fervently hope they will shelter the same sturdy spirits and modest happiness, the same kind of people I have here presented with affectionate care.

FREDERICK WILLIS, *A BOOK OF LONDON YESTERDAYS*

This typical occupant of a seat in the stalls is of course Willis himself, who was perfectly content to live out his days as a modest hatter whose regular pleasures included the music hall. Willis was also a proud and resolute suburbanite, with a touching loyalty to local amenities. Both as a small boy in Victorian London, not so far from the Crystal Palace, and as a young man with a young wife, living in a small, snug house in Camberwell, he revelled in the sophistication of the productions in the halls close to his home. Nor was it simply a question of allegiance to his own district; once they took their seats, Willis and his neighbours could never be sure whom they might recognise on the stage. Time and again in his reminiscences, he brings out the point that the demarcation lines between artist and audience were very often smudged by the sheer volume of talent required to fill all the stages in England. In addition to the renowned professionals and the regular touring acts on one side of the footlights, and spectators like Willis on the other, there was also a great drifting army of part-timers whose services were called upon occasionally, and very often seasonally. Most surprising of all, the machinery for recruiting this casual labour was of the simplest. Instead of seeking the help of casting agents and managers, the local impresario would go out and do the job for himself.

London suburban theatres depended mostly upon the touring companies, but their Christmas pantomimes were entirely their own productions. Few of us could regard our local pantomime with an impartial eye, since we were all very jealous of our native prestige. A Holloway man might rave about his local pantomime and we listened tolerantly to his ravings, but when he paused for breath we smugly pointed out how wrong he was. *Our* pantomime was recognised by the press as the best in suburban London. That we referred to the local press was not necessary to dwell upon.

All suburban pantomimes presented one famous music-hall star supported by a galaxy of lesser lights. This was before the time when every artiste was described as a star. The chorus girls and show ladies were our own local product, and we in Camberwell considered the Camberwell beauties second to none.

Of our two theatres, the Theatre Metropole was small and charming, so charming that Bernard Shaw said it was better than the West End at half the price; the Crown was so large and imposing that the proscenium arch was only a foot or two smaller than Drury Lane, and the depth of the stage was such that it could and did accommodate easily a coach and four in one of its melodramas. The Crown always had Marie Lloyd as principal boy, and a host of talent to support her – the Two McNaughtons, Alice Lloyd, Daisy Wood, Dan Crawley are some I remember. Naturally all the nice girls of Camberwell had an urgent ambition to appear as members of the chorus or show ladies, and as there were such a lot of nice girls in Camberwell the management could afford to be very choosy. The result was so dazzling that my heart misses a beat only to think of it after sixty years. As for scenery, Drury Lane had to look to its laurels when the curtain went up on a Crown pantomime.

However, despite the grandeur of the Crown and the charm of the Metropole, the Surrey Theatre, which, alas, was not in Camberwell but in Southwark, was the acknowledged Drury Lane of South London. Unlike our own local theatres it was old with tradition, and tradition was respected at that time. In grandeur the Surrey Theatre was excelled by the Crown. The curtains draping the proscenium of the Surrey were not real curtains, only curtains painted on canvas; but what curtains they were, with massive gold ropes and tassels! I was brought up on the Surrey pantomimes and I viewed with distaste the real plush curtains, furnished at fabulous cost, at our Crown Theatre. I confided to my theatrical Uncle James, who was my escort, that they were not a patch on the painted curtains at the Surrey. It was a case where reality fell far short of imagination. Besides, I argued, everything about a theatre should be make-believe, not real. Instead of laughing at my views my uncle agreed with them. Arriving home he said, 'What you want in theatrical matters is *effect*, and spending great sums of money is no guarantee that you will get it.'

George Conquest and the Surrey Theatre were as inseparable as Sir Augustus Harris and Drury Lane. What George Conquest did not know about pantomime was not worth bothering about. He was the originator of the Flying Ballet, and suspended his most shapely damsels on wires more or less invisible so that they floated airily over his historic boards. Nobody admired those flying nymphs more than I did when I was a child, and by great good luck it happened in later years that I made the intimate acquaintance of one of these charmers. True, it was rather a prosaic reunion because she was my landlady when I had snug lodgings at Brixton.

Being full of good humour and anecdotage, she told me how she came to join Mr Conquest's company. It seems that when Mr Conquest began to exercise his mind about pantomime he strolled about the neighbourhood of the Blackfriars Road like a recruiting agent in search of likely recruits. On one such occasion my friend, then a girl of eighteen, was walking with another girl when they were accosted by the famous impresario. He regarded them with a critical eye and asked, 'How would you like to go on the stage?' My friend's companion was very indignant at being spoken to in this way by a total stranger, but my friend was made of sterner stuff. She tossed her head and replied indifferently, 'I have never thought about such a thing!' Mr Conquest was impressed, as well he might be, for, judging from my friend's appearance when I came to know her I can well imagine what she looked like at the age of eighteen. She used to call me Basil, and one of her stock phrases was, 'Basil, when I was a girl I was a platinum blonde!' Well, Mr Conquest did not casually come across good-looking platinum blondes every day, so he approached closer and said in a stage whisper, 'Have you got a good leg?' This finished my friend's companion; she walked away, either in disgust or perhaps she had not much confidence in her leg. But the platinum blonde stood her ground and, her leg being satisfactory, she never looked back.

She remained with Mr Conquest until her marriage. As she was twelve years my senior it was clear to me that she was one of the damsels who had so stirred my childish imagination, and I was deeply moved. But I must confess I was equally moved by her other accomplishments. She had a very pretty hand at making beefsteak puddings, and when she placed a helping before me with the thick gravy issuing from its rich interior I was not sure in which capacity I loved her best, a flying nymph or a maker of beefsteak puddings. Possibly an over-indulgence in this delicacy had made her less aerial than formerly. Mind you, she was still very comely, but I think it would have taxed the ingenuity of Mr Conquest to find a wire, at least an invisible wire, that was capable of bearing her weight when she was my landlady.

FREDERICK WILLIS, *A BOOK OF LONDON YESTERDAYS*

The pantomime hamadryad who evolves into the buxom landlady is a stock character in the mythology of the profession, although none the less real for that. But it was not just in local domestic circles that men like Willis encountered those who had had the magic experience of slipping through the looking-glass into the enchanted world of professional music hall. At the hatters where he worked, Willis would take his lunch with his colleagues on the premises, where the basement would be prepared each day by one of the odd-job boys employed by the firm. It would be the boy's responsibility to whiten the stone round the gas-fire, clean the cutlery, spread the table with sheets of white paper, and even on occasion abstract from unknown sources a vase of flowers. Willis recalls that this paragon had enjoyed a childhood so exotic that for the rest of his life Willis remembered its details.

He was a real Cockney, living where he was born, in Bedfordbury. He had been partly educated at Drury Lane Theatre, where he was once one of forty or fifty children who annually became imps, sprites, rabbits, bigheads, and many other delightful objects in the Lane pantomimes. At the age of sixteen or seventeen he was as full of reminiscence as I am now in my dotage, and from the ample store of his experience he enriched my knowledge of the world many an afternoon while I was having my tea and eating his stale cakes. I gathered then that his favourite role during his theatrical life was that of a wave in a merciless sea. It seems that for this purpose the whole host of children crawled under a blue painted canvas of immense size and by dint of each child heaving up and down to his or her heart's content the audience were presented with a wonderful illusion of the trackless ocean. He summed up the

140

experience in the crisp sentence, 'It wasn't 'arf a bloomin' lark'. I quite believed him.

Between rehearsals and performances he and the other children pursued their studies in the schoolroom provided for that purpose at the theatre, and every afternoon Dan Leno and Herbert Campbell treated the assembly to cakes and tea. He regarded Bedfordbury as a kind of village and St Martin's Church, where he attended Sunday-school, as the village church. It seemed that everybody knew everybody in Bedfordbury. He was very proud of his village and his church, and lost no opportunity to remind me that Nell Gwyn and Jack Sheppard were buried in the churchyard. From the Drury Lane Academy he graduated to the Old Mo, and regaled us with brief excerpts from the programme each week. Before coming to us as a junior porter he had been a district messenger, and his adventures in that fascinating occupation in the dead of night, on night duty, were full of meat. It was clear that our employment was only an episode in a promising career. I lost him years before the 1914 war, but I feel confident that he was one of the first in the Flanders trenches.

FREDERICK WILLIS, *A BOOK OF LONDON YESTERDAYS*

In recalling a past so deeply cherished and yet so utterly vanished, Willis is no more than gently fatalistic about his sense of irrevocable loss. Emotional deprivation was felt at a much deeper level, and in a very different way, by a man born out of wedlock in the back streets of Manchester, destined to become the most accomplished autodidact of his generation. Unlike Willis, who enjoyed the music hall as a boy and looked back with sweet regret as a grown man, Neville Cardus was so inclined to the retrospective view that even as a small boy witnessing the miraculous delights of Christmas pantomime, he was acutely conscious of the transcience of what he was witnessing. Sceptics may feel that Cardus the old man, peering down the long corridor of the years at his own young self, was grafting on to the small boy subtleties of perception far beyond the sensibilities of so callow a witness. Anyone who was ever acquainted with Cardus will know this to be untrue. In any case, the sense of time passing, of irrecoverable loss, of the fleeting nature of deep joy, so far from being a metaphysical refinement, is a perfectly commonplace attitude, well enough known to any schoolboy who has ever had his heart pierced by the final whistle at a football match, or to any small girl reduced to tears by the realisation that the ballet has ended. Cardus was a romantic from the day he was born, but he had that duality of vision which told him that the price of the romanticism was a sense of irony which somehow made the romance all the sweeter, the irony of the knockabout comic walking solemnly through the streets on his workaday business unaware that an idolater is dogging his tracks shaking with laughter, of the beauteous heroine who will never know that long after she has packed her bags and moved on to the next engagement, one small street urchin will remain steadfast to her image for the rest of his life. One aspect of his appreciation Cardus certainly did acquire much later, and that was the understanding of what music hall represented, the degree of excellence of its great virtuosi, the grievous loss to national culture when it was all over and done with.

I was not more than twelve years old when I first entered a theatre. It was one of Robert Courtneidge's Christmas pantomimes in Manchester, *Robinson Crusoe*, I think, with Vesta Tilley as the principal boy. I was not 'taken' to this pantomime; I went by myself and watched from the highest gallery in the world. After long waiting in a queue until you would hear the lifting of a bar at the door, you placed your sixpence under a wire-netting, from behind which the girl or woman in charge pressed a lever, and a heavy square deposit of lead came out of a slot. That was your ticket.

The climb to the gallery was arduous, even to an eager boy. Round and round, with acute angles all the way; at every step upwards one's body became more bent on the purpose, the knee action more deliberate, the breath more sternly drawn. Then, at the top of the steps was a dark refreshment bar (not yet opened) to pass through, and now at last the theatre itself was attained. At great distance below was the stage, the curtain alluringly down. To find a front place in the gallery involved some agility and nerve; there were no seats, only long rows of wooden ledges, and to save time and to get there first we did not walk gingerly down a central staircase but leaped from cliff to cliff. We would lean over the rail of the gallery and watch the stalls and pit assembling. Sometimes a programme fluttered down, like a visitant from another hemisphere.

When I write that 'we' would lean over the gallery rail, I am using the 'we' metaphorically; for I went alone to the theatre in my boyhood, as indeed I went alone everywhere, walking through the city streets reading a boy's paper and by some instinct always coming out of my enchantment just in time not to bump against a lamp-post. I do not know how I contrived to get money for admission to the theatre gallery week by week; on one occasion at least I committed petty theft. I stole a volume out of the limited and discursive family library, which comprised *East Lynne*, the Bible, somebody's Dream Book, and one other novel, this by Marion Crawford. The volume I stole was a collection of poems by Coleridge, and I am at a loss to this day to understand how it came to find a place in the household. I took it to a second-hand bookseller's in Oxford Street owned by a man of immeasurable age, who made me think of the Old Testament. His clothes were shiny and he smelt; his name was Coleman; and in his front window, amongst a ruin of ancient literature, was a phrenologist's bust, the head marked into squares like the counties on a map. The interior of the shop was gloomy; piles of books, and the odour of damp and slow decay. There was another Coleman, reputed to be a son, with skin of vellum and eyes tightly stuck together by what my fearful imagination visualised as blindness.

Coleman senior looked at the Coleridge, rumbled in his stomach, and offered me a shilling. I took it and fled straight up the brow of Oxford Street, under the railway arch, past the corner shop with birds in cages around the door and gold-fish in globes in the window. It was Saturday afternoon; there was a pantomime matinée. It may have been the sale of Coleridge that enabled me to see Ada Reeve as Aladdin, G.P. Huntley as Widow Twankey, and Horace Mills as Abanazar. I did not go to the pantomime in the innocence of most boys of ten or eleven years old. In those days boys and girls were not encouraged to enter a theatre at all in a provincial English city; the pantomimes of the period were severely sophisticated in their outlook both towards the particular theme of *Cinderella* or *The Forty Thieves* and towards life in general. Maggie Duggan and George Robey occasioned much concern in the councils of the Manchester Watch Committee, protectors of public morals. There was also a suspicion in many families that theatres were peculiarly combustible and likely to catch fire; in brief, for a boy to set foot in a theatre alone was thought a certain means sooner or later either of going to the devil or of being burnt alive. The danger to my morals seldom occurred to me, but frequently I felt a vague apprehensiveness when I stood looking down over the gallery rail on the delights below, forbidden delights, delights deceitfully enjoyed; for I always lied whenever I was asked where I had been when I got home again. Electricity was more or less a new and experimental department of science forty years ago; and Robert Courtneidge invariably brought the first part of his pantomime to an end by a long 'transformation' scene, in which furnaces of magnificences were unfolded as one flimsy gauze curtain after another ascended on high, beginning with the narrowest strip of the stage on which the Fairy Queen stood, in company with the principal boy; and she would wave her wand saying:

> And now Aladdin take me by the hand
> And I will show you all the joys of Fairyland.

Opalescent deeps of the sea; caves of turquoise and rubies; apocalyptic sunrises and radiance of every boy's dream of the Arabian Nights, all accumulating in a lavish expense of electricity. It was with an amount of relief that one witnessed at the apotheosis a temporary lowering of the fireproof curtain.

As I say, I did not attend my pantomimes in the innocence of childhood; the fairy-tale basis of a pantomime had for me but a secondary interest. I marked the distinction between Robinson Crusoe and the principal boy who happened to be playing the part; I knew that Abanazar was Horace Mills, and once when I saw Horace Mills walking in a Manchester Street looking exactly like any man of business wearing gloves and a bowler hat, I followed secretly behind him and laughed to myself at his every movement though he did nothing that was the slightest bit funny off the stage. Ada Reeve was Aladdin one year; I remember that when she couldn't remember the world 'Abracadabra', and she realised she was locked in the cave more or less for ever, she immediately consoled herself and the rest of us by singing 'Good-bye, Dolly Gray', the popular song of the Boer War. But the point is that she didn't sing the chorus but spoke it, in a husky dramatic monotone. This was revolutionary; this was new method. The cognoscenti in the dress circle, I was informed years afterwards, were taken aback, and they shook their heads until by force of art Ada Reeve conquered a lifetime's principles. Round about this time of my life I saw Ada Reeve in *Floradora* the very week after the last performance of the pantomime; and pantomime ran from Christmas to Easter; and now she was a fashionable society darling, in a big brimmed hat, and she sang a song called 'Tact' in front of a row of long-trousered top-hatted young men with silver-mounted walking sticks. One week Aladdin's cave and the splendour of the Orient, but in a few evenings it had all gone. Now, living and moving and having being on the same boards, walking in the same places where Widow Twankey and Abanazar had shaken the theatre into reckless and eternal laughter, were elegance and romance in a setting of tea-planters or what not; palm trees and deodar, and the melodies of Leslie Stuart. The palimpsest of the stage! I didn't know of such a word but I remember a sudden feeling of sadness coming to my eyes when, once at a pantomime somebody sang 'Is your Mammy always with you?' and as I looked at the singer's movements in the round circles of limelight that followed her, throwing two dancing shadows, the thought came to my mind that some day somebody else would perhaps be dancing on the same spot, and all would have become different; all would then be new and this would be forgotten long ago.

The old pantomimes observed a strict set of unities; the identity and comparative importance of the author of the 'book' – as it was called – was recognised. The 'book' was composed mainly in rhymed couplets, more or less heroic, uttered by the Demon (or Storm) King:

> Ride on thou proud and saucy ship
> But soon I'll have this Crusoe in my grip.

These lines were invariably pronounced at the beginning of Act I in Davy Jones's Locker, which was a drop-scene calling for merely what Mrs Gamp would have called a 'parapidge' of stage. The Demon King was a baritone, and the chances might be that we had last heard him on the pier in August at Southend singing the 'Bedouin Love Song' with the pierrots. Now in a more dramatic environment under the sea and in the dark he probably struck a deeper and more ambitious vocal note; 'Rage thou angry storm' from Balfe was not beyond the dream of possibility.

An inviolate decree held that in the programmes of classical pantomime the dramatis personae and the cast should be denoted and set forth in a running

143

parenthesis of wit, such as: 'Mrs Sinbad (who has sin-badder days) ... George Robey.'

From the murky element of the Storm King we would be changed in the twinkling of an eye to Pekin (maybe); or if the pantomime were of the occident the scene would be the village green outside the 'Bull and Bush'. It was in Scene 2 that the pantomime really began and the stalls filled up. The Storm King didn't appear again for hours, or the Fairy Queen. I often wondered what they were doing all the time. In Scene 2 the important personages of the pantomime made their appearance in order of renown. The Baron (or the Emperor) was allowed to hold the centre of the stage for a few minutes; perhaps he was even given a song, but nobody listened to him; he was merely a part of the connived plot of suspense. First came the principal girl – Amy Augarde or even Gertie Millar; then the more substantial principal boy (the best of all was Ada Blanche); and the principal boy would dash down the footlights and embrace the principal girl, kicking his left leg backwards as he did so.

At last, when the 'House Full' boards were put up in the theatre's main entrances – terrible to see if you were outside in the fog trying to catch a glimpse of something behind the brilliant lights of the *foyer* – now was the moment: the stage was left significantly vacant for a brief pause. From the wings came sounds of brawl and derision and racket. And the Dame would arrive in some state of dishevelment, out of breath, having, for some reason never explained, been chased. Dan Leno or Robey or Harry Randall or Wilkie Bard – it might be any of them! – in elastic-sided boots, hair parted straight down the middle and tied in a bun, towards which the right hand would absent-mindedly stray when she came down the stage and spoke to us intimately about 'Her First' and of the vicissitudes of matrimony. An incomparable school of great English comic-actors created a Dickensian gallery of Dames. The greatest of them was Robey's 'Mother Goose', who swerved from the unities of pantomime in her entrance to that most matchless of all pantomimes at the Manchester Theatre Royal, Christmas, 1904; and I saw it many times before it vanished into air the following March.

The scene was Mother Goose's cottage, and the Landlord had called for the rent. George Bastow was Mother Goose's son, and he endeavoured to keep the enemy at bay. (All landlords in our pantomimes and melodramas were enemies, as a matter of democratic course.) 'The rent was not paid last week, or the week before, or the week before,' raged the tyrant; 'this is the last straw and final notice. Into the streets you all go!' At this moment George Robey appeared, bland, with kindly recognition, wiping imaginary soap-suds from the hands on an apron. 'Ah, there you are, landlord,' said Mother Goose in Robey's fruitiest voice; '*there* you are – such a lot wants doing to the house!'

It was in this same pantomime that George Robey held the stage for half an hour (while the scene-shifters were noisy and active behind a drop-scene, often causing it to bulge from contact with some royal dome or pinnacle) and created the immortal Mrs Moggeridge, a next-door neighbour, who, because never seen, has lived for ever. Robey came on from the side of the stage in a condition of agitation, fingers twitching, nose sniffing. He cast glances to the direction whence he had entered; they were glances poignant with contumely and injured pride. Simmering a little, but still on the boil, he folded arms, gave another toss of his head sideways and said, simply but obliquely. 'Mrs Moggeridge!' Nothing more than her name to begin with, but the intonation, with a descent of pitch at 'ridge', was contemptuous. Then he bent to us over the footlights, and in a sudden hysteria of ridicule, stated (or rather he conveyed) this information: 'Fairy Queen in a Christmas pantomime!' After another snort and a pause he added, in a voice pitched to a deeper note of irony, 'Her!'

Satisfaction and triumph here became evident in Robey's eyes and gestures; but suddenly he stiffened, and the neck was thrust again towards Mrs Moggeridge's garden wall, whence obviously some Parthian thrust had been aimed. 'And what of it?' asked Robey, the voice rising in mingled menace, disdain and clear conscience. 'What of if?' (pronounced 'What arvert').

Speculation sought in vain to deduce the nature of Mrs Moggeridge's innuendo that it should have compelled this final bridling and this unanswerable fiat. Enough to say that after the pronouncement of it Mrs Moggeridge was heard no more. It is hard to believe we did not actually hear her or see her; there wasn't never indeed 'no sich a person'; it was a conjuration of comic art.

Robey was a master of tantrums, or in other circumstances, of spasms. In *Jack and the Beanstalk,* when Jack returned home with beans for the sale of the cow, Robey as the Dame achieved an awe-inspiring expression of twitching incredulity, woe and mortification, all evenly blended. He (or she) hurled the beans through the window, and at once the stalk began to grow upward. Robey caught sight of it out of the corner of his eyes as he was suffering another wave of distress. And he began to giggle, to experience hysteria ... but no words can describe this masterpiece of comic acting. It was done by imaginative absorption into a character and a scene; and here is the difference between the old great pantomime comedians of my youth and the comedians of to-day, who get their laughs by the things they say and are not funny in themselves, and are certainly not actors. Robey and Leno and Wilkie Bard and Little Tich and Harry Weldon were most nights in the year performers in the music hall, red-nosed and holding an audience for three-quarters of an hour, holding the theatre single-handed, with song and patter; and from time to time they would leave the stage to return as a new character – Robey's Lord Mayor of Muckemdyke, Leno's pathetic little Cockney just married, the victim of a building society; he had bought a house, and he leant over the footlights to tell us in husky confidence of his pride of possession. It was a nice house, with the river at the bottom of the garden; that is, when the garden wasn't at the bottom of the river. But I must use a platitude now; it was not what these old drolls said, it was the way they said it. Little Tich, breathing on his tall hat before giving it a rub round with his elbow, made a noise that emptied his lungs, fraught with bronchitis. Gusto and faith in a complete surrender to extravagance; no smart-cracks but natural nonsense – as when the Ugly Sisters in *Cinderella,* having been refused admission at the ball, Tom Foy said to Malcolm Scott, 'Let's walk in backwards and they'll think we're coming out.' It was these comedians of the music hall who peopled our memories of pantomime with a gallery of Dames, each as rich in identity as Betsy Prig and Mrs Gamp and the nurse in *Romeo and Juliet.*

The convention of pantomime persisted that the Dame and her son should begin poor and end wealthy. All the good characters, in fact, shared ample fortune as a reward of virtue; and during the last scene they came before us most opulently garbed – Robey's magnificence was like a fantastic dream or apotheosis of a riotously lunatic Schiaparelli. The lesser male luminaries of the show, Idle Jack or Tinbad the Tailor, would wear terrific check suits with huge buttons of gold, and their choice in walking sticks was *rococo.* Nobody was harshly treated in this last of all the pantomime's consummations of glory and electricity; even the Demon King received a burst of applause when he appeared, apparently a reformed character, in morning-coat and grey topper. And the children crowed their delight as the Cat came on for his share of the general recognition and acclamation, wearing a fur coat most likely.

Then the final chorus and the last ruthless descent of the curtain. Nothing left but the return to the world, to find oneself again in the streets outside, where life had been going on just the same on a winter day; it was dark now, with the gas-lamps burning, and when we had entered in realms of gold it had been afternoon and broad daylight.

In the street at the back of the Manchester Theatre Royal was a long narrow door through which the scenery was carried to the stage. At night I would go there, when nobody was looking, and peep through the slit and try to catch the glimpse of the

145

magic interior. I would hear the pantomime in the distance, the laughter and the striking up of the band; and I knew exactly what was happening at this moment – Daisy Jerome was coming on to the stage as a Dutch girl in sabots and stamping them with stiff ankles and singing something about diamonds in Amsterdam, Amsterdam, Amsterdam. I knew the pantomime word- and music-perfect, with all the patter and action, so that on any afternoon or evening wherever I happened to be – probably walking the Manchester streets – I could follow any performance and live in it by proxy, so to say. As I mumbled to myself and imitated Robey's eyebrows and bulging cheeks, I was probably regarded by passers-by as an idiot boy.

Joy beyond the dream of avarice came to me when I obtained a job selling chocolates in the Comedy Theatre, where Eugene Stratton was Pete the page-boy in *Cinderella*. Every afternoon at two o'clock, every evening at seven, for three months – and I could see it all for nothing, in fact was actually paid a few shillings weekly. I would ply my trade until the curtain rose, then stand at the side of the pit, my tray still strapped over my shoulders, and as time went on I acquired a professional casualness even to the point of leaving the auditorium during certain of the less momentous scenes, and going to the bar to count my proceeds and replenish stock in time for the interval. I would contemplate the audience, the majority of them new to the show, with the tolerance of the 'deadhead' towards the *dilettante;* if the principal boy happened to be below her best form I could put a proper value on loose uninstructed applause.

I was actually spoken to once by Eugene Stratton, who came through a door covered with green baize into the front of the theatre after a matinée. He wore a tweed overcoat and a soft hat and he called me 'Sonny'. He was a little man with a careworn but kindly face, and he had about him a strange odour of limelight and Havana cigar. It was in this pantomime that Stratton presented his 'scena' of the negro horse thief, 'I may be crazy, but I love you.' 'So won't you come right here and say good-bye, bekase I may not see you any more.' He stood with his slouch hat hanging down from his right hand, looking at the bedroom window of the shack where his lady-love dwelt; he lifted himself slightly on tip-toe to get his high notes.

When at last the pantomime came to an end winter was changing to spring. On the Monday following the last performance on a Saturday night, I was a wandering spirit. The theatre was closed, and I walked about the streets, melancholy in the twilight. The cloud-capped towers and the gorgeous palaces, the great globe itself, had dissolved. The principal girl, whose portrait on a post-card I had carried in my pocket since Christmas, until the edges frayed, was far away in London, rehearsing for a George Edwardes' musical comedy. Stratton was top of the bill at the Hippodrome in Newcastle. The Fairy Queen had returned to her home in Balham, where her invalid mother lived. On the front page of *The Era* was a brief statement to the effect that the Demon King was 'resting' in Acacia Road or Maida Vale.

Pain which I could not define came into my heart and stomach when I wondered where at this very minute all the scattered glories might chance to be. The dispersion of forces brought together, God knows how, for a moment! – no, I was not sophisticated enough to understand this ironic flavour in my boyish sense of loss, as the old pantomimes dispersed, or whenever school broke up and the playing-fields stood empty in the evening's afterglow and I thought of all I had known there only a day or two since, and everybody somewhere in a void to-night.

So with the high galleries of the theatres from which I looked down and experienced hours of happiness which, while they were passing, cheated us into believing they were far beyond the touch of time. Absorbed in pleasure, the romance and tinsel of the stage entering the mind and blood like a medieval chemist's magic distillation. Applause that came from rapture and love – for we loved those that played for us week by week. And at the last night we sang from gallery and pit and circle and stalls 'Shall Auld Acquaintance be Forgot'; and Mother Goose and the Demon King and her son Jack and the Principal Boy and the Baron and the Fairy

Queen held crossed hands and jerked them to the tune's rhythm, before the last inexorably obliterating curtain.

After one such farewell I went the next evening into a Manchester park, and sat on a bench and tried to read a book. My imagination winged the entire face of England looking and listening. Then the bell tolled, announcing the time for the closing of the gates, and the pathways became misty and vacant and I heard the park-keeper's cry 'All out, all out!' From another direction came echoes: 'All out, all out!' In the smouldering Manchester sunset I tried to see the symbol of London and all its lights; Shaftesbury Avenue and Leicester Square – and Drury Lane itself, where the Christmas pantomime was even yet, in late March, running twice daily, though the boards were up announcing the 'Last Weeks', and the confectioners' shop windows were already full of Easter eggs.

NEVILLE CARDUS, *SECOND INNINGS*

Willis and Cardus, the hatter and the aesthete, members of the same generation, have only one thing in common, a conviction that the apparently casual art of the music hall has given them something they might not have found anywhere else, a celebration of the vitality of the working classes, a sublimation of the humours of mean streets. Of the two, Willis was a little closer to the reality of music hall life, being blessed with one or two family connections with the performers, and also, it seems, rather good at insinuating himself into the company of the artists. Yet again he conveys the sense of an art form picking up and then gently replacing ordinary people for service on the stage. He also discloses the way that dynastic tendencies occasionally began in the old halls. His friendship with a long-forgotten but once well-known Demon King has built a bridge across which the recollections can advance further forward into the age of Noël Coward.

English pantomime may not be very great theatrical fare but it is unique, having no parallel in any other country. A Canadian variety artist said on the radio that she could not understand why the principal boy in pantomime is so obviously a girl, and claimed that her own children resented this position. That is the whole point. From my youngest days I always knew the principal boy was a girl, and far from resenting it I revelled in it. I remember that the experiment of having a man for principal boy was tried once at Drury Lane with disastrous results. Nobody liked it. A principal boy has to be dashing and fairy-like. No man could do this in pantomime without being ridiculous, and to have a ridiculous principal boy is opposed to all tradition. I like to think English pantomime is a survival of the ancient Roman Saturnalia, a time of wild revelry and a reversal of the order of things; a time when intelligence is put in cold storage. After all, the Romans were here for four centuries and perhaps England, isolated by the sea from the Continent, holds or held more of the spirit of that great race than any other country.

The Crown Theatre, which I have mentioned before, produced some gorgeous pantomimes, and, as with all pantomimes, originality in jokes (unless they were topical) was discouraged. I remember one writer of pantomime books who so specialised in ancient jokes that even the management protested. He defended himself by saying, 'Look here! That joke has always raised a laugh as long as I remember, so in it goes!' One particular scene represented, according to the

147

programme, 'Camberwell Green in the Olden Times'. It was very beautiful and the curtain went up on an empty stage to give the audience a chance to absorb its beauty. To a subdued chorus of 'Oooooh! Isn't it lovely!' the orchestra played soft music and simulated bird song, and then two rustic characters appeared, and after gaping around in admiration the comedienne gasped, 'It IS lovely! So romanteek and pictureskew!' This step from the sublime to the ridiculous raised a good laugh, but my grandmother told me this was a stage joke of her girlhood. Of course in the kitchen scene there was the usual slapping about of paste and flour, and Alderman Fitzwarren entered in time to stop a great dollop of wet dough with his face. This, and the resounding slap, gave me great satisfaction and I am happy to say still does. Then there was the well-established wash-tub scene in which the dame, busily engaged in washing clothes, fishes out an intimate garment of women's underwear and hurriedly pops it back again, while Alderman Fitzwarren, standing by, says impatiently, 'Don't show them, you old fool – put them back and hum – HUM to show indifference!'

When 'A Little Bit off the Top' was the song of the year, I remember one first night at the Crown pantomime when, in response to the enthusiasm of the audience at the conclusion, the manager appeared to offer his thanks. He was a tall, dignified man, slightly bald on top, and as he stood before the applauding audience he made an imposing appearance. Unfortunately he was no speaker and the enthusiasm had unnerved him. He stammered a few unintelligible words, but Marie Lloyd, standing just behind, was instantly alive to the situation. She tripped forward, said a word to the musical conductor, and then with that arch look of impudence for which she was famous, reached up and tapped the manager on his bald pate with the words, 'Just a little bit off the top!' Instantly the orchestra started the tune, and no speech the manager could have made would have brought the incident to a more satisfactory conclusion.

Marie Lloyd was always principal boy at the Crown, but at Drury Lane she was always principal girl. At the Crown she had a first-class company to support her, and among the lesser lights was Arthur Lawrence. He was Demon King for years at this theatre, and being a bass singer was usually billed as 'A bold bad Demon with a (bass) voice in everything'. He delighted us with 'Asleep in the Deep' and other old favourites, and held us spellbound as he descended lower and lower down the musical scale. When he reached rock bottom he breathed a sigh of relief. In those days I rejoiced in the acquaintance of theatrical folk and I had many a drink with Arthur (he loved a drink!). He was very thin, very active, and very social, and always had a new story. None of us had much hope that he would ever reach the top rank, but farther still from our thoughts was the fact that his daughter, then waiting in the wings of time to be born, would get her name in the big lights of London and New York as the justly acclaimed Gertrude Lawrence. The last time I saw Arthur was in the Strand, when he told me he was among the choristers at the new Coliseum, a novel and short-lived feature of that house in its early days.

The chorus girls of the Crown were drawn mostly from local talent. The qualifications required were a good figure, a good voice, a pretty face, and a brain – in that order. When we boys saw the chorus in all its glory of tights and tinsel, when we hear them sing 'The Honeysuckle and the Bee', we felt that life had no more to offer. After the last performance of the season the management gave a supper to the whole company and their selected friends, and in the true spirit of Saturnalia the stars waited upon the company. I remember Marie Lloyd as an active and attentive waitress radiating good fellowship. It was a riotous evening, and as supper never started before midnight it was a case of going home with the milk in the morning, but as the festival was always on Saturday night this did not inconvenience me at all.

FREDERICK WILLIS, *A BOOK OF LONDON YESTERDAYS*

It is revealing that the song 'The Honeysuckle and the Bee' figures so potently in so many reminiscences. As a small boy Charlie Chaplin came home to his mother's rooms in Lambeth one Saturday night to find the place deserted and the larder bare. Unable to endure the silence in the rooms, he went out into the street and sat on the kerb near the house in case one of the family should turn up. By midnight nobody had appeared, and all the lights had gone out except those of the chemist and the pubs. The boy felt hopeless and wretched.

Suddenly there was music. Rapturous! It came from the vestibule of the White Hart corner pub, and resounded brilliantly in the empty square. The tune was 'The Honeysuckle and the Bee', played with radiant virtuosity on a harmonium and clarinet. I had never been conscious of melody before, but this one was beautiful and lyrical, so blithe and gay, so warm and reassuring. I forgot my despair and crossed the road to where the musicians were. The harmonium player was blind, with scarred sockets where the eyes had been; and a besotted, embittered face played the clarinet. It was all over too soon, and their exit left the night even sadder.

CHARLIE CHAPLIN, *AUTOBIOGRAPHY*

The genesis of the song is unusual. Written in 1901 by the lyricist Albert H. Fitz and the composer William H. Penn, it became popular overnight when sung by Ellaline Terris in *Bluebell in Fairyland*, a children's musical about a London flower-girl who has assorted adventures with the Little Folk. The poignancy of Chaplin's recollection may be compromised slightly by the fact that he was twelve years old before the song was written, thirteen before it became popular, and yet his recollection of the blind harmonium player is placed when he was some years younger. But there is certainly poetic truth in his story, because 'The Honeysuckle and the Bee' does possess that quality which is indefinable but which Chaplin gets close to when he talks of its melody being 'reassuring'. What was odd about the song was that having achieved such felicity the team of Fitz and Penn should never have struck again. An explanation was forthcoming only with the death of a distinguished American political hack called Sol Bloom, who had for twelve years been Chairman of the Foreign Relations Committee of the United States House of Representatives. Bloom had apparently written 'The Honeysuckle and the Bee' when in his early twenties and acquired a lifetime's income from it as Albert H. Fitz. The 'H' in that name never stood for anything. Neither, it appears, did Bloom. Among other surprising contexts in which the song appears is Robert Tressell's 'The Ragged-Trousered Philanthropists', in which some workmen render it as part of an impromptu singsong, no doubt for that reassuring quality in its structure which Chaplin mentions. No enduring song ever enjoyed a long life with a more insubstantial lyric.

You are my honey, honeysuckle,
I am the bee.
I'd like to sip the honey sweet from those red lips, you see.
I love you dearly, dearly, and I want you to love me,
You are my honey, honeysuckle, I am the bee.

In due course, a new generation of popular songs duplicated with striking preciseness the sentiments of Albert H. Fitz with 'Honeysuckle Rose', by Thomas 'Fats' Waller and a nephew of the Queen of Madagascar called Andreamenentania Paul Razafinkeriefo, professional name Andy Razav. As for Fred Willis, at least once the glittering enchantment of the halls lapped at the very doors of his life. Artists in those days often sustained a precarious career through the exercise of some small talent. In the case of Willis's aunt, this talent was so small as to be very nearly non-existent. Its saving grace was that although small, it was very loud. The aunt is another instance of one generation of performers begetting a second.

One of my theatrical aunts, Aunt Bess, was, I heard later, the best screamer on the English stage. She flourished in touring companies, where screamers were valuable, and we received her letters from the most unlikely places. She was a plump, jolly woman with a comely, florid face and comfortable figure that must have looked very well over the footlights. She had a daughter much older than myself who made her theatrical debut in *Constantinople* at Olympia, where she was one of the nymphs who appeared and danced at various stages of the show and sustained the characters of English, Spanish and Turkish beauties in the various scenes. I was taken to the show, which at that time was the talk of London, and I was dazzled with the splendour of it all, although I failed to identify my cousin. She was a very pretty girl with charming manners, and I fell in love with her even at that tender age. I felt quite cut up years afterwards when she married a sergeant in the Scots Guards and went abroad, and so out of my life.

FREDERICK WILLIS, *A BOOK OF LONDON YESTERDAYS*

Another enchanted beggar at the music-hall feast was Thomas Burke, a product of the working-class courts of South London. As a lad around the turn of the century, his modest aspirations echo strongly the sentiments of Willis's hypothetical Londoner. He dreamed of one day rising to the eminence of a clerk's stool in the City, wearing stand-up collars and a frock-coat, living in a six-room house with a small garden, and able to afford occasional visits to the theatre – and then, Burke tells himself, 'the other boys at the Board School would look up to me'. None of this was Burke's eventual fate. By educating himself at the local library, and by persecuting magazine editors with a doggedness which eventually broke their resistance, he rose to the precarious independence of free-lance journalism, publishing novels, volumes of short stories, reviews and essays. Today he is totally forgotten except for a book of lurid short stories about London's Chinese community,

Limehouse Nights, one of which, *Broken Blossoms,* enjoyed world currency as a motion picture in Silent days. Unlucky in love and never a part of any literary coterie, Burke developed into an opinionated sentimentalist for whom all the olden days were golden days. He remained passionately in love with London all his life, and came to know the back-stage intricacies of the music hall rather better than most of its celebrants, as we shall see. For the moment we find him reminiscing about the deep joy he found in the halls in the opening years of the century.

My chief recreation at that time, next to reading, was the music hall, and I spent many an evening, not at the local Imperial Palace nor at the Alhambra or Empire, but at the Tivoli, the Oxford and the London Pavilion. There one could see in one evening, for a matter of two shillings, eighteen or twenty stars. One could see Ernest Shand with his grotesque curates; Chirgwin, the White-Eyed Kaffir, who was as Cockney as Camberwell; Sam Mayo, the Immobile One; Gus Elen, with his coster songs; Marie Lloyd, who was Marie Lloyd; George Robey, who was George Robey; Mark Sheridan, with bell-bottomed trousers and French stove-pipe hat; T.E. Dunville, a sort of Saturday-night back-street pierrot; Phil Ray, with spluttered songs made up of abbreviated words; Harry Tate, with his adventures in Motoring, Golfing or Fishing presented in dishevelled sketches of everyday life shot with lucid intervals of lunacy; Ella Retford with her Lancashire-Irish songs; Wilkie Bard creating a world of his own in which nothing could be taken for granted; Dutch Daly with a concertina and a stream of stories; Harry Lauder, who was Harry Lauder; Cinquevalli, who turned juggling into poetry; George Mozart, with shrill, acid sketches of types from any suburban High Street; Little Tich, who was indescribable; Vesta Tilley with her young-men characters; the American R.G. Knowles, with the husky voice and the machine-gun hail of broad anecdote – all these you could see in one bill, in the circle for two shillings, in the pit for a shilling, and in the gallery for sixpence.

From those evenings of grotesquerie I caught again the thrill of contact with real life that I had found in those moments of my childhood. It was not the real life of the poets and musicians, but it was more alive than anything in the routine of streets and houses. It held the essence of man's daily war with all the things that are against his realisation of dignity and godship; his circumstances, his clothes, his furniture, his appetites, his friends, all were shown as conspiring against him, tripping and impeding every approach to his noble estate just below the angels. In all that apparent idiocy, behind all those macabre masks, was the passion of life itself, felt and lived. In the angels and arabesques of that contorted world I found more truth than in the theatre or the street. Under the lunatic jargon of the songs and the monstrous costumes was a logic not of intellect but of poetry, drawn from the midnight deeps of the subconscious. When the music halls died I lost a source of delight. Nothing of the kind is to be had today. Our deliberately 'crazy' comedians and 'crazy' shows, imitations of American vaudeville, have nothing of the true, native, spontaneous lunacy. You cannot reduce logic to the irrational or carry lunacy to the height of sense by deliberation; it must spring, as it did from those older men, from life and habit.

THOMAS BURKE, *SON OF LONDON*

Burke's view of the music-hall stage is strikingly similar to that of Cardus; neither man ever tired of returning again and again to the theme of the Empires and Palaces of their lost youth. In both cases there was much of the modern world which came in for heavy punishment for having banished so felicitous a form of popular entertainment. Burke never had much time for the glossy Americanised commercial cinema which so completely obliterated the Halls. Cardus went much further, so exulting in the triumphant assertion of will inherent in the lives of the great music-hall artists that he lost his balance somewhat and concluded that because a few exceptional people – like himself – had overcome all the frightful economic and social obstacles standing in the way of a career in the arts, then it was grossly unfair for the state to have deprived future generations of that same triumph by helping them. In old age Cardus' glowing recollection of the halls encompasses the unintentionally comic incongruity of a slashing attack on the Welfare State.

In my youth, around 1905, the music hall was abundant, a mirror held up to the life and habits of the nation, notably reflecting the joys, trials and domestic frustrations of the 'lower classes'. In every large city a Moss and Stolls Empire or Hippodrome was erected. The old Victorian variety saloon, with its affable, loquacious 'Chairman', became obsolete; into these new Empires and Hippodromes of plush and gilt, the family could respectably venture; comparatively venture, that is to say. There would be for them to view the presence and wink of Marie Lloyd, the 'Flossie' of the period in apotheosis, as though leaning over the gold bar of Heaven, beer-pumps of Paradise beside her. She would sing and tell us that 'our lodger's such a nice young man, a nice young man he is, so kind, so good to all our familee; he's never going to leave us, oh dear, oh dear, no. He's so sweet, so very sweet, – mother tells me so.' All sung and acted with glances and gestures of unprintable imputations. George Robey, eyebrows admonishing; Eugene Stratton, 'coon' singer, with his husky voice, dancing on air and haunting our ears with 'Little Dolly Daydream' and 'Lily of Laguna', melodies still in the air. Only yesteryear I heard 'Lily of Laguna', sung in the near distance, wafted over the moonlit water, as the liner I was voyaging in was anchored outside Colombo, and I leant over the ship's side.

There was Cinquevalli juggling with heavy (or they looked heavy) cannon balls; there was the funny man, supposed to be a waiter in a restaurant, who came on the stage carrying a terrific pile of plates. He held the plates in his hands, trying to keep them in position with pressure from his chin. He swayed this way, that way. The plates wriggled, describing a mark of interrogation. Then they crashed, split asunder, to the exalted liberation of our born, innate and tyrannical regard for order and the eternal fitness of things; also, at the same time, liberating the imp of destruction residing in everybody worthwhile. The funny waiter, after contemplating the wreckage of pottery minutely, extricated a hammer from his coat-tails and proceeded to smash each plate that had somehow escaped intact from the general destruction.

Every week we would, towards Friday, look at the hoardings in Manchester to find out what allurements had been conjured for us next Monday and following nights. The music-hall announcements on the hoardings contained three decisive classifications; top of the bill, middle of the bill and bottom of the bill. Top and bottom were representative, or indicative, of performers supposedly possessing equal powers of box-office attraction. I have known music-hall posters heralding Robey at the top of the bill, with Wilkie Bard or Gertie Gitana at the bottom. Yet between 'top' and 'bottom' there was some subtle, almost feudalistic difference; Robey, Vesta Tilley, Little Tich never were names at the bottom. The nomination for the 'middle' of the bill usually referred to some talent potential enough to remain for a time being weighed in the balance, in a sort of purgatory of public esteem.

Little Tich! His name was really Relph and, I believe, he had some French blood in him. He was small in physical stature, but he did not exploit dwarfish traits. He wore long, flapping boots, over which he would lean as he took the audience into his confidence. He presumed baldness, sported a bow tie and a top, shiny hat, upon which he would breathe, then polish with a sleeve. And, as he breathed, he would advertise his bronchitis. Like most of his famous contemporary comedians, Robey, Weldon, George Formby and Harry Tate, Tich was an actor; he did not set out obviously 'to be funny'. He did not, in the manner of most latter day T.V. comedians, laugh at his own humour. In fact, the T.V. comedians are usually the first to laugh. And Tich, and the rest of the music-hall makers of fun, did not use a microphone. Imagine Robey reprimanding an audience via microphone: 'Desist! I am not here as a source of public flippancy. I'm surprised at *you,* Ag-er-nes!' Only to think of Stratton gliding over the boards as though bodilessly thrown by the limelight; only to think of him, microphoned, singing 'Little Dolly Daydream, pride of Idaho – to think thus is blasphemy of cherished memories. Tich, like his colleagues, was essentially serious; the laughter he provoked came as a by-product of an accurately observed impersonation of life.

I remember his presentation of a prosecuting counsel, bewigged and gowned, ironically obsequious before the court, unctuous in speech with 'M'luds', and grappling with briefs and precedents. He had charm, a common characteristic of the comedians of his period. Whenever he took a curtain he would bow quickly and capaciously over his extended boots, and his bow would be so suddenly grateful and acknowledging that he would knock himself out as his bald head collided with the stage. Once I laughed at him so convulsively that I fell off my seat at a pantomime at the Manchester Palace theatre (I confess I was then only ten years old). Tich was one of the Ugly Sisters in *Cinderella,* and they had not received tickets of invitation for the ball. A flunkey attendant refused them admission. In a swift burst of inspiration, Tich said: 'I know! – let's walk in backwards, and they'll think we're coming out.'

Wilkie Bard, as a charwoman, came down the stage, carrying a bucket of soapsuds and a cleaning cloth. He went down on his (or her) knees, and made a wide wet circle on the floor with the cloth, indicating the immediate sphere of the cleansing operations. Then, suddenly, he would rise from her knees, come before the footlights, and announce by song, in a soft contralto voice, that 'I want to sing in Opera', thus confiding in us a lofty but natural ambition.

Harry Tate, as a 'city' man, came bustling into his office, moustaches working rapidly, and saying to the staff: 'Good morning, good morning, good morning!' 'No letters this morning?' he said. 'Very well, then; we must write some.' All done very seriously and not apparently conscious of an audience.

There is only one comedian alive today, as I write on Sunday, January 25, 1970, who could go into the company of the masters of the high-noon of the music hall. He is Frankie Howerd. Maybe I should add the names of Harry Worth and Al Read.

George Formby (senior) certainly mingled with the greatest depicters of Lancashire character and climate of the 'depression' years. He was Lowry in advance of Lowry, pale of face, scarecrow thin, muffler and shapeless clothes covering his undernourished frame. Probably his major meal at night before bedtime, as a boy, had been 'pobs'; to produce 'pobs' a thick round of white loaf was cut into cubes and put into a basin. Tea was then poured into it, with sugar and condensed milk added, the whole of these constituents churned by a spoon into a congested mess, nicely calculated to keep hunger at bay till morning – as I can well testify. George Formby would come on to the stage tentatively, look around and find the conductor of the music-hall orchestra, find him rather to his surprise. 'Good evn'in', Alf', he would say, adding, 'Ah'm a bit tight on chest tonight, but Ah think Ah can mannidge.' The voice quavered as it put up the fight. Laughter contested pathos. He would sing that he was standing at the corner of the street, starry-eyed, hoping for romance in the guise of a blonde. When he danced it was as though he was recurrently seized by dizziness and weakness of the legs. As I say, Lowry pre-Lowry. Lowry himself emerged from the Lancashire scene which Formby made visible. Lowry knocked at doors, as I did, trying to sell insurance burial policies to slum denizens who could hardly afford to keep alive.

Welfare State! Grants for students of art, literature and culture in general? R. H. Spring sold evening newspapers in a Welsh town when he was at school in the daytime, supporting a widowed mother. Who writes and paints for us now, knowing anything fundamental about life at the bone? University dons who have never sung 'Lily of Laguna', or avidly eaten (or drunk) 'pobs', or stood at the corner of the street, tight on chest, but dreaming dreams of escape?

Every night, up and down the land, these old-time comedians had to hold the attention of vast audiences by means of individual talent and presence, and by their own unmicrophoned voices. And the audiences in the Empires, Tivolis, Palaces and Hippodromes could be brutal in response. Pennies were thrown from the galleries to the stage occupied by some lonely, pitiful, incompetent performer. I have myself thrown an egg at an unfunny comedian in the Tivoli theatre, once situated in Peter Street, Manchester. A small company of us boys, housed in bathless, unlavatoried houses in Rusholme and Moss Side, would go to the Tivoli gallery. We saved weekly from our earnings as carriers and fetchers, handcart pullers, sub-clerks, newspaper sellers in the streets; and before invading the Tivoli, we 'clubbed' our financial assets and bought a supply of eggs, sharing them equitably. In those days there were, as Dan Leno (greatest of comedians next to Charlie Chaplin) pointed out, three categories of eggs: new laid, fresh – and eggs. It was an 'egg' that I threw at the unfunny man on the stage of the Manchester Tivoli Theatre in 1905; and I hit him in his middle-stump with a brilliant throw from long-on in the gallery.

The three greatest comedians, Chaplin, Leno and George Formby (senior), shared the secret of mingling pathos with comic appeal; each showed us the 'little' man, the product of an un-affluent State, rich as Croesus or poor as church mice, according to the position in life to which one had been called, so we were clerically informed, by God. The 'little man' looking for some sign of romantic colour in his encircling drabness of environment, waiting and waiting, catching a glimpse; then, like Chaplin in his first 'silent' and most cherishable showings, departing to the distance, alone, shoulders hunched and depressed until, suddenly, he flicked his cane, thrust one foot outward, as another romantic hope stirred him.

If the comedian, or music-hall performer of any kind, did not have true powers of the actor, he was soon herded among the 'middle of the bill' mediocrities. As I say, Chaplin, Leno and Formby could be humanly touching. At the extreme of these was Grock, an entirely unexpected and fantastic visitation to the music halls of Britain; foreign, of course. Grock was the most complete and consummatory of all clowns, tall with an egg-shaped forehead, and with a long chin which he would project to express determination or coyness, according to changing circumstances. The first impression he conveyed to us was of shyness, as he sidled on to the stage from the rear, wearing trousers tight and long, a large collar with a striped bow, coat-tails and flat oversized boots. As he came before us, he staggered under the weight of a fiddle-case big enough to contain a double-bass. After he had removed from his back his apparently insupportable burden he opened the case and produced from it the tiniest violin imaginable. This was not a trick obviously contrived to get laughter of the unexpected from the audience alone. Grock himself was clearly as much surprised and delighted as ourselves at his discovery of so enchantingly tiny a violin.

He made soft gurgles of delight; his red mouth described the outlines of a quivering letter V. He never spoke an organised dictionary language; but he could be expressive and eloquent with onomatopoeia. Only once did he utter, during his performance, a recognisable verbal sound. He performed with what the programme named as his 'Partner', a sleek, tailored young man who played a violin (a standard violin, if not a Strad). Grock, at the piano, was concerned with something or other wrong about the concert grand, opening the lid and looking within. The 'Partner', impatient to begin a piece, struck the top of the piano with his bow, whereat Grock, looking up sharply and over his shoulder, cried out: 'Come in!'

Grock's 'Partner' was a perfect foil to Grock, shiny and well-oiled of hair, serious and manifestly ambitious as a solo violinist; but finding Grock not an easy, adjustable collaborator. A problem arose as soon as 'Partner' joined Grock on the stage, a problem arising from the positions of the piano and the piano stool, standing yards apart. Grock, with all the good-will in the world, put his strength and shoulders to the bulk of the 'Steinway' grand pianoforte and strove, might and main, to push it towards the stool. When the sleek young 'Partner' very condescendingly lifted up the stool, carried and placed it in front of the keyboard, the most embracing smile of illumination spread over Grock's face. He was enchanted. Grock, indeed, was constantly finding out things for the first time. From the moment he came into the scene, Grock unmistakably was a being out of another dimension, yet nonetheless a visitant humanly related, and willing to learn. He sat down at the piano, the 'Partner' chafing to impress us on his violin. Grock ran his fingers over the keyboard. The 'execution', the fingering, seemed not to please him, the tone was lacking in brilliance. Then he discovered that he was wearing thick woollen gloves. So he took them off and played the scales again. His smile now became beatific. He drew his 'Partner's' attention – and, indirectly ours – to the phenomenon; with his bare fingers he could play much better. We could infer that he had, until this very revelatory moment, played the piano all his life in gloves.

'Partner' here left the stage to Grock, who produced from somewhere a concertina. He climbed onto a chair, an ordinary cane chair, and sat on the curved back of it, knees crossed, a most precariously balanced position. He leaned towards the footlights, and, after deep intake of breath, blew them out, left to right. A single 'lime' shone on his face in the prevailing darkness. He prepared himself to play the concertina. His fingers pressed the keys; and, faintly, we could hear the beginning of the quartet from *Rigoletto*. What is more, Grock was hearing it too. He listened intently. He looked around and up and down, seeking the source of the music. When he had traced it to the concertina, which he held far from his body in the truly professional manner, his chuckle of enchanted surprise was more and more gurglingly onomatopoeic.

Next, he indicated to the conductor that he was, at long last, really ready for serious playing, with full orchestral accompaniment. The conductor raised his arms and baton. And before the orchestra could begin a note, there was a crash, a splitting noise, not merely of wood and of cane, but as of a whole universe, the bottom dropping out of it. Grock had crashed clean through the chair at this moment of the conductor's, the orchestra's, and everybody else's suspense.

Clowns have from time to time immemorial sat on chairs and fallen off, have sat on hats. Grock sat on his own violin, exactly as he fell through the chair. The traditional clown played practical jokes on other folk, scoring over them because of superior knowledge. The clown's traditional 'booby traps' were played by Grock on Grock himself; they didn't score over *him*. He was happy to run into them. He found his tiny fiddle in the enormous case like a child finding its little toe for the first time, bubbling with pleasure. Grock made the fantastic – and the humanly likeable – companionable. In our strange complicated world he was willing to learn, but often rather at a loss. In private life, Grock was Swiss. He broke off relations with and engagements in this country because he objected to our ideas about income tax. He was, at any rate, not going to be taken in by that.

NEVILLE CARDUS, *FULL SCORE*

B ut for all Cardus's fine dreams of a world redeemed by the romance of rags to riches, it was quite impossible for the music hall, even in the days of its flamboyant greatness, to opt out of the real world. Cardus makes no mention of the fact that in 1905, the very year in which he locates his recollection of a better world, the gods and goddesses of his pantheon were mustering for the biggest public fight in their history. By 1906, with the landslide victory of the Liberals at the year's General Election, a head-on collision between artists and management was unavoidable. Two events quickly followed that election, the formation of the Variety Artists' Federation as a Trade Union, and the passing through Parliament of the Trade Dispute Act. Within a month of the passing of that act, the crisis inside the profession exploded. The asperities of a life where control of the halls had fallen into the hands of two or three financial manipulators controlling their 'circuits' soon led to the unthinkable – a withdrawal of labour.

On December 21st 1906 the Trade Disputes Act became law. A month had not gone by before a strike broke out in London which attracted the attention of the general public, not only because it occurred in the capital, but even more by its unexpected nature. It was a strike of music-hall artists which soon spread to the entire staff. The artists objected to certain conditions, in their opinion too severe, which the managers inserted in their contracts. The musicians and mechanics – in fact music-hall employees of every description – followed suit. The great music halls of London were obliged to close. In a hall which happened to be vacant the strikers organised a monster entertainment in aid of their strike and 2,500 pickets triumphantly asserted the right of peaceful persuasion the law had just conferred upon them. The strike, during which strict discipline was maintained, and which did not interfere with the material welfare of the nation, had the sympathy of the public. The managers gave way, and a 'board of conciliation' decided to ask for the services of the Board of Trade's professional arbiter, George Askwith. When the twenty-two variety theatres concerned had reopened, the arbitrator had twenty-two meetings, heard a hundred witnesses and finally drew up and got accepted to both parties the Music Hall Award of 1907 which, though altered several times later, constituted the first labour code for all music-hall employees. It comprised a standard form of contract and regulations for settling future disputes. It would seem that the President of the Board of Trade, Lloyd George, was tempted at first to give the intervention of his Board a more picturesque garb and had therefore offered the post of arbitrator to a personage much in the limelight in London, T.P. O'Connor, a man half Irish, half English, half politician, half journalist and man of letters. O'Connor refused.

ELIE HALEVY, *HALEVY'S HISTORY OF THE ENGLISH PEOPLE IN THE 19TH CENTURY*

Throughout the strike, *'The Daily Telegraph'*, the newspaper which had so involved itself in the Ormiston Chant scuffle, once again kept its readers abreast of developments inside the music-hall world. In the case of Mrs Chant, the paper had decidedly taken up the fight on behalf of the halls. This time there was hardly any need for it to state any very strong opinions at all. Merely by publishing the demands of the VAF, it was making clear to its readers that it was the managements and impresarios who were at fault.

War has been declared between those who control and those who provide the entertainment given in the music halls of the country. No time has been lost in bringing matters to a crisis in London. On Monday evening there was no performance in five of the six variety houses under the direction of Mr Walter Gibbons. At one of these, the Holborn Empire, a performance was given, but there was no 'second house'. The artists, orchestra, the stage hands, and most of the other employees, had decided to strike because of an alleged breach by the management of an agreement which was arrived at between the parties. Yesterday there were rapid and serious developments, of which the most notable was the determination to induce the artists engaged at all the halls belonging to the syndicate of which Mr G. Adney Payne is the head to join in the movement and to refuse to perform. The effect of this decision was that the area of dispute was immediately widened...

Until the end of last week there existed three separate organisations formed to safeguard the interests of those employed at music halls – the Variety Artists' Federation, the National Association of Theatrical Employees, and the Amalgamated Musicians' Union. These, while retaining their independent machinery, have now combined under the title of the National Alliance of Music-hall Artists, and this combination was solidified on Sunday evening at the meeting held in the Surrey Theatre under the presidency of Mr W. Crooks, MP. Before this combination was effected the Variety Artists' Association had entered into negotiations with Mr Walter Gibbons, and maintain that he agreed to the payments of half a day's wage for matinees – all the halls controlled by Mr Gibbons are run on the two houses a night system – to artists engaged at all the halls belonging to him and to incorporate in contracts certain other demands put forward on behalf of the employees. Apparently no agreement was arrived at with regard to unexpired contracts, and Mr Gibbons, holding that the arrangement should only apply to contracts after July 14, declines to sign contracts of which the terms have been fixed by the association. Accordingly the artists and others engaged at the six halls mentioned were 'picketed' by representatives of the federation, and many of them refused to take their turns...

Now as to the demands of the employees ... As summarised in the 'Performer', the official organ of the Variety Artists' Federation, the terms which they ask all music-hall proprietors to agree to are as follows:

1. That at all their halls, or halls under their contract, working two shows a night, all matinees shall be paid for at the rate of one-twelfth salary for each matinee.

2. That no artist shall be transferred from one hall to another without his, her, or their consent.

3. That 'times' shall not be varied after Monday in each week without the artist's consent.

4. That all disputes shall be referred to a board of arbitration, such board to consist of two nominees of the proprietors and two nominees of the VAF executive

157

committee, and an independent chairman to be nominated by the above four nominees.

5. No commission to be stopped where artists are booked direct.

6. No bias or prejudice to be shown to any artist who has taken part in this movement...

THE DAILY TELEGRAPH, 23 JANUARY 1907

Two days later, readers were able to perceive that the dispute had crystallised into the demands of strike leaders like Marie Lloyd against the denials and protestations of angelic innocence by the impresarios. The most offensive of these, the oleaginous Oswald Stoll, attempted to blacken the names of the strikers by implying mental incapacity on their part. The stupidity of Stoll's attitude was only compounded by his belittlement of Marie Lloyd, who by this stage in her career had become the most popular woman in the country. Even had she been wrong, public opinion would have been inclined to side with her against the likes of Stoll; in fact, the case she propounded was watertight.

MARIE LLOYD, who is taking a very active part in the struggle, stated emphatically that the Alliance meant to fight tooth and nail, and she had every hope that they would win. 'A wrong impression has got abroad,' she remarked, 'as to the position of the "star" artists. It is said that they are quarrelling with the managers on their own behalf. That is not so. We can dictate our own terms. We are fighting not for ourselves but for the poorer members of the profession, earning from 30s to £3 per week ...' ALEC HURLEY (reducing the issue to a more personal level). What we are really fighting ... is a music-hall trust. If the policy which has caused all the trouble succeeds, it will be impossible for artists to earn a living in London at all. At present the average artist is really at the mercy of the manager. He has to sign a contract to appear at a certain hall for six nights, and he is not allowed to perform at any other hall in the neighbourhood for twelve months thereafter. In many cases it practically means ruin. I myself have an engagement at a North-East London hall, and I have been asked to undertake another shortly afterwards in a neighbouring district. I mean to accept it ... VESTA TILLEY. Personally, she had no grievance, nor had any of the leading artists, but she knew of the grievances of those whose turns were in less demand ... HARRY RANDALL. This agitation has been going on underground for ten years, and now that it has come to the surface the matter is not likely to be allowed to rest until a substantial change has been secured ... HARRY FRAGSON was strongly of opinion that the artists are entitled to a re-adjustment of terms, although even now they are not quite so hardly used as their brethren in France used to be...

Invited to explain the situation [OSWALD STOLL] ... declared that very few of the artists knew what they were fighting for, and many were appalled at the result of their secret meetings, held in the true spirit of irresponsible adventure. Verbal fireworks by similar men had caused sad havoc in the United States, and it was a vital article in the constitution of the present American federation that they must not be on strike.

Questioned as to the reason for the strike, Mr Stoll said: 'It is an indisputable fact that every performer with an iota of real entertaining power is getting, not only a living, but a handsome living, while many whose vocation should be anything but that of public entertainers are able to maintain a standard of living which thousands of trade unionists would envy.'

Have you noticed the statements of Miss Marie Lloyd? – 'Oh, yes: Her utterances are so grossly exaggerated that it is to be hoped they are due to an innate partiality for dramatic effect, rather than to that truth which constitutes her value as an artist...'

Do the public quite understand the meaning of what is called the 'barring clause' in the agreements of artists? – 'The barring clause is really the foundation of the "variety" superstructure. It means that managers pay a large salary for the exclusive services of an artist. Performers who appear anywhere and everywhere soon tire the public, but when they play at one place alone they speedily assert their true value...'

THE DAILY TELEGRAPH, 25 JANUARY 1907

Music Hall War

Twinkle, twinkle, brilliant Star!
Oh, I wonder where you are.
With the V.A.F so bright,
You will **not** show here to=night.

The following Stars will not appear at the Payne and Gibbons' Halls till the dispute is settled:—

MARIE LLOYD	MARIE KENDALL
MARIE DAINTON	VICTORIA MONKS
VESTA VICTORIA	GUS ELEN
ARTHUR ROBERTS	R. A. ROBERTS
JOE ELVIN	ALEC HURLEY
CLARK & HAMILTON	PAUL MARTINETTI
JOE O'GORMAN	FRED GINNETT
JOCK WHITEFORD	WAL PINK
HERBERT SHELLEY	Leonard MORTIMER

Printed by the Co-operative Printing Society Limited, Tudor Street, London, E.C., and Published by J. B. Williams, 9, Great Newport Street, W.C.

Although, as Marie said in her riposte, the strike was almost exclusively to do with the treatment handed out to the run-of-the-mill artists rather than the big names, the star attractions were solid in their support of the newly-formed Federation, and maddened managements still further, not merely by withholding their labour, but by giving whimsical reasons for doing so.

Harry joined the Variety Artists' Federation on its formation in 1906, and was among the stars who supported the London music-hall strike in the following year by helping to picket the offending theatres and refusing, or rather, failing, to appear. He sent a telegram to the Tivoli, one of the 'blacked' houses, where he was top of the bill with Marie Lloyd, saying, 'I am learning a new cornet solo. Cannot tear myself away.' Marie Lloyd's telegram said, 'I am busy putting a few flounces on my dress so I cannot appear tonight.'

RICHARD FINDLATER, *LITTLE TICH*

At first managements tried to outface the strikers by booking obscure acts willing to work no matter what the circumstances. Every district was combed for retired performers, every agency investigated. Artists who would in the normal course of events have been ignored by the circuits were suddenly offered flattering terms if only they would agree to appear. In retrospect it seems extraordinary that managements should have believed that it made little difference what was presented so long as the stage was occupied by someone. The public, gullible as it sometimes was, never quite became as gullible as all that, and soon realised that much the best show could be seen free outside the theatre.

A performance was attempted at 'The Holborn' by some artists hastily pressed into service. An accompanist was found, and the place of the limelight man was filled by the cinematograph operator with his lantern. The audience took the situation good-temperedly in the main; though there was a noisy demonstration at the opening. Rusty, long-forgotten acts were dragged from obscurity, and old stars tempted out of retirement for a 'come-back'. At The Oxford the manager Mr Blythe-Pratt addressed the audience. 'I am sorry to tell you that the VAF is endeavouring to prevent our artists working here tonight. I regret that it will be quite impossible to present our regular programme, but I am going to put forward an entertainment which I hope will really entertain you.' This consisted of: Mrs Brown Potter, who gave a recitation; Mr Ten Thomas, who sang a jockey song; Mlle D'Aubigny from the Paris Opera House who sang Tosti's 'Goodbye' – 'with much taste'; a Hungarian violinist and a diminutive Continental mandolinist, 'a decidedly good player'.

Not surprisingly the liveliest entertainment was found outside the theatre, where pickets distributed leaflets proclaiming: 'Music Hall War. Mr Gibbons says his companies consist of picked artistes and musicians. Mr Joe Elvin says: 'Unfortunately he picked them before they were ripe'. Down With The Trusts.

Artists stopped the passers-by and asked for their support.

'Blacklegs,' Marie shouted gaily at Lockhart's troupe of elephants, the only turn to go on at one hall, and when Belle Elmore, a second-rate artist, forced her way through pickets to cries of 'Stop her!', Marie shouted back, 'Don't be daft. Let her in and she'll empty the theatre.'

DAN FARSON, MARIE LLOYD AND THE MUSIC HALL

Marie's joke at the expense of poor Belle Elmore was soon to be eclipsed in the most macabre way. At the Water Rats Dinner Dance at the Vaudeville Club in 1910, a place was laid for Belle and her husband, an insignificant-looking man called Dr Crippen. When the doctor arrived, it was with a much younger woman wearing Belle's jewellery. By the time the dinner took place, Belle had been lying dead in the cellar for nearly three weeks. As for the strike, it was settled at last, more or less to the satisfaction of the artists, after signs of a split in the ranks.

DAILY TELEGRAPH, 28 and 30 January 1907, reported that the Alliance had held mass meetings. At the first enthusiasm was unbounded, especially when the announcement was made that a lease had been taken of the Scala Theatre, with a view of running it as a music hall, and turning the adjoining buildings into a music-hall exchange. But at the second it was resolved to postpone the opening of the Scala Theatre performances until Monday, Feb. 11. The decision is significant in perhaps more ways than one. In the first place, it seems to indicate that the resolution to open the Scala to-morrow had been taken without adequate regard to the facts of the situation. In the second, it may be taken as showing that at the variety artists' headquarters the view is held that the end of the strike is not quite so near as some of the more enthusiastic members of the alliance profess to believe.

. . . the music-hall strike is practically at an end. For five hours yesterday representative managers and 'star' artists discussed the question of a settlement, and at the conclusion of the meeting it was announced that an agreement had been reached . . .

There is little doubt, however, that the action of the 'stars' must lead to the collapse of the strike movement. As a result of the unbending attitude of the National Alliance officials, a strong third party has been formed . . . [Including] Arthur Roberts, Marie Lloyd, Little Tich, Vesta Tilley, Harry Randall, Wilkie Bard, George Robey . . .

Late last evening the alliance issued the following statement, signed by the chairman, Mr Mountford, and the joint secretaries, Mr Johnson, Mr Williams, and Mr Gerald:

There is no truth in the rumours of an approaching settlement of the music-hall war. There is no 'third party' in the National Alliance. The result of the conference between certain members of the Variety Artists' Federation and the managers has in no way affected the strike. The happenings of the next few days will doubtless convince everybody of the fact that the strike is still in progress . . .

The strike was one of the first examples of that application of arbitration machinery to become so familiar to twentieth-century electors. The Liberal government, in the flamboyant person of its President of the Board of Trade, David Lloyd George, certainly took the VAF seriously, and was anxious to show that its own new legislation was practicable. The extent to which the strike settlement constituted a victory for the rebels is revealed by a comparison of the demands stated in *The Daily Telegraph* for January 23rd, and the arbitration judgement agreed on five months later.

The great entertainment with which the National Alliance of Variety Artists hope to set London agog ... [took place] at the Scala Theatre last night amid plenteous signs of enthusiasm. If one were to be severely critical, one might say at once that the performance was disappointing. If by 'stars' are meant variety artists of the first rank, then was the title somewhat of a misnomer. It might more appropriately have been designed 'A Night Without the Stars', for the stellar array was by no means of the first magnitude ... Nevertheless, there were plenty of 'stars' scattered about the house ... Miss Marie Lloyd viewed the performance from a box ...

On 15 February THE DAILY TELEGRAPH had to report that last evening the Music Hall War entered upon a new phase, when all the pickets were withdrawn from the twenty-two halls 'barred' as a result of the strike ... Mr George R. Askwith was yesterday ... asked to officiate as arbitrator. It is understood that he has accepted.

He took four months to make his final arbitration. THE DAILY TELEGRAPH carried a precis of his report on 15 June: Mr [G. R.] Askwith declares that where, under the terms of an engagement, an artist may be transferred from one to another theatre of an associated group with the consent of the artist, such consent shall not unreasonably be withheld.

Existing contracts often provide that managers may in their absolute discretion close their houses, when salaries shall not be payable. The arbitrator decides that such withholding of salaries shall only be justified where the theatre is closed by reason of national mourning, fire, epidemic, strikes, lock-outs, disputes with employees, or order of the licensing or any local authority. No salary shall be payable if the artist is ill or in default ...

Where the contract says the artist shall appear at all matinees weekly without the payment of any additional remuneration, artists shall in future only be called upon to perform at such matinees as were the usual weekly practice at the time the contract was made; any additional matinees to be paid for ...

[On the barring clause] which was largely the cause of the music-hall artists' strike, the arbitrator gives a number of most important decisions:

(a) The barring of theatres of varieties for a period after the termination of any engagement, except for not more than two weeks after the termination of an engagement in provincial towns, is abolished.

(b) In a London West-end theatre of varieties, if the engagement be for at least fourteen weeks during any period of twelve months, and a salary of at least £40 per week, the contract may include conditions that the artist can be barred from performing at other theatres ...

His award was the basis for all future contracts and agreements. Improved awards were made in 1913 and 1919.

162

By the time the music-hall strike was settled, there was no doubt in the minds of the British public who was the first lady of the profession. She was Matilda Alice Victoria Wood, one of eleven children of a Hoxton artificial flower-maker. At the age of fifteen she took to the stage under the name of Bella Delmore, making her debut at the Grecian, in City Road, at a salary of fifteen shillings a week. One day a manager gave her some advice. Her chosen name was unsuited to the no-nonsense attitude of the music-hall audiences. She must think of something a little less pretentious.

Inspiration came in the form of a big poster on the walls, what is known to advertising people as a 'forty-eight sheet pictorial'. That poster bore a picture of an old gentleman in his shirt-sleeves, with a circular smoking-cap on his grey hair and a kindly, if rather superior, expression on his face. His right hand was raised in admonition, the index finger extended; he was evidently laying down the law and giving people the benefit of his wisdom, whether they wanted it or not. The caption was 'The Family Oracle', and in his left hand he held the source of the information he could impart. It was the fountain of all the wisdom which he was prepared to disclose; in his opinion it was quite infallible. That encyclopaedia of knowledge was a newspaper and its name was 'Lloyd's Weekly News'. The name screamed at you in enormous type. Bella saw it and was riveted to the spot. There it was. And it fitted so well with Marie. Marie Lloyd – that was the name, and from that moment onwards Marie Lloyd she was.

W. MACQUEEN POPE, *MARIE LLOYD*

As Marie Lloyd her rise was phenomenal. The debut at the Grecian took place in 1885. Within a year she was famous, earning as much as ten pounds a week. Soon she was making ten times that money, but remained gauche in the ways of the profession. It was an unwritten law of the 1880s that no performer stole or borrowed the material of a professional rival, but took the trouble instead to find her own material for which she paid the songwriter for exclusive rights. Marie knew little of this convention. To her a song was a song, to be sung by whoever took a fancy to it. Her fancy was touched by a popular piece currently being featured by yet another doomed young singer, Nelly Power. In 1887 Miss Power died, but not before there had been a clash over the disputed musical territory.

Marie 'borrowed' a song from Nelly Power, 'The Boy in the Gallery', and made it into a favourite of her own. Unlike most music-hall songs, it's a simple, beautiful ballad with a wistful charm that still captivates today:

> The boy I love is up in the gallery,
> The boy I love is looking now at me.
> There he is – can't you see,
> Waving his handkerchief
> As merry as a robin that sings in the tree.

Nelly Power died two years later at the age of thirty-two, and was so poor that the undertaker sued her agent George Ware for £8.19.6 for the funeral expenses.

DAN FARSON, *MARIE LLOYD AND THE MUSIC HALL*

So spectacular was Marie's private life that it has sometimes since threatened to eclipse her art. Two of her weaknesses could be said eventually to have destroyed her: her reckless generosity, almost as though she felt a secret guilt at receiving such huge salaries, and her sad failure to make a good marriage. Her first attempt, at the age of seventeen, to a race-track lizard called Courtney, was never much of a marriage, apart from the daughter it produced. Courtney, who was deeply interested in ready money, was driven to distraction by Marie's habit of flinging it around indiscriminately, to every acquaintance with a hard-luck story. As for the career, it was going beautifully, except on those very rare occasions when Marie failed to take account of the subtle gradations in humour from district to district and from hall to hall.

'I'm going to the Paragon next Monday. It's the first time I've ever appeared there. I reckon I shall have to "lay it on a bit thick" down Whitechapel way, what?'

'My dear girl,' I replied, 'I marvel at *you* – an East End native – making such a statement to *me*, with all my inside knowledge of East End shows and show-goers. Now, speaking from that experience,' I continued, 'and from the manner in which I have seen Hoxton, Whitechapel, and Mile End playgoers and music-hall goers treat "blue" singers and undressed actresses, I warn you that if you dare to sing at the Paragon any of your very "shady" songs you are now singing in the West End, that East End audience will balloon you off the stage.'

As I entered the Paragon I heard a noise. It was the sound of an audience giving a not too favourable reception to our wonderful little pal. In fact so unfavourable was it that Marie dashed off in a mixed state of rage and weeping. Happily she pulled herself together and returned to give one of her cleverest character studies.

H. CHANCE NEWTON

In Sheffield she clashed verbally with the audience. After a cool reception at the end of the first house, she turned on them angrily. 'You don't like me, well I don't like you. And you know what you can do with your stainless knives and your scissors and your circular saws – you can shove 'em up your arse.' She stormed off to her dressing-room, refusing to go on for the next house. With superb diplomacy, the manager knocked on her door and said he'd come from the audience who wanted to apologise.

'Don't try to schmooze me,' she called.

'They'll do what you say with the knives and scissors,' he assured her, 'but can they be spared the circular saws?' There was a moment's silence, then a burst of laughter as she relented.

'All right, then, play "God Save the Queen" and tell 'em she's here.'

DAN FARSON, *MARIE LLOYD AND THE MUSIC HALL*

M arie's regal pretensions were no joke, even though she may have expressed them in ribald terms. She was intensely proud of the position she had won of undisputed pre-eminence in her profession. She even transcended stardom by becoming one of the great Englishwomen of her epoch. She was as famous on Broadway, in South Africa, in Australia, as at home, and it was this prestige which created problems which proved insoluble in her private life. The same feeling of inadequacy which had caused her first husband to feel humiliated was eventually to destroy her relationship with his successor, Alec Hurley. They should have been ideally suited, Marie the Queen of the Halls, Hurley her Coster Consort, a talented performer with a considerable career of his own, if not remotely in the class of Albert Chevalier or Gus Elen. But the time came when Hurley too drifted away, forced outside the enchanted circle by the exclusivity of Marie's genius, and her insatiable appetite for parties and socialising. Marie took to the life represented by Romano's as though born to it; Hurley remained loyal to his pint at the local pub. Inevitably he came to feel that he was extraneous. He and Marie lived openly in sin, as the Victorians so quaintly put it, from 1900, married in 1905 once Marie's divorce became absolute, and stayed together till 1910, when the great tragedy of Marie's life occurred. She fell in love with an Irish jockey called Bernard Dillon, one of nature's rats, a drunk whose sporting speciality was getting into fights with lesser opponents, including Marie's father, who took him on when the old man was seventy-four years old. But his most famous victories were those scored over his own wife, whose injuries grew more and more horrific and, at last, impossible to hide. In a sense Dillon killed Marie with his brutality, even though the biographers have generally resorted to euphemism in defining the disease which killed Marie as 'a broken heart'. Long after her death, Dillon was still at it, beating up his latest mistress and stealing money from her; prosecuting counsel came as close to the truth as anyone when he observed, 'You are nothing more than a pot-house blackguard.'

Why, then, did Marie Lloyd, who might have had almost any man in the kingdom, select so odious a lout? She appears simply to have fallen madly in love with him, and was, according to her sisters, immensely flattered that so much younger a man should find her sexually attractive – Marie was forty when they met, Dillon twenty-two. Dillon's scandalous behaviour makes a discordant counterpoint to the triumphal march of Marie's career up to the start of the Great War. In 1913 they sailed together for New York as Mr and Mrs Dillon. The Port authorities soon discovered that they were not legally married and, anxious to preserve the pristine reputation of their nation, placed the couple on Ellis Island preparatory to sending them back to Britain. At the last moment the authorities were persuaded to let them enter, but the sequence of events drew out one of her more renowned witticisms. When asked by a local journalist what she thought about America, she pointed at the Statue of Liberty and said, 'I love your sense of humour.' In December 1913, while Marie was conquering Chicago, Hurley died; in February 1914 Marie and Dillon were married in Portland, Oregon. The world which had created and supported the music hall had almost run its course. Perhaps the most vivid and convincing portrait of Marie in full and delighted control of her art, achieving that legendary fusion of spirit with every worldling on the premises, is the one painted by the annalist of the men-about-town.

In imagination put the clock back to a Saturday afternoon some thirty years ago, before wars, the internal combustion engine, and the film changed our lives and habits, and come with me to the Saturday matinée at the Tivoli. These Saturday afternoons are a feature of London's theatre world; to them go half the music-hall profession, in or out of collar; men from Fleet Street and the Temple; members of that curious population which rarely seems to leave the old Strand; racing men, men about town, journalists, a mixture of coteries who all seem to know one another, and who are regular in one thing at least, their attendance at the Tivoli and Oxford matinées.

It is still the age of 'looking-in'; one looks in at a music hall, not so much in search of a seat, in which to sit out a performance, as to meet a few friends, watch a particular turn or two, chat, hear the latest news of the town, and wander about in perfect freedom. We are not as yet in a generation which is content to occupy an exiguous seat in a gigantic picture palace and sit in darkness gazing at an American film. Dozens of the Tivoli and Oxford, Empire and Alhambra habitués never occupy a seat, but see all they wish to see from the promenades. As we enter the Tivoli promenade from the few steps which lead out of the vestibule from the street level we see at once it is more crowded than usual, in spite of the fact that the turns include such stars as Eugene Stratton, George Robey, Vesta Victoria, Florrie Ford, and others famous in music-hall land, but the reason is soon learnt. Marie Lloyd is to try out a new song so the usual matinée has become an event.

With a supreme disregard for the performance on the stage, we turn to the right of the promenade, and enter the big saloon which is both bar and rendezvous for the coteries. The cigar-scented atmosphere is filled with the murmur of voices, as the groups melt into one another, and dissolve anew. A swing door is pushed open, and a head protrudes.

'Marie's number!', cries a voice; glasses are put down, and the big room empties in a trice. We elbow our way to the promenade at the back of the circle, and lean our arms on the partition dividing it from the back row of the seats to watch. The orchestra has struck up a typical Marie Lloyd number, jaunty, debonair, catchy, and the house waits in silence. Then, from the wing, comes a little fair-haired woman, blue-eyed, with an indescribably friendly smile, and there is a roar of welcome from ceiling to floor. A cheery nod of recognition and salute, a tiny wave of the hand, and Our Marie begins.

The song? Nothing in particular. As with most of the great artists of the halls it is simply a vehicle, but, make no mistake, trite as it may seem, there is method in it. It is cleverly designed for its purpose, and it fulfils that purpose better than a more aesthetic composition could do. We are still in the age of the great personalities; just as Irving could and did make badly-written work such as 'Louis XI' or 'The Dead Heart' the medium for a superb performance, so do the supreme artists of the halls make of their obvious and crude material a ground-work for the display of their powers of impersonation and characterisation. So, the song is nothing in particular. The singer is everything.

Watch the play of the hands, the eyes, the controlled and perfect gesture; listen to the intonation of the tritest words, and, in spite of all attempts at criticism and dissection, you yield yourself to the artist. In some indescribable way she has gathered her audience to her; they are hers, to do with as she pleases. They laugh with her, they chuckle with her, they wink with her. 'We're all pals together,' she

166

seems to say, 'and, strictly as pals, what do you think of this?' And she proceeds to tell us 'this'. Yet she remains the Queen, 'Marie Lloyd, the Queen of Comediennes', and we are her adoring subjects.

Bearing all this in mind, we who saw and heard Our Marie can fill in the picture as we recall the words of those songs of hers, but, I wonder, do they convey anything to the unfortunates who did not live under that reign? Take, for example, the famous trip to Paris:

We went to a music 'all, and a lady she was singin'
And all the blokes was laffin'. Bill says 'Come art!'
I says 'Shan't! first I can't make out what they got to laff abart.'
And some bloke turns to me an' says, 'Well, it's a good job that you can't!'

Still, I'd like to go again, to Paris on the Seine,
For Paris is a proper pantomime,
And if they'd only shift the 'Ackney Road and plant it over there,
I'd like to live in Paris all the time.

Or again, 'I Shall Never Forget the Days When I Was Young', with the crinoline-like bustle which performed incredibilities of grotesque, and the tiny parasol which had such an emphasis of its own:

I shall never forget the days when I was young.
Oh, it don't seem so very long ago,
Since I used to twist my feet to the organ in the street,
I shall never forget the days when I was young.

Granted the supreme artist, can you see the possibilities? Her range was a wide one, from the Cockney girl on holiday to the sophisticated woman of the world, and to the disreputable old dear:

Great, oh, she's great, is the woman of umpty-eight,
A lot she's endured from the thing they call man.
Still, if to live o'er again she began
Would she live it again, would she play the same game?

And then came the last line, delivered as only Marie Lloyd could half-sing, half-speak it, in that adorable husky breathiness of voice she shared with Ellen Terry: 'Well – and that unforgettable half-laugh, half-chuckle – *'Rather!'*

And into that entirely undistinguished doggerel Marie Lloyd infused wit, humour, worldliness and sheer fun. She never ceased to study her audiences. It had been an ambition of hers to appear at the Palace, then at the top of its fame as a variety theatre, and when at last she did appear there, she found its rather specialised type of audience did not seem to grasp her first character studies. An excess of refinement is probably a bar to an appreciation of pictures of lower-class life. But indefatigably she tried song after song, and at last succeeded with:

There they are,
The pair of them on their own!
There they are,
Alone, alone, alone.
They gave me half a crown
To run away and play –
But – umpty iddle-y, umpty iddly
Umpty iddle-i-ay.

167

And with that absurdity, dressed by Marie Lloyd, she captured the ultra-smart, ultra-sophisticated stall floor of the Palace Theatre.

Her middle-aged and elderly baggages were gems of characterisation. The disreputable old dear who held that 'a little of what you fancy does you good':

> I always 'old with 'aving it, if you fancy it,
> If you fancy it, that's understood.
> But if that's your bloomin' game, I intend to do the same,
> 'Cause a little of what yer fancy does yer good.

The merry old soul who went for a walk with a gentleman friend, came over queer, and sat down on the grass, not alone. When she woke up she was alone, and looked for her purse. 'I've been buzzed!' exclaimed one of the ruins that Cromwell knocked about a bit sadly. 'That's what comes of sitting on the grass with a commercial traveller.'

And best of all, perhaps, with the best song, the cheery old dame who carried the old cock-linnet in its cage as her contribution to the removal:

> Away went the van with the 'ome packed in it,
> And I followed on with the old cock linnet,
> But I dillied and dallied, dallied and dillied,
> Lost me way and don't know where to roam,
> An' of course I'd to stop an' have a little drop of tiddley –
> Now I can't find my way 'ome.

As she herself said of Dan Leno, 'If we didn't laugh at him, we'd cry our eyes out.'

J.B. BOOTH, *THE DAYS WE KNEW*

Booth's glittering description of Marie Lloyd in full flow raises the old bone of moral contention which the world kept flinging at her throughout her working life: was she or was she not vulgar? It seems obvious beyond any reasonable doubt that she was, that she strained to be vulgar, that vulgarity lay at the very heart of her whole aesthetic, that she celebrated vulgarity, perfected its expression and eventually arrived at the paradox of vulgarity refined to the ultimate degree. But the question is bedevilled by Marie's need to protect herself from Mrs Grundy, and the consequent dissimulation which she adopted as her standard defence. In the early years of the century a committee was formed to 'clean up' the stage, its members evidently being unaware that the only way of improving the moral tone of a performance is to monitor every production of it, and that the written text hardly ever discloses any suggestiveness contained therein. In music hall, where often there was no written text at all, and where so much was achieved with the wink and the nudge, the committee was bound to come a spectacular cropper, which it did when it summoned Marie Lloyd.

She was furious at what she considered an insult to herself, her profession, and her public by people who had no right to judge anyone. But she kept her temper. She went along, with a pianist, and she waited her turn. In due course it came. There was a dangerous gleam in her eye, but outwardly she was all smiles and charm. She sang her songs to that committee; all her popular songs, so that they could judge fairly and squarely. She sang them 'Oh, Mr Porter', 'The Two of Them On Their Own', 'A Little Bit of What You Fancy', 'Everything In the Garden's Lovely', and many, many more. She sang them without an inflection, a nod, wink or smile. The committee was taken aback. This was not what they had expected, and maybe not what they had hoped for. If any of them had ever seen her on the halls, they did not say so. They found nothing wrong. They had a short confabulation among themselves, and then the chairman informed Miss Lloyd with condescension, that she had their permission to continue to sing her songs. She could go. That was the last straw. The fine, healthy temper, so long subdued, flashed out. She was going to get her own back.

'Oh, I can go, can I?' she hissed. 'Thank you for nothing. You've had me here over an hour. I've sung song after song and you've found no fault with them. I can go on singing them, can I? All right. A fat lot you know about anything. A fat lot you know about songs and singers, or what they mean. You've heard those songs of mine you thought so dreadful, and they are all right. Splendid. Now I'll show you. I'll sing you some of the songs your wives sing in your drawing-room. They are clean enough, aren't they? All right, you just see what you think.'

Marie sang two of the popular ballads which were warbled at pretty well every musical evening at the time, when musical evenings were very popular indeed. They were 'Come into the Garden, Maud' and 'Queen of my Heart'. What she did with those songs was nobody's business; the men who wrote them would have been amazed; Alfred Lord Tennyson would probably have expired of heart failure. Every little word had a meaning of its own, when Marie so willed. Leaving the poor committee stunned and gasping, she wished the members good afternoon and swept out.

W. MACQUEEN POPE, *MARIE LLOYD, QUEEN OF THE MUSIC HALLS*

In composing this highly idealised account of an incident at which he was not present the author would appear to be showing Marie Lloyd behaving in an unwise and perhaps untypical way. Yet the story has been circulated so widely and has been accepted by so many of those who knew Marie intimately, that she really does seem to have blown the gaff, as she might have put it, on her own tactics. It is impossible to believe that anyone could have doubted for a moment that Marie chose the sort of songs which were about the kind of life lived in the mean streets which had raised her. And yet her standard defence was always that she sang of innocent people, and was only to be misinterpreted by those with lewd and corrupted minds. Her most detailed defence of her own professional morality was laid down on her visit to America in 1897.

'I might as well say right here that my songs are not blue – at least not half as blue as they are painted. Just because I sing them, they are suggestive and vulgar and nasty and everything else your cheap little reporters can think of to call them. I'll bet if I sang the Songs of Solomon set to music, I would be accused of making them bad, just because people at the halls want songs that are not quite dead marches and I give in to them. You take the pit on a Saturday night or a Bank Holiday. You don't suppose they want Sunday School stuff do you? They want lively stuff with music they can learn quickly. Why, if I was to try to sing highly moral songs they would fire ginger-beer bottles and beer mugs at me. They don't pay their sixpences and shillings at a music hall to hear the Salvation Army. But mind you, I don't say that my songs are thick simply because they are lovely. The trouble is that people are looking for blue, and I can't help it, you know, if they want to turn and twist my meanings.'

(Marie then defends a song called 'Saturday to Monday', and insists that 'even a parson couldn't see it was blue unless someone told him'.)

It's the same with 'The Railroad Song'. It's not at all thick, and yet the people get clever and say it means all sorts of things. I can't help that, can I? I can't make people think straight. People are awful queer, and I don't see the use of trying to please them. You Americans are awfully clever, but you are too smart here, for you find things blue and thick that an Eton boy could hear without being hurt by. And I guess I don't hurt the music-hall audiences much, even if they do see a whole lot in my songs that isn't there.'

Having said which she then, presumably, winked the other eye. 'The Railroad Song' was the Americanised title of a song whose original title made its ambivalent overtones so obvious that no explanation was required and no defence effective. It was revelled in by British audiences as 'She'd Never Had Her Ticket Punched Before':

> She arrived at Euston by the midnight train.
> But when she got to the wicket, there was someone wanted to punch her ticket.
> The guards and the porters came round her by the score,
> And she told them all that she'd never had her ticket punched before.

In those days the railway was a prolific symbol of the flighty life. Once the cheap day excursion eliminated the chaperone from the race, a working-class girl was free to nip off to Brighton or Southend and do whatever she pleased away from the prying eyes of the neighbourhood. Hence Florrie Ford's 'They're All Single by the Seaside' and Mark Sheridan's 'You Can Do a Lot of Things at the Seaside That You Can't Do in Town'. Among Marie Lloyd's group of railway songs, the most notorious was perhaps one with the identical double-entendre to the ticket saga, 'I've Never Lost My Last Train Yet'. A young girl goes to Boulogne on a day-trip, and has such a good time that she misses the ferry home.

> For when looking at the clock,
> I received a dreadful shock
> On discovering that the sun had gone and set.
> So a telegram I wrote:
> 'Dear Mama, I've missed the boat!'
> But I haven't lost my last train yet, Oh No!
> I haven't lost my last train yet.

Oddly enough, the most famous of all Marie's railway songs, and one of the most durable music hall songs of all time, has lost much of its innuendo through years of hearty chorus singing by amateurs who revel so much in the sound of the words and the lilt of the melody that they hardly ever stop to think what the song might once have meant to so complete a mistress of the art of sly suggestion as Marie Lloyd. This song is 'Oh! Mr Porter', the story of a young innocent girl who boards a train and forgets to get off at the stop she had in mind – or to put it another way, a girl who is persuaded by an elderly gentleman she meets on the train to go very much further than she had intended. 'Oh! Mr Porter' was only the most successful of a whole group of songs following this scenario; another was 'Bradshaw's Guide', in which yet another innocent maid is picked up on a train by yet another kind gentleman, and is so overcome by his kindness that 'She could not recollect the town to which she'd wished to ride'. She returns to his rooms with him; 'And all the livelong day, the both of us, we tried to find the town she wanted in the Bradshaw's Guide'.

'Oh! Mr Porter' was by far the best of all the railway songs, by virtue of its irresistible march-swing. It was composed by one of the best musicians who worked in the music hall, George Le Brunn, an engaging man with delightfully flamboyant habits. He had begun by writing for the first of the Mashers, Charles Godfrey, and soon became his inseparable companion. It was Godfrey who first established the method by which artists might find a way to counter Le Brunn's slapstick professional ethics. He was in the habit of arriving at band calls with only part of the new orchestration, and sometimes none of it. Inquiries would then be made as to where Le Brunn was staying. A map was consulted and all the public houses between the digs and the theatre marked. An emissary was then sent to visit all these hostelries and retrieve the band parts which Le Brunn had left behind in a fit of beery forgetfulness, perhaps the trombone music at The Royal George, the second clarinet at The Green Man, the vocal line at The Dog and Duck and so on. No report has come down to posterity as to who went to retrieve the emissaries, but at any rate, Le Brunn's habits were endured because he was capable of writing the kind of songs which would stay with an artist for the rest of his or her career, and even, in one or two cases, of entering national folklore.

Oh! Mr Porter

Lately I just spent a week with my old Aunt Brown,
Came up to see the wondrous sights of famous London Town.
Just a week I had of it, all round the place we'd roam,
Wasn't I sorry on the day I had to go back home?
Worried about with packing, I arrived late at the station,
Dropped my hatbox in the mud, the things all fell about,
Got my ticket, said Good-bye, Right away, the guard did cry
But I found the train was wrong and shouted out:

Oh! Mr Porter, what shall I do?
I want to go to Birmingham and they're taking me on to Crewe.
Send me back to London as quickly as you can,
Oh! Mr Porter, what a silly girl I am.

171

The porter would not stop the train but laughed and said, 'You must
Keep your hair on, Mary Ann, and mind that you don't bust.'
Some old gentleman inside declared that it was hard,
Said, 'Look out of the window, Miss, and try to call the guard.'
Didn't I, too, with all my might I nearly balanced over,
But my old friend grasped my leg and pulled me back again.
Nearly fainting with the fright, I sank into his arms a sight,
Went into hysterics but I cried in vain:

Oh! Mr Porter, *etc.*

On his clean old shirt front then I laid my trembling head.
'Do take it easy, rest awhile,' the dear old chappie said.
'If you make a fuss of me and on me do not frown,
You shall have my mansion, dear, away in London Town.'
Wouldn't you think me silly if I said I could not like him?
Really he seemed a nice old boy, so I replied this way:
'I will be your own for life your imay doddleum little wife,
If you'll never tease me any more I say.'

Oh! Mr Porter, *etc.*

WORDS BY THOMAS LE BRUNN, MUSIC BY GEORGE LE BRUNN

Although Marie Lloyd was never seriously challenged as the Queen of the Halls, there were several rival ladies whose reputations have survived, deservedly so. One was Vesta Victoria, a singer of wryly comic songs whose American success was even greater than the considerable acclaim she enjoyed at home. The trade papers seem to have had an insatiable appetite for interviews with Miss Victoria, with the result that following her fortunes conveys to perfection the cosy prose conventions of the kind of journalism so keenly followed inside the profession.

Chats with Celebrities
No. LXXVII Miss Vesta Victoria

Happy, right happy is the nation which has no history. Therefore, surely equally fortunate must be the young artiste whose life has been so uneventful, so destitute of exciting incidents, so unclouded in its prosperity, that she is forced to exclaim, as she sits herself opposite my unworthy self, 'I am afraid this will be a silly kind of interview, for I have very little to tell.' The young and most charming lady of whom I write is Miss Vesta Victoria.

After having sat down warily, with one optic secretly watching a canine beauty who was standing on the rug in the tasteful drawing-room of Miss V. V.'s abode, I assured my hostess that I was certain our chat would, when recounted in the columns of the 18-months-old ENCORE, be found highly interesting to my readers. I then inquired as to her birthplace.

'I am a native in Leeds,' quoth Miss Vesta.

'Oh, yes, that's in Westmoreland, isn't it?' put in the member of the staff who usually accompanies me, thereby showing that geography is not one of his strong points. After the Yorkshire-born miss had exhibited a pearly set of white teeth – the dog I was watching so anxiously also had teeth: oh, such teeth! – she (Miss V., not the animal) continued:

'Yes, my parents were both in the profession, my father being Joe Lawrence, while my mother was well known on the halls as Marian Nelson.'

'How old were you when you commenced to appear in public?'

'I was working with my father when five years old, my first appearance being at Gloucester, where papa had a music hall which was previously a circus. It was called the Pavilion. I used to go on every Friday night, in order to become accustomed to an audience. At that time I used chiefly to depend on my dancing.'

'And who taught you that art?'

'Well, my father gave me an insight of dancing as a baby; the rest I learnt myself.'

'Quite so,' I remarked absently, with a sidelong glance at that 'dawg', who would, I felt sure, teach me how to dance in no time, if he felt so inclined.

'My first paid engagement was at Mr Dan Lowrey's Star, Dublin, when I was five. I used, I recollect, to sing a little servant's song called 'Sarah Scrubbs', and a factory girl ditty, but I was too young to introduce much. I was, of course, engaged with my father, and received £3 a week.'

I think this is the amount Miss Victoria said, but it may have been £30, for my hands were trembling so with nervousness at the sight of that beast of prey, who wouldn't even bark, for, remembering the ancient adage, I was afraid he would bite, and I could tell by that glancing eye that he had thoughts of a good meal from my calf.

'After remaining in the provinces for a while I came to London when I was six, and opened at Sam Collins's, the Cambridge, and the South London, with songs and dances. I stayed in London for some time, and then returned to the provincial halls again.'

'Your most famous dog – beg pardon, I mean song, of course – was "Daddy wouldn't buy me a Bow-wow"?'

'Of course that caused a lot of talk, but it didn't do me the slightest amount of good as far as raising my salary. My greatest song has been the "Good-for-nothing Nan", which doubled and trebled my salary.'

(I do wish people would keep their dogs chained up. When I go into Parliament I shall introduce a Bill to that effect.)

'Who was this song by?'

'Tom and George Le Brunn. I first sang it at the Trocadero. The idea of the song and of the dance was, I may say, quite my own. Before that I had several big successes, notably "The Dutch Girl"; a Tyrolean song, "The Mountain Guide", and "My Old Man".'

'Now what of "Daddy, etc."?' (Oh, that dog! Evidently Miss Victoria's worthy parent had been so worried with the song that he bought her this STAR-GAZER-distresser, this large-eyed-and-mouthed animal now in such close propinquity to me.)

'I first sang it at the South London, eighteen months ago. It was written and composed by Joseph Tabrar. By the way, there is a coincidence about it worth telling, I think. I was working at the London Pavilion as well at that time, and one Saturday afternoon, I saw Mr Tabrar, who told me he had an idea for me, and he sang the chorus over. I took a big fancy to the song at once and said, "Will you write it up and bring it to me to-morrow?" Well, on the Saturday night, at the South London, I was presented, on the stage, with a little black kitten inside a basket. It came from Miss Alice Conway, of Conway and Clark.'

'Have you still got it?' I asked, trembling, as I wondered if this lady's partiality for animals extended to the domestic lion, or some other tame pet.

'Oh yes, and big cat it is now. I was offered a lot of money for it, in America, but wouldn't part with it for anything. On Sunday, Mr Tabrar came up and finished the song, and I told him of my present. He said, "Take the kitten on with you". I learnt the song that day, the band parts were arranged at eleven at night, and I sang it at the South London on the Monday. The cat went to America with me, and back again. It has been lost three times, and once was away for four days. We then found an old maid had it who had a mania for cats. That was in Hull.'

'And shortly after the time you first sang the song with the piteous refrain you visited the States, did you not?' I asked, as I silently and cautiously changed places with my friend, to be nearer Miss Victoria, and a little farther from that thing – the dog.

'Yes, a few weeks after. I sang the song first in the latter part of October, and on the 3rd of December sailed, by the S.S. *Etruria*, for New York.'

'How did you enjoy the voyage? Had you a pleasant time, eh?'

'No, I was very ill all the way, and I kept asking to be thrown overboard. Mother, who was with me, was ill too. I never went into the saloon for a meal once during the whole voyage, and when I got to New York I was as thin as a rail. The sailors and all on board were very kind to me.'

'You appeared with Mr Tony Pastor, did you not?'

'Correct. I was at his theatre for twelve weeks, and three weeks at Buffalo. On my opening night in New York the flowers presented to me covered the stage. Mr Pastor made a speech and there was quite an ovation. It was a grand reception, and I could have cried with joy.'

'Do you have to sing more songs over there than in this country?'

'No, it is not like the provinces. One is supposed to do three songs a night, but I had to do six, and all the time I was in America I was suffering acutely from catarrh. The only thing I didn't like was the quick changing. Mr Pastor said I was the biggest success of any artiste who had gone over there except Bessie Bonehill. On my first night I received bouquets from her, from the Howard Athenaeum Co., Mr and Mrs Pastor, the '5A's' Club, and all the aristocracy of America.'

'I suppose everyone was delighted with "Bow-wow", the song I mean, *not* the animal.'

Miss Victoria smiled saucily and said –

'It was the biggest success ever known there. Over five thousand copies of it were sold in New York alone in one month. The cat got splendid notices in the papers, and, as I told you, I had many good offers to sell it. One was from a member of the Vaudeville Club, who offered me 125 dollars (£25), but I wouldn't part with it for any money.'

'You must have been sorry to come back, if you were treated so well.'

'Yes, I should have liked to have stayed a little longer, but I could not postpone my English engagements. I appeared at the Vaudeville Club, as well as at Pastor's Theatre, for six weeks. They generally engage artistes for only one week; most of them have also to appear on Sundays, but I did not. The Club consists of four hundred members, who are the pick of the aristocracy. I fulfilled three weeks before I went to Buffalo, and, on returning, had another three weeks. The Club gave me a brougham, coachman, and footman to work my "turns" with. I used to go there after I had finished at the Theatre, and had to sing three or four songs. I generally went there about twelve o'clock, the performance being over about one.

'I was one evening at this club presented with what was, I think, quite a unique gift. It was a horseshoe of flowers, in the middle of which were the words "Good-bye, Bow Wow", and below, in a garden of flowers, stood the dog you have been admiring.'

Some years later Miss Victoria was interviewed by the most prestigious and representative of the trade papers, *The Era*.

Chat with Miss Vesta Victoria
(by our own commissioner)

Miss Vesta Victoria, who is, at the time these lines are being penned, fulfilling contracts at the Tivoli, Oxford, and Paragon, speaks in enthusiastic terms of her recently-concluded American engagement. 'They say I made the greatest success that has ever been known there,' she says in her vivacious manner. 'The Press and the public were awfully good to me; in fact, I have never even been treated so well in my own country. I was away from home for three months, and I performed all the time in New York, appearing under the management of Messrs Percy Williams, Hammerstein, and Proctor. Had it not been for the fact that I had arranged to open in London on June 4 I should undoubtedly have stayed much longer in the States. Mr Louis Fields wanted me to play the leading comedy part in his new play at the Herald-square Theatre in New York. If I had been able to comply with his wishes, I should have been with him for thirty-five weeks – the period for which the piece is to run.'

Miss Victoria's statement as to the hearty reception she experienced in New York is fully borne out by certain Transatlantic newspaper extracts which have been placed at our disposal. Here is one from the *Brooklyn Daily Eagle:* 'The little English music-hall star, in her eccentric characters and comic songs, has proved the best vaudeville attraction Mr Williams has ever had.' That is saying a good deal, but there is no doubt that it is the truth, as a consensus of Press opinions indicates. Miss Victoria is going back to America in October. She tells us that the salaries given in the land of dollars and dimes are far better than those to be got in England, and she herself has such an admiration for American people that she is already looking forward with keen pleasure to the renewing of their acquaintance. She finds very little difference between the variety theatres of the two countries. 'Our high-class music halls,' she says, 'may be somewhat more elaborate in their appointments and decorations, but that is about all. No; I did not play in any of the theatres where continuous performances are given. My longest appearance for one night? Well, I was on the stage for forty-seven minutes, that was my record. Every night there were continual shouts for encores, and I had to make speeches to the people.'

'Then they were not satisfied with two or three songs, Miss Victoria?'

'I used to sing six or seven songs at each performance, my repertoire including "It ain't all Honey", "The Artist's Model", "Waiting at the Church", the "Hunting Song", "The Country Girl", and "The Turkey Girl". All of them proved immensely popular. I happened just to take out the stuff they particularly liked. American audiences are most demonstrative. I had no end of bouquets, flowers, presents, and congratulatory letters.'

A reference by Miss Victoria to a couple of new songs she was producing at the London halls suggested a question.

'I suppose the bringing out of a new song is something akin, from the artist's point of view, to the playing of a new part?'

'I am always very nervous', replies the lady, 'concerning the singing for the first time in public of a new song. Of course, I know that, having been on the stage since I was four years of age, I ought to have got used to the work by now. But the fact is, you never can foretell how a song is going to turn out at its introduction before a

175

crowded house. I sang songs in America that lots of people said would fall flat there. The only way to test a song is to render it before an audience, for there are lots of songs which the artist may think are suitable, but which do not appeal to the audience. Another set of verses which, in one's own opinion, possesses no artistic merit, may go splendidly with the house. Now, the songs I prefer are those which afford opportunities for plenty of comedy work and burlesque acting. Anybody can sing a chorus song. I think my new song, "Waiting at the Church", will prove almost, if not quite, as popular as "Our Lodger's Such a Nice Young Man". I only put that song on just before I sailed for America, and it was the most succcessful thing I did over there.'

'How long will you be away from us the next time?'

'I have engagements in the States offered me for six months. I should probably remain in New York for four months, and the rest of the time would be spent in some of the other big towns.'

Miss Victoria made her first big hit with the song of 'Good for nothing Nan', when she was a child of ten. She dressed and made up as a wayward, Topsy-like character. From that she went on to do broad low comedy as well as light comedy. But a greater triumph came with 'Daddy wouldn't buy me a Bow-Wow', which created a sensation in variety circles. The tune was whistled and hummed in the streets of every town and city in the Kingdom, as well as in America, where Miss Victoria was rewarded with rapturous applause. The clever artist could have made a nice little sum of money by the sale of dogs, for specimens of every breed of the canine family were presented to her while the 'Daddy wouldn't buy me a Bow-Wow' craze was at its height. She had a similar experience, though the presents were not of the livestock order, when she sang the song 'Just because they put me into Trousers', a song which, among many others, that became equally popular, was written by Miss Victoria's brother, Mr Lawrence Barclay.

Admirers of Miss Victoria may be interested to learn that the grotesque dresses which she has been seen wearing on the stage have been designed by herself, and made by her mother.

THE ERA, 16 JUNE 1906

Vesta Victoria's repertoire has about it a curious sequential felicity. Her most famous song, 'Waiting at the Church', tells of premarital catastrophe, as does 'Our Lodger's Such a Nice Young Man', so nice, in fact, that he marries the singer's mother, which subsequently inspires the disappointed young maiden to complain that 'Now We Have to Call Him Father'. But at last wedding bells chime, and the bride finds it a mixed blessing to be married into the world of art.

It's Alright in the Summertime

My old man is a very funny chap,
He's an artist in the Royal Academy.
He paints pictures from morning until night,
Paints 'em with his left hand, paints 'em with his right.
All his subjects, take the tip from me,
Are very very Eve-and-Adamy,
And I'm the model that has to pose,
For his pictures ev'ry day.

And it's alright in the summertime, in the summertime it's lovely.
While my old man's painting hard, I'm posing in the old back yard,
But oh, oh, in the wintertime, it's another thing you know,
With a little red nose,
And very little clothes,
And the stormy winds do blow, oh, oh.

One day I am Cupid with a dart, and another day a fairy beautiful,
I pose as Venus arising from the sea, in the water-butt with the
    water to my knee.
Then he hangs me out upon the line, you see, I have to be so dutiful,
As I hang there, oh, he paints me as an angel in the sky.

My old man, oh, he plays a funny game,
And I've only just begun to tumble him.
All day long he's a-running out of paint
But the paint is whisky, don't you think it ain't.
These are all the clothes I've got to wear,
But I've made up my mind to humble him.
I'll take a walk up the West one day,
Just dressed up as I am.

WORDS AND MUSIC BY FRED MURRAY AND GEORGE EVERARD

Vesta Victoria's most successful songwriters were the team of Henry Pether and Fred Leigh, who, apart from writing 'Waiting at the Church', provided her with yet another song illustrating the unforeseen difficulties in the way of a young lady hoping to get a husband. This song has a curiously extended history, no doubt due to the long-standing reputation Vesta earned in America. In the early years of the century she made this song of Pether and Leigh's famous on both continents. Long after her retirement Columbia Pictures produced one of the most successful musical pictures of all time, *Cover Girl*, starring Gene Kelly and Rita Hayworth, with songs by the distinguished team of Ira Gershwin and Jerome Kern. The convolutions of the plot dictated that at one point Miss Hayworth, as a New York nightclub dancer, should become her own grandmother, a one-time star of the music hall. In this flashback sequence the older Hayworth sings Vesta Victoria's song, without acknowledgement. The credits for the picture simply say 'Songs by Ira Gershwin and Jerome Kern'. A whole generation of young film-goers was duped into thinking that those two writers had achieved the remarkably accurate pastiche of the grandmother's song. In fact, it was by Pether and Leigh; its inclusion in the picture is almost certainly explained by Kern's intimate familiarity with vaudeville and his frequent working periods in Edwardian London, where he haunted the musical theatres and music halls and must have seen Vesta doing her stuff. Certainly the song was of the sort which sticks in the mind.

Poor John

I ought to think myself a lucky girl, I know,
'Cos I'm engaged, but still, somehow, I don't think so.
John – that's the name of my finnonce, you see,
There's no mistake he's very fond of me.
He took me out for walks and oh, he was so nice.
He always used to kiss me on the same place twice.
Often in the park we would sit and spoon,
And I was oh, so happy till the other afternoon.

John took me round to see his mother, his mother, his mother,
And while he introduced us to each other,
She weighed up ev'rything that I had on.
She put me through a cross-examination,
I fairly boiled with aggravation.
Then she shook her head, looked at me and said,
'Poor John. Poor John.'

As soon as she could get me all alone, oh dear,
She asked so many questions that I felt quite queer.
Thought John too young to take a wife just yet,
Asked when and where it was that we first met.
She said no girl could help but worship her dear son,
And told me pretty plainly what a prize I'd won.
Started fairly slow, then she made a spurt,
And hoped that I knew how to put a tailpiece on a shirt.

John took me round to see his mother, *etc.*

She said, 'Young girls today are all for outside show,
The clothes you see may look all right, the rest, oh no.'
What she was driving at I soon made out,
My style of dress was too refined, no doubt.
Then all at once she gave a sigh and cried, 'Oh, lor',
I wonder what on earth he wants to marry for?'
That was quite enough. Up my temper flew,
Says I, 'Perhaps it's so that he can get away from you.'

John took me round to see his mother, *etc.*

HENRY PETHER AND FRED LEIGH

There was a whimsical postscript to Vesta Victoria's sequence of songs leading into a marriage with mixed blessings. When widowed, she reminisced in song with an item called 'He Was a Good, Kind Husband', whose most telling lines were:

> There he would sit by the fireside,
> Such a chilly man was John.
> I hope and trust there's a nice warm fire
> Where my old man's gone.

Miss Victoria lived on until 1951, by which time Frederick Willis was already beginning to compile his account of what was now a truly lost age. Taking as his vantage point the fiftieth anniversary of the arrival in Britain of Queen Alexandra, he compiled one of the most comprehensive accounts of the music hall ever published, yet again drifting from the red plush and gilt of the great West End halls to the lesser but still considerable pomp and circumstance of the suburban theatres.

The fiftieth anniversary of Queen Alexandra's arrival in England was celebrated in 1912. A few of my older shopmates could remember her arrival at Bricklayers Arms Station, which was then the London Terminus of the South-Eastern Railway, and all were agreed about her beauty and the welcome she received. Alexandra Day was established on June 26th of that year and celebrated by selling artificial wild roses in aid of the hospitals. In the early years of Alexandra Rose Day all roses were uniform in size and material, and no matter how much you gave you had only one rose and wore only one. It would have been considered bad form to wear more. I remember the beautiful weather of that day very clearly. It was what we call (erroneously) typical English June weather, blue sky, soft breezes and glorious sunshine. The streets were gay with pretty girls in the graceful flowery dresses and picture hats of the period, selling roses from trays decorated with pink satin ribbons and garlands of the flowers. Many famous beauties were among the sellers in the West End and there was keen competition to get roses pinned into buttonholes by those fair hands. It was at this time that the Music Hall came into its own. The first command performance was given at the Palace Theatre before King George and Queen Mary. The Music Hall had, however, received royal approval in 1901 when Dan Leno was commanded to Sandringham. He gave a selection from his repertoire before a Christmas family party which included King Edward. Until then the Music Hall had been under a cloud and was not spoken of in respectable circles, but afterwards there were long queues outside the Pavilion where Dan was appearing.

Music Hall proper is a purely English institution. It grew out of the sing-songs held in Victorian taverns and the singers were drawn from the common people. They made local and intimate topics the themes of their jokes and songs. It was a kind of family party where the jokes were family jokes. That is why the old music-hall artists had little success abroad; even Dan Leno was a failure in America. The music-hall artist turned the tragedy of life into comedy. He knew, no one better, all about the ups and downs of the poor and near-poor of London; the pawnshop, the pub, fried fish, and mothers-in-law were the stock jokes, and efforts to keep up appearances provided an endless theme for mirth. From the earliest days music-hall songs reflected the mood of the people. Sometimes they were sentimental, sometimes patriotic and political. At times they were poor in quality but they were never meaningless as so many songs are to-day. In the early years of this century music halls had emerged from the pot-house and entered the palace. The stars of the palaces had graduated in the pot-houses, and the old timers had an air of honest vulgarity and simple ostentation that was inoffensive because of their obvious sincerity. Many were reckless and thriftless, but all had attractive personalities. There was something about them emanating from that peculiar genius which had made them what they were. Such was the genesis of the Music Hall, represented at the time I am writing about by the Tivoli, Oxford, Pavilion, Canterbury and Middlesex.

The Hippodrome and Coliseum belonged to another type of house altogether. They were entirely new and, in the entertainment world, were the last word in architectural and engineering ingenuity. I was privileged to go behind the scenes of the Coliseum before it was opened to the public, and I was most impressed with the

179

machinery for manipulating the revolving stage, the conveniences for the performers, and the general efficiency; everything was designed to ensure a perfect performance. The Coliseum started with four performances a day, two of them quite distinct, an achievement that has never been excelled in the theatre. But neither the Coliseum nor the Hippodrome had any connection with true Music Hall. They went right back to Astley's Circus and the ancient Bartholomew Fair for their inspiration. Acrobats, performing animals, educated horses, Houdini the gaol-breaker, giants, trick cyclists, dancers, and 'Grand Zoological and Aquatic Spectacles' were the sort of shows that had assembled at Bartholomew Fair. Messrs Moss and Stoll, those remarkable men of the variety theatres who gave us the Hippodrome and Coliseum, brought them all up to date, cleansed them, made them honest and respectacble, and presented them in handsomely-equipped houses at popular prices.

In their efforts to create an atmosphere of grandeur the management of these houses sometimes overdid it. Normally a turn is, and was, announced in an ordinary music hall by slipping a number-plate into a panel at the side of the proscenium. This office was usually performed by a stage hand. Moss's management tried to improve the method. A golden easel stood on each side of the stage and the number of the turn was placed upon it by a dignified footman, dressed in the full glory of the livery of an eighteenth-century nobleman's servant, wig, silk stockings, plush breeches all complete. This was too much for the Cockney's sense of humour. Every time this grand figure appeared to change the number the house rocked with ironical cheers. No star could ever hope for a more tremendous ovation than this simple operation of changing the number on the board drew from the audience. The management soon saw that pomp and circumstance has its limits and the old system of number boards was restored. Later, these houses had a much higher form of entertainment, the Coliseum even going so far as to have a Sarah Bernhardt season, in which that great French actress appeared in extracts from some of her most famous plays. Before this, however, the Hippodrome presented Machnow, the Russian giant. Machnow arrived at the Hippodrome in a pantechnicon on which was a flaming poster saying: 'Machnow The Russian Giant Is In Here'. Whether he was or not I am unable to say. I have no taste for freak-gazing so I didn't see Machnow in his professional capacity, but I went to measure him for a top hat. He was certainly an enormous man. I forget his exact height – something well over eight feet, I think – but I remember the size of his hat, which was eight. This was extremely small for so big a man, and to make the hat more proportionate we gave it a very wide and 'wingy' brim. It added to his stature considerably. Machnow could speak no English and he gave me the impression of being a simple peasant. 'Shake hands with the gentleman!' said his manager, as I was leaving him. This was a phrase that Machnow evidently understood. He held out a mighty hand with a gentle smile and I did the best I could with it.

The Alhambra, Empire, and The Palace belonged to another type of house. The Empire, in Leicester Square, described itself as 'The Premier Variety Theatre, Cosmopolitan Club and Rendezvous of the World'. The Alhambra was satisfied with the more modest description of 'National Theatre of Varieties'. Both houses specialised in Ballet and although I have no particular liking for this form of dramatic art I was much impressed with the genius, efficiency and discipline that were striking features of ballets at both houses. It gave me the satisfaction that I always get from a really first-class piece of craftsmanship. For some years I had rather close contact with the Alhambra and I was astonished at the amount of hard work the *corps-de-ballet* had to get through. Rehearsals were strenuous and frequent, and the girls appeared each morning with the regularity of factory workers. Their life seemed one incessant hurrying backwards and forwards from home to theatre. In private life they were quiet and reserved and gave no hint of their profession in their appearance. Later, the Empire made a feature of Revue which really *was* Revue. It burlesqued current affairs in a way that would not be possible to-day. The spirit of the Empire and Alhambra was continental, and neither house had any connection with real Music Hall. Our two greatest music-hall artists, Dan Leno and Marie Lloyd, never appeared at either of the Leicester Square houses.

During the last few years Londoners have seen their music halls disappear and cinemas spring up in their places. In the days I am dealing with, theatres were disappearing and the all-conquering music halls taking their places. It was a great shock to theatregoers to see the Lyceum, so long the scene of Sir Henry Irving's triumphs, become a 'Palace of Varieties', with two performances a night. Thomas Barrasford attempted to give a show something between those of the Leicester Square houses and the Hippodrome and Coliseum. His chief item was an excerpt from Grand Opera, with a first-class company of Continental singers. It was a praiseworthy attempt to raise public musical taste, but it failed because English people never had much liking for opera. The Royal English Opera House was conquered by the variety theatre and became The Palace, one of the most beautifully decorated houses in London. Here Maud Allen took the town by storm, but her fame was short-lived. Her 'Salomé Dance' was really a good joke to those who knew how this hitherto unknown young woman was rocketed to stardom by the power of advertisement. The best thing that came out of Maud Allen's act was Will Evans's 'Saloppi Dance'. While the arty people were showing off their newly-acquired knowledge of classical dancing, in high-flown discussions in the press and elsewhere, Will Evans was making the Tivoli rock with laughter with his clever burlesque of the act. The music hall audience, with its native common-sense, guessed rightly that Maud Allen's 'Salomé Dance' was bunk.

In the heyday of the halls the term 'music hall' was rarely used, 'palace of varieties' never. People referred to the hall by name. They went to the 'Tiv', 'Pav', or 'Mo'; they did not generalise the whole lot as 'music hall' as people now talk about 'the pictures'. Each hall had its individuality. The Tivoli was in its prime in the days of Adney Payne, a big, ex-military type of man with a heavy, drooping moustache, who was a familiar figure in the Strand and was known as 'The Guv'nor' to everyone. He was the only man the star showed any respect for. He made the name of the Tivoli famous, so that it was spoken of with affection in all parts of the world where Englishmen met, although its whole history did not exceed twenty-five years. I refer to a Tivoli programme over forty years old and find that out of seventeen turns twelve are stars commanding salaries of from £100 to £250 per week – Will Evans, Happy Fanny Fields, George Robey, Wilkie Bard, G.H. Elliott, Harry Fragson, Little Tich. I could never understand how the Tivoli did it, for it was only a tiny house. Perhaps this accounts for its short but brilliant life.

The Middlesex, in Drury Lane, was a bit of an anachronism. A hall built on the site of the old Mogul Tavern, it lingered on for a few years in the Victorian manner. It was referred to by its patrons as 'the Old Mo', and a variety artist who got through his turn there without incident was very good indeed. The Old Mo had no use for incompetence. Audiences were not afraid to hiss in those days and a performer getting 'the bird' was not a pleasant sight. There was no polite applause; either it was genuine or it was absent altogether. The painful silence that followed an unsatisfactory turn was often camouflaged by a crashing chord from the orchestra. Sometimes the reception was mixed and the 'Encores' of those who approved were counteracted by cries of 'No More!' from the opposing school of thought. In the din it was not always possible to distinguish one from the other, as they sounded much alike. But one could never mistake a 'raspberry', and I regret to say that some members of the audience were masters of this expressive signal of contempt.

My funniest recollection is of Harry Tate in 'Motoring'. When he first presented this sketch at the Tivoli he literally stopped the show. I have never seen anything funnier. Harry Tate's burlesques were not just nonsense; they were cartoons of real life, exaggerated but recognisable. Eugene Stratton brought us the legendary romance of the Southern States of America. He was astonishingly light and graceful, his eyes and teeth gleamed out of his black face as the limelight followed him round the stage, and he sang the melodies of Leslie Stuart, 'Lily of Laguna', 'Little Dolly Daydream', and other lovely tunes which will bring pleasure to generations still to come. Bransby Williams's Dickens impersonations carried more conviction to me, an ardent Dickensian, than those of any actor, but it is only fair to point out that Bransby Williams's sketches were almost too short for faults to be noticed. Bransby Williams made Dickens known to thousands of people who had never read a word of Dickens in their lives. Paul Cinquevalli (who was really an Englishman) was the greatest juggler of all. Every performance he gave was an object lesson in human dexterity. I never saw him bungle a trick and I never heard of anyone who did. All who saw him lost interest in any other juggler.

G.H. Chirgwin was another unique variety artist. His special features were a one-string fiddle, a black face (with one white eye) and a falsetto voice. Originally the whole of his face was blackened, but one night he accidentally rubbed off the black round one eye and this attracted so much notice that he made the white eye his trademark and billed himself 'The White-Eyed Kaffir'. His turn was not my cup of tea – I usually adjourned to the bar until he had finished – but his popularity was enormous and rarely was he allowed to leave the stage without singing the song that the audience loved best, 'The Blind Boy'. Cries for 'Blind Boy' would come from all parts of the house and the plaintive wail of the song that so distressed me must have given pleasure to hundreds of thousands during the Kaffir's career.

My two greatest memories are, of course, Dan Leno and Marie Lloyd. I shall always remember Dan Leno, a queer little figure, coming on with a trot and stopping close to the footlights with a characteristic little dance. One night, at the time when another comedian was imitating this dance, Dan came forward, gave his little dance with great deliberation, and bringing his foot down finally with an emphatic slap he glared at the audience and exclaimed, 'That's mine!' It was the only time I saw him serious on the stage and the audience roared its approval. He had a way of peering forward at the audience as if he were taking the whole house into his confidence and his eager face always seemed hopeful that everyone would believe his preposterous stories. 'When I got married,' he used to say with ludicrous dignity, 'I always said there would only be one master in my house!' Here he paused and glared sternly at the audience before adding, 'And so there is, that's the missis!' While he waited for the laughter to stop his face would become wreathed in that famous smile and then he would add, reassuringly, 'But I'm a sort of foreman!' He spoke in a mild, conversational voice that could be heard distinctly all over the house. This was a gift of all successful music-hall artists, the priceless gift of audibility without effort. When I hear some of the modern variety artists doing their stuff in one long shout from start to finish, I think of this. I saw one of Dan Leno's last performances at the old Pavilion and although I detected a deflection in his style I had no suspicion that he was seriously ill. His early death came as a great shock, for there were few men held in more affectionate esteem.

Dan Leno and Marie Lloyd, in common with other old-time music hall artists, acquired their remarkable success on their merits alone. They worked their way up from the lowest grade of entertaining to stardom without the assistance of press agents, producers, expensive scenery, or beauty choruses. They stood alone in front of a painted canvas, and it was only their genius and personality that won the audience and maintained its support. Poor Dan Leno always had dreams of playing tragic parts and he loved to dress as Irving's characters and have his photograph taken, but Marie had no ambition to be anyone but herself. Dan and Marie were not actors, far from it. They were just outstanding characters in a country rich in individualism, and they had the genius to exploit their personalities for all they were worth. Marie Lloyd was a frank and generous soul who hated humbug like the plague. Her dazzling smile and Cockney personality won all hearts. She appeared so audacious that one expected her to say the most outrageous things, but she didn't.

The character she presented on the boards, a rather full-blown, prosperous, vulgar woman of the period, was one that could be seen all over London, especially in the market places, and the comedy she got out of it was inexhaustible.

Adney Payne was not only a highly successful music-hall manager, he looked the part to perfection, but Oswald Stoll (afterwards Sir Oswald) a greater manager still, looked like the last person in the world to have anything to do with music halls. He might have been a respectable, small business man, with a little suburban house and an interest in the local nonconformist church. He spoke slowly and softly while surveying you benevolently through his glasses. Yet this remarkable man had been in the variety business since childhood, in partnership with his mother, who was frequently seen in the box-office at the Coliseum. He thoroughly transformed the music halls of the whole country. He was most particular that the spotlight on top of the Coliseum should shine on the clock of St Martin-in-the-Fields. He neither drank nor smoked, and as far as I know never took a holiday. For relaxation he wrote a study of Herbert Spencer and an essay on high finance, which authorities tell me is remarkable.

Of course, the Music Hall had some severe critics. Worthy people, who had never been inside a music hall in their lives, strongly condemned them. All social evils, especially among the young, were laid at their door. (People say the same sort of thing to-day, about cinemas.) Mr W.T. Stead was a journalist who made a great noise in the world. He announced rather pompously that he had never been inside a music hall in his life, but he intended to go and give his verdict to an anxiously-awaiting world. He did, and gave his opinion in four words, 'Drivel for the dregs'. To-day, looking back through the rosy clouds of memory, we are inclined to go to the other extreme and think that in the old music halls everything in the garden was lovely. The truth, of course, lies in between. Music halls made no pretence to have any aim other than that of providing amusement and bearing this in mind I should think a normally intelligent member of the audience found that in the best halls seventy-five per cent of the show was good and the rest poor. In the other halls the proportion was about fifty-fifty.

Music hall artists were a distinct type, shrewd in many ways, simple in others. Fond of flattery, they became easy prey for the hordes of cadgers and scroungers that flourish in every age and country. They were happy-go-lucky, hard working and surprisingly abstemious. A large part of their lives was spent in travelling all over the country from one hall to another. Sunday was the day for travel. On Sunday evening, after they had settled their lodgings for the coming week, they would make Brixton Road their promenade. Here they would meet one another and adjourn to the Old White Horse for an hour or two of sociability. They loved to advertise the fact that they were 'Pros'; their dress was distinctive, their hair cut differently. What strutting and posing there was, what tales of sensational ovations at Wolverhampton or Wigan were told, what wonderful notices from the local press all over England were quoted! They presented a sad picture of dissipation to the prudes and killjoys but an object lesson to the observant of that glorious Mark Tapley spirit that is cheerful in very unfavourable circumstances. The greater part of their lives consisted of hard work, dull lodgings, wandering from town to town, and fighting all the time to keep their periods of 'resting' down to a minimum. Who would grudge them a few hours' cheerfulness in a comfortable pub?

As old age came on, a lot of these cheerful souls fell upon hard times. Many were helped by the admirable organisations they created themselves, and some went into comfortable retirement. I remember Whit Cunliffe, a top-liner who, dressed as a Georgian Dandy, sang topical songs, a refined and tuneful turn. After the First World War he would take off his hat and show me that he was getting a bit thin on the top, although he looked no more than five-and-twenty on the stage. 'And when,' he used to say, 'when I raise my hat on the stage and that bald spot is large enough for the audience to see, then I say good-bye to the footlights for ever and retire to my little farm in Kent.' Whit Cunliffe was so young and virile looking that on two occasions (he told me) during the first war, a girl presented him with a white feather on a railway station platform. Needless to say he was quite flattered. Harry Randall I knew on and off the stage in the days when he appeared in baggy frock coat and scrubby top hat, singing about all the tricks he practised to 'make things hum' in his little general shop. Years afterwards I met him in comfortable retirement. He was still a dapper little figure faultlessly dressed, he still had the alert face and bright eyes. He lived in a residential hotel on the northern heights of London. The hotel was a fine Georgian house in extensive grounds which had once been the home of David Garrick. 'I live here,' Harry used to say, with a twinkle in his eye, 'to keep up the theatrical prestige of the neighbourhood.'

Out in the wilds of suburbia, the 'Empires', offshoots of the Hippodrome, were springing up. Beautifully decorated and equipped, they provided a condensed Hippodrome show at very moderate prices. They had the same disadvantage, however, of other great organisations – lack of individuality. If individuality was what one wanted there were still a few of the independent type from which to choose, notably the 'South London', 'Bedford', 'Collins's', 'The Forresters' (where, it is said, Dan Leno first appeared), 'The Star', Bermondsey, locally known as 'The Rats' (where Charlie Chaplin appeared, unknown and anonymous, in a Fred Karno sketch) and the 'Metropole', Camberwell. The latter had been a theatre, and a very charming little house it was. In its music-hall days the managing director was Mr Jesse Sparrow, a shrewd man of the theatre who had Music Hall in his blood. He gave a consistently good show and had a special flair for collecting unknown turns of merit from all over the country. Unlike Carroll Levis's 'Discoveries', these were all qualified artists who had not yet hit the top line although many of them deserved to do so. The cosy elegance of this little theatre was ideal for the music-hall spirit and here one could always be sure of a pleasant evening with 'Versatile Comediennes', 'Musical Eccentrics', 'Society Entertainers', and 'The Girl You Can't Forget'. The 'Met' also put on some first-class sketches. I recall 'The Spy', a dramatic episode written by Percy Ford, who was the acting manager of the theatre. This was an incident of the American Civil War and the theme was the conflict between a mother's private feelings and her duty to the State. The scene was a domestic interior that could easily be fitted up from any scenic storeroom, the cast two actors and one actress, the acting time twenty minutes. Yet it held the house, and it was powerful enough to linger in my memory for over forty years. The 'Met' had a very live orchestra of half a dozen members including the conductor. To watch this orchestra and listen to the music was alone worth the price of admission. The spirited overture would be a potpourri of popular songs, in which every man was responsible for at least two instruments; the conductor, in his spare moments between attending to the piano and violin, conducted the orchestra with much aplomb, using the bow of his fiddle.

The gallery of the Metropole was the stronghold of the Camberwell boys, as good a test audience as any artist could wish for. They gave an honest, unmistakable verdict, and no sounder judges could be found in London. In my youth I was as fond of a bit of fun as anyone and, accordingly, three friends and I booked a box (price 5s) at the 'Met' one evening and turned up in evening dress. The Camberwell boys took it for granted that the management should be seen in the grand entrance in evening dress, as indeed they were, but when they saw us entering the box with dignity they were severely shaken. Shrill inquiries sounded across the auditorium: 'Which one of yer is Burlington Bertie?' followed by the command, 'Turn rarnd yer swankers, yer ain't got no backs to yer coats!' We bore this in dignified silence. As the evening advanced the air became more electric until, at last, during a pause in the programme, one of my friends, the wag of the party, leaned forward in the box and, shooting his cuffs, fitted a monocle into his eye and surveyed the gallery with an icy stare. The result was pandemonium, and amid cries from the chuckers-out of 'Order

PLEASE!' we discreetly withdrew. I did not fully appreciate this joke until a penny bus journey was between us and the infuriated populace.

FREDERICK WILLIS, *101 JUBILEE ROAD*

Willis tended to admire the scantily-clad young ladies of the chorus from afar, almost as though they were mysterious creatures from another planet, even though they were, as we know, often members of his own family, or residents of the same street as his own. Arthur Symons enjoyed tormenting himself into paroxyms of unrequited passion in the stalls, in the wings, at the stage door, anywhere where the tension could inspire his muse to write of forbidden fruits and perfumed nights. A much brisker approach was the one adopted by that cheerful amorist Hesketh Pearson, most urbane and confidential of biographers, whose book about his own life presents a portrait of robust and thoroughly enjoyable explorations into the riddle of the relationship between lust and love. One of the interludes in his youth when he was living in Brighton involved a visit to the local theatre whose conclusions must have made many of his readers envious.

Every Christmas the Grand put on a pantomime, and Robinson Crusoe was the theme of the one produced on Boxing Day, 1908. I went with a business acquaintance to a performance in the first week of 1909, and saw a chorus-girl who made my heart miss a few beats. She was a brunette with large dark eyes, a Grecian profile, and a perfectly proportioned figure. I learnt her name from an attendant, and in the interval sent her a note with the largest box of chocolates I could buy in the theatre. The note said that I would be at the stage-door after the show. That began an affair that lasted for two years. For all I know she may still be alive, so I had better change her name to Bella. She lived in Brighton with her family and had a sister almost as pretty as herself. I cannot honestly say that she had much intelligence, and as far as I could make out the only book she had ever read was *Alice in Wonderland*, but her sense of fun made her good company and her sudden rages made her look extraordinarily beautiful, so that I sometimes provoked them for the pleasure of beholding a tempestuous Venus and the satisfaction of mollifying her.

HESKETH PEARSON, *BY MYSELF*

Pearson's cheerfully amoral approach to the halls would have borne out the very worst fears of families like C.H. Rolph's, which combined a conviction that it knew best with a blanket ignorance of what it suspected represented the very worst. Rolph's description of the opposition inside his family to his having anything to do with music hall evokes thoughts of H.L. Mencken's definition of Puritanism, which is the worry that somebody somewhere might be enjoying himself. Rolph was introduced to the forbidden joys of the halls by his brother Jim, in the days before the Great War when the family was part of the working-class population of Fulham. His recollections are of particular interest to me for the lurid light they shed on the approach to comedy of my distant ancestor Sam Mayo, and for his corroboration of my suspicion that Harry Lauder may not quite have been all that his own generation cracked him up to be.

I simply could not understand what could be evil about a hall with music in it. I did understand that the music halls had bars where you could drink during the intervals or (if you preferred it) throughout the evening; and my mother had sad memories of what drunkenness had meant to some of her childhood friends. It was her belief, and Grandma Speed's, that the theatre and music hall were mere devices for encouraging people to drink. Charlie Chaplin records in his autobiography that every music-hall entertainer, after his act, was expected to go to the bar and drink with the customers – and would get no further engagements if he didn't. Many of the Fulham pubs advertised 'musical evenings', and those with gardens made a special feature of open-air concerts in summer. My mother thought this was where a great number of young people began a lifetime, usually a short one, of drunkenness. And she was probably right.

But the music hall, having begun as a sing-song in a pub, had already become the Palace of Varieties, and its progress from drunken knees-up to theatrical respectability was nearly complete. Charles Booth had written as early as 1889 in his *Life and Labour of the People in London* that 'the story of progress in this respect may be traced in many of the existing places which, from a bar parlour and a piano, to an accompaniment on which friends "obliged with a song", have passed through every stage to that of music hall; the presiding chairman being still occasionally, and the call for drinks in almost every case, retained. But the character of the songs on the whole is better, and other things are offered: it becomes a "variety" entertainment.' In 1912 King George V decreed (or perhaps merely acquiesced in) the first of all the Royal Command Performances. But if this was intended as the music hall's final accolade of respectability it was not so regarded in our house, and indeed it may well have been that the reputation of royal households was such that even a King of England couldn't decree anything into respectability.

By 1911 the 'presiding chairman' was a thing of the past; and for my part, far from being seduced into drunkenness, I never even saw the bar. (Jim was a non-drinker.) I think the biggest surprise of my first music-hall visit – at the Hammersmith Palace of Varieties – was the orchestra. I was accustomed by this time to the sound of a band or orchestra tuning up, and to me it has always been a strangely pleasant and exciting cacophony, full of mouth-watering promise and chaotic splendour. The orchestra at the Hammersmith Palace spent less time over this than I had expected, but it was still effective enough as a musical aphrodisiac. And then it played! Its speed was ludicrous, maniacal, contemptuous. The raucous 'Overture' lasted about thirty deafening seconds and ended with an irrelevant crash of cymbals. I was extremely disappointed and scornful, but I was to discover that all music-hall orchestras did it; and that, indeed, these places were not halls of music but theatres where entertainers told funny stories, enacted funny sketches, abused each other, conjured, juggled, contorted themselves, sang and danced, performed highly dangerous acrobatics and – very occasionally – played popular classics on piano, violin, trumpet, or mouth-organ. I thought they were all utterly enchanting.

Fred Karno was then at the height of his fame as producer of the 'Birds' series of comedy sketches – *Early Birds, Jail Birds, Mumming Birds,* and others; and on these he constructed a huge theatrical empire of over thirty companies, fostering such outstanding performers as Charlie Chaplin, George Graves, Harry Weldon and Billie Reeves. On that first evening at the Hammersmith Palace we saw Bransby Williams in a series of the impersonations for which we was renowned – Uriah Heep, Micawber, and the Abbé Liszt. In the last-named, for some reason, he staggered about the stage playing a concertina, and someone in the gallery threw a coin on to the stage. A dropped coin in those days made a bright and unmistakable ringing sound. Bransby Williams stopped playing. 'That,' he shouted, 'is an insult, and I'm not accustomed to insults.' I was petrified. He strode off the stage to cries of 'Come back Bransby', 'Come on mate, get on with it', 'Good old Bransby', etc. And after a while, encouraged no doubt from off-stage, he graciously came back to complete his act.

On other Saturday evenings in those exciting years I was taken to the Granville at Walham Green, the Putney Hippodrome and Shepherds Bush Empire, seeing the same variety artistes (as they liked to be called) time after time: Ernie Mayne, Sam Mayo, T.E. Dunville, Ernie Lotinga, and a host of less famous names. I have before me a Granville Theatre of Varieties programme for 18 August 1911, in which Fred Karno presented 'Mumming Birds', with a cast including the now forgotten names of Fred Arthur, Wheeler and Wilson, The Martins, Terry and Birtley, Arthur Clifton, Madeline Rees (most of whom I saw on other occasions) and 'The Cinematograph Showing New Pictures'. Seats in the Orchestra Stalls cost one shilling, Pit Stalls ninepence, Circle sixpence, Gallery threepence. 'Mumming Birds' was the mildly bawdy sketch in which, three years earlier, Charlie Chaplin had played, at the age of eighteen, the part of a comedy drunk in a highly individual way that ensured his future and his fortune. But I never saw Charlie Chaplin on the stage.

I remember being astonished at the coarseness and the sexual innuendos of T.E. Dunville and Sam Mayo; I could outdo them both (I believed) in suitable company, but it was probably because of them and their imitators that, while I was uncomfortable when female artistes were on the stage (I suppose I didn't like to think they had to associate with the Dunvilles and the Mayos), I positively hated the females who impersonated males, the Vesta Tilleys and the Hetty Kings. I was unable to see why all comedians couldn't be as unembarrassing as Billy Merson. I never saw pantomimes until I took my own children to them, and even then they were spoiled for me by the transvestite principal boy and pantomime dames, theatrical eccentricities I have simply never understood. To this day Danny La Rue, gifted as I'm sure he must be, makes my flesh crawl. George Robey was reputed to be the supreme pantomime dame, but his double handicap was that I regarded him anyway as a self-satisfied bore. And although I saw Harry Lauder only once, I thought him a bore too: his success and réclame have always mystified me.

Now I felt certain that my growing addiction to the music hall would be frowned upon not only by my parents but also by Mr Herbert. Mr Herbert, therefore, must not be allowed to know and my life was becoming complicated. And although this involved none of the deception practised upon my parents, for there was absolutely no reason why I should tell Mr Herbert, today I find it strange that I felt more conscience-smitten about him than about them in relation to it. A recurring nightmare was the fear that I might get caught by one of them listening to someone like Nellie Wallace.

C.H. ROLPH, LONDON PARTICULARS

The fear which Rolph describes, that respectability might be tainted by a single visit to a music hall, received a killing blow in 1912 when the new monarch, George V, and Queen Mary sanctioned the first Royal Command Performance. The king's father, Edward VII, had paid open but not formal visits to the Empire and the Alhambra, accompanied by Queen Alexandra, but the events of 1 July 1912, at the Palace Theatre, constituted the first official recognition that the halls had become respectable. Indeed so respectable that more than one historian has suggested that the nod of approval from the monarch was not so much an accolade as a death blow, for how can any institution built on ribaldry and calculated vulgarity become a diversion for the Establishment? It had always been clear that Edward VII had a genuine affection for the halls and a positive lust for the night-life they symbolised. His son, in contrast, was not quite the man to wink at a chorus girl, and it is revealing that his only cultural achievement, according to the Oxford History of England, was the wearing of trousers creased at the sides instead of at front and back. The omens were, then, not good, and they were rendered much worse by the appointment of three men to supervise arrangements for the Command Performance: Edward Moss, Oswald Stoll and one Walter de Frece, a music-hall manager better known to posterity as Mr Vesta Tilley.

The final selected list of artists drawn up by these three dubious men was as inept as any disinterested observer might have expected. Stoll and Moss had already established a sort of monopoly over the halls, but by 1912 Moss was already a dying man, and there is little doubt that it was Stoll's influence which mattered. In any contest for the title of the most odious man in the history of the popular theatre, a great many votes would go to Bernard Dillon for his string of knockout victories over the women he lived with. A great many more would go to Fred Karno, who appears to have been suffering from some sort of psychosexual disorder, as we shall see. But Stoll was probably worse than either of them. Dillon and Karno never spread their brutalities far beyond the family hearth, whereas Stoll, whose dementia was impersonal, reduced to despair whole generations of performers and writers. He achieved this difficult trick by gaining a stranglehold on the profession and then displaying a parsimony and lack of charity which grew so acute that it engendered jokes at his expense.

Oswald Stoll was quite a man. A ruler with a rod of iron. He wouldn't have this and he wouldn't have that. I played Chiswick once, and on the wall was a notice which said, 'Artists are requested not to ask for free seats. If their friends won't pay to come and see them, how can they expect the public to?' He used to wear a frock coat and silk hat every day. He lived at Putney and walking through Putney Hill one time, so the story goes, there was a poor man standing in the gutter selling matches. He said, 'Buy a box of matches guv.' 'Why?' says Stoll. 'Well, I've only taken fourpence all day.' 'Really?' says Stoll, 'Tell me, how does that compare with the corresponding week last year?'

STANLEY HOLLOWAY, BBC SOUND ARCHIVES

Technically the Coliseum was a music hall but Stoll saw it as something grander. There were no drinking bars and there were signs in the dressing rooms: 'Please do not use any strong language here. Coarseness and Vulgarity are not allowed in the Coliseum. Gentlemen of the chorus are not allowed to take their whips to the dressing room.'

Unattractive, with gold pince-nez, deploring the use of expletives, Stoll was not only a teetotaller but a non-smoker. He patrolled the Coliseum picking up cigar ends off the carpet with the rebuke to the customer, 'Pardon me, sir, but you wouldn't have done that in your own home, would you?' When an artist complained about his position as last on the bill, explaining that he lived outside London and it was hard to find transport so late, Stoll had the simple solution: 'Move'. When a manager dared to criticise him, Stoll warned 'Do not ever dare tell me that I am wrong. If it happens again you will be dismissed.' A considerable time later the man had forgotten the incident, and pointed out another mistake. 'Mr Manager,' said Stoll, 'I told you once before never to dispute my orders. Kindly now go and draw three months' salary from the cashier in lieu of notice.'

DAN FARSON, *MARIE LLOYD AND THE MUSIC HALL*

There are only two possible explanations for the antics indulged in by Stoll and de Frece when compiling the programme for the first Royal Command Performance on 1 July 1912. Either they were both demented, or they were taking advantage of their situation to settle some old scores. Six years earlier, Marie Lloyd had been prominent in the strike against the managements, an occasion on which Stoll, after making public statements impugning her level of intelligence, had been roundly beaten. The defeat still rankled, and in spite of the opinion of H.G. Hibbert that the truth of the affair will never be known, it seems clear enough that Stoll was so keen to gain his revenge that he was willing even to reduce his own credibility to nil by omitting his enemy from the list. But there were other omissions which were less understandable, those of Eugene Stratton and Albert Chevalier. What is unfortunate about these breaches of justice is the reaction of the victims, who, instead of dismissing the whole silly episode with a ribald aside, made a public display of their sense of outrage. Chevalier even took a whole page in *The Era* to insist how worthy a choice he was, quoting the *Morning Post*: 'Historically as well as artistically his omission is a blunder of the first magnitude.'

Marie's reaction was even more pointed, and has become one of the most notorious gestures of defiance in the history of the English stage. She decided to hold a rival command performance of her own in a nearby theatre, and must have been enraptured to hear what a fiasco the official function turned out to be. Predictably *The Times* maintained the pretence that everything in the royal garden had been lovely.

THEIR MAJESTIES AND MUSIC HALLS
COMMAND PERFORMANCE
THE ART OF THE VARIETY THEATRE

Last night the art of the variety theatre received a new and a signal honour – an honour, too, which the art has thoroughly earned by its steady progress from obscurity (not unmixed with obscenity) in 'caves' and 'cellars' to general favour as an indispensable form of harmless amusement housed in sumptuous palaces . . .

The scene in the house to which they lent their distinction must have convinced them that vulgar display is by no means a characteristic of the modern music hall. Three million roses sounds, we admit, like overdoing it; but the three million roses used . . . in decorating the house – not to mention the wisteria, the flower-wreathed coloured lights, the beautiful marble decked with baskets and other Renaissance ornament in gold – were disposed with so much fine taste that the effect was one of light and airy elegance. The Royal box itself, with its roses, carnations, and other real flowers, its exquisite painted panelling and graceful pillars, was a work of art of which no age or place, however courtly, need have been anything but proud. And as for the audience, if, in boxes, stalls, and dress circle, it was not absolutely representative of the average music-hall audience at one of the larger houses – if the men wore tails and white ties instead of jackets and black ties, and the ladies appeared in something even more elaborate than the elaborate evening dress which is familiar in the stalls of a variety theatre – the audience looked, on the whole, more

189

like an average music-hall audience than an audience at a gala night at the opera.

And overhead tier upon tier was packed with the genuine enthusiastic music-hall audience – some of whom had been waiting since the small hours of the morning to gain admittance . . . .

The Programme

The Palace Orchestra, overture, 'Britannia'
Pipifax and Panlo ('Humpsti Bumpsti')
Barclay Gammon, 'Rule Britannia' and 'In the Shadows'
The Palace Girls, 'A Fantasy in Black and White'
G.H. Chirgwin
Joe Boganny's Opium Fiends, 'Five Minutes in China Town'
Fanny Fields, 'The Happy Little Dutch Girl'
Cinquevalli, 'The Human Billiard Table'
Harry Tate, 'Motoring'
Vesta Tilley, 'Algy, the Piccadilly Johnnie'
La Pia, 'The Dance of Fire' and 'The Spirit of the Waves'
Little Tich, 'Popularity' and 'Big Boots'
Arthur Prince and Jim, nautical ventiloquial scena
The Palace Orchestra, selection, 'Melodious Memories'
Alfred Lester and Buena Bent, 'The Village Fire Brigade'
Clarice Mayne with J.W. Tate, 'I'm Longing for Some One
    to Love Me'
George Robey, 'the Mayor of Mudcumdyke'
Charles T. Aldrich, eccentric humorous juggling
David Devant, sleight of hand
Wilkie Bard, 'The Night Watchman'
Anna Pavlova, assisted by L. Novikoff and members
    of the Imperial Russian Ballet, 'Le Cygne', 'Papillon',
    Divertissement, 'Valse Caprice'
Harry Lauder, 'Roamin' in the Gloamin' '
Cecilia Loftus, 'Impressions of Artists'
Variety's Garden Party. Produced by Albert Toft
'God Save the King', solo by Harry Claff

That list includes no one who is not among the most talented and eminent of the thousands who provide nightly amusement in the music halls of the country; and though it would be possible to point to omissions of famous names and of popular branches of the art (no one will regret the absence of performing animals, but there are no trick bicyclists and no wire-walkers), the programme is pretty thoroughly representative . . . Their Majesties followed the whole programme with evident interest and amusement; though, like most of us, they must have found some items far too short and others far too long. Indeed, not a few of the performers seemed to be a little overawed by the august occasion, and to lack the sparkle of the oddity which endears them to the nightly patrons of the music hall; and the slowness of some meant drastic reduction of the time allotted to others . . .

THE TIMES, 2 JULY 1912

The truth was very different and a great deal more entertaining, to posterity if not to the audience on the night. Neither the artists nor their royal audience was entirely at ease, the artists no doubt inhibited by Stoll's announcement in the newspapers on the morning of the show that there was no room for vulgarity in music hall, and the royals uneasy lest the lower orders parading on stage should commit some breach of etiquette too shocking for the delicate sensibilities of the members of the royal houses of Germany and Russia who were watching.

The Command began on a Monday evening at 8.05 before a welter of Royalty; the Grand Duchess George of Russia, Princess Henry of Battenberg, and Princess Christian were received by Alfred Butt at the Royal entrance. Even Conan Doyle, who reported the evening, succumbed to obeisance, describing King George V as 'a lover of true Bohemianism'. He described the inside of the theatre, glowing with red roses, as a 'floral fairyland', but unfortunately the show itself was chilly. Just like today, the artists were stiff and indulged in that embarrassing play to the Royal Box which the Royal Family must find more tedious than anyone.

Harry Tate said afterwards, 'I was all right after I had got out the line about taking my son back to the Naval College, with the accent on the 'naval'. The King smiled and then I was quite comfortable.

Happy Fanny Fields, though 'fresh and bonny as ever', was so nervous that she made the mistake of telling the audience, 'I'm suffering just as much as you are.'

Wilkie Bard was described as 'dreadfully dull' by *The Daily Mail*, and Pippax and Paulo were trembling with anxiety.

Chirgwin, 'The One-Eyed Kaffir', a performer in the true music-hall tradition, was out of his element. 'Somehow or other,' reported *The Daily Chronicle*, 'before that brilliant company, Mr Chirgwin's performance on the one-stringed gramophone-fiddle was a curious reminder of the music hall's unambitious days.' He cracked a joke towards the Royal Box, 'but somehow or other it had not quite the answering laugh from on high that was expected.' 'Sorry it didn't go,' said Mr Chirgwin, like the fine old fellow that he is.

Ida Crispi walked out at rehearsals when Stoll said it wouldn't be 'nice' to have her rolled up in a carpet at the end of Yankee Tangle, and Little Tich was so nervous that he refused to go on at the end when Harry Claff in a suit of white shining armour and a white helmet strangely like a policeman's led the whole company in the National Anthem.

But for all the pains he took to render the evening's entertainment excruciatingly respectable, Stoll might just as well not have bothered. For he had made the deadly mistake of endowing Queen Mary with rather more tolerance than she in fact possessed. It was somehow poetic justice that the artist guilty of the most shocking misdemeanour of the night was the lady who only recently had had the piquant experience of being courted by Stoll and de Frece at the same time. Vesta Tilley, whose main claim to fame is that she appeared on stage dressed as a man, was evidently too much for the delicate sensibilities of the crowned heads in the audience.

So far as Queen Mary and the other Royal ladies were concerned, one little fact was curiously inescapable. They obviously did not like the appearance of Miss Vesta Tilley in her familiar male costume as the inimitable Algy. Queen Mary and the Grand Duchess George of Russia consulted their programmes almost severely throughout the song and studiedly looked away from the stage ... there was an expression on Queen Mary's face that she does not approve of actresses appearing in masculine clothes.

THE CHRONICLE

M eanwhile, as the crowned heads cringed in the face of the jolly coarsenesses of the working classes, what of Marie Lloyd? Five minutes' stroll down Shaftesbury Avenue from the Palace Theatre stood the London Pavilion, where something rather more diverting was taking place.

A packed house greeted Marie Lloyd at the London Pavilion, cheering her to the echo, demanding song after song, shouting encouragements and assuring her of their love and loyalty. On the bills outside, a special slip was pasted which proclaimed her 'The Queen of Comediennes'. It proclaimed that 'Every Performance Given by Marie Lloyd is a Command Performance by order of the British Public'. She had her revenge. From then on, Marie's billing hardly ever varied. She was either 'Queen of Comediennes' or 'Queen of Comedy'.

W. MACQUEEN POPE, *MARIE LLOYD, QUEEN OF THE MUSIC HALLS*

We shall never get the inner history of the Command Performance of 1912, a fierce contortion of personal ambition, a bitter antagonism of jealousies, a triumph for nobody in particular. In the event there was a picturesque crowd, a rather dull performance which could not, by the wildest stretch of the imagination, be called typical of the English music hall, but above all, there was another brilliantly contrived worldwide and sensational advertisement for the Palace Theatre.

H.G. HIBBERT, *FIFTY YEARS OF A LONDONER'S LIFE*

T he aftermaths were piddling. Conan Doyle was never again to achieve such inspired heights of fatuousness as his claim that King George V approved of Bohemianism, nor did *The Times* improve very often on its decision that on the night of the Royal Command the programme was 'pretty thoroughly representative'. Stoll and de Frece received knighthoods in 1919, an honour which so overcame poor de Frece that he succumbed instantly to delusions of nobility, retired from the music hall and sank to the indignity of a seat at Westminster. Lady de Frece, no longer Vesta Tilley, followed him into dignified retirement from the vulgarity of earning a living, allowing posterity to draw its own Freudian conclusions about an act whose only distinction was the ambivalence of a shapely young lady impersonating a shapely young man.

This kind of impersonation was skilfully ambivalent. The imitation of the male was as exact and convincing as the artiste could make it, but the essential feminity of the performer was nevertheless subtly and often intriguingly apparent. Thus the knowingness which goes with such a line as 'How many lemonades we had, My word! I really couldn't tell' is not only made innocent of the leer that might otherwise lurk therein but, through irony, such knowingness is gently ridiculed. But is the ridicule too gentle? Is there in the song an affectation of innocence? Is the adopted pose of youthful raffishness cheeky enough?

PETER DAVISON, *THE BRITISH MUSIC HALL*

It seems strange that neither Stoll nor de Frece seemed aware that Miss Tilley's transvestite performance might give offence to the members of a court still deeply embalmed in the bandages of Victorian propriety. At any rate Lady de Frece, who had begun life in rather more modest circumstances, brazened out the imposture of nobility and refinement to the bitter end.

What was known to one past generation as the 'fop' and to another as the 'dandy' became the 'dude' and the 'masher', the 'swell' and the 'toff'. There was also the 'chappie', who was of less social consequence, the 'fellah' who had just turned sixteen, and the 'Piccadilly Johnny With The Little Glass Eye.' That indicates the range of Vesta Tilley's male impersonations. Among them are soldiers, sailors, militia-men, policeman and messenger-boy, as well as a curate or two, but even these belonged to that side of masculinity which is clothes-conscious. All the young men she has pretended to be are proud of what they wear – all of them, from the one in 'Etons' to the one in khaki.

For fifty years she paraded such types before our delighted eyes. There was more than imitation in her mannerisms. There was more than caricature. She was always a very ordinary youth, but she portrayed him in an extraordinary manner. We saw him not as we saw him in real life, or as he imagined himself, but as he appeared in the eyes of a clever, critically observant woman. Conjure up in your memory the portraits she painted of youth in the 'seventies, 'eighties, 'nineties, nineteen-hundreds, pre-war years and war years; in that picture gallery which now fills your mind there is the history of a period. And it is a history with a noteworthy moral.

Since there have been debates concerning how she began, we must refer to her own account of it in *Recollections of Vesta Tilley*. When she was three years of age – she was born on May 13, 1864, at Worcester – her father, Harry Ball, was chairman of a music hall in Gloucester. On the night of his departure, he was given a complimentary benefit:

'It was a red-letter night in my life, for my father decided that I should make my first public appearance on that occasion. It comes back to me as though it were yesterday. I remember the Hall filled with tobacco smoke and the fumes of beer, my father carrying me to the side of the stage, straightening my little skirts, the band striking up the music of my little medley, and his words of encouragement: "Don't be frightened. Sing as if you meant it. Don't cough, and speak clearly."'

They moved to Nottingham, where he had been engaged as chairman of the St George's Hall, and there she was billed as 'The Great Little Tilley'. Not until she had 'run through the whole gamut of female characters, from baby songs to old maids' ditties', was she caught posturing before the glass in her father's hat and coat – the well-known incident which gained for her the little evening suit, big enough for 'an ordinary rabbit', that she treasures still. At the age of five she wore this and a large moustache in mimicry of Sims Reeves, at Birmingham. She also wore it on a return visit to Leicester, only to hear the chairman announce, 'Ladies and gentlemen, I regret this interruption, but the band will play a selection while Little Tilley retires to take off her trousers and appear as we expect to see her.' That set-back forgotten, she made such progress in her studies that on her arrival in London at the age of ten, audiences could not tell whether she was boy or girl. 'Great Little' had to go. Three names, chosen from a list at the end of a dictionary, were written on slips of paper and put in her father's hat. The one she drew had written on it, 'Vesta'.

Truth to nature was so much her aim that her art might have been deemed contrary to the spirit of pantomime. Yet an engagement as Robinson Crusoe at Portsmouth, when she was thirteen, was only the first of many Boys, sometimes Second, but usually Principal. She prided herself on acting emotional scenes seriously and sincerely, but she entered into the spirit of topsy-turveydom all the same. There are photographs of her in all the feathers, fleshings, and feminine finery of Prince Charming, and there is a picture of her in doublet, hose – and bowler hat. She might have changed our idea of the Principal Boy if she had a mind to, but she was too good a trouper to upset its frolics. In all the scenes of the fairy-tale she obeyed its rules and sang her own songs in between-whiles: 'Quite a Toff in My Newmarket Coat', written and composed by her father, she sang in *Beauty and the Beast* at Birmingham in 1881. To compose songs for her was an honour many sought. Leslie Stuart provided her with 'Sweetheart May', George Dance with 'Angels Without Wings' and 'Daughters', Walter de Frece with 'A Simple Maiden' and Oswald Stoll with 'Mary and John'. Thus she numbered among those whom she inspired to write words and music three who were to be knighted.

Now is the time to describe the characters she created, for some of them are being forgotten. One such is 'Burlington Bertie', with the Hyde Park drawl and the Bond Street crawl, whose memory has been obscured by Ella Shields' 'Burlington Bertie from Bow' – a very different person. We must remember 'Burlington Bertie' because he is the clue to Vesta Tilley's opinion of men. 'He'll fight and he'll die like an Englishman', she sang in the midst of her mockery of his follies, which is a plain hint that Vesta Tilley's understanding sympathy for her victims has never been very far beneath the surface. That is precisely why we have always been hypnotised by them.

Go back to her portrait of one of the 'rollicking, frolicking, devil-me-care young blades', who knocked down postmen and threw the village 'slop' into the horsepond. It is inspired by frank admiration of the young male, no matter how rowdy, which was probably her first feeling about him. You might also imagine she envied him his zestful nights out on the spree; she even let him get tipsy with an air, whether or no that was true to life. But 'A Nice Quiet Week', in which all these things happened, belonged to the days before she found herself.

Some of her songs in the 'eighties hardly bear the imprint of her personality at all. Some are of the kind any red-nosed comic or serio comic might have sung. It was after she had become the London Idol, with full assurance of the public's loyalty, that she gave us something more than entertainment, something that has direct bearing on life!

At the beginning of the 'nineties she was still singing the praises of those who were 'ready at night fir a row or a fight', but a little later came 'Algy – The Pic-ca-dil-ly John-ny With the Lit-tle Glass Eye'. He was as rollicking as his forerunners right until the last line of the last verse when you heard that behind the scenes the girls called him a 'jay'. Then there arrived the young man named Brown, who went to Paris for a weekend with a fair demoiselle who turned out to be his wife. Once again, you see, Vesta Tilley was telling the story against the masher she mimicked.

Henceforth, instead of merging her own personality into that of the character she acted, she brought her wits to bear upon him critically. By pretending to be young men for so long, she had come to understand them as well as they did themselves.

Now she went further, and understood them better than they did themselves. That is why we saw them, not as we could see them in real life but as they were when viewed through a clever woman's eyes.

'By the Sad Sea Waves' illustrated this process. She picked on the poor little London 'chappie' earning fifteen shillings a week and spending every penny he could spare on haberdashery for a week at Brighton, where he hoped to pass muster on the promenade as a real masher. Again, the story goes against the hero of the song. Back at business, he found that the beauty he met at Brighton was the girl in the cook-shop. No doubt the songwriter had a little mockery in mind. In performance, however, this was magically translated. What we felt when Vesta Tilley showed him to us was not derision but pathos. She felt for him and with him, and her tenderness over that little scrap of humanity was evident in all the portraits she painted from that time onwards.

Crochety veterans might wonder what on earth the younger generation was coming to, and hold the youths of 1909 up to ridicule in contemptuous sketches (such as the one which appeared that year on the programmes of *An Englishman's Home*, at Wyndham's), but Vesta Tilley knew. She knew the heart of the junior clerk as well as she knew the heart of young Tommy Atkins, with his throaty shout of 'Jolly good luck to the girl that loves a soldier' – such a pocket marvel of military precision that nothing of him remained when his place came to be taken by the civilian soldier of the War. No, there was no resemblance whatever between the two. But we recognised the weedy youth in khaki; we had seen him in 'By The Sad Sea Waves'. Unknown to the crochety veterans in club armchairs, there had always been in him the stuff heroes are made of. He was to win the battles they would do their damnedest to lose. He would man their trenches as cheerfully as he once lined seaside esplanades: and the only one to have prophetically recognised it in the past was not he himself – for he died without gaining consciousness that he was a hero – but Vesta Tilley.

Looking back on the junior clerk, we can see how she had discerned pluck even in his drudgery to buy haberdashery. She had always read what was in him. When the time came to answer those cartoons of him as a tailor's dummy with a novelette, she signalised his vindication with, 'I joined the Army yesterday, so the Army of to-day's all right'. On the surface it was a joke – but only on the surface. As that meagre figure in khaki clumped across the stage in heavy ammunition boots, we might echo Figaro's line which Byron translated in *Don Juan* – 'And if I laugh at any mortal thing 'tis that I may not weep'.

WILLSON DISHER, *WINKLES AND CHAMPAGNE*

But knighthoods and ladyships notwithstanding, the music hall continued to reflect the life of those back-streets from which it took all its vitality. By its very nature it could not help but be unrefined much of the time, which is not to say that it lacked infinite subtleties of its own. But the laughter was inherent in the vitality, which is why the periodic attempts by the Chants and the Stolls to 'clean up' the halls had no point. How strange it is that de Frece, who was so concerned to keep the music-hall stage respectable, never once made a speech in the House of Commons, or ever made any political gesture, which implied that working-class life itself might be cleaned up, in the sense that its dwellings, hygiene, standard of living etc, might be uplifted to the point where a reigning monarch with the creases in his trousers going the wrong way might find them acceptable. The entertainers of the working class meanwhile went about the humbling practicalities of their work.

Among these was the poetess of the Cockney life, Kate Carney, who spoke in her act of the pleasures of 'playin' tanner marf organs'.

Several of Kate Carney's coster sketches included real animals, and 'Three Pots a Shilling' featured a donkey:

'One night the donkey trained for the part got lost somehow, but I sent a man with a brougham to get another, and in due course he reached the hall with a young ass standing broadside on in the carriage, his head out at one window, his tail through the other, and the inside like a stable. On another occasion, to get the donkey in at a certain stage door we had to fix up a little gangway over the narrow passage leading to it, the approach being flanked by a couple of rather high walls. One night the donkey made a misstep and rolled off the gangway over the wall, and before we recovered him it was necessary to go and ask the owner of the plot of ground on the other side, 'Please can I get my donkey, it's gone over your garden wall.'

NOTTINGHAM FOOTBALL NEWS, 24 MARCH 1906

In a world where the passage of the donkey was a major philosophic problem, it was understandable that the finer points of the aesthetic life should go untouched. It is true that Little Tich was a sensitive soul off-stage, with a wide range of knowledge, true also that George Robey used a fleeting acquaintance with Cambridge University to pass himself off as someone familiar with the groves of academe. But Robey, for all his pretensions, was never quite in control of the social nuances. In *Follow On*, E.W. Swanton recalls Robey's election as a member of the MCC; at the Anniversary Dinner, the new member turned up wearing a frock coat, 'a sad case of a funny man trying not to be funny at all'. More typical than Robey's pose were the down-to-earth candours of his fellow-workers.

Sickert was ruthless, and once, when Mrs Sickert enquired of him what had become of his celebrated life-size canvases of musical-hall artistes painted in his early days, he told her he had destroyed them because they took up too much room. He added that he had offered one of them, a portrait of herself, to Katie Lawrence, and she had refused it with a classic phrase of contempt:

'What! That thing! ... Not even to keep the draught out from under the scullery door.'

OSBERT SITWELL, *A FREE HOUSE*

The Beggarstaff Brothers had been commissioned to produce a poster for the Drury Lane Pantomime, 1895-96. The result was that classic among posters, the 'Cinderella'. But the work did not find favour with Sir Augustus Harris; and the famous manager was supported in his dislike by Dan Leno, who thought the poster looked as though someone had spilt ink down it. The situation was saved by the fortunate arrival of Phil May, who, realising the state of affairs, turned the position by innocently congratulating Sir Augustus on having been so fortunate in obtaining such an effective advertisement.

HOLBROOK JACKSON, *THE EIGHTEEN NINETIES*

There was, however, one insurmountable problem in the social sense, and that was that many of the unrefined young ladies of the world of music hall were irresistibly attractive, as a great many heirs to plentiful estates discovered, to the acute embarrassment of mater and pater. The story of Belle Bilton is a case in point. Belle, the daughter of an army recruiting sergeant, went on the stage, accompanied by her sister Flo, when only thirteen years old. What should have been the rest of her girlhood was a tough apprenticeship served in provincial shows and pantomimes. By 1882 the Bilton Sisters were playing at the Empire, Leicester Square, where Belle's faery charms, her rampant bosom and tiny waist made her the talk of the hour. She was interviewed, photographed, publicised through postcards, pursued by young men and fêted by old ones. Seymour Hicks described her as 'sweetly pretty, her beauty being of the wistful delicate type'. Of the musical content of the family act, Hicks said, 'the little ditties they warbled were inane, and always followed with a stereotyped class of simultaneous movement chivalrously called dancing by their hosts of admirers'. The most famous song in their act ran:

> We're fresh, fresh as the morning,
> Sweeter than new-mown hay.
> We're fresh, fresh as the morning,
> And just what you want today.

At the end of 1887, still claiming in song to be as fresh as the morning, Belle was pregnant by what was known in those days as a cad. She was then befriended by one Isidor Wertheimer, who asked her to marry him and, when she refused, continued to protect her from all the perils surrounding a girl in her situation. But Isidor's family was not as charitable as he was.

In the spring of 1889, they decided to send Isidor to New York on business for the family firm. It was then that Belle met Viscount Dunlo, heir to the Earl of Clancarty. She seems to have been as violently attracted to him as he was to her. It is hard nowadays to understand what a title meant to people lower down the social scale. It had a glow, an attraction – behind the ordinary-looking young lord trembled escutcheons, knights in armour, and all the panoply described by Sir Walter Scott. Belle was a simple girl, and she believed all Lord Dunlo told her.

Vesta Tilley said that she remembered the courtship of Viscount Dunlo – how he used to call for the beautiful Belle after the show, and outside in the street he kept his private hansom cab – waiting to drive her off to supper. Miss Tilley was, of course, wrong. It was not the noble lord's private hansom cab, it was Isidor's, Isidor, who had been banished to the other side of the Atlantic by his family. While Isidor was absent, William le Poer Trench, Viscount Dunlo, known to his friends as Fred, was whispering sweet nothings into the ear of Belle, feeding her after the show (on credit), and then driving her home to the grand house in the fresh air of St John's Wood, paid for, and staffed, by the faithful Isidor. He seems to have made extensive use of Isidor's carriages, as well as proposing marriage to Isidor's loved one.

MADELEINE BINGHAM, *EARLS AND GIRLS*

B elle and Fred were soon secretly married, but not secretly enough. *The Pall Mall Gazette* published the news, and the Earl immediately decided to step in and save the family name by parcelling Fred off on a two-year world cruise. Fred, the dutiful son rather than the dutiful husband, went off as instructed, leaving Belle to struggle on under the auspices of Isidor, who had now returned, unaware that the Earl's detectives were watching his every move. At last Belle came to court accused of adultery. Her triumph was so absolute that even *The Times* sided with her, saying of the Earl that he had behaved towards this darling of the halls 'hardly, unfeelingly and almost cynically. It is Lord Clancarty's own fault if his conduct is set down in some quarters as a piece of sharp practice.'

Outside the court Belle received the ovation from the crowd. The case had made her into a heroine. When she came on to the stage of the Empire Theatre that night, the stalls, the pit, and the gallery rose to her. From hundreds of throats and words 'Welcome back!' drowned the orchestra. Enormous floral tributes were handed on to the stage, the *corps de ballet* thronged round to congratulate her, and the scene-shifters and call boys joined in the general rejoicings. The theatre orchestra played a triumphant march to drown the cheers, and the Press representative finally addressed the audience in a 'few well-chosen words'. It was as if Belle had won a victory, not only for herself, but for the whole of her profession. Beauty had defeated the Beast in the best pantomime tradition.

MADELEINE BINGHAM, *EARLS AND GIRLS*

Augustus Harris had planned to exploit a society scandal into a stage sensation. All the world knew about the romantic marriage of Belle Bilton. When singing with her sister on the halls as the Sisters Bilton, she had won the heart of Lord Dunlo, both at twenty years of age. There had been a secret ceremony and a quiet honeymoon at a hotel in Northumberland Avenue before the Earl of Clancarty brought such pressure to bear that the bridegroom set out for Australia only nine days after the wedding. 'I love you dearly,' he wrote to his wife, but on his return he was persuaded by his father to sign a petition for divorce. Directly the case was heard he declared his belief in her innocence so firmly that there was applause in court and outside.

'Druriolanus' saw his chance. With a sudden change of plans he chose 'Beauty and the Beast' as the subject of his pantomime for the Christmas of 1890, and announced that Lady Dunlo would be Beauty, leaving the public to guess whether any reference to her husband's 'change of face' was intended by the story of a hero temporarily changed into a beast. She returned to her old life so simply and naturally that Whimsical Walker (so that fine old clown told me) often sat by her side while they dined at the bar of a ham-and-beef shop. When the nine days' wonder died, Lady Dunlo was not such a great success as had been expected and her engagement ended when she was slightly hurt in an accident – a few months before her persecutor died and she left the stage to become Lady Clancarty.

M. WILLSON DISHER, *WINKLES AND CHAMPAGNE*

Caught between the prigs of the aristocracy and the sprigs of the music hall were the intellectuals and men of genuine sensibility. Like Shaw and Beerbohm, they sensed that the halls at their best displayed a verve and imagination sadly lacking in the legitimate theatre, and were not afraid to say so. Among the most vociferous supporters of the halls were Edward Gordon Craig, son of Ellen Terry, and Ford Madox Ford, novelist, memoirist, editor and critic. Craig tended to be intense about anything to do with the Arts, and may partly have been taking the opportunity to aim a punch at the commercial theatre which had great difficulty taking him seriously. Ford was a different case. A man of the world, experienced in several spheres, he had been raised in an atmosphere heady with the excesses of the Pre-Raphaelites, who had circulated around their father-figure, Fordie's grandfather, Ford Madox Brown. Fordie's father had been the music critic of *The Times*, and now Fordie, a precocious novelist grown into one of the most distinguished editors in the history of literary periodicals, was finding delights in the halls which were sadly missing in his usual cultural round. He has been called the biggest liar of English cultural life in the last hundred years, but always defended himself, as Cardus did, by saying that there is such a thing as poetic truth, which transcends mere facts. He was at any rate an irresistible raconteur, and he certainly was a known frequenter of the music hall.

The modern theatre is worn out; it never was so worn out as it is today. The music hall, cherishing as it does so much creative talent of a somewhat exaggerated order, is very much alive. Half, if not more, of the music hall turns may be called creative. Madam Yvette Guilbert's performances are the finest examples of the living music hall. Madame Bernhardt, the most distinguished of those who have turned from the theatre to the music hall, does no creative work of the kind, but the fact of so celebrated a performer appearing on the music-hall stage must be accepted as the 'legitimate' theatre's recognition of the force of what is known as the Variety stage.

EDWARD GORDON CRAIG, *THE MASK*

During the daytime, Ford's office was perpetually inundated with visitors, so that it was chiefly at night that the actual job of editing the Review could be carried on. But even at night, callers dropped in casually to see how the work was going forward. In order to avoid them, at least for an hour or two, it was Ford's singular practice to attend the second house at the local music hall. At least once a week my first task, on arriving at Holland Park Avenue, was to secure a box or two at the Shepherd's Bush Empire. After dinner I went out and stopped a hansom, and editor and 'sub' drove down to Shepherd's Bush with the manuscripts which had accumulated during the day. During the performance, or rather during the duller turns, Ford made his decisions and I duly recorded them. But when someone really worth listening to – the late Victoria Monks for example, or Little Tich or Vesta Victoria – appeared on the stage, the cares of editorship were for the moment laid aside. After the show, we went back to the flat and worked on, sometimes until two in the morning. There must have been a good deal to be said for the Shepherd's Bush Empire from Ford's standpoint. The atmosphere was conducive, there was no one to worry him and he could think undisturbed. When he stayed at home, on the other hand, there was always the prospect of some illuminated friend arriving to drink his whisky and to proffer advice, suggestions or complaints. By contrast, the music hall must have seemed a haven of peace.

DOUGLAS GOLDRING, *SOUTH LODGE*

B ut Fordie, for all his interest in the better turns on the bill, kept himself apart from the stalls, the pit and the gallery, where ordinary citizens sat enjoying the spectacle of the artistic reflection of their own lives. Once inside a music hall, a man might meet anyone, stumble into all sorts of adventures. In novels and shows he almost always did, although they were not quite the sort of adventures which happen in H.M. Tomlinson's retrospective novel of Edwardian days, *The Day Before*. Early on in the story, Clem, who has recently been signed on as a reporter by a national morning newspaper, and put under the charge of the veteran Mr Todd, persuades Todd that the beautiful young woman they are trying to find in connection with a mystery of vital importance to national security is somewhere in Plymouth. Once arrived at the town, Clem decides to kill an hour or two at the local music hall.

The audience was bright and quick with a large admixture of blue-jackets, soldiers, and marines. It was young, hearty, and responsive. It was ready to laugh when tickled. Its cries and movements never hesitated through nice consideration. The orchestra knew what was wanted, and could never get beyond three bars without starting the crowd off, when rhythmic feet became additional percussion instruments. Existence was prime to those people, and they didn't care who knew it. Why, an artist would feel satisfied, without pay, if he could keep that crowd laughing all the time. And how easy that might be, if only one knew enough about physiology. A little happiness goes a long way when the taskmaster is absent. The auditorium was misty with tobacco smoke, and the masses of distant faces, embayed by the faded ormolu rockery of the theatre, were restless in the tides of the fun, but blurred. It was as if humanity were out of reach, and to be seen only through almost invisible fathoms of the unapproachable.

The trim diminutive figure of Vesta Tilley in the uniform of a militiaman, with swagger cane and cheroot, came tripping into the brightness of the boards on light feet unknown to parade grounds. 'Jolly Good Luck to the Girl That Loves a Soldier'. She parodied immature abandon with a strut round the stage, while the audience let her know that everybody there belonged to her. Clem's gaze wandered at ease approvingly over the entranced crowd below. Presently he fixed it, stressing his eyes against distance and haze.

Could he be mistaken? If only he had a pair of binoculars! That must be her below. He might be a sanguine fool, yet the girl down there must have many advantages to get so near the image of Mrs Pitta. Now if she would only turn her face, to show her profile, that might settle it. That presently she did, and all but resolved his doubt. He remembered that he owed a sort of duty to Mr Todd, and kept watch, till the girl, idly surveying the people aloft, met his direct look, and held it coolly. She seemed to frown, as she averted her face. That was what a girl would do, if she intercepted a bold stare, but Clem was not rebuked. There was no further need to make sure of it, for now he knew. He was going to talk to her. He backed out, losing no time, but when he approached that seat below it was vacant. She had gone again. There was not even a disappearing cab.

H.M. TOMLINSON, *THE DAY BEFORE*

In the real world melodrama did not come quite so cheap. And yet Frederick Willis too nurtured his impossibly romantic dreams, even though they were of a very different kind to Clem's in Tomlinson's story. Willis's recollections of Edwardian London ache with nostalgia for a world irrevocably lost and beyond recall; none of the hundreds of episodes in his memoirs is more poignant than the following, which tells how one night, out on the town with three of his mates, he meets up with a couple who have clearly spent most of their lives working in the halls. Modest though their professional record apparently is, they retain that bouquet of magic which all performers hold for all members of the audience. Willis and his pals are clearly flattered to be treated as equals by these veterans. What lights the story is the reckless dream of the couple. They have worked out a route to fame and fortune, and believe in it so implicitly, and have furnished it so comprehensively down to the last fol-de-rol, that Willis is fascinated by the whole business. Forty years on he can still recall every detail of that night, even down to the sense of loss and desolation at the end of it all.

On Christmas Eve we usually went for a mild rag round the town. I remember one such evening when four of us, including Leslie, went into a Brixton tavern. The bar was crowded with a noisy, jolly company and, noticing a piano in the corner, I suggested that Leslie might oblige with a tune. He agreed with alacrity, and walking over to the piano removed his hat, displaying a fine head of curly, auburn hair, and sat down. Glancing round at the company he realised that it would require an item of special merit to get attention in that genial uproar, so he struck a few rousing chords and then began singing 'Captain Ginger', a song that was just beginning to attract attention. We were all gratified by the hush that came over the noisy conversation, and when he came to the chorus and we three supported him in spirited style the customers really began to take notice. By the time he got to the end the whole bar was roaring,

> 'I love – the ladies –
> Not one of 'em would I injah!
> All the girls are fond of Gin –
> Gin, Gin, Gin, Gin, Ginjah!

There followed an ovation. Everybody in the bar, observing the colour of his hair, was shouting, 'Good old Ginger!', 'Give us another, Ginger!', 'Have one with me, Ginger!' I forget how many songs we sang that night but we were there until 'Time, gentlemen, *please!*' We were played out with a hearty chorus of 'Good night Ginger!', 'Merry Christmas, Ginger!' and I found myself between a jolly-looking man and woman who were pressing all four of us to return with them to their home for supper.

We walked down sundry dark back streets and were finally halted by our new friends before a grubby little house. Our host opened the front door with a latch key and we all crowded into a poky little 'hall', the most striking features of which were a pair of voluminous but dusty red-plush curtains and a framed photograph of Dan Leno with make-up and signed simply 'Leno'. Our host and hostess, who were, presumably, husband and wife, although they always referred to one another as 'my partner', led us into a living-room, and the gentleman immediately sat down before a piano which bore evidence of many a concert party campaign and started a seasonable selection, including 'The Rowdy-Dowdy Boys' and 'Let's All Go Down

201

the Strand'. This was followed by a remarkable display of pianoforte gymnastics, which duly resolved itself into 'God Rest You Merry, Gentlemen!' fervently sung by all of us and concluded with tumultuous applause.

Meanwhile our hostess, with astonishing dexterity, attended to the purely material side of the entertainment. A slumbering fire was roused into action, an extra gas point (with a broken incandescent mantle) was lit, and the table cleared of a lot of impedimenta, including an old umbrella, a bundle of holly, and a dirty towel, and we all sat down to an ample supper of cold ham and tongue, pickles, and bottled stout. Our hosts were highly entertaining people, he having the breezy good fellowship of a prosperous bookmaker and she the engaging personality of the typical Edwardian variety artiste. I understood in a vague sort of way that they were in the Profession, and I knew instinctively that they were thoroughly good-hearted people. Under the benign influence of the ham, tongue, and stout we were soon bosom friends, and our host got down a bulky volume which, he explained after blowing the dust off, contained press cuttings, every one of which was in praise of his partner and himself. He next showed us a file of letters from important people and organisations whom he had approached, so far without success, with his Great Scheme, which he proceeded to explain.

He started by telling us that he was a Man With An Idea which was, in short, a fortune in embryo. The Idea was named, provisionally, London by the Sea, and was to consist of an extensive building about the size of the Albert Hall in the West End of London. It was to have a sky-blue ceiling and to be illuminated with myriads of hidden amber lights to give the illusion of sunshine, and it was to be fitted up with a fully-licensed buffet with tables and chairs dotted about in continental fashion at one end of the hall and a well-equipped stage at the other. The whole hall was to be decorated with the finest scenic effects of sea and landscape, and round the walls were to be stalls with gay awnings where fancy goods and novelties were to be sold. In the centre was to be an ornate bandstand surrounded by a promenade. The whole was to be opened daily all the year round from midday to midnight, and throughout that period there were to be alternate band performances and stage shows. 'No fear of weather, boy, everything under cover!' he assured us, and said he could fill the variety bill every week with clever but unknown turns who would be glad to give a show in London for 'next to nothing'. He prattled on, holding us all spellbound with the magnificence of The Scheme. 'The stalls will be let out on lease, thus providing an assured income, and the stage shows will become a proper school for variety, the only place of importance in England where an unknown act can get a chance, boy!'

The only obstacle that prevented the Scheme from being put into operation was lack of Capital. Each time our host came to that ominous word he pursed his lips and a cloud of profound melancholy overshadowed his normally cheerful face. But he soon brightened up and continued, 'All great ideas spring from absolutely rock bottom, boy – then something comes along and whizzzz! Off you go up among the Kiralfys, with the public eating out of your hand and Drury Lane putting on a scene from 'London by the Sea' in the new melodrama. Come on, boys, drink up, don't let the beer get cold. I'll open another bottle!' The enthusiasm of our host was infectious and we all discussed the Scheme as if it were ten o'clock in the evening instead of two o'clock in the morning, and I began to think that I was a member of the committee putting the finishing touches to a project that was in active preparation. I have a misty recollection that the stalls with fancy awnings were my suggestion, but I do remember very distinctly that I was passionately concerned about the immense electric sign that was to be outside this admirable centre of entertainment. It was to be set up in amber-coloured bulbs and read, 'Come into the Sunshine'. Our host looked at me admiringly, and cried, 'Boy, you've hit it! Look here, we mustn't lose sight of one another, you're a man with inspiration. 'Come into the sunshine!' It couldn't be more apt! People mooning about London on a cold night – or, say, a foggy night! That's it, a foggy night! They look up and see 'Come into the Sunshine' –

marvellous! In they come, you couldn't stop 'em!'

Our hostess, however, was more practical. She seemed to live mainly in the present, and interrupted this splendid dreaming with references to Christmas dinner which, since it was about three o'clock, was a thought for today. She led us out to an off-stage region in the rear where there was a curious smell – a potpourri of paraffin, onions, and carbolic soap – and introduced us to an immense goose hanging ready for the feast. She enlarged upon the virtues of sage and onion stuffing and apple sauce, and clearly anticipated a real, old-fashioned Christmas, due, as she darkly hinted, to a 'lucky deal' on the part of her esteemed partner. The fact that she knew the names of none of us caused her no inconvenience, as she addressed each one of us as 'Dear' or 'Darling'.

At last it occurred to us that it was time to go. 'Look here!' exclaimed Leslie, 'what about making a move, must be getting rather late!' 'Not until you've had a drop out of the bottle for old times' sake!' said our host decisively. 'Come on, what's it to be, gin, whisky, or rum?' 'Give the boys, rum, Partner!' said the lady. 'It'll keep the cold out. I'll have a drop of white satin.' So rum it was. We sang 'Auld Lang Syne' with no idea of the words but with much feeling and crossed hands, there was a deal of hand-shaking and Merry Christmassing, the lady embraced and kissed us warmly, and we trooped noisily out into the silent street. We never saw them again, did not know their name, and forgot where the house was.

FREDERICK WILLIS, *A BOOK OF LONDON YESTERDAYS*

It must not be thought that either Clem down in Plymouth or Willis in the local hall at Camberwell ever sensed an inferiority rooted in the shortcomings of the architecture or the decor around them. One of the most striking features of the rule of the syndicates was that there was a mean below which elegance was not allowed to sink. While uniformity was never quite achieved, nor perhaps even desired, most of the provincial Palaces and suburban Empires shared a certain splendour of conception reflected in the red plush upholstery, the cherubim and seraphim dancing on the ceiling, even the occasional hamadryad supporting the box office.

In December 1909 Arnold Bennett, about to embark on the most ambitious work of his career, the *Clayhanger* trilogy, which traces the life of a young boy as he grows to manhood in the Five Towns, went back to Hanley to check some local facts. On the 8th of the month he confided to his journal, 'After dinner I went to the Grand Theatre, 9.15 p.m. I was profoundly struck by all sorts of things. In particular by the significance of clog-dancing, which had never occurred to be me before. I saw a "short study" for *The Nation* in this. Towards the end I came across Warwick Savage and walked home with him. This was a pity because I had got into an extraordinary vein of "second sight". I perceived whole chapters. Of all the stuff I made sufficient notes.' Bennett duly wrote his 'short study' for *The Nation,* changing only the name of the town, into Hanbridge, and of the theatre, into the Empire.

When I came into the palace, out of the streets where black human silhouettes moved on seemingly mysterious errands in the haze of high-hung electric globes, I was met at the inner portal by the word 'Welcome' in large gold letters. This greeting, I saw, was part of the elaborate mechanics of the place. It reiterated its message monotonously to perhaps fifteen thousand visitors a week; nevertheless, it had a certain effectiveness, since it showed that the Hanbridge Theatre Company

Limited was striving after the right attitude towards the weekly fifteen thousand. At some pit doors the seekers after pleasure are received and herded as if they were criminals, or beggars. I entered with curiosity, for, though it is the business of my life to keep an eye on the enthralling social phenomena of Hanbridge, I had never been in its Empire. When I formed part of Hanbridge there was no Empire; nothing but sing-songs conducted by convivial chairmen with rapping hammers in public-houses whose blinds were drawn and whose posters were in manuscript. Not that I have ever assisted at one of those extinct sing-songs. They were as forbidden to me as a High Church service. The only convivial rapping chairman I ever beheld was at Gatti's, under Charing Cross Station, twenty-two years ago.

Now I saw an immense carved and gilded interior, not as large as the Paris Opera, but assuredly capable of seating as many persons. My first thought was: 'Why, it's just like a real music hall!' I was so accustomed to regard Hanbridge as a place where the great visible people went into to work at seven a.m. and emerged out of public houses at eleven p.m., or stood movelessly mournful in packed tramcars, or bitterly partisan on chill football grounds, that I could scarcely credit their presence here, lolling on velvet amid gold Cupids and Hercules, and smoking at ease, with plentiful ash-trays to encourage them. I glanced round to find acquaintances, and the first I saw was the human being who from nine to seven was my tailor's assistant; not now an automaton wound up with deferential replies to any conceivable question that a dandy could put, but a living soul with a calabash between his teeth, as fine as anybody. Indeed, finer than most! He, like me, reclined aristocratic in the grand circle (a bob). He, like me, was offered chocolates and what not at reasonable prices by a boy whose dress indicated that his education was proceeding at Eton. I was glad to see him. I should have gone and spoken to him, only I feared that by so doing I might balefully kill a man and create a deferential automaton. And I was glad to see the vast gallery with human twopences. In nearly all public places of pleasure, the pleasure is poisoned for me by the obsession that I owe it, at last, to the underpaid labour of people who aren't there and can't be there; by the growing, deepening obsession that the whole structure of what a respectable person means, when he says with patriotic warmth 'England', is reared on a stupendous and shocking injustice. I did not feel this at the Hanbridge Empire. Even the newspaper lad and the match-girl might go to the Hanbridge Empire and, sitting together, drink the milk of paradise. Wonderful discoverers, these new music-hall directors all up and down the United Kingdom! They have discovered the folk.

The performance was timed as carefully as a prize-fight. Ting! and the curtain went unfailingly up. Ting! and it came unfailingly down. Ting! and something started. Ting! and it stopped. Everybody concerned in the show knew what he and everybody else had to do. The illuminated number-signs on either side of the proscenium changed themselves with the implacable accuracy of astronomical phenomena. It was as though some deity of ten thousand syndicated halls was controlling the show from some throne studded with electric switches in Shaftesbury Avenue. Only the uniformed shepherd of the twopences aloft seemed free to use his own discretion. His 'Now then, order, *please*', a masterly union of entreaty and intimidation, was the sole feature of the entertainment not regulated to the fifth of a second by that recurrent ting.

But what the entertainment gained in efficient exactitude by this ruthless ordering, it seemed to lose in zest, in capriciousness, in rude joy. It was watched almost dully, and certainly there was nothing in it that could rouse the wayward animal that is in all of us. It was marked by an impeccable propriety. In the classic halls of London you can still hear skittish grandmothers, stars of a past age unreformed, prattling (with an amazing imitation of youthfulness) of champagne suppers. But not in the Hanbridge Empire. At the Hanbridge Empire the curtain never rises on any disclosure of the carnal core of things. Even when a young woman in a short skirt chanted of being clasped in his arms again, the tepid primness of her manner indicated that the embrace would be that of a tailor's dummy and a pretty head-and-shoulders in a hairdresser's window. The pulse never asserted itself. Only in the unconscious but overpowering temperament of a couple of acrobatic mulatto women was there the least trace of bodily fever. Male acrobats of the highest class, whose feats were a continual creation of sheer animal beauty, roused no adequate enthusiasm.

'When do the Yorkshire Songsters come on?' I asked an attendant at the interval. In the bar, a handful of pleasure-seekers were dispassionately drinking, without a rollicking word to mar the flow of their secret reflections.

'Second item in the second part,' said the attendant, and added heartily: 'And very good they are, too, sir!'

He meant it. He would not have said as much of a man whom in the lounge of a London hotel I saw playing the fiddle and the piano simultaneously. He was an attendant of mature and difficult judgement, not to be carried away by clowning or grotesquerie. With him good meant good. And they were very good. And they were what they pretended to be. There were about twenty of them; the women were dressed in white, and the men wore scarlet hunting coats. The conductor, a little shrewd man, was disguised in a sort of *levée* dress, with knee-breeches and silk stockings. But he could not disguise himself from me. I had seen him, and hundreds of him, in the streets of Halifax, Wakefield, and Batley. I had seen him all over Yorkshire, Lancashire, and Staffordshire. He was a Midland type: infernally well satisfied with himself under a crust of quiet modesty; a nice man to chat with on the way to Blackpool, a man who could take a pot of beer respectably and then stop, who could argue ingeniously with heat, and who would stick a shaft into you as he left you, just to let you know that he was not quite so ordinary as he made out to be. They were all like that, in a less degree; women too; those women could cook a Welsh rarebit with any woman, and they wouldn't say all they thought all at once, either.

And there they were ranged in a flattened semi-circle on a music-hall stage. Perhaps they appeared on forty music-hall stages in a year. It had come to that: another case of specialisation. Doubtless they had begun in small choirs, or in the parlours of home, singing for the pleasure of singing, and then acquiring some local renown; and then the little shrewd conductor had had the grand idea of organised professionalism. God bless my soul! The thing was an epic, or ought to be! They really could sing. They really had voices. And they would not 'demean' themselves to cheapness. All their eyes said: 'This is no music-hall foolery. This is uncompromisingly high-class, and if you don't like it you ought to be ashamed of yourselves!' They sang part-song music, from 'Sweet and Low' to a *Lohengrin* chorus. And with a will, with finesse, with a pianissimo over which the endless drone of the electric fan could be clearly distinguished, and a fine, free fortissimo that would have enchanted Wagner! They brought the house down every time. They might have rendered encores till midnight, but for my deity in Shaftesbury Avenue. It was the 'folk' themselves giving back to the folk in the form of art the very life of the folk.

But the most touching instance of this giving-back was furnished by the lady clog-dancer. Hanbridge used to be the centre of a land of clogs. Hundreds of times I have wakened in winter darkness to the sound of clogs on slushy pavements. And when I think of clogs I think of the knocker-up, and hurried fire-lighting, and tea and thick bread, and the icy draught from the opened front-door, and the factory gates, and the terrible time-keeper therein, and his clock: all the military harshness of industrialism grimly accepted. Few are the clogs now in Hanbridge. The girls wear paper boots, for their health's sake, and I don't know what the men wear. Clogs have nearly gone out of life. But at the Hanbridge Empire they had reappeared in an art highly conventionalised. The old clog-dancing, begun in public-houses, was realistic, and was done by people who the next morning would clatter to work in clogs. But this pretty, simpering girl had never worn a clog seriously. She had never regarded a clog as a cheap and lasting protection against wind and rain, but as a contrivance that you had to dance in. I daresay she rose at eleven a.m. She had a Cockney accent.

She would not let her clogs make a noise. She minced in clogs. It was no part of her scheme to lose her breath. And yet I doubt not that she constituted a romantic ideal for the young male twopences, with her clogs that had reached her natty feet from the original back streets of, say, Stockport. As I lumbered home in the electric car, besieged by printed requests from the tram company not on any account to spit, I could not help thinking and thinking, in a very trite way, that art is a wonderful thing.

ARNOLD BENNETT, *THE NATION*

B ennett's perception about the clogs was too good to be frittered away on a mere magazine, so he transferred the idea to the first book of his *Clayhanger* trilogy. In Chapter Ten we encounter Florence the clog-dancer, but in surroundings nothing remotely like the stage of the Hanbridge Empire. In order to incorporate the dancer, and the theory, into the time-scale of his story, Bennett has placed Florence a generation earlier in the evolution of music hall, and has her performing in a public house, the occasion being 'a jollity of the Bursley Mutual Burial Club'. The most striking difference of all between the two passages is that whereas in the essay Bennett tells us that the girl danced, in the novel he describes the dance itself.

She danced; and the service-doorway showed a vista of open-mouthed scullions. There was no sound in the room, save the concertina and the champion clogs. Every eye was fixed on those clogs; even the little eyes of Mr Peake quitted the button of his waistcoat and burned like diamond points on those clogs. Florence herself chiefly gazed on those clogs, but occasionally her nonchalant petulant gaze would wander up and down her bare arms and across her bosom. At intervals, with her ringed fingers, she would lift the short skirt – a nothing, an imperceptibility, half an inch, with glance downcast; and the effect was profound, recondite, inexplicable. Her style was not that of a male clog-dancer, but it was indubitably clog-dancing; full of marvels to the connoisseur; and to the profane naught but a highly complicated series of wooden noises. Florence's face began to perspire. Then the concertina ceased playing – so that an undistracted attention might be given to the supremely difficult final figures of the dance. And thus was rendered back to the people in the charming form of beauty that which the instinct of the artist had taken from the sordid ugliness of the people. The clog, the very emblem of the servitude and the squalor of brutalised populations, was changed, on the light feet of this favourite, into the medium of grace.

ARNOLD BENNETT, *CLAYHANGER*

B ennett, with his preference for French culture, does not seem to have interested himself much with one of the more flamboyant products of Parisian show-business, the dancer Gaby Deslys. On the only occasion she is mentioned in his journals, in March 1915, when he went to see her in a forgotten show called *Rosy Rapture* by of all people Sir James Barrie, he noted only two facts, first, that there were 'tons of flowers for Gaby Deslys at the end', and second, that on entering the theatre, there were cries of his name from the pit: 'I think this never happened before to me'. Miss Deslys, on the other hand, was quite used to such receptions, and probably expected them. In 1913 Miss Deslys, indulging her habit of making brief but sensational appearances on the London stage, caught the eye of a young army officer with a gift for effusiveness of style.

With the sumptuousness of the entertainments at my Aunt Londesborough's and at Mrs Keppel's, I could contrast the archiepiscopal austerities of Lambeth, with its cohorts of curates devouring the modern equivalent of locusts and wild honey. But even the wild honey would have proved, I apprehend, to be tame. After dinner, at 10.15 or 10.30 in the evening, many guests repaired to the Chapel, which had been so hideously frescoed in the time of my Tait relative. I remember with what relief – for the company of the clergy sometimes intimidates me, who am frightened by no other men – I used to ask for a taxi, and tell the driver to take me to the Alhambra, where I arrived just in time to hear the last half-hour of a revue, entitled, if I remember rightly, *Swat That Fly!* And there I would meet all my friends from the Brigade, admiring the serried ranks of beauties on the stage, the curls and legs and eyes in line. Or else I would hurry away from Lambeth in order to see the performance of Gaby Deslys at the Palace Theatre or elsewhere – a star, in her kind, of European celebrity. And here the reader and I will escape for an instant to discuss her – though there is a connection in memory betwen her and the Church, as will become evident in a moment, for this artiste held strict views on the clergy, or, at any rate, on Bishops. Though she possessed a house in London, facing the Park, with a tall, demure-looking painted façade, the window-boxes of which blazed with formal flowers, geraniums and their predecessors and successors throughout the spring and summer months, and though she was often to be seen driving in a motor, Paris was her headquarters and her appearances on the London stage were short in duration and infrequent. They occupied about ten minutes or a quarter of an hour each night for a special engagement of ten days or a fortnight, every few months. Moreoever, it must be admitted that when she essayed a bigger act on the English stage, and a longer run – as, for example, when Sir James Barrie wrote for her the whole of a revue, entitled *Rosy Rapture,* which was produced at the Duke of York's Theatre in 1915 –, she was not so successful. But in her brief songs, dances, and scraps of acting and conversation, all of which she entered upon and executed with a sort of casual deliberateness, she was curiously effective. There was no-one to approach her in her own form of stage glamour, and strange yet banal allurement. To a flourish of elementary ragtime, very French in its accent, on the part of the theatre orchestra – usually to *The Gaby Glide,* a tune possessed of a peculiarly inappropriate and naïve gaiety – would come from the wings a flutter of silk, feathers, flesh and jewels, drenched in light, and the star would have arrived to join her partner Harry Pilcer, who, by a convention, would already be looking for her ('Where can she be?' 'Where is she?') everywhere except in the direction from which she advanced. The moment she was there, rather heavy shouldered for her body, and crested like a bird, for she was wearing on her head a tight-fitting cap loaded with ostrich feathers, she seemed, with her fair hair and tawny fair skin, to absorb every ray of light in the theatre, to exist only in that flaring, sputtering brightness of another world, to be outlined with the icy fires of a diamond. She would sing a little, dance for a moment, as if she were almost too fragile, and too much in need of protection, to execute the steps, sing in her voice with the rolling r's of her French throat, unmusical but provocative, and the whole result was perfect of its kind, a work of art, but specialised as the courtship-dance of a bird, with the same glittering and drumming vanity, except that here the female and not the male played the chief rôle.

Though both Gaby Deslys and Harry Pilcer could, in their looks and their personality, no less than in the turn they gave, have belonged to no other period than their own, and albeit Gaby Deslys was so famous a music-hall artiste, yet, in addition, there pertained to her the interest of a specimen: the last surviving example – though the type, no doubt, is recurrent – of a certain kind of almost legendary stage figure, most usually to be seen in the Paris of the Second Empire and more generally to be found in the Europe of the nineteenth century. In this resembling Lola Montez, she had helped to upset a throne, and famous as an artiste, was no less notorious for the part she had played, and for which Fate had cast her, in the downfall of the Braganza dynasty. The infatuation of the youthful King Manoel – who had become sovereign after the terrible assassination in a Lisbon thoroughfare of his father King Carlos, and of an elder brother – had, a year or two before, been for many months the subject of eager but condemnatory report in the Press of the world, and in Portugal the stories that the new King was lavishing money on a French dancer, and had bestowed upon her pearl necklaces and gems said to be heirlooms, had certainly done much to inflame Portuguese opinion against him. Now, the King was an exile in Twickenham; and as for Gaby Deslys, it can be imagined that while the stories had increased her notoriety in England, they had by no means influenced the Nonconformist flocks or the Anglican congregations in her favour. On the first morning after her reappearance on the London stage, a Bishop, I recollect, made a public protest in an interview, against her performance, alleging that her clothes were too scanty (though actually it was in the precise opposite, in the richness and style of her clothing, that the whole essence of her appeal resided). Ten days subsequently, on her return journey to Paris, Gaby Deslys, too, gave an interview to journalists assembled at Dover, in which she would only say, 'Tell your Bishops, I love them – but they show too much leg!'

After her death, some five years later, she was found to have left a large fortune to the poor of Marseilles, which she declared to be her native city: though when her will was published several French papers contained statements that she had been brought to France at a very early age from a town in Roumania, where she had been born, and in which still lived various relations of hers who intended to claim their inheritance, under the *Code Napoléon*. This origin, however, has never been established, and would seem for her an improbable one – since nobody more French, in her way of moving, speaking, or wearing clothes, can be imagined.

OBSERT SITWELL, *GREAT MORNING*

Miss Deslys, who flitted to such great effect in that hinterland between ballet and the music hall, had a devastating effect on most of the men who saw her in action. She was one of the most romantic personalities of her day, with a reputation boosted by scandal, gossip and a notoriety which appears to have been well earned. When Sitwell saw her for the first time at the Alhambra, she had been preceded by deliciously wanton stories which evoked recollections only of purely fictitious *femmes fatales* like Antoinette de Mauban in *The Prisoner of Zenda*.

It was at this time that Gaby Deslys first came to Leicester Square, after playing a part in the overthrow of the Portuguese monarchy. When the assassinations were being plotted, public unrest was fanned by accounts of the wealth bestowed on her and of the price paid for her 'ropes of pearls'. When fanatics rushed the palace and killed the king, her life might have been taken had she not escaped from the city by hiding in a hay-cart. She came back to London where she had previously appeared at the Gaiety as the Charm of Paris. Now, with a legend around her name as well as those pearls around her neck, she became a star at the Alhambra in the year of the revolution in Portugal when the republic was proclaimed after battle and siege in Lisbon.

Her manner was disarmingly frank, especially when she turned earnestly towards you with a childlike look, and though she had earned a reputation for being mercenary through and through, a sense of mischief might impel her to flaunt her bewitchments upon some old, dry, hard-headed businessman during a trifling debate over her theatrical concerns, and leave him bewildered. She quarrelled in her love affairs and could blaze into picturesque fits of bad temper. Away from this side of her life she inspired strong liking even among those who did not admire her stage performance – her fixed smile, her dancing that was mainly posing, and her little cries that suggested a dulcet parrot. With her it was the legend that mattered. Her death from cancer of the throat in 1920, when she was thirty-six years of age, marked the end of London's belief in such feminine glamour and the beginning of the period of disenchantment.

M. WILLSON DISHER, *WINKLES AND CHAMPAGNE*

Disher's view that with the death of Gaby Deslys, so died all feminine allure on the London stage, may sound just a shade overwrought, but the testimonies of others who saw her in action certainly go some way to confirming this view.

On the right of the little black-coated group there was a barman of sound-effects in a gilt pergola full of bells, triangles, boards and motor-cycle horns. With these he mixed cocktails, adding from time to time a dash of cymbals, all the while rising from his scat posturing and smiling vacuously. Mr Pilcer, in tails, thin and rouged, and Mlle Gaby Deslys, like a big ventriloquist's doll, with a porcelain complexion, corn-coloured hair and a gown with ostrich feathers, danced to this hurricane of rhythm and drumbeats of a kind of domesticated cataclysm which left them completely drunk and dazzled under the streaming glare of six air-raid searchlights. The house stood and applauded, roused from its torpor by this extraordinary number, which is to the frenzy of Offenbach as a tank is to an 1870 *calêche*.

JEAN COCTEAU

Though it is true that I never imitated anybody, this did not prevent me from eyeing what Gaby Deslys bought, and buying what she had her eye on. It began with her chemises in the rue de Douai, and ended up with her dancing partner. He had caught my eye when I first saw him, very much as he had caught hers in New York. Pilcer was very much in love with her by this time, but Gaby was never short of swains. The most famous of her loves was Manoel of Portugal, who lost his crown for her, so they say. However, there is a story that Manoel suddenly put in an appearance at a restaurant where Gaby was dining with a party of friends. Gaby turned white. 'What do I do now?' she muttered. 'We've never even met. They're going to call my bluff.'

Manoel walked calmly over to the table and addressed one of the party. 'Will you introduce me to Mademoiselle Deslys? I should be happy to ratify this most entrancing of falsehoods.'

MISTINGUETT

209

I saw Gaby Deslys at the Globe Theatre, which was a rather daring thing to do, but my mother thought it would be good for my education to see Harry Pilcer do his drunkard's dance on the staircase, which was very famous. Afterwards, allowed by my mother who waited at a café around the corner, I went back and waited outside the stage door for Gaby Deslys to come out. There was this great white Rolls outside the door and out she came; it was after a matinée and she was screaming for Harry who was dallying in the theatre somewhere. They were going back to the house they had in Knightsbridge. I was lucky enough to get her autograph before she swept off in the Rolls. But I knew Harry Pilcer well. When Gaby died, he was left a little money. He was a great favourite in Cannes. He ran the Palm Beach Casino and whenever I wanted a table I just rang and he gave it to me, but as I couldn't afford to pay those prices I always went as his guest. He was a very kind person, and we could all see exactly why she adored him.

ANTON DOLIN
(ALL THREE ARTISTS QUOTED IN CHARLES CASTLE, THE FOLIES BERGÈRE)

Long after her death, Gaby Deslys continued to exercise the minds of those who had experienced her stage technique and the effect of her personality. During her time in London in the Great War, she defiantly continued to show all the outward manifestations of peace and plenty, for which she was adored more than ever, except by a small minority which took exception to a flamboyance which it considered unpatriotic.

During the Great War, when she was at the Alhambra in *5064 Gerrard,* she seemed to embody the reckless gaiety of that London of dark streets, air raids, and soldiers from the three corners of the earth. She had so flamboyant a way with her that she acted the same part on the stage and off. Everything about her, from her pearls and huge fans to the white car she drove continuously despite petrol restrictions, caught the public eye. Her enemies added to the effect by sending roughs to throw pennies on the stage when she was at the Globe Theatre; one of them held so desperately that he could not be dragged from the dress-circle by four men until the manager, Mr MacQueen Pope, brought an ebony ruler hard down upon his wrists.

M. WILLSON DISHER, WINKLES AND CHAMPAGNE

Ten years after her death, the confusion to which Osbert Sitwell alludes regarding her origins was still a bone of contention in the Paris law-courts, where claimants to her fortune battled it out to nobody's satisfaction.

The government is continuing its efforts to find out whether Gaby Deslys was Marie-Elise Gabrielle Caire of Marseille or Hedwige Navratil of Hatvan in Hungary. If the latter was the case, she was one of three Hedwige Navratils, as it seems there were a couple of others, one of whom has just turned up in the Paris courts. The fight, of course, is for money: Gaby Deslys left a fortune of nine million francs, a quarter of which went automatically to her family, the Caires; a quarter-million unautomatically to the American dancer Harry Pilcer, and the rest to the poor and tubercular of Marseilles. The Navratils now say the Caires were not her family; neither Pilcer nor the poor of Marseilles know what to think, and the government gets nowhere.

Gaby Deslys's star ascended in 1904; she was a gay brunette whose voice, as the French say, was full of 'yes'. She starred at the Folies-Bergère, at the Olympia, and introduced American dancing here on the arm of Harry Pilcer. She had a pavilion in the Rue Villebois-Mareuil, a private *hôtel* in the Rue de Bornier, and a magnificent London establishment in Kensington, where the bed lay on a dais beneath an arch of black marble supported by marble pillars. She refused to marry the Duc de Crussol, stating that no man was rich enough to buy her liberty.

JANET FLANNER, *PARIS WAS YESTERDAY*

But when Gaby Deslys first hit London, neither she nor anyone else gave a thought to the possibility that the world was about to come to an abrupt and bloody end. The tinsel universe of the West End, with its great performers, its vast palaces of entertainment, its indulgence in plenty in the midst of squalor, seemed likely to go on for ever. It was the heyday of the men about town and the bohemian journalists who drifted from stalls to club to race-track to restaurant, citizens of a privileged world-within-a-world.

In those days, great was the rivalry between the two great Leicester Square houses, and at luncheon-time the Cavour, the restaurant patronised by the rival staffs, was wont to hum with rumours of attractions and counter-attractions. So keen was the competition that it was reported that when at last the exhumation order was made which was to decide for good and all whether the coffin contained the mysterious Duke of Portland, or merely Druce of the Baker Street Bazaar, George Scott had stolen a march on his brother manager by camping outside the cemetery gates with a cast-iron contract in his hand, ready to book the occupant of the coffin for the Alhambra in the event of his turning out to be the eccentric Duke.

In the kitchen-garden behind the Cavour the very rhubarb beds were marked out by champagne flagons thrust neck downwards into the grateful earth, a noble sight. 'The rhubarb? Oh, I cannot charge you for it!' old Philippe would say with a smile. 'You would protest at the price. It cost me to grow it nine-pound-ten a stick.'

In those days of intense theatrical rivalry the Cavour was the music-hall restaurant *par excellence* for lunch. Not only was it frequented by the powers behind the scenes, the impresarios, managers, and music-hall agents and their curious entourages, mysterious gentlemen who sold jewellery to rising stars, and the sporting element, but the performers themselves were also in evidence.

The two great Leicester Square halls by no means had things their own way, for under the Butt regime the Palace was a formidable rival, and, from the social point of view, a Society with the big S, the Palace led. The Maud Allen boom brought the Asquiths and their political and artistic set, and the early triumphs of the Russians, with the incomparable Pavlova and Mordkin, placed the Palace at the head of affairs in its own particular line. It soon acquired a reputation for beauty and wit, and lived up to it. One night as poor, merry, golden-haired little Gaby Deslys shot her final dazzling smile at the orchestra and tripped off the stage, an enthusiast in the upper circle woke from his reverie, and, turning, eyed the somewhat shapeless bundle at his side with savage contempt.

'An' you,' he sneered, '*You* wear flannel! You would!'

'But flannel's 'ealthy, Jim,' the patient creature wailed.

'Damn health!' he snarled.

The Russian successes at the Palace produced the inevitable crowd of imitators, and one such, a large and lavish lady from Oldham, Wigan, or some such Tartar backblock, was disporting herself at a trial rehearsal with a band of assistant coryphees. Poor George Bull, a member of the Palace staff, watched with serene disapproval.

'Well,' observed someone, 'what do you think of the new Russian?'

'Funny without being Volga,' observed George calmly.

J.B. BOOTH, *OLD PINK 'UN DAYS*

In the years leading up to the Great War, the debate continued to rage between those who applauded the ascent up the social scale effected by the music hall, especially since the accolade of the Royal Command Performance, and those who feared that it had been not so much an accolade as a concussing blow to the brain. There were even those like Beerbohm who believed, or affected to believe, that the rot had set in long before that, back in the distant Victorian times when the simple jingoism of the Great MacDermott had been replaced by the ribaldry of the slapstick comedians. On the whole, though, the feeling seemed to be that the music hall was a much more respectable, much cleaner, much more comfortable place to be than in the old days. Yet there is something disconcertingly prudish about this account by a famous Liberal newspaper columnist-editor, with its implication that *double-entendres* are to be regretted, and that to be insulted from the stage is a damaging experience. Gardiner's widest fame was as a pseudonymous essayist called Alpha of the Plough, whose collected volumes lay at the foot of many a post-war Christmas tree. Alpha, who specialised in essays with titles like 'On Being Called Thompson' and 'In Praise of Maiden Aunts', is hardly read today, but his better work retains that bouquet of charm which once commended him to so many readers.

The other afternoon I went to a music hall, one of those wonderful palaces that have sprung up in such abundance in the last twenty years, places where for a shilling or so you may sit on velvet, and pass through purple hangings, and be shown to your seat by magnificent persons in gold lace, and have tea brought to you between turns by maidens whose manners are as spotless as their caps. The music hall of our youth was a thing of tinsel and orange-peel, reeking with smoke and obscenity. There are people who affect to deplore its disappearance. They exalt its freedom, its carelessness, its honest mirth. What they fail to recall is the fact of its filth. It was a noisome sewer, and one of the best signs of the times is that the sewer has been cleansed. You may go into any music hall today without being insulted from the stage.

The fact is due to many things – education, the growing sense of public decency, Mrs Ormiston Chant, and the LCC from without. I am not sure that the appearance of Albert Chevalier, a quarter of a century ago, was not a revolutionary event. It certainly marked the beginning of the modern music hall. He touched a new and richer note. He showed that the music hall audience was hungry for something better than the *double-entendre,* that its tastes and its demands had been grossly depreciated by ignorant or base-minded managers. He gave his hearers wholesome laughter and honest tears, and his success purified the music hall. It has never looked back since. Today you will find there not merely plush-covered seats and gold-laced attendants, but the art of Barrie and Bernard Shaw.

A.G. GARDINER, PILLARS OF SOCIETY

While Gardiner was waxing enthusiastic about the state of the halls, another, more modest Londoner was wandering through the West End with his new bride, casually taking in the sights and sounds of the city they loved so passionately. Fred Willis was a married man of a few weeks' standing when he and Mrs Willis went off one Saturday to find a good second-hand bookcase to fill a barren corner in their sitting-room. Eventually they found what they wanted in Camden Town, 'a bookcase that might have been made for us, Jacobean, leaded-glass panes, dull brass fittings, cunning drawers, everything in fact that one would expect to find in a cultured, neo-Georgian home'. But the escapade had been exhausting, and the young couple found refuge in a once-famous public house.

Through this familiar scene Elaine and I went, feeling that all around us was permanent and secure, and triumphant in the success of our expedition we entered the Blue Posts for refreshment. This was in a side-turning adjoining the Oxford Music Hall, very familiar to us but overlooked by the casual visitor. We thought that old tavern and the Oxford were there for ever, but it has all been swept away long since and a palatial Corner House now occupies the site. It was as quiet and peaceful in that saloon bar as an exclusive West End club, and in the intervals when we were not talking about our wonderful bookcase we watched the select company, mostly music-hall artistes, talking about their triumphs, past and to come.

While we were drinking Joe Elvin came in. I wonder if anyone remembers Joe today. His sketches were very popular then, pure slapstick but very funny. He was a striking figure, rather tall, with a rosy, clean-shaven face and white close-cut hair. He usually dressed in a blue melton overcoat with velvet collar, and wore a black bowler hat. He was one of the cleanest-looking men I have known, the picture of good health and spirits. During the music-hall strike, which happened a few years earlier, I was talking to him in this same house when a party of minor music-hall artistes came in. Joe was on strike in their interests, not his own, and I admired him very much for this. One of the artistes said, 'Have you seen the bills outside the Tivoli, Mr Elvin? They say "We have a company of picked artistes".'

'Picked artistes,' exclaimed Joe scornfully. 'Yes, picked before they were ripe.'

In the little court outside, a trio of minstrels was giving a sensitive rendering of 'In the Shadows', while the brightly-dressed crowds in Oxford Street sauntered past, and the Oxford audience applauded Harry Randall. It would be difficult to picture a more peaceful and harmless community of people, but as I look back on that scene it occurs to me that about this time three young men with bombs were being smuggled

213

across the frontier of Bosnia intent on blowing the lid off hell. If we had heard about this incident that night our first question would have been, 'Where is Bosnia?' When we were told that it was in the Balkans we should have regarded the business as a good joke because 'Trouble in the Balkans' was such a familiar headline that newspapers must have kept a stock of posters ready printed for use as occasion demanded.

But of course we knew nothing about this. We went home across Westminster Bridge, and as we surveyed our familiar London we should have thought, if we *had* known, that it would take a very special bomb to disturb the strong but placid bloodstream of the British Empire. The motor-bus whirled us past the Canterbury, with its red-and-blue posters announcing Marie Lloyd and Eugene Stratton, and through the maze of the Elephant and Castle rising to the crescendo of Saturday night traffic with electric signs flashing Bovril, Vinolia and Johnny Walker, Still Going Strong. Newspaper vans were dashing about bearing their urgent message, 'Close of Play', trams lumbered over the tangle of points, and the tailor's shop adjoining the tavern on the island site announced in flaming capitals, 'Fashionable Suits, to measure, Latest Styles, 30s, No Extras. Finished in a Week'.

FREDERICK WILLIS, *A BOOK OF LONDON YESTERDAYS*

Willis shared with millions of his fellow-countrymen an inability to become reconciled to the earthquake of the Great War. Pointedly he calls the closing chapter of his book of reminiscences 'The Scarlet Line': 'Nineteen hundred and fourteen is to people of my generation like a Scarlet Line drawn across the story of their lives' – scarlet because of the blood which would soon stain every street in the four kingdoms. A man of his opinion was Thomas Burke, by now busily at work on the collected discursive essays which would do much to establish his reputation with both readers and publishers. This book, *Nights in Town*, did not appear until 1915, but its spirit is of the days before the war, when the silent wanderer could drift into the various villages which comprise London, mix with its habitués, and draw neat, colourful conclusions. Burke was something of a solitary, who never found his perfect mate, and who seems to have consoled himself by falling in love with his home town instead, especially at night. His first book was composed of descriptions of his forays into the different districts and what he found there, drugs in Limehouse, squalid bedsitters in Hackney, whist drives in Surbiton, trouble with the law in Hoxton, and so on. The most interesting of the twenty accounts is the one which opens the book. It shows not only Burke's abiding affection for the genre, but the trouble he had taken to discover a little more about the workings of the profession than could be discerned from a seat in the stalls. It is also, quite unintentionally, a fond farewell to that metropolitan merry-go-round about to be wrecked by the coming of a great war.

An Entertainment Night
Round the Halls

Of course, every night spent in London is an entertainment night, for London has more blood and pace and devil than any city I know. Thick as the physical atmosphere is with smoke and fog, its moral atmosphere is yet charged with a sparkle as of light wine. It is more effervescent than any continental city. It is the city of cities for learning, art, wit, and – Carnival. Go where you please at nightfall and Carnival slips

214

into the blood, lighting even Bond Street – the dreariest street in town – with a little flame of gaiety. I have assisted at carnivals and festes in various foreign parts – carnivals of students and also of the theatrically desperate apaches in the crawling underworlds. But, oh, what bilious affairs! You simply flogged yourself into it. You said, as it were: 'I am in Vienna, or Berlin, or Paris, or Brussels, or Marseilles, or Trieste; therefore, I am gay. Of course I am gay.' But you were not. You were only bored, and the show only became endurable after you had swallowed various absinthes, vermuths, and other rot-gut.

All the time you were – or I was – aching for Camden Town High Street, and a good old London music-hall. I cannot understand those folk who sniff at the English music-hall and belaud the Parisian shows. These latter are to me the most dismal, lifeless form of entertainment that a public ever suffered. Give me the Oxford, the Pavilion, or the Alhambra, or even a suburban Palace of Varieties. Ever since the age of eight the music hall has been a kind of background for me. Long before that age I can remember being rushed through strange streets and tossed, breathless, into an overheated theatre roaring with colour. The show was then either the Moore and Burgess Minstrels or the Egyptian Hall, followed by that chief of all child-life entertainments – tea at a tea-shop. But at eight I was initiated into the mysteries of the Halls, for a gracious *chef d'orchestre* permitted me to sit in the orchestra of an outlying hall, by the side of a cousin who sawed the double bass.

I have loved the music-hall ever since, and I still worship that *chef d'orchestre*, and if I met him now I am sure I should bow, though I know that he was nothing but a pillow stuffed with pose. But in those days, what a man! Or no – not a man – what a demi-god! You should have seen him enter the orchestra on the call: 'Mr Francioli, please!' Your ordinary music-hall conductor ducks from below, slips into his chair, and his tap has turned on the flow of his twenty instruments before you realise that he is up. But not so Francioli. For him the old school, the old manners, laddie. He never came into the orchestra. He 'entered'. He would bend gracefully as he stepped from the narrow passage beneath the stage into the orchestra. He would stand upright among his boys for a little minute while he adjusted his white gloves. His evening dress would have turned George Lashwood sick with envy. The perfect shirt of the perfect shape of the hour, the tie in the correct mode, the collar of the moment, the thick, well-oiled hair, profuse and yet well in hand, the right flower in the buttonhole at just the right angle – so he would stand, with lips pursed in histrionic manner, gazing quietly before him, smiling, to casual friends, little smiles which were nothing more unbending than dignified acknowledgement. Then he would stretch a god-like arm to the rail, climb into his chair, and spend another half-minute in settling himself, turning now and then to inspect the house from floor to ceiling. At the tinkle of the stage-manager's bell the grand moment would come. His hand would sail to the desk, and he would take the baton as one might select a peach from the dessert-dish. He would look benignly upon his boys, tap, raise both resplendent hands aloft, and away he would go into the 'Zampa' overture.

His attitude to the show was a study in holy detachment. He simply did not see it. He would lean back in his chair at a comfortable angle, and conduct from the score on his desk. But he never smiled at a joke, he never beamed upon a clever turn, he never even exchanged glances with the stars. He was Olympian. I think he must have met Irving as a young man, and have modelled himself on his idiosyncrasies. Certainly every pose that ever a musician or actor practised was doubled in him. I believe he must have posed in his sleep and in his bath. Indeed, my young mind used to play upon the delicate fancy that such a creature could never do anything so common as eat or drink or pursue any of the daily functions of we ordinary mortals. I shrank from conceiving him undressed . . .

Once, I remember, he came down from his cloudy heights and stood my cousin a drink and myself a lemonade. I didn't want to drink that lemonade. I wanted to take it home and stand it under a glass shade. He himself drank what I was told was a foreign drink in a tiny glass. He lingered over it, untouched, while he discussed with us the exact phrasing of the symphony for the star man's song; then, at the call, with a sweep of his almighty arm he carried the glass to his lips with a 'To you, my boy!' held it poised for a moment, set it down, and strode away, followed by rapt gazes from the barmaids.

A stout fellow. He took the conductor's chair with all the pomposity of a provincial borough official. He tapped for the coda with the touch of a king knighting an illustrious subject. And when he led the boys through the National Anthem, standing up in his place and facing the house, all lights up – well, there are literally no words for it . . .

At twelve years old I grew up, and sought out my own entertainment, prowling, always alone, into strange places. I discovered halls that nobody else seemed to know, such as the Star at Bermondsey, the Queen's at Poplar, and the Cambridge in Commercial Street. I crawled around queer bars, wonderfully lighted, into dusky refreshment-houses in the Asiatic quarter, surely devised by Haroun al Raschid, and into softly lit theatres and concert-halls. At eighteen, I took my pleasures less naïvely, and dined solemnly in town, and toured, solemn and critical, the western halls, enjoying everything but regarding it with pale detachment. Now, however, I am quite frank in my delight in this institution, which has so crept into the life of the highest and the lowest, the vulgar and the intellectual; and scarcely a week passes without a couple of shows.

The mechanism of the modern hall is a marvellous thing. From the small offices about Leicester Square, where the big circuits are registered, men and women and children are sent thousands and thousands of miles to sing, dance, act, or play the fool. The circuits often control thirty or forty halls in London and the provinces, each of which is under the care of a manager, who is responsible for its success. The turns are booked by the central booking manager and allocated either to this or that London hall, or to work the entire syndicate tour; and the bill of each hall, near or far, is printed and stage-times fixed weeks in advance. The local manager every Saturday night has to pay his entire staff, both of stage and house; that is, he not only pays programme girls, chuckers-out, electricians, and so forth, but each artist, even the £200 a week man, is paid in cash at each hall he is working. When a new turn is booked for any given hall, the manager of that hall must be 'in front' and watch that turn and its success or non-success with the house; and, at the end of the week, a confidential report has to be sent to headquarters in which the manager tells the cold truth: whether the show is good, whether it 'went', how much salary it is worth, and whether it is worth a re-booking.

It is, like journalism, a hard, hard life and thankless for every one concerned, from bill-topper to sweeper; yet there is a furious colour about it, and I think no one connected with it would willingly quit. The most hard-worked of all are the electricians. First in the hall of an evening, they, with the band and the janitors, are the last to leave. Following them, at about half-past five (in the case of the two-house halls), come programme girls, barmaids, call-boy, stage-manager, shifters, and all other stage hands.

All are philosophers, in their way, and all seem to have caught the tang of the profession and to be, sub-consciously, of the mummer persuasion. I once had a long, long talk with the chief electrician of a London hall, or, to give him the name by which he is best known, the limelight man. I climbed the straight iron ladder leading from the wings to his little platform, with only sufficient foothold for two people, and there I stood with him for two hours, while he waggled spots, floods, and focuses, and littered the platform with the hastily scrawled lighting-plots of the performers.

The limes man is really the most important person in the show. Of course, the manager doesn't think so, and the stage manager doesn't think so, and the carpenter doesn't think so, and the band doesn't think so. But he is. Many of the music-hall favourites, such as La Milo and La Loie Fuller, would have no existence but for him.

Skilful lighting effects and changes of colour are often all that carries a commonplace turn to popularity; and just think of the power in that man's hands! He could ruin any young turn he liked simply by 'blacking her out'; and, if he feels good, he can help many beginners with expert advice. The young girl new to the boards, and getting her first show, has hardly the slightest idea what she shall give him in the way of lighting-plot; very generously, she leaves it to him, and he sees her show and lights it as he thinks most effective.

Long before the doors open he is moving from box to box, in wings and flies, fixing this, altering that, and arranging the other; and cursing his assistants – usually lads of sixteen – who have to work the colours from wings, roof, circle, and side of the house. Lights are of three kinds: spot, focus, and flood. The spot is used on a dark stage, and lights only the singer's head and shoulders. The focus lights the complete figure. The flood covers the stage. Each of these is worked in conjunction with eight or nine shaded films placed before the arc light. Here is a typical lighting-plot, used by a prominent star:-

'First song. Symph.; all up stage and house. Focus for my entrance. White perches and battens for first chorus. Then black out, and gallery green focus for dance, changing to ruby at cue, and white floods at chord off.'

The limelight man never sees the show. In his little cupboard, he hears nothing but the hissing of his arcs and the tinkle of the stage-manager's prompting bell at the switchboard which controls every light in the theatre before and behind. He has to watch every movement of the artist who is on, but what he or she is doing or saying, he does not know. He is, perhaps, the only man who has never laughed at Little Tich.

John Davidson, I think, wrote a series of poems under the title of 'In a Music Hall', but these were mainly philosophical, and neither he nor others seem to have appreciated the *colour* of the music-hall. It is the most delicate of all essences of pleasure, and we owe it to the free hand that is given to the limelight man. You get, perhaps, a girl in white, singing horribly or dancing idiotically, but she is dancing in white against a deep blue curtain, filigreed with silver, and the whole flooded in amber light. And yet there are those who find the London music-hall dull!

The modern music-hall band, too, is a hard-working and poorly remunerated concern; and in many cases it really is a band and it does make music. It is hard at it for the whole of the evening, with no break for refreshment unless there be a sketch in the bill. There are, too, the matinées and the rehearsal every Monday at noon. The boys must be expert performers, and adaptable to any emergency. Often when a number cannot turn up, a deputy has to be called in by 'phone. The band seldom knows what the deputy will sing; there is no opportunity for rehearsal; and sometimes they have not even an idea of the nature of the turn until band parts are put in. This means that they must read at sight, that the conductor must follow every movement of the artist, in order to catch his spasmodic cues for band or patter, and that the boys must keep one eye on music they have never seen before, and the other on their old man's stick.

The conductor, too, works hard at rehearsals; not, as you might think, with the stars, but, like the limelight man, with the youngsters. The stars can look after themselves; they are always sure to go. But the nervous beginner needs a lot of attention from the band, and it is pleasant to know that in most London halls he gets it ungrudgingly. A West End *chef d'orchestre* said to me some time ago: 'I never mind how much trouble I take over them. If they don't go it means such a lot to the poor dears. Harry Lauder can sing anything anyhow, and he's all right. But I've often found that these girls and boys hand me out band parts which are perfectly useless for the modern music-hall; and again and again I've found that effective orchestration and a helping hand from us pulls a poor show through and gets 'em a return booking. Half the day of rehearsing is spent with the beginners.'

An extraordinary improvement in the musical side of vaudeville has taken place within the last fifteen years. Go to any hall any night, and you will almost certainly hear something of Wagner, Mendelssohn, Weber, Mozart. I think, too, that the songs are infinitely better than in the old days; not only in the direction of melody but in orchestration, which is often incomparably subtle. It is, what vaudeville music should be, intensely funny, notably in the running chatter of the strings and the cunning commentary of woodwind and drums. Pathetic as its passing is, one cannot honestly regret the old school. I was looking last night at the programme of my very first hall, and received a terrible shock to my time-sense. Where are the snows of yesteryear? Where are the entertainers of 1895? Not one of their names do I recognise, and yet three of them are in heavy type. One by one they drop out, and their places are never filled. The new man, the new style of humour, comes along, and attracts its own votaries, who sniff, even as I sniff, at the performers of past times. Who is there to replace that perilously piquant *diseur* Harry Fragson? None. But Frank Tinney comes along with something fresh, and we forget the art of Fragson, and pay many golden sovereigns to Frank to amuse us in the new way.

Where, too, are the song-writers? That seems to me one of the greatest tragedies of the vaudeville world: that a man should compose a song that puts a girdle round about the globe; a song that is sung on liners, on troopships, at feasts in far-away Singapore or Mauritius; a song that inspires men in battle and helps soldiers to die; a song that, like 'Tipperary', is now the slogan of an Empire; that a man should create such a thing and live and die without one in ten thousand of his singers knowing even his name. Who composed 'Tipperary'? You don't know? I thought not. Who composed 'Let's all go down the Strand', a song that surely should have been adopted as The Anthem of London? Who composed 'Hot Time in the Old Town to-night' – the song that led the Americans to victory in Cuba and the Philippines? We know the names of hundreds of finicky little poets and novelists and pianists; but their work never shook a nation one inch, or cheered men in sickness and despair. Of the men who really captured and interpreted the national soul we know nothing and care less; and how much they get for their copyrights is a matter that even themselves do not seem to take with sufficient seriousness. Yet personally I have an infinite tenderness for these unknowns, for they have done me more good than any other triflers with art-forms. I should like to shake the composer of 'La Maxixe' by the hand, and I owe many a debt of gratitude to the creator of 'Red Pepper' and 'Robert E. Lee'. So many of these fugitive airs have been part of my life, as they are part of every Cockney's life. They are, indeed, a calendar. Events date themselves by the song that was popular at that time. When, for instance, I hear 'The Jonah Man' or 'Valse Bleu', my mind goes back to the days when a tired, pale office-boy worked in the City and wrote stories for the cheap papers in his evenings. When I hear 'La Maxixe', I shiver with frightful joy. It recalls the hot summer of 1906, when I had money and wine and possession and love. When I hear 'Beautiful Doll', I become old and sad; I want to run away and hide myself. When I hear 'Hiawatha' or 'Bill Bailey', I get back the mood of that year – a mood murderously bitter. Verily, the street organ and its composers are things to be remembered in our prayers and toasts.

Every London hall has its own character and its own audience. The Pavilion programme is temperamentally distinct from the Oxford bill; the Alhambra is equally marked from the Empire; and the Poplar Hippodrome, in patrons and performers, is widely severed from the Euston. The same turns are, of course, seen eventually at every hall, but never the same group of turns, collectively. As for the Hippodrome and the Coliseum – non-licensed houses – their show and their audience are what one would expect: a first-class show, and an audience decorous and Streathamish. I think we will not visit either, nor will we visit the hall with its world-famous promenade. The show is always charming, for it has a captivating English première ballerina; but the audience is so much more insistent than the performance that it claims one's attention; and when you have given it attention you find that it is hardly worth it. For this would-be wicked audience is even duller than the decorous. It is the woman of forty trying to ape the skittish flapper. It is the man who says: 'I will be Bohemian! Dammit, I will; so there!' It is jejeune, and as flat as last night's soda-water. There is nothing in it.

Let us try the Oxford, where you are always sure of a pleasant crowd, a good all-round show, and alcoholic refreshment if you require it. There are certain residentials, if I may so term them, of the Oxford, whom you may always be sure of meeting here, and who will always delight you. Mark Sheridan, for example, is pretty certain to be there, with Wilkie Bard, Clarice Mayne, Phil Ray, Sam Mayo, Frank and Vesta (what a darling Vesta is!), T.E. Dunville, George Formby, and those veterans, Joe Elvin and George Chirgwin.

There is a good overture, and the house is comfortable without being gorgeous. There is a sense of intimacy about it. The audience, too, is always on form. Audiences, by the way, have a great deal to do with the success or non-success of any particular show, quite apart from its merits. There is one famous West End hall, which I dare not name, whose audience is always 'bad' – i.e. cold and inappreciative; the best of all good turns never 'goes' at that house, and artists dread the week when they are booked there. I have seen turns which have sent other houses into one convulsive fit, but at this hall the audience has sat immovable and colourless while the performers wasted themselves in furious efforts to get over the footlights. At the Oxford, however, the audience is always 'with you', and this atmosphere gets behind and puts the artists, in their turn, on the top of their form. The result is a sparkling evening which satisfies everybody.

It is a compact little place, as the music-hall should be. In those new caravanserai of colossal proportions and capacity, it is impossible for a man to develop that sense of good-fellowship which is inseparable from the traditions of the London hall. Intimacy is its very essence, and how can a man be intimate on a stage measuring something like seventy feet in length, a hundred feet in depth, with a proscenium over sixty feet high, facing an auditorium seating three thousand persons, and separated from them by a marbled orchestra enclosure four or five times as wide as it should be? It is pathetic to see George Mozart or George Robey trying to adapt his essentially miniature art to these vasty proportions. Physically and mentally he is dwarfed, and his effects hardly ever get beyond the orchestra. These new halls, with their circles, and upper circles, and third circles, and Louis XV Salons and Palm Courts, have been builded over the bones of old English humour. They are good for nothing except ballet, one-act plays with large effects, and tabloid grand opera. But apparently the public like them, for the Tivoli, when rebuilt, is to be as large again as its original, and London will be deprived of yet another home of merriment.

There is always an acrobat turn in the Oxford bill, and always a cheery cross-talk item. The old combination of knockabouts or of swell and clown has for the most part disappeared; the Poluskis and Dale and O'Malley are perhaps the last survivors. The modern idea is the foolish fellow and the dainty lady, who are not, I think, so attractive as the old style. Personally, I am always drawn to a hall where Dale and O'Malley are billed. 'The somewhat different comedians' is their own description of themselves, and the wonder is that they should have worked so long in partnership and yet succeeded in remaining 'somewhat different'. But each has so welded his mood to the other that their joint humour is, as it were, a bond as spiritually indissoluble as matrimony. You cannot conceive either Mr Dale or Mr O'Malley working alone or with any other partner. I have heard them crack the same quips and tell the same stories for the last five years, yet they always get the same big laugh and the same large 'hand'. That is a delightful trait about the music-hall – the *entente* existing between performer and audience. The favourites seem to be *en rapport* even while waiting in the wings, and the flashing of their number in the electric frame is the signal for a hand of welcome and – in the outer halls – whistles and cries. The atmosphere becomes electric with good-fellowship. It is, as Harry Lauder used to sing, 'just like being at home'. It must be splendid to be greeted in that manner every night of your life and – if you are working two or three halls – five times every night; to know that some one wants you, that some one whom you have never seen before loves you and is ready to pay good money away in order to watch you play the fool or be yourself. There they are, crowds of people with whom you haven't the slightest acquaintance, all familiar with you, all longing to meet you again, and all applauding you before you have done anything but just walk on. They shout 'Good boy!' or 'Bravo, Harry, or George, or Ernest!' It must indeed be splendid. You are all so – what is the word? – matey, isn't it? Yes, that's the note of the London hall – mateyness. You, up there, singing or dancing, have brought men and women together as nothing else, not even the club or saloon bar, can do; and they sit before you, enjoying you and themselves and each other. Strangers have been known to speak to one another under the mellow atmosphere which you have created by singing to them of the universal things: love, food, drink, marriage, birth, death, misfortune, festival, cunning, frivolity and – oh, the thousand things that make up our daily day.

There is just one man still among us who renders these details of the Cockney's daily day in more perfect fashion than any of his peers. He is of the old school, I admit, but he is nevertheless right on the spot with his points and his psychology. His name is Harry Champion. Perhaps you have seen him and been disgusted with what you would call the vulgarity of his songs. But what you call his vulgarity, my dears, is just everyday life; and everyday life is always disgusting to the funny little Bayswaterats, who are compact of timidity and pudibonderie. The elderly adolescent has no business at the music-hall; his place is the Baptist Chapel or some other place remote from all connection with this splendid world of London, tragic with suffering and song, high endeavour and defeat. It is people of this kidney who find Harry Champion vulgar. His is the robust, Falstaffian humour of old England, which, I am glad to think, still exists in London and still pleases Londoners, in spite of efforts to Gallicise our entertainments and substitute obscenity and the salacious leer for honest fun and the frank roar of laughter. If you want to hear the joy of living interpreted in song and dance, then go to the first hall where the name of Harry Champion is billed, and hear him sing 'Boiled Beef and Carrots', 'Baked Sheep's Heart stuffed with Sage and Onions', 'Watcher, me Old Brown Son!', 'With me old Hambone', 'William the Conqueror', 'Standard Bread'. If you are sad, you will feel better. If you are suicidal, you will throw the poison away, and you will not be the first man whose life has been saved by a low comedian. You may wonder why this eulogy of food in all these songs. The explanation is simple. In the old days, the music-hall was just a drinking den, and all the jolly songs were in praise of drink. Now that all modern halls are unlicensed, and are, more or less, family affairs to which Mr Jenkinson may bring the wife and the children, and where you can get nothing stronger than non-alcoholic beers, or dry ginger, the Bacchanalian song is out of place. Next to drinking, of course, the Londoner loves eating. Mr Harry Champion, with the insight of genius, has divined this, and therefore he sings about food, winning much applause, personal popularity, and, I hope, much money.

Watch his audience as he sings. Mark the almost hypnotic hold he has over them; not only over pit and gallery but over stalls as well, and the well-groomed loungers who have just dropped in. I defy any sane person to listen to 'Whatcher, me Old Brown Son!' without chortles of merriment, profound merriment, for you don't laugh idly at Harry Champion. His gaiety is not the superficial gaiety of the funny man who makes you laugh but does nothing else to you. He does you good. I honestly believe that his performance would beat down the frigid steel ramparts that begird the English 'lady'. His songs thrill and tickle you as does the gayest music of Mozart. They have not the mere lightness of merriment, but, like that music, they have the deep-plumbing gaiety of the love of life, for joy and sorrow.

But let us leave the front of the house and wander in back of a typical hall. Here is an overcharged atmosphere, feverish of railway-station. There is an entire lack of any system; everything apparently confused rush. Artists dashing out for a second house many miles away. Artists dashing in from their last hall, some fully dressed and made-up, others swearing at their dressers and dragging baskets upstairs, knowing that they have three minutes in which to dress and make-up before their call. As one rushes in with a cheery 'Evening, George!' to the stage-door keeper, he is met by the boy – the boy being usually a middle-aged ex-Army man of 45 or 50.

'Mr Merson's on, sir.'

'Righto!'

He dashes into his dressing-room, which he shares with three others, and then it is *Vesti la giubba* ... The dressing-room is a long, narrow room, with a slab running the length of the wall, and four chairs. The slab is backed by a long, low mirror, and is littered with make-up tins and pots. His dresser hurls himself on the basket, as though he owed it a grudge. He tears off the lid. He dives head foremost into a foam of trousers, coats, and many-coloured shirts. He comes to the surface breathless, having retrieved a shapeless mass of stuff. He tears pieces of this stuff apart, and flings them, with apparent malice, at his chief, and, somehow, they seem to stay wherever he flings them. The chief shouts from a cloud of orange wig and patchwork shirt for a soda-and-milk, and from some obscure place of succour there actually appears a soda-and-milk. A hand darts from the leg of a revolving pair of trousers, grabs the glass and takes a loud swig. The boy appears at the door.

'Mr Merson coming off, sir!'

'Right-*o*! and blast you!'

'No good blasting me, sir!'

From far away, as from another world, he hears the murmur of a large body of people, the rolling of the drum, the throbbing of the double-bass, the wail of the fiddles, sometimes the thud of the wooden-shoe dancer, and sometimes a sudden silence as the music dims away to rubbish for the big stunt of the trapeze performer.

He subsides into a chair. The dresser jams a pair of side-spring boots on his feet while he himself adjusts the wig and assaults his face with sticks of paint.

The boy appears again. He shoots his bullet head through the door, aggressively. 'Mr Benson, *please!*' This time he is really cross. Clearly he will fight Mr Benson before long.

But Mr Benson dashes from his chair and toddles downstairs, and is just in time to slip on as the band finishes his symphony for the fourth time. Once on, he breathes more freely, for neglect of the time-sheet is a terrible thing, and involves a fine. If your time is 8.20, it is your bounden duty to be in the wings ready to go on at 8.17; otherwise ... trouble and blistering adjectives.

While he is on, the boy is chasing round the dressing-rooms for the 'next call'. This happens to be a black-face comedian, who is more punctual than Mr Benson. He is all in order, and at the call: 'Mr. Benson's on, Harry!' he descends and stands in the wings, watching with cold but friendly gaze the antics of Mr Benson, and trying to sense the temper of the house. Mr Benson is at work. In another minute he will be at work, too. Mr Benson is going well – he seems to have got the house. He wonders whether he will get the house – or the bird. He is about to give us something American: to sing and dance to syncopated melody. America may not have added great store to the world's music, but at least she has added to the gaiety of nations. She has given us ragtime, the voice of the negroid Bacchus, which has flogged our flagging flesh to new sensations; she has given us songs fragrant of Fifth Avenue, and with the wail of the American South; and she has given us nigger comedians. Harry doesn't much care whether he 'goes' or not. They are a philosophical crowd, these Vaudevillians. If one of them gets the bird, he has the sympathy of the rest of the bill. Rotten luck. If he goes well, he has their smiles. Of course, there are certain jealousies here as in every game; but very few. You see, they never know ... The stars never know when their reign will end, and they, who were once bill-toppers, will be shoved in small type in obscure corners of the bill at far distant provincial halls.

That is why the halls, like journalism, is such a great game. You never know ... The unhappiest of the whole bill of a hall are 'first call' and 'last call'. Nobody is there to listen to 'first call'; everybody has bolted by the time 'last call' is on. Only the orchestra and the electricians remain. They, like the poor, are always with them.

After the show, the orchestra usually breaks up into parties for a final drink, or sometimes fraternises with the last call and makes a bunch for supper at Sam Isaacs'. After supper, home by the last car to Camberwell or Camden Town, seeking – and, if not too full of supper, finding – a chaste couch at about two a.m. The star, of course, does nothing so vulgar. He motors home to Streatham or St John's Wood or Clapham Common, and plays billiards or cards until the small hours. A curious wave of temperance lately has been sweeping over the heads of the profession, and a star seldom has a drink until after the show. The days are gone when the lion comique would say: 'No, laddie, I don't drink. Nothing to speak of, that is. I just have ten or twelve – just enough to make me think I'm drunk. Then I keep on until I think I'm sober. Then I *know* I'm drunk!' They are beginning, unfortunately for their audiences, to take themselves seriously. This is a pity, for the more spontaneous and inane they are, the more they are in their place on the vaudeville stage. There is more make-believe and hard work on the halls to-day, and I think they are none the better for it. As soon as art becomes self-conscious, its end is near; and that, I am afraid, is what is happening to-day. A quieter note has crept into the whole thing, a more facile technique; and if you develop technique you must develop it at the expense of every one of those more robust and essential qualities. The old entertainers captured us by deliberate unprovoked assault on our attention. But to-day they do not take us by storm. They woo us and win us slowly, by happy craft; and though your admiration is finally wrung from you, it is technique you are admiring – nothing more. All modern art – the novel, the picture, the play, the song – is dying of technique.

I have only the very slightest acquaintance with those gorgeous creatures – the £200 a week men – who top the bill to-day; only the acquaintance of an occasional drink in their rooms. But I have known, and still know, many of the rank and file, and delightful people they are. As a boy of fifteen, I remember meeting, on a seaside front, a member of a troupe then appearing called The Boy Guardsmen. He was a sweet child. Fourteen years old he was, and he gave me cigarettes, and he drank rum and stout, and was one of the most naïve and cleanly simple youths I ever met. He had an angelic trust in the good of everything and everybody. He worshipped me because I bought him a book he wanted. He believed that the ladies appearing in the same bill at his hall were angels. He loved the manager of his troupe as a great-hearted gentleman. He thought his sister was the most radiant and high-souled girl that Heaven had yet sent to earth. And it was his business to sing, twice nightly, some of the smuttiest songs I have heard on any stage. Yet he knew exactly why the house laughed, and what portions of the songs it laughed at. He knew that the songs went because they were smutty, yet such was his innocence that he could not understand why smut should not be laughed at. He was a dear!

There was another family whom I still visit. Father and Mother are Comedy Acrobats and Jugglers. Night by night they appear in spangled tights, and Father resins his hands in view of the audience, and lightly tosses the handkerchief to the wings; and then bends a stout knee, and cries 'Hup!' and catches Mumdear on the spring and throws her in a double somersault. There are two girls of thirteen and fifteen, and a dot of nine; and they regard Dad and Mumdear just as professional pals, never as parents. This is Dad's idea; he dislikes being a father, but he enjoys being an elder brother, and leading the kids on in mischief or jolly times.

I was having drinks one Saturday night, after the show, with Dad, in a scintillating Highbury saloon, when there was a sudden commotion in the passage. A cascade of voices; a chatter of feet; the yelping of a dog.

'What's that?' I murmured, half interested.

'Only the bother and the gawdfers,' he answered.

'Eh?'

'I said it's the bother and the gawdfers ... Rhyming slang, silly ass. The Missus and the kids. Bother-and-strife ... wife. Gawd-forbids ... kids. See? Here they come. No more mouth-shooting for us, now.'

They came. Mumdear came first – very large, submerged in a feather boa and a feathered hat; salmon pink as to the bust, cream silk as to the skirt. The kids came next, two of the sweetest, merriest girls I know. Miss Fifteen simply tumbled with brown curls and smiles; she was of The Gay Glow-worms, a troupe of dancers. Miss Thirteen tripped over the dog and entered with a volley of giggles and a tempest of light stockinged legs, which spent themselves at once when she observed me. In a wink she became the demure maiden. She had long, straight hair to the waist, and the pure candour of her face gave her the air of an Italian madonna. She was of The Casino Juveniles. We had met before, so she sidled up to me and inquired how I was and what's doing. Within half a minute I was besieged by tossing hair and excited hands, and an avalanche of talk about shop, what they were doing, where they were this week, where next, future openings, and so forth; all of which was cut short by the good-humouredly gruff voice of the landlord, inquiring –

'That young lady over fourteen?'

'Well ... er ... she looks it, don't she?' said Dad.

'Dessay she does. But is she?'

'Well ... tell you the truth, Ernest, she ain't. But she will be soon.'

'Well, she can come back then. But she's got to go now.'

'Righto! Come on, Joyce. You got the bird. Here, Maudie, take her home. Both of you. Straight home, mind. And get the supper ready. And don't forget to turn the dog out. And here – get yourselves some chocolates, little devils.' He pulled out a handful of silver. 'There you are – all the change I got.'

He gave Maudie four shillings, and Joyce half a crown – for chocolates; and Maudie tripped out with flustered hair and laughing ribbons, and Joyce fell over the dog, and the swing-doors caught her midwise, and there was a succession of screams fainting into the distance, and at last silence.

'Thank God they're gone, bless the little devils!' And Dad raised his dry ginger in salutation; while Mumdear allowed me to get her a port-and-lemonade. It had apparently been a stiff show.

'Funny, but ... if you notice it ... when one thing goes wrong everything goes. First off, Arthur wasn't there to conduct. His leader had to take first three turns, and he doesn't know us properly and kept missing the cues for changes. See, we have about six changes in our music, and when you kind of get used to doing a stunt to 'Mysterious Rag', it sorts of puts you off if the band is still doing 'Nights of Gladness'. Then the curtain stuck, and we was kept hanging about for a minute, and had to speed up. Then one of our ropes give, and I thought to myself: 'That's put the fair old khybosh on it, that has.' Gave me – well, you know, put me a bit nervy, like. We missed twice. Least, George says I missed, but I say he did. So one thing and another it's been a bad night. However, we went all right, so here's doing it again, sonny. Thumbs up!'

She beamed upon me a very large stage beam, as though she had got the range of the gallery and meant to reach it. But it was sincere, and though she makes three of me, she is a darling, very playful, very motherly, very strong-minded. Indeed, a Woman. She fussed with the feathers of her boa, and sat upright, as though conscious of her athletic proportions and the picture she was making against the gilded background of the saloon. She had an arm that – but I can say no more than that paraphrase of Meredith: She Had An Arm. When you remember that often four times nightly she holds her husband – no lightweight, I assure you – balanced on her right, while, with her left, she juggles with a bamboo-table and a walking-stick, you can realise that She Has An Arm, and you can understand the figure she cuts in

223

commonplace intercourse. You are simply overwhelmed physically and morally.

'But look here, sonny, why not come home and have a bit of supper with us? That is, if there is any. But come round, and have a plate of grab-what-you-can-and-make-the-best-of-it, eh? I think we got some claret and I know George's got a drop of Three-Star. Young Beryl's off to-morrow on the Northern tour with the White Bird Company, so of course we're in a devil of a muddle. George's sister's round there, packing her. But if you'll put up with the damned old upset, why, come right along.'

So we drank up, and I went right along to a jolly little flat near Highbury Quadrant. As we entered the main room, I heard a high, thin voice protesting –

> But there were times, dear,
> When you made me feel so bad!

And there, flitting about the room in dainty lace petticoat, and little else, was young Beryl, superintending her aunt's feverish struggles with paint and powder-jars, frocks, petties, silk stockings, socks, and wraps, snatching these articles from a voluminous wardrobe and tossing them, haphazard, into a monumental dressing-basket, already half-full with two life-size teddy-bears.

She was a bright little maid, and, though we had not met before, we made friends at once. She had a mass of black curls, eyes dancing with elfin lights, a face permanently flushed, and limbs never in repose. She was, even in sleep – as I have seen her since – wonderfully alive, with that hectic energy that is born of spending oneself to the last ounce unceasingly; in her case, the magnetic, self-consuming energy of talent prematurely developed. Her voice had distinctive quality, unusual in little girls of nine. When she talked, it was with perfect articulation and a sense of the value and beauty of words. Her manners were prettily wayward, but not precocious. She moved with the quiet self-possession of one who has something to do and knows just how to do it, one who took her little self seriously but not conceitedly.

On the stage she has been the delight of thousands. Her gay smile, her delicate graces, and her calm, unfaltering stage manner have touched the hearts of all sorts and conditions, from boxes to bar. Eight times a week, six evenings and two matinées, she was booked to take the stage from the rise of the curtain and leave it for scarcely more than two minutes at a time until the fall. This was by no means her first show. Before that she had been pantomime fairy, orphan child in melodrama, waif in a music-hall sketch, millionaire's pet in a Society play, a mischievous boy in a popular farce, dancer in a big ballet, and now the lead in a famous fairy play, at a salary of ten pounds a week. No wonder Dad and Mumdear, and even the elder girls, regarded her with a touch of awe and worship. But, fêted as she is, she has never been spoilt; and she remains, in spite of her effervescent life, a genuine child. The pet of the crowd behind the scenes, the pet of the house in front, she is accustomed, every night, to salvoes of applause, to flowers left at the stage-door, and to boxes of chocolates handed over the footlights. Night after night, in dance or make-believe of life, she spends herself to exhaustion for the pleasure of the multitude; night after night, in a tinsel-world of limelight and grease-paint, she plays at being herself.

I rather wondered what she thought of it all, and whether she enjoyed it; but, like most little girls, she was shy of confidences. Perhaps she wondered at it all, perhaps sometimes she felt very tired of it all – the noise, the dust, the glamour, and the rush. But she would not admit it. She would only admit her joy at the ten pounds a week, out of which Mumdear would be able to send her favourite cousin Billie to the seaside. So I had to leave it at that, and help with the packing; and at about a quarter to one in the morning supper was announced as ready, and we all sat down.

I forget what we ate. There was some mystery of eggs, prepared by Joyce and Maudie. There were various preserved meats, and some fruit, and some Camembert, and some very good Sauterne, to all of which you helped yourself. There was no host or hostess. You just wandered round the table, and forked what you wanted, and ate it, and then came up for more. When we had done eating, Dad brought out a bottle of excellent old brandy, and Joyce and Maudie made tea for the ladies, and Beryl sat on my knee until half-past two and talked scandal about the other members of the White Bird Company.

At three o'clock I broke up a jolly evening, and departed, Maudie and Joyce accompanying me to Highbury Corner, where I found a vagrant cab.

Perhaps, after the cleansing of the London stage, its most remarkable feature is this sudden invasion of it by the child. There has been much foolish legislation on the subject, but, though it is impossible artistically to justify the presence of children in drama, I think I would not have them away. I think they have given the stage, professionally, something that it is none the worse for.

All men, of course, are actors. In all men exists that desire to escape from themselves, to be somebody else, which is expressed in the nursery, by their delight in 'dressing up', and, in later life, by their delight in watching others pretend. But the child is the most happy actor, for to children acting is as natural as eating, and their stage work always convinces because they never consciously act – never, that is, aim at preconceived effects, but merge their personalities wholly in this or that idea and allow themselves to be driven by it. When to this common instinct is added an understanding of stage requirements and a sharp sense of the theatre, the result, as in the cases of Iris Hawkins, Bella Terry, and Cora Goffin, is pure delight. We live in a little age, and, in the absence of great figures, we are perhaps prone to worship little things, and especially to cultivate to excess the wonder-child and often the pseudo-wonder-child. But the gifted stage-children have a distinct place, for they give us no striving after false quantities, no theatricality, and their effects are in proportion to the strength of their genius. Of course, when they are submitted to the training of a third-rate manager, they become mere mechanical dolls, full of shrill speech and distorted posings that never once touch the audience. You have examples of this in any touring melodrama. These youngsters are taught to act, to model themselves on this or that adult member of the company, are made conscious of an audience, and are carefully prevented from being children. The result is a horror. The child is only an effective actor so long as it does not 'act'. As soon as these youngsters reach the age of fifteen or sixteen the dramatic faculty is stilled, and lies dormant throughout adolescence. They are useless on the stage, for, beginning to 'find themselves', they become conscious artists, and, in the theatrical phrase, it doesn't come off. It is hardly to be expected that it should, for acting, of all the arts, most demands a knowledge of the human mind which cannot be encompassed even by genius at seventeen. That is why no child can ever play such a part as that of the little girl in Hauptmann's 'Hannele'. Intuition could never cover it. Nor should children ever be set to play it. The child of melodrama is an impossibility and an ugliness. Children on the stage must be childish, and nothing else. They must not be immature men and women. Superficially, of course, as I have said, every child of talent becomes world-weary and sophisticated; the bright surface of the mind is dulled with things half-perceived. But this, the result of moving in an atmosphere of hectic brilliance, devoid of spiritual nourishment, is not fundamental: it is but a phase. Old-fashioned as the idea may be, it is still true that artificial excitement is useful, indeed necessary, to the artist; and conditions of life that would spoil or utterly destroy the common person are, to him, entirely innocuous, since he lives on and by his own self. And, though some stage children may become prematurely wise, in the depths of their souls, they must preserve, fresh and lovely, the child-spirit, the secret glory shared by all children. If they lose that, they have no justification of any kind.

There was a little girl on the London stage some few years ago whom I have always remembered with joy. I first saw her accidentally at a Lyceum pantomime. That pantomime, and every subsequent show, I saw again and again; and I went always for the dancing of this little girl – Marjorie Carpenter.

I had had, on that first occasion, a long and boring Saturday in Fleet Street, writing up difficult stuff for a North Country Sunday paper. At seven o'clock we turned out, and had one of those completely bad dinners of which Fleet Street alone holds the secret. We loafed in and out of various places, and eventually reached Wellington Street, and some one suggested dropping in. So we dropped in, drugged with wine and other narcotics, and, being young, we saw ourselves pathetically, as it were, a little too conscious of the squalor of it all. Frankly, the show bored me, though, as a rule, I love pantomime and all other vulgar things; and I was suggesting a retreat when they suddenly rang down on the funny man, and the theatre was plunged in a velvet gloom. Here and there sharp lamps stung the dusks. There was a babble of voices. The lights of the orchestra gleamed subtly. The pit was a mist of lilac, which shifted and ever shifted. A chimera of fetid faces swam above the gallery rail. Wave after wave of lifeless heads rolled on either side of us.

Then there was a quick bell; the orchestra blared the chord on, and I sat up. Something seemed about to happen. Back at the bar was a clamour of glass and popping cork, and bashful cries of 'Order, please!' The curtain rushed back on a dark, blank stage. One perceived, dimly, a high sombre draping, very far up-stage. There was silence. Next moment, from between the folds, stole a wee slip of a child in white, who stood, poised like a startled fawn. Three pale spot-limes swam uncertainly from roof and wings, drifted a moment, then picked her up, focusing her gleaming hair and alabaster arms. I looked at the programme.

It was Marjorie Carpenter.

The conductor tapped. A tense silence; and then our ears were drenched in the ballet music of Délibes. Over the footlights it surged, and, racing down-stage, little Marjorie Carpenter flung herself into it, caressing and caressed by it, shaking, as it seemed, little showers of sound from her delighted limbs. On that high, vast stage, amid the crashing speed of that music and the spattering fire of the side-drums, she seemed so frail, so lost, so alone that – oh! one almost ached for her.

But then she danced: and if she were alone at first, she was not now alone. She seemed at a step to people the stage with little companies of dream.

I say she danced, and I must leave it at that. But I have told you nothing . . . nothing. Little Twinkletoes gave us more than dance; she gave us the spirit of Childhood, bubbling with delight, so fresh, so contagious that I could have wept for joy of it. It was a thing of sheer lyrical loveliness, the lovelier, perhaps, because of its very waywardness and disregard of values. Here was no thing of trick and limelight; none of the heavy-lidded, wine-whipped glances of the adult ballerina. It was Blake's 'Infant Joy' materialised. She was a poem.

In the heated theatre, where the opiate air rolled like a fog, we sat entranced before her – the child, elfish and gay and hungry for the beauty of life; the child, lit by a glamorous light. Far below the surface this light burns, and seldom is its presence revealed, save by those children who live very close to Nature: gipsy and forest children. But every child possesses it, whether bred in the whispering wood or among sweetstuff shops and the Highbury 'buses; and I, for one, recognised it immediately this lovely child carried it over the footlights of the Lyceum Theatre.

Hither and thither she drifted like a white snowflake, but all the time . . . dancing; and one had a sense of dumb amazement that so frail a child, her fair arms and legs as slender as a flower-stem, should so fill that stage and hold the rapt attention of a theatreful of people. Here was evidence of something stronger than mere mastery of ballet technique. Perfect her dancing was. There was no touch of that automatic movement so noticeable in most child dancers. When she went thus or so, or flitted from side to side of the stage, she clearly knew just why she did it, why she went up-stage instead of down. But she had more than mere technical perfection: she had personality, that strange, intangible something so rare in the danseuse, that wanders over the footlights. The turn of a foot, the swift side look, the awakening smile, the nice lifting of an eyebrow – these things were spontaneous. No amount of rehearsal or managerial thought could have produced effects so brilliantly true to the moment.

She took five calls; and the orchestra gave her a final chord off. Then a sudden tempest of lights shattered the dusks, a rude chorus was blared, the 'rag' was rung up for the principal boy, and I and a few others tumbled out into the glistening lamplight of the Strand.

THOMAS BURKE, *NIGHTS IN TOWN*

And so the troops marched off to war, singing in time to the ditties which appealed to them the most. Of the two great hymns of that war, 'Pack Up Your Troubles in Your Old Kit Bag', was a rare example of a song written for a competition becoming genuinely popular. But it was the history of the other which constitutes an oddity. 'It's a Long Way to Tipperary' was first heard in the halls in 1912, where it was sung by its part-author, Jack Judge. There it achieved a modest fame, contributing thereby to the truth of an observation made half a century later by J.B. Priestley, 'As soon as the English go to music halls, they love the Irish'. In 1914, at the start of the war, the song was revived by Florrie Forde with much greater success. When the volunteers swung down the lanes towards Flanders and death, it was this ditty about an Irishman's visit to London to which they marched, although, as more than one commentator has since observed, they cared much less about Tipperary than about being taken away from the fleshpots of the West End — 'Goodbye Piccadilly, farewell Leicester Square'. The vogue for this adapted marching song proved to be as brief as the optimism which sent volunteers dashing to join the colours in their tens of thousands. By the end of 1914 'It's a Long Way to Tipperary' was a painful reminder of the naïveté of those first days of fighting, when, the experts assured everyone, it would 'all be over by Christmas'. All that was over by Christmas in the event was the hope of a short, sweet battle. And because of the curiously evocative power of music to conjure up a specific moment and a specific mood, there were soldiers who remembered their experiences in the war to end wars in terms of the musical accompaniment to it which they had themselves provided.

I saw British infantry, in the early weeks of that war, swinging along towards it singing 'Tipperary'. The song was not sung in France after the September of that year, though it remained a favourite at home. To this day, when I hear that foolish and sentimental air, I know very well why a man has been known to go apart, to think over what might have been, and what is, and to weep in secret. That song, and the swift dissolving of our accustomed scene, the bright illusion we had mistaken for the everlasting hills, chanced to come together. The England we knew, once upon a time, vanished with the men who marched away in an autumn that seems to be a century gone . . .

Back we go, beyond 'Tipperary' and Mons, to the Somme and 'The Bells of Hell go Ting-a-ling a-ling'. Beyond again to the Boer War, when, as I remember it, nobody sang the 'Absent-Minded Beggar', but all preferred 'I'll Be your Sweetheart if you will be mine'. Back still more to trouble by the Nile, and 'Over the Burning Sands of Egypt, under a Scorching Sun'; and to a confusion of Burmese, Chinese, Zulu, and Afghan upsets. 'We Don't Want to Fight but by Jingo if we Do' was only a threat that we might join in a fight that was going on. I was about then. It was that Disraeli again. To say nothing of incidentals, such as 'Good-bye, Dolly Gray' and the Spanish-American war. Is there yet an end in sight? I noticed, though, there wasn't much of an inclination to sing a new song during the last great war.

H.M. TOMLINSON, *A MINGLED YARN*

227

One junior officer in the Welsh Fusiliers, destined to become renowned some years later, recorded the revealing fact that the troops tended not to sing overtly patriotic songs at the front, but preferred instead the obliquities of ribaldry and satire.

That night we marched back again to Cambrai. The men were singing. Being mostly from the Midlands, they sang comic songs rather than Welsh hymns: 'Slippery Sam', 'When We've Wound Up the Watch on the Rhine', and 'I Do like a s'nice S'Mince Pie', to concertina accompaniment. The tune of 'S'nice S'Mince Pie' ran in my head all next day, and for the week following I could not get rid of it. The Second Welsh would never have sung a song like 'When We've Wound Up the Watch on the Rhine'. Their only songs about the war were defeatist:

> I want to go home,
> I want to go home.
> The coal-box and shrapnel they whistle and roar,
> I don't want to go to the trenches no more,
> I want to go over the sea
> Where the Kayser can't shoot bombs at me.
> Oh, I
> Don't want to die,
> I want to go home.

There were several more verses in the same strain. Hewitt, the Welsh machine-gun officer, had written one in a more offensive spirit:

> I want to go home,
> I want to go home.
> One day at Givenchy the week before last
> The Allmands attacked and they nearly got past.
> They pushed their way up to the Keep,
> Through our maxim-gun sights we did peep,
> Oh, my!
> They let out a cry,
> They never got home.

But the men would not sing it, though they all admired Hewitt.

ROBERT GRAVES, *GOODBYE TO ALL THAT*

Another young infantry officer confirms the view offered by Graves. One day, sorting out the company food rations in a front-line trench, the officer was blown up by a bomb and buried in the wreckage of the trench. When he awoke he was in a Leicestershire hospital, where he found the musical privations at least as painful as his injuries. He was to become a recognised connoisseur of the music hall, so his views on the suitability of various songs for the troops, and his insistence that jingoism still associated with the Great Macdermott was rejected out of hand, are especially revealing.

There may be people who enjoy a hospital life, but at no time have I been one of them. Once my temperature began to come down and I was no longer wandering in the land of delirium, I longed to be out of that bed, that ward. Opposite my bed was a table on which there was a gramophone, and on the turntable of this gramophone was a record of a baritone singing 'Sussex, Sussex by the Sea!'. Everybody who went past halted a moment or two to start the gramophone going, but nobody ever changed the record. Lying there, forbidden to move, indeed in no condition to take action, I had to endure hours of that cursed instrument grinding out 'Sussex, Sussex by the Sea!' Now and again a small piano arrived and with it some well-meaning but not brilliant local talent, mostly wobbly sopranos. One of them, not remarking how we glared from our beds, nearly always sang that drivelling refrain:

> We don't want to lose you
> But we think you ought to go,
> For your King and your Country
> Both need you so.

The First War, unlike the Second, produced two distinct crops of songs; one for patriotic civilians, like that drivel above; the other, not composed and copyrighted by anybody, genuine folk song, for the sardonic front-line troops. Of these some were bawdy, like the famous 'Mademoiselle from Armentières' and 'The Ballad of Bollocky Bill the Sailor and the Fair Young Maiden'; some were lugubrious and homesick, without patriotic sentiment of any kind, like 'I Want to Go Home'; others were sharply concerned with military life from the standpoint of the disillusioned private. The best of these, with its rousing chorus of 'I know where he is', asked in one lilting verse after another if you wanted the officer, the sergeant major, the quartermaster-sergeant, and so on, and then told you what these nuisances were up to. The last verse and chorus, however, changed the form and the mood, for here the battalion was the subject, and after 'I know where it is' was repeated quietly there came the final reply:

> It's hanging on the old barbed wire.
> I've seen 'em, I've seen 'em
> Hanging on the old barbed wire.

229

And to this day I cannot listen to it unmoved. There is a flash of pure genius, entirely English, in that 'old', for it means that even that devilish enemy, that death-trap, the wire, has somehow been accepted, recognised and acknowledged almost with affection, by the deep rueful charity of this verse. I have looked through whole anthologies that said less to me.

J.B. PRIESTLEY, *MARGIN RELEASED*

While the soldiers in the field were ruthlessly excising any trace of stage heroics from their songs, on the Home Front it was Jingo, Jingo all the way, from the crocodile tears of 'Keep the Home Fires Burning' to the white-feathery implications of songs like 'We Don't Want to Lose You but we Think You Ought to Go'. It is one of the commonest facts about the Great War that between the fighting soldiers and the civilians left behind there was a gulf of sensibility so vast that no returning soldier felt capable of even beginning to bridge it. Disgusted by the cheap heroics of those who still pursued more or less normal lives, the soldiers left the civilians to their own devices, which included the persecuting of anyone with a vaguely mittel-European name, the outlawing of German Measles, and sundry other imbecilities, like the pillorying of those suspected of being traitors, or turncoats, or laggards. On at least one occasion this led to a musical incident which saw the troops and the civilians adopting diametrically opposed positions. The point at issue was the conduct of the greatest of all music hall artists, a man described in the Oxford History of England as 'England's gift to the world in this age, likely to be remembered when her writers, statesmen and scientists are forgotten, as timeless as Shakespeare and as great'. During the Great War this paragon was not in France, nor even in Britain, and it was his absence in California and the work he was doing there which brought about so remarkable a dichotomy in the views of Englishmen.

As soon as Chaplin had established his no-nonsense political credentials, he fell into reminiscences of the old music-hall songs and, cued by my mention of some of the great names, he went off into a bout of marvellous total recall, ballooning before my eyes into the bosomy swagger of Marie Lloyd and bawling out, 'A Little of What You Fancy Does Y'Good', then shrinking into the exquisite shape of Vesta Tilley, the pocket Astaire, and singing 'I'm Colonel Coldfeet of the Coldstream Guards' and 'Into a cookshop he goes dashin', Who should bring his plate of hash in, But the girl he had been mashin', by the sad sea waves'. I told him that my father had kept for me, and I still had, a wartime record of 'Oh, the Moon Shines Bright on Charlie Chaplin'.

'That', he said in sudden alarm, 'scares the hell out of me.'

What I'd forgotten in mentioning that song, though it was neither hard nor pleasant to recall, was the insensate jingoism of wartime Britain, the hounding of German shopkeepers, the cretinous women patriots handing a white feather to young men in civilian clothes, and the holy indignation of comfortable editorial writers against any famous Englishman abroad who had not dashed home to join Our Boys Out There On Flanders Fields. Chaplin was a glaring target, and there was much doltish sarcasm at his expense, until it was discovered that few imports from England bucked up Our Boys Out There like the Chaplin films shown behind the lines. For a nasty spell he was Chaplin the Slacker in the London press and 'Good Old Charlie' in the trenches, after which the hunt was abandoned. At its height, somebody sent Chaplin the new song. In its American original it was about an Indian maiden called 'Little Red Wing', but the lyrics were changed in the British version, whose chorus went:

230

Oh, the moon shines bright
On Charlie Chaplin,
His boots are crackin'
For want of blackin'

And his little baggy
Trousers they need mendin'
Before we send him
To the Dardanelles.

'I went home', said Chaplin, 'and read about the Dardanelles after that, and for a time I was certain they were out to get me.' He laughed now, but he remembered it as a threat long enough to begin hustling around addressing war bond rallies with bouncing enthusiasm, once the United States was in the war.

The songs led naturally to the old vaudeville days in England and the seedy rooms, in dark provincial towns, that he had shared with Stan Laurel. I don't think he saw much of Laurel in Hollywood, certainly not in my time, but he spoke affectionately of him, and told me why. There was a time during a provincial tour when Chaplin was often absent from his lodging, till one Saturday night he came back petrified with fright that his girl in the show was pregnant. Laurel evidently confronted this life crisis as mildly as he contemplated the crasser ordeals of Oliver Hardy. He went off to his trunk and fumbled around in it for a while and came back with a handful of pound notes. They were such savings as he could have scratched up from a fifteen-shilling-a-week salary. Chaplin never said whether the offer had to be taken up, but the memory of it made him more indulgent to the antics of Laurel and Hardy than to any other of the Hollywood comedians, of whom he was uniformly contemptuous.

ALISTAIR COOKE, *SIX MEN*

Chaplin's career embodies paradox within paradox. The greatest genius to rise through the ranks of the music hall, he had left it forever by the time he was twenty-one years old. And yet having forsaken it for the newfangled entertainment invention which was to crush the halls out of existence, he deployed his arts in that new all-powerful destructive industry in such a way that in retrospect his achievement can be said to be the preservation of the fleeting art of impromptu performance in a medium more or less imperishable. When we read of the impossibility of describing in words the art of Little Tich and Dan Leno, we bask in the consolation of knowing, and being familiar with, the thousands of feet of celluloid upon which Chaplin has left an indelible print of their art. When he went to make moving pictures and found himself obliged to improvise a new plot and a new set of gags each day, it was his music-hall experience which saw him through. And, as his world fame grew and his power as a film-maker increased he was able, through full-length features like *Modern Times, City Lights* and especially *Limelight*, to demonstrate once and for all the balletic art of slapstick pantomime raised to its very highest point.

The main criticism levelled at Chaplin is that in imposing a narrative form on his arabesques and tumbles, he was guilty of such arrant sentimentality that there were moments when the mawkishness ruined the comic effects. In the archetypal Chaplin fable, the waif seeks true love amid abject poverty. The forces of capitalism in the Big City all but destroy his hopes; in the end he has fought no more than a draw with the forces posed against him, and takes his leave of us by waddling off into another sunset, bravely prepared to fight and lose one more time. The fates are almost always brutally unkind. Honest men are driven to the gutter; good women are broken by an indifferent world; small children are left to go hungry, the end result of all this brave laughter in the face of catastrophe being an extraordinary blend of laughter and tears, with the tears sometimes too much for the sophisticated viewer. The culminating work in this genre is *Limelight*, in which the gifted young dancer is crippled, the talented comic deprived of employment, and suicide constantly beckons from the waters of the Thames. At what point does pathos devolve into bathos?

Are there moments when the laughter of the audience is an uneasy defence against the spectacle of a man exposing false emotions a little too glibly? The problem for Chaplin, as well as for his audiences, is typified by the caption to a photograph in his *Autobiography*, showing the kind of Victorian slum street which will remain, so long as there is such a thing as history and students to study it, a reproach to the governing classes. Only a moral defective could have designed such dwellings, and only a thief could have extracted rents from them. Under this disgraceful fragment of evidence, Chaplin has written, 'Where we lived, next to the slaughterhouse and the pickle factory, after Mother came out of the asylum'. It is inspired comic caption writing. Placed in the context of one of Chaplin's one-reelers, it would have raised hoots of knowing laughter.

The only difficulty here is that this street *was* where they lived, Chaplin's mother *did* go into an asylum. The first seven chapters of the autobiography comprise a masterpiece, one of the greatest accounts of working-class life in the English language. And from it we learn that all his broken clowns are his father, all his sad waifs his mother. When we are about to arraign Chaplin on charges of slapping on the sentimentality a little too thick, what are we to say of his stage debut, an episode so wonderful and yet so terrible that our sense of what is and what is not fitting in the realm of public entertainment is flung into hopeless disarray. No artist, except possibly Dickens, in another age nurturing a more lachrymose sensibility, would dare concoct such a tale.

It was owing to her vocal condition that at the age of five I made my first appearance on the stage. Mother usually brought me to the theatre at night in preference to leaving me alone in rented rooms. She was playing the Canteen at Aldershot at the time, a grubby mean theatre catering mostly to soldiers. They were a rowdy lot and wanted little excuse to deride and ridicule. To performers, Aldershot was a week of terror.

I remember standing in the wings when mother's voice cracked and went into a whisper. The audience began to laugh and sing falsetto and to make catcalls. It was all vague and I did not quite understand what was going on. But the noise increased until Mother was obliged to walk off the stage. When she came into the wings she was very upset and argued with the stage manager who, having seen me perform before Mother's friends, said something about letting me go on in her place.

And in the turmoil I remember him leading me by the hand and, after a few explanatory words to the audience, leaving me on the stage alone. And before a glare of footlights and faces in smoke, I started to sing, accompanied by the orchestra, which fiddled about until it found my key. It was a well-known song called 'Jack Jones' that went as follows:

> Jack Jones well and known to everybody
> Round about the market, don't yer see,
> I've no fault to find with Jack at all,
> Not when 'e's as 'e used to be.
> But since 'e's had the bullion left him
> 'E has altered for the worst,

For to see the way he treats all his old pals,
Fills me with nothing but disgust.
Each Sunday morning he reads the 'Telegraph',
Once he was contented with the 'Star'.
Since Jack Jones has come into a little bit of cash,
Well, 'e don't know where 'e are.

Halfway through, a shower of money poured on to the stage. Immediately I stopped and announced that I would pick up the money first and sing afterwards. This caused much laughter. The stage manager came on with a handkerchief and helped me to gather it up. I thought he was going to keep it. This thought was conveyed to the audience and increased their laughter, especially when he walked off with it with me anxiously following him. Not until he handed it to Mother did I return and continue to sing. I was quite at home. I talked to the audience, danced, and did several imitations, including one of Mother singing her Irish march song that went as follows:

Riley, Riley, that's the boy to beguile ye,
Riley, Riley, that's the boy for me.
In all the Army great and small,
There's none so trim and neat
As the noble Sergeant Riley
Of the gallant Eighty-eight.

And in repeating the chorus, in all innocence I imitated Mother's voice cracking and was surprised at the impact it had on the audience. There was laughter and cheers, then more money-throwing; and when Mother came on the stage to carry me off, her presence evoked tremendous applause. That night was my first appearance on the stage and Mother's last.

CHARLIE CHAPLIN, *AUTOBIOGRAPHY*

Why was his mother driven to such desperate and humiliating expedients? Where was her handsome husband, an accomplished entertainer earning up to £40 a week on the halls? Why did his wife need to work at all? Once again, the truth has no regard for the fastidiousness of modern taste. In 1886, three years before Chaplin was born, there appeared in the music shops a Temperance ballad called 'Don't Go Out Tonight, Dear Father', in which a small child implores his drunkard of a father to stay home and comfort his dying wife. The sentiments embodied in the lyric are excruciating, but it is probable that one artist who could have identified with them, and perhaps did, was Chaplin, whose father drank himself into an early grave within a few years of abandoning his wife and children to their own pathetic devices.

I was hardly aware of a father, and do not remember him having lived with us. He too was a vaudevillian, a quiet, brooding man with dark eyes. Mother said he looked like Napoleon. He had a light baritone voice and was considered a very fine artist. Even in those days he earned the considerable sum of forty pounds a week. The trouble was that he drank too much, which Mother said was the cause of their separation.

It was difficult for vaudevillians not to drink in those days, for alcohol was sold in all

233

theatres, and after a performer's act he was expected to go to the theatre bar and drink with the customers. Some theatres made more profit from the bar than from the box-office, and a number of stars were paid large salaries not alone for their talent but because they spent more of their money at the theatre bar. Thus many an artist was ruined by drink – my father was one of them. He died of alcoholic excess at the age of thirty-seven.

CHARLIE CHAPLIN, AUTOBIOGRAPHY

Already our misgivings about the relentless wretchedness of the world of the poor depicted by Chaplin in his productions begin to falter. The sadness we can dismiss in art is not so easy to dismiss in real life. Yet Chaplin has hardly started yet. In telling the harrowing tale of his childhood he maintains a quiet, controlled tone which is far more moving than any anger he might have expressed. He simply talks quietly to us, leading us through a succession of shocking privations which culminate in the collapse of his mother's health. A doctor later told Chaplin that her mental stability disintegrated not through some congenital affliction or cerebral degeneracy, but simply, if that is the right word, from malnutrition. Her distractions are strongly reminiscent of the behaviour of some poor victim in one of the later novels of Dickens, and it is a point worth considering by those critics who were and are in the habit of dismissing the working-class madness of some Dickens characters as crude caricature, that their creator may have been reporting on the medical effects of not having anything to eat. The earlier chapters of Chaplin's autobiography are certainly Dickensian in several aspects, especially with regard to his mother, who drifted in and out of institutions and hospitals while Charlie and his elder brother Sydney coped as best they could. One Saturday evening Charlie came home to find the place deserted and the cupboard literally bare. It is the first moment in the autobiography when he becomes conscious of those sentimental melodies for which he was one day to become famous.

When I returned, it was night; I knocked at the door, but no one answered. Everyone was out. Wearily I walked to the corner of Kennington Cross and sat on the kerb near the house to keep an eye on it in case someone returned. I was tired and miserable, and wondered where Sydney was. It was approaching midnight and Kennington Cross was deserted but for one or two stragglers. All the lights of the shops began going out except those of the chemist and the public houses, then I felt wretched.

Suddenly there was music. Rapturous! It came from the vestibule of the White Hart corner pub, and resounded brilliantly in the empty square. The tune was 'The Honeysuckle and the Bee', played with radiant virtuosity on a harmonium and clarinet. I had never been conscious of melody before, but this one was beautiful and lyrical, so blithe and gay, so warm and reassuring. I forgot my despair and crossed the road to where the musicians were. The harmonium-player was blind, with scarred sockets where the eyes had been; and a besotted, embittered face played the clarinet. It was all over soon and their exit left the night even sadder.

CHARLIE CHAPLIN, AUTOBIOGRAPHY

A tiny light begins to gleam at the far end of the tunnel when Chaplin's father, performing the last and perhaps the only paternal gesture of his life, uses his influence to gain his son entry into a workaday touring troupe called the Eight Lancashire Lads, managed by a Mr Jackson and his wife. It was one of the first promising things ever to happen to Chaplin, but in telling the story he cannot keep away from the tragic melancholia attaching to the life of a man paid to make people laugh, that occupational hazard which goes with the duty to make others forget their troubles no matter how acute your own. Chaplin witnessed this kind of despair in his very first professional engagement, and never forgot it.

Father knew Mr Jackson, who ran the troupe, and convinced Mother that it would be a good start for me to make a career on the stage and at the same time help her economically: I would get board and lodging and Mother would get half a crown a week. She was dubious at first until she met Mr Jackson and his family, then she accepted.

Mr Jackson was in his middle fifties. He had been a school-teacher in Lancashire and had raised a family of three boys and a girl, who were all a part of the Eight Lancashire Lads. He was a devout Roman Catholic and after his first wife died had consulted his children about marrying again. His second wife was a little older than himself, and he would piously tell us how he came to marry her. He had advertised for a wife in one of the newspapers and had received over three hundred letters. After praying for guidance he had opened only one, and that was from Mrs Jackson. She too had been a school-teacher and, as if in answer to his prayer, was also a Catholic.

Mrs Jackson was not blessed with abundant good looks, nor was she a voluptuary in any sense of the word. As I remember her she had a gaunt, skull-like, pale face with manifold wrinkles – due, perhaps, to having presented Mr Jackson with a baby boy rather late in life. Nevertheless, she was a loyal and dutiful wife and, although still nursing her son at the breast, worked hard at helping with the management of the troupe.

When she told her side of the romance, it varied slightly from that of Mr Jackson. They had exchanged letters, but neither one had seen the other until the day of the wedding. And in their first interview alone in the sitting-room while the family waited in another room, Mr Jackson said: 'You're all that I desire,' and she avowed the same. In concluding the story to us boys, she would primly say: 'But I didn't expect to be the immediate mother of eight children.'

The three sons' ages ranged from twelve to sixteen, and the daughter was nine, with hair cut like a boy in order to pass as one in the troupe.

Each Sunday, everyone attended Catholic church but me. Being the only Protestant, I was lonely, so occasionally I went with them. Had it not been for deference to Mother's religious scruples, I could easily have been won over to Catholicism, for I liked the mysticism of it and the little home-made altars with plaster Virgin Marys adorned with flowers and lighted candles which the boys put up in a corner of the bedroom, and to which they would genuflect every time they passed.

After practising six weeks I was eligible to dance with the troupe. But now that I was past eight years old I had lost my assurance and confronting the audience for the first time gave me stage fright. I could hardly move my legs. It was weeks before I could solo dance as the rest of them did.

235

I was not particularly enamoured with being just a clog dancer in a troupe of eight lads. Like the rest of them I was ambitious to do a single act, not only because it meant more money but because I instinctively felt it to be more gratifying than just dancing. I would have liked to be a boy comedian – but that would have required nerve, to stand on the stage alone. Nevertheless, my first impulse to do something other than dance was to be funny. My ideal was a double act, two boys dressed as comedy tramps. I told it to one of the other boys and we decided to become partners. It became our cherished dream. We would call ourselves 'Bristol and Chaplin, the Millionaire Tramps', and would wear tramp whiskers and big diamond rings. It embraced every aspect of what we thought would be funny and profitable, but, alas, it never materialised.

Audiences liked the Eight Lancashire Lads because, as Mr Jackson said, we were so unlike theatrical children. It was his boast that we never wore grease-paint and that our rosy cheeks were natural. If some of us looked a little pale before going on, he would tell us to pinch our cheeks. But in London, after working two or three music halls a night, we would occasionally forget and look a little weary and bored as we stood on the stage, until we caught sight of Mr Jackson in the wings, grinning emphatically and pointing to his face, which had an electrifying effect of making us suddenly break into sparkling grins.

When touring the provinces we went to a school for the week in each town, which did little to further my education.

At Christmas time we were engaged to play cats and dogs in a Cinderella pantomime at the London Hippodrome. In those days, it was a new theatre, a combination of vaudeville and circus, elaborately decorated and quite sensational. The floor of the ring sank and flooded with water and elaborate ballets were contrived. Row after row of pretty girls in shining armour would march in and disappear completely under water. As the last line submerged, Marceline, the great French clown, dressed in sloppy evening dress and opera hat, would enter with a fishing rod, sit on a camp stool, open a large jewel-case, bait his hook with a diamond necklace, then cast it into the water. After a while he would 'chum' with smaller jewellery, throwing in a few bracelets, eventually emptying in the whole jewel-case. Suddenly he would get a bite and throw himself into paroxysms of comic gyrations struggling with the rod, and eventually pulling out of the water a small trained poodle dog, who copied everything Marceline did: if he sat down, the dog sat down; if he stood on his head, the dog did likewise.

Marceline's comedy was droll and charming and London went wild over him. In the kitchen scene I was given a little comedy bit to do with Marceline. I was a cat, and Marceline would back away from a dog and fall over my back while I drank milk. He always complained that I did not arch my back enough to break his fall. I wore a cat-mask which had a look of surprise, and during the first matinée for children I went up to the rear end of a dog and began to sniff. When the audience laughed, I turned and looked surprised at them, pulling a string which winked a staring eye. After several sniffs and winks the house-manager came bounding back stage, waving frantically in the wings. But I carried on. After smelling the dog, I smelt the proscenium, then I lifted my leg. The audience roared – possibly because the gesture was uncatlike. Eventually the manager caught my eye and I capered off to great applause. 'Never do that again!' he said, breathlessly, 'You'll have the Lord Chamberlain close down the theatre!'

Cinderella was a great success, and although Marceline had little to do with plot or story, he was the star attraction. Years later Marceline went to the New York Hippodrome, where he was also a sensation. But when the Hippodrome abolished the circus ring, Marceline was soon forgotten.

In 1918, or thereabouts, Ringling Brothers' three-ring circus came to Los Angeles, and Marceline was with them. I expected that he would be featured, but I was shocked to find him just one of many clowns that ran around the enormous ring –

a great artist lost in the vulgar extravagance of a three-ring circus.

I went to his dressing-room afterwards and made myself known, reminding him that I had played Cat at the London Hippodrome with him. But he reacted apathetically. Even under his clown make-up he looked sullen and seemed in a melancholy torpor.

A year later in New York he committed suicide. A small paragraph in the papers stated that an occupant living in the same house had heard a shot and had found Marceline lying on the floor with a pistol in his hand and a record still turning, playing *Moonlight and Roses*.

Many famous English comedians committed suicide. T.E. Dunville, an excellent funny man, overheard someone say as he entered a saloon bar: 'That fellow's through.' The same day he shot himself by the River Thames.

Mark Sheridan, one of England's foremost comedians, shot himself in a public park in Glasgow because he had not gone over well with the Glasgow audience.

Frank Coyne, with whom we played on the same bill, was a gay, bouncy type of comedian, famous for his breezy song:

> You won't catch me on the gee-gee's back again,
> It's not the kind of horse that I can ride on.
> The only horse I know that I can ride
> Is the one the missus dries the clothes on!

Off stage he was pleasant and always smiling. But one afternoon, after planning to take a drive with his wife in their pony and trap, he forgot something and told her to wait while he went upstairs. After twenty minutes she went up to see what was causing the delay, and found him in the bathroom on the floor in a pool of blood, a razor in his hand – he had cut his throat, almost decapitating himself.

Of the many artists I saw as a child, those who impressed me the most were not always the successful ones but those with unique personalities off stage. Zarmo, the comedy tramp juggler, was a disciplinarian who practised his juggling for hours every morning as soon as the theatre opened. We could see him back stage balancing a billiard cue on his chin and throwing a billiard ball up and catching it on the tip of the cue, then throwing up another and catching that on top of the first ball – which he often missed. For four years, he told Mr Jackson, he had been practising that trick and at the end of the week he intended to try it out for the first time with the audience. That night we all stood in the wings and watched him. He did it perfectly, and the first time! – throwing the ball up and catching it on the tip of the billiard cue, then throwing a second and catching that on top of the first. But the audience only applauded mildly. Mr Jackson often told the story of that night. Said he to Zarmo: 'You make the trick look too easy, you don't sell it. You should miss it several times, then do it.' Zarmo laughed. 'I am not expert enough to miss it yet.' Zarmo was also interested in phrenology and would read our characters. He told me that whatever knowledge I acquired, I would retain and put to good use.

And there were the Griffiths Brothers, funny and impressive, who confused my psychology, comedy trapeze clowns who, as they both swung from the trapeze, would ferociously kick each other in the face with large padded shoes.

'Ouch!' said the receiver. 'I dare you to do it again!'

'Do yer?' ... Bang!

And the receiver would look surprised and groggy and say: 'He did it again!'

I thought such crazy violence shocking. But off stage they were devoted brothers, quiet and serious.

CHARLIE CHAPLIN, *AUTOBIOGRAPHY*

Illness forced Chaplin to leave the Eight Lancashire Lads, but after trying a succession of menial occupations, he was hired to play a small part in a touring production of *Sherlock Holmes*. The next engagement was with a vaudeville act called Casey's Circus, in which Charlie did a burlesque of Dick Turpin the Highwayman. When the act appeared in London, six of the boys boarded in the Kennington Road with the Field family, a widow lady, and her three daughters. The atmosphere was so congenial that after the engagement with Casey's Circus ended, Charlie went back to stay with the Fields. While he was out of work his rent was paid by his brother, earning four pounds a week with Fred Karno. It was now that Charlie decided to invest in a solo act of his own.

At the time Jewish comedians were all the rage in London, so I thought I would hide my youth under whiskers. Sydney gave me two pounds, which I invested in musical arrangements for songs and funny dialogue taken from an American joke-book, *Madison's Budget*. For weeks I practised, performing in front of the Fields family. They were attentive and encouraging but nothing more. I had obtained a trial week without pay at the Foresters' Music Hall, which was a small theatre situated off the Mile End Road in the centre of the Jewish quarter. I had played there previously with Casey's Circus and the management thought I was good enough to be given a chance. My future hopes and dreams depended on that trial week. After the Foresters' I would play all the important circuits in England. Who knows? Within a year I might rise to be one of Vaudeville's biggest headliners. I had promised the whole Fields family that I would get them tickets towards the end of the week, when I was thoroughly at home with my act.

'I suppose you won't want to live with us after your success,' said Phoebe.

'Of course I will,' I said graciously.

Twelve o'clock Monday morning was band rehearsal for songs and cues, etc.; which I carried out professionally. But I had not given sufficient thought to my make-up. I was undecided how I should look. For hours before the night show I was in the dressing-room experimenting, but no matter how much crêpe hair I used I could not hide my youth. Although I was innocent of it, my comedy was most anti-Semitic, and my jokes were not only old ones but very poor, like my Jewish accent. Moreover, I was not funny.

After the first couple of jokes the audience started throwing coins and orange-peel and stamping their feet and booing. At first I was not conscious of what was going on. Then the horror of it filtered into my mind. I began to hurry and talk faster as the jeers, the raspberries, and the throwing of coins and orange-peel increased. When I came off the stage, I did not wait to hear the verdict from the management; I went straight up to the dressing-room, took off my make-up, left the theatre and never returned, not even to collect my music books.

It was late when I returned home to Kennington Road and the Fields family had all gone to bed and I was thankful they had. In the morning at breakfast Mrs Fields was anxious to know how the show went. I bluffed indifference and said, 'All right, but it needs a few alterations.' She said that Phoebe had gone to see me, but had told them nothing, as she was too tired and wanted to go to bed. When I saw Phoebe later she did not mention it, neither did I; nor did Mrs Fields or any of the family ever mention it again, or show any surprise at my not continuing the week.

CHARLIE CHAPLIN, *AUTOBIOGRAPHY*

It was Sydney who now opened the last of the doors for his younger brother and finally set him on his way. By now their mother was in the asylum where she would remain for some years, until her two sons were in a position to remove her and care for her themselves. It was Sydney's connection with Fred Karno that was the vital link in Chaplin's chain of progress.

As a result of seeing an advertisement in *The Era*, a theatrical paper, he joined Charlie Manon's troupe of knockabout comedians. In those days there were several of these troupes touring the halls; Charlie Baldwin's Bank Clerks, Joe Boganny's Lunatic Bakers, and the Boicette troupe, all of them pantomimists. And although they played slapstick comedy, it was performed to beautiful music *à la* ballet and was most popular. The outstanding company was Fred Karno's, who had a large repertoire of comedies. Each one was called 'Birds'. There were 'Jail Birds', 'Early Birds', 'Mumming Birds', etc. From these three sketches Karno built a theatrical enterprise of more than thirty companies, whose repertoire included Christmas pantomimes and elaborate musical comedies, from which he developed such fine artists and comedians as Fred Kitchen, George Graves, Harry Weldon, Billie Reeves, Charlie Bell and many others.

One day Sydney told me that Mr Karno wanted to see me. It appears he was dissatisfied with one of the comedians playing opposite Mr Harry Weldon in 'The Football Match', one of Karno's most successful sketches. Weldon was a very popular comedian who remained popular up to the time of his death in the 'thirties. Mr Karno was a thick-set, bronzed little man, with keen sparkling eyes that were always appraising. He had started as an acrobat on the horizontal bars, then got together three knockabout comedians. This quartet was the nucleus of his comedy pantomime sketches. He himself was an excellent comedian and originated many comedy roles. He continued playing even when he had five other companies on the road. One of the original members tells the story of his retirement. One night in Manchester, after a performance, the troupe complained that Karno's timing was off and that he had ruined the laughs. Karno, who had then accumulated £50,000 from his five shows, said, 'Well, boys, if that's the way you feel, I'll quit!' then, taking off his wig, he dropped it on the dressing-table and grinned, 'You can accept that as my resignation.'

Mr Karno's home was in Coldharbour Lane, Camberwell; annexed to it was a warehouse in which he stored the scenery for his twenty productions. He also maintained his offices there. When I arrived he received me kindly. 'Sydney's been telling me how good you are,' he said. 'Do you think you could play opposite Harry Weldon in "The Football Match"?'

Harry Weldon was specially engaged at a high salary, getting £34 a week.

'All I need is the opportunity,' I said confidently.

He smiled. 'Seventeen's very young, and you look even younger.'

I shrugged off-handedly. 'That's a question of make-up.'

Karno laughed. That shrug, he told Sydney later, got me the job.

CHARLIE CHAPLIN, *AUTOBIOGRAPHY*

239

Chaplin had little affection for Karno, and sounds at times as though he is gaining belated literary revenge for the indignities flung at him by his autocratic master. In fact, Chaplin was letting Karno off very lightly. It seems impossible that, working for him as he did, Chaplin was not aware of the bestial side of Karno's nature. All he says of his old boss is that he could be brutal with his tongue.

Karno could be cynical and cruel to anyone he disliked. Because he liked me I had never seen that side of him, but he could indeed be most crushing in a vulgar way. During a performance of one of his comedies, if he did not like a comedian, he would stand in the wings and hold his nose and give an audible raspberry. But he did this once too often and the comedian left the stage and lunged at him; that was the last time he resorted to such vulgar measures. And now I stood confronting him about a new contract.

'Well,' he said, smiling cynically, 'you want a raise and the theatre circuits want a cut.' He shrugged. 'Since the fiasco at the Oxford Music Hall, we've had nothing but complaints. They say the company's not up to the mark – a scratch crowd.'

'Well, they can hardly blame me for that', I said.

'But they do', he answered, pinning me with a steady gaze.

'What do they complain about?' I asked.

He cleared his throat and looked at the floor. 'They say you're not competent.' Although the remark hit me in the pit of the stomach, it also infuriated me, but I replied calmly: 'Well, other people don't think so, and they're willing to give me more than I'm getting here.' This was not true – I had no other offer.

'They say the show is awful and the comedian's no good. Here,' he said, picking up the phone, 'I'll call up The Star, Bermondsey, and you can hear for yourself ... I understand you did poor business last week,' he said over the phone.

'Lousy!' came a voice.

Karno grinned. 'How do you account for it?'

'A dud show!'

'What about Chaplin, the principal comedian? Wasn't he any good?'

'He stinks!' said the voice.

Karno offered me the phone and grinned. 'Listen for yourself.'

I took the phone. 'Maybe he stinks, but not half as much as your stinkpot theatre,' I said. Karno's attempt to cut me down was not a success. I told him that if he also felt that way there was no need to renew my contract. Karno in many ways was a shrewd man, but he was not a psychologist. Even if I did stink it wasn't good business of Karno to have a man at the other end of the phone tell me so. I was getting five pounds and, although my confidence was low, I demanded six. To my surprise Karno gave it to me, and again I entered his good graces.

CHARLIE CHAPLIN, *AUTOBIOGRAPHY*

Not on the whole an altogether unprepossessing sketch, and Karno would no doubt have been pleased to settle for it. The truth was that he was the most odious person in the entire history of music hall, perhaps of the English stage. Indeed, his biographer, J.P. Gallagher, cannot bring himself to be explicit about Karno's bestiality, but merely says that Mrs Karno was 'unwilling to submit to his perverse fancies'. Karno married Edith Cuthbert, a box-office girl, in 1889; within a year the doctor called in to treat Mrs Karno for extensive injuries inflicted by Karno threatened action if Karno persisted in his brutalities. Edith was pregnant at the time, but the fact only seemed to add a certain flavour to Karno's sport. Later he scarred Edith for life by stamping on her face, and found solace with as many other women as he could find who were willing to put up with his appalling subhuman behaviour. The palm for beating up women in the Music Hall has always gone to Bernard Dillon, but it is doubtful if even that rat was quite as detestable as Karno. Dillon's crimes were compounded by the fact that they shortened the life of the most popular woman in England, while Karno's outrages were inflicted on a theatrical nonentity. But the sheer horror of Karno's conduct puts him in a different league from Dillon, and suggests strongly that in a more enlightened age he would have been certifiable. Meanwhile Chaplin, who was evidently able to cope with Karno's excesses, developed quickly in the troupe, but soon felt constricted by the limitations of the work.

I was almost nineteen and already a successful comedian in the Karno Company, but something was lacking. Spring had come and gone and summer was upon me with an emptiness. My daily routine was stale, my environment dreary. I could see nothing in my future but a commonplaceness among dull, commonplace people. To be occupied with the business of just grubbing for a living was not good enough. Life was menial and lacked enchantment. I grew melancholy and dissatisfied and took lonely walks on Sunday and listened to park bands. I could support neither my own company nor that of anyone else. And of course, the obvious thing happened: I fell in love.

We were playing at the Streatham Empire. In those days we performed at two or three music halls nightly, travelling from one to the other in a private bus. At Streatham we were on early in order to appear later at the Canterbury Music Hall and then the Tivoli. It was daylight when we started work. The heat was oppressive and the Streatham Empire was half empty, which, incidentally, did not detract from my melancholy.

CHARLIE CHAPLIN, *AUTOBIOGRAPHY*

A welcome distraction came in 1909 with an engagement with the Karno troupe at the Folies Bergère. One subject Chaplin never mentions is Little Tich, whose work he studied in close detail in Paris, closely enough to lift Tich's entire stage persona of the Little Man in the tattered, dusty clothes. It has been said that Chaplin's failure to mention Tich, in an autobiography covering over 500 densely-packed pages, constitutes one of the most lamentable lapses of the charitable instinct in the

241

history of the popular arts. But in a sense it is this very omission which shows how deeply rooted in Tich's art was Chaplin's own. The egotist could bear to discuss comics to whom he knew he was infinitely superior. Tich he could not bear to mention at all. He came back from Paris inspired by what he had seen Tich doing, and soon began duplicating a great many elements of his art. His great rival in the Karno troupe was a much more famous comedian who was no better than Chaplin when it came to the charitable instinct.

Weldon's comedy character was of the cretinous type, a slow-speaking Lancashire boob. That went very well in the North of England, but in the South he was not too well received. Bristol, Cardiff, Plymouth, Southampton, were slump towns for Weldon; during those weeks he was irritable and performed perfunctorily and took his spleen out on me. In the show he had to slap and knock me about quite a bit. This was called 'taking the nap', that is, he would pretend to hit me in the face, but someone would slap their hands in the wings to give it a realistic effect. Sometimes he really slapped me and unnecessarily hard, provoked, I think, by jealousy. In Belfast the situation came to a head. The critics had given Weldon a dreadful panning, but had praised my performance. This was intolerable to Weldon, so that night on the stage he let me have a good one which took all the comedy out of me and made my nose bleed. Afterwards I told him that if he did it again I would brain him with one of the dumb-bells on the stage, and added that if he was jealous, not to take it out on me.

'Jealous of you,' said he contemptuously, on our way to the dressing-room. 'Why, I have more talent in my arse that you have in your whole body.'

'That's where your talent lies,' I retorted, and quickly closed the dressing-room door.

CHARLIE CHAPLIN, *AUTOBIOGRAPHY*

Weldon was certainly a difficult man. His speciality was impersonating a series of antiheroic types. When Chaplin refers to the football sketch he is recalling one of the most celebrated of all sporting lampoons, in which Weldon becomes Stiffy the Half-witted Goalkeeper. Later Weldon used another famous sketch involving him as a great pugilist, 'with a two-stone body and a twelve-stone head'. In this sketch his manager would invite the members of the audience to dare to box three rounds with his man, saying, 'Will any gentleman?', to which Weldon would add, 'Will any lady?'. In the period immediately after the Great War he was the most popular comic on the music-hall stage, but, in the words of Willson Disher, 'he felt the strain that overwhelms so many comedians in middle age'. 'Feeling the strain' is a euphemism for drinking. Around 1924 my father was working with a small jazz orchestra which did the occasional week in the halls. For four weeks they shared the bill with Weldon, and my father would stand in the wings every night to watch this hilarious man impersonate a cowardly prize-fighter. But even more wondrous than the comic technique was the man's ability to exercise it at all. For each night, as he stood in the wings preparing himself to go on, Weldon would sway from side to side, recklessly drunk and hardly able to control his movements. Yet the moment he strode out into the lights and the applause, he regained control. When telling this story, my father would add that until he saw Weldon, he had believed that this ability to dispense your art while under the influence was confined to jazz musicians.

Six months had drifted by in England and I had settled down to my usual routine, when news came from the London office that made life more exciting. Mr Karno informed me that I was to take the place of Harry Weldon in the second season of 'The Football Match'. Moreoever, we were to open at the Oxford, the most important music hall in London. We were to be the main attraction and I was to have my name featured for the first time at the top of the bill. This was a considerable step up. If I were a success at the Oxford it would establish a kudos that would enable me to demand a large salary and eventually branch out with my own sketches, in fact it would lead to all sorts of wonderful schemes.

CHARLIE CHAPLIN, *AUTOBIOGRAPHY*

An attack of laryngitis ruined the appearance at the Oxford, and soon Chaplin was touring around with Karno in what has become the most renowned sketch in music-hall history, not simply because it was a classic sketch but because it was Chaplin's last contact with the music hall. A talent scout spotted Chaplin in Karno's company and offered him the chance he coveted so desperately.

The chance to go to the United States was what I needed. In England I felt I had reached the limit of my prospects; besides, my opportunities there were circumscribed. With scant educational background, if I failed as a music-hall comedian I would have little chance but to do menial work. In the States the prospects were brighter.

The night before sailing, I walked about the West End of London, pausing at Leicester Square, Coventry Street, the Mall and Piccadilly, with the wistful feeling that it would be the last time I would see London, for I had made up my mind to settle permanently in America. I walked until two in the morning, wallowing in the poetry of deserted streets and my own sadness.

CHARLIE CHAPLIN, *AUTOBIOGRAPHY*

At this point Chaplin takes his leave forever of the music-hall stage, armoured for the struggle with Hollywood by the techniques acquired with Karno, with Casey's Circus, with his mother, and above all by his contact with the art of Little Tich. Chaplin's prescience regarding his prospects in America was extraordinary. It was as though he sensed that one era was closing and another just beginning, and that he was destined to rise alongside the new form of entertainment. In the deeper sense, the change in personality from the Kennington waif to the Californian virtuoso was nothing short of calamitous. By the end of Chapter Seven of the autobiography, this clown, writing his first book at the age of seventy-four, seems likely to achieve a masterpiece, one of the few great classics of British working-class life. From the very first lines of the next chapter, the book swiftly disintegrates into a vast compendium of platitude, self-glorification and potted philosophy. Gone is the quiet, beautifully controlled style, gone the rationale of humility and common sense. In its place is a tiresome, routine showbiz job, which scatters the names of the irrelevant great in every chapter.

But not the great of Chaplin's past. The most lamentable thing of all about the failure to sustain the magnificent quality of the early chapters is the almost total dismissal of the Music Hall. Once Chaplin is away there is hardly a mention of anyone working the halls. That Little Tich should never once be referred to is unfortunate but understandable. That Stan Laurel, with whom Chaplin had a special link, and for whom he felt genuine admiration, should never be mentioned is much more remarkable. Even when he can bring himself to refer to the giants of the art which nurtured him, Chaplin clearly has great difficulty in being complimentary; when saluting Dan Leno, in whose comic approach Chaplin's own was rooted, there is something ungracious about it all, as though Chaplin, irritated by the need to mention the man, gains revenge by the insertion of 'I suppose' and 'so Mother told me'.

Dan Leno, I suppose, was the greatest English comedian since the legendary Grimaldi. Although I never saw Leno in his prime, to me he was more of a character actor than a comedian. His whimsical character delineations of London's lower classes were human and endearing, so Mother told me.

CHARLIE CHAPLIN, *AUTOBIOGRAPHY*

Yet it is Chaplin alone who performed the miracle of preserving in permanent form the fleeting grace of a transient art. Of all the hundreds of films he made, there is not one which does not bear testimony to his music hall roots, not one which is not embellished with some little comedic trick or gesture acquired in the halls of the Edwardian epoch. When in *Limelight* Chaplin has trouble making his arms the same length: when in *City Lights,* gloved for a boxing match, he needs to go to the lavatory and holds out his hands to his second in a gesture of dumb appeal; when, dressed in a pathetic hooped swimming costume in *Modern Times,* he takes an extravagant dive into two inches of water; when in *The Gold Rush* he makes an epicure's banquet of an old boot; when in *Shoulder Arms,* caught in the trenches of Flanders, he holds a bottle of wine over the rim of the parapet so that the enemy snipers can open it for him by shooting off its neck, Chaplin is demonstrating the vocabulary of the pantomimic art picked up in the Alhambras and Palaces of his youth.

That it was essentially pantomimic was a point which Chaplin might have raised in his own defence when charged with the appropriation of Little Tich's stage persona. Both Tich and Dan Leno relied heavily on language, especially its slapstick misuse, to amplify the comic impact of their dress and gestures. Chaplin needed to say nothing at all. There were no funny songs, no patter, no monologues, attached to his reputation. He sensed that once he opened his mouth the purity of his interpretation was compromised. For Chaplin not only had an inadequate high-pitched voice, but, much more serious, could not write half-way reasonable dialogue. His dogged defiance of the Talkies was more than mere perversity. It was a fight for survival. Even when he did finally bow to the need for talk in his productions, he most ingeniously reduced the spoken word to inspired gibberish. In *The Great Dictator*, lampooning Hitlerian rant, Chaplin screams out tirades of rubbish which sound so convincing that not until hearing the speech for the second or third time does the listener realise that Chaplin is not actually saying anything at all, but merely mouthing crazy noises which make the point of Hitler's insanity more eloquently than the most inspired rhetoric or the most cunning satire.

When confining himself to dumb-show, Chaplin was able to take the classic devices of the music hall and place them in a context which would last for as long as the celluloid on which they were printed. Probably the most creative of all his assaults on mere wordage can be found in a scene wherein the nonsense-syllables become an essential part of the character's predicament, almost as though showing us that at the point where the human being is obliged to resort to speech, the fact that too often he has nothing worth saying will guarantee spectacular fiasco. Chaplin is a waiter in a crowded dance-hall restaurant. He makes his entry carrying a tray on which is packed a huge meal, including half a chicken. His customers are sitting at a table on the far side of the crowded floor. Holding the tray far above his head and displaying miraculous powers of balance and dexterity, he succeeds in reaching the table without disaster. But when he lowers the tray the chicken has vanished, impaled on the protruding spike of a chandelier suspended low over the dance-floor. But this is only the start of the waiter's discomfiture. He is not only serving meals, but has been hired to sing also. Before making his entry he has ensured against drying up in mid-song by scribbling the lyrics of his chosen aria on the starched cuffs of his white shirt. The moment comes for his song. The floor is his. There is a chord from the orchestra. He announces himself by flinging out both arms in acknowledgement of the applause. Both cuffs fly off into the crowd and play no further part in the story. The song begins, and the waiter, trapped without words, improvises a sort of garbled bogus-Italian, the Latin equivalent of the Mock-Teutonic rubbish in *The Great Dictator*. Speech, says the waiter, is a last and very unsatisfactory resort.

That this was true for Chaplin, if not for the rest of the industry, was proved by *Limelight*, Chaplin's last great attempt to record once and for all the art of the halls. But as Calvero, the broken old clown, Chaplin mouths such platitudes regarding great art and great artists that the onlooker squirms with embarrassment. In the end Calvero makes his last great public appearance and symbolically dies in the wings. We are back to the beginning, to the clown-father who died of drink before he was forty, to the pretty soubrette-mother whose mind disintegrated under the strain of failure. Somewhere among all the clutter and bric-a-brac of *Limelight* lies the evidence of Chaplin's own past.

In the autobiography Chaplin names his source for Calvero, an American comic who suffered the same fate as Chaplin Senior, to lose the only accomplishment which stood between him and destitution.

Frank Tinney I saw when I first came to New York. He was a great favourite at the Winter Garden, and had a gregarious intimacy with his audience. He would lean over the footlights and whisper: 'The leading lady's kind of stuck on me', then surreptitiously look off-stage to see that no one was listening, then back at the audience and confide: 'It's pathetic; as she was coming through the stage door tonight I said "Good evening", but she's so stuck on me she couldn't answer.'

At this point the leading lady crosses the stage, and Tinney quickly puts his finger on his lips, warning the audience not to betray him. Cheerily he hails her: 'Hi, kiddo!' She turns indignantly and in a huff struts off the stage, dropping her haircomb.

Then he whispers to the audience: 'What did I tell you? But in private we are just like that.' He crosses his two fingers. Picking up her comb, he calls to the stage manager: 'Harry, put this in *our* dressing-room, will you, please?'

I saw him again on the stage a few years later and was shocked, for the comic Muse had left him. He was so self-conscious that I could not believe it was the same man. It was this change in him that gave me the idea years later for my film *Limelight*. I wanted to know why he had lost his spirit and his assurance. In *Limelight* the case was age; Calvero grew old and introspective and acquired a feeling of dignity, and this divorced him from all intimacy with the audience.

CHARLIE CHAPLIN, *AUTOBIOGRAPHY*

In this passage Chaplin seems to be suggesting that the windbaggery of Calvero's talk about great art was intentional, and meant to point the moral of an artist grown too precious for his audience. Certainly what Calvero needed for his redemption was a touch of the old Kennington vulgarity, as exemplified in an early exchange in the autobiography between Chaplin's mother and the woman from whom she had rented a room.

Mrs Taylor's one desire was to convert her husband, who, according to her Christian scruples, was a sinner. Her daughter, whose features were of the same cast as the mother's except that she was less sallow and, of course, much younger, would have been attractive but for her *hauteur* and objectionable manner. Like her father, she never attended church. But Mrs Taylor never gave up hope of converting them both. The daughter was the apple of her mother's eye – but not of my mother's eye. One afternoon, while on the top floor watching Mr Taylor at work, I heard an altercation below between Mother and Miss Taylor. Mrs Taylor was out. I do not know how it started, but they were both shouting loudly at each other. As I reached our landing, Mother was leaning over the bannisters: 'Who do you think you are? Lady Shit?'

'Oh!', shouted the daughter. 'That's nice language coming from a Christian!'

'Don't worry', said Mother quickly, 'It's in the Bible, my dear: Deuteronomy, twenty-eighth chapter, thirty-seventh verse, only there's another word for it. However, shit will suit you.'

After that, we moved back to Pownall Terrace.

CHARLIE CHAPLIN, *AUTOBIOGRAPHY*

It is tempting to speculate on what the great Calvero would have made of that exchange, but at least Mrs Chaplin's vocabulary rings true. Once he had established his reputation, Chaplin adopted a new personality to go with it, which might be a partial explanation why, once his autobiography leaves Britain, the past is hardly ever referred to again. The fact would have interested the second of the three master comedians who had reached the sanctuary of the United States by the time the Great War began. He was a comedian whose early career was entangled with Chaplin's in the most fortuitous way. Arthur Stanley Jefferson (1890-1965), a Lancashire comic born into a theatrical family, played alongside Chaplin in Karno's most renowned sketch, 'Mumming Birds', understudied his rival, later took over his roles, and later still augmented his stage act with an impersonation of Chaplin dressed as the Tramp. When Chaplin went to America with Karno's troupe, Jefferson, known professionally as Stan Laurel, went along. The two performers were much closer than Chaplin in his autobiography would have us believe.

The vaudevillian was a breed apart. His loneliness was often acute, and after hours there was the constant search for companionship, usually in some bar. Although Chaplin has recalled those days with a stately melancholy in his prose, a mood quite appropriate to the vaudevillian's sense of alienation, he continued sharing cheap boarding-houses with Stan while on tour. They sought out cheap restaurants together, and Stan remembered many a meal cooked on a gas-ring, an art Chaplin had learned from his mother. Stan continued to refine his craft in his room at night, and Chaplin proved to be a brilliant critic, for which Stan was lastingly grateful. But Stan was reluctant to get too close to Chaplin, and there is no evidence that Chaplin would have allowed it. Stan never told interviewers of their experiences together on the road; he told his wives. There was a fierce ambition in Chaplin, greatly exceeding Stan's own, that coloured all his relationships.

Before they left England, Chaplin had turned down the title role in a Karno production entitled 'Jimmy the Fearless', and the part had gone to Stan. Chaplin then sat out front for a week watching Stan's performance and liked what he saw. On the following Saturday, he informed Karno that he had changed his mind and would accept the role. Stan was fired from the production that weekend, although he was kept on as a regular member of the company. He never forgot the incident. It made him keep his guard up for a while after their arrival in America, but Chaplin was simply too gifted to be anything but admired.

FRED LAWRENCE GUILES, *STAN*

After the tour, Chaplin stayed on in America, but Laurel came home. In 1912 he returned again with Karno, and this time followed Charlie's example. It is through Laurel's biographer that we are able to grasp the comic principles on which the famous 'Mumming Birds' was built.

'Mumming Birds' was a burlesque of sorts. It was composed of a series of noisome routines mercifully panned by an audience, actually members of the Karno troupe, sitting in a box on the stage. One of the audience members was 'an inebriated swell' played by Chaplin and understudied by Stan. Although Stan was to play nearly every part in the sketch at least once, the plum role of the drunk was not one of them since Chaplin never missed a performance. Even though the slight lad from the Lambeth slums had suffered from poor nutrition throughout his boyhood and skipped countless meals, he was virtually indestructible as an adult and outlived Stan by twelve years.

The opening of 'Mumming Birds' was a rousing tune *in fortissimo*, 'Let's All Go to the Music Hall', which gave way to a waltz. An usherette showed a boy and his uncle into a box, then brought the drunk into another. Girls entered, dancing on stage in a dreadful, out-of-step way. They were followed by two comics with song, dance and patter, interrupted by catcalls from both the boy and the drunk. A pompous actor then recited 'The Trail of the Yukon', slogging stubbornly through a barrage of insults from the drunk and the boy. When Karno first described his idea for the revue to his actors, he told them that they had all suffered rudeness and abuse from audiences, no matter how fine their performances, 'so we're going to give them the kind of performance such audiences deserve'. And he did. As the evening unravelled, the drunk got out of his box frequently to chase an off-key quartette from the stage, and to take on an obese and inept wrestler, Marconi Ali, and win the bout. There were numerous falls on stage by the drunk, and when Stan took over the role after Chaplin

247

was summoned to Hollywood, he claimed he injured his head in falling. He was to become very wary of comic falls and was constantly worried about a hazard common to boxing but not usually associated with the theatre, the possibility of 'bruising his brain'. He mistakenly believed that had caused the mental collapse of Dan Leno.

Dan Leno was born thirty years ahead of Stan – exactly a generation separated them. Very early in Stan's stage career, once he had discarded the boy comic routines, he began borrowing from Leno. They had identical physiques except that Stan was a little taller, both of them were slight, slender, with double lines around the mouth and surprised eyebrows. M. Willson Disher, in a charming study of the nineteenth-century halls, describes Leno in performance as having 'a perpetually startled look in his bright, merrily gleaming eyes, framed in semi-circular brows, and in his jerky movements; there is eagerness in every part of him from the disconcerting legs to the straight, strained mouth set in the curious double-rim formed by the lines of the cheeks'.

Anyone familiar with Stan's screen image will recognise the borrowings – he retained them to the end of his long career. There were also other, more disquieting resemblances. Leno never relaxed. He had to be joking even off the stage. Gags abounded. No one felt really safe around him. Stan's behaviour off-stage and later off-camera was remarkably similar. Leno had sudden bursts of anger and would rage at his friends, then abjectly beg their forgiveness within hours. His behavioural history reads very much like the charges against Stan in the three divorce proceedings in which he was involved.

Dano Leno did not 'lose his mind on stage', as Stan frequently stated, but began giving away money and valuables to strangers. He set in motion a long-cherished ambition, shared by most comics, to play Shakespeare, pulling a company together and starting rehearsals. He begged Constance Collier to be his leading lady. Naturally enough, she declined, and he went to pieces, unable to perform again for months. When he did return to the stage of the Drury Lane, audiences were too fascinated by his recent instability to laugh. Instead, they stared uneasily at him. So Leno retired that year and died soon afterwards. If one believed in spiritualism, a strong case could be made for the influence of Dan Leno beyond the grave. He died in 1904, shortly before Stan's initial appearance on the professional stage in a panto revue. According to show business rumour, comedian Peter Sellers believes that Leno has also been orchestrating his career, and Sellers' international success followed Stan's by only a slight interval. There seems no doubt that Dan Leno's spirit is not at rest; his image has been seen in his old dressing-room mirror at the Drury Lane by a number of noted performers, including Noël Coward. Stan would have laughed at such phenomena and speculation. He was never a church-goer, although he was nominally a member of the Church of England, and he considered spiritualism a harmless pursuit of crackpots.

FRED LAWRENCE GUILES, *STAN*

Later, when he became one of the most popular film actors in the world, Laurel appears to have been more generous than Chaplin could ever bring himself to be in acknowledging his professional debts. Like Chaplin, Laurel's screen business was born directly out of what he had learned on the music-hall stages of Edwardian England. But although he was obviously a derivative stylist, he certainly succeeded, in the long partnership with Oliver Hardy, in finding a muse all his own.

Stan brought many of the movements, gestures and *look* of his screen character with him from the stages of variety houses and music halls. There was a great deal of Dan Leno, something of Chaplin, and much else picked up along the way. Very early on in his stage career Stan had made an interesting discovery: he found that audiences laughed at him before he ever said or did anything. It had something to do with the good intentions that were inherent in his smile, a trap to catch everyone off guard. It had even more to do with the way he looked at people. There was no eyeball contact. He could have been looking at a herd of seals or a cage of primates. His blink was slow, in some dim hope that comprehension might be there when he opened his eyes again but it was forever beyond him.

FRED LAWRENCE GUILES, *STAN*

Considering that they were working in the same industry in the same small town, it is remarkable that Chaplin so successfully managed to keep Laurel at arm's length. Indeed, meetings between them were so rare that when one took place, accidentally, in 1936, it was described by Stan's biographer, although not Chaplin's. By this time Chaplin was revelling in the sensation of being a rich and powerful man, and among his indulgences was a 55-foot motor cruiser with three state rooms and a small crew. Laurel, with none of Chaplin's drive or business acumen, practised his beloved hobby of fishing from the modesty of his boat the *Ruth L*. On an afternoon in 1936, Chaplin, the owner of a vast house with Japanese servants, and proprietor of his own studio, was sailing his cruiser in the Pacific off Catalina when he recognised Laurel in the *Ruth L*.

Chaplin recognised Stan and had one of his crew toss him a line. Stan chose to forget the time he had tried to talk to Chaplin by phone 'just for a get-together' when Chaplin could not be reached. There followed a hearty reunion at sea, and as first one, then the other recalled incidents from their early days with Karno, the awkwardness of the years of separation fell away. The ladies lapsed into a chatty rapport; they both had husky, little girl voices, permanently sustained by being treated – when the mood struck their partners – like over-indulged children. Ruth and Paulette Goddard became a delighted audience for a couple of hours as the men competed with each other in dredging up the hoariest of music-hall ballads. Chaplin roared with laughter as Stan sang what he described as being a song for Mother's Day:

> Don't go in the poorhouse
> Until I come home
> And we'll go in together.

Chaplin accepted a gift of freshly-caught fish and they parted, vowing to keep in better touch. But their lives were running on different tracks and years would go by before they would meet again.

FRED LAWRENCE GUILES, *STAN*

The most striking contrast of all between Karno's two apprentice-comics is that while Chaplin never even considered stepping on to the music-hall boards once he had left London and become a world figure, Laurel, in harness with Hardy, returned to the live theatres of England twice, in 1947 and again in 1952. The 1947 trip was one of the first peace-time exercises in nostalgia offered to the theatre-going British, who were entertained by a newspaper photograph one morning showing Laurel and Hardy queuing for ration books being doled out by clerks working by candlelight.

Delfont had booked them throughout the British Isles in the major music halls. When they reached Newcastle, there was no heat either in the theatre or in their hotel, and they sat together bundled in heavy coats and phoned Lucille [Hardy] in California to tell her of their huge success and cheer her up. Stan put the last piece of coal in the grate and said, 'There'll always be an England.'

FRED LAWRENCE GUILES, STAN

At the time of this meeting, with Chaplin poised on the brink of *Monsieur Verdoux*, in which he would finally discard Little Tich's disguise, and Laurel's career almost at an end, the third great comedian to come from Britain and preserve his art in a medium more durable than anything the stage could offer was about to achieve a very different sort of accolade: shared star-billing with Shirley Temple. But whereas both Chaplin and Laurel spent the rest of their lives refining the craft first picked up in the halls, Archie Leach, later to become famous as Cary Grant, passed through his music-hall phase so quickly that his connection with it was later forgotten by most of his followers. After one or two failed attempts to get employment in one of the local Bristol theatres, Leach succeeded through the good offices of a friend. It was not long before the boy found himself living at the very heart of the music-hall dormitory, in South London.

His mentor got him a non-paying job aiding the electricians who worked the arc lamps (or lime lights) at a rival music hall, the Empire, where for some weeks he happily risked burning fingers helping to change and adjust the carbon arcs, an occupation that came to an abrupt end when, working the follow-spot from the booth in the front of the house, he accidentally mis-directed its beam, revealing that one of an illusionist's best effects was done with mirrors (as, to this day, most of them are). He thereupon beat a retreat back to the Hippodrome, where he made himself useful, as a general errand-boy, working backstage.

It was there that he heard that a troupe of boy acrobats, managed by one Bob Fender, was regularly being depleted as the performers reached military age, which was sixteen. Archie Leach was not quite at school-leaving age, which was fourteen, but he wrote a letter to Pender, in his father's name, offering his services and enclosing a picture that showed a chap tall for his age and well-built, someone who could easily pass for older than his years. Pender replied favourably, telling Archie to report to Norwich for a tryout, and even enclosing his rail fare. Archie stole away in the middle of the night, caught the train, and was placed in training with the troupe. It took his father a week to find him, but whatever anger he felt over the incident was disarmed by the agreeable and responsible Pender who, with his wife, ran his company with due regard for the proprieties. Besides which, he was a Mason, which reassured Elias Leach. They agreed that Archie could return to the troupe as soon as he could legally leave school, an event Grant would later claim he tried to hasten by getting himself expelled for cutting classes and general bad behaviour. Whatever the case, he was soon back with Pender, and working on stage with the rest of the boys.

Dancing, tumbling, even stilt-walking became part of his repertoire. And above all mime, the ability to convey mood and meaning without resort to dialogue, which was to be so much a part of his genius as a film actor. But for fourteen-year-old Archie Leach it was the life of the company off stage that was significant, the camaraderie of it. When they were not on tour, or when they were playing one of the London variety circuits, the lads lived, dormitory-style, in the Penders' house in Brixton, in the South East of the capital, an area that provided digs for performers by the hundreds, since it was handy both to the great city and to the many theatres of the south coast. There was training in the morning, and the boys were expected to help with communal chores, the cooking, cleaning and washing up, before going to work. The hours were regular – breakfast every morning at 7.30, lights out every night at 10 – the structure of his days firmer than he had ever known, and he thrived on that.

RICHARD SCHICKEL, *CARY GRANT: A CELEBRATION*

W hen the Pender troupe was offered the chance to tour the American circuits, Leach duplicated Chaplin's strategy and stayed on after the rest of the Pender team had returned to England. Pender sounds like the perfect obverse of Karno, a kindly, considerate employer who helped Grant as best he could to make the difficult transition from the English to the American stage. On the surface, there seems little left of the music hall in Grant's suave urbane style. Yet his mastery of timing, and, in the great comedies of the 1930s, that suggestive gleam in his eye and a tendency to perform extravagant gestures, are seen by some of his critics as evidence of those lost Alhambras and Empires.

The business first at hand was establishing the Pender troupe on new ground. It was a little frightening, despite the fact that the theatre to which they were ordered to report had a comfortably familiar name, the Hippodrome. But what a contrast it was to the Bristol Hippodrome! Located on Sixth Avenue between 43rd and 44th Streets, its revolving stage stretched virtually the entire distance between the numbered thoroughfares. It had a ballet corps of eighty, a chorus of one hundred and required backstage employees numbering around eight hundred to mount a show that might have a cast of a thousand performers – drawn from all over the world. It could, and often did, present water ballets on stage and it required its performers to check in for work at a time clock, not so much because the management was mean-spirited, but because this was the only way to keep track of everyone. The auditorium seated ten thousand people, making it the largest theatre in the world.

The little Pender troupe, with its unpretentious if expert knockabout routines, was afraid it would be lost in these overwhelming precincts, but they were not, and they

251

settled in for a run that lasted the season, and then were booked on the Keith circuit, the leading vaudeville wheel, for a tour that took them to the major eastern cities and well into 1922, when, finally, they returned to New York and the top of their profession – they played the Palace. Along the way the boys met a former President, Woodrow Wilson, and on the beach at Atlantic City, Archie saw Jack Dempsey, out for a peaceful swim, swarmed by a mob of autograph seekers who seemed to appear out of nowhere.

The tour forms one of Cary Grant's fondest memories – everything was so new, everything was so interesting and the familial ties he felt to the Penders and the rest of the boys were unabated. Yet he had, as well, a gift for independence – the best legacy of his former life – and a forceful if unfocussed ambition. When the tour ended, he and a couple of the other boys decided to stay on in America. And the fair-minded Pender staked them with the cash equivalent of their homeward fares, without mentioning the inconvenience and expense of finding and training replacements.

For Archie Leach his first months on his own were a bit of a scuffle. An Australian who would later become well known as the costume designer, Orry-Kelly, hand-painted neckties which Archie hawked for him on the streets. A little later, recruited to escort the opera singer Lucrezia Bori to a dinner party (she sensed his poverty and kindly insisted on walking to and from it to spare him the cab fares) he met George Tilyew, the entrepreneur who owned Steeplechase Park, and got a job from him as a stilt-walker, advertising that Coney Island attraction by stalking up and down in front of it, and trying to avoid the little boys determined to trip him up. After that he joined forces with some other Pender refugees and some Americans, and they worked up an act for the Hippodrome, which they then toured on a circuit somewhat less grand than the Keith, working their way through Canada, and along the American west coast, where they played Los Angeles among other cities. The act broke up some time in 1924, and for a time Archie did a bit of this and a bit of that in vaudeville – he worked with jugglers and a unicycle rider, he was the audience plant in a mind-reading act, and he was a straight man for comedians. If there is anything that unifies this diversity it is that all his jobs required impeccable timing, a good-natured ability to keep your eyes open and your mind alert for the cues, and a talent for self effacement. If, as one believes, he has the best comic timing of any leading man in film history, and if, as Pauline Kael suggests, he is also the least narcissistic of actors, those admirable qualities were polished in this period.

RICHARD SCHICKEL, *CARY GRANT: A CELEBRATION*

There is some evidence to suggest that Grant, for all his long and successful career in Hollywood, never forgot his English music-hall beginnings, and may even have missed them a little from time to time. At any rate, he has the unexpected distinction of being responsible for the creation of a typical English song of the halls written a generation after the parade had passed by.

Coleman and Leigh went to Hollywood in 1965 and wrote 'Pass Me By' for the film *Father Goose*, starring Cary Grant and Leslie Caron. 'Cary would always be singing me these marvellous old English music-hall songs and I guess it finally got to me', says Cy, who reveals further that the correct tempo for 'Pass Me By' can be gleaned from Cary Grant's inimitable walk.

EDWARD KLEBAN, FROM A SLEEVENOTE FOR COLUMBIA, *COLEMAN SINGS COLEMAN*

252

'Pass Me By', a jaunty pseudo-variety song written in 6/8 time, has lyrics which might have been composed to fit the wardrobe of Leno, Tich or Chaplin:

> Behold me two great shoes that never saw a shine,
> Trousers I can hold up with a laundry line,
> A lovely ash that has an awful lot of spine,
> Shirt-tails flyin'
> Well, I'm a bloomin' dandelion.

Apart from the curious temporary British disapproval of Chaplin during the Great War, expressed in 'The Moon Shines Bright' squib, none of the three English comedians who spent the years of the Great War in America was ever seriously criticised for his absence. Whether that absence was deliberate or accidental is perhaps less important now than it might have seemed then. Certainly it sounds like an excellent arrangement that men like Chaplin, Laurel and Grant were able to pursue long and brilliant careers instead of suffering a pointless and obscene death in the mud of Flanders. Not all the great performers on the halls were as fortunate, but it is only fitting for the music hall to take its farewell of that war, not with a solemn salute but with a gesture of inspired ribaldry.

Billy Bennett was one of the most accomplished composers of nonsense verse of his day. Billing himself as 'Almost a Gentleman', and looking from a distance a little like a humanised version of Hitler, Bennett would recite rambling catalogues of rhymed gibberish with the air of brisk commensense:

> The little sardines had gone into their tins
> And pulled down the lid for the night.

Before enjoying great acclaim on the halls, Bennett had been a cavalryman in the regular army. The lavatorial nature of his last military action is worthy of the music hall at its very finest.

Before the First World War Billy Bennett was a cavalryman and his father eventually bought him out. In the good old days of riding, Billy used to go over the jumps with arms folded, no saddle or stirrups, and he said you'd come a terrific purler, the horse as well. They didn't care about the man, only the horse. They could get another man for a shilling a day, but the horse cost £30. At the end of the war he and another soldier were in a certain village where they had a big NAAFI place, and they were told to clear this NAAFI place up. So they gave the various articles to people. In the end all that was left was two big sacks of Epsom Salts. 'We didn't know what to do with them,' Billy said. 'So one night we took the stuff and emptied it down the village well. After that the place became famous as a health spa.'

STANLEY HOLLOWAY, FROM THE BBC SOUND ARCHIVES

When the war ended at last, British life had changed irrevocably, and the music hall with it. There is a curious passage in one of Thomas Burke's discursive essays in which he grumbles about the replacement of unadulterated Englishness by a mixing at once less insular and vaguely disturbing. It is 1917, and Burke, wandering round the town in search of some cosy pre-war refuge from the fighting, is dismayed to learn from the advertisements for the halls that 'here again England was frozen out. There were comedians from France, jugglers from Japan, conjurors from China, trick-cyclists from Belgium, weightlifters from Australia, buck-dancers from America . . . A stranger arriving from overseas might suppose that the war was over, and that London was in the hands of the conquerors.' Burke's hysteria is hardly justified; he knew better than most men that there had always been a cosmopolitan flavour to the music-hall stage. According to one best-selling novelist, the night the war ended a music-hall song mysteriously appeared from nowhere to swagger into the hearts of the celebrants.

As they found their way along a path, the silent blanket of fog was pierced by a murmur and then by a paleness ahead, the two presently merging into a vague impression of the Owl on this night of November the eleventh, 1918. A two-storied, ivy-clustered, steep-roofed building, ablaze with shouting celebrants of victory; a friendly pub, traditional without being self-consciously old-world. Established in the forties, when neighbouring Bockley was a small country town, it had kept its character throughout an age that had seen the vast obliterating spread of the suburbs and the advent of motor traffic; it had kept, too, the sacred partitions between 'private' and 'public' bars – divisions rooted in the mythology of London life, and still acceptable because they no longer signify any snobbish separation, but merely an etiquette of occasion, dress, and a penny difference in the price of a pint of beer. Even the end of a great war could not shatter this etiquette; but with the sacred partitions still between, the patrons of both bars found community in songs that were roared in unison above the shouting and laughter and clatter of glasses. They were not especially patriotic songs; most were from music halls of the nineties, a few were catchy hits from the recent West End revues. But by far the most popular of all was 'Knees Up, Mother Brown', a roaring chorus that set the whole crowd stamping into the beer-soaked sawdust . . .

The crowd were still singing 'Knees Up, Mother Brown' in the bars below. It sounded new to him, both words and tune, and he wondered if it were something else he had forgotten. He did not know that no one anywhere had heard it before – that in some curious telepathic way it sprang up all over London on Armistice Night, in countless squares and streets and pubs; the living improvisation of a race to whom victory had come, not with the trumpet notes of a Siegfried, but as a common earth touch – a warm bawdy link with the mobs of the past, the other victorious Englands of Dickens, Shakespeare, Chaucer.

JAMES HILTON, *RANDOM HARVEST*

When the war ended the country settled down to do what it could to reconstitute the smashed fragments of the old life, and naturally cherished more warmly than ever any symbols of the old days still available. Of these, none was more prized than Marie Lloyd, who had by now graduated from saucy soubrette to the archetypal middle-aged working-class matriarch. She was still a comparatively young woman, only forty-eight when the war ended; unfortunately Bernard Dillon had almost completed his work of destruction by this time, and although Marie continued to work regularly and with more brilliance than ever, her poor health and its cause were public knowledge.

A friend has described Marie's disintegration those last few years: 'Alone, sobbing, eating virtually nothing, completely exhausted and broken, the touch of arrogance, all the fight in her had gone. All she had left was to go out on stage and work. At least the public still wanted her and loved her.'

It's the loss of that vital 'touch of arrogance' that seems so sad. That was Dillon's crime.

Walter Barfoot was a call-boy at the Finsbury Park Empire from 1915-20, and remembers that Marie was always given Dressing-Room 7 because it was on the ground floor and she was so often 'under the weather'. By the interval after the first house on Tuesday, she already needed a sub of £70 for the three shows she had played: 'Only what's due to me, cock.' She had to climb wearily up the stairs to the manager's office at the back of the circle, for Coleman Hicks refused to pay out the money in front of the hangers-on that cluttered her dressing-room, along with the bottles of whisky and Guinness and the smell of fish-and-chips. There was always a crowd of women, and the odd man or two, but when they pressed Walter to come in and have a drink with them he never noticed anything 'immoral'. The only time he heard Dillon's name mentioned was her reply when her brother asked if he would be coming in that night – 'No, the bastard isn't.'

Before the first house she would take a drink for Dutch courage, but Barfoot says she was invariably the worse for drink after the second house. Only the staff and those who knew her could really tell. Walter noticed it became more and more difficult to get her on stage: 'Ten minutes, Miss Lloyd', then 'Five minutes, Miss Lloyd', followed by a frantic 'On stage, Miss Lloyd' with the answering cry of 'Oh, bugger off'. To make things easier, they built her a special dressing-room in the wings, concealed by scenery, but even so they had 'to watch her somewhat'. A reputation for unreliability began to spread. Finsbury Park was on the Number One Moss circuit. Soon she was playing the Number Two circuit and lesser halls.

DAN FARSON, *MARIE LLOYD AND THE MUSIC HALL*

Marie staggered on until 1922, persecuted by a husband described by one of her biographers as 'a gangster'. The last of her great songs was one which came dangerously close to the truth of her condition, 'It's a Bit of a Ruin That Cromwell Knocked About a Bit'. The lyrics describe how the lady is asked for information about the local ruin by a gentleman with whom she goes strolling in the woods. She later realises he has stolen her purse, but knows that the blame is partly hers, for before the stroll the pair of them had enjoyed some drinks at the Cromwell Arms. In delivering the song, Marie was required to portray a woman whose best years are past her and who is slightly the worse for drink. The date was 4 October 1922.

She waited listlessly in the wings, holding on to the scenery. Then came that inimitable intro music, bright and tantalising as ever, and suddenly there was Marie. Her last song was one of those remarkable 'character' numbers that distinguished the climax of her career: 'It's a Bit of a Ruin That Cromwell Knocked About a Bit'. Marie appeared as a worn-out old dear, scrummaging through her handbag for a drop of gin. With lines like 'a relic from a bygone age', it was agonisingly appropriate. 'Hold on', she said, opening her bag. 'Half a mo', I've come over funny. Here, ain't you ever bin like it? Well, if you ain't I must have copped the lot. It's a sort of feeling that says to you – 'look, old girl, it's time you had one'. And that reminds me, I've got a little drop of you-know-what which does the we-know-how in here ... I shan't detain you a moment, while I have a little search for it.' Panic in her eyes, as the battered bag was left swinging open. 'Hello, it's gone. Would you believe it, when I came out of my house this morning I had a nice little drop of gin in here. But you can see for yourself, can't you? Bottle, cork and all, gone. You know what's happened to me? I've been buzzed. That's what comes from sitting in the long grass with a stranger. I'm the unluckiest girl in the world – Sooki Hardcastle. It doesn't matter what I go out with, I'm bound to go home without it.'

Then she began to sing, or speak, this extraordinary song:

> I'm very fond of ruins, and ruins I like to scan,
> And when you talk of ruins,
> Why, you should see my old man.

In keeping with the character, she staggered, and the audience laughed, not realising she was ill:

> In the gay old days, there must have been some doin's,
> No wonder that the poor old abbey went to ruins.

She staggered, uncontrollably, and the audience roared. Then she fell and the curtain was lowered while the audience continued to laugh and cheer. When the curtain rose again the stage was empty and the audience was still unaware that the curtain had fallen on 'Our Marie' for the last time. When she died, three days later on October 7, 1922, the bills were already going up at the Alhambra: 'Next week, welcome return of Marie Lloyd'.

DAN FARSON, *MARIE LLOYD AND THE MUSIC HALL*

Lunching some years ago at Mrs Aria's I espied among the contents of her beautiful drawing-room a ridiculous, even a preposterous, little table – a rickety little thing about two feet square and which yet contrived to 'let down' on both sides. Both its design and the gilt scroll-work adorning the legs betokened the late 'seventies, though the top had obviously been painted and varnished at a later date and according to the Japanese whimsy of the 'nineties. Eliza told me that she had bought the table in the street from a man coming away from the sale at which the effects of Marie Lloyd were disposed of. We spent an hour talking about the One and Only, and making my adieux I left the room casting a longing, lingering look at what had become, despite the Irving relics, its most treasurable possession. Next day one of Carter Paterson's vans stopped outside my house and disgorged this exquisite *objet d'art* with Mrs Aria's card attached to its soundest leg. It is in front of me as I write, though I write not upon it, since it would hardly bear the strain of composition.

In an essay on another incomparable artist Mr Maurice Baring has said that what she was like will be among the permanent guesses of mankind, and this is also true of Marie Lloyd. So long, of course, as there are people living who saw her and can communicate their recollections to each other, so long will Marie Lloyd still live, because there will still be a corporate sense of her. But the time will come when she will be a thing of the past, old dear – the old words but with a tragic difference. What, then, will remain? A few faded photographs and a few records stored away in the libraries of the gramophone companies. Presumably the day is at hand when one will be able to buy records and even films of great players as easily as one can buy copies of *Tom Jones* and *Adam Bede*. But that day is not yet come, and in any case the demand for such records and films must first exist. What the eye does not see the heart cannot rejoice at, and I am persuaded that the public would only have to hear the old records of Marie Lloyd to want to buy them. It is not thought that there would be any demand for Marie, and therefore the opportunity to know whether this demand exists is not provided. Yet that there is a demand for the essence of Marie Lloyd is proved by the rapturous reception recently accorded to her three sisters and one daughter who, in an entertainment largely composed of Marie's old songs, contributed here a sketch for a facial resemblance, and there the hint of an intonation or flick of a gesture, the whole amounting to less than the shadow of a shade.

What, then, were Marie Lloyd's characteristics? What was she like? Our grandchildren will doubtless be told that she was a vulgar singer of indecent songs, whereby she will be confounded in the general mind with the big-bosomed, broad-buttocked, butcher-thighed Principal Boys who could look as Harriet Vernon looked but lacked her magnificent voice. Now, though Marie filled every corner of the stage, she was a little woman poised upon tiny, elegant feet. She was chic in the way that Réjane was chic. If Sans-Gêne was the mirror of an Empire, Marie was the looking-glass of the Promenade. Whatever she wore took on the gleam of white satin, though that which dazzled most was her smile, to which front teeth like those of a jovial horse gave an air of luxury in the Elizabethan, riotous, and best sense of the word. Was Marie Lloyd vulgar, and were her songs indecent? I can best answer by quoting something I wrote in *The Saturday Review* for October 14, 1922:

'When in the Tottenham Court Road, I saw, tucked under the newsboy's arm, the sheet which announced that Marie Lloyd was dead, everything around me became still. The street lost its hubbub, and for a space I was alone with a personal sorrow. In moments of emotion one is apt to notice the little things, and at once I remarked that, on the poster, the artist's name was prefaced with the word "Miss." Death, it seemed, laying his hand upon her who was known over the whole English-speaking world as "Marie", must use more ceremony. "Marie" – pronounced with the broad vowel beloved of the Cockney – was in everybody's mouth that day, in club and barrack-room, in bar-parlour and in modest home. On the high seas "Marie's dead" would be droned from ship to ship. Returning from Kempton a party of bookmakers

257

fell to speaking of the dead artist. One said, with tears in his eyes, "She had a heart, had Marie!" "The size of Waterloo Station," another rejoined. Her abounding generosity was a commonplace of the profession. She would go down to Hoxton, where she was born, and make lavish distribution to the street-urchins of boots and shoes which she fitted with her own hands. She had numberless pensioners dependent upon her charity. She earned some two hundred thousand pounds, and gave it all away. "God rest her," said the bookmaker who had first spoken, and bared his head. That night, at Blackfriars Ring, a bruiser with the marks of many fights declared: "We shan't none of us see the likes o' Marie again. She wur a great artist.". . .

'From any cold-blooded, reasoned immorality her songs were entirely free. Flaubert, you remember, makes one of his characters conjure up the red lamp of a brothel with the reflection that of all life's experiences this youthful one has been the most truly happy. Marie Lloyd's honest spirit would have utterly disdained so pitiful a philosophy. The sailor of whom she sang might, as the result of an encounter in Piccadilly, miss his ship, but a mere incident would not turn him, like Flaubert's sentimental fellow, eternally adrift. There was no decadent Latin taint about Marie; she was almost saltily British. Villadom accepted her in the way it accepts the gay dog who makes no secret of his gaiety. Villadom will have nothing to do with the sad fellow whose pleasure is furtive, and it recognised that there was nothing sad or secret about its idol. Marie knew that the great English public will open its arms to vice, provided it is presented as a frolic. She knew, though she could not have put her knowledge into words, that her art was one with the tradition of English letters, which has always envisaged the seamy side of life with gusto rather than with deprecation. Yvette Guilbert harrowed the soul with the pathos of her street-walkers; Marie Lloyd had intense delight in her draggle-tails. She showed them in their splendour, not in their misery; the mopishness and squalor of their end were not for her. And that is why, when she came to the portrayal of elderly baggages, she refrained from showing them as pendants to her courtesans. A French artist would have insisted upon the inevitable descent to the procuress; the English artist rejected even Mother Peachum. Instead she gave happy life to battered harridans ludicrous in the sight of man, if not of God; diving into their very entrails for the unstilled riot which made old Jenny steal from her husband's bed to dance at the ball. Again she proved herself an infinitely greater realist than others more highly esteemed. She depicted the delight of humble life, the infinite joy of mean streets. When some jovial crone, emerging from the wings, flung at an unseen, routed foe a Parthian, "And it wouldn't take me long, neither!" you settled in your stall to listen to a reading from the Book of Low Life. There was unction here, and a smack of the lips over a Vulgate the accuracy of which, divined by the boxes, was eagerly confirmed by the gallery. Was Marie Lloyd vulgar? Undoubtedly. Vulgarity was her darling glory; she relished and expounded those things which she knew to be dear to the common heart.

'Marie's "dial", as the Cockney would put it, was the most expressive on the halls. She had beautiful hands and feet. She knew every board on the stage and every inch of every board. In short, she knew her business. But it is not my purpose to write now of technical excellence. Rather would I dwell on the fact that she was adored by the lowest classes, by the middle people, and by the swells. "I hope," she said in a little speech before the curtain at her last appearance at the Alhambra, "I hope I may, *without bigotry,* allude to my past triumphs." Poor soul, it is we who should ask to be delivered from that vice. Marie broadened life and showed it, not as a mean affair of refusal and restraint, but as a boon to be lustily enjoyed. She redeemed us from virtue too strait-laced, and her great heart cracked too soon.'

Daughter of John and Matilda Wood, Marie was born at Hackney on February 12, 1870, and had conferred upon her the names of Matilda Alice Victoria. He father was a waiter at the Old Greek, and was commonly known as 'Brushwood', from his habit

258

of continually brushing his clothes. She used to declare that she had a narrow escape from becoming a school-teacher, and the mind boggles at what she might have taught! While still at school she produced with the aid of friends an entertainment of her own in the shape of 'The Fairy Bell Minstrels'. Marie's first professional appearance was on May 9, 1885, at the Eagle Music-hall, City Road, run by Mr Thomas Broom, formerly mine host of a public house off Drury Lane. Here she appeared under the name of Bella Delmere, and sang two songs entitled 'My Soldier Laddie' and 'Time is Flying'. She went sufficiently well to secure a return engagement, and when she reappeared at the same house on June 22, 1885, she was billed as Marie Lloyd. At the old Falstaff Music-hall, Old St., E., she was spotted by George Belmont, who did so much to popularise the twice-nightly system at 'Sunny Old Sads', as he used to call old Sadler's Wells, and the Sebright Music-hall, Hackney. 'Barnum's Beauty', as Belmont christened himself, stated afterwards that he gave Marie Lloyd no fewer than eight engagements at salaries ranging from 50s. to £50 per week. It was at the Sebright that Marie appeared in February 1886. Shortly afterwards she was entertaining at the old Star, Bermondsey, which recently, after a period of picture shows, went back to variety. Her songs in these early days were 'And the Leaves began to Fall', 'Sure to Fetch Them', 'Harry's a Soldier', and 'She has a Sailor for a Lover'.

Her work and success with the outlying London halls soon became known, and after an engagement at the Bedford Music-hall in Camden Town, she came nearer the West End, and appeared at the Middlesex in Drury Lane. It was at this hall that Marie Lloyd first became famous, and the town talked so much about her song, 'The Boy that I Love sits up in the Gallery', that an engagement at the Oxford Music-hall followed, where she appeared for twelve months together. She was described on the bills as a serio-comic, and on August 6, 1887, a critic wrote of her: 'She saucily told us that the good young men are not built that way now, and she found no one to dispute that dictum. Who, indeed, would have thought of contradicting so pleasant and vivacious a lady?' Of her dancing, the same critic said: 'She gave a welcome specimen of her saltatory skill, for she is decidedly one of the cleverest step dancers on the stage. She was enthusiastically applauded.'

Marie Lloyd had often appeared at the Middlesex in Drury Lane, and the story is told how, when Augustus Harris offered her the job of principal girl, she asked him, 'Which theatre?' 'The Lane,' he replied, whereat she retorted that she had already played in the Lane. She pretended not to be thrilled at the prospect, but actually this was one of the proudest moments in her life. She played 'The Princess All Fair' in *Humpty-Dumpty*, produced on Boxing Day, 1891, and scored heavily with the number 'Whacky Whacky Whack'. In the same cast were Dan Leno, Herbert Campbell, and Little Tich. The following year she again appeared at Drury Lane, this time as Little Red Riding Hood in *Little Bo-Peep, Little Red Riding Hood, and Hop 'o My Thumb*. Her quaint fun in this production was specially mentioned by the critics. Dan Leno, Little Tich, Herbert Campbell, and Ada Blanche were also in the cast. On Boxing Day, 1893, Marie Lloyd once more appeared at the Lane, in pantomime, this time as Polly Perkins in *Robinson Crusoe*. A chronicler of the period refers to her as 'dainty, arch, and exquisitely attractive in the pretty costumes, acting, dancing, singing – aye, and undressing too – without a word or an act which could bring the blush of shame to the cheek of consciousness, and yet piquant withal as the best pimento. Her songs are encored, and her Polly is adored'. The principal artists were the same in the previous years' pantomimes. Her salary at Drury Lane was now £100 a week. When Arthur Collins did *The Sins of Society* at the same theatre, he tried hard to persuade Marie Lloyd to play the music-hall heroine 'opposite' Albert Chevalier, but she declined, as she had declined revue, declaring her conviction that variety was her job.

Marie Lloyd once appeared in revue; this was at the Tivoli, and was called *The Tivoli Revue*. It was produced by Charles Raymond and Philip York, the lyrics being by Roland Carse, and the music composed and arranged by Maurice Jacoby. Little Tich and George Gray were in the cast, and Marie appeared as Sarah Bernhardt and afterwards Marguerite Sappho, the prehistoric woman. Her very clever caricature of Sarah and excruciatingly funny performance as the Prehistoric Woman vastly amused George Robey, who elsewhere was depicting Prehistoric Man. Marie was promoted to the part of principal boy in 1898, when she played the title-rôle in *Dick Whittington* at the Crown, Peckham, one of the newly-built suburban theatres which have since gone over to the pictures. The pantomime ran for over two months. The following Christmas she also figured as principal boy at the Crown, playing Prince Heliotrope in *Cinderella,* with her sister Alice as Cinders. That production also ran for two months. Marie appeared at other London and provincial theatres in pantomime, and in variety at every leading hall in the United Kingdom, America, South Africa, and Australia. In those old and palmy days, the three leading halls were the Oxford, London Pavilion, and Tivoli, known as the Syndicate Halls. Marie was booked there for months on end, her times being:

Oxford	9.40
Pavilion	10.10
Tivoli	10.35

Her admirers used to go from one hall to the other in order to enjoy over and over again a performance which was frequently identical. These houses were one-show-a-night-halls, and she used to fit in a suburban hall as well.

Marie Lloyd first appeared at the Palace, Shaftesbury Avenue, then under the management of the veteran Charles Morton, on December 26, 1897. Boxing Day was not a busy day with the ordinary Palace audience. For the most part this was made up of a fashionable after-dinner crowd, not found in the other halls in London, but on that night the building was probably more closely packed in every part than any other in town. The audience was largely composed of those who regarded Marie as the bright particular star in their amusement sky, all eager to welcome her back after her absence – and triumphs – in America, while others wanted to see the result of what they regarded as Mr Morton's daring experiment. The wiseacres shook their heads ominously and prophesied failure. Marie, they declared was not suited to a smart audience. She must tone down her songs, they declared, asking sagely what would then be left. But Marie was just as daring as ever, giving with redoubled gusto songs whose riskiness was accentuated by the spirit of gaiety and sophistication. Then came her imitators, and in shoals. So much so that prior to a provincial tour she delightedly published the following:

'Miss Lloyd, having no further use in town for her hats and sticks and sunshades, will be very pleased to give any original lady either or both of the above mentioned articles (who are thinking of giving the public something new) on receipt of their addresses, as it will save them a lot of trouble and expense. Don't worry, girls. I am on tour, thinking out something fresh for you in my spare moments. It might be expensive, but it shall be original.'

Eight years after her first stage appearance Marie went to Paris, and was received with greater acclamation than any English comédienne who had preceded her. When she returned to England she brought back a song entitled 'The Naughty Continong'. It was not often that Marie's sense of humour deserted her, but it did on the occasion of her French début. After she had sung her song there were ecstatic cries of '*Bis! Bis!*' Take me back to England at once,' she said. 'Take me back to where they love me, away from these hateful people. I have done my best and they called me a beast!'

One of the proudest moments of her life was when she went to Germany and topped the bill over all the continental stars at the Winter Gardens, Berlin. She had the opportunity of studying the attitude of the Germans towards the English, and found that, while the ordinary people held the British in the highest regard, the Junkers were never tired of sneering at us. 'I used to go about Friedrich Street,' she said, 'with my fists clenched at some of the remarks that were made. One day I overheard a burly officer with a scar on his cheek say something insulting about the British, and I promptly retaliated by giving him a blow in the face, accompanying the act with the remark "There's one for the other side!" And then I went back home.'

Marie's Australian trip at the beginning of 1901 was preceded by a banquet at the Tivoli Restaurant. Managerial and other admirers were present in great number, and glowing speeches were made in her honour. She was welcomed home the following November with a flourish of trumpets, special bills to announce her return being posted all over the town. At the Oxford Music-hall her reception was overpowering. She stood in the centre of the stage bowing and smiling, while the hall rang with tumultuous cheering. The reception was too much for the sensitive artist. Voice and memory both failed her, and in the middle of her song she broke down utterly. She tried again, and again broke down. 'It's no good,' she said, 'I can't go on,' and walked off the stage. Bouquets were handed up, and demands for a speech were made. Marie came on again with moist eyes, and was heard to say that she had come from a beautiful climate into the London fogs. 'And if there is a cold going,' she added, 'your Marie is sure to catch it. I ought not to have come to-night, and I must get well before I appear again.' Malicious people asserted that Marie was played out, but time proved them to be wrong, for she continued her triumphs shortly afterwards in a scene entitled 'The Bond Street Tea-Walk,' which became the rage.

When the Royal Performances in aid of the Variety Artists' Benevolent Fund were started at the Palace Theatre, the name of Marie Lloyd did not figure in the list, and she made no secret of her annoyance at the omission. The organisers were nervous as to whether a little of what you fancy does you good would be acceptable to the distinguished visitors.

Marie Lloyd took an active interest in the music-hall strike in 1907. Her house in King Henry's Road, N.W., was used as a meeting-place where the stars could air their grievances. But time was getting on, and so was Marie. She had always been fond of numbers about coster maids 'coming over goosey' on the bridal morn and now the time was ripe for studies in later celebration. So we had the two songs by which she will probably be best remembered, the one entitled: 'I'm One of the Ruins that Cromwell knocked abaht a Bit,' and that one whose chorus ran:

> My old man
> Said 'Follow the van,
> Don't dilly-dally on the w'y!'
> Orf went the van
> With the old man in it;
> I walked behind
> With my old cock linnet.
> I dallied and dillied,
> Dillied and dallied,
> Lorst my w'y and don't know where to roam,
> 'Cos you can't trust the speshuls like the old-time coppers,
> When you can't find your way home.

Marie's fiftieth birthday was celebrated at the Bedford Music-hall, Camden Town, on February 12, 1920, and it was a night without parallel. Standing amidst great banks of flowers, she made a characteristic speech of thanks. She recalled that when she first appeared at the Old Bedford her salary was the modest one of 15s weekly. Though she had had her share of the hard knocks of life Providence had been good to her, and her earnest wish was that she might be spared a few years longer both to please the public and to do in private life what she could for the poor. Marie might well have claimed that if she had headed many a bill she had also footed many – a not inconsiderable number out of charity to her brother and sister artists who had fallen on hard times. To an interviewer she once said:

'I have no desire to brag – or, as the modern word is, swank – but I think I can justly say that no artist can claim more consistent popularity, and therefore I am very grateful to the public who have loyally supported me through all these years of strenuous starring. It is wonderful, by the way (she continued), how artists grow old by repute. People imagine that "pros" have a birthday every month. The other day an old man with long white whiskers tottered up to me and said – "How well you wear! Why, my mother used to take me as a little boy to see you in pantomime at Drury Lane!" "Well," I replied, "then I must be wearing better than you do!" On another occasion at a suburban hall an elderly man, with a grey beard down to his knees, asked, "Do you remember me?" "No," I replied. "Oh," he said, "I used to be call-boy at the Bedford when you made your first appearance there." Well (she went on), I have had a crowded hour of life – work and worry, sorrow and joy. People do not always get the credit for the good they do, and some get more than they deserve. The wounded Tommies know what I do for them, and the gratitude which I know they feel is more to me than diadems and decorations. Personally, I feel as youthful as ever and can enjoy life with the best of them.'

Marie Lloyd's house at Golders Green was the resort of celebrities of the profession, and many a merry gathering was held there. They called her house 'The Flies', and its meaning was epitomised in an anthem set to the rhythm of 'Where do Flies go in the Winter Time?' It ran thus:

> They all go round to Marie Lloyd's
> In the winter time,
> And tickle a tune upon her tickolee.
> There's something nice
> Always on the ice,
> And you never have to ask her twice
> For a drink of her kickolee.
>
> Her front door is never known to lock,
> It's always standing open, so you never have to knock.
> Nobody knows what time it is, for the hands are off the clock
> And we don't go home till morning
> At good old Marie Lloyd's.

Marie Lloyd figured occasionally on the films. Her last picture was for the Gaumont 'Round the Town Weekly Budget', and the officials will never forget her visit to the studio. There was no lift, and she had to climb four flights of stairs to get to the scene of operations. Marie, who like Hamlet was then 'fat and scant of breath', roundly abused everybody, declaring that it had 'never taken her so long to reach the "gods".' She invited all present to share a bottle of champagne which had providentially been provided for her, then dressed, sang her song 'Round the Town' and gave a show as bright and amusing as if she had been facing her usual vast and admiring audience.

Marie Lloyd was three times married 'with varying unhappiness'. Her first marriage was with Percy Courtney, and was dissolved. She married Alec Hurley, the popular coster comedian, on October 27, 1906, and they went to America together the following year. Hurley died on November 30, 1913, at the age of forty-two. Marie was in Chicago at the time, and expressed herself shocked at the news. Her third marriage was to Bernard Dillon, the jockey.

On October 7, 1922, the great comédienne passed away. She collapsed on the stage of the Edmonton Empire while singing her character song, 'I'm One of the Ruins that Cromwell knocked abaht a Bit'. When she swayed about on the stage in the song the audience thought she was realistically imitating a drunken woman; but actually she could have had little idea of what she was doing. She was buried at Fortune Green Cemetery, Hampstead, on October 12. The progress to her last resting-place was semi-royal. All the way from her home in Golders Green to the grave side the road was lined with a crowd so dense that police had to be summoned to keep the way clear, and so many crowded into the cemetery that the gates had to be closed an hour before the interment was timed to take place. The cortège was led by six large motor-cars heaped with floral tributes from leaders of the profession, jockeys, boxers, costermongers, stage hands, dressers, and all sorts of people high and low in the social scale. That morning Ellen Terry had herself taken to the house a laurel wreath of which the inscription ran: 'In memory of a great artist. She gave lightness of heart to many a heart bowed down'. Kate Carney, her contemporary, who is still with us, sent a wreath bearing the words, 'A real white woman – From her oldest friend'. A floral horseshoe with whip, cap, and spurs inscribed 'From her jockey pals' was signed by Steve Donoghue, B. Carslake, and other exponents of the 'sport of kings'. A spectacular touch was given to the cortège by Marie's own car following the hearse – empty except for the chauffeur, who had driven her to and from her engagements for so many years. The public filed past the open grave in their hundreds, showering flowers on one whose genius had so often taken them out of their drab and difficult lives.

J. P. Harrington, who had written so many of her songs, paid tribute to her in the following homely but sincere verses.

> Marie, the final curtain's down, old friend,
> And in your ears has rung the last encore.
> Right in the limelight to the very end
> I see you standing. Now your part is o'er
> Eternity has claimed you evermore.
>
> Loyally will ten thousand lips attest
> The love and good deeds that cling round your name.
> Only your many pensioners know best
> Your generous heart. How, seeking no réclame,
> You gave by stealth and blushed to find it fame.

It was Marie Lloyd's boast that she was very, very lucky in the songs she got. She had not many failures, but she always said that there was a good deal of picking and choosing to be done. 'You cannot say to yourself that you want a new song and just buy it.' She spent a large amount every year on songs, and, of course, bought an immense number that she could not sing. 'You may take it that one has to buy ten songs before one finds a really good one. A song,' she said, 'is often hit on by the merest accident.' 'Then you Wink the Other Eye' was said to have been suggested at a convivial gathering. George Le Brunn, sitting at the piano playing anything and everything, whispered to Marie about something that was going on. 'Oh, wink the other eye, George,' she said. He repeated the words to a kind of accompaniment – and thus was evolved one of Marie's biggest song successes. Marie was all in favour of keeping a song to herself and not publishing the number. Here are some of her successes.

> 'Oh! Jeremiah, don't you go to Sea.'
> 'Never let a Chance go by.'
> 'That was Before My Time.'

'Don't Laugh!'
'How Dare you Come to London!'
'Poor Thing!'
'What do you take Me for?'
'Actions Speak Louder than Words.'
'Then you Wink the Other Eye.'
'Oh! Mr Porter.'
'The Naughty Continong' ('You should go to France').
'Whacky, Whacky, Whack.'
'Keep off the Grass.'
'Twiggy Voo?'
'Among My Nick-Nacks.'
'Johnny Jones.'
'There They are, the Two of Them on Their Own.'
'Salute My Bicycle.'
'Hulloa! Hulloa!! Hulloa!!!'
'Everybody Wondered how He Knew.'
'Clever, Ain't You?'
'The Coster's Christening.'
'Everything in the Garden's Lovely.'
'Folkestone for the Day.'
'Garn Away.'
'It's a Jolly Fine Game Played Slow.'
'Rum-tiddley-um-tum-tay.'
'Silly Fool.'
'As if She Didn't Know.'
'The Geisha Girl.'
'Tiddley-om-pom.'
'Tricky Little Trilby.'
'The Wedding Bells were Ringing.'
'You can't Stop a Girl.'
'You're a Thing of the Past, Old Dear.'
'Customs of the Country.'
'Maid of London, Ere We Part.'
'She'd Never had Her Ticket Punched Before.'
'Millie.'
'The Bond Street Tea-Walk'
'I'd Love to Live in Paris all the Time.'
'A Little of What You Fancy does You Good.'

Arthur Roberts was a great admirer of Marie Lloyd, and makes several references to her in his book *Thirty Years of Spoof.*

'As she was in her youth [he writes], so she was to the day of her death – the most improvidently generous woman I have ever met. She used to ask me to wait for her after the show to protect her from the sharks who were always hanging about the wings ready to seize her earnings. While she was on the stage – busily earning money for people – she was the spirit of life and buoyancy. When she had thrown her last magic smile to the audience she would often totter to the wings. As an artist there is, of course, no limit by which one can gauge her répertoire. She could be everything and anything. She touched pitch, and it was immediately refined. If she sang about rags she made them into silk.'

In his loyalty dear old Arthur is here talking nonsense. Marie never refined anything; what she did was to take a tiny segment of life, discover its true colour, and then raise it to its highest power of vividness. Where other artists in the same line needed an ell, Marie took only an inch. This, because she was a great enough actress to make an inch do an ell's job, and sufficient of an artist to know when the job had been done. Her powers of facial expression were extraordinary, and she had no need of words to tell you that she was a girl just up from the country whom all her dad's horses would never get back to the farm. Or that the streets were not what they used to be. Or that whatever the sport she would be game to the last. Through part of the 'eighties and all the 'nineties and nineteen-hundreds she was all that young men thought and Pitcher wrote.

To sum up, Marie within her range was one of the greatest artists who has ever stepped on the English stage, legitimate or otherwise, while on the boards of the music-hall she never had or ever could have any rival with the single exception of Vesta Tilley. . .

How did Marie stand in relation, shall I say, to Yvette Guilbert? This is like asking whether Bernhardt or Duse stood higher? – a question said to be the authentic mark of futility in critics. 'You cannot measure infinities against one another; any artist in whom genius rises as high as it has done in these two women partakes, in a sense, of infinity, for that genius admits you to states of feeling in which there is no less or more but only a sense of boundless release of heart and mind.' If this be true, there is no need for comparison in any estimate of Marie Lloyd. She had genius, and it shall stand at that.

JAMES AGATE, *THE POST-VICTORIANS*

A much-loved but naïve singer once shared a dressing-room with her. They seldom appeared on the same bill, for both were 'headliners', but this was a charity benefit. 'Have a drink', was Marie's greeting. The artist refused primly and Marie, with a muttered 'Too bloody pure to live', downed the glass herself. Then she produced a really filthy chamber pot that she carried around with her, for she was too big a star to share the communal lavatory, and used it, stark naked. 'As an artist, yes,' said the shattered singer afterwards, 'but as a person, never mention her name to me again.'

She made a point of teasing Ada Reeve, who was also rather proper. Sailing into Romano's one lunchtime, Marie spotted her in a corner sitting with an important Manager. 'That's a nice bit of cock you've got there', she cried out pleasantly as she passed them.

DAN FARSON, *MARIE LLOYD AND THE MUSIC HALL*

The famous Marie Lloyd was reputed to be frivolous, yet when we played with her at the old Tivoli in the Strand never was there a more serious and conscientious artist. I would watch her wide-eyed, this anxious, plump little lady pacing nervously up and down behind the scenes, irritable and apprehensive until the moment came for her to go on. Then she was immediately gay and relaxed.

CHARLIE CHAPLIN, *AUTOBIOGRAPHY*

There was a naïve innocence in her songs of those days. She made her first advance towards the suggestiveness encouraged in her later life with 'Keep off the Grass' and 'Then You Wink the Other Eye', and displayed a rather rare tact in her accommodation of her art to her years. She was only fifty-two when she died. She was so young when she first impressed herself on the popular imagination that there was a disposition to believe she was much older. The first song in which she admitted the passing of the years was entitled 'You're a Thing of the Past, Old Dear'. It was at once recognised that in the dashing serio-comic singer we had a character actress of rare insight. It was a little amusing to note the reluctance with which Marie Lloyd gave herself up to the art of 'low comedy'. She would alternate a conventional 'serio' song, 'The Cosmopolitan Girl', with such 'rough stuff' as 'One of the Ruins Cromwell Knocked About a Bit'. The Cromwell, let it be explained, figured on the signboard of a public house: the ruins were its too-frequent frequenters. It was in this character of a drunken woman, staggering on the stage of the Edmonton Empire, that Marie Lloyd fell. The audience shrieked with laughter at the realism of the scene. It has often laughed at such an incident, from Peg Woffington's seizure onwards. The stricken actress was carried home to die.

H.G. HIBBERT, *FIFTY YEARS OF A LONDONER'S LIFE*

The most perceptive of all the analyses of Marie LLoyd's stage persona was the one made by H.M. Tomlinson, who measured the new-fangled American cinema by the standards Marie had set, and found it sadly wanting. In placing Marie on a level with the Shakespearean sluts and the Dickensian draggletails, Tomlinson was quietly making the point that Marie, for all the modesty of her background and the unpretentious nature of her professional setting, was an expression of the English genius. His feelings have been duplicated by thousands of people who remembered seeing her. My father, who started out in life by mastering the gentle art of truancy in order to attend regular lectures at the Oxford Music Hall, and ended it by savouring the art of Frank Sinatra, Noël Coward, Barbra Streisand and others, had no hesitation when I asked who he thought was the greatest entertainer he had ever seen. The reply was as quick and as certain as Tomlinson's: 'Marie Lloyd'. When I asked him why, again his response was Tomlinson's: 'Because she was all of us.'

Our theatres have been diminished, our music halls retired, and Charlie Chaplin advised that he is out of date, and the latest mechanism from the physical laboratories secured by men with too much money, in order that we should be gratified in a spacious new building by a display less appropriate than the label on a jam pot. It was not possible for me to get out of the palace at once, so I mused and regretted the past, while waiting. I remembered that, not far from this modern vacuous wonder of a picture palace with its puppets, and its dismal magnitude in which all communion with one's fellow sinners was lost, I had heard Marie Lloyd for the last time. It was in a dingy little music hall. You could have recognised a friend in its remotest corner; and the hall was full that night. Marie Lloyd was coming.

I had never seen her, but I knew the legend. When I was a boy I had heard men gossiping in an office, who should have been intent upon ledgers and commercial documents, and the subject, which animated them more than duty, was a young lady, unknown to me, but probably most attractive, named Marie Lloyd. One of the men would lower his voice when he came to the point of an anecdote, and presently they were all loudly gay. Not seldom in later life stories about her were enticingly outlined to willing listeners, so that she was shadowed forth, and it was easy to believe she was a character. Still, here I was in a suburban music hall, in another age, and Marie Lloyd, though gifted with the complete art of femininity, would be getting on; I thought that night, while waiting for her, that I must be all too late for her full charm; I was expecting too much. A lanky figure in a diminutive bowler hat, his trousers too short, his loose hands and wrists dangling well beyond his coat-sleeves, with a cane, and a red nose, appeared on the platform. He tottered round it in agitation twice, and

266

then stopped to inform us that his wife had gone away with the lodger. He made a song about it. Nobody present seemed to suffer very much, perhaps because they had heard something like it before. Another man followed, and jeopardised a number of dinner plates. Then a kilted figure appeared, whose recommendation was his Scotch accent; that is the only suggestion I can offer. The audience maintained its amiability.

There was some hesitation on the part of the management – the stage remained empty too long, while the audience murmured its expectancy and a growing impatience. Then an electric Number 10 suddenly flashed beside the proscenium. The audience stirred, became quiet, and settled itself. The orchestra played an air which everybody but myself appeared to know well. Interrupting the music, a woman, wearing a dress that was an absurd caricature of the raiment supposed to appertain to a naughty lady, paraded insolently to the footlights. She only looked at us, in handsome weariness. There was a merry call from the 'gods'. She sang a song in careless confidence, a little hoarsely, making hardly a movement, except of a shapely arm and an eloquent hand; sometimes there was a show of an ankle, which a woman might give who could do more, but merely wishes to annoy us. This was Marie Lloyd. Nothing was certain about her then except that my neighbours were fully under her control. She knew them, but she was as indifferent as a sultana in a tedious court. She lifted slightly her cloud of silk, mocked us with the prelude to a dance, and abruptly left us, with a grace that was contumelious. Just as she reached the wings she turned her head, and gave us a look.

The immediate cry of delight which greeted the empty stage did not take me unaware. It is possible that I was in it. It is not easy to be dumb when taken by a glad surprise. If this was elderly Marie Lloyd, then she was eternal youth. Age she would never know…but was this all? For she could do more than this. Would she come again? We could wait. It was far from midnight; or next morning would not be too late.

She appeared again, but I was not prepared for her. I knew at once I had not seen her before. Who was she now? A little shabby London woman, whose household was flitting, and somehow she had taken the wrong road. She had been following the van but had lost it. She was carrying the family canary in a cage and a handbag. She was tired, too, and I suspect she had been thirsty. She complained, in a droll way, in a language known to that house, of her tribulations. We laughed with her. What was she now? She was London. She was all the Cockneys. We laughed at ourselves.

Yet what is a Cockney? It is so hard to say that you will rarely find one in a book. There is Sam Weller, but not enough in literature to give Sam adequate companionship. The Cockney is a dangerous subject, who betrays most artists and authors. He is nearly as old as the Chairman, and is sometimes like that fellow, because of the antiquity of his civilisation and its stress. He has worked for two thousand years, and still works, so he does not expect much. He is a hereditary unbeliever. He resists conversion to a new faith; the gods have upset his apple barrow too often. He has seen the death of many kings, and of so many great causes that he thinks it enough if he can keep his own barrow on two wheels for one day. He is sentimental, but protects his easy pity with a dry derision. He wears the mask of a cynic, and comments on affairs through restrained lips. Things have so often gone awry for him, notwithstanding the laws and the prophets, that it has ceased to be amusing; but this has given him patience, and his philosophy a bleak humour. He loves his fellow men, but he has no faith in them; he has seen too many of them, and too much.

How did Marie Lloyd convey this, and more? Well, how did Dickens manage it? And how often has Dickens been born again? Marie Lloyd, somehow, held communion with us. She did not have to speak. When she assumed that we knew, most certainly we knew, and chuckled. As a Cockney lady who had lost the van conveying her household goods, which was a grievous thing, though not without its

267

fun, she would hesitate in an explanation of the accident, tongue-tied, and at once our sympathy flowed. Or she would, failing in her tired state to remember what it was she really wanted to do, ask us an innocent and irrelevant question. It was our own moving job that was lost. But when she came, not to the fine points of conduct, such as the way one may innocently behave after several calls on a dry road in the hope of conjuring up a heart refreshed, but to the elements of life, Marie Lloyd's deranging candour would have moved Sir John Falstaff to one of his grand and moving periods. Her sallies shocked the house into wonder as deep as silence, just before it shook with laughter. We had heard the truth, and knew it almost at once. We understood each other better, as we went home.

H.M. TOMLINSON, *OUT OF SOUNDINGS*

M arie's death left several members of her family to carry on her work. To one of them, her sister Alice, she even bequeathed her songs. During her lifetime Marie had much to endure from gossips and fools who did what they could to spread the canard that she was older than she pretended. One weekly paper, *The Referee*, supported her cause by publishing every week the line: 'Miss Marie LLoyd was born on February 12th, 1870'. This statement, reiterated week after week, became something of a journalistic joke, and Marie subscribed to it by inserting in that periodical what she called a

Combined Certificate.
MISS MARIE LLOYD
Notice to All.
Miss Marie Lloyd has only one daughter – and she is not on the stage.
In Answer to all inquiries –
Marie LLoyd, born February 12th, 1870.
The following are her brothers and sisters and their respective ages:
John Wood (not in the profession),
born December 17th, 1871.
Alice Lloyd, born October 20th, 1873.
Grace Lloyd (not in the profession),
born October 13th, 1875.
Daisy Wood, born September 15th, 1877.
Rosie Lloyd, born June 5th, 1879.
Annie Wood (not in the profession),
born June 25th, 1883.
Sydney Wood, born April 1st, 1885.
Maud Wood, born September 25th, 1890.
This is final. Will anyone disputing this kindly apply at Somerset House.
Wood is the family name. Lloyd stage ditto.

Some years after Marie's death the echoes of her art were heard in New York City, where the eldest of her surviving sisters enjoyed a considerable reputation. She was reviewed by the most perceptive American critic of the century.

Miss Alice Lloyd, the music-hall singer, has been appearing at the Palace. Though always somewhat overshadowed by her more famous sister Marie, Alice Lloyd has had her own reputation. She was prettier and less coarse than Marie; and she diversified flirtatious young-girl songs, such as 'May, May, May – She Lives in Mayfair so Gay', with pathetic Cockney plaints such as 'Never Introduce Your Bloke to Your Lady-Friend'. It is agreeable to hear her again – and all the more because she now brings with her some of the best of Marie's old songs, the rights to which were bequeathed her by her sister.

Marie Lloyd was one of the most memorable of the music-hall performers of her generation. She was not a success in New York; on the occasion of her first visit, fifteen or twenty years ago, she was denounced by a newspaper critic in some such language as 'a combination of French salacity with English vulgarity'; and when she tried to visit us again, during the War, she suffered the same fate as Gorki and was at first not allowed to land. But in London her position was supreme. As Mr T.S. Eliot wrote in the *Dial* on the occasion of her death, 'whereas other comedians amuse their audience as much and sometimes more than Marie Lloyd, no other comedian succeeded so well in giving expression to the life of that audience, in raising it to a kind of art. It was, I think, this capacity for expressing the soul of the people that made Marie Lloyd unique and that made her audience, even when they joined in the chorus, not so much hilarious as happy'.

Her Cockney characterisations were wonderful. They were not the impersonations of a virtuoso like Albert Chevalier, who incorporates himself so completely in the dialect and make-up of his role that we lose sight of a basic personality. Marie Lloyd was primarily herself and always remained unmistakable through the variety of ages and conditions which she assumed in her various songs and which sounded the different keys of her instrument. This instrument was certainly as vulgar as Marie's grinning mouth of English horse teeth and yet as fine as the artistic instinct which enabled her to appreciate their value.

It is interesting to compare 'Good Old Iron', a song which Alice Lloyd has been singing at the Palace and which must, I think, be one of Marie's, with the somewhat similar number – 'Although they used to call me Gladstone's Pet, There's life in the old girl yet!' – performed with so much success by Miss Beatrice Lillie in Charlot's Revue. Funny as Miss Lillie is, she does not succeed, or try to succeed, in making her superannuated star comic opera star into a three-dimensional human being: her effectiveness, indeed, depends to a great extent on the mere business of the rest of the company, who are supposed to be helping the old lady out. Nor – what is also to the point here – did Miss Lillie really do very much with the waitress in the restaurant scene: she did not even 'live' the role sufficiently to keep up its Cockney accent; whereas either Marie or Alice Lloyd would have fallen into the accent with the character, and the main strength of the character would have lain, not in its jokes, but in its humanity. Good Old Iron is a lady of pleasure who has seen her best days – 'Of course I can't deny I may have lost a pound or two – lost me purse – lost me way – but what is that to you?'. With her prunellas, her little parasol and her high-necked black gown of the nineties, she would be distressing or gruesome were it not for her unwithered good humour and her indomitable British spirit: 'Come on, fellows! Take a chance! Have a dip in the lucky bag!' –

> Good old iron! Never was known to rust!
> Never was known to rust!
> A little fruity on the crust!
> I'm no chicken – but everything's complete.
> The fellows think I'm no good becuz
> I'm not so plump as I useta wuz.
> But don't forget, the closer to the bone – the sweeter the meat!

EDMUND WILSON, 21 OCTOBER 1925

eediness pervades the world of the traveller-essayist Stephen Graham, whose journalistic tendencies may be gathered accurately enough from a selection of his published works: *A Vagabond in the Caucasus; A Tramp's Sketches; With Poor Immigrants to America; The Gentle Art of Tramping; New York Nights; London Nights*. In the latter volume, published in 1925, Graham drifts among the dispossessed of a great city, observing carefully what might have seemed to be trivialities at the time, but which, now that they have vanished from London life, serve as beacons in the fog confronting the social historian. Graham had a theory about London, that 'our days are democratic; our nights are feudal', by which he meant that his travels had taught him that in the big city, poverty is bearable by day, intolerable once the dark creeps in. Predictably Graham picks the most modern halls he can find, patronised by the poor, who are vaguely aware, as Graham is acutely aware, that now that the music hall is in decline, its morals have been cleaned up to the point where the vigorous impertinence of the great days, the swagger of arrogance, the defiant cocking a snook, has faded away, to be superseded by mere professionalism.

In the Fourpenny Gallery

A street leads into East India Dock Road. It has eight fried-fish shops, and on Saturday night clouds of white vapour and smelly steam of boiling fat roll upward to the Poplar sky. Happy buyers with satchels jostle one another getting into shops where notices inform you that 'Relief tickets are taken here'. The public-houses have arcades wherein an overflow of customers stand and tope. One walks along to what may be called 'Eel Pie Corner' – for there is so much eel pie for sale. It is just by Blackwall Tunnel and the dock gates. Thereunto I frequently resort to see life at the other end of town.

My wife and I went to a music hall one Saturday night to see the fun. 'Show yer the stalls, lidy?' said a small boy, hopefully.

The stalls cost a shilling. But we made our way up the gallery stairs, followed by the jeering mirth of loafers who thought us to be 'out on the cheap'. It only costs fourpence in the gallery, and I had made the mistake of wearing an overcoat. No galleryite down there possesses an overcoat.

Still, we paid our coppers and went in. An attendant, seeing that we were 'clars', made a place for us to sit down, though scores were standing. The theatre was thronged with the denizens of dockland. The floors were covered with peanut shells. There was a whispering, grating chorus from the whole gallery, of the cracking of hundreds of monkey-nuts, a rustling sound which never ceased. We sat down on nut-shells, and our feet dangled among them. One could imagine one was sitting on the seashore.

A revue was showing. Bare-legged girls marched past as soldiers; elegantly dressed concert-parties sang glees in the light of shaded lamps, while the 'wandering violinist' crept and crooned about the stage; a third-rate Robey dialogued with a third-rate Grossmith; a naughty girl pointed a giddy toe at the circles and made love to the men. The male audience love-called to her, whistled, mewed. They blew penny trumpets, they sang the choruses.

They greeted with derisive laughter some of the 'things we see in dreams'; for instance, a tableau of a wet day in Poplar and a clerk coming from the Labour Exchange to a man's home to bring him the dole and save him going out into the wet.

270

And when an ambitious soprano indulged in romantic crescendo they caterwauled at her, told her to take her voice home and fry it. They picked upon the gawky dancing-girl who did not quite do her part, and called out to her, 'Go it, long 'un!' There were coster flappers wedged among the lads, and they tittered nervously at the exploits of half-naked girls upon the stage. Youth round about kept referring to what they called 'tarts'. When an actor incautiously remarked that he had had a dream last night it was the signal for ribald shouts to him from self-conscious males. What an odour in the theatre! The stalls reeked upward to the circles; the circles to us. A notice said that any bringing bottles would be instantly expelled. Less dangerous missiles went back and forth from the stage. Luckily tomatoes were dear at the time. There were many men engaged trying to keep order and stopping wilder forms of excess.

Many songs were drowned in noise wherein the shelling of nuts was the persistent background. But every one settled down and was happy when the orchestra struck up, 'Oh, how I love my darling!' Dock youth sang, rolled their bodies rhythmically, beat time with their feet, got together, and forgot everything else. This was the best moment – the interval between first and second acts – a persisting music, a persisting happiness. Young fellows who had come in with newspaper wisps of chips sang this song even with potatoes in their mouths. Before the end of the performance, however, many bethought themselves of the 'pubs', and struggled out to get a drink.

The theatre was like a Moscow theatre after the revolution, with the eaters of sunflower-seeds invading the haunts of the intelligentsia and spitting seed husks all over the floors. It is a Red crowd; not Suburbia; real London, the alternative London. I thought, as I sat there among the nut-shells, how curious it would be to see that audience filling Covent Garden, with a demagogue speaking to it from the Royal box.

I returned to the fourpenny gallery, and had an even more amusing night. Before sitting down I swept the peanut shells from the seat. Away down below on the stage a pretty young vocalist was singing 'Nobody has ever kissed me', and the youths of the gallery were whistlng to her and calling, 'Give us 'arf a chance'.

She sang a little and danced a little. It was one of the innumerable variants of 'There's a man wanted here,' and was a typical music-hall turn.

But it became even more typical when she was interrupted by a supposed member of the audience acting the part of being the worse for liquor and intent on breaking the girl's innocent record. New mirth enkindled as the vocalist flirted with him across the footlights. The youths in the gallery guffawed.

But still it improved when another supposed member of the audience also began to interrupt; this time a bellicose and beery middle-aged lady in a lurid bonnet.

'I'll teach you,' she said. 'I'll teach you to interfere with other women's men. Keep yer 'an's orf 'im, I tell yer, or it'll be the worse for yer.'

The orchestra stops playing.

The girl sways helplessly, and pretends to look much scared and annoyed.

Then the old woman goes for her supposed husband. They show their devotion by out-slanging one another, till the old woman sobs and the old toper sobs also, and they dry their eyes together and make it up. Then at last the injured wife is able to look with triumph at the daring young thing waiting helplessly on the stage.

'Proceed with your song,' says she.

The girl seems to cheer up.

'But, one minute,' says the old woman in a thick, solemn, beer-sodden voice. 'Before you continue, young woman, I'd like to tell you something about your voice. It is this. As a singer, as a sing-ger, mark you, I think that *you* are a very good dancer.' The youths in the gallery are infinitely pleased. They had forgotten that expression – 'as a singer you're a very good dancer' – but they've got it again now. For, of course, it is not original; it is part of the general stock-in-trade of music-hall

271

comedy. The whole make-believe interruption was also something well understood and quite expected. Seldom does one sit through a programme without make-believe interruptions from the audience. No one is deceived by them, unless, perchance, a country girl just up from the village, one who 'hasn't been in London long'.

A comic star is singing on the stage, but a bloated and most disagreeable theatre attendant has appeared amid the stalls calling in a dreadful voice:

'Programmes! Programmes!'

Or it is another well-known comedian singing and some one in collusion with him starts a supposed scandal, calling out in an authoritative voice: *'I forbid you to sing that chorus.'* Or two men are playing on the stage, and one pretends to faint. Then a supposed doctor in the audience cries out with the tones of outraged science:

'It's a scandal, sir; I say it's a scandal.'

'What's the matter?'

'I say it's a scandal; that man is dying.'

Or it is a comedian as an airman, and some supposed Air Force officer, or dandy enthusiast in a box, begins to interrupt all the comedian's patter by remarks of exaggerated enthusiasm.

All that is stock-in-trade. But it is interesting how, even apart from the manner of presentation of humour, there is a set of jokes which are the common property of all the comedians. You may hear them as easily in Leicester Square as in Mile End Road. It strikes the unwonted visitor to the Pavilion as very original when Stanley Lupino says of some one: 'He has bats in the belfry.' It is not always grasped that the expression belongs to the music-hall at large, and is used by any comedian as occasion offers. It is currency at both ends of town, at Piccadilly Circus or in West India Dock Road.

It is like the expression, 'I've got that Kruschen feeling,' which never fails to evoke mirth and scarcely ever fails to be used by some one in the programme.

> 'I am going to the most beautiful city in the world.'
> 'Where's that?'
> 'Wigan.'
> 'What do I look like?'
> 'You look like the son of Tarzan.'
> 'No, you're wrong; I'm the Sheikh!'
> 'He's got no money; he comes from Maida Vale.'
> 'I'll have to consult my solicitors: Salmon and Gluckstein.'
> 'Let's go over to Sam Isaacs.'
> 'I'd like to have one, wouldn't you? Yes, *I'd like to have one;* let's go to the old "Red Lion" instead.'

The supposed stinginess of the Scots and of Sir Harry Lauder in particular, are greatly exploited themes; nearly every Scotch turn or joke being no more than a variant of the other.

All successes are endlessly imitated. I do not know that the original songs and patter suffer by being imitated, but it is sometimes painful to listen to a would-be Scottish comedian with rouged face and bright green tartan kilt trying to re-hash Lauder songs, making sly remarks about his sporran all the while.

One of the most clever of the humorous songs of the past is 'Burlington Bertie from Bow'. It was astonishingly popular in the Army, and especially with the Guards, perhaps because of the priceless lines:

> I'm Burlington Bertie,
> I rise at ten-thirty,
> To Buckingham Palace I go.
> I stand in the yard

While they're changing the guard,
And the King shouts across 'Toodloo.'

Burlington Bert, if you remember, had not got a shirt; he was Burlington Bertie from Bow. When the Queen asked him to stop to lunch, he said, 'Thanks, no! I had a banana with Lady Diana, I'm Burlington Bertie from Bow'.

And now one hardly visits a music hall without hearing some sort of re-cast Burlington Bertie. The audience does not necessarily detect it. It sits back and enjoys it, revelling in the mirth of 'Wandering Walter from Wimbledon Way', or 'I'm Charlie Golightly – what-ho!'

Charlie Golightly dines with Sassoon at the 'Ritz'. 'Sassoon' has now become as much a music-hall property as Tarzan. But Charlie Golightly inevitably explains in his chorus that it was not the 'Ritz', after all, it was the Hotel Rowton House, for he's 'Charlie Golightly – what-ho!'

I have no doubt that all the real live comedians keep enriching the general stock-in-trade of the music hall. Directly a hit has been made with a certain joke, the joke goes round and gets somehow into the repertoire of all and sundry. When Vesta Tilley left the stage she bequeathed her wonderful conception of the young man, the gay spark, the giddy son following in father's footsteps. It is almost as if there were a Vesta Tilley seed which had been sown; there are little Vestas growing on every stage.

Unfortunately, this makes for some monotony at last. People expect to have old jokes to laugh at, but do not want to laugh too often at the same ones. Wigan and Tarzan have to be dropped in time. The day will come when it will be useless for a comedian to explain:

'It was that last Guinness did me,' or 'Where are the doin's?' or 'I'm Mademoiselle from Armentières.'

They will have been said at too many places at the same time too often.

I believe the success of the negro comedians in their Plantation Revue was due more to a complete absence of the English stock-in-trade than to their own personal originality. They are drawing from another stock.

Florence Mills's wonderful song –

He may be your man,
But he comes to see me SOMETIMES;
And when he's with you
He's got ME on his mind –

is by no means unlike a whole host of funny songs which I have heard from coloured comedians in negro music-halls in America. The negroes are very good and have now several modern imitators. Not the least clever a white girl who, having the whole negro intonation, made a great hit with song entitled:

I'm the one-man woman
Lookin' for the one-woman man.

There were not a few negroes in the audience, out with their white coster girls. They seemed to appreciate it as much as any.

The coon romance seems dying; the quaint Southern burlesque seems to be taking its place.

So, hey for Creole gumbo! It tastes well in New Orleans, but it is a greater novelty in London. It is a wonderful soup, with all sorts of things in it, and its quality depends on the stock.

It would be a mistake to think that the use of the general stock is the sign of a second-rate comedian. Observe closely the patter of the greatest of 'stars'; you will see much of their cleverness depends on using the well-known jokes and catches more adroitly. In the music-hall you seldom hear new things; you hear the old more cleverly re-set.

At The Other End Of Town

It comes rather as a jar to a young man and his girl when a boy in buttons, examining his tickets B1 and B2, says: 'B for Boob, second row from the front.' It is no use reporting him to the girl who sells the programmes. She will get a laugh out of it also. 'Your ticket is B, isn't it – well, what yer worryin' about?' It's all part of the fun.

Watch the dancing chorus. Every one of the girls seems to have her eyes on some one, one even on you, trying to make you laugh. They are all in camisoles and struggling to put on frocks. Rather shocking? No, only laughter-seeking. *The leading lady will ask male help.*

All the girls come among the audience and request young men to do up their fastenings behind, and not one returns to the stage till she is 'done up'. Some old grouser has a powdered darling almost on his knee. Does he not loosen up and grin? All are conquered by mirth.

Two men in Palm Beach suits come on the stage and give a 'take-off' of American 'hoofers', comedy step-dancers, chewing tobacco or gum, while they speak as if their noses were trumpets, paddle their feet, and see-saw with their shoulders.

'Say, you gink, you bonehead, d'y'know who we are? We're just two melancholy murderers, we-are-the-ass-ass-ins-of-gloom! Gloom hasn't got a snowball's chance in Hades with us. Should have seen how we went over in Dayton, Ohio. Oh, boy, they're laughing yet. Ye can hear them howling on the wireless.' Truly they make American vaudeville artists seem more funny than they really are.

Americans get their humour by tall talk and brag; we get ours by swank and laughing at ourselves. So Colonel Coldfeet of the Coldcream Guards walks in and blows out his cheeks, and swings his cane and rubs his monocle and gives himself away. The Coldstream Guards is one of the most famous regiments, but it would be thought beyond words if some Coldstreamer in the audience stood up and protested against the fun and the funny Colonel.

> We're never afraid when we're on parade;
> We're the idols of the nurse and parlourmaid,

as a popular ditty once expressed it.

The brave man who is not brave, and the man who won't fight are inexhaustible sources of mirth. 'Oh, dear, I'm getting very deaf. A feller arst me to 'ave a drink the other night. I could 'ear that all right. We 'ad one or two. He begins to tell me of the girls 'e'd known. When 'e'd done ah descrabes to 'im a girl ah noo. What d'yer think? He puts dahn 'is glass an' sez:

'"I'll punch your bloomin' 'ead. That's the girl I'm going' to wed. I'll punch your bloomin' 'ead, I will."

'I said "Oo?"

'He said "You."

'I said "Me?"

'He said Yes."

'I said "Oh!"'

I heard the other night Charles Coborn sing 'Two Lovely Black Eyes' – an oldish man now, for he was the original singer of it a quarter of a century ago, sang it every night for a year:

> Only for telling a man he was wrong,
> Two lovely black eyes.

It was the same sort of humour; the laugh at oneself, a quick facial expression suggesting the blows and the swollen eye-sockets and a peeping mirth at his own expense.

The same man sang originally 'The Man that Broke the Bank at Monte Carlo'. He sang it thirty years ago. It almost succeeded as a comic song in 1923:

> I walk along the Bois de Boulogne
> With an independent air.

The eyes of a great young audience were fixed upon that comic strut. They did not know the song very well, but it was good. Coborn tried to get them to sing the chorus with him, and there, I thought, was a moment of strange pathos. For, surely, more than half of those who sang it with him in the Tivoli so long ago are dead by now, or in any case far from the music hall.

In his day the music hall was not what it is now. There was a feature which has been quite removed. It may still seem to be sometimes an annexe of a public-house. But the *demi-monde* no longer plies its trade therein.

The cleaning up of the audience has helped to clean up the stage. There has been a long and steady progress away from impropriety. The saloon-bar and smoking-room is no longer legal tender across the footlights. Even the features of low burlesque disappear. The male comedians no longer infallibly split the seats of their trousers in every act and walk sideways in mock distress.

There is much cleverness on the music-hall stage to-day, humorous personation, and upon occasion quite Dickensian scenes. Indeed, there is a much truer reflection of the mind of the English people in the music hall than in the 'legitimate' theatre.

The comedians of to-day are not content to fill up their time with old gags; they have so much to make fun of. If it's not the 'garden subbub',

> Away from the noise and the hubbub
> Where we make our own stewed rubbub,

it is the absurd ticket-collector at the entrance to the lift, saying 'All-tickets-please, all-tickets-please, further-down-the-lift, further-down-the-lift, further-down-the-lift', or it is a take-off of the nursing home with the absurd nurse saying every time she is in the room: 'By the way, while I'm here, I think I'll make your bed'.

What skits there were during the War on every aspect of our unusual public life! Surely, it showed us what a funny lot of people we really are, and what an appetite we have for fun. Nero, the terrible lion, eats a man alive at every performance. His blood-red cage stands on the stage. Dreadful feeding-time howls resound from within. And the new attendant discusses the situation: 'Here I am playing second fiddle to Nero-ohhh! Would any gentleman or . . . lady like to step up and try our lion?'

Some one tired of life staggers on to the stage. 'No, it's hardly fair on the lion,' says the attendant. 'I'll make the sacrifice; I'll go in. Remember me to friends at the vicarage. Say I made a good end. Let my wife know only to make tea for one. It's a far, far better thing that I do now . . .'

The attendant goes in to Nero. There is horrible squelching and roaring. The owner of the lion puts up a notice: 'New Attendant Wanted'. And then the surprise: out comes the attendant from the cage and rolls down his sleeves and turns the notice round to the reverse side on which is written: 'New Lion Wanted'. Curtain.

Even little children – and many are taken to the halls – call to the stage or ask father about it all, and laugh and clap with the rest. It is a family outing. It is no longer the beer-sodden audience which in the old days a magnetic little Vesta, singing 'Following in Father's Footsteps', could alone vitalise and make one, but a lively, eager, expectant crowd, mostly young, it is true, between the ages of five and fifty.

There are few people left to-day who would condemn the music-hall as a low pleasure. To them we might say, in the words of a Lancashire comedian, 'You big lump o' nowt, go and have a look at it for yourself!'

STEPHEN GRAHAM, LONDON NIGHTS

It would be interesting to know if Graham, on the night when he went out into the darkened streets of the town to follow the antics of the electorate, ever stopped to consider the proposition that he was not so very far from the halls after all. Two generations later, the idea that the art of public entertainment and the game of politics are swiftly merging is commonplace enough. But in the days of Graham's quaint reportage, the two were still thought to be aeons apart, even though there was no leading politician who could hope to maintain his position without presenting to the electorate a persona just as contrived in its own way as the mask donned by the stage performer. At least one historian has commented on the gradual shift away from the orotundity of the formal address to the more relaxed pleasures of informal conversation. The influence of the music hall, he points out, had much to do with the colloquialising of the art of political claptrappery.

For Lloyd George, parliament was less important than the public meeting. He said: 'My platform is the country'. This was the time when all political leaders did a great deal of public speaking. The period opened in the 1880s, after Gladstone's Midlothian campaign; it tailed off in the 1930s, perhaps because interest in politics declined, perhaps because of the radio. Lloyd George came just at the top of the wave. His style was all his own. Other statesmen spoke in formal terms, carefully prepared. Churchill, for instance, learnt his early speeches, word for word, by heart and read his later ones. Lloyd George spoke with his audience, not to them, and snapped up phrases as they were thrown at him. 'Ninepence for Fourpence' was the result of one such interruption; making Germany pay to the uttermost farthing, the less happy result of another. Most public speakers seemed to be the contemporaries of Henry Irving or Beerbohm Tree. Lloyd George gave a music-hall turn, worthy of Harry Lauder or George Robey, the prime minister of mirth, and the great days of the music hall, roughly from 1900 to 1930, corresponded exactly with his. In 1923 Lloyd George was persuaded to use a microphone for the first time, and he accepted it ever afterwards. I suspect that it ruined his public style, as it certainly ruined the music hall.

A.J.P. TAYLOR, ESSAYS IN ENGLISH HISTORY

Slowly, inch by inch, theatre by theatre, the music hall was fading into the past. Once the talking pictures arrived, any faint hope of its survival finally vanished. But it had other enemies, including the revue, a form of stage entertainment midway between a variety bill and a musical comedy. When J.B. Priestley first came to London after a boyhood in Yorkshire and a four-year vacation in Flanders by kind permission of the government, he noticed that there was still something of the old spirit left, although the encroachments of revue were already making inroads on the once vast audiences for the halls. Some of the greatest stars were already either dead or retired by the time Priestley came to live in London. Yet when he looked back, at the end of a long life, he saw the post-war years as an Indian summer for the halls.

During the last few years the intimate revue, which I have always preferred to musical comedy, has been revived with considerable success, and I fancy it offers us more genuine satire and wit than it did thirty years ago. But I do not think it is mere age that makes me believe the original *Nine O'clock Revue* at the Little and the early Charlot revues were much better, filled with richer talent, bigger personalities, funnier sketches, more artful tunes. And what is certain is that the music hall of today is nothing but the ghost of what it was in the early 'twenties in London. It had already passed its peak even then, but some of the ripe old turns were still with us. You could look in at the Coliseum, as I often did on a winter afternoon, and see Little Tich and Harry Tate, and there were still some glorious drolls at the Holborn Empire (a sad loss; it had a fine thick atmosphere of its own), and the Victoria Palace, and the rest. There were no microphones and nobody needed them. There were no stars who had arrived by way of amusing farmers' wives and invalids on the radio. There were no reputations that had been created by American gramophone records for teenagers. The men and women who topped the bills had spent years getting there, learning how to perfect their acts and to handle their audiences. Of course, there was plenty of vulgar rubbish, but all but the very worst of it had at least some zest and vitality. And the audiences, which laughed at jokes and did not solemnly applaud them as BBC audiences do now, were an essential part of the show; they too had vitality, and were still close to the Cockneys who helped to create, a generation earlier, the English music hall of the great period, the folk art out of which, among other things, came the slapstick of the silent films, especially those of Chaplin.

J.B. PRIESTLEY, *COMING TO LONDON*

By this time young Neville Cardus, the one-time programme-and-chocolate sales-man at the Manchester Gaiety Theatre, had graduated to the Valhalla of the *Manchester Guardian* reporters' room, from which ivory tower he was sent out to review anything which might take the fancy of Haslam Mills, his hero and Chief Reporter. Mills had a deep affection for the halls, regarding them as a legitimate pretext for cerebral prose of the more profound kind. But Cardus's sense of humour often saved him from the preciousness of which he later accused his own apprentice self.

After I had reported annual meetings and what-not for a fortnight, Mills asked me to attend a Manchester music hall, a secondary affair, outside the city. But it meant that next day my initials would be printed in the *Manchester Guardian* – that is, if the notice got in the paper at all. The occasion was a programme at the Ardwick Empire, headed by a fat comedian named Ernie Mayne. I went to the 'first house' and arrived back at the office at nine o'clock, and set to work at once, isolating myself in an office fastness called the 'library'. I wrote three hundred words, and I took three hours over them. I was so late with my copy that Arthur Wallace, who that night was editing the theatre notices, missed his last tram home and had to take a taxi. He passed the notice without a 'cut' or the disturbance of a comma. It began 'Mr Ernie Mayne is indigenous to the music hall.' A more authentic *Guardian* touch was this: 'Two individuals, whose names we cannot remember, did an astonishing variety of things with a violin and piano – did everything, in fact, except play on them.' The notice pleased Mills, and it won me my spurs; but on looking back at it I blush. I think it was crudely imitative, and I suspect that Mills was a victim of indirect flattery. A week or two later Mills came to me one Friday evening. 'You are off-duty tomorrow, aren't you? It's your free week-end,' he said. I replied that it was. 'Well', he continued, 'on Monday, Little Tich appears at the Manchester Hippodrome, and I shall put you down to write about him.' He paused to note the effect on me. 'But', he went on, 'I want you to spend tomorrow in suitable preparation. Go into the country. Take a long walk. But take it alone. And meditate upon Little Tich.' I followed the instructions to the letter.

Another instance of what young lions we were in the Mills circus: a certain Max Erard came to the Manchester Hippodrome. He played an organ in coloured electric light, and he advertised that it weighed eight tons. My notice jumped at the obvious opportunity for satire. He retaliated with a strong letter to the Editor, theatening horse-whipping. A few weeks afterwards he was back at the Manchester Hippodrome, top of the bill – 'Return of the Great Max Erard'. Mills again sent me to write of him; but as I thought it might seem cheap to go over the same ground, I omitted mention of Erard at all, concentrating on some more or less anonymous first turn of the show. As it happened, Sidebotham was this time taking (that is, editing) the music-hall notices, and I had attended a Monday matinee. Just before six o'clock Sidebotham came into the reporters' room and touched me gently on the arm. 'You've not discussed Erard and his organ,' he said. I explained that I could add nothing to my notice of a month earlier. 'But', persisted Sidebotham, 'if you don't mention him again he'll think his threatening letter has dismayed us.' He took me below to the Thatched House and stood me the first whisky and soda of my life. It flew to my head, and I went back to my Manchester Hippodrome notice and added, 'Max Erard returns this week with his organ. It still weighs eight tons.' Whether the remark is funny today I doubt; it was a great success in 1917. I was credibly informed that Scott himself smiled at it, after a comprehensive explanation had been given him of all the antecedents – which must nearly have involved somebody in a short history of the British music hall.

NEVILLE CARDUS, AUTOBIOGRAPHY

How far is Cardus justified in claiming the flattery of imitation of Mills? Certainly Mills was the fastidious prosodist that Cardus eventually became, and was a dominant influence on the paper at that time. In Cardus's autobiography, the handsome, saturnine Mills looks steadily from a dark background at the camera which catches the silvering front locks, the dark, deep-set eyes, the strong jawbone resting on the white silk scarf, the casual ease of the overcoat, the stick and bowler hat held between gloved hands. Cardus describes how he used to watch Mills in the act of composing a notice, and how, one night, he went into the sanctum of his office after Mills had gone home. 'On the floor at the base of Mills's desk I saw many crumpled balls of copy-paper. I picked up all the crumpled papers, unrolled them, straightened them out, and studied them. There were at least a dozen, and each contained no other words than, neatly written as ever: 'Palace of Varieties'.

The modern reader has little chance of savouring Mills's style, but in 1924 he did publish a collection of essays called *Grey Pastures,* which had appeared from time to time in his newspaper. They tell of his boyhood in a small Lancashire country town, and, among other things, of his acquaintance with one of the local musicians who worked in the music hall.

The First Violin

It had once been a chapel. So much was clear from its oblong configuration – a building in which it had been more important to hear than to see, with two shallow galleries and a deep one facing the stage. And as they were still using up quantities of maroon brocade with tassels, I judged it to have a been a Dissenting chapel, belonging to one of the more recondite sects, small in number and very dainty of belief, for maroon hangings are the mark of the higher Nonconformity, just as white lawn is the mark of the Church of England and purple velvet that of Rome. When and at what conjecture in the rise and fall of its faiths it became a music hall I hardly know, but if one came early, when the audience was still arriving in ones and twos, it might still have been a chapel, and the tilting of the plush seats punctuated one's reverie very much like the desultory opening and shutting of pew doors – the same note of preparation for a quiet, customary event. But here the illusion ceased, for instead of the pulpit with its plush and morocco, the carafe of water with the down-turned glass, and the demure glimmer of light through an egg-shell globe, there was a drop-curtain, and on the drop-curtain a highly seductive view of life on the North Coast of Africa, with the god Pan playing some part.

For my part I never thought he had enough elbow-room for a mannered instrument like the violin. The brass rail which cut off the orchestra from the stalls irked him, and his hand used to beat softly against the curtain when he was hard at work on his top string. Once when I was on the front row of the stalls he even smote me on the knee with his knuckle. The assault occurred in the fluent passage of 'Raymond', and he opened his pale-blue eyes and glanced at me along the slope of his instrument, hoping that I should understand. And then when he was on his low string he had to allow for the neck of the other 'first', a pathetic figure so placed as to have no view whatever of the stage, though when the house was convulsed he would pop up and peer over the stage, still sawing.

And yet the First Violin was not without learning in the techniques of his art, and particularly was he skilled in the reading of obscure and not infrequently corrupt musical text. Much journeying to and fro in the jungle of song and badinage and dance had given him fortitude for the doubling back of the path and a kind of instinct for the right way through. And this, though the finger-posts were laconic and far between! Several sheets of blank music-paper and then in the middle of a page in a spiky hand the words 'Father Brings the Milk Home in the Morning' and two thumb-marks! The treble of the refrain pushes on with sudden volubility for several bars, and then a long passage has been scored out by someone who seems to have been in a temper, and the thread is resumed over the next page but one, and is pursued through a good deal of ambiguity and some sticking-plaster, until suddenly out of the mist there shoots an alarming rocket of semi-quavers. The chorus is repeated as often as it suffices Miss Wax Vesta to change for the next song. The First Violin has got to know it – he lets go. And Vesta having signalled that she is ready, the conductor taps twice and stops matters on a chord which is still unresolved. The First Violin makes no protest. He turns over his manuscript. 'I'm a Dashing Militaire', remarks the spiky hand, and Miss Vesta herself appears – a very final corroboration of the announcement. She walks several times the breadth of the stage to induce that *rapport* between herself and the audience which is a condition of her art. Incidentally she hums the melody hard through her teeth, bringing the orchestra by the scruff of its neck into the rhythm. The First Violin glances from her to his music and back to her again, anxious to be taught. By and by he has it right. His violin is frosty with resin-dust for a considerable area around the bridge.

But I admire him most at those moments when the orchestra, having made a false start, gathers round and becomes, parliament of clashing and conflicting views; when the voice of an unseen presence in the wings is hissing, 'No, no, the Spring Song'; when the dancer on whom the curtain has just risen is held up against a black velvet background in an effective preliminary attitude of some constraint which in the anatomical nature of things she cannot preserve much longer. The conductor is receiving suggestions from right and left, from the cornet player who has removed his instrument an inch from his mouth to enforce a theory which he holds rather strongly – from everybody except the broad-backed man at the piano, who sits deep down and in some detachment, and to whom, however they settle it, it is sure to resolve itself into 'pom' with the left hand and 'pom-pom' with the right. I suspect the First Violin on such occasions of a tendency to giggle; certainly there is in his eye a cheerful recognition of the fact that in art as in life the ideal is always some way ahead. He glances to this effect at the derisive audience over his brass rail, and when eventually they find the right place and the voice at the wings is appeased and the lady on the stage released, he goes on as though nothing worth mentioning had occurred – a happy warrior!

Two ducks shouldered through the ornamental water, sitting deep – saying something fretful. They left four oblique curling rollers behind them as they swam. On this Sunday morning they were the only entertainment in the recreation ground, for a third duck in deep apathy on a stony island was not spectacular. The smoke from a row of new houses over the palings beat down over the geometrical flower-beds, and on everything beneath a grey, racing sky there was an unevaporated ooze – on the metal battledores which warned one off the grass, on all the cast-iron in which the recreation ground is rich, on the swings which stood like the gallows in an asphalt annexe. Down the path, the centre of a fidgety family group, came the First Violin. His right hand was on the brass rail of a perambulator; in his other hand there was a newspaper with a slab of reading matter turned up. But the reading went slowly, for the youngest but one, who was coming to years of indiscretion, exhibited a stubborn preference for walking over the benches along the path, a mode of progression which involved a good deal of quarrelling with his kindred and some risk. The First Violin intervened in the dispute at regular intervals. Once he was busy for some time extracting damp gravel from the knees and palms of the youngest but one. And none of those who looked on but I, knew that he led a band, sat night by night in the draught which comes from the little door under the stage, the draught which is nectarously flavoured with an escape of gas; that he co-operated in public with the accepted wits – that ladies who were 'the rage' dragged him by the scruff of his neck into the rhythm of a song. Slowly the family group worked its way home – twice round the ornamental water and into the road, the perambulator agitated violently on the stones. Progress was hampered all the way home by the inability of the youngest but two to be satisfied until he had touched with his five fingers each separate garden railing they passed. More than once the First Violin turned and called him on, urging the nearness of dinner-time. And then he was gathered into the empty distances of rather a long street. It was off hours with the First Violin.

WILLIAM HASLAM MILLS, *GREY PASTURES*

Mills is describing the grimy tugs and freighters of the music-hall fleet. What of its great flagships, and especially those twin bastions of glamorous ballerinas and knowing gentlemen sauntering through its bars? Their days too were numbered. The torpedos of Hollywood were soon to sink them forever. In October 1936 the Alhambra was demolished; within a few months the Odeon Cinema had risen in its place, announcing its arrival with Ronald Colman in *The Prisoner of Zenda*. By then the Empire had long since gone. It had closed in January vc1927 after enjoying the swan-songs provided by the Gershwin Brothers for Fred and Adele Astaire to sing in *Lady Be Good,* and now vied with the newer Odeon as the venue for the Royal Command Film Shows. But long before then the change in styles had begun to undermine the world which had once so delighted J.B. Booth and his friends. In a novel whose characters reminisce about the ill-fated heroine Jenny in *Carnival,* Compton MacKenzie charts the decline of the old Leicester Square music-and-dance headquarters.

So Maudie dressed herself in the white tail suit which was supposed to mark the extreme dressiness of night on the river, and in which the first line of boys would dance their final number to the whirring reds and blues and greens of the firework display that would bring the ballet divertissement to a brilliant conclusion.

When this was over there would be a long interval before the ballet proper began, an interval filled in for the audience by jugglers, acrobats, musical acts, and perhaps some entertainer of international reputation. In these years immediately before the War the Orient provided for its patrons what was in essentials precisely the same entertainment it had been providing for a generation. The success of the Russian Imperial Ballet at Covent Garden had for a while slightly shaken the complacency of the board of directors; but it was soon felt that the Orient could hold its own by importing a *prima ballerina assoluta* from Russia instead of relying on France or Italy as for so long. Yet somehow this simple solution did not work. Night after night the most comfortable stalls in London – stalls as individually wide and well-sprung as the armchairs of the clubmen who frequented them – grew emptier. Death and illness and age were telling upon the habitués of the older generation, and the younger men of the new generation were not taking their places. The promenade was still full enough; but the hobbled skirts of 1910 had cramped the style of peripatetic harlotry. Large hats, long trains, ample busts, sequins and silk petticoats gave the women of the Alhambra and Orient and Empire promenades that five-pound look which for thirty years had been accepted as the standard of a luxury article. When hobbled skirts came in they might as well have frequented the Leicester Lounge or one of the cafés nearby: full-rigged whores were going the way of full-rigged ships: the promenade at the Orient was not what it was.

Old Mr Moberley, the managing director, assured the members of the board, all elderly city men like himself, that he had spared nothing to make the new ballet a success, and his fellow directors looking at the costs of production and the salary list did not doubt it. Yet the ugly fact remained that the Orient was getting emptier and emptier, and that unless some way was discovered of winning back its audience the Orient would have to close its doors. The thought of that huge aggregation of domes and minarets and coloured tiles, which had been the most prominent feature of Piccadilly Circus for fifty years, standing dark and desolate struck a chill even into the warm capon-lined paunches of the city fathers who were responsible for its management and maintenance. There must be some way of making the Orient

281

prosperous again. Perhaps the public was tired of ballet. The director who first put forward that possibility was stared at by his colleagues. Nevertheless he had merely stated aloud what they were all wondering to themselves, and once the morbid doubt had been clothed in words the directors began to consider what should take the place of ballet. Revue seemed to offer the best chance; but there was one bold old gentleman who actually suggested turning the Orient into a cinema theatre.

'A cinema theatre?' exclaimed Mr Moberley. 'Good god, why not turn it into a kaleidoscope while you're about it? I've never been inside one of these so-called cinema theatres myself, but they tell me the craze is already showing signs of dying down. The five minutes we give them of the bioscope to let people get their coats on is all *our* audience wants of that kind of thing,' Mr Moberley concluded with a snort.

Nevertheless, as if the crimson and gold flock walls of the board-room had heard the secret, a rumour went round the theatre that the present ballet founded upon the novel *Aphrodite* by Pierre Loüys was to be the last of the long line of them and that the Orient would presently be closed, reconstructed, redecorated, and opened next autumn as a cinema theatre. To more than half the ladies of the corps de ballet who had danced at the Orient since they were almost children and whose mothers had danced there before them an announcement that the end of the world would succeed the run of *Aphrodite* would have been less alarming. To the majority of the dressers, many of whom had themselves danced once upon a time in the ballet, the rumour of the closing of the Orient was like the approach of death. Scene-shifters, wardrobe-women, musicians, programme-girls, they all grew queasy at the notion. Every night they looked at the empty stalls with a growing sickness at the heart, so completely had everybody in that musty old warren of a theatre become identified with it. There had been new girls who had boasted openly that they had no intention of remaining long at the Orient; but somehow they always did remain. They might grumble at the fines, moan over the ill-lighted and ill-ventilated dressing-rooms, groan over the stone stairs up and down which they had to rush a dozen times every night, slang the quality of the food provided in the canteen, and denounce the disgracefully long hours they were kept waiting at rehearsals; but they always succumbed to the influence of the half grim, half kindly genius of the place. Girls who had come for one ballet had remained for twenty; and on the day the managing-director had patted their heads in fatherly fashion and told them that they were no longer young enough to stand the strain of the life of a ballet girl they had many of them burst into wild sobs and entreated him not to give them their notice unless he wished them to consider their life at an end. To such overwrought females Mr Moberley had made a habit of offering as a prize to be attained in a few years' time, the possibility of returning to the Orient, when there was a vacancy among the dressers. And the woman who had come to the Orient as a bright-eyed girl of eighteen would leave it at thirty-eight with the hope of coming back to it again at fifty as a blowsy bonneted Mrs Pilkington.

On this fine evening the chief topic of conversation had once again been the rumour that the Orient was to be closed and the ballet disbanded. The news of the death of Jenny Pearl, one of the very few girls who had left the Orient of her own accord, seemed like an omen of what might happen to all of them if the theatre in which they lived, laughed, ate, drank, undressed, dressed, danced and gossiped should close its doors upon them.

So during the interval between the two ballets when her companions talked about the dead dancer it was in the light of their own future compared with what now seemed the perfect security of a happy and humdrum past.

'I remember like as if it was last week the night Jenny told us she was going to be married,' said Gladys West.

'It'll be three years ago this November,' supplemented Maudie Chapman. 'Because I married my Walter the Christmas after Jenny left, and Ivy was born the November after that and she'll be two next November.'

'That's right,' Lucy Arnold confirmed. 'Because I first came to the Orient just before that Christmas, and I took Jenny Pearl's place.'

'No, you didn't,' Irene Dale contradicted, 'you took Elsie Crauford's place.'

'A lot you know about whose place I took,' retorted Lucy. 'You was away in Paris with your Danby when I came to the Orient and you wouldn't be here again now if Jenny Pearl hadn't have left.'

Irene Dale crossed the floor of the dressing-room, a threat louring in her blue eyes.

'I've stood enough from you, Lucy Arnold. Because you look like a bad imitation of Jenny Pearl you needn't think you *are* Jenny Pearl. You needn't think you can talk like *her* and get away with it. I've had it in my mind for a long time to jolly well punch into you, and I'll ...'

But before she could strike, two or three of the girls caught hold of Irene and pulled her back to her own place.

'Shut up, Irene Dale,' said Maudie. 'What a time to start in quarrelling about Jenny! And you shut up too, Lucy Arnold.'

Madge Wilson and a lissom gypsy-faced girl with short curly hair, called Queenie Danvers, were inclined to encourage the fight, but the majority for peace was too large, and they were disappointed of their excitement.

'I remember when we were all standing by the stage-door and waving good-bye to her as she ran down the court into Jermyn Street,' said Gladys West, 'she turned round and called back, "See you all soon," and we never have seen her, and now we'll never see her. She was a lad. When I think of all the girls in the Orient there has never been one like Jenny Pearl. There was something about her none of us have got.'

COMPTON MACKENZIE, *FIGURE OF EIGHT*

The young men who had once frequented the real-life Orients were now middle-aged and in some cases eminent gentlemen who had never forgotten the ambience and the repertoires of the old music hall. None had achieved more for the halls by the exercise of his own art than the painter Walter Sickert, whose surviving portraits of that world are the most evocative evidence to survive. Sickert had found genuine enjoyment in his performer-models and in later life still indulged in the habit of expressing his most forthright views in the whimsical form of a quotation from some faded music-hall text. One day his close young friend Osbert Sitwell went to visit him in his studio.

As I approached, I saw a tall, bearded man standing in the road. He stood in the middle of this silent and empty road, looking through the archway in the wall, with its iron gate, into the large, green area of the Physic Garden, its strips of lawn varied with early flowering magnolias and other shrubs, and with old mulberry trees, as yet hardly in leaf. Out of all these things the sun was weaving a thousand intricate and living designs, and it shone, too, full upon the face of the stranger, showing it in detail against a background of sooty brick. He did not see me; he thought himself alone; his face wore a peculiarly keen look of observation, or of comprehension, as of someone in the act of saying, 'Oh, I understand!' and his eyes held a rapt and penetrating expression. His curling – or rather, waving – grey hair showed at the sides of the half tall hat of rough black felt he was wearing – and then I recognised this stranger. It

283

was Sickert! And the diverse effects I have mentioned were merely a part of a new disguise he had adopted since I had seen him a month previously ... For the rest, it consisted of a dark poacher's coat with large pockets with flaps, and a pair of shepherd's plaid trousers. Under his arm he carried a square parcel done up in brown paper. The fan-shaped beard spread out over his stiff single collar and bow tie, and it perhaps made the finely cut face, with its concavities, unusual at his age, seem broader than it was. It blurred, too, a little the boldness of the features, but nothing could obscure the cool keenness of the grey-blue eyes, full of light, or the acuteness of the whole head, which constituted part of its invariable handsomeness ... Suddenly he saw me approaching, gave a charming, friendly smile and at once began to sing a verse of a comic song that he knew amused me. It was, he had told me, a song that was said to have been popular with ex-soldiers after the Crimean War, when talk of starting a new conflict filled the air, and it certainly expressed my own views about the current dispute:

> If you'll excuse me
> We've 'ad some!

There he stood, in the middle of the empty road, in the sunlight of a spring evening, most carefully rendering the words, deliberately, as if it were a matter of importance, and converting his whole appearance into a box, as it were, for the production of this song.

OSBERT SITWELL, *NOBLE ESSENCES*

Yet another essayist not prepared to let the music-hall tradition fade away without committing some of his thoughts to paper was J.B. Atkins, a writer of such quality that at various periods in his career the readers of *Punch, The Spectator, The Manchester Guardian* and *The Westminster Gazette* learned to look out for his reports. He was especially good on the subject of London, although James Bone, who wrote the introduction to the collection called *Side Shows,* has a point when he writes that to him Atkins 'seems to me rather a visitor than a Londoner, bringing standards and perspectives of the sea and country into his London studies. Perhaps for that the London part of his book gives me peculiar pleasure, bringing back something of the country-town London of Mr Spectator, although to most of his friends Atkins may seem the most townlike modern who walks Pall Mall'. One of the tiny alleys which appealed to Atkins, as it has to many others, is Maiden Lane, which to this day retains its bouquet of first nights and floral tributes through the stage doors of the Adelphi and Vaudeville Theatres which still spill out into its narrow path, and through Rules' Restaurant, at whose midnight napery I once saw Professor Higgins himself, munching roast beef while deep in contemplation of a book, no doubt on Phonetics. At Atkins's time the lane was renowned for a reason which has, alas, lost its relevance in the modern age.

Bathyllus and His Art

Just before Christmas there is a change in the appearance of shop-windows which we all know: more lights throw a fierce glare into the streets; delicious eatables are piled one upon another, with a gaiety of appearance which they are notoriously unable to

284

impart to their consumers; and nearly everything invites judgement upon itself by its suitability for a Christmas present. This is a conspicuous change, to be sure, but there are other changes which, if not conspicuous, are more significant. Let me recommend a walk round about Covent Garden, in the upper part of Wellington Street, in Maiden Lane, and then on the Rialto, which is the southern slope from Waterloo Bridge.

Here you see the changes which announce the season of the pantomimes. Crowns, tiaras, breast-plates, cuirasses, Zouaves, helmets, cocked hats, masks, glass jewels for Aladdin, glass slippers for Cinderella, enormous beads for Man Friday, uniforms, muslin skirts, ballet-dancers' shoes, Moorish clothes for Dick Whittington, and I know not what, are shaken free of the dust which has lain on them all the summer, and are rearranged in shop-windows. No fierce light beats upon them. The jewels look like the dull glass they are, and the sequins cannot raise a glitter among them. No need to attract the eye of the passer-by. The manager of the country pantomime, who is going to cut a dash with the cast-off raiment of London pantomimes, knows exactly where to go. There is a sermon in every one of these shop-windows, but it is too trite to be mentioned. But I may remark upon the impressive juxtaposition of Bow Street and the fine collection of shepherdesses' crooks in one shop.

Not only the shops announce the season. Accomplished but unsuccessful practitioners of the dramatic art take heart again, and lift up tired eyes glowing with a new ambition. It is here that they throng the recognised meeting-places, where an agent may, at any moment, throw an engagement at them, and give them the opportunity of at last bringing a stupid town to their feet. Here you may mark hope springing eternal in the breast of an artist who has been of no particular importance since twelve months ago, when he was dressed in red, drew three pounds a week, and was nightly fired into popularity from a trap below the stage. Ah, those were great days, and they are upon him again!

Maiden Lane at this time of year is the only place where an enormous percentage of the men are heroes, and of the women heroines. There is a Roman Catholic Church at the corner, which was more used before the Irish colony was driven out of Clare Market, and to come into the lane at this end is perhaps the most suitable introduction. But there is a great deal to be said for coming at it from one of the alleys – cracks between houses – which lead up from the Strand.

The chief beauty of these alleys after dark is the way they are illuminated by concealed lights filtering out from windows which you cannot see till you come up to them. Going up one alley, I looked in at a lighted window, and beheld a bicycle repairer at work among such a litter of iron as one might expect to see in a village shop. He worked under a flare of gas. I was so astonished to see him and his shop – I felt as though I were looking in at the forge of a village blacksmith – that I stood and gazed. He came to me and said: 'If you go up to the top and turn to the left, you will get out.' I did not want to get out in the least, but I obeyed his instructions. I suppose the people who dwell in these cracks think that every stranger who comes there has got in by mistake, and that the true hospitality of the quarter is to show him out. But this only deepens the mystery of the bicycle repairer. Why does he repair bicycles in this spot, if, when a possible customer comes, he only runs out and says: 'Go up to the top and turn to the left'?

Maiden Lane, I said, is frequented by heroes and heroines. The heroines may also be heroes, as this happens in pantomime. Maiden Lane is also the only place where I ever heard of prosperous people in fur coats stopping their conversation when a policeman came in sight, politely whistling 'A Policeman's Life is not a Happy One', and gravely continuing their conversation when the policeman had passed on. There is an excellent tea-shop in Maiden Lane, and here the principal boys, principal girls, star-trap jumpers (first grade – and there are not many left), high-class demons, and the most important fairies congregate. I think the waitresses brighten their occupation by temporary incursions into pantomime. You can hire rooms in this lane to drill a chorus. There are also rooms for fitting on pantomime clothes.

Here, too, is Rule's saloon, full of ancient prints, cartoons, and theatrical reminiscences. Round the walls are little shrines, where electric light illumines the busts of Charles Mathews and Dan Leno, and the figures of Hyperides and Phryne. Hyperides, having failed to clear Phryne of a charge of impiety, is indicating to the judges the beauty of his client, for all the world like a French lawyer.

The York Hotel at the bottom of the Rialto is also full of old prints, old play-bills, and theatrical cartoons. To be important here, you must be a star or an agent. You must have money to buy talents or talents to offer. You may hear a man offer to make the fortunes of a theatre in the unadorned words, 'I do fifteen minutes with twelve gags,' and you may hear the agent of the music-hall reply that the minutes are too many and the gags too few. The Rialto has perhaps a larger spirit than Maiden Lane. Here a man might say, with the easy confidence of perfect appropriateness: 'Well met on the Rialto, signor!' It would also be easier to broach the subject of a loan in this free air. It encourages the large manner. But, on the whole, the vogue is with Maiden Lane, and it was there I met my friend Bathyllus, who has written pantomimes.

'Tell me, Bathyllus,' I said, 'do you like writing pantomimes?'

Bathyllus passed his hand over his brow. 'A terrible business!' he said. 'You can't be literary – you have to write down. I'm always saying to myself, "Don't be literary, Bathyllus, my boy, or this blooming show will be a frost." Think of the people I've got to deal with on the stage – superstitious, bad memories, no art! And then think of the public who want the same old subjects year after year. Why don't they let one write a bit? But they won't. What are you to do?'

'I know the subjects are limited, Bathyllus,' I said, 'but which do you think is the best?'

'Why, Whittington, of course,' he said. 'That's real good business. Just think of it. First scene: London – fifteenth century – costumes, and all that. There you have your picturesque touch. Next scene: Highgate Heath – rural – peasants – milkmaids, and all that. There you have your simple, good-old-England business. Next scene: The voyage to Morocco – nautical business. Next scene: Morocco Oriental splendour – grand ballet – pile it on as much as you like – can't make a mistake. Besides, there's the cat.'

'Is a good cat difficult to get?' I asked.

'Very,' said Bathyllus. 'I remember one year when there was a boom in Whittingtons. All the old retired men at the acrobatic business came back as cats. Then there weren't enough! One man had a wooden leg. He was a cat somewhere down in the country.'

'Why do you say pantomime people are superstitious?' I asked.

'Because they are,' said Bathyllus. 'Peacocks' feathers! They won't have 'em on the stage. What are you going to make of a Chinese scene without peacocks' feathers? Sickening! Then they won't say the last two lines of the book till the first night, and then, perhaps, they forget 'em. Suppose I write for the ending –

Aladdin wishes you good luck and cheer,
A very happy and a bright New Year!

Well, they want to keep that till the first night. Out come the words, down goes the curtain, crash goes the band – all for the first time! That's going to bring them good luck. "Bluebeard's" unlucky, too.'

'And their stupidity?' I said.

Bathyllus became very gloomy. 'Add two lines to a part,' he said, 'and they're done for. Alter the cue, and they don't know where they are for days. I remember one year when I wrote the words for "Bo-peep," I made Bo-peep say she was going to advertise for her sheep. The Baron said: "Why are you going to do that?" Bo-peep said: "To attract attention." The Baron answered: "To attract attention nowadays you ought to refrain from advertising." If you'll believe me, I couldn't get the Baron to say this bit. I kept saying: "Why do you leave those lines out?" "All right, old chap," he used to say, "I can't get the run of them all at once." Days passed, and at last I said: "Don't you think you might have learnt that little bit by now?" "Well, to tell you the truth, old chap," he said, "I don't quite see the point of saying it."

'But the managers,' said Bathyllus, 'are often the worst of the lot. One year I wrote "Bluebeard". The manager came to me and said: "I've got a fine thing – a full size model of the Rocket, the first locomotive. It cost one hundred and sixty pounds." "Very good," I said. "You'll put it on in the Harlequinade, I suppose? You can make some good fun out of the Rocket." "Harlequinade!" he said. "Harlequinade be blowed! Do you think I'm going to put my best thing on when half the people have gone? No, sir, it must go on in the second act." "But that's the Boudoir Scene," I said. "You can't have the Rocket in the Boudoir Scene." "Can't I?" he said. "You see." Well, he did give way about that, but he'd made up his mind to have it on somewhere. I said I'd rather have it in the Palm Grove Scene than in the Boudoir; so every night the Rocket was shoved on in the Palm Grove.

'I didn't write any words about it; I hadn't got the heart. It just came on. What made it worse was, it used to stick nearly every night.'

'At last I went to the manager, and I said: "Look here, I've thought of a real good thing. When the Rocket stops Bluebeard shall say: 'Well, you can't have a rocket without a stick!'" Will you believe it, the manager said he didn't put the Rocket there to have it laughed at, and he should take it off altogether. And he did – he did!'

Bathyllus buried his face in his hands.

J.B. ATKINS, *SIDE SHOWS*

Although the music hall was disappearing fast, its stars were still alive and well and still obliged to earn a living. This the lucky ones did by playing in the surviving halls, appearing in radio or musical comedy and even in a few cases in the cinema. One who enjoyed a long and successful career without diluting the calculated lunacy with which she had made her reputation in the halls was the extraordinary Nellie Wallace, 'the Essence of Eccentricity', who was born in the same year as Marie Lloyd and was still famous as a comedy performer when she died in 1948. Nature had endowed her with a profile which ruled out anything except slapstick, and this she mastered as well as any female clown of her times.

Just to be let loose on the stage gives her so much joy that she performs an *entrechat* in each corner. She is free from the indelicacy of the ballerina. Instead of frills and laces, she exposes what seems to be an expanse of lurid wallpaper. 'It's excitement, all excitement,' she cries. 'If you're fond of anything tasty, what price me?' She performs all the tricks of feminine allure in a skin-tight evening gown that puts her at a disadvantage when she drops her fan and has to lie full length, because she cannot bend to pick it up. 'Strange', she exclaims, looking at the clock, 'he promised to be here at 9.30. It is now twelve o'clock.' With that she looks towards us to excite our sympathy with a despairing sniff over protruding teeth and a heart-rending squint.

She was born at Glasgow, during a lecture tour given by her father, with her mother as pianist. Her first appearance on the halls was as a child clog-dancer, before she became one of the Three Sisters Wallace. She acted in theatres with her parents until her success as a comedian while playing Little Willie's death scene in *East Lynne* sent her back to the boards as a single turn.

M. WILLSON DISHER, *WINKLES AND CHAMPAGNE*

A nd it was as a single turn that Nellie, with a nose that looked capable of opening a can of sardines, a pair of painted eyebrows which endowed her with an expression of kindly imbecility, and a general comprehensive mastery of the arts of eccentricity which established her as one of the first and most successful female Dames in a branch of the profession so thoroughly dominated by men, was seen one afternoon by a small boy who was instantly and utterly crushed into idolatry.

The only positive enjoyment I discovered was being allowed, occasionally, to work the hotel's water-lift, a slow and stately machine which gurgled its way up and down when you pulled on a greasy rope. Into this contraption, on a morning when I was operating it, there lightly stepped a large foreign lady of advanced years, dressed in threadbare black. I had doubts whether the water could replace her immense weight; I eyed her like a hangman and then hauled on the rope manfully and successfully. When eventually we reached her floor, after a little upping and downing, she complimented me on my skill; so we became instant friends. She told me, among other interesting things, that she used to be a champion pole-punter in Russia, oh, long before the Revolution; that she had once given a gymnastic display before the Tsar and that as a small girl she walked the tight-rope. A vision filled my head of this new and welcome friend high in the air, wearing a sort of spangled bathing costume, balancing on a rope with the aid of her punt-pole, while, way down below, crowned heads rose in tumultuous applause. She asked me if I had ever been to the circus. The answer was 'No'. Had I, perhaps, ever been to the theatre? Well, I had seen *Chu Chin Chow,* which I had enjoyed very much; and I gave her half a verse of 'The Cobbler's Song'. I had also seen *Puss in Boots* but had hated it. 'This must be remedied', she said and instantly proposed taking me the following week to a matinée at the Coliseum, where there was a variety show. She was as good as her word. She bought seats for the two of us in the Dress Circle. I hate to think, now, what economic heart-searching she must have gone through, rummaging in her vast black bag to see if she had sufficient funds, and wondering, perhaps, if she would have to draw on her meagre savings.

The Coliseum offered jugglers, clowns, maidens in flimsy frocks who danced in flickering lights, attempting to look like flames; a man, with his hands and feet shackled, in a glass tank of water, from which he just managed to escape in a flurry of bubbles; some funnyish men in squashed hats and baggy trousers; acrobats, of course, of whom my hostess was sternly critical; some boring singers; and then – and then – the Top of the Bill, Nellie Wallace.

I don't believe I laughed at Miss Wallace on her first appearance. Truth to tell, I was a little scared, she looked so witch-like with her parrot-beak nose and shiny black hair screwed tightly with an enormous, bent pheasant's feather, and dark woollen stockings which ended in neat, absurd twinkling button boots. Her voice was hoarse and scratchy, her walk swift and aggressive; she appeared to be always bent forward from the waist, as if looking for someone to punch. She was very small. Having reached centre stage she plunged into a stream of patter, not one word of which did I understand, but I am sure it was full of outrageous innuendos. The audience fell about laughing but no laughter came from me. I was in love with her.

Later in the afternoon she turned up in a bright green, shiny and much too tight evening gown. She kept dropping things – bag, fan, handkerchief, a hairbrush – and every time she bent to retrieve them the orchestra made a rude sound on their wind instruments, as if she had ripped her dress or farted. Her look of frozen indignation at this pleased me enormously, but my companion clearly thought the whole act very vulgar and something which would not have been tolerated by the crowned heads of Russia. I laughed a lot but didn't fall out of my seat until Nellie's next act, in which she appeared in a nurse's uniform ready to assist a surgeon at an operation. The patient, covered with a sheet, was wheeled on stage and the surgeon immediately set about him with a huge carving knife. Nellie stood by, looking very prim, but every now and then would dive under the sheet and extract with glee and a shout of triumph some quite impossible articles – a hot water bottle, a live chicken, a flat-iron, and so on. Finally, she inserted, with many wicked looks, a long rubber tube which she blew down. The body inflated rapidly to huge proportions and then, covered in its sheet, slowly took to the air. Nellie made desperate attempts to catch it, twinkling her boots as she hopped surprisingly high, but all in vain. The orchestra gave a tremendous blast as she made her last leap; and that is when I fell off my plush seat and felt faintly sick.

I left the theatre in a daze, trying to walk like her, catching imaginary corpses in the air, glaring with wildly shocked eyes at innocent passers-by and generally misbehaving myself. My kind friend cannot have been very put out, as she offered me an ice-cream soda at Lyons. I liked the idea but asked the price. She said it would cost about two shillings but that was all right as personally she only needed a cup of strong tea. I asked if I might please spend the two shillings on something else. 'On what?' Without hesitation I said I would like to buy some flowers for Nellie Wallace. Those were the days when flower women could be found almost anywhere in London, so somewhere near Trafalgar Square we bought a small bunch of yellow roses which I proudly carried to the stage door of the Coliseum, where a note was written by my hostess and signed in a scrawl by me. The flowers were sent up straight away – I stood around to make sure of that – to my dotty new heroine. 'You shall have the ice-cream all the same', I was told. It was proving a far more expensive outing than had been intended, I fear. At Lyons I slowly got through an enormous ice, giggling from time to time with blissful memories of the afternoon in the theatre and then thinking, with reverence, of those button boots and the impertinent feather in Nellie's hat.

Perhaps the ice-cream was a mistake; the whole experience had been too much for me. By the time we got back to Cromwell Road I was feverish and put straight to bed. By nightfall I had a temperature of 104 (which impressed me no end) and my mother, in a panic, called for a doctor. I was kept in bed in the gloomy hotel for a month and was fairly ill, on and off, for a year.

That might have been the end of my over-excited matinée, but it wasn't quite. After I had been in bed a week I received a great bunch of yellow roses together with a note which read, 'I hope the little boy who sent me flowers gets better soon. Love, Nellie Wallace.' The kind Russian lady had gone to the theatre, explained my passion and asked Miss Wallace to send me a postcard. The flowers came instead. I can remember protesting loudly when the water was changed in the vase; I was under the impression that Nellie had provided not only the roses but the vase and water as well. And perhaps she had fired an ambition in me as well. I was determined that one day I also should have a hat with a broken feather. I never met her. Later in life I saw her a few times, but it was never quite so magical as when I was seven. No doubt, with the years, her vitality had diminished, her hoarse voice grown feebler and her brand of vulgarity become too familiar. Yet the boots seemed to live on. I would like to think they are well cared for in some eccentric museum and, when darkness falls, that they shed their primness, take up idiotic positions and tap out some old, raucous, ribald music-hall song.

ALEC GUINNESS, *BLESSINGS IN DISGUISE*

For those less famous than Miss Wallace, and less accomplished, refuge from a dying profession was often found in some modest theatrical boarding house or country pub, its parlour walls scattered liberally with photographs of the great departed, fulsomely inscribed to 'Dear Old Marge, in Memory of Cleethorpes Pav, 1913', or 'What ho, Georgie boy, it's your old Dan, The Tivoli – again'. These Marges and Georgie-boys, clinging to their flimsy rafts, were stock fictional types even before the talking pictures finally wiped out the profession; as early as 1905 Artie Kipps is scrutinising the walls of the actor Chitterlow's room and finding 'chiefly photographs of ladies, in one case in tights which Kipps though a "a bit 'ot"; but one represented the bicyclist in the costume of some remote epoch. It did not take Kipps long to infer that the others were probably actresses'. And they were all, like Chitterlow, slightly larger than the life they had tumbled into, always clinging grimly to the faded freemasonry of their old ways, and forever torn between wistful dreams of a return to the old-time tinsel and relief at the workaday security they had discovered. When the Second World War started and live entertainers were suddenly in demand again, if only to distract soldiers killing time in the garrison theatre, or each other in a different kind of theatre, the old timers sometimes found themselves offered a new lease of professional life.

By now a mere stage career was no longer enough to guarantee any considerable fame. The advance of the primitive cinematograph into the worldwide movie industry, added to the circulation of millions of gramophone records, meant that careers had to be tilted away from the personal appearance towards the machine. The Americanisation of the halls was very nearly complete. In the summer of 1931 a young athlete was taken to see a variety show, and it is revealing that the impresario whose guest he was introduced him, not to a local performer, but to an American visiting entertainer.

Gubby remembers his fourth Test best for the fact of his meeting with the great jazz singer Sophie Tucker, through R. H. Gillespie, the impresario who controlled the theatre chain known as Moss Empires. RH was a cricketer and a great friend of cricketers and he had dined well before telling Gubby and Tom Webster, the cartoonist, that they must come round to the Hippodrome and hear and meet her. Installed in a box RH had a hard job keeping awake and at times dropped into a noisy slumber. Round they went at the end to the star's dressing-room, the impresario, now fully awake, going through the conventional routine:

'Soph darling, you were simply marvellous.'
'You great big bum', was the lady's reply,' 'I heard you snoring up there.'

E.W. SWANTON, *G. O. ALLEN*

It is a dramatic irony that even as the music hall was melting away into history, an artist should have flourished who is thought by a great many good judges to have been the most brilliant comic of them all. Thomas Henry Sargent (1894-1963) was born in Brighton, son of a builder's labourer. The family finances were more or less non-existent, and every known account of his childhood paints a portrait of penury relieved by laughter. His choice of the stage name of Max Miller has misled some later biographers into the belief that he was Jewish; according to his biographer, John M. East, Max 'did not discourage this belief. Indeed he thought it would help him in his theatrical career where the Jewish fraternity held key positions'. In fact his father was of Romany stock, a tough, hard-drinking man whose idea of an eventful night was to get into a pub brawl. The details of Max's early life are an accidental testimony to the truth lying at the heart of so many great music hall songs. 'My Old Man Said Follow the Van' is evoked in Max's reminiscence about his childhood: 'Dad would run up as big a bill for the rent as possible and when the landlord started to threaten him, we'd do a midnight flit. Out with the old barrow and we usually made for under the pier where we'd camp out until we could get fixed up with a new flat the next day.' Then there is Dan Leno's routine in 'The Swimming Master', with its remark, 'My brother, he's passionately fond of water. He's a milkman', beautifully refined by Max's, 'My first job was as a milk boy at three shillings a week and commission. When I was delivering milk I used to drink some out of a dozen bottles and fill up the rest with water. I was taking an interest in my work, see?'

As a soldier in the First World War, Max began entertaining professionally; later he graduated to seaside shows and concert parties, all too aware that England was no longer a land fit for pierrots to live in. It was the early 1930s before he became a leading star of a declining profession, winning national notoriety for the blueness of his material and a rabelaisian approach to everything. Raised in the overcrowded, often brutalised courts of the working class, Max drew much of his material from the habits and problems of that life, particularly illegitimacy. As an example, a bogus autobiographical anecdote: 'When I was a boy my mother noticed I was looking miserable. She said, "What's up?" I said, "I told Dad I wanted to marry Miss White. Dad said, 'You can't. She's your half-sister. When I was young I had a bike and I got about a bit'. Then I told him I wanted to marry Miss Green and he said, 'You can't. She's your half-sister'. My mother said, "Don't you take no notice of him. He's not your father anyway."' And another: 'Bloke wins £25,000 on the Pools. When his father asks him what he's going to do with the money, he says, "Well, dad, I'm giving you a pound for a start." His father says, "Thanks very much. What you going to do with your half?". "I think I might take a trip round the world. What about you?". "Oh, I think I'll marry your mother."'

But Miller's best-loved material was about sex. There was hardly a phrase in conversational English which he could not render suggestive: 'I rang the doorbell. A woman answers it and says, "Yes?" I said "Wait a minute. I haven't asked you yet".' All over the country, but especially in London, audiences roared with laughter and cheered their hero even before his act had started. He was one of the great folk heroes of modern history, perhaps the greatest English actor of the twentieth century, an ad-libber of astonishing speed and resource, and a complete master of the art of orchestrating the reactions of any audience he faced. To read his jokes on paper tells only half the story, for he was inimitable in the style of his delivery, which breathed the very essence of chirpy London back-streets and the impudence of a triumphant survivor in an indifferent universe.

I'd tell you the story of the red-hot poker, only I don't think you'd grasp it.

That reminds me of the chorus girl who married a rich old invalid. She promised to take him for better or worse. She really took him for worse, but he got better.

As I always say, lady, some girls are like flowers. They grow wild in the woods.

The missus said to me yesterday, 'Every time you see a pretty girl, you forget you are married.' 'No', I told her, 'I remember.'

I saw a girl who was proud of her figure. Just to make conversation I asked her, 'What would you do if a chap criticised your figure?' 'Well', she said, 'I wouldn't hold it against him.'

A pal of mine married his typist. They got along just the same as before. When he dictates to her she takes him down.

My young nephew Roland was having a lesson in grammar and his teacher wrote on the blackboard, 'I didn't have no fun at the seaside.' She turned round and said, 'Roland, how should I correct that?' 'Get a boy friend,' he told her.

JOKES BY MILLER, PUBLISHED IN *THE SUNDAY DISPATCH*

In private life Miller's parsimony was a legend. But outweighing any tendency to stinginess was his admirable contempt for the microscopic men whose entrepreneurial activities put them nominally in charge of his career, latterday Stolls with little grasp of the very art from which they were making their money. Miller laughed in the faces of such people, showing them the same supreme arrogance which was at the heart of his stage performances. He knew he was a law unto himself, that between him and his enormous public there was a bond which was quite untypical of the usual artist—audience relationship. Miller was Their Man. He was, in some glorious way, the back-street Londoner personified, and this status gave him license to do more or less as he pleased once he stepped on to a stage. It is significant that whenever he clashed with what one might laughingly call authority, the essentially private nature of the encounters was soon altered. The whole of Britain was fairly quickly apprised of the facts.

The juggler, Billy Gray, described one night at the Holborn Empire.

Max was a riot that night. He just went on and on and the audience wouldn't let him go. He overran his time so much the stage manager brought the house tabs down on him. Unfortunately for Max, Val Parnell was out front. I was standing in the wings as Parnell came storming through the pass door, his face as black as thunder. 'You'll never work the Moss Empires again as long as you live,' he stormed.

'Mr Parnell,' said Max, 'you're thirty thousand pounds too late.'

JOHN EAST

In Max Miller the music hall, in its death throes, underwent an apotheosis which saw it become the allegorical representation of the nation which had nurtured it. The collapsing Empires of the theatre circuits and the collapsing empires of the British in the postwar period became one. In John Osborne's play *The Entertainer* we see an ageing comic spitting defiance at a world which has deserted his craft for the picture palaces, and is even now poised on the brink of deserting the picture palaces for the small screen. Why pay to see rubbish when you can watch it free in the discomfort of your own home? The leading character of *The Entertainer* is modelled closely on Miller, except that, as Miller was very quick to point out, Osborne's Archie Rice has become a failure, whereas Miller retained his easy ascendency to the very last. The role of Rice was originally played by England's premier actor, Laurence Olivier. Having played most of the great classic roles with distinction, Olivier was now turning his hand to something beyond his experience. His portrayal of Archie Rice was acclaimed by all those dramatic critics whose experience of Miller's background was nil, but it would only have embarrassed the habitués of the old Holborn Empire and the Met, Edgware Road. Among those unimpressed was Miller himself.

My wife went to see Sir Laurence Olivier after she saw him appear in *The Entertainer*. He said he was a great admirer of mine. Never met him myself. I understand he studied me closely before he played the part of this dud comic – to be insulted by Sir Laurence, that's a compliment in my book. I could have straightened him out on a few things if he'd asked me.

MAX MILLER, QUOTED BY JOHN EAST

The creator of Rice, the playwright John Osborne, later denied having modelled his hero on Miller. If he did not, then somebody certainly did. Olivier's style of delivery was so blatantly based on Max that comparisons at Olivier's expense were unavoidable. The absurdly loud stage costume, the cadences of the sentences, the tap-dancing, the patter songs, everything was in the tradition of the Cheekie Chappie. But Osborne is right enough when he says that while Rice was a man, Max was a God. His essay on Max, published soon after Max's death, gives some idea of how much the son of a Brighton builder's labourer came to mean to the urban poor who flocked to see him, who revelled in every blasphemy against prim caution, who exulted in the sight and sound of an artist who threw back at them their own witticisms polished to the highest pitch of perfection. In Max Miller the working classes saw themselves raised to truculent godhead, for which reason he has become, like Marie Lloyd before him, part of English social history.

He was a popular hero more than a comic. He was cheeky because he was a genius. All genius is cheek. You get away with your nodding little vision and the world holds its breath or applauds. Max took your breath away altogether and we applauded. When I was at school he was popular only with the more sophisticated boys, and girls

293

seemed bored by him altogether although I suspected that the girls I longed to know
– big, beautiful WAAFs or landgirls – would adore an evening with him. I loved him as
fiercely as I detested the Three Stooges and Abbott and Costello. He was not a great
clown like Sid Field nor did he make me laugh so much. The Cheeky Chappie was not
theatrically inventive in any profound sense. His fantasy was bone simple, traditional,
predictable and parochial.

It is said that he hit his insolent peak during the early forties at the Holborn
Empire. I saw him there only twice, but during the next twenty years his style
slackened very little and he never looked less than what he was – the proper
champion of his type.

What type?

He was the type of flashiness. He was flashiness perfected and present in all things
visible and invisible. The common, cheap and mean parodied and seized on as a style
of life in face of the world's dullards. Maxie would have been in his element in the
Boar's Head. Just to begin: his suits were superb. My favourite was the blue silk one
with enormous plus-fours and daisies spluttered all over them. With his white
upturned hat on one side and correspondent shoes he looked magnificent, perfectly
dressed for bar parlour or Royal Enclosure. In those days of clothing coupons, I
longed to wear such suits, although a weakness for clothes was likely to get you
called nancy boy. Someone called out after me in the street once because I was
wearing a dull but yellow pullover. No doubt he grew up to be a customs officer or on
the staff of the *Daily Telegraph*. No one would have dared to jeer at anyone who could
wear a suit like Maxie's. He was constantly being banned by the BBC, then the voice
of High Court Judges, Ministries and schoolteachers. Sometimes he was fined £5 for
a blue joke which became immediately immortal. I knew the truth was that Max was
too good for the BBC, and all the people like it. But this was just.

He went on telling them from the *Blue Book,* wearing his smashing clothes,
looking better than anyone else, and smelling of sea air, the open doors of public
houses and whelks. He talked endlessly and with a fluency that made me spin. He
was Jewish, which made him racy and with blasphemy implicit in his blood. He sang
his own compositions in an enviable voice and with a pride I thought both touching
and justified. 'This little song ... this little song I wrote ... you won't hear anyone
else singin' it. No one else dare sing it!" Nor would they.

He seemed to talk supercharged filth and no one could put him in prison or tell him
to hold his tongue. He appeared to live in pubs, digs, race-courses and theatre bars.
Naturally, he never worked. On top of all this, he had his own Rolls Royce and a
yacht, and was rumoured to own most of Brighton. I discounted stories about his
alleged meanness and never buying anyone a drink. He was simply holding on to what
he'd got and he deserved it more than anyone else in the world.

Above all, he talked about girls. Unwilling girls, give-her-a-shilling-and-she'll-be-
willing girls, Annie and Fanny, girls who hadn't found out, girls on their honeymoon,
fan dancers minus their fans, pregnant girls and barmaids the stork put the wind up
every six weeks. You always felt with Maxie that he didn't go too much on birth
control, but if anything went wrong the girls would be pretty good-tempered about it.
As for their mothers, he could always give them a little welcome present, too. In the
same way, the wife was complaisant, just another cheerful barmaid at home, reading
the *News of the World* till Max felt like coming back for 'coffee and games'. Except
that Max could always do without the coffee.

One always acknowledged his copyright to a joke. You could do nothing else. Some
of his jokes are still school folklore. There's the immortal story of the man on a
narrow ledge and didn't know what to do about it. That one cost £5 and worth every
penny of it. There are incomplete lines like:

When roses are red
They're ready for plucking.
When a girl is sixteen.
She's ready for –'ere!'

You could repeat the line but not the master's timing over his swivelling grin of outrage at the audience. 'You can't help likin' him, can yer?' They couldn't. They daren't. He handled his rare shafts of silence like – a word he would have approved – a weapon. When he paused to sit down to play his guitar and watched the detumescent microphone disappear, he waited till the last bearable moment to thrust his blade with 'D'you see that, Ivor? D'you? Must be the cold weather!' He was a beautiful, cheeky god of flashiness who looked as if he'd just exposed himself on stage. 'There'll never be another!' There wouldn't, and he knew it and we knew it.

As soon as the orchestra played 'Mary from the Dairy', I usually began to cry before he came on. And when he did appear, I went on doing so, crying and laughing till the end. Even his rather grotesque physical appearance couldn't belie his godliness. You could see his wig join from the back of the stalls and his toupé looked as if his wife had knitted it over a glass of stout before the Second House. His make-up was white and feminine, and his skin was soft like a dowager's. This steely suggestion of ambivalance was very powerful and certainly more seductive than the common run of manhood then. He even made his fleshy, round shoulders seem like the happy result of prodigious and sophisticated sexual athletics – the only form of exercise he acknowledged.

Some people have suggested to me that I modelled Archie Rice on Max. This is not so. Archie was a man. Max was a god, a saloon-bar Priapus. Archie never got away with anything properly. Life cost him dearly always. When he came on, the audience was immediately suspicious or indifferent. Archie's cheek was less than ordinary. Max didn't have to be lovable like Chaplin or pathetic like a clown. His humanity was in his cheek. Max got fined £5 and the rest of the world laughed with him. Archie would have got six months and no option.

I loved him because he embodied a kind of theatre I admire most. His method was danger. 'Mary from the Dairy' was an overture to the danger that he might go too far.

And occasionally he did, God bless him, and the devil with all nagging magistrates and censors and their wives-who-won't. Whenever anyone tells me that a scene or a line in a play of mine goes too far in some way then I know my instinct has been functioning as it should. When such people tell you a particular passage will make the audience 'uneasy' or 'restless' they seem as cautious and absurd as landladies and girls-who-won't. Maxie was right. And hardly a week passes when I don't miss his pointing star among us.

JOHN OSBORNE, *MAX MILLER – THE CHEEKY CHAPPIE*

I am glad to have the opportunity of telling you that you are to me a great genius.

LETTER FROM JOHN BETJEMAN TO MAX MILLER

U nlike most of his great predecessors, Max is preserved more or less unblemished on two or three long-playing recordings of actual performance. There is one night in particular, in October 1938 at the old Holborn Empire, which captures the subtle nature of the balance between artist and audience. Max toys with the house, playing their roaring laughter as an expert angler plays a spectacularly large catch. This is London celebrating itself on the eve of its own dissolution. Just as World War I swept away the world which was indigenous to the halls, so World War II destroyed whole tracts of the town, including so many of the theatres which artists like Max were always able to fill. The outbreak of the second war brought back to England one of its more eccentric exiles, Max Beerbohm, who had for the last thirty years fought to preserve his vision of Edwardian London by leaving it before the destruction could begin. In Rapallo in Italy he scribbled and doodled away, returning again and again to the same few Edwardian themes. When he came home to share the Blitz with the rest of the town, taking great care to describe himself as a Cockney, he mastered a new art by becoming one of the outstanding radio voices at Broadcasting House, where he delivered a series of retrospective talks which included one on the halls he had never forgotten.

Music Halls of My Youth

Sunday 18 January, 1942
Ladies and Gentlemen, or – if you prefer that mode of address – G'deevning.

It is past my bed-time; for when one is very old one reverts to the habits of childhood, and goes to bed quite early – though not quite so early as one went to one's night-nursery; and not by command, but just of one's own accord, without any kicking or screaming. I always hear the nine o'clock news and the postscript; but soon after these I am in bed and asleep. I take it that my few elders and most of my contemporaries will have switched off and retired ere now, and that you who are listening to me are either in the prime of life or in the flush of enviable youth, and will therefore know little of the subject on which I am going to dilate with senile garrulity.

Would that those others had sat up to hear me! In them I could have struck the fond, the vibrant chords of memory. To instruct is a dreary function. I should have liked to thrill, to draw moisture to the eyes. But, after all, you do, all of you, know *something* of my theme. The historic sense bloweth where it listeth, and in the past few years there has been a scholarly revival of interest in the kind of melodies which I had supposed were to lie in eternal oblivion. Some forty years ago that enlightened musician, Cecil Sharp, was ranging around remote parts of England and coaxing eldest inhabitants in ingle-nooks to quaver out folk-songs that only they remembered. It was a great good work that Cecil Sharp did in retrieving for us so many beautiful old tunes and poems – poems and tunes in which are enshrined for us a happier and better life than ours, a life lived under the auspices of Nature. I salute his memory. And I take leave to think that he would have been as glad – well, almost as glad – as I am to hear often, on the wireless, revocations of things warbled across the footlights of music halls in decades long ago. For these too are folk-songs, inalienably English, and racy of – no, not of the soil, but of the pavements from which they sprang. I even take leave to think that if Shakespeare had lived again and had heard them warbled in the Halls he might have introduced them into his plays, just as he had introduced – with magical variations, of course – the folk-songs of his own time. He might have done so. Or again, he might *not*. For he was very keen, poor man, on

296

amidst salvoes of fervid expectation. A very elastic and electric little creature, with twists and turns of face and body and voice as many as the innumerable pearl buttons that adorned his jacket and his breeches. Frankly fantastic, but nevertheless very real, very human and loveable in his courtship of 'Arriet by moonlight, or in his enjoyment of the neighbours' good wishes as he drove his little donkey-chaise along the Old Kent Road. I was at that time too young to appreciate the subtleties of the technique that he had acquired and matured on the legitimate stage. But in later years I knew enough to realise that he was becoming rather a slave to these subtleties. He was no longer content to merge his acting in the singing of a song. He acted outside the song, acted at leisure between the notes, letting lilt and rhythm go to the deuce. But his composition of words and music never became less good. There was always a firm basic idea, a clear aspect of human character. 'My Old Dutch', 'The Little Nipper', 'You Can't Get a Roise out o' Oi', and the rest of them, still live for that reason. I had the pleasure of meeting him once, in his later years, and was sorely tempted to offer him an idea which might well have been conceived by himself: a song about a publican whom the singer had known and revered, who was only. One and only, but great: none other than The Great Macdermott, of whom I had often heard in my childhood as the singer of 'We Don't Want To Fight, But, By Jingo, If We Do'. And here he was, in the flesh, in the grease-paint, surviving and thriving, to my delight; a huge old burly fellow, with a yellow wig and a vast expanse of crumpled shirt-front that had in the middle of it a very large, not *very* real diamond stud. And he was still belligerent, wagging a great imperative forefinger at us across the footlights, and roaring in a voice slightly husky but still immensely powerful a song with the refrain 'That's What We'd Like To Do!' In Russia there had been repressive measures against Nihilists, and Mr Joseph Hatton had written a book entitled *By Order of the Czar*– a book that created a great sensation. And in consequence of it the Great Macdermott had been closeted with the Prime Minister; nor did he treat the interview as confidential. I remember well some words of his song.

> 'What would you like to do, my Lord?'
> I asked Lord Salisburee'

but the words need the music; and I remember the music quite well too. A pity I can't sing it. But perhaps I could do a croaking suggestion of it . . .

(Sung)   'What would you like to do, my Lord,'
I asked Lord Salisburee.
'The great Election's very near,
And where will then you be?
The English people have the right
To fight for those who are
Being oppressed and trodden down
By Order of the Czar.
That's what we'd like to do!
Beware lest we do it too!
To join those aspirants
Who'd crush Russian tyrants –
That's what we'd like to do!'

And I do assure you that the audience would have liked to do it. You may wonder at that, after hearing my voice. You would not have wondered had you heard the Great Macdermott's.

But the fierce mood was short-lived. There arose in the firmament another luminary. Albert Chevalier, as new as Macdermott was old, came shining forth

297

a thing which many of the younger poets of our day disapprove of, as being rather bad taste: the element of beauty. And I cannot claim that this element was to be found in the songs of the *lion comique* or of the *serio* of my day, or of the days before mine. Indeed, I cannot claim for these ditties much more than that there was in them a great gusto. But gusto is an immense virtue. Gusto goes a huge long way.

'My day', as I have called it, dawned exactly fifty-one years ago. I was a callow undergraduate, in my first Christmas vacation. I had been invited to dine at the Café Royal by my brother Julius, whose age was twice as great as mine; and after dinner he proposed that we should go to the Pavilion Music Hall, where a man called Chevalier had just made his début, and had had a great success. I was filled with an awful, but pleasant, sense of audacity in venturing into such a place, so plebeian and unhallowed a den, as a music hall; and I was relieved, though slightly disappointed also, at finding that the Pavilion seemed very like a theatre, except that the men around us were mostly smoking, and not in evening clothes, and that there was alongside of the stalls an extensive drinking bar, of which the barmaids were the only – or almost the only – ladies present, and that the stage was occupied by one man now dead, whose business was carried on by his son, Ben, an excellent young man, – 'But 'e'll never be the man 'is father woz'. The chorus was to be something of this sort:

(Sung)

> I drops in to see young Ben
> In 'is tap-room now an' then,
> And I likes to see 'im gettin' on becoz
> 'E's got pluck and 'e's got brains,
> And 'e takes no end o' pains,
> But – 'e'll never be the man 'is Father woz.

But nothing so irks a creative artist as to be offered an idea, good or bad. And I did not irk Chevalier.

A man who introduces into an art-form a new style of his own has usually to pay a high price for having done so. Imitators crop up on all sides, cheapening his effects. This price Chevalier did not have to pay. He escaped in virtue of being partly French. His manner and method were inimitable in our rough island Halls. Singers of coster songs began to abound but they were thoroughly native and traditional. Gus Elen defied the conventions only by the extreme, the almost desperate glumness of his demeanour, and the bitterness of what he had to say, on a stage where cheeriness against all odds was ever the resounding key-note. Immensely acrid was the spirit of his "E Dunno where 'e Are' and of his 'Well, it's a Grite Big Shime'; but even these were mild in comparison with the withering pessimism of a later song of his. Often in reading the work of some of those younger poets whom I have mentioned I am reminded of that other famous song, 'What's the good of ennyfink? Why, nuffink!'

Very different was the philosophy of Dan Leno. Fate had not smiled on him, his path was a hard one, he was beset by carking troubles and anxieties, he was all but at his wits' end, the shadow of the workhouse loomed, but there was in his little breast a passion of endurance, and a constant fount of hope, that nothing could subdue. His meagre face was writhen with care, but the gleam in his eyes proclaimed him undefeatable. He never asked for sympathy: he had too much of Cockney pride to do that; but the moment he appeared on the stage our hearts were all his. Nature had made him somehow irresistible. Nor do I remember any one so abundant in drollery of patter. He was, by the way, the inaugurator of patter. In his later years he hardly sang at all. That was just a perfunctory gabble of a stanza and a chorus, and the rest was a welter of the spoken word – and of imaginative genius.

He used to appear yearly in the Drury Lane pantomime, with the enormous Herbert Campbell as foil to him. But there he was wasted. Team-work nullified him. He could shine only in detachment. Besides, Drury Lane was too big for anybody but

298

Herbert Campbell; and for him, it seemed to me, any music hall was too small. But I was very fond of him, that Boanergetic interpreter of the old tradition, with Mr James Fawn as his only peer or rival. Physically somewhat less great than these two, Mr Charles Godfrey had a wider range. He could be heroic as well as comic; and he abounded also in deep sentiment. 'After the Ball' is indeed a classic; but alas, as I found some years ago in a modern song book, the text has been corrupted, to suit tastes less naïve than ours were. The unsophisticated syntax of what Godfrey sang in his baggy dress-suit has been wantonly changed. No doubt you know the opening words of the present version. But what Godfrey gave us was

(Sung)   Came a small maiden,
         Climbed on my knees,
         'Tell me a story,
         Do, Uncle, please!'
         'Tell you a story?
         What shall I tell?
         Tales about giants?
         Or in the dell?'
         After the Ball was over,
         After the –

and so on. But 'Tales about giants? Or in the dell?' That's the thing to remember and cherish.

Mr Harry Freeman, dear man, sounded no depths, and scaled no heights of sentiment, and indeed had no pretensions of any kind, except a thorough knowledge of his business, which was the singing of songs about Beer, about the Lodger, about being had up before the Beak, about the Missus, about the sea-side, and all the other safest and surest themes. He never surpised one. He never disappointed one. He outstood in virtue of being a perfect symbol and emblem of the average. I delighted in him deeply. I think he had a steadying influence on me. To this day, whenever I am over-excited, or am tempted to take some unusual and unwise course, I think of Harry Freeman.

A saliently sharp antithesis to him was R. G. Knowles, surnamed 'The Very Peculiar American Comedian'. Nothing restful, everything peculiar, about *him!* He alone had a 'signature tune'. He was the inventor of that asset. The opening bars of Mendelssohn's Wedding March were played as he rushed on from the wings, hoarsely ejaculating 'I've only a moment to linger with you': a tall man with a rather scholarly face, wearing a very shabby frock-coat, an open collar, and not very white duck trousers, much frayed at the heels of very large old boots; also an opera-hat, flat-brimmed and tilted far back from the brow. He spoke rather huskily, with a strong native twang, at the rate of about ten words to the second. I tremble to think how many anecdotes he must always have uttered before he broke into a brief song and rushed away to linger for a moment with an audience in one of the other Halls. From some of his anecdotes one gathered that he was no prude. But there one wronged him. Some years ago my dear friend William Archer, the famous dramatic critic, and introducer of Ibsen to our shores, told me that he had recently met, travelling in India, a man of whom I probably knew a good deal, R. G. Knowles, a music-hall performer. 'He told me,' said Archer, 'that he had definitely retired from the music halls; and I asked him why. He said that the tone of them had fallen to a very low level: there was so much that was ob-jectionable. He said, "Mr Archer, in *my* turns there was never anything ob-jectionable. Sudge-estive – *yes*."'

I am not in a position to deny that ob-jectionability may have supervened. I had ceased to attend the Halls because the virus of 'Variety' had come creeping in: conjurors, performing elephants, tramp-bicyclists, lightning calculators, and so on, and so forth. The magic had fled – the dear old magic of the unity – the monotony, if you will – of song after song after song, good, bad, and indifferent, but all fusing one with another and cumulatively instilling a sense of deep beatitude – a strange sweet foretaste of Nirvana.

I often wondered, in the old Tivoli and elsewhere, who wrote the common ruck of the songs I was listening to, and what the writers bought one half so precious as the wares they sold. As to their tariff, I once had a queer little sidelight on that in a newspaper report of a case in the County Court at Hastings. The defendant stated that he earned his living by writing the words and music for music-hall songs. He was asked by the Judge how much he earned in the course of a year. He replied promptly, 'Three hundred and sixty-five pounds.' And then, the Judge being astonished at such exactitude, he explained that he was paid one pound for every song, and wrote one every day.

I should have liked to learn more about him. That he was not of the straitest sect of Sabbatarians is obvious. For the rest, what manner of man was he? Was he entirely a creature of habit? Or had he sometimes to plod without aid from his Muse, while at other times she showered inspiration on him? Was it in the comic or in the sentimental vein that he was happier? And was he a discerning judge of his own work? For aught I know, he may have written and composed 'Daisy, Daisy, Give me your Answer True'. On the evening of that day, did he say to himself, 'Not marble nor the gilded monuments of princes shall outlive this powerful rhyme'? And this question leads to another. Why, exactly, has 'Daisy, Daisy' triumphed perennially, holding her ground against all comers? There is a reason for everything in this world, there is a solution of every mystery. And, with your co-operation, I should like to – but time forbids. I should like also to have said a great deal about Marie Lloyd, whose funeral was less impressive only than that of the great Duke of Wellington; about Little Tich, who took Paris by storm; about Vesta Tilley and Mark Sheridan; also about Miss Ada Reeve, and about Mr George Robey. To her, and him, and to the shades of those others, I apologise for my silence. The work of all of them gave me great delight in my youth. Perhaps you will blame me for having spent so much of my time in music halls, so frivolously, when I should have been sticking to my books, burning the midnight oil and compassing the larger latitude. But I am impenitent. I am inclined to think, indeed I have always thought, that a young man who desires to know all that in all ages and in all lands has been thought by the best minds, and wishes to make a synthesis of all those thoughts for the future benefit of mankind, is laying up for himself a very miserable old age.

Good night, children ... everywhere.

MAX BEERBOHM, *MAINLY ON THE AIR*

By now the music hall was sufficiently passé to begin to be the object of a succession of revivals which continue to this day. The echoes of the original grow fainter, and the attempts of a dedicated few to save something from the wreck inspire essays in reconstruction. Soon after the last war Bernard Shaw, now in his ninety-first year, fulminated against one such attempt at revival, although the logic of his case reads rather shakily. Unable to bring himself to acknowledge that the inferior versifying of the old-time songwriters could have had anything to do with the appeal of the great stars, Shaw built up a case quivering with Shavian ingenuity, which proved that had Marie and Bessie and the rest of them sung the national anthem, the result would have been the same. Posterity takes the liberty of disagreeing, but Shaw's statement is revealing for the heat with which he defends the stars of his younger days.

The elderly members of the BBC Advisory Council who had fallen to the charm of music-hall singers, like Marie Lloyd, Bessie Bellwood, and Vesta Tilley, tried to revive them by broadcasting their songs. Now these songs, with their interpolated patter, were not only vulgar but so silly as to be hardly intelligible. And the BBC made the outrageous mistake of thinking that the secret of their popularity lay in their vulgarity, though a moment's consideration should have convinced them that vulgar and silly girls could be picked up in any poor street for a few shillings a week. The real secret was that their intonation and rhythm were so perfect as to be irresistible. When Marie Lloyd sang 'Oh, Mr Porter, what shall I do? I want to go to Birmingham and they're taking me on to Crewe', nobody cared tuppence about Birmingham or Crewe; but everybody wanted to dance to Marie's exquisite rhythm, and found the sensation delightful. Bessie Bellwood's patter, assuring us that she was not going to 'gow on the stije and kiss her ijent', did not draw sixpence into the pay boxes; but she, too, could sing in perfect tune and measure. Chirgwin earned his salary, not for his make-up as the White-Eyed Kaffir or his substitution of a kerosine tin with one string for a Stradivarius, but for his infallible musical ear, which kept him always exactly in tune. Sir Harry Lauder, still with us, triumphed, not because of his Scotch accent, but because he has a very fine voice and never sings a false note nor misses a beat. The sham Maries and Bessies strove their hardest, not too successfully, to be vulgar in the Cockney manner, and took their passable intonation for granted. The revival was a disgraceful failure.

GEORGE BERNARD SHAW IN MUSICAL TIMES, JANUARY 1947

S haw's old successor at the *Saturday Review,* now Sir Max Beerbohm, would no doubt have echoed those sentiments had he bothered to notice them. The only considerable critical contemporary of Shaw's still in the firing line, Max had remained in the home country long enough to ensure the defeat of the Axis, and then returned to the time-warp of Rapallo, where he sketched and resketched the heads of George Moore, Pinero, Henry James and the rest of the victims of his youth. As the repository of rapidly fading history, Max attracted the curious, including the American journalist S.N. Behrman, who first visited him at Rapallo in 1952, returning several times until Max's death in 1956. Behrman extracted a great deal of witty malicious reminiscence from Max, including recollections of his days as a follower of the music hall. Although some of what Behrman reports is the stock Beerbohm response, it is worth reproducing if only to underline how the artists on the halls seem to have been almost the only group of which he approved so thoroughly that his restless impulse to lampoon and ridicule was for once controlled.

My remark set Max off. He began to sing from the repertory of one of the favourite music-hall comedians of his youth, George Robey. When Max sang, he leaned far forward in his chair, his expression immensely solemn. Assuming an air of honest indignation and injured innocence, he sang, in full Cockney but with unimpaired diction. Max's eyebrows became very active; they twitched in Pecksniffian outrage. The burden of the song was that Robey had been accused by malevolent spirits of playing Peeping Tom at the bathing machines at Brighton. When Max came to the end of the song, his voice and eyebrows cried out in gruesomely lascivious protest:

'Did I go near the bathing machine?
Naow!'

Max had adored Robey. He smiled as he spoke of Robey's impersonation, in a sketch, of Queen Berengaria; evidently she was putting on the royal raiment in a bathing machine, and the sudden startled expression, half reluctant, half experimental, indicated that the Queen was herself suspicious that George Robey was lurking somewhere in the vicinity. When Robey died, Max said, he had been given a memorial service at St Paul's. This had afforded Max intense amusement, and, he said, it would have afforded the same to Robey. 'Pity he couldn't have been informed'.

Max then imitated Marie Lloyd singing 'Oh, Mr Porter, What shall I do? I want to go to Birmingham and they're taking me on to Crewe'. To Marie, Max, a few years before, had paid an obituary tribute over the BBC. 'It is strange', Max had said, 'that of all the women of the Victorian era the three most generally remembered are Queen Victoria herself, and Miss Florence Nightingale, and – Marie.'

When Max was sixteen, his half-brother Julius, who was then twice his age, had taken him to dinner at the Café Royal and then to his first music hall, the Pavilion, to hear the Great Macdermott – 'a huge old burly fellow, with a yellow wig and a vast expanse of crumpled shirt-front that had in the middle of it a very large, not *very* real diamond stud'. It was at a moment of anti-Russian tension, because of repressive measures taken by the Tsar against the Nihilists, and The Great Macdermott, it appeared, had had an interview with the Prime Minister about it. This was odd – as if Eisenhower were to consult Jimmy Durante about certain Russian tensions now – but it was so. Macdermott, Max says, did not regard the interview as confidential. He sang about it the night Max first heard him:

> 'What would you like to do, my Lord?'
> I asked Lord Salisburee.

Fond of tracing words to their sources, Max remembered that the word 'jingo', as a symbol of effervescent patriotism, had been introduced in a music-hall song by this same Macdermott. It was at a moment when Russia appeared to be threatening Turkey, then (as now) England's ally. Max, imitating Macdermott, became quite bellicose, unusual for him:

> We don't want to fight, but by jingo, if we do,
> We've got the ships, we've got the men, we've got the money too!
> We fought the Bear before, and while Britons shall be true,
> The Russians shall not have Constantinople!

I chided Max for being so possessive about Constantinople. He relaxed from his belligerence and said that he didn't want it for himself, he just didn't want the Russians to have it.

I remembered that Miss Jungmann had told me he had once written a song for the music hall entertainer Albert Chevalier, and I asked him about that. 'Oh', he said, 'I wrote it, but I never offered it to Chevalier. I did meet him though. Macdermott was enormous, Chevalier small and electric. He did coster songs and wore pearlies. He had a song, which I can't sing – it would be an injustice to him – called 'You Can't Get a Roise Out o' Oi'. But I'll try two lines from another'. Max sang:

> It isn't so much what 'e sez,
> It's the nahsty way 'e sez it.

'Chevalier's songs', he went on, 'always had a clear form. They were well constructed. I knew them all by heart once. I got into his mind, don't you know, and, embolded by this, I ventured to construct a song that, it seemed to me, he might have written himself. It tells about an old barman whom Chevalier had known and loved and who was dead and whose pub was now being run by his son. The song I wrote was called 'But 'E'll Never Be the Man 'Is Father Woz', and the chorus went like this.' Max treated me to a private performance of the song, which he had also sung on his broadcast.

> I drops in to see young Ben
> in 'is tap-room now an' then,
> And I likes to see 'im getting on becoz
> 'E's got pluck and 'e's got brains,
> And 'e takes no end o' pains,
> But – 'e'll never be the man 'is father woz.

On the BBC Max told his audience why he had never submitted the song to Chevalier. 'Nothing so irks a creative artist as to be offered an idea, good or bad,' he said. 'And I did not irk Chevalier.'

But Max's special affection, in the teeming past that so crowded his present, went out to two Lilliputians who were giants of the old music halls – Little Tich and Dan Leno. These two were friends of his. 'Little Tich!' Max said. 'He was tiny. I felt gross beside him, and yet, you know, I couldn't have been so much larger, because I remember the time I was asked to appear and speak at some charity or other organised by the Playgoers' Club. The presiding officer was just about to call on me when some bigwig, some Eminence or other, made his sudden appearance. The Chairman was so bowled over by this irruption that he quite lost his head. 'And now I have the honour to announce Sir Tich!' It made it easy for me to speak, you know. I apologised, I believe, for having forgotten my great boots. He used to slosh about – Little Tich – in great boots. They were as long as himself. He had them specially made, and the walk he managed in them was – well incommunicably funny. It was...' Max's feet did a slosh on the carpet. 'No, it cannot be imitated. He had a sad face. So did Dan Leno – the saddest face, I believe, I have ever known. Little Tich told me this story himself. When his son was born, he was in a state of great anxiety, and he was sitting on the stairs, with his head bowed in his hands and wondering how everything was going, and presently the doctor came along and comforted him. 'It's all right, my little man', he said, 'you've got a baby brother.' When the baby brother grew up, Little Tich worried dreadfully about him. He wanted his son to take holy orders. I met him in a pub near His Majesty's and found the dear man in a state of particular depression. 'Oh!', he said. 'My boy! I don't know what will become of him. He is not serious. He is not religious. I am afraid he hasn't a vocation. Instead of studying, he prefers to hang around your brother's theatre. He's probably in there right this minute. If he can't get a seat, he stands at the back of the stalls.' He was a marvellous mime, Little Tich. He was a *succès fou* in Paris – even more than in London. But Dan Leno was a great artist, the greatest of them all.'

Not having to worry about boots, Max was able to imitate Dan Leno. He did it with his fingers. 'The greatest thing he ever did – at least, to my taste – was a scene in a shoeshop. He made you see everything. He wrote his patter himself, and it was trenchant and shattering. Well, in the shoeshop, a mother comes in with a little boy. Dan skips over to her.' Max did the skip with his hands, in miniature staccato jumps. 'He asks the mother how old the little boy is. Three. THREE! Leno is lost in admiration. He can't repress his amazement and wonder, don't you know, that a little boy of three could be so precocious, so mature, so altogether delectable. Then he skips up the stepladder.' Max's fleet fingers skipped up the stepladder. 'And he rummages around for the shoes. Red boots with white buttons she wanted. While he's up there, on top of the stepladder, he keeps looking down at the boy, as if he had never seen such a cynosure. But he can't find the proper shoes. He rummages around with increasing desperation among the boxes.' Now both of Max's hands were rummaging around wildly and helplessly among the shoe-boxes. 'He produces a multitude of shoes, but the mother won't accept them. But this time, his attitude towards the little boy has changed, don't you know. He becomes somewhat critical of the little boy – even homicidal. Oh, it was wonderful, but it is impossible to describe,' said Max as he finished describing it.

Max continued to talk about Dan Leno. 'You know, Constance Collier – she was a member of Herbert's company at His Majesty's – once told me an extraordinary story about Leno. She came home late one evening, after her performance – it was very late; she had been out to supper, I imagine – to her flat, in Shaftesbury Avenue. She noticed a brougham before her door as she went in. There in her sitting-room was Dan Leno. He had been there for hours. Constance had never met him, but, of course, she was thrilled to see him. What do you suppose he wanted? Now, mind you, you must remember that at this very moment Dan Leno was the idol of England; he could do no wrong with his public, which adored him. Well, he wanted to play Shakespeare. That is why he had waited, and kept a brougham with a coachman on the seat waiting – because he wanted to enlist Constance's sympathy for his ambition to play Shakespeare. He wanted to meet my brother. Constance arranged it. She brought Dan Leno to Herbert. But nothing came of it. Why wouldn't Herbert employ him? He would have been wonderful – Dan – as one of Shakespeare's clowns. I didn't know about it, or I should have pleaded with Herbert'.

Max looked at me sorrowfully. 'He was a sad man, Dan Leno. Wildly generous. Surrounded always, don't you know, by a crowd of hangers-on and sycophants, to whom he gave freely whenever they asked.'

S. N. BEHRMAN, *CONVERSATIONS WITH MAX*

When Beerbohm died he could have claimed with some justification to have outlived the institution which had once given him such great pleasure. By 1960 there remained only one last refuge of the old halls. At the Victoria Palace, a theatre whose dispositions echoed the expansiveness of the old halls, was installed one of the most extraordinary companies of comics ever to animate British life. Charlie Naughton and Jimmy Gold had formed their alliance in 1908; Jimmy Nervo and Teddy Knox had become a double act in 1919. But Flanagan and Chesney Allen joined forces in 1920, after a brief meeting in an estaminet while serving with the army in the Great War. Flanagan, the dominant influence within the group, had imbibed the art of Alec Hurley when, as a boy, his job was to fetch fish-and-chips for the artist appearing at an Aldgate theatre not far from his father's shop. It was not till 1931 that he and Allen left revue for variety, using a composition by Flanagan, 'Underneath the Arches', as their theme song. In 1932 an impresario called George Black, wishing to speed up the pace of comedy at the London Palladium, advertised a 'Crazy Week', in which the audience was repeatedly mixed up with the performers, and comics kept interrupting each other's acts. From this successful experiment evolved the six-man team, The Crazy Gang, whose embryonic brand of humour may be gathered from an extract printed in the Palladium programme.

You must all have heard the story of Sweeny Todd, how one day his father caught him with a Nax and said, 'What are you a doing of?' 'I want to be a sailor like you, Mother,' answered the child, and they gave him a yo-yo and sent him to the Labour Exchange, where he became three times Lord Mayor (and *how* he could Lord Mayor!). However he met a Madammois – a Madammois – a woman, and she said, 'If you can find the one that owns this slipper I will make you a Millionaire.' It would be a shame to give the plot away on a five years' lease, so they built on the ground and it was the curse of India. Years afterwards people will look up to his monument and say, 'There was a brave man who mastered his yo-yo.'

Lacking the sharpness of wit of Max Miller, the Crazy Gang compensated with a sort of child-like innocence whose rebelaisian overtones were dedicated to the art of knockabout rather than to the knowing wink of the Cheekie Chappie. All six were variations on the theme of the clown. Nervo, a member of the once-famous Holloway circus family, took his professional name from a monkey. His partner was a son of well known *improvisateur* called G.T. Cromwell. Before they joined forces with Flanagan and Allen and Naughton and Gold, they were well known for their lampoons of ballet dancing and their slow-motion wrestling matches. The Crazy Gang, flung together through a caprice of George Black, cohered magically, soon becoming the most famous and successful comic team in the entertainment business. Until 1940 their home was the Palladium. After the war, when Allen retired, the Gang reformed at the Victoria Palace in 1947. In 1956 one of the comedians associated with them in their early days, Monsewer Eddie Gray, rejoined them. Forever perched on the brink of retirement, the Gang always committed itself to one more show, and by the time they really did call it a day, in 1962, they had become a national institution, having appeared in fourteen Royal Command Performances, becoming popular film stars and, in the case of Flanagan and Allen, successful recording artists, and generally accepted as the last guardians of a dead genre. Their retirement, when at last it came, was a highly emotional affair. The whole country sensed that in some indefinable yet unmistakable way things would never be quite the same again. Nor were they, in the popular theatre. It was someone's stroke of inspiration at Broadcasting House to despatch to the Victoria Palace on the last night of the Crazy Gang one of the finest ad lib reporters the Corporation ever possessed. This was René Cutforth. whose range of expertise stretched from modern warfare to ancient and modern laughter. After watching the scenes of roaring affection and sentiment at the Victoria Palace, Cutforth hot-footed it back to Broadcasting House and delivered one of the most cherished items in the Corporation's vast sound archives.

It had been a notable night. The house lights kept coming on and turning off again in a capricious way. So many pocket cine-cameras were turning that sometimes you could hardly hear the show. The house was solid with warm, affectionate, roaring fans, and a manic gentleman in front of me kept leaping up and and shouting 'Never!' whenever the word retirement was hinted at. When finally, in a decently-ordered chaos, the Crazy Gang crashed to its conclusion at about midnight, we were all agreed in my part of the house, some of us with tears, that something English, human, and admirable had departed from this mortal scene.

Well, what?

On the face of it, the glamour that was Piccadilly and Leicester Square had meant nothing to anybody outside the theatre since my father was a young man. But watching the Gang's final performance, I suddenly realised why, in the theatre, it had lasted so long and so well. This was a convention which assumed that everybody in the house was a fully paid-up member of the human race, and it implied that the membership fee was pretty stiff, involving a good deal of time spent in the lavatory for instance, or wishing you were upper-class. The hard, cold face of success or the

305

petulant self-pitying one got short shrift here. In this world the human condition was presented undistorted. The formula was simple. Take any basic human wish. Take, for instance, that universal dream, the eastern harem, where coveys of gorgeous girls six feet high, in transparent trousers, swanned around in an ecstasy of acquiescence. Inject into this paradise the awesome figure of Charlie Naughton. It's not what he does, it's what he is. There, deplorably, stands the human race, a wreath of laurel around its brow, three-quarters naked. He looks like a hamster who's swallowed a tennis ball. 'He's a eunuch,' Bud Flanagan patiently explains, 'he's got no scruples.'

There was a young, snooty girl made up like an owl in a coal-hole in the bar, where I was in the interval. Most of the fans were middle-aged, middle-class and middle-browed, but she was made of sterner stuff. 'Sexual infantilism', she said, and went on to propound the theory that life was real and life was earnest, and nothing more real than bottoms and breasts, so where was the joke? The fans' eyes glazed. They were too civilised to tell her that as a member of the human race she was obviously not fully paid up, but you could see them reflecting that every new attitude since the old music halls had been colder than the last, and that the latest was a proper freezer, and not, more's the pity, what the Gang would have made of it, a bum-freezer. So she went off in a cold fury of superiority and we settled down to an exposition by Monsewer Eddie Gray on the vanity of human wishes, and the moment when his anxious, irritable, terrible dignity, as his fifth or sixth trick comes miserably to pieces, drove him to ask, 'Well, what is it you want, then. Love?' When the curtain finally fell, it was a colder and more meagre world we were left in.

RENÉ CUTFORTH, *BBC SOUND ARCHIVES* 19 MAY 1962

Four years after that memorable night, Flanagan and I collaborated on a thirty-minute script in which Flanagan remembered his career and discussed some of his favourite recordings. It was revealing that in composing 'Underneath the Arches', which is a very fetching melody, he had merely started to whistle and soon found himself with a complete tune. Being untrained as a musician, Flanagan was obliged to sing it over and over to himself to make sure the tune did not evaporate. Some time later, after Flanagan died, the following appreciation appeared in *The Times*.

Bud Flanagan, OBE, a comedian so popular that he became an English institution, died on October 20th, 1968, at the age of seventy-two. As the leading partner in the double-act of Flanagan and Allen, as the leading spirit in the now legendary Crazy Gang, and, since the Crazy Gang ceased its operations in 1962, as a solo artist, Bud Flanagan provided a combination of the outrageous, the inventive, and the endearing which made him a universal favourite.

Bud Flanagan was born Robert Winthrop – his Polish-Jewish father had taken the name Winthrop when he settled in England – in Spitalfields, London, in 1896. The future comedian began his working life as a call-boy at the Cambridge Music Hall, in the East End of London, where he became aware of the tradition of English humour of which he was to become a part. At the Cambridge he saw most of the great performers of the period, amongst them Alec Hurley, 'The Coster Comedian', upon whom he modelled his stage voice. Eventually the young Winthrop ran away to America, where, after casual jobs and a career as a boxer (which, he claimed, lasted for one fight) he toured in Vaudeville until he returned to England to enlist in the Army during the First World War.

It was in an estaminet at Poperinghe that he first met Chesney Allen when they were both resting out of the line, and a reunion some years later, as members of one of Florrie Forde's touring revues, led to their partnership as Flanagan and Allen. For a time before this, Robert Winthrop had been touring as Chick Harlem the blackface comic; the new name, Flanagan, was in part a compliment to Florrie Forde, whose maiden name was Flanagan, and in part a good-humoured revenge upon an Irish Sergeant-Major Flanagan who 'didn't like Jews'; Robert Winthrop had promised the Irishman that he would make the name famous as a joke, and he spent the rest of his life doing so.

The act of Flanagan and Allen was a combination of songs with cross-talk in the tradition of the down-and-out Flanagan confronting the elegantly aristocratic Allen. It allowed both the partners room for surprising invention, and Flanagan, with his broken straw hat, enormous shabby clothes he could not possibly fill, and vast Hebraic leer, showed himself to be an extremely resourceful comedian. The act began in the provinces but soon brought the pair to London, where they starred in a number of revues at the Holborn Empire and the Palladium. The Depression of 1931 nearly drove them from the stage into full-time bookmaking, for they both were devotees of racing, but instead, with the double-act teams of Naughton and Gold and Nervo and Knox, and with Monsewer Eddie Gray, they became the Crazy Gang and added a new dimension to comedy in the variety theatre. Their antics did not stop at the rude interruption from the gallery or the plaintive objection from a stage box, but were likely to occupy the foyer as well as the aisles of a theatre. Popularity with the Royal Family, whom they subjected to inoffensive and usually quite respectful cheekiness, gave them a position parallel to that of a medieval court jester. Flanagan's delight in periphrastic mistakes – 'Goodwood' was usually 'Fine Timber' to him – opened a vein of surrealist fantasy which, perhaps, helped to make them favourites with the intelligentsia. As well as that, in their sixties they were all capable of acrobatic hilarities. The vulgarity of their humour – Flanagan objected to the idea that his jokes were ever 'dirty' but admitted that he enjoyed what he described as 'broad' – was often interrupted by his shout of 'Oi!', leaving the shocking dénouement to the audience's imagination.

In all this, Flanagan was the ringleader, and his approach to comedy was entirely professional and painstaking. The anarchy which he inspired on the stage was carefully built up to a climax, just as his jokes were taken over from every possible source and then polished until they seemed entirely his own. His singing of the popular songs of four decades was a pleasure his admirers will not quickly forget, but his own 'Underneath the Arches', a salute to the down-and-outs of the Depression, is perhaps the only one of the dozens he sang to have the quality of a classic.

Bud Flanagan received the Order of the British Empire in 1958, and after the Crazy Gang broke up in 1962 he continued to appear in pantomime, for the idea of retirement did not appeal to him. With Chesney Allen and others of his colleagues he appeared in a number of films which did not succeed in conveying the warmth and liberating power of his personality, which dissolved inhibitions in the shortest possible time. If his humour, like his personality, had something about it which was essentially Jewish, he fed this quality into the tradition of the music hall, and he came to exciting vivid life through interplay with an audience.

THE TIMES, 21 OCTOBER 1968

By this time, anyone wishing to research the music hall found himself pursuing the elusive ghosts of ancient history. By 1974 my own attempts to save whatever reminiscences I could for the Sound Archives of the BBC resolved themselves at last into visits to Neville Cardus and Stanley Holloway. Most of Cardus's talk was a recapitulation of what he had already written several times. Holloway had spent most of his career in the straight and musical theatres, but his 'Albert' monologue had taken him into Variety for a while, and certainly in his boyhood he had seen several of the great artistes of the halls. Holloway exulted in the eat-drink-and-be-merry approach of the old turns, and even though it was all now ages ago, he could not help laughing out loud as some tiny moment came back to him from a past which spanned every sort of theatre from *The Co-Optimists* to *My Fair Lady*. He was talking to me at one point about the farcical attempts at recasting *My Fair Lady* indulged in by Jack Warner, when he suddenly remembered one of his old comrades from the days when an artist toured the circuits and made what he could of domestic bliss.

Do you remember Stanelli? He was staying in some small hotel, and the little chambermaid used to come in every morning to bring him his breakfast in bed. About the middle of the week Stanelli's wife came up to join him, so she was lying in the double bed with him. The maid came in and took a bit of a look and said, 'Good morning, sir.' So he said, 'Oh, bring two breakfasts ... wait a minute.' He looked at his wife and said, 'Do you take sugar?' and she said, 'Yes, please.'

STANLEY HOLLOWAY, BBC SOUND ARCHIVES

I was working in the pit of the then Company Theatre, which later became Miss Horniman's famous Gaiety Theatre. I was selling chocolates and they were called Bovril Chocolates, penny a bar. I saw Eugene Stratton in a pantomime called *Robinson Crusoe* and he sang 'I May Be Crazy But I Love You', I remember. An escaped negro making love to his girl. And then he sang 'Lily of Laguna', and danced to it. His dancing was so light-footed, I've never seen anything quite like it. Only once, when Pavlova came to the Free Trade Hall, Manchester, with no scenery, just a black curtain. She had a Ballet Corps there, and on the platform was a loose plank and when the rest of the ballet danced you heard this plank go plonk, and when she danced, not a sound. And they used to go twice daily, you know, two o'clock and seven, and it was hard work for these people. There was a girl in this pantomime named Daisy Jerome, and I was then about sixteen or so and I fell in love with her. Never spoke to her of course in my life. But in those days they used to have picture postcards, so I got a picture postcard of Daisy Jerome and oh, I could see her every day on the stage and I wore it always next to my heart. And one day I was in the theatre early, before the matinée began, and through the Dress Circle came Eugene Stratton and Daisy Jerome and he said 'Hello, sonny', and nothing in my life has ever thrilled me so much as Eugene Stratton in the company of this beautiful musical comedy star saying 'Hello, sonny'.

People used to go to the pantomime as a sort of ritual. They went every week. You'd see almost the same people every Thursday, the same people every Friday, and sometimes, when it had been running about eight weeks, they would change the script. People would write letters to the papers about changing the script in a pantomime. It was as though somebody had changed the script in *Hamlet*. They didn't like the comedians to change their scripts.

I remember the music hall when it was not quite respectable. They talk today about streaking. I went to a pantomime when I was quite young, taken to it by my beautiful and marvellous Auntie Beatrice, and every girl on the stage was quite naked. But they were all posed like classical statues. And George Robey arrived in the midst of this nude statuary and I can see now his eyebrows going up and him saying 'Well, I mean to say, I mean to say.'

The popular comedians were not vulgar. Robey spoke beautiful English. Wilkie Bard, beautiful English. Bard sang one of the most beautiful of popular songs, 'I Want to Sing in Opera'. Wilkie Bard as a charwoman comes out on to the empty stage with a pail of water, with a dish cloth. Got down on his knees, made a great circle of wetness, which was the sphere of operations to clean the floor. Then wrang out the dish cloth and then walked down the stage, leaned over the footlights and began to sing 'I Want to Sing in Opera'.

NEVILLE CARDUS, BBC SOUND ARCHIVES

So long as *The Manchester Guardian*, now reconstituted as *The Guardian*, was willing to grant him the space, which was not nearly as often as it should, Cardus was ready to draw on his recollections of the halls. One of the last features of his to appear in the paper included a line or two not encountered in previous essays on the subject.

Little Tich

This is the year, so I am told, of the centenary of Little Tich. And who – a natural question nowadays – was Little Tich? He enjoyed universal renown as a music-hall comedian in the late Victorian, and throughout the Edwardian, years, a name as famous then as Ken Dodd's now – and Tich got his reputation unaided by television and radio. He 'topped' the bill at Empires and Hippodromes and Palaces and Tivolis everywhere, holding his vast audiences with no microphone to lend him acoustical aid.

His real name was Relph, and there was something French in his make-up, a diminutive physical make-up, some four feet. He wore long flapping boots, over which he would lean towards us whenever in intimately communicative mood. Also he simulated baldness, giving an occasional appearance of – to quote a meta-physically minded music-hall reviewer of 'The Manchester Guardian' – 'an egg-shaped personality.' (I think the writer was Donald Boyd.)

But Little Tich didn't trade on dwarfishness. Like most of his famous contemporary comedians, Robey, Leno, Weldon, Wilkie Bard and Harry Tate, he was an actor, a comic actor, with a keen eye for character. Also, like Robey and the rest, he was essentially serious; the laughter he caused came as a byproduct of his impersonating art.

I remember him playing the part of a prosecuting counsel, bewigged and gowned, full of patronising 'M'luds', and grappling with briefs and precedents. Or he would come before us as an insurance agent for a burial society, breathing loudly on his tall hat, then polishing it with his sleeve, and while breathing, letting us hear that his lungs were full of bronchitis. I can't remember that he ever sang; yet he must have sung. Some sort of song (with an 'ad. lib.') was part of the music-hall convention, if only as an excuse to digress into 'patter'. Little Tich had great charm, a common characteristic of comedians of his day, a characteristic terribly lacking in the comedians of 1967, most of whom begin their acts or funny stuff by guffawing themselves at us, a cue or clue to the fact that they really are about to be funny. Whenever Tich took a curtain he would bow quickly and effectively right over his long flapping boots, knocking himself out as his bald forehead collided with the stage. Once, I laughed at him so convulsively that I fell off my seat at a pantomime at the Manchester Palace (I confess I was then only eight years old). Tich was one of the Ugly Sisters in 'Cinderella'. They had not received tickets of invitation to the ball, and the flunky attendant refused admission. In a sudden burst of inspiration Little Tich said, 'I know! – let's walk in backwards and they'll think we're coming out.'

The great comedians of this epoch told us of what was then known as the low life of the man in the street, 'low' with certain social aspiration. George Robey could be, in his accent, more Oxford than Balliol. And, as I say, these funny men went to work in all seriousness. An interruption of a laugh, in a Robey discourse, sent his eyebrows indignantly up. 'I am not he-arr,' he would expostulate, 'to be made a laughing stock.' Then, with a glare into the remote parts of the audience, 'I'm surprised at you, Ag-er-ness!'

Wilkie Bard, as a charwoman, came down the stage carrying a bucket full of soap-suds and holding a cleaning cloth. He went down on his (or her) knees, making a wide wet circle with the cloth, an indication of the immediate sphere of her cleansing operations. But then he would rise suddenly from her knees and, coming before the footlights, announce by song, sung in a husky and excessively refined voice, 'I want to sing in Opera,' thus confiding to us a laudable and natural ambition.

I didn't place Little Tich in the company of the greatest comedians of his heyday, not with Robey, or even with Harry Tate, who in a sketch called 'City Man' came bustling into his office, his moustaches like bristling radar, saying, 'Good morning, good morning! Any letters?' And, on being told there were no letters this morning, said: 'Very well, then, we must write some.' All very serious, and not conscious of an audience. Only one comedian of today could go into the company of the masters of the high-noon of the music-hall. He is Frankie Howerd. Maybe, I should add the names of Harry Worth and Al Read (at his best and *solo*).

Every night, up and down the land, these comedians had to entertain enormous audiences by means of their own individual talents and their own un-microphoned voices. (Imagine Robey, or Tate, or Little Tich, tied to a microphone – all appearances destroyed of the characters they were 'taking-off'!) And the audiences in the Empires, Tivolis, Palaces and Hippodromes could be brutally frank in criticism. Pennies were thrown from the galleries on to the stage occupied by some pitifully incompetent clown. I have myself thrown an egg at a particularly unfunny man at the Tivoli, in Peter Street, Manchester. In those distant times there were, as Dan Leno pointed out communicatively over the footlights, three categories of eggs – new laid, fresh and – eggs. It was strictly an 'egg' that my young right arm unerringly aimed at the unfunny man at the Manchester Tivoli, in 1905, hitting him in the middle-stump with a throw from long-on in the gallery.

Again, I say, they had charm, these Victorian and Edwardian comedians. Little Tich abounded in it. Closing an interview he said, 'And then, after the show, a quiet supper, a whisky, a page or two of Montaigne – and bed-oh!'

They put life as they knew it on the stage, living-pictures (a period term) from 'Punch' and Phil May. I repeat, these comedians were actors – remember Robey's Sancho to Chaliapin's Don Quixote: The greatest of all makers of laughter, Chaplin of course, could touch us to amiably sentimental huskiness in the throat. And, later than Tich, came the incomparable Grock, a grotesque lovable being from another dimension, clown in *apotheosis*, discovering with childlike glee a new habitation. He sat down and played the piano with gloves on his hands. Noticing the gloves, he took them off. His delight at finding he could play better without gloves was a joy to behold. And – I insist, and repeat a word out of date now, and even distrusted – they had 'charm' – a characteristic, I say it once more, not immediately apparent among the TV gigglers with their microphones.

NEVILLE CARDUS IN THE GUARDIAN

Cardus's contemporary, J.B. Priestley, also had a few things left to say about the old halls. Late in the day, in 1965, he published a novel whose fictitious music-hall performers occasionally cross paths with real artists of the time before the Great War. For Priestley as for Fred Willis, a scarlet line was drawn across the map of his life on 4 August 1914, which is where, for all practical purposes, the story of *Lost Empires* ends. The authorial voice of the tale belongs to an aged successful painter looking back to a brief season in youth when he accompanied a music-hall company on its tour. At one point the painter suddenly dispenses with the make-believe characters in the story and turns to the real thing.

Twice, topping our bill, we had a comedian who I think has been under-valued. This was Harry Tate, whose Motoring, Fishing, Billiards sketches contained the sprouting germ of so much surrealist comedy, and whose glaring and bellowing sportsman, always reduced to stunned silence by the enormity of events, was a creation touched with genius, a lunatic caricature of a real and horrible type of Englishman. And once we had Little Tich, released from the Tivoli to dazzle the suburbs. Uncle Nick, who had appeared with him abroad, knew him well, and I was introduced to him, a solemn little Mr Relph, who talked to me about painting. On the stage he might be a barrister in court, a tipsy man-about-town, a regal lady encumbered with an enormous train, but always he set these miniature beings blazing with a mad energy, as if, coming from a different species, they were flaming burlesques of our own larger dim idiocies. And just once we had Grock, who hadn't been long in England then and hadn't reached the height of his fame, but even then was the best clown I ever saw except Chaplin. He was like a serious, humble but hopeful visitor from another planet, and like Chaplin he brought your laughter close to the beginning of tears. I was ready to pour out my admiration and gratitude to him, but off the stage he seemed aloof, rather grim, perhaps because he couldn't feel at ease and at home in England, a divided country, one part of it in love with comic genius, the other part cold and hostile to it. To this day, if my arthritis allows it, I can do a very rough imitation of Grock's act, just a poor sketch of it, that makes people laugh who never saw him in all his comic glory.

J.B. PRIESTLEY, LOST EMPIRES

Even today the occasional book of childhood reminiscence appears which cites the music hall as the source of deep pleasure remembered. Not always is the witness some famous novelist or critic like Cardus and Priestley. In the late 1970s the BBC presented a series of five-minute broadcasts by an unknown writer called Rose Gamble, who had been raised in the back streets of Chelsea between the wars. The vividness with which she was able to conjure her past led to the publication of a fuller text in the form of an autobiography of childhood in which the annual pantomime loomed large.

After the wonder of Christmas Day came the final treat, the pantomime. As soon as tea was over on Boxing night, we went up our street in the crackling cold to get into the front of the queue for the gallery. The Chelsea Palace glowed red and yellow lights all over the road, and people spilled in and out of all of its doors. There was music from the buskers and cries from the pedlars, hot chestnuts, peanuts-all-roasted, hot taters and toffee apples. Great posters lit with spotlights showed the fairy queen and the long-legged principal boy, shining and glittering above the crowds. We dragged Mum across the Kings Road in a panic that we shouldn't get in, and joined our queue that huddled in the darkness of Sydney Street, willing the doors to open. At the squeak of the crash barrier we edged forward and the queue began to move until we caught the airless smell of the grey stone stairs. Up and up we went, Mum breathing heavily, and Lu and Georgie racing ahead to grab our places.

The first sight of the gods was a shock, for the steepness of the setting took your breath away. There were no real seats, just slightly curved layers of stone, each covered with a strip of thin matting. People squeezed up together and leaned back on the feet and knees of those squashed in behind them. We bounded down the tiers to the iron bar, filled in with wire mesh, that separated us in the gallery from the proper red seats of the upper circle, and sat on our folded coats so that we could see over the top. The stage was covered by a shiny stiff curtain painted all over with advertisements, and we twisted round to watch the crowd pouring in and filling every space, pleased and excited that we were in the front. There was such a noise with everyone talking and moving about and kids running up and down to the lav, not using the stairs but pushing between the seated people. Lu pointed out the bald heads bobbing in the orchestra pit, and families settled in the gold boxes each side of the stage. One large lady sat prominently forward displaying a sparkling necklace.

'Diamonds', hissed Dodie. I stared at the sumptuous box, red curtains glowing in the golden light, and I saw the glittering jewels. It was all marvellous and magic, and there we were in the same place as a lady wearing diamonds.

Immediately below us the upper circle was packed full, and further down were even more sweeping curves of people in the dress circle. We could just see the first few rows of the stalls behind the curtain of the orchestra pit. People began to clap when the conductor suddenly appeared. He nodded his head to them over his shoulder and held up his arms. I clutched Dodie's hot hand and leaned forwards, pressing my head to the wire mesh. The orchestra burst into a jiggy tune, making a thin loud noise so that you could hear every instrument. The advertisements disappeared upwards and the great, gold-fringed curtains took their place. Softly, slowly the lights dimmed, the people grew very still, the footlights sprang into a line. Like lightning the red curtain flew away and I almost fell on to the great open stage,

312

brilliant with light and colour, painted trees and cottage, and awhirl with identically dressed dancing villagers in tap shoes. The panto had begun, and I was already intoxicated.

ROSE GAMBLE, *CHELSEA CHILD*

When Dan Leno died, there were Compton Mackenzie and Max Beerbohm to preserve his living memory. Little Tich and Wilkie Bard remained active in the mind of Cardus and Priestley. Stanley Holloway had virtual total recall of whole songs, whole acts, whole bills. In the wistful singing of Bud Flanagan might be discerned faint overtones of the coster art of Alec Hurley. And for a long time after her mother's death, Marie Lloyd Junior bravely invited the deadliest comparisons by keeping Marie's repertoire and style of delivery alive. But in time not only the great stars but also the great reminiscers who remembered them were gone too. There are no more Carduses and Holloways and Mackenzies from whom to seek information, or with whom to consort with the old stars at only one remove. The music hall has become ancient history, and it has required conscious, perhaps even self-conscious attempts at revival movements to keep it alive. However successful these revival attempts may be, not even the most obdurate defender of the halls would pretend that the art of the music hall any longer arises naturally, as it once did, out of the ebullience and sublime sense of the ridiculous of the working class.

Yet the audience for such entertainment remains with us yet awhile. For more than thirty years the BBC television programme *The Good Old Days,* although sometimes a feeble echo of the real thing, remained one of the most popular of all long-running shows. Even more interesting, at the Player's Theatre in Villiers Street, just by Hungerford Bridge at Charing Cross, may be discovered, or rediscovered, not merely the entertainment, but the style of audience behaviour which was once the norm. J.B. Booth, were he to come back to pay a visit to the Player's, or Mackenzie, or Cardus, or any of the witnesses to music hall's cheerful confrontation with the real world, would sense a bouquet of the old days, in the freedom of movement to and from the bars, the informality of the audience, the sharing of convention between the paying customer and the paid performer. But one TV show and one theatre is, after all, not very much, the very last stronghold of a crumbling fortress. Music hall as an active, evolving, developing art, is as dead as the bombazine and bustle skirts which once filled its seats. Entertainment has moved on, as it and everything must. But the relics of the halls are particularly affecting.

A few gramophone records audible enough to convey the spirit of the original. Books and photographs, even a few feet of film on which the likes of Lily Morris and Gus Elen come magically alive for a minute or two, and we can get an inkling of what our grandfathers used to enthuse about. But the memorabilia survive only through good luck or the fanaticism of some eccentric collector. In 1958, working as a professional saxophonist, I was recruited into an execrable orchestra to be featured every Saturday evening in a popular music programme. The shows were shot in the old Hackney Empire, only very recently converted into studios. The conversion had been done brutally, crudely. Bits of walls, halves of rooms, segments of ceiling, had been left suspended in their own rubble. On the first day I was passing from a dressing-room to a tea-trolley when I noticed, in a small section of wall left standing between two small rehearsal areas, a glint of brass. When I went closer, I saw it was a

313

plaque screwed into the wood. The inscription said 'Presented to Her Majesty Queen Victoria by His Majesty the Shah of Persia on the occasion of his visit'. There followed a date. For the next few days I thought about that plaque, and at last decided that on my return on the following Saturday I would steal it on behalf of posterity. When I returned, it, and the wall, had vanished. I cannot imagine that the Queen of England and the Shah of Persia ever enjoyed an assignation at so modest a venue as the Hackney Empire. But I saw the plaque, and I was a witness to its evaporation. Like the music hall, it had simply disappeared into the past, leaving behind no more than a puff of dust.

The music hall is dying, and, with it, a significant part of England. Some of the heart of England has gone, something that once belonged to everyone, for this was truly a folk art.

JOHN OSBORNE, INTRODUCTION TO *THE ENTERTAINER*

Mitchener: 'How is your daughter?'
Mrs Farrell: 'Which daughter?'
Mitchener: 'The one who has made such a gratifying success in the music halls.'
Mrs Farrell: 'There's no music halls nowadays: they're variety theatres.'

BERNARD SHAW, *PRESS CUTTINGS*

Now is it all over, and the laughter and good fellowship of those days only echo in the corridors of time. Those London suburban theatres had a short life but a merry one, and all that is left are a few grandmothers who were once beautiful chorus ladies, a host of memories, and one or two anachronisms like myself to recall them.

FREDERICK WILLIS, *A BOOK OF LONDON YESTERDAYS*

INDEX

315

317

ACKNOWLEDGEMENTS

The author and the publishers wish to thank the copyright holders for permission to reprint extracts from the following copyright material:

Max Beerbohm, *Mainly on the Air*, © William Heinemann Ltd; Madeleine Bingham, *Earls and Girls*, © Hamish Hamilton Ltd; All contributions by Neville Cardus © The Estate of Neville Cardus; Charles Castle, *The Folies Bergère*, © Methuen & Co. Ltd; David Cecil, *Max*, © Constable & Co. Ltd; Charles Chaplin, *My Autobiography*, © The Bodley Head Ltd; Winston Churchill, *My Early Life*, © Hamlyn Publishing Group Ltd; C. B. Cochran, *A Showman Looks On*, © Messrs Harbottle & Lewis (Solicitors); Alistair Cooke, *Six Men*, © The Bodley Head Ltd; M. Willson Disher, *Winkles and Champagne*, © Batsford Ltd; John East, *Max Miller–Cheekie Chappie*, © W. H. Allen & Co. plc; Eleanor Farjeon, *A Nursery in the Nineties*, © David Higham Associates Ltd; John Felstiner, *The Lies of Art*, © Victor Gollancz Ltd; Janet Flanner, *Paris was Yesterday*, © Angus & Robertson Ltd; Rose Gamble, *Chelsea Child*, © BBC Publications; Victor Glasstone, *Victorian and Edwardian Theatres*, © Thames & Hudson Ltd; Robert Graves, *Goodbye to All That*, © Jonathan Cape Ltd; Fred Lawrence Guiles, *Stan* © Michael Joseph Ltd; Alec Guinness, *Blessings in Disguise*, © Hamish Hamilton Ltd; Elie Halevy, *History of the English People in the Nineteenth Century*, © A. & C. Black Ltd.; Aldous Huxley, *Point Counterpoint*, © Chatto & Windus Ltd; Rudyard Kipling, *Something of Myself*, © Macmillan Publishers Ltd; Compton Mackenzie, *My Life and Times*, *Echoes*, © Chatto & Windus Ltd; Paul Nash, *Outline*, © Faber & Faber Ltd; Hesketh Pearson, *By Myself*, © William Heinemann Ltd; J. B. Priestley, *Margin Released*, *Great Morning*, *Lost Empires*, © William Heinemann Ltd; Christopher Pulling, *They Were Singing*, © Harrap Ltd; S. N. Rehrman, *Conversations with Max*, © Hamish Hamilton Ltd; C. H. Rolph, *London Particulars*, © David Higham Associates Ltd; L. C. B. Seaman, *Life in Victorian London*, © Batsford Ltd; all contributions by George Bernard Shaw, © the Society of Authors; Osbert Sitwell, *A Free House*, *Great Morning*, *Noble Essences*, © Macmillan Publishers Ltd; E. W. Swanton, *Gubby Allen*, © Century Hutchinson Ltd; A. J. P. Taylor, *Essays in English History*, © Penguin Books Ltd; H. M. Tomlinson, *All Our Yesterdays*, *The Day Before*, © William Heinemann Ltd, *A Mingled Yarn*, © Gerald Duckworth & Co. Ltd. Every effort has been made to trace the holders of copyright material used in this anthology. We apologise for any omissions in this respect, and on notification we undertake to make the appropriate acknowledgement in subsequent editions.